Foreign Policies of
Northern Europe

Also of Interest

† Available in hardcover and paperback.

Westview Special Studies in International Relations

Foreign Policies of Northern Europe
edited by Bengt Sundelius

This cross-national treatment of the foreign policies of Northern Europe—Denmark, Finland, Iceland, Norway, Sweden—is organized by substantive policy areas rather than by country, thus allowing most-similar-case analyses of several dimensions of the countries' international relations. The authors make comparisons among the countries in each area of investigation and present details of security, international development, and neighborhood and foreign policy processes. They also describe and explain international and domestic forces that shape the region's external policies. The combination of sound, empirically based data and attention to broader international and theoretical interests allows relevant comparisons with other advanced industrial states.

Bengt Sundelius, a native of Sweden, is associate professor of international studies at Bradley University. In 1980–1981 he was visiting research associate at the Swedish Institute of International Affairs, Stockholm. He is the author of *Managing Transnationalism in Northern Europe* (Westview Press, 1978) and several articles on European affairs.

Foreign Policies of
Northern Europe

edited by Bengt Sundelius

Westview Press / Boulder, Colorado

082 126

Westview Special Studies in International Relations

Copyright © 1982 by Westview Press, Inc.

Published in 1982 in the United States of America by
  Westview Press, Inc.
  5500 Central Avenue
  Boulder, Colorado 80301
  Frederick A. Praeger, President and Publisher

Library of Congress Cataloging in Publication Data
Main entry under title:
Foreign policies of Northern Europe.
  (Westview special studies in international relations)
  Bibliography: p.
  Includes index.
  1. Scandinavia—Foreign relations—Addresses, essays, lectures. 2. Finland—Foreign relations—Addresses, essays, lectures. I. Sundelius, Bengt. II. Series.
DL55.F67   327.48   81-24062
ISBN 0-89158-909-0   AACR2
ISBN 0-86531-137-4 (pbk.)

Printed and bound in the United States of America

Contents

Figures and Tables

Acknowledgments

This volume would not have been possible without the steadfast support of a number of institutions and individuals. The Board for Research and Creativity at Bradley University helped initiate the project. The Nordic Cooperation Committee for International Politics supported two workshops where the authors could come together to discuss their contributions. The publication of the studies was made possible by grants from the Letterstedtska Foreningen, Stockholm, the Nordic Cooperation Committee for International Politics, and the Swedish Institute. Westview Press believed in the project and manifested great patience with us. Jeanne Clayton, Charles Miles, and my loving wife provided invaluable assistance in the preparation of the manuscript. They, as well as the individuals associated with the named institutions, deserve considerable credit for the completion of this project.

Bengt Sundelius

1
Introduction to North European Foreign Policies

Bengt Sundelius

Three basic ambitions have guided the work on this volume about North European foreign policies. Primarily, we hope that this collection of papers will prove pedagogically useful and will help disseminate knowledge about the North European countries. Secondly, the essays represent a limited but concerted effort to improve our substantive comprehension of foreign policy behavior. We also hope the book will be theoretically interesting and relevant to the broader field of foreign policy studies.

As a student and teacher of North European affairs working in North America, I have been struck by the lack of good teaching materials. Works in English are often very specific in their orientations, being the end product of a dissertation or other scholarly research. Generally, these studies are of limited use as introductions to the problems of the area, but the more general surveys available too often focus on only one country and do not directly lend themselves as introductions to the entire region. This lack of comprehensive introductory texts is particularly regrettable, as outsiders often instinctively view the area as a unit. Their interest, previous knowledge, and need for additional training pertain to the North European or Scandinavian region as a whole. Those who teach comparative political analysis also find it difficult to take advantage of the many enriching examples available from the North European region.[1]

One of the ambitions of this project is to help fill the present gap in available pedagogical tools. This is attempted by making available to an international reading audience a volume addressing an important dimension of North European affairs in a cross-national, comprehensive manner.

Each chapter in this book is an original contribution and was commissioned especially for the volume. We hope that teachers and students will find the collection of papers useful and informative. Although the domestic arena is left relatively untouched, students of Scandinavia should be able to place each country's international position and relations in perspective after reading these overviews. Similarly, students primarily concerned with specific types of foreign policy, and only secondarily with Scandinavia, should profit from the reviews of the North European policies. We hope that this book, in a limited way, will alleviate the widely perceived need for additional education materials in this field. It may also stimulate colleagues to address other aspects of North European developments in a similar fashion.

Comparative Approach

Many surveys of Danish, Finnish, Icelandic, Norwegian, and Swedish foreign policy are available.[2] In most instances, the authors of these works have concentrated on one political entity or one single case of unique events or developments. The dominance of single-case analysis is also illustrated by some recently edited volumes, with materials from all the North European countries.[3] These collections indicate clearly the opportunities available for detailed comparative analyses of various aspects of the countries' foreign policies. However, they tend to consist of separate-country studies with very limited comparisons across the cases.[4] As a result of the preference for single-case analysis, few attempts at formulating empirical theory have been made. Conclusions drawn seldom reach beyond the specific case, generalizations made do not include essential features of neighboring policies, and a general understanding of the subject does not appear to evolve in a cumulative fashion.

With regard to North European domestic politics, the situation is somewhat different. In this field, several Scandinavian scholars have been engaged in explicitly comparative Nordic studies.[5] Although nationally oriented works clearly dominate here also, a more deliberate attempt to reach across state lines has been made. No doubt, the many obvious similarities found in the domestic arenas have stimulated this effort. Comparisons with neighboring societies can improve understanding of one's own political system. Possibly the divergent Nordic foreign policy orientations may have made similar comparative exercises appear less useful in the foreign policy field. Yet the desire to emphasize the common Nordic social and political heritage in the face of different cold war alignments may also have been a motivating force behind some cross-national presentations.[6]

In addition, the Scandinavian domestic area has been more directly incorporated into the mainstream of international social science research, partly through the work of native scholars such as the late Stein Rokkan and Erik Allardt.[7] A fruitful interchange seems to have developed in this arena of comparative inquiry. Much of North European research has influenced the general thrust in the field, whereas many Scandinavian specialists rely on common theoretical assumptions and general conclusions drawn elsewhere. As a result, the study of North European society, domestic politics, and domestic policy is more closely intertwined with the larger research concerns in the field of comparative politics.

It is not surprising that most "outsiders" studying North European developments are found in the domestic rather than in the international politics field.[8] The international reputation of Scandinavia for advanced, industrial, welfare societies with successful records of solving socioeconomic issues has stimulated a broad interest in their domestic lives. Again, the motivation for comparative study has often been to learn something of value from their success. Naturally, U.S. and British researchers have found North European foreign policies in general less relevant to their own national conditions and external objectives.

If North European foreign policy studies are to contribute to the advancement of the comparative study of foreign policy, more analysts must break away from their traditional preoccupation with single-country studies. By adopting a more comparative perspective, using variables in a more deliberate manner, offering more explicit hypotheses, and expressing conclusions in more easily transferable terms, specialists on Scandinavia could make an important contribution to the foreign policy field. Its impact could be similar to the impact the work of Scandinavian specialists in the field of domestic politics has made in the study of industrial societies, electoral and interest group politics, and public policy. Subsequently, one objective behind this volume is to generate North European foreign policy studies with relevance beyond the specific cases or events analyzed. We try to present studies that are useful and interesting for the larger international community of foreign policy specialists.

Most Similar Systems Design

Inspired by James Rosenau, a leading American school of thought on foreign policy is characterized by theoretical sophistication, methodological rigor, and the inclusion of a large number of cases. The works of this school have made an important contribution to the field by sharpening definitions of concepts and variables, by using novel methods, and by offering new, thought-provoking hypotheses about possible relationships between variables.[9] In addition, these studies are truly comparative in design. Their emphasis is not merely on analyzing a number of countries' external policies, but more importantly on systematic and explicit comparison of various facets of their behavior. A constant search for similarities, differences, and regularities is included as a vital part of the analysis. Unquestionably, other scholars engaged in efforts to enhance the understanding of national foreign policies could profit from the experiences of the Rosenau group. Specifically this is the case in northern Europe, where most specialists have engaged in more traditional modes of foreign policy analysis.

The comparative study of foreign policy, as pursued by the Rosenau school, is not without its limitations. The concern with scientific rigor sometimes leads to a preoccupation with data manipulation. The high level of abstraction in the analysis can make for conclusions almost void of substantive content. The frequent reliance on many questionably categorized cases limits the persuasiveness of the conclusions offered. The dependence on relatively few variables, analyzed in isolation from their contextual environment, weakens the strength of the subsequent findings. The classical problem of the validity of operational variables and of the data used is not uncommon here either. In sum, what is gained in theoretical sophistication and methodological rigor is at times lost in empirical validity and relevance. If the objective is to formulate empirically founded theories of foreign policy behavior, both these components should be included in the research enterprise.

The most similar systems design is a possible avenue toward constructing empirically based theories of foreign policy behavior.[10] Here, a few selected cases are explored in depth to ensure empirical validity within an explicit comparative framework. The theoretical and methodological strengths of comparative inquiry are combined with the empirical accuracy and comprehensiveness of the area specialist. The result of this approach should be findings that are empirically solid and yet expressed in transferable, general terms. Although the substantive content of the conclusions is high, the suggested relationships suffer from limited scope of applicability. Thus, it is crucial that the results of each research effort can be transferred to another empirical setting for retesting and, hopefully, for an extension of their scope of validity. It seems that the most similar systems design can generate truly empirical theories that can be extended and modified to cover an even larger number of cases. No claim can be made that universally applicable relationships have been discovered. One can only assert that for the type of nation analyzed one has considerable confidence in the validity and accuracy of one's findings.

The North European region offers a rich testing ground for the most similar systems design approach. In this area, an unusually tempting opportunity exists for comparative inquiries leading to empirically sound theories of foreign policy behavior. The nations' foreign relations and internal features differ enough to make comparisons meaningful and interesting. In addition, the common characteristics of the area are significant enough to make cross-national analysis manageable without losing empirical credibility. Ib Faurby comments:

> On this background it is surprising, and worthy of notice in a Nordic journal of international politics, that the number of comparative studies of the foreign policies of the Nordic countries, is extremely small. Here is clearly an untried potential for testing the value of the most similar systems design in comparative foreign policy. The number of political, economic, and cultural factors which could be eliminated from the analysis is large and on the other hand there are still important differences in foreign policy to be accounted for, particularly in alliance policy and in foreign economic relations. One of the arguments against the most similar systems design is that such systems often do not show sufficient variation of the dependent variable, but that is not the problem with the Nordic countries as far as the major foreign policy issues are concerned.[11]

In line with this view, a final objective of this volume is to explore the usefulness of the most similar system design as an approach to the comparative study of foreign policy and to show that this method can generate limited empirical theories. Of course, studies in a reader that aims primarily at providing basic substantive knowledge have to cover a vast ground in a small space and cannot develop theoretical arguments more than in rough outlines. Within these limits, however, we hope to help "advance comprehension of the dynamics whereby most nation-states in the modern period somehow manage to benefit from and cope with—or at least remain distinct from—their environments."[12]

Basic Outline

The organization of this book is rather simple. Two introductory chapters deal primarily with the forces that help shape foreign policy behavior. The first essay analyzes the relationship between the changing international system and national policies. Here, a rather long-term perspective is used to show how different international conditions, largely beyond national control, have contributed to shifting national policies and created differences among nations during the twentieth century. Chapter 3 discusses the role of domestic factors and structures in foreign

FIGURE 1.1

Organizing Perspective

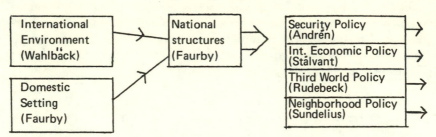

policymaking. The importance of cultural, social, economic, political, and administrative variables is highlighted in an effort to help explain existing similarities and differences in national policies.

Four chapters treat separate dimensions of the foreign policy behavior of the North European countries. Their purpose is to describe in comparative terms the content, style, and orientation of national security policy, international economic policy, third world policy, and neighborhood policy. These policy sectors are chosen with the view that they represent the main thrust of contemporary North European foreign relations. Each chapter maps out important commonalities and variations among national policies and provides an overall assessment of the characteristic features of the policy area.

In the concluding section, an effort is made to pull together the findings of the previous studies. By using illustrative tables, each nation's characteristic features are summarized and accentuated. Similarly, linkages between foreign policy behavior in separate sectors and distinctive determining factors are made. We hope this exercise has generated some propositions of more general interest. Although these propositions are of very limited geographical validity, they should serve as hypotheses for testing in other regional settings.

Finally, we present a selected bibliography of North European foreign relations. Here, the interested reader can find additional works on the various policy dimensions covered in this introductory volume.

Notes

1. Although most Scandinavian texts suffer from similar pedagogical shortcomings, an important exception is noteworthy: Ingemar Lindblad, Krister

Wahlbäck, Claes Wiklund, *Politik i Norden* (Stockholm: Aldus, 1974). Here, each political feature is discussed on a cross-national basis, giving a comprehensive understanding of the entire North European area. The result is a book that not only is rich in detail, but also enables its readers to place each society in perspective of the others. One can only regret that this valuable text has not yet been translated into English and made available to American students.

2. See the numerous works listed in the bibliography.

3. For example, Johan Jorgen Holst (ed.), *Five Roads to Nordic Security* (Oslo: Universitetsforlaget, 1973); Gunnar Jervas (ed.), *Utrikespolitik i Norr* (Lund: Studentlitteratur, 1973); "Nordic Aid to Underdeveloped Countries," *Cooperation and Conflict* 2(1970); "Scandinavian and Western European Economic Integration," *Cooperation and Conflict* 1(1969).

4. Some notable exceptions are Ake Landqvist (ed.), *Norden pa Varldsarenan* (Stockholm: Tema, 1968); Nils Andrén, *The Future of the Nordic Balance* (Stockholm: Defense Research Institute, 1977); "The Nordic Countries in the United Nations," *Cooperation and Conflict* 3-4(1967); Barbara Haskel, *The Scandinavian Option* (Oslo: Universitetsforlaget, 1976); Tiovo Miljan, *The Reluctant Europeans* (Montreal: McGill University Press, 1977); Ib Faurby, "Foreign Policy-Making in Scandinavia," in William Wallace and William Paterson (eds.), *Foreign Policy Making in Western Europe* (Farnborough: Saxon House, 1978); Nikolaj Petersen, "Danish and Norwegian Alliance Policies, 1948-49: A Comparative Analysis," *Cooperation and Conflict* 14, No. 4 (1979): 193-210.

5. Among the studies some books can be noted: Nils Herlitz, *Elements of Nordic Public Law* (Stockholm: Nordstedt, 1969); Nils Andrén, *Government and Politics in the Nordic Countries* (Stockholm: Almqvist-Wiksell, 1964); Erik Allardt, *Att Ha, Att Alska, Att Vara: Om Valfard i Norden* (Lund: Argos, 1975); Sten Berglund and Ulf Lindstrom, *The Scandinavian Party System* (Lund: Studentlitteratur, 1978); Ingemar Lindblad, Krister Wahlbäck, Claes Wiklund, *Politik i Norden* (Stockholm: Aldus, 1974); Nils Elvander, *Skandinavisk Arbetarrorelse* (Stockholm: Liber, 1980).

6. For example, Henning Friis (ed.) *Scandinavia Between East and West* (Ithaca: Cornell University Press, 1950); George R. Nelson (ed.), *Freedom and Welfare, Social Patterns in the Northern Countries of Europe* (Copenhagen: Ministries of Social Affairs, 1953); Joseph A. Lauwerys (ed.), *Scandinavian Democracy* (Copenhagen: Danish Institute, 1958); Jorgen Bukdahl (ed.), *Scandinavia: Past and Present* (Odense: Arnkrone, 1959); Franklin D. Scott, *Scandinavia* (1950; 2d ed., Cambridge: Harvard University Press, 1975); Folmer Wisti (ed.), *Nordic Democracy* (Copenhagen: Danish Institute, 1981).

7. Note the participation of these scholars in large international research projects pulling together findings from several areas. For example, Stein Rokkan and Richard Merritt (eds.), *Comparing Nations* (New Haven, Conn.: Yale University Press, 1966); Stein Rokkan and Suart Eisenstadt (eds.), *Building States and Nations* (Beverly Hills, Calif.: Sage, 1973); Stein Rokkan and Seymour Lipset (eds.), *Party Systems and Voter Alignments* (New York: Free Press, 1967); Erik Allardt and Stein Rokkan (eds.), *Mass Politics* (New York: Free Press, 1970). Also note

the contributions by Stein Rokkan and Nils Stjernqvist in Robert A. Dahl (ed.), *Political Oppositions in Western Democracies* (New Haven, Conn.: Yale University Press, 1966).

8. Of the 173 members of the North American Conference Group on Nordic Society only 16, or nine percent, list their major research interest as international relations or foreign policy. Similarly, the British Association for Scandinavian Studies in 1978 included 34 members of which merely 4 indicated a similar orientation.

9. Some examples are James Rosenau (ed.), *The Scientific Study of Foreign Policy* (New York: Free Press, 1971); idem (ed.), *Comparing Foreign Policies* (Beverly Hills, Calif.: Sage, 1974); idem (ed.), *In Search of Global Patterns* (New York: Free Press, 1976); Patrick McGowan (ed.), *Sage International Yearbook of Foreign Policy Studies*, Vols. 1– (Beverly Hills: Sage, 1973–   ); P. McGowan and H. Shapiro, *The Comparative Study of Foreign Policy* (Beverly Hills, Calif.: Sage, 1973); Charles Kegley et al. (eds.), *International Events and the Comparative Analysis of Foreign Policy* (Columbia: University of South Carolina Press, 1975); Maurice East et al. (eds.), *Why Nations Act* (Beverly Hills, Calif: Sage, 1978).

10. This method is discussed in Adam Przeworski and Henry Teune, *The Logic of Comparative Social Inquiry* (New York: John Wiley, 1970); Arend Lijphart, "The Comparable Cases Strategy in Comparative Research," *Comparative Political Studies* 8, No. 2 (July 1975): 158–177; Ib Faurby, "Premises, Promises, and Problems of Comparative Foreign Policy," *Cooperation and Conflict* 3(1976):139–162.

11. Faurby, op. cit., p. 154.

12. Rosenau (ed.), *Comparing Foreign Policies*, p. 22.

2

The Nordic Region in Twentieth-Century European Politics

Krister Wahlbäck

A Comparative Introduction

One way to characterize the position of the Nordic region in European politics is to compare the region with other areas in a reasonably similar situation. Are there any such areas? With some imagination we may conceive of the map of Europe as a triangle with three corners: the Nordic region, the Iberian peninsula, and the Balkans. These three regions share the geographic position of being attached to the continent, but situated at some distance from the European heartland. At the same time, they are vastly different in other respects.

A comparison of Europe's Nordic corner with the two other corners may help us to recognize some of the basic factors setting the Nordic region apart in the European context. These factors may be too elementary and too self-evident to be noticed by those who live in the Nordic area and take its situation for granted. In addition, many people, in the area and elsewhere, may resist a comparative perspective on areas they are not accustomed to seeing as comparable. Still, if we want to take a detached outsider's view of the Nordic area in European politics, it seems natural to start by observing how this region differs from the other two corners of Europe. Some of these differences are as follows.

1. *The Nordic countries never had colonies of any significance in the third world.* Thus, conservative and militaristic forces in their societies were not strengthened by the operation of colonies, as they were within the Iberian nations. The Nordic countries were also spared the agonies of decolonization that Portugal and Spain have experienced in recent decades.

2. *The Nordic countries were never subject to a foreign empire, as the Balkan countries were under Ottoman rule.* Thus they were able to develop as independent nations and change their political systems

9

gradually according to their own values and customs. Finland is a special case as it was part of the Russian empire from 1809 to 1917, though it retained a significant autonomy even under the czar.

3. The Nordic countries were never greatly influenced by feudalism. The peasants retained their political rights, dating back to the birth of the nations in early medieval times. Denmark was an exception, but it caught up with the others by the middle of the nineteenth century. This tradition contributed to a comparatively smooth transition to democracy. The industrial workers had the advantage of the democratic spirit generated by the peasants' continuous role in national politics for centuries.

This spirit was important also in the area of foreign relations. In contrast to both the Iberian and the Balkan nations, the Nordic countries developed a national consensus on democracy, which prevented foreign powers from exploiting political and social divisions to increase their influence. By the same token, foreign powers were not drawn into Nordic domestic struggles by some social group eager to bolster its position by leaning on foreign support.

Finland is again a special case. As part of the Russian empire it was particularly affected by the Bolshevik revolution. A Socialist revolt after the declaration of independence in December 1917 was followed by a hundred-days civil war in 1918, which was won by the White anti-Communists. The Reds were supported by the Soviets, the Whites by the Germans. The war left social scars for the future and opened some possibilities for the Soviets and the Germans to play on domestic divisions. Up to 1944 there was a rivalry for control over Finland in which the Soviets could exploit Red die-hards in the underground Communist party and the Germans could exploit White die-hards among Conservatives.

4. In contrast to the Iberian and Balkan nations, the Nordic countries—with high literacy, efficient administration, and the Protestant ethic of individual initiative—were able to industrialize rapidly at the end of the nineteenth century. Consensus on democracy as well as domestic stability stimulated economic expansion and development of the welfare state. Being rich and egalitarian, the Nordic countries have been more successful than most other small states in dealing confidently with powerful nations.

5. The Nordic region is divided among nations reasonably equal in size and power. Thus each is fairly willing to enter into regional cooperation, as witnessed by the vast network of Nordic organizations. It may safely be assumed that the different situation on the Iberian peninsula is partly due to Spain's dominance.

Regional cooperation in the Nordic area has not been hampered by territorial disputes comparable to those dividing the Balkan nations. There are no minority problems to complicate relations. The Swedish-speaking minority in Finland (some 6 percent of the population) has always had a prominent role in Finnish society and has never regarded itself as a Swedish irredenta. In the 1960s and 1970s many Finns moved to Sweden to find jobs, but they are scattered all over the country and have yet to develop a clear minority consciousness. For more than two centuries the only intra-Nordic border disputes have concerned islands of minor significance. The Swedes and Finns disputed the Åland Islands in 1918–1921, and the Danes and the Norwegians quarreled about Greenland in 1930–1933. Both issues were settled peacefully through international adjudication.

The Nordic harmony is certainly not perfect. For one thing, there are historical memories that still have some divisive effect. Norway was under Danish rule between 1380 and 1814, and it was forced into a union with Sweden that lasted from 1814 to 1905. Finland had never been independent before it was included in Sweden in the thirteenth century. It remained so until the Russian conquest of 1809, after which it was a grand duchy under the czar. Iceland came under Danish rule in the fourteenth century and gained full independence only in 1944.

Historically, Denmark and Sweden are the old and preponderant powers in the area. For centuries they were locked in a struggle for dominance, ending with a treaty in 1814 by which the Swedish king acquired Norway. The antagonism gradually gave way to a feeling of Scandinavian kinship in the middle of the nineteenth century, when Denmark came under pressure from Germany. Norway, Iceland, and Finland, the younger states, have felt the need to assert their identity apart from Denmark and Sweden, particularly in cultural and linguistic matters. Of course, national sensitivities are more acute in countries where the struggle for independence is well remembered.

Traces of such resentment and jealousy still exist. It is also a fact that the equality in size and power is only relative. Sweden is twice as powerful as each of its three neighbors on most indicators of national resources. It is sufficiently strong to irritate its neighbors, but not to dominate them. Its superiority was most marked in the two decades after the end of World War II, when the Swedes enjoyed the advantages of having stayed out of the war. The problem is gradually becoming less important as Sweden's neighbors—in particular the oil-rich Norwegians—are catching up.

To sum up, the outlook for regional cooperation in the Nordic area is much more promising than in the Iberian and Balkan regions. A reasonable and equitable distribution of power, an absence of territorial disputes, and strong cultural similarities combine to make possible the role of the Nordic states as pioneers in regional cooperation. Rather than consume their resources in fighting each other, these countries try to pool their action and influence, significantly increasing the relative power of the Nordic area as a whole.

6. *Two of the Nordic countries have long had common borders with big powers—Denmark with Germany and Finland with Russia.* Neither has clear-cut geographical or ethnological dividing lines to indicate a natural frontier to their big neighbors. Both have had to face crises and wars over border issues. Thus the Nordic area has been less fortunate than the Iberian peninsula, where the Pyrenees constitute a significant frontier-barrier to the single big power neighbor, France. The Nordic situation is rather similar to that of the Balkan countries, where both the Romanians and the Yugoslavs have had border conflicts with the Russians and the Italians.

7. *The Nordic area has only partially been able to keep out of the struggle for mastery of Europe during this century.* In World War I, Sweden, Denmark, and Norway all managed to stay neutral. In World War II, only Sweden did. The Nordic area was more directly affected by big power calculations. Both the Soviet attack on Finland in 1939 and the German attack on Norway and Denmark in 1940 were to some extent preventive wars. The Soviets feared that Finland might come under German influence, and the Germans feared that Norway might come under British influence. In the cold war, finally, the trend toward an increased role for the big powers in the area was reaffirmed. Norway, Denmark, and Iceland joined the North Atlantic Treaty Organization (NATO) in 1949 (although Norway and Denmark did not accept foreign bases in peacetime). Finland entered a limited security pact with the Soviet Union in 1948. Only Sweden remained without formal ties to any big power.

Thus, even if the Nordic countries have managed to limit the role of the big powers, the area has been increasingly affected by crossing Russian, German, and Anglo-American strategic interests. The Iberian countries have been more fortunate. They are placed well behind the French-Anglo-American front. They have been conveniently protected both from the Soviet ambitions in postwar Europe and from German ambitions before 1945 (except of course in 1936–1939, when the Italians and the Germans gave massive support to Franco in the civil war in the hope of using Spain against the Western powers in a future war).

Nevertheless, the Nordic area has not been as exposed as the Balkan countries have been. They were *all* drawn into both world wars, finding themselves in a cross fire of Austrian, German, Russian, Italian, and

British ambitions. In postwar Europe, Yugoslavian nonalignment after 1948 and Romanian assertiveness within the Warsaw Pact after 1958 have not sufficed to stabilize the region. There has not developed a situation of relatively low-level big power involvement of the kind that has prevailed in the Nordic area even after 1949. One reason for the difference is that Sweden, the central country in the Nordic region, was able to stay neutral during World War II and emerged richer, stronger, and more stable than ever in the postwar world. It served as a core of neutrality in the center of the region. Thus, it facilitated the efforts of its Nordic neighbors to limit their ties to the big powers.

The overall picture that emerges from the preceding pages is clear. On the whole, the Nordic countries have been exceptionally fortunate. They have not failed to exploit their comparative advantages over the two other corners of Europe. They have managed to preserve their independence, develop rich and egalitarian societies, handle their mutual relations in a cooperative way, and keep their region reasonably free from the tensions on the continent.

These experiences have produced a domestic political culture and an attitude to foreign policy that differ from those of the Iberian and Balkan nations. Today, public debate and official declarations display a strong belief in the need to change international conditions and in the prospects for doing so. There is much pleading for disarmament, development assistance to poor countries, and an end to big power dominance. There is not much discussion of structural obstacles to international change or of security problems for the Nordic region itself. Not unnaturally, the Nordic peoples project their experience of rational and peaceful reform onto the international scene. This inclination grew in the 1960s and 1970s when the memories of wartime experiences receded.

To what extent political leaders share this view of the world, rather than assert it for tactical reasons, is an open question. Also, there are subtle differences in outlook among the Nordic countries themselves, reflecting differences in their recent history. Finnish and Norwegian statements reveal some pessimism and concern for problems of national security. But they do not change the general picture.

The tenor of public debate on foreign policy is a factor of political importance. It is also an expression of historical experiences. Today's differences among the Nordic, Iberian, and Balkan ways of discussing foreign policy are a natural result of the differences in their social development and geographical situation.

Let us return to where we started. We decided to compare three regions vastly different but with something in common with respect to geopolitical situation. We based this decision on several considerations. Two of them not mentioned so far should be spelled out.

One is the conviction that comparison is an unsurpassable pedagogical technique. In this case it is a lever to make us look beyond the particular region we are interested in. It is a means to make us search for some more general perspectives on the Nordic region.

Another consideration concerns theory. When we selected the three regions to compare, we emphasized the common features in their geopolitical position. This implies a certain view as to what are the main determinants of foreign policy. Obviously, we consider geography to be one of them. We believe that it has a major explanatory value for analysis of long-term policies, particularly within subsystems of minor nations like the ones we have identified in Europe's three corners. This is a theoretical postulate and, as such, subjective. That is why it is important to spell it out.

In this introduction we have mapped out some characteristics of the Nordic region compared with two other European areas. In the process we have also indicated some of the differences between the five countries within the Nordic area. Our next task is to present a more comprehensive outline of the main foreign policy problems each of these five nations has confronted.

Five Countries in Search of Security

The question of survival and security is paramount in the foreign policy of almost all countries in Europe. The Nordic area is no exception. It may appear otherwise in peaceful times, which permit the nations to turn their attention to other concerns. But the basic question arises in each crisis as long as Europe remains split between competing alliances and political systems. It sets the framework for the nations' international activity. For this reason we shall stress in the outlines that follow problems related to the Nordic nations' search for security.

Norway

Norway is traditionally a pro-British nation, controlling an important coastline on the North Sea. Originally, its anglophile sentiments did not prevent it from wanting to keep out of the conflicts between the big powers. Neutrality was its immediate stance upon independence in 1905. In World War I it succeeded in staying neutral.

Norway faced a serious problem, however. The British wanted to complete the naval blockade of Germany by mining the territorial waters of Norway in the North Sea. This, of course, would have been a violation of Norwegian neutrality. The British knew that the Norwegians would protest, but hardly fight, to prevent British mine laying. The Germans suspected the British intentions and in fact would have liked to establish naval bases in Norway to improve their submarine warfare against the British. But the Germans lacked resources for an attack on Norway. Thus they could do little more than wait anxiously. In the end, the Norwegians yielded to British pressure and mined their waters themselves in 1918.

This crisis is worth consideration, particularly because it highlights the credibility problem of a neutral country. If a neutral country is too sympathetic to one of two opposing parties, it invites that party to take self-interested action against the neutral country on the assumption that it will never seriously fight back. Thus the neutral country is forced to make the choice it wished to avoid by neutrality. Further, it invites suspicion within the opposite camp, which may in fact be the first to strike.

However, the problem of neutrality never developed to that extent for Norway during World War I. Instead Norway emerged even more convinced of the merits of its position. Like the other Scandinavian countries, it viewed the League of Nations as a solution to its security problem and reduced its defense accordingly. But in World War II the old problem materialized again.

The British wanted to mine the Norwegian territorial waters to cut off German transports of Swedish iron ore along the Norwegian coast. (In winter the Norwegian port of Narvik functioned as an export outlet for the Kiruna iron ore fields in northernmost Sweden.) For a while in early 1940 the British hesitated to violate a neutral country and thus provoke a hostile reaction of public opinion in the "Big Neutral" at the time, i.e., the United States. The British also toyed with the idea of launching a military expedition to Finland, ostensibly to help the Finns in their Winter War against the Russians, but in fact to occupy the Swedish ore fields on the way. The Finns made peace in March 1940, however, and the pretext vanished. Finally the British decided to go ahead with the mine laying in early April 1940, expecting only a show of resistance on the part of the Norwegians.

On the German side, the navy had long advocated an attempt to seize Norway as a means of waging a more effective submarine war against the British. Hitler became receptive to this plan when he learned about the British designs against his vitally important iron ore supply route. This time the Germans had sufficient naval and air power for a daring surprise attack. The Norwegians, who had not mobilized the minimal military resources they had, still chose to fight, and the British attempted to improvise a military expedition to support them. These efforts failed, however, and after two months of fighting, the Norwegian king and government fled to London. Norway was occupied for five years. In exile the king became a much respected symbol of Norwegian resistance.

In 1948–1949 the Norwegians faced the choice of uniting with the British and Americans against the perceived Soviet threat or of staying neutral in a defense alliance with the Swedes and the Danes. Now the strategic situation was very different than it had been during the world wars. The Soviets had no navy of any importance. At least in the short run they could hardly constitute any military threat to the core area of Norway unless they first occupied Sweden, which would be a major operation. What officials in Oslo feared were political pressure and intimidation. Since 1945 Norway had had a short border with the Soviet Union in the far North. (From 1920 to 1944 a slice of Finnish territory had served as a buffer, but the Russians had seized this area during the war.) Thus the Soviets might apply local military pressure in a way the Germans had never been able to do. The Norwegian government felt that U.S. backing was necessary. The decision to join NATO also reflected moral and psychological uneasiness with conducting a strict and credible policy of neutrality in a conflict between the Soviet Union and Norway's old allies in the West.

In recent years Norway's strategic position in the Soviet-NATO conflict has in fact begun to resemble its old position in the German-British conflict. To the Soviets, with their expanding naval and air capabilities, the attractiveness of the Norwegian airports has increased. If they could use these airports, or at least deny them to the West, it would be much easier to fight NATO's lines of communication across the Atlantic and to protect their own bases in the Murmansk area on the Kola peninsula. Here, close to the Norwegian border, the Soviets have their powerful northern fleet, including most of their submarines with strategic missiles. To the West, accordingly, it is vital in the event of a war to deny the Russians access to the airports in Norway, using them instead to attack the Soviet bases in the Murmansk area and to contain the Soviet fleet in the Barents Sea.

In another respect there is no resemblance to either the 1918 or 1940 situation. With Norway in NATO, there will be no more watching in the twilight for who will be the first to violate Norwegian neutrality. The problem will rather be at which stage in a crisis the Norwegians would want to call on the Allied reinforcements that are planned.

The tradition of neutrality seems to resurface, however, in a basic Norwegian dilemma. It is sometimes difficult for Norway to decide on the extent of its participation in NATO programs. Some of the programs may be important for the alliance as a whole, but may complicate relations between Norway and the Soviet Union and make Norwegian territory more exposed in the event of a war. Norway wants to combine security and reassurance. One such reassurance of course was Norway's decision in 1949 to rule out the stationing of NATO troops on its territory unless it was threatened by attack. But to strike the right balance is a permanent concern. Military developments pose the problem in new forms. The government's decisions are often criticized. Some of the opponents would in fact prefer neutrality for Norway, although this preference is only implicit in their argument. Some of Norway's allies, however, resent what they regard as attempts to have full NATO security without full NATO solidarity.

Norway's problem has remained the same for a very long time, whether it is neutral or a NATO member, whether it fears Germany or Russia. Its coastline is too important. However, an entirely new factor has been added in the 1970s by the development of the law of the sea. Norway has established an enormous economic zone and begun to exploit the oil riches of the continental shelf. The common Norwegian-Soviet border in Finnmark has been extended far into the Barents Sea, and the exact delimitation remains to be settled. But it is still too early to tell how this will affect Norway's international position.

Denmark

Denmark fought against Prussia in 1848–1849 and in 1863–1864 to keep Slesvig and Holstein. These two provinces in the southern part of the Jutland peninsula had originally been attached to the Danish kingdom, and large parts of Slesvig had a Danish-speaking majority. Both provinces were lost. Denmark spent the next fifty years trying to establish a consistent policy toward its increasingly overwhelming neighbor, the German Reich under Bismarck and the kaiser. The Danish government on the whole preferred a policy of appeasement and adaptation. A serious defense effort and attempts to draw British, Russian, or Scandinavian support might have been possible alternatives, but they became more and more doubtful.

During World War I the Danes did their best to satisfy the Germans and convince them that Germany's essential security interests could be taken care of without occupying Denmark. Two of the approaches to the Baltic Sea that Denmark controlled were closed by Danish mine laying. This action in violation of the rules of neutrality was done to keep the British fleet out of the Baltic in accordance with German wishes.

After the German defeat, Denmark was able to get back most of the Danish-speaking parts of Slesvig in 1920 as a result of a plebiscite. The effects of fifty years of German efforts to germanize Slesvig could not be

undone, however, and most Danes accepted that a reasonable compromise was preferable in view of Denmark's long-term interests and the
inevitable resurgence of German might. In fact, when Hitler came to
power he avoided reopening this particular border settlement imposed
by the Treaty of Versailles. During the interwar period the Danes maintained a very small defense, which was not intended to repel a serious
enemy attack. They studiously avoided any foreign policy moves, either
in the League of Nations or in their relations with the British or their
Scandinavian neighbors, that Berlin might resent. Nevertheless, German
control of Denmark was necessary for the attack on Norway, and in April
1940 Denmark was occupied in a matter of hours. The Danish king and
government accepted the occupation under protest, and it was not until
August 1943 that the legal government definitely resigned. To the end of
World War II the regular Danish administration functioned well.

Denmark emerged from the war without the prestige of gallant Norway; however, it was comparatively undamaged from sabotage by
resistance groups or from German exploitation or repression. After much
internal debate the Danes resisted the temptation to improve on the 1920
border with Germany. They realized the risk of creating resentment
among the Germans.

The strategic importance of Greenland to the United States had
become evident during World War II and was a major reason why the
United States was anxious to see Denmark join NATO in 1948–1949. The
Danes felt the impact of Soviet might more intensely than the
Norwegians. Soviet troops in Germany were very close to the vital parts
of Denmark. But the Danes were also more doubtful than the
Norwegians about the Western capacity to support Denmark militarily
in case of need. Of course, Denmark's geography and topography make
her particularly vulnerable to an attack. Thus, the Danes joined NATO
with more internal doubts than the Norwegians. In general, Denmark
has remained a somewhat less wholehearted member of the alliance than
Norway.

At the same time, it would seem that Denmark's historical security
problem has been taken care of in a rather favorable way, perhaps better
than at any previous period after the rise of Germany. Denmark has no
common border with the power it now fears, the Soviet Union. Its main
supporting power, the United States, is far away and thus poses no threat
to Danish identity. Its traditional enemy, Germany, is divided. The
Federal Republic is its ally, but only as a partner in a vast alliance system
to which they both belong. The pressure from Denmark's rich and
energetic neighbor to the south remains in the economic sphere, but its
military aspect has been contained.

Iceland

Iceland is very different from the other Nordic countries. It displays many of the characteristics of a third world country in a Nordic cultural setting. A remote era of greatness still stimulates national self-confidence. Beginning in the ninth century, Iceland was the center of a flourishing material and literary culture for a few hundred years. But a drastic decline began well before Iceland came under Danish rule in the fourteenth century. The Icelanders remained poor, dependent upon Danish trade monopolies and ravaged by catastrophes and diseases up to this century. A kind of home rule was gradually granted by the Danes, but independence was not attained until 1944, when Denmark was under German occupation.

The economy is still wholly dependent on one single resource—fish—which is unreliable in quantity and subjected to volatile prices. The ups and downs of the economy have been dramatic, and inflation rampant. Many third world countries have experienced conflicts with the West after nationalizing their natural resources. The Icelanders have had similar controversies with Western powers—in particular Britain—as they have gradually expanded the exclusive fishery zone around Iceland. They have tried to protect the resources on which their livelihood is based and to reserve as much of these as possible for themselves.

The Icelanders are proud of the vitality of their modern culture and of their distinct Nordic character. At the same time, they are situated far away from the Nordic core area. Thus in matters of security they can receive no assistance from their Nordic friends. To the extent that they perceive a threat from the Soviet Union, they are completely dependent upon U.S. support. The central problem of Iceland's foreign policy is to reconcile an intense national identity with the geographical position as a stepping stone between the United States and Europe. The half-reassuring, half-threatening U.S. presence symbolizes the problem.

The Americans have maintained a military base at Keflavík outside the capital, Reykjavík, since July 1941. The membership in NATO since 1949 relieves Icelanders of any expenditure for military purposes. Their contribution to the alliance consists of a few square miles for the base facilities. The base, in fact, generates substantial economic benefit through the purchasing power of some 4,000 resident Americans. However, a substantial minority of the Icelandic population perceives the presence of such a relatively large number of foreigners (the entire native population being only 230,000) as a threat to the indigenous culture.

For NATO, the Keflavík base is vital for peacetime surveillance of crucial sea areas. In case of war it is necessary for defending the Greenland–Iceland–Great Britain barrier against Soviet attempts to project naval power into the Atlantic. If Keflavík could not be maintained, there would have to be some substitute. The Norwegian policy of not accepting peacetime NATO bases may in fact depend on Iceland maintaining the opposite policy. Thus Iceland is important for the entire Nordic security pattern.

Finland

Finland has had the same overriding foreign policy problem as Denmark: to develop an acceptable relationship to an adjoining big power, in this case Russia. But Finland has also had to cope with the problem of a stronger neighbor to the west, Sweden.

When Finland became independent in 1917, its Swedish problem was largely a matter of history and psychology. For 600 years before 1809, Finland had been part of the Swedish realm. This had determined the character of Finnish society and culture in a way the young nation found difficult to recognize. The Western values that set Finland apart from its eastern neighbor and that it was proud to represent had, after all, been implanted through Swedish rule.

Moreover, a Swedish-speaking minority remained in Finland. It still held an important position, and the Swedish language was recognized as one of the two languages of the bilingual Finnish state. Finnish-speaking nationalists, however, wanted to curtail or destroy this arrangement. The language issue grew to be prominent in Finnish domestic politics during the interwar period. Most Finnish politicians were unwilling to fulfill the ambitions of the nationalists partly through fear of Swedish reaction. Thus the relationship to Sweden was linked to a most sensitive domestic issue.

Finland's relationship with Russia in the Swedish era had consisted of centuries of border wars, until the Russian conquest of 1809 transferred Finland to the other side of the border. Czar Alexander I granted Finland considerable autonomy. The nation probably was better able to develop its own culture than would have been possible within the Swedish realm. The czar was repaid with the loyalty of the Finns. From the 1890s on, however, Russian nationalists persuaded the czar to embark on a policy of Russification and destruction of Finnish autonomy. This process was well advanced by the time of the Russian defeat in World War I, which made possible the Finnish declaration of independence on December 6, 1917.

Alone among major Russian parties, the Bolsheviks were willing to recognize Finnish independence. But Bolshevik support of the Reds during the Finnish civil war from January to May 1918 more than offset any goodwill gained. There was also a conflict over the border in Karelia. It was settled by a compromise in 1920, but irredentism among Finnish right-wing groups and Soviet support to the Communist underground in Finland continued to damage the relationship.

The Finns rejected the Danish model of an adaptive foreign policy toward their big power neighbor. Instead they opted for a stance of rather stiff independence. Some Finns even wanted to enlist German support. Any such signs touched a raw nerve on the Russian side. The Germans had intervened in the Finnish civil war in the spring of 1918 and tried to use Finland as a bridgehead against northwestern Russia. With Hitler's rise to power any indications of Finnish links with the Germans were given intense attention in Moscow.

However, the Finnish government never contemplated a German orientation during the 1930s. Instead they wanted to extend cooperation with Sweden to defense matters. The Swedes thought that a Finnish orientation toward neutral Sweden would serve to allay Soviet fears by keeping Finland at a safe distance from Germany. Stalin, however, decided that Finland had to be brought into the Soviet sphere of interest. He gained Hitler's agreement in the pact of August 1939. In October 1939, Stalin asked for a few slices of Finnish territory, but also for a naval base in southwestern Finland. Granting him such a base would have brought Finland out of the circle of Nordic neutrals. When the Finns refused, the Red Army attacked. Stalin picked a prominent Finnish Communist, O. V. Kuusinen, who had lived in Moscow since 1918, and appointed him as head of a "people's government" of Finland. Kuusinen was scheduled to enter Helsinki after two weeks of fighting. After two months of costly battles, Stalin dropped Kuusinen and began to negotiate with the government in Helsinki. After another six weeks, the Winter War ended in March 1940 by Finland ceding Karelia, a tenth of her territory, as well as the naval base Stalin wanted. But the Finns retained their independence, demonstrating to Moscow how well they could fight for it.

When Hitler prepared to attack the Soviet Union, the Finns joined him. Without concluding a formal alliance with Germany they waged the so-called Continuation War of June 1941 to September 1944 in order to get Karelia back and confirm Finland's fully independent position toward the Soviet Union. Instead, in the end they had to accept the same territorial losses as in 1940 and to enter a new relationship with the Soviets. Again, a Soviet naval base was established in southwestern Finland.

In 1948 a Finnish-Soviet pact of mutual cooperation was concluded. The pact recognized a special Soviet interest in Finland by its two main provisions: the possibility of Soviet military assistance to Finland in case of an attack from Germany or countries allied to Germany and consultations between the two parties in case of a threat of such an attack. The defense of Finland remained of course the task of the Finnish armed forces, and the pact recognized Finland's wish to stay outside of the conflicts between the big powers. The Finnish policy of reconciliation was based on the assumption that Soviet interest in Finland was defensive and strategic, not offensive and ideological. The Finns would be able to keep their domestic system provided they took Soviet security needs as perceived by Moscow into account. The proclaimed goal was to gain the confidence of their big eastern neighbor. In short, the Finns opted for a "Danish" policy at the very moment when the Danes were finally able to abandon it.

The Finns have pursued this policy for more than thirty-five years, first under President J. K. Paasikivi and then under his successor U. K. Kekkonen. It has succeeded in its main goal. Finland has developed into a rich, modern Nordic and Western democracy, in full economic and cultural contact with the West, while extending far-reaching cooperation with the Soviet Union. In addition, there have been some striking successes. In 1955, the Soviets returned the naval base to Finland. This made it possible for the Finns to embark upon a policy of neutrality. In 1956, the Finns were also able to join the Nordic Council, the organization for economic, social, and cultural cooperation that the four other Nordic countries established in 1953.

Nevertheless, there have been some strains in the Soviet-Finnish relationship. The most important occurred in the autumn of 1961, when the Soviets asked for consultations in accordance with the 1948 pact, citing West German activities as a threat of attack on Finland. However, Khrushchev eventually agreed to postpone the consultations, which in fact never took place.

With the improvement of relations between Moscow and Bonn since the late 1960s, the traditional spillover to Finland of the Russo-German conflict has become much less important. The problem for the future is rather the repercussions of NATO's role in Norway. It may be difficult to maintain an agreed balance between the Soviet buildup on the Kola peninsula and the Norwegian efforts to improve NATO's capacity to deploy rapid reinforcements in Norway. For Finland, situated between the Soviet Union to the east and Scandinavian neighbors to the west, even minor irritants in Soviet-Scandinavian relations are cause for concern.

In the 1970s, the most publicized aspect of Soviet-Finnish relations was what some Western commentators call Finlandization. This term is shorthand for the complex problem of Finnish sensitivity to Soviet thinking. On such issues as the composition of the Finnish government, the tenor of press comments, and the bias of foreign policy initiatives, it is no doubt possible to make a case that Soviet points of view have sometimes had their influence. But the larger issue must be seen in proper perspective. Finland is situated close to vital parts of a superpower that has a different political and economic system. Finland was once part of that power, and not long ago Finland lost two wars against it. With such a background, is it really unreasonable for Finland to pay attention to Soviet views? Still, there is a lingering suspicion even among Finns that more regard than necessary is sometimes paid to Soviet wishes. Such suspicions by their very nature cannot be proved wrong. They are bound to cause a certain malaise in a people as proud as the Finns.

Generally, it may be said that Finland has submitted itself to an exacting standard by claiming a foreign policy of neutrality. This means that Finnish policies are compared with those of other neutrals like Sweden or Switzerland that do not have a long common border with a superpower or a historically complicated relationship with it. Nevertheless, the Soviets have accepted Finland's efforts to pursue a policy of neutrality, implicitly acknowledging that there are certain kinds of proposals they cannot put forward to the Finns.

Sweden

The problems of Sweden's foreign policy have largely been indicated in the preceding discussion of the problems of its neighbors. Sweden has often found itself "in the eye of the cyclone," watching the smaller countries to the east and west being drawn into wars or entering into cooperation with different big powers. Its instinct has been to try to keep out of conflicts, to sustain neutrality, and to maintain as much Nordic cooperation as possible while waiting for better times.

In World War I, Swedish neutrality had a pro-German tilt. Since the loss of Finland in 1809, Sweden had lived with Russia as a close neighbor. The Russians controlled the Åland Islands not far from Stockholm. In a Russo-German war, Sweden could not wish for a Russian victory. As Denmark and Norway had very different problems, the most the three countries could hope for was to avoid ending up in different camps. In this regard they succeeded. There was also some cooperation in facing their main common problem: how to uphold the rights of the neutrals to trade with both camps in the war as the British tightened the blockade against Germany.

With both Russia and Germany defeated in World War I, with Finland independent and Denmark strengthened, the position of Sweden and of the whole region was better than anyone had dared to hope. Some

Swedes thought that this favorable Nordic situation ought to be consolidated by a defense alliance among the four countries. But at the end of the 1930s these countries feared different powers, and they believed in different methods to divert the threat. The Norwegians felt secure on their own; the Danes appeased the Germans; the Finns opposed the Russians; and the Swedes, who feared both the Germans and the Russians, pursued a cautious and armed neutrality.

Only the Finns were eager to cooperate militarily with Sweden. They seemed prepared to adjust to Sweden's idea of strict neutrality. However, it turned out that Stalin thought that Swedish-Finnish cooperation was contrary to Soviet interests. The Swedes tried to make him understand that this view was shortsighted. When they failed, they decided that even a limited military cooperation with Finland would be too risky.

During the two Soviet-Finnish wars of 1939–1940 and 1941–1944, the Swedes followed basically the same policy. Sweden refused to intervene militarily in Finland, but supported it with arms, bread, and money. Sweden also tried to mediate a Soviet-Finnish peace and limit the German influence in Helsinki. On the whole, this policy succeeded in both wars. Sweden did nothing to support the Norwegians upon the German attack in the spring of 1940. Germany was a more formidable power than Russia, and the Norwegians were less effective in defending themselves than the Finns. Surrounded by German divisions from June 1940 on, Sweden made some concessions to German demands, mainly by granting them rights to use Swedish railways for transport of soldiers on leave from Norway to Germany and back. This proved enough to avoid a German attack, but also enough to alienate the Norwegians. The Swedes played for time, rearming and waiting for a restoration of the balance of power when the Soviets and the Americans entered the war. On the whole, this policy succeeded as well. Of course, the decisive factors were always the course of the war and the interests of big powers. For Stockholm, the task was to assess correctly the narrow margin these factors provided for safeguarding Sweden's independence.

When the cold war between the United States and the Soviet Union began in 1947, the Swedes made a more determined effort than in the 1930s to keep their Nordic neighbors together by offering a defense alliance. Finland was not included this time; its special relationship with the Soviet Union was formalized in April 1948, just before the discussions with the Norwegians and Danes started. Sweden was spurred to abandon isolated neutrality only by the fear that its western neighbors might otherwise seek security by joining the big powers. If they did, this would transmit international tensions to Sweden's borders and make it more difficult to stay out of a future war. However, the Norwegians preferred to accept the U.S. offer to join the Atlantic alliance. A neutral

Scandinavian alliance the Swedes offered was not considered to provide enough security in a world of superpowers. The Danes followed the Norwegians into NATO.

The Swedes continued their own policy of neutrality as a matter of course. They thought that the strategically attractive parts of the Nordic region were situated outside Sweden's borders. Thus, Sweden would stand a chance to keep out of another war, at least for a time, if by maintaining a strong defense it ensured that the costs of violating its territory would be substantial. Further, most Swedes were convinced that if Sweden joined NATO, it would divide the Nordic area sharply between the blocs and extend the confrontation line on the European continent to the north. It would jeopardize Finland's attempt to limit its ties to the Soviet Union and keep its domestic system intact. Even many Swedes who were inclined to let ideology decide foreign policy were reluctant to run such risks.

Finally, neutrality had succeeded in two world wars. Public opinion would not easily switch to something new. In the United States, the traditional faith in isolationism was at this time overcome by the realization that any balance of power without the United States was inconceivable. By contrast, a small power like Sweden was free to carry on a policy that was largely based on the same premises as the former U.S. position. On the whole, these considerations would seem to be as relevant in 1980 as they were in 1950.

The Nordic Pattern Reconsidered

Let us return to the overall perspective once again and consider the present situation in the light of trends in the past and of prospects for the future. Since the early 1950s, the pattern of Nordic security has remained basically unchanged. It is often called the Nordic balance. What does this term mean?

It was first used after the Finnish-Soviet "note crisis" in 1961. After the Soviet note requested consultations according to the 1948 treaty, the Norwegian government hinted that if such consultations were to result in a change of Finland's military situation, the Norwegians would have to reappraise their own policy of refusing NATO bases in peacetime. A few days later Khrushchev met with Kekkonen and agreed to postpone the proposed consultation. The joint communiqué stated that Kekkonen had stressed the risk of "war psychosis" in the Scandinavian countries if consultations were to take place. In a sense, this confirmed the notion that the Soviet-Finnish relationship must be shaped with due regard to repercussions in other parts of the Nordic area.

Thus, the term *Nordic balance* refers to a politically favorable but

delicate situation that demands care and attention in order to be maintained. It does *not* denote a military balance. For one thing, the correlation of military forces between the two blocs cannot be calculated on the
basis of the situation in the Nordic area alone. Instead, it depends on the
military strength of the Nordic members of NATO on the one hand and
on the military strength of that part of the Soviet Union bordering the
Nordic area on the other. This correlation of forces is heavily weighted in
favor of the Soviet Union, which is not unnatural. The Soviet Union is a
big power with some of its most vital areas situated in the northwest. A
local imbalance is considered acceptable in Norway and Denmark, provided that the overall balance in Europe and between the superpowers is
preserved. But how great can this imbalance be? The parties have
managed to maintain an implicit understanding. The increasing importance of the Kola base complex since the 1960s has made this task
gradually more difficult, as the Soviet conventional forces in the base
area and on the sea have increased in power. If the U.S.–USSR détente of
the early 1970s were in the future to weaken further, some observers fear
that an escalation of military measures by NATO in Norway and by the
Soviet Union on the Kola peninsula would result. Some even fear that
such a development might "spill over" into Soviet moves to establish
some form of peacetime military cooperation with Finland. But it is
unlikely that the Russians would see their interests served by a move that
would provoke major reactions in Scandinavia and Western Europe.

Sweden faces the traditional responsibility of a neutral state. It has to
maintain a sufficiently strong defense to deter any temptation on the part
of the big powers to use Swedish territory or airspace in an armed conflict over Scandinavia. Obviously, the weight of this responsibility is affected by developments in northern Europe.

Sweden may also have a responsibility that derives from the present
situation of northern Europe as a low tension region. Both superpowers
maintain modest military profiles in the region. On the Western side, this
is demonstrated by the recognized Norwegian and Danish policy with
regard to foreign bases and nuclear weapons. On the Soviet side, it is illustrated not only by Moscow's acquiescence to Finland's view that
peacetime military cooperation with the Soviet Union would be incompatible with its international position, but also by the nature of the
Soviet buildup on the Kola peninsula. Its massive naval forces based in
this area are vital for maintaining a global balance of power with the
United States. However, considering the importance of the Kola bases,
Soviet ground forces assigned to secure the bases are not very large.

Even if both superpowers maintain modest military profiles in the
region, their efforts to do so may not represent self-evident policies on

their part. That Sweden constitutes a well-defended area between the blocs may be an important factor. Military planners in Brussels and Moscow know that vital parts of the territories under their responsibility in northern Europe will not easily be attacked by the other side, as long as Sweden is able to repel any attempts to use its land and airspace. The more the Swedes want to preserve the present situation in the region, the more they may have to take care to preserve their military capabilities.

The increasing importance of the Soviet Kola base complex since the early 1960s is the biggest change in the immediate security environment of the Nordic area in this century. Before World War I, there was a continuous growth of the German navy and of the capacity of its bases at the North Sea, but this growth mainly affected Denmark. The Kola bases have moved the lines of confrontation of the big powers to the northern parts of the Nordic area in a way that is historically new and that affects the entire area. In that sense, Admiral Gorchakov of the Soviet navy has been more sinister than Admiral Tirpitz of the kaiser's navy as a symbol of big power ambitions.

The Nordic countries do not live in fear of Soviet designs, however. In fact, they have some confidence in Soviet common sense and capacity to look beyond the immediate situation when it comes to northern Europe. This confidence is based on the historical record.

It is true that the record is by no means flawless. Stalin made a number of fateful mistakes. In the 1930s he overestimated pro-German sentiment in Finland and underestimated Finnish determination to defend their independence. By launching the Winter War he set in motion a sequence of events in the Nordic region in 1939–1940 that ended in the German occupation of Norway and Denmark. This experience, in turn, made the Norwegian and the Danish peoples willing to abandon neutrality and join NATO in 1949. In addition, Stalin scared the Scandinavians by a rather ominous policy toward Finland in 1948. Thus, he further prepared the ground for U.S. military influence in western Scandinavia, which has developed into a major headache for Moscow.

Since then, however, Soviet leaders seem to have learned the risks of challenging the status quo in northern Europe. Besides, the mistakes committed should not conceal the fact that Soviet ambitions have been comparatively modest in the Nordic area. This becomes clear if we take a long-term view. Since 1910, Russia has risen from the rank of one of six major European powers to the status of one of two superpowers. Compared to the czar's empire in 1910, Brezhnev's realm has advanced in central Europe from Warsaw to Rostock and Prague, and in southern Europe from Odessa to Budapest and Sofia. In northern Europe, however, it has receded. Finland has become independent. In addition, Norway and Denmark, which were friendly neutrals at the czar's time, are now allied to Russia's main adversary.

Nations learn by their own experiences, not by those of other peoples. For the Nordic governments, the decisive factor is Soviet attitudes toward the Nordic region, not toward other parts of Europe. The Soviet leaders may in fact have accepted the present Nordic situation. They may realize that if by careless actions they were to force a more clear-cut division of the Nordic area between the military blocs along the lines on the Continent, it would not be to their advantage. In the final analysis, this should serve to deter any temptation to challenge the present Nordic security pattern. By the same logic it cannot be taken for granted that the United States would necessarily dislike such Soviet actions against Finland that would move the other Nordic states closer to the West. In fact, in 1948–1950, when many Americans wanted Sweden to join NATO, one reason was the feeling that even if this would mean Soviet control of Finland, the net effect would be positive to the West. However, this was long ago, and before Finland's international position had been strengthened. Also, with thirty years' tradition of Nordic stability as a recognized part of the European situation, there are important checks against radical change. So the overall picture is mixed. Gradual changes are taking place that demand increasing skill and care on the part of all powers concerned in order to preserve the pattern of Nordic security. Still, this pattern is based on rather solid historical traditions and long-term interests. It should be sufficiently established to withstand the strains of the foreseeable future.

Five Nations Facing Interdependence

So far we have dealt with problems of security in the traditional sense. There is another kind of challenge to security, however. In the jargon of the 1970s, it is usually referred to as interdependence. This is a modern euphemism, but the underlying reality is as old as the first peaceful contacts between big and small powers. The problem is well illustrated by the Nordic region.

The Nordic nations want to be rich and open societies. They want to concentrate their production in the narrow sectors where they enjoy comparative advantages on the world market. Thus, they believe in free trade. They also want to take advantage of the cultural and technological vitality and inventiveness that some great nations display. Thus they believe in free exchange of ideas and knowledge.

They have developed these convictions gradually, as they have come to realize that they belong to the fortunate nations that stand to gain by free international exchange. However, some of the Nordic countries,

primarily Iceland, and to some extent Norway and Finland, were less enthusiastic than the others. They had less favorable competitive positions,
and they retained somewhat stronger defensive nationalist reflexes. But
on the whole, the Nordic nations clearly belong to those who want to
open their borders to the challenge of international contact and competition.

During the 1970s, however, they have become increasingly conscious
of the costs of throwing themselves open to foreign influence. One issue
often raised in academic and intellectual debate concerns how this influence affects a people's freedom to decide how its own society should
develop. Private industry in the Nordic countries has to operate under
conditions about as favorable as in other Western countries, if it is to be
competitive and keep capital and talent in the country. But what remains
then of the prospects for developing a society different from the average
Western type, of creating a society that is, for example, more socialist,
decentralized, or ecologically balanced? Such alternatives can be realized
only gradually and in a rather marginal fashion if they are to be compatible with the interests of industry. Of course, the voters are free to
disregard these limits. But they will hardly do so if they fear that in the
process private industry will suffer and they themselves will have to
forgo amenities to which they have grown accustomed under, as some
would say, "the corruptive influence of Western capitalism."

From the point of view of foreign policy, however, a related aspect is
more important. The Nordic countries have limited resources and an
eclectic culture, and they confront big powers with vast markets, giant
corporations, and pervasive cultural strength. Even in such relatively
strong and confident nations as the Nordic countries, the influence acquired by the big Western powers can be overwhelming. In fact, this
becomes by far the most pressing security problem for those who would
define a nation's security as the protection of its social and industrial
structure and its cultural heritage against "undue foreign influence." Of
course it is always a question of degree. In today's Europe perfect isolation is as impossible as a total dismantling of the instruments for controlling the exchange with other nations. Even for an ambitious middle-
sized power like France under de Gaulle it was a question of striking a
balance. But this does not make the problem any less important.

However, the issue easily escapes the attention of the public. It is a
creeping process that is difficult to pin down and does not depend on formal public rulings. At the same time, the issue raises very basic value
questions concerning attitudes toward internationalism versus isolationism and toward the Anglo-American culture that has dominated the
postwar world.

If the voters really resented present trends, some of the main political parties would no doubt make it a prominent issue. Iceland is the only country where this has happened. Otherwise this is not a question the political parties are eager to address. It may be a divisive issue for almost all of them. Only on the extreme Left can it be dealt with in a manner consistent with general policy. Planned economy, strict control of trans- actions with foreign countries, orientation toward the COMECON area and the third world—such traditional left-wing advice may be said to promote an increased sovereignty, at least in a certain sense and under certain conditions.

But sovereignty or security is not the only goal of society. This would lead to a garrison state isolated from the rest of the world. A high stan- dard of living and free exchange with other nations are objectives that most peoples are unwilling to curtail in order to attain the rather abstract aim of increased sovereignty. Also, transnational ties may be seen as in- struments for peace. They increase the risks for any state contemplating defying the international community. Finally, to engage fully and con- fidently in international exchange may be a means to promote a nation's culture and values abroad.

The result of these conflicting impulses is a vague declaratory policy and an interpretation of security that in practice permits a further under- mining of sovereignty in the absolute sense. The dilemma is existential, but it is not very different for the Nordic nations than for other small states in Western Europe. However, in two respects their situation is a special one.

First, the alternative of regional, Nordic arrangements is available in some instances as a means to reduce the impact of Western influence. By combining their resources the Nordic countries may establish a "home market" of sufficient size to provide a basis for these arrangements. Formerly, such proposals were sometimes regarded with suspicion in the smaller Nordic countries, particularly in Norway. Many people feared Swedish designs to dominate its neighbors by keeping them within a limited Nordic framework. Today, this is much less of a problem.

Second, Sweden and Finland as neutrals have to consider carefully the extent to which they are interdependent with big NATO countries. They have to make credible their capacity to withstand Western political pressure by economic and other means in time of crisis or war.

Sweden, with its tradition of surviving for years world wars close to its borders, is making elaborate and expensive preparations for another period of isolation. Its society must be ready to function without much exchange with other countries. This readiness, however, is becoming in- creasingly difficult to arrange for more than a few weeks, as dem- onstrated in a number of "vulnerability studies" in recent years. Yet a future war would hardly last for more than a few weeks, and even if it did it would no doubt be less unpleasant to starve than to fight. It is true that drawn-out crisis periods may precede a war and that NATO may then contemplate economic sanctions to force Sweden to grant some political or military concessions. But it seems unlikely that NATO would conclude that such attempts would be effective. Besides, the alliance might well be unable to enforce and coordinate sanctions among member countries.

Finland does not quite share the Swedish belief in the chances of staying out of a war. Its pact with the Soviet Union indicates its sensitive strategic position. There is another way in which the Finnish situation differs from that of Sweden. About 20 percent of Finland's foreign trade is with the Soviet Union (compared to some 4 percent in Sweden's case). Foreign observers often suspect the Soviets of using trade as an instrument of pressure. However, they are unlikely to apply it in this case. The Soviets are probably as dependent on Finnish industrial products as the Finns are on Soviet commodities. In addition, the Soviets have consistently presented the Soviet-Finnish relationship as an attractive example to the world, not least in its economic aspects. It represents an investment that the Soviets are unlikely to jeopardize.

The emergence of the European Communities (EC) raised the problem of interdependence in a new way for all the Nordic countries. They had to consider membership in an organization aiming not only at interdependence but at integration. The alternative was to stay outside the arena where decisions of major importance to them would be made in any case and thus abandon the idea of trying to influence these decisions from within.

The Swedes finally opted for the second alternative. However, the argument was not that Sweden opposed economic integration, but that the foreign policy coordination as well as the economic and monetary union envisaged by the Common Market countries would be detrimental to the credibility of neutrality.

For Finland, membership was out of the question. The main problem was to convince the Soviet Union that the Finns had to secure the same tariffs for Finnish exports as their Swedish and Norwegian competitors. The Soviets finally agreed, and a free trade agreement was signed between Finland and the EC. For Norway and Denmark there were no foreign policy obstacles to full membership. The economic arguments in favor of full membership were stronger for Denmark, however, with its substantial exports of agricultural products; agriculture is of course the most strictly regulated sector of the economy of most European states. In both Denmark and Norway the opponents argued mainly in terms of

safeguarding national independence by staying out of the EC. They won
the referendum in Norway, but lost in Denmark. The Norwegian
government signed a free trade agreement, and Denmark became the
only Nordic member country of the EC.

Less than a decade has passed since these events. It is too early to tell
whether the different decisions the Nordic countries have made with
regard to EC membership have really had much impact on their degree of
dependence. In any case, the problem of reconciling unavoidable dependence with national values remains.

Small is beautiful, according to a theory popular among sociologists
who stress the advantages of a manageable society. But small nations
face difficult tests with regard to traditional security and the challenge of
interdependence. Max Jakobson, the Finnish diplomat and analyst,
recently asked which of his country's two neighbors would prove to be
more dangerous to the national identity of the Finnish people in the
1980s, "the conservative superpower behind the closed Eastern border or
the bright lights of the open society in the West." And his final comment
applies to all the Nordic nations:

> The military virtues displayed by the Finnish people in the 1940s have no
> relevance to defense against the threat of a gradual dilution of national
> identity in a world dominated by a few powerful entities able to exploit the
> new "supertechnologies." The survival of Finnish independence will de-
> pend on the ability of the Finns to continue to maintain the high degree of
> social cohesion, self-reliance and originality of national spirit they have
> shown in the past decades.

3
Decision Structures and Domestic Sources of Nordic Foreign Policies

Ib Faurby

Introduction

The foreign policy of any state is the product of external as well as internal demands and influences. The specific nature and the relative weight of these demands and influences can vary from one state to another and from one issue to another.

The purpose of this chapter is twofold. First, it describes the domestic institutions through which internal and external demands are processed and the foreign policy decisions that are made in the Nordic countries. Second, it discusses at a very general level the main domestic influences on the making of foreign policy in the five countries. But because foreign policy is the result of external as well as internal factors, the perspective of this chapter cannot alone provide explanations of the countries' foreign policies. Such explanations must be sought in the chapters on specific foreign policy issue areas.

It is also important at the outset to emphasize that it is misleading to talk about *the* foreign policy–making process. There is not a single process, but a number of different policymaking processes depending on the issue in question. Thus, the institutions mentioned in the following discussion are not all activated every time a foreign policy decision is made. The foreign policy–making process varies with the substance and the importance of the issue in question and with the time available for decision making.

The details of these processes can only be accounted for through specific case studies, which are outside the scope of the present essay. When a concrete decision is referred to in the following pages, it is only for the purpose of illustrating a general phenomenon or a deviant case.

At a more general level, however, we can say that there are governmental bodies formally responsible for making or assisting in the making
of foreign policy decisions and that various "outside" groups try to influence those decisions. Although the distinction may be difficult to draw
in practice, the "inside" groups consist of persons and institutions endowed with formal responsibility, through law or politico-
administrative practice, for the making of policy within the issue area in
question. They will characteristically be the cabinet, a minister and his
department, and in certain cases the parliament or one of its committees.
The extent to which the formally responsible persons or groups dominate
the decision-making process depends partly on formal rules and partly
on the nature of the issue.

If outside groups are strongly affected by the decision in question
and/or the issue generates widespread disagreement, the dominance of
the formally responsible decision makers tends to decline. Yet the less
time available for decision making, the less likely is the direct involvement of outside groups, though their interests and views may be known
to the decision makers and may still be taken into consideration.

At this very general level we can, using Stein Rokkan's terminology,
distinguish between two main "channels" of influence on the decision
makers, i.e., the "numeric" (or "democratic") channel (voters-parties-
parliament-cabinet) and the "corporate" channel (members-interest
organizations-bureaucracy-cabinet).[1] Whether one or the other of these
channels or both are activated again depends on the issue in question,
i.e., who is affected by the decision and in what way. The more
specifically an issue affects a limited group, e.g., the producers of a certain product, the more likely it is that the importance of the corporate
channel will increase and the role of the numeric channels decrease.
However, the stronger and more widespread disagreement concerning
policy, the more likely that the numeric channel will dominate over the
corporate channel; thus the issue becomes "politicized."[2]

The major part of this chapter is a general description of the formal
decision-making structures and the potential domestic actors in the making of Nordic foreign policies. It is organized into four main topics: the
executive; parliaments and parties; economic structure and interest
representation; and press and public opinion. In each section the
characteristic features of and the main differences among the five countries, considered to be of some importance in the making of foreign
policy, are discussed. Naturally, no single chapter can deal with every
feature of the decision-making machinery nor with the activities of every
group trying to influence the process.

The Executive

Historically, the conduct of foreign policy has in all countries been regarded as a special executive privilege. The traditional dominance of the executive in the making of foreign policy is, of course, also reflected in the constitutions and political practices of the Nordic countries. Even today, foreign policy is to some extent considered a special issue area, where different procedures apply than those in the making of purely domestic policies and where the executive still has a dominant position.

Heads of State

The three Scandinavian countries are constitutional monarchies, whereas Finland and Iceland are republics with presidents serving as heads of state. Parliamentary democracy was established in the three Scandinavian countries during the second part of the nineteenth and the early years of the twentieth century. There are cases, however, of royal influence on foreign policy making after this time period, particularly during times of crisis. Examples can be found in all three countries during the two world wars. But in the post–World War II era, the period primarily dealt with in this book, the monarchs could not be considered as belonging to the institutions and groups involved in the making of foreign policy. Monarchs have only certain representative functions vis-à-vis foreign governments.

Since its final independence from Denmark in 1944, Iceland's head of state has been a president. The political powers of the president are strictly limited and quite comparable to those of the Scandinavian constitutional monarchs.

In clear contrast to this, the president is the paramount foreign policy maker in Finland. The reasons for this central role of the president are to be found in the formal rules of the constitution, as well as in political circumstances reinforcing formal powers.

The Finnish president is elected for a six-year period (and without limits on the number of terms each president can serve) by an electoral college appointed by the electorate. Like the U.S. and French presidents, he has his own mandate from the voters independent of parliament. Furthermore, the relatively long term of office makes the president an important element of stability and continuity in a political system with rapidly changing cabinets.

The president appoints and dismisses ministers, whereas parliament can only declare its nonconfidence in these ministers. The often complicated parliamentary situation gives the president strong influence on the composition of cabinets.

He also has a number of other independent powers. Of particular importance in the present context are the special powers that the president holds in the area of foreign policy. The constitution states that the president has responsibility for the overall direction of foreign policy. The political developments since 1944 and particularly during Uhro Kekkonen's presidency have strongly increased the president's role in the making of Finnish foreign policy. Kekkonen has been accepted as having particular abilities in conducting relations with the Soviet Union and has come to be seen as a personal guarantee for amiable Soviet-Finnish relations.

This development has meant that foreign policy has become the special domain of the president to a larger extent than was foreseen in the formal constitutional rules. His increasing role in foreign policy making has in turn contributed to a general strengthening of the president's position in domestic politics, particularly in the years following the so-called note crisis of 1961.[3]

The Cabinet

In Iceland and the three Scandinavian countries, the governmental body chiefly responsible for the making of foreign policy is the cabinet, which in turn is responsible to parliament. In Finland, the role of the cabinet is circumscribed by the powers of the president just mentioned.

The cabinets are collectively responsible for government policy, and although the press might speculate about internal disagreements, cabinet members are expected to support the common policy line in all public pronouncements. A special problem, however, arises with coalition governments, which is typical in Finland and in Iceland. This type of government is quite common in Denmark. Here the participating parties may feel a need to present the policies that they pursue within the coalition and thus make public the internal controversies of the government. The traditional norm of cabinet unanimity is as a result not always observed. In Finland, in fact, it is accepted that the parties in a coalition government can disagree over minor policy matters. This is also reflected in the fact that the Finnish system makes use of majority decisions in the cabinet on matters not considered important enought to break up a coalition.

A most remarkable example of internal cabinet disagreement on a major policy issue is to be found in Iceland. The Keflavík Agreement of 1946 between the United States and Iceland was negotiated by Prime Minister Olafur Thors, who was also foreign minister in a three-party coalition government that included the Popular Alliance of Communists and other left-wingers. The agreement, which was unquestionably the most important and far-reaching political issue at the time, was negotiated without the cabinet being informed. When the agreement came up for ratification in parliament, the prime minister was strongly criticized by the Popular Alliance for his handling of the issue. This disagreement naturally led to the breakup of the government, which nevertheless had to continue for another five months as caretaker government until a new coalition could be forged.[4]

In other respects there are variations in the internal workings of the cabinets. The Danish, Finnish, and Norwegian cabinets have a number of committees, which prepare decisions for the full cabinet. Thus, for example, the Danish and the Norwegian cabinets have a security committee, the Danish cabinet also has a common market committee, and the Finnish cabinet has a foreign affairs committee. This has not been the practice in Sweden. The size of the Icelandic cabinet is so small (normally about six ministers) that there is no need for a committee system.

There are also procedural differences as to which decisions have to be taken in meetings where the head of state is present, in meetings presided over by the prime minister, and decisions made by the individual ministers. The distinction between the first two is mainly of a formal nature, except in Finland, whereas the distinction between collective cabinet decisions and individual ministerial decisions is more important. In the Swedish system of government, a smaller number of decisions are formally made by the individual minister than are in the other countries.

Although lacking exact information about the time spent by cabinets on questions of foreign policy, it is reasonable to assume that in periods of international stability, cabinets spend relatively little time on foreign policy. Most matters of foreign policy are left to the foreign minister and, if he is so inclined, to the prime minister. In Denmark, however, membership in the European Community makes it necessary for the prime minister to be rather continuously engaged in matters of foreign policy since he regularly participates in the meetings of the European Council, i.e., the formalized summit meetings held three times a year between the leaders of the ten countries.

The role of individual ministers in the cabinet naturally depends on a number of circumstances about which it is difficult to generalize. The relationship between the prime minister and the foreign minister, between these and other ministers, between the foreign minister and his civil servants depends among other things on their personal political strength, competence, and interest in foreign policy. We have already mentioned President Kekkonen's unrivaled role in the making of Finnish foreign policy, which substantially limited the personal role played by frequently changing prime ministers and foreign ministers.

Differences in government stability in the other countries have also influenced the role of individual politicians. During the forty-year period from 1936 to 1976, Sweden only had three prime ministers and one of them, Tage Erlander, served in this capacity for twenty-three consecutive years. The longest serving Norwegian prime minister, Einar Gerhardsen, served for sixteen years, whereas J. O. Krag only served seven years as Danish prime minister, but he had previously been foreign minister. Anker Joergensen had by 1980 served the same length of time as Mr. Krag.

In Iceland, as well, there has been a remarkable continuity of political leaders. Olafur Thors, leader of the Independence party for almost a quarter of a century, served five times as prime minister, starting before independence and finishing in 1961. Herman Jonasson of the Progressive party, who was prime minister from 1956 to 1958, had his first term in the office in 1934–1938.

In Sweden, Östen Undén was foreign minister from 1924 to 1926 and then again from 1945 to 1962, whereas in Norway, Halvard Lange was foreign minister from 1946 to 1965. Both men, like their prime ministers, gained an immense amount of authority in relation to their civil servants, their cabinet colleagues, their political parties, and their parliaments as a whole. No compatible situation has existed in Denmark since Peter Munch was foreign minister in the 1930s.

The Bureaucracy

The day-to-day administration of foreign policy is handled by the ministries of foreign affairs and a number of other ministries. Here the foreign policy decisions are prepared and executed. A large number of decisions on routine matters are also made by the civil servants without the direct involvement of the political authorities.

The ministries of foreign affairs have been constantly expanding throughout the twentieth century, particularly during the years following World War II. The rapidly increasing number of independent states, the equally rapidly growing number of international organizations, plus the continued inclusion of new issues in international negotiations and regulations have placed an ever-growing demand on the ministries of foreign affairs.

This development has also meant that ministries other than the ministries of foreign affairs have become directly involved in international negotiations. In most countries it has raised the problem of how relations between foreign ministries and other ministries should be organized. Once virtually monopolizing contacts with foreign countries and international intergovernmental organizations, ministries of foreign affairs now primarily coordinate external relations. This development is, however, less pronounced in Iceland than in the other Nordic countries due to the limited size of its administration.

The dominant concepts of civil service and civil servants in the Nordic countries are based upon the classical European notion of the politically neutral administrator who loyally serves the government of the day. A "spoils system" similar to U.S. practice, where a relatively large number of top administrators are appointed by the chief executive, is unknown. This does not mean, however, that political party affiliations never influence the appointment of civil servants to certain positions. In Norway, both the minister of foreign affairs and the minister of defense have politically appointed assistant secretaries. There are also a number of examples, particularly from Sweden and Finland, of politicians becoming ambassadors or of politically active academics entering the foreign service and being placed in relatively important positions.

There are, however, both similarities and important differences in the administrative structures and traditions of the five countries, some of them reflecting the historical links between the countries. The main difference is between what could be called the west Nordic (Denmark, Norway, and Iceland) and the east Nordic (Sweden and Finland) administrative traditions. In the east Nordic, particularly the Swedish, tradition the legislative body only makes general laws and not decisions on specific cases. This tradition is not found in Denmark, Norway, and Iceland where the parliaments often regulate individual cases. This formal distinction is, however, not always clear in practice.

In Denmark, Norway, and Iceland the individual minister is responsible for and can intervene in the administrative processes under the jurisdiction of his ministry. This is not so in Finland and particularly not so in Sweden, where a sharp division is found between the minister's department and the underlying, quite independent agencies that are responsible for the actual administration of laws and decrees. These agencies can only be instructed from above through formal decisions the cabinet makes. This, of course, means that the civil servants have larger individual responsibilities for matters that in the west Nordic systems are the responsibilities of the minister.

The most important exception to this system in Finland and Sweden is, however, the ministries of foreign affairs. As in the three other countries, this ministry, together with the diplomatic service, forms a departmental unit under the immediate direction of the minister of foreign affairs.

Besides the ministries of foreign affairs, the most important ministries in the field of foreign policy are those of defense (except in Iceland, which is totally without a national defense establishment) and of trade. But, as already mentioned, the international developments have meant that a number of other ministries have become directly involved in international affairs. This development has been most far-reaching in Denmark due to its membership in the European Community. Only one ministry, the ministry of ecclesiastical affairs, does not participate on a continuous basis in international affairs.[5]

The traditional monopoly on external contacts held by the ministries of foreign affairs has been eroded and replaced by a coordinating role. How coordination is carried out varies, however, from country to country. It seems as if the Swedish, Finnish, and Icelandic ministries of foreign affairs have been more effective in the coordinating role than the Danish. There can be several reasons for this difference. Central coordination may be more important in Sweden and Finland to maintain credible neutrality. The limited size of the Icelandic administration may make coordination less burdensome. Finally, Denmark's more comprehensive and continuous involvement in international affairs through membership in NATO and the EC may make the task far more complicated than in the two neutral countries.

Concluding a study of the impact of interdependence on foreign policy making in Norway, Maurice A. East points to the strong informal ties that cut across boundaries within the central administration and minimize the negative consequences of limited formal coordination. Similar observations can be made about the administrative systems in the other Nordic countries. East, however, fears that a crisislike situation would demonstrate the vulnerability of the Norwegian system.[6]

In the field of security policy the relations among the ministries of foreign affairs, ministries of defense, and the military leadership seem in all the four relevant countries to rest on a well-established division of responsibilities and procedures of coordination. Rivalries between the different armed services undoubtedly exist in all countries. In Denmark, they have at times been rather strong and public and thus limited the impact that united military recommendations could have on the decision makers.

In foreign economic policy the division of responsibilities varies among the Nordic countries. The Norwegian ministry of trade has a rather strong independent position as regards foreign economic relations. This seems also to be the case in Sweden, but here foreign economic policy is handled by joint bureaus of the ministry of trade and the ministry of foreign affairs. The Finnish ministry of foreign affairs has a section that deals with trade policy, and in Denmark the ministry of foreign affairs consists of two departments. One of these departments has responsibility for many of the issues that, for example, in Norway belong to the ministry of trade.

A third general issue area is that of development assistance, though this area is marginal in the case of Iceland. In the four other countries development assistance administrations were established in the 1950s and early 1960s. In Finland, the development assistance administration was from the beginning a bureau and later a section within the ministry of foreign affairs. In the three Scandinavian countries the development assistance administrations originally enjoyed considerable independence. Through the late 1960s, the 1970s, and the early 1980s these administrative units have, through a series of reforms, become more directly subject to the direction of the ministries of foreign affairs as development assistance has increasingly been seen as just another aspect of the countries' economic policies.[7]

By way of concluding this section, how can the role of the bureaucracy be summarized? The general literature on foreign policy making published in the 1970s strongly emphasizes the role of bureaucracies, hence the term *bureaucratic politics*.[8] Naturally the size, permanence, and expertise of the bureaucracy indicate that it has an important role in policymaking, particularly so in the field of foreign policy with its traditional executive dominance. But the power of the bureaucracy is not unlimited. It functions in a certain political climate and in extensive interaction with ministers, parliamentary committees, and other departments and interest organizations.

The size of the bureaucracy can be one factor influencing the nature of the decision-making process. Not necessarily all the features of bureaucratic politics found in the large U.S. bureaucracy can be found in the smaller Nordic bureaucracies. The very small Icelandic bureaucracy works differently not only from the U.S. bureaucracy but also from those of the other Nordic countries.

Yet bureaucratic battles are also fought in the Nordic countries. The battle for control over coordination of Common Market policies in Denmark[9] or over the decision to build the Swedish Viggen multipurpose military aircraft[10] are cases in point.

Crucial for the role of the bureaucracy is the political nature of the issue in question. As we shall see in a later section, the socioeconomic interest organizations are closely integrated in the decision-making system in the Nordic countries. This means that all foreign policy issues of importance to the organizations are prepared and often executed in close cooperation with these organizations. Such participation is evident in issues relating to foreign economic policy, but also to weapons production.

Another factor has to do with the politicization of issues, i.e., whether they become topics for public debate or partisan disagreement. When that happens the role of the minister or of the entire cabinet increases. But even when issues are not politicized, the civil servants must consider the potential tactical problems and the minister's possibilities of securing support in the cabinet and of finding a majority in parliament in case the issue should become politicized at a later stage.

So, even if the bureaucracy is an important actor in the decision-making process it does not act in a political vacuum. Thus it is difficult to characterize its "independent powers" in a meaningful way.

Parliaments and Parties

Parliaments and Foreign Policy

As mentioned in the preceding section, foreign policy in the Nordic countries, as in most other countries, is primarily an executive matter. Throughout the twentieth century, however, the role of parliaments in the making of foreign policy has increased. Two of the the most important factors explaining this development are the principle of parliamentarism and the critique of the secret diplomacy that arose in the years following World War I. After the war many countries established special parliamentary bodies for increased control over foreign policy. In the Nordic countries special foreign policy committees were established in Sweden, Norway, and Denmark in the years from 1921 to 1923.

Also during the years following World War II the role of parliaments in the making of foreign policy seems to have been increasing, partly as a consequence of the increasing importance of foreign economic questions with their directly observable consequences for the domestic economy—not least in small developed states with a large amount of foreign trade. This is probably also occurring as a consequence of an increased public interest in international questions in general. From time to time there have been debates over the role of parliaments in the making of foreign policy. In Finland, where the influence of parliament is weaker than in the four other countries, there was in the late 1960s and early 1970s quite an extensive debate over what was called the democratization of foreign policy. Commissions were formed and reforms proposed, but apart from some rather marginal changes, the fundamental relation among parliament, cabinet, and president remained unaltered.[11]

The extent to which foreign policy issues are debated in the plenary sessions of the parliaments varies considerably. Dag Anckar found that during the nine-year period from 1955 to 1963, which was quite an active period in Finnish foreign policy, the total number of speeches made on foreign policy issues in the Finnish parliament was only 263.[12] Even without comparable data from the four other parliaments, it seems clear that foreign policy is debated much less in the Finnish parliament than in the other Nordic parliaments. At the other extreme of foreign policy debate, we would probably find Denmark. In the 1957–1964 period the Danish parliament voted 120 times on a foreign or defense policy issue, and in most cases the votes were preceded by debates where at least one representative from each party spoke at least once.[13]

Besides debates, addressing questions to the minister is another way to raise issues in the plenary sessions of the parliaments. A Norwegian study concluded that relatively few questions were asked about foreign policy (3.5 percent) and that since Norway became a member of NATO, the number of questions dropped during periods of international tension.[14] This finding does not correspond to the situation in Denmark, which has had a constant and very dramatic raise in the number of questions on foreign policy. This development seems part of a general tendency to ask more questions, but in the parliamentary session of 1977–1978 the foreign minister was nevertheless asked more questions than any other minister with the exception of the minister of justice.[15]

An important part of the work of parliaments goes on in committees. We have already mentioned the establishment in the early 1920s of special foreign policy committees in the three Scandinavian parliaments. Similar committees exist in Finland and Iceland. Their primary function is to serve as advisory bodies that the government can—and under certain circumstances must—consult before important foreign policy decisions are made. The membership normally consists of senior members of parliament—often party leaders—and thus is potentially powerful. Yet, although the deliberations of these committees are secret, their role in the making of foreign policy seems quite limited. Critics have claimed that through these committees the opposition becomes hostages of the government by being informed without being able to use the information in public criticism. This view has led observers to characterize the Swedish foreign policy committee as a golden mousetrap.[16]

A number of other parliamentary committees with responsibilities for particular areas related to foreign policy can be found, as, for example, the defense committees in the three Scandinavian countries and Finland. Of particular interest is the Market Policy Committee of the Danish parliament, which was first established in 1961 to follow the government's negotiations for membership in the European Community. In 1972–1973 it was turned into a permanent committee with exceptionally wide powers vis-à-vis the government.[17] None of these committees are, however, as powerful as congressional committees in the United States. They have very limited staff assistance and do not conduct public hearings.

Besides these formally established procedures for consultation and decision making there are, of course, also informal channels through which members of parliament discuss matters of foreign policy with the cabinet. In times of crisis, one finds examples of cabinet consultations with opposition party leaders before decisions are made. In Sweden, informal consultation of opposition leaders (with the exception of the Communists) became a regular and almost formalized practice until it was discontinued by the three-party coalition government in 1976.

Party Systems

The formal rules delineating the functions of the parliament in the making of foreign policy cannot stand alone in a description of the roles of parliament. The political parties and the party systems are fundamental for any understanding of how the parliaments function vis-à-vis the cabinets. Under a parliamentary system of government with cohesive political parties (i.e., with strong party discipline), the relationship between government and parliament is very much a question of the general partisan basis of the government and the relationship between the governing party or parties and the opposition, a relationship that in the Nordic multiparty systems is quite different from the relationship between parties in a two-party system.

The traditional socioeconomic cleavages of the early twentieth century are reflected in the structure of the party systems. Changes in the socioeconomic structure of the population is only slowly reflected in the party system either through adaptation by the existing parties or by changes in the composition of the system itself.

Though all five countries have multiparty systems, the Finnish and the Icelandic systems differ in important respects from those systems in the three Scandinavian countries. Each of the latter countries have a Social Democratic party (in Norway called the Labour party) as the largest political party and the party having most often been in government. Particularly in Norway and Sweden the Social Democrats have been dominant for a very long period. The alternative to the Social Democrats or to predominantly Social Democratic governments has almost always been a bourgeois coalition of three (in Norway four) parties.

The main bourgeois parties are the Conservatives and the Agrarians, in Norway and Sweden called the Centre parties and in Denmark the Liberals. Then in Norway and Sweden we find the Liberals and in Denmark the Radicals, a social-liberal party. Norway also has a Christian People's party.

To the left of the Social Democrats we find the Communists, never a very large and influential party in Scandinavia, though in Sweden its votes have been necessary to keep Social Democratic minority governments in office. In 1960 the Danish Communists were succeeded on the left wing by the Socialist People's party, which in 1968 split to form the Left Socialists. Also in Norway there is a Socialist People's party and other left-wing groupings to the left of the Social Democrats.

One may also distinguish between the party systems in the Scandinavian countries themselves. On the one hand, the Social Democrats have been dominant in Norway and Sweden. On the other hand, in Denmark a less dominant Social Democratic party has been in opposition several times. It has either been in government in coalition with other parties or comprised a minority government dependent on support from opposition parties from issue to issue.

Finally, major changes, particularly in the Danish system, have taken place during the 1970s. In 1973, Denmark witnessed a landslide election where an outgoing parliament of five parties was succeeded by a parliament of ten parties. All the "old" parties suffered considerable losses as have a number of completely new parties, and two small parties that had not been in parliament for thirteen years entered parliament. One of the new parties, the antitax Progress party, strongly in opposition to traditional political values, became the second largest party. This fragmentation and polarization combined with the economic crisis opened a period of governmental and parliamentary instability leading to successive and rather inconclusive elections throughout the 1970s.

In the other Scandinavian countries, a number of changes took place during the 1970s, although they were less dramatic than in the Danish case. The polarization over the Common Market issue in Norway led to the breakup of the Liberal party, dividing it into two parties defined according to attitudes toward membership of the European Community. The referendum campaign was likewise instrumental in creating the Socialist Alliance of the Socialist People's party and other left-wing groups and caused the heavy losses of the Labour party in the 1973 election.

For quite different reasons, Sweden also experienced changes in the 1970s. No new parties found their way into the Swedish parliament and only relatively few votes determined the fall of the Social Democratic government in 1976. The election led to the creation of the first non–Social Democratic government in forty-four years. The three-party government broke up on the issue of nuclear energy, but was reestablished following the 1979 election when the three parties barely secured a majority.

The Finnish party system differs in a number of important respects from the Scandinavian pattern. In Finland, we find a much stronger Communist party (electorally cooperating with others in the Finnish People's Democratic League) and a weaker Social Democratic party. The pivotal position in the party system is held by the large and very influential Agrarian party, since 1965 called the Centre party. The main right-wing party is the conservative National Coalition, which has been rather uninfluential. There is both a Finnish People's party (a liberal party) and a Swedish People's party, considered to be a liberal party but mainly defined along nationality lines. In the first half of the 1970s a right-wing protest party, the Rural party, had a shortlived success.

No party has had a majority in parliament, and Finland has often been governed by very shortlived coalition governments. The Centre party has participated in most of these coalitions and often supplied the ministers for the most important posts in the government. It was also the party of President Kekkonen. From 1944 to 1948, the Communists participated in the governments, but were then kept out until 1966. Since then they have participated in a number of coalition governments. Also, the Social Democrats were out of government from 1959 to 1966 mainly because the party's leadership and foreign policy position were unacceptable to the Soviet Union.

As in Denmark and Finland, no party has ever held an absolute majority in the Icelandic parliament. The largest party is the conservative Independence party. Its main rival is the mainly rural Progressive party. The Social Democratic party is weak by Scandinavian standards and has suffered from a number of breakaways from its left wing. On the Left we find the Popular Alliance, which includes Communists and non-Communist left-wing groups. On the left wing there has been different small parties, mainly splinter groups from either the Social Democrats or the Popular Alliance. Icelandic cabinets have been based on changing combinations of these parties, including coalitions of ideologically strongly divergent parties, in order to secure majority government.

In very general terms, the party systems in the three Scandinavian countries can be described as multiparty systems with two-bloc competition, although one bloc traditionally has been stronger than the other. The Finnish system could be characterized as a center-bloc system, and the Icelandic as a changing majority-bloc system.

Yet, the party systems cannot be satisfactorily described using merely the classical dichotomy between government and opposition. Studies in legislative behavior have shown that the overwhelming majority of parliamentary decisions are made with the support of more than just the governing party or parties.[18] Divisions following a strict government/opposition dimension are relatively few. This seems to be particularly true within the field of foreign policy.

There is a general tendency to keep foreign policy "above party politics," though in Iceland and in Denmark foreign and defense policy traditionally has been more politicized than in the three other countries. But even when foreign policy becomes politicized, the dividing line on the major issues seldom coincides with the division between government and opposition. In Denmark and Norway, for example, the Social Democrats and the large bourgeois parties have, with very few exceptions, been the bearers of NATO membership and defense policy in spite of the aforementioned two-bloc competition. On Common Market membership, the bourgeois parties in Norway differed while the Conservatives and the Labour party leadership were in agreement. In Denmark, Common Market policy is primarily made through compromises between the Social Democrats and the Liberals. The real opposition to prevailing foreign policies comes from the extreme Left and, where such parties exist, the extreme Right.

The Parties

Although there are important similarities among the Nordic party systems, the fact that we find parallel parties and even parties having the same name, e.g., the Social Democrats and the Center parties, does not necessarily mean that there are corresponding similarities in the policies pursued by them. This is particularly true when we look at the foreign policy stands the parties take.

For example, there may be many common ideas and attitudes among the Nordic Social Democratic parties in favor of increased Nordic cooperation; nevertheless, even with Social Democrats in power in two or three of the countries at the time, divergent foreign policy interests have led to failure of all the most ambitious schemes for Nordic integration.

TABLE 3.1

PARTIES REPRESENTED IN THE NORDIC PARLIAMENTS 1980

Country Party	No. of parliamentary seats	Popular Vote %	Country Party	No. of parliamentary seats	Popular Vote %
Denmark			**Finland**		
Social Democrats	68	38.2	Social Democrats	52	24.0
Conservatives	22	12.5	Democratic League	35	17.9
Liberals	22	12.5	(incl. Communists)		
Progress Party	20	11.0	Centre	36	17.4
Centre Democrats	6	3.2	Conservatives	47	21.7
People's Socialists	11	6.0	Swedish People's	10	4.5
Radicals	10	5.4	Party		
Christian People's Party	5	2.6	Liberal Party	4	3.7
Justice	5	2.6	Christian League	10	4.8
Left Socialists	6	3.6	Rural Party	6	4.6
Fareo Islands representatives	2		Total	200	
Greenland representatives	2				
Total	179				
Iceland			**Norway**		
Independence Party	22	37.9	Labour Party	76	42.3
Popular Alliance	11	19.7	Conservatives	41	24.7
(incl. Communists)			Centre	12	8.6
Social Democrats	10	17.4	Christian People's	22	12.2
Progressive Party	17	24.9	Party		
Total	60		Socialist Alliance	2	4.2
			Liberals	2	3.2
			Total	155	
Sweden					
Social Democrats	154	43.2			
Centre	64	18.1			
Conservatives	73	20.3			
Liberals	38	10.6			
Communists	20	5.6			
Total	349				

Source: Nordisk Kontakt, No. 12/80 (1980) p. 585.

The Conservatives in Finland have been very positive toward increased economic cooperation in the Nordic region, seeing it as a way to modify the country's dependence on the Soviet Union. The Danish and particularly the Norwegian Conservative party have by contrast been among the parties most skeptical on this issue, fearing it as a possible detraction from wider European economic integration.

The most striking, but not at all surprising, example of parallel parties having strongly divergent policies can be found in the attitudes toward Common Market membership among the Agrarian or Centre parties of the four countries, with the Danish party being extremely promembership and the Finnish and Norwegian parties, for quite different reasons, strongly against. Here, of course, the different prospects for Danish and Norwegian agriculture in the EC and, in the case of Finland, incompatibility with the fundamental doctrine of the country's foreign policy explain the differences.

Space does not allow for a discussion of each political party nor for a discussion of the internal policymaking in the political parties. Only two more general points will be made in this respect. First, the organs of the ruling party (party conference and, more often, executive committee) are from time to time the locus of important decisions also in the area of foreign policy. For example, the Norwegian decision to join NATO was made by the Labour party conference in 1949, and once the conference had decided overwhelmingly in favor of joining, the question was, for all practical purposes, settled. The subsequent decision by parliament was never in doubt.[19]

Second, and closely related, is the fear of the leadership of splitting its own party on a major issue. The mere anticipation of a split will influence policy. Since the Social Democratic parties have been dominant in the three Scandinavian countries and since the dividing line on many controversial issues seems to go right through these parties, they provide a host of examples of how a governing party modifies its position, at least in part, out of fear of open disagreement. One example is the Swedish government's attitude toward the development of Swedish nuclear arms. In the early 1950s, development of tactical nuclear weapons was advocated by the military leadership and by the Conservative party. The question would no doubt have split the Social Democratic party had the government decided to go ahead with a nuclear program. An extensive public debate took place, but a committee of the Social Democratic party representing all shades of opinion proposed a postponement of the decision. The question was postponed by the government until international developments such as the test ban and nonproliferation treaties had made it irrelevant for all practical purposes.[20]

Another example might be the internal disagreement in the Danish and Norwegian Social Democratic parties in 1979 on the proposed modernization of NATO's theater nuclear forces in Europe. Although different positions were taken by the Danish and Norwegian governments, both decisions could to a very large extent be explained in terms of the internal disagreements in the two ruling parties.

The Common Market issue, however, provides an important exception to this method of arriving at major policy decisions. In Sweden in 1970–1971, the government's initial relatively positive attitude of at least considering full membership was modified in the course of the debate because of, among other things, opposition within its own ranks. This was not the case in Norway and Denmark. Here the Social Democratic governments went ahead, determined to join the EC in spite of strong internal party opposition. The Danish party leadership had originally tried to overcome internal opposition by making its positive attitude dependent upon Norwegian membership, but as the final decision approached and the uncertainty of the Norwegian referendum became apparent, it tried quietly to drop the "Norway proviso."[21] However, from a purely party political point of view, the experience of the Danish and Norwegian party hardly encourages repetition.

Economic Structure and Interest Representation

Economic Structure

Four of the five countries analysed in this book belong to the highly industrially developed countries, whereas Iceland, though highly developed in some sectors, shares some of the features characteristic of developing countries. All five are among the countries most dependent on international trade. With foreign trade accounting for about one-third of the net factor income, external economic relations become the most important aspect of domestic as well as foreign policy in periods of military stability and noncrisis. In spite of these general common characteristics, there are a number of important differences in their economic structures that influence their foreign policies.

The main agricultural areas are in Denmark, southern Sweden, southwestern Finland, and the middle of Sweden. From an economic point of view, agriculture is most important in Finland and Denmark and least important in Iceland and Sweden. Denmark is the only one of the five countries that is a net exporter of agricultural products. About 60 percent of the land is cultivated, compared to 9 percent in Finland, about 7 percent in Sweden, less than 3 percent in Norway, and only about 1 percent in Iceland. But at the same time, the proportion of the population employed in agriculture is about the same in Denmark and Norway, a little more in Finland, and only a little less in Sweden. The holdings in Norway, Finland, and northern Sweden are on the average smaller in size than those in Denmark, whereas those in southern Sweden are bigger.

Until the late 1950s, agriculture accounted for more than 50 percent of Denmark's total exports, but this percentage steadily declined due to the agricultural protectionism of the EC, the industrialization of the Danish economy, and the growth in industrial exports during the European Free Trade Association (EFTA) period. Sweden, partly for strategic reasons, has tried to curb the decline in agricultural production in order to retain about 80 percent self-sufficiency. In Norway, unfavorable climatic and topographical conditions necessitate a high degree of protectionism and subsidy of agriculture. In Finland and northern Sweden the climate is also unfavorable to several crops. Icelandic farming consists mainly of sheep farming and the growing of fodder crops. These differences in the preconditions for agricultural production are a major explanation for the different market policies of the Nordic countries.

The major fishing nations among the four Nordic countries dealt with here are Norway and Denmark; fisheries are of very limited importance to the Finnish and Swedish economies. Yet fisheries are of overwhelming importance to the Icelandic economy. In 1965, fish and fish products accounted for 95 percent of the country's export earnings. Although a determined effort has been made to build up other industries and diversify exports, fish and fish products still dominate, by 1973 still accounting for 74 percent of all exports. This heavy and one-sided dependence on one type of product makes the economy very sensitive to the fluctuations of the international market. It is, of course, this explanation for the country's policy on fishing limits that has brought Iceland into fierce disputes with other countries, primarily Britain, in the so-called cod wars.

The Norwegian catch is about the size of the catch of all other Nordic countries (including Iceland) put together. The Danish catch is about 60 percent of the Norwegian. Coastal fisheries are particularly important in Norway, whereas the major part of Danish fishing is done in distant waters, mainly in the North Sea. Each type of fishing creates its particular problems vis-à-vis other fishing nations, as for example the disagreements between Britain and Denmark over fishery policy within the European Community.

Forestry and its associated industries are of considerable importance to Sweden and Finland. Wood and wood products, particularly paper, weigh heavily in the exports of these two countries. The amount of productive forests are much smaller in Norway, insignificant in Denmark, and nonexistent in Iceland.

The industrial basis of the five countries differs considerably in other respects as well. Denmark and Iceland have hardly any natural resources and must import almost all raw materials for their industry, though in Iceland all electricity is produced from water power or hot springs. The three other countries, particularly Norway, have large actual and potential hydroelectrical resources, which in Norway provide all electricity consumed and even some for export. In Sweden about 60 percent of all electricity is produced from hydroelectrical sources. Add to this the well-known discoveries of large oil and gas reserves on the Norwegian part of the continental shelf, which have dramatically changed Norway's economic prospects and are at the same time a reason for Norway's special status within the International Energy Agency. Much less well known is the fact that recent discoveries of oil and gas resources on the Danish North Sea shelf, though of a much smaller size, could cover a substantial part of the energy consumption in a country hitherto completely dependent on imported energy.

Of other mineral resources of importance, iron ore should be mentioned. It is found in Sweden, Finland, and Norway, with the Swedish resources being the most important and supplying the basis for both light and heavy industry. Some producible copper, lead, and zinc also exist in Sweden and Finland, and in the latter nickel can be found as well. Considerations of foreign policy and the existence of natural resources have both contributed to the establishment of an arms industry in the two neutral countries. Sweden, in particular, has a large independent weapons industry. Yet the steeply increasing costs of modern arms production and foreign policy considerations that place limits on sales abroad raise doubt about the future of the country's efforts in this field.

One final branch of industry to be mentioned in this brief overview of Nordic economies is that of shipping. Norway has one of the world's largest merchant fleets. The Swedish fleet is the second largest among the Nordic countries with about a quarter of the tonnage of the Norwegian, whereas the Danish is the second by number of ships. For all the three countries, foreign currency earnings from international shipping is of considerable importance. This is particularly true in the case of Norway, which is strongly involved in all issues of international shipping, such as those raised at the United Nations Conference on the Law of the Sea or at the United Nations Conference on Trade and Development (UNCTAD).

The relative importance of shipping in the Norwegian economy has, however, been declining in the latter part of the 1970s due to the crisis in international shipping and the increasing earnings from oil exports.

Size and concentration of industry vary considerably between the five countries. In Denmark, there is a large number of relatively small firms, often working as subcontractors to foreign firms. In Sweden, the firms

are larger but relatively fewer in number, although only few Swedish industries would be considered large by international standards. Industry
in Finland and Norway falls between these two extremes.

Without being a comprehensive account of the economic structures of
the Nordic countries, this section is intended to show that in spite of the
often stated large similarities among them, there are a number of differences that are important for understanding their foreign policies and
for evaluating the relative strength of different economic interests and interest organizations in the making of foreign policy.[22]

Interest Organizations

The Nordic countries are among the most thoroughly organized countries in the world. Almost any conceivable aspect of social, economic,
political, and cultural life has its formal organizations. The membership
ratio (that is the ratio between actual and potential members) of the
socioeconomic interest organizations is high compared to other countries. It is somewhat higher in the three Scandinavian countries than it is
in Finland. It is lowest in Iceland.

In all the five countries, the head organizations of employers and
workers are among the most important interest organizations. In the
three Scandinavian countries, the private employers are organized in one
national organization, while in Finland, where the employers within
commerce have their own organization, there are two organizations at
the national level. On the other side of the negotiating table, the workers
in the three Scandinavian countries are joined in one organization at the
top level, whereas in Finland the competition between the Communists
and the Social Democrats led to the establishment of two national
organizations, which were again united in one organization in 1969. In
Iceland, the division in Communist and Social Democratic organizations
and a decentralized structure make organized labor relatively weaker
than in the other Nordic countries. The Scandinavian labor organizations are closely aligned politically with the Social Democratic parties.
Also, public employees, including the military, and the professions have
strong national organizations.

Each of the four countries has a general industrial organization
representing the urban industries. In Finland, however, the wood-
processing industry has its own independent organization due to the
traditional divergence of views on free trade between the wood-
processing industry and the industries primarily producing for the Finnish market. Each country also has a national organization for crafts and
small industry. Also, the banks have their common national organiza-

tions. Trade and commerce, however, are handled by several different
organizations, the main dividing line being between wholesale and retail
trade.

Finally, there are the agricultural organizations. In Denmark, three
organizations represent the small landholders, the farmers, and the large
landowners respectively. Politically the small landholders have had
relatively close ties to the Radical party, the farmers to the Liberal party,
and the large landowners to the Conservative party. They cooperate,
however, in the politically very influential Agricultural Council.

In Finland, the organizational division is between the large and influential Central Association of Agricultural Producers on the one hand and
the smaller Swedish Agricultural Producers on the other. They too
cooperate over a wide area where they have common interests.

In Norway, as in Denmark, the main organizational division is between the small landholders and the farmers; the former tend to support
the Labour party, whereas the latter have been closely associated with the
Centre party. The organizations cooperate in an organization similar to
the Danish Agricultural Council, but without its political strength.

In Sweden, however, there have not been similar organizational divisions within agriculture. All agricultural producers belong to one national organization politically associated with the Centre party.

These are the main organizations covering the broad sectors of the
economy. Besides these, there are a multitude of producer organizations
representing specific sectors of production. The main pattern of the
organizational structure in each of the four countries is, of course, partly
a reflection of the industrial structure. We have, for example, already
noticed the existence of an independent organization for the wood-
processing industry in Finland. It is not surprising to find the very influential Norwegian Shipowner's Association, which takes an active interest in a number of foreign policy issues.

Besides these organizations, major firms can independently play roles
in the making of foreign policy on issues that are of special concern to
them. This is particularly the case with large (by Nordic standard)
multinational corporations or other firms with a large share of the country's exports or other foreign currency earnings.

We have so far been concerned only with the socioeconomic interest
organizations. But there is another type of interest organization, the so-
called promotional group or organization. Normally formed around a
single issue, a promotional group has a rather loose organizational structure and a "membership" of anyone who is interested in participating.
Such groups have existed in relation to several foreign policy issues. The
most famous example from the 1950s and early1960s is the Campaign for

Nuclear Disarmament, which existed in many countries and was also active in the Nordic countries. One of the older and more established organizations is the Norden Association, which promotes Nordic cooperation. Particularly in Denmark it has a large membership. Undoubtedly the most influential promotional groups have been the Danish and the Norwegian people's movements against the Common Market. These were formed with the primary purpose of securing a negative majority in the referendums on membership in the European Community. They played an important role in the mobilization of voters, and the Norwegian organization definitively contributed to the negative result of the referendum. The two organizations were not, however, typical promotional groups. Their campaigns were closely linked with the activities of certain political parties and, in Norway in particular, socioeconomic interest organizations, which gave them organizational and financial resources seldom available to promotional groups. The situation in which they were active was also unique in the sense that a foreign policy decision was made through a referendum. The further development of the Danish organization was also atypical in that the organization ran its own candidates for the direct election to the European Parliament in 1979, four of whom were elected.

Corporate Pluralism

How do the interest organizations influence the making of foreign policy? The socioeconomic interest organizations are closely integrated in the political-administrative structure and decision-making processes. The extent of this integration has occasionally been the subject of political debate, but it is formalized through rules and practices. Generally, the involvement is accepted as not only legitimate and useful but most often as politically and administratively necessary. In Sweden, this process gave rise to the term *Harpsund Democracy*, named after the prime minister's holiday resort, where many meetings between government and leaders of the organizations were held. This integration of the interest organizations into the political process is often referred to as corporate pluralism.

Direct organizational participation is not restricted to a small number of major interest organizations. A very large number of organizations have contacts with the bureaucracy in one way or another. Yet there are admittedly great variations in the intensity and scope of the relationship between organizations and bureaucracy. Socioeconomic producer organizations dominate the system of corporate decision making. Other types of organizations also participate, but at a lower level and in a more casual way.

Organizational resources are also important. According to a Danish study, no less than 92 percent of the organizations with a permanent staff of more than twenty-five participate daily in the work of the public administration. The degree of corporate decision making also varies with the kind of public policy in question. It is highest in the area of specific regulations of individuals or organizations within specific sectors of society.[23]

The development of a system of corporate pluralism within the area of foreign policy making is primarily a reflection of the general corporatization that has taken place in the Nordic societies over a long span of time. Within foreign policy it is particularly in relation to foreign trade that this development has been most noticeable. Since balance-of-payments issues are general problems with effects on the entire society, the promotion of foreign trade has become an obvious area for close cooperation between state and industry.

The process of economic integration in Western Europe has in all states irrespective of their formal relations to Western European organizations for economic cooperation also been a force in the development of domestic corporate decision structures. This has particularly been the case for Denmark.

In Finland, the extensive trade with the Soviet Union and the other COMECON countries where trade is conducted by the state has been a separate factor in the development of corporate structures in the area of foreign trade.[24]

In the case of Denmark there is the particular question of the involvement of interest organizations in the making of policies and decisions on the broad range of EC-related matters both at the national and the community level. The involvement is most intensive in the fields of agriculture, fisheries, and associated areas where EC regulations may have direct and very substantial consequences for the organizations and their members. According to the previously cited Danish study, 22 percent of the organizations within the field of agriculture and fisheries that reported having contact with public authorities claim to have daily contact on EC matters.[25] The organizations try to influence EC policy primarily through contacts with the Danish administration and only secondarily through contacts with EC institutions. The most important interest organization at community level is COPA (Comité des Organisations Professionelles Agricoles de la CEE), the agricultural interest organization. For the nonagricultural national interest organizations, activity at the EC level is primarily collecting information.

The socioeconomic interest organizations are thus closely integrated in the policymaking process. Their influence is primarily achieved through representation on a number of public boards and committees and through a regular process of consultation by the administration. In this way, they influence legislation at the preparatory stage and affect specific administrative decisions through direct participation in the decision-making processes.

The promotional groups, which are not given a similar direct access, try to influence decisions, primarily those made by parliament, through a mobilization of the public and the press. They hope in this way to press political parties to accept the views of the groups.

Press and Public Opinion

Press

The importance of the press in the policymaking process is generally recognized by observers and politicians alike. Yet, there is very little systematic empirical evidence about the ways in which this influence is exercised and how strong it is.

A characteristic feature of Nordic newspapers has been their political party affiliations. Even quite small towns used to have more than one newspaper. In Denmark, for example, around the time of World War I, thirty towns had three or more often four newspapers, each aligned with one of the main political parties.[26] Since then, and particularly since 1945, the number of newspapers had declined dramatically. A growth in readership has been accompanied by a constant decline in the number of newspapers. Most of the small papers, and a number of the large ones, have disappeared.

In the Scandinavian countries, the direct political party affiliations of the remaining papers have been weakened. In an attempt to attract a broader readership there have also been changes in the content of newspapers; relatively greater emphasis is being placed on general interest articles. Although this development is a general one, the structuring along political party lines is still a prominent feature of the press in Iceland and Finland.

In all the Nordic countries, the "bourgeois" press has a much larger readership than the Social Democratic and left-wing press. The newspapers on the Right have a far larger percentage of newspaper sales than the percentage of votes going to the parties of the Right. This means that, for example, many Social Democratic voters read a non–Social Democratic paper. The importance of this is difficult to evaluate, but a Swedish study has shown that Social Democratic voters reading bourgeois papers were more critical of the Social Democratic government's handling of the 1973–1974 oil supply crisis than those who read a Social Democratic paper.[27] There may, however, be different ways of explaining this finding.

The number of newspapers in the Nordic countries is high by international comparisons. Sweden actually has the highest newspaper rate in the world with fifty-five copies per 100 inhabitants in 1968.[28] It is also very high in Iceland, where the small population has a choice of six dailies.

The electronic media are publicly owned, which does not mean, however, that they are instruments of the government of the day. They are under obligation to be politically "comprehensive" in their coverage. But it is a perpetual issue of heated public debate in several of the Nordic countries whether in fact the public media do live up to this obligation. At one time, foreign minister Arthi Karjelainen proposed that the statute of Finland's Radio should commit it to follow the foreign policy views of the government. This formal proposal was, however, never passed.[29]

Compared to most other Western nations, the amount of broadcasting, particularly by television, is very limited. Only Sweden and Finland have two TV channels. In the border areas of the other Nordic countries, it is possible to receive one or more foreign TV programs. This possibility is going to be extended considerably in the near future due to satellite transmission of TV programs by a number of European states. A common Nordic satellite has been discussed, but not yet decided on. In the public debate it is taken for granted that satellite transmissions will have wide-ranging effects. Yet, it is difficult to foresee the exact nature of the political consequences.

The coverage by the written as well as by the electronic media is predominantly domestic. This is clearly the case in local newspapers. The rate of foreign news in the electronic media is relatively high, but the absolute amount is still limited by the very nature of the media. In both the national dailies and the electronic media, however, the amount of foreign news has been increasing throughout the period since World War II.

For its foreign news the Nordic press is very dependent on the large international news agencies. The four countries (not counting Iceland) do have their own national news agencies, but they also depend on the international agencies for the vast majority of foreign news. The number of foreign correspondents sent out by individual Nordic papers and by radio and television is quite limited. A few of the larger national dailies from different Nordic countries share correspondents in some places abroad.

The particular international position of Finland does place some limits on what and how the Finnish press—and not just the publicly owned part of it—can write about the Soviet Union. These limits are observed through "self-censorship" or, as some prefer to call it, "considerations of realpolitik."[30] This is in certain respects a parallel to the Danish situation in the late thirties when the government actively tried to restrain criticism of Germany in the Danish press.

The press is both a channel of communication between the other actors and an independent actor in the foreign policy process. At least in the short-term perspective, the press seems to be less influential in making people change their attitudes than in "setting the agenda" of the political debate, i.e., influencing what becomes a political issue and what does not. But this is certainly not a minor role, since the substantial content of political decisions can be very dependent on which actors are mobilized to participate in the policymaking process.

Social Cleavages

Generally speaking, the Nordic countries are ethnically very homogenous, and they are probably also among the most socially and culturally homogenous countries in the world. Nevertheless, there are cleavages, some of which are also important in terms of foreign policy.

In Iceland there are no ethnic or national minorities. Safeguarding the purity of Icelandic culture and language is an important political issue and seems to be a central issue involved in the controversies over the U.S. base at Keflavík. Ethnic or national minorities can be found, however, in the other four Nordic countries. In northern Norway, Sweden, and Finland we find the Lapps, an originally nomadic people primarily breeding reindeer. Although their total number in the three countries is only 30,000 to 35,000, they have increasingly made themselves heard in domestic politics.

In Denmark, there is a small German minority on the Danish side of the Danish-German border. There is also a Danish minority on the German side. In the 1930s and during the German occupation, there existed a quite vocal German minority that gave rise to fears for a German demand for border regulations. No demands were made to that effect, however. Since World War II the existence of the two national minorities have from time to time been an issue in Danish-German negotiations, as, for example, when Germany joined NATO in 1955. Though not formally connected with Danish acceptance of German membership, negotiations between the two countries resulted in an electoral law increasing the electoral possibilities of the Danish minority in Slesvig-Holstein.

In the case of Denmark the two partly self-governing areas of Greenland and the Faroe Islands must also be mentioned. The population of these areas is very small, less than 50,000 and 40,000 respectively. However, due to their distinct ethnic or national composition, their geographical location and—in the case of Greenland—size, and their economic structure and constitutional status within the Danish state, these two peoples are of far greater political importance within Denmark than the size of the population would otherwise indicate. To mention just one important example, the Faroe Islands are not members of the European Community, and, considering the negative attitudes in Greenland toward the Community, it is quite possible that Greenland may choose to leave the Community within a few years. The increased political awareness of and cooperation among the arctic peoples can also be seen in the creation of the Inuit Circumpolar Conference in 1980.

In Finland there is a Swedish-speaking minority, which prior to Finnish independence provided the majority of the social and political elite. Throughout the twentieth century the size and the political influence of the Swedish minority has been declining. Today, it makes up about 6 percent of the total population. But as shown in the preceding sections of this chapter, the existence of two linguistic groups has left its mark on political and organizational structures. In Finland we also find the self-governing Åland Islands. Like the Faroe Islands, they have even gained representation in the Nordic Council. Recently the question of representation of Greenland and the politically more touchy issue of Lapp representation have been raised.

The relative ethnic homogeneity, as discussed earlier, must also be modified in another respect. In recent years Denmark, Norway, and particularly Sweden have allowed very substantial immigration from southern Europe and the Middle East. Out of 8 million inhabitants in Sweden, 1 million are immigrants. The largest group, however, consists of Finns (between 300,000 and 400,000), but it is the other groups that have caused an intensive public debate over how immigrants should be integrated in Swedish society. There can be no doubt that this massive immigration is going to have far-reaching consequences for Swedish society. Whether or how it will have any effects in relation to foreign policy is too early to tell.

The strongest regional cleavages in the Nordic region are undoubtedly to be found in Norway. The cleavage between the center and the periphery is politically important. Fundamentally different political cultures are to be found in Oslo and on the south and west coasts. The traditional issues separating the two have been temperance, fundamentalist religion, and language. The split asserted itself most clearly in the debate and referendum over membership in the European Community, where the "traditionalists" (in coalition with the political Left) fought and won the fierce battle.[32]

Historical Experience

Situated in the same geographical region, the Nordic countries have shared many historical experiences. Some of them have even shared history as one country or as a union under the same monarch. Yet, as pointed out by Barbara Haskel, the historical legacy is ambiguous.[33] What looks like common history has only rarely been common experience. This is clearly the case when looking at the most important historical situations during the nineteenth and twentieth centuries which have had a bearing on foreign policy.

Sweden's more than 150 years of successful armed neutrality has given the doctrine of neutrality a status in Swedish political thought that has no equivalent in the other countries including Finland. The Finnish policy of neutrality is different from the Swedish and based on quite another historical experience. The Swedish doctrine of "nonalignment in peace aiming at neutrality in war," as it is officially stated, is the ideological basis of all Swedish foreign policy and is supported by almost all sectors of the population. Thus any foreign policy move by government or opposition must be demonstrated to be in accordance with the doctrine in order to gain acceptance and credibility. Yet the doctrine is sufficiently broad and vague to allow for a wide range of policies. This can be seen in the change from a relatively passive to a much more active and outspoken foreign policy that took place in the 1960s.

Besides the experience of successful neutrality, it is difficult to point out historical experiences that have influenced foreign policy attitudes in Sweden like the traumatic experiences of many other European countries. For this reason, Sweden has occasionally been called a country without history.[34]

Three historical situations are of particular importance for the development of general foreign policy attitudes in Denmark. A hazardous foreign policy based on unrealistic assumptions of the country's military strength led to the war of 1864 and the subsequent loss of two-fifths of the kingdom. This experience laid the foundation for the image of Denmark as a small and powerless state very dependent on Germany. In some political circles it led to the belief that any Danish defense effort was inherently futile. In the 1880s and until the turn of the century, defense policy furthermore became the major issue in domestic politics. The political Left used this issue in its battle with the government over the principle of parliamentarism and parliament's sole right to appropriate money. It could thus be said that Denmark has a tradition of partisan infighting over defense appropriations unknown in the other Nordic countries.

The policy of the interwar years was one of almost unarmed neutrality. The immediate surrender and the following German occupation during World War II made the Social Democrats give up unilateral disarmament. It also set in motion the development that, following the advent of the cold war, made the Social Democrats, the Liberals, and the Conservatives give up neutrality. The small but influential Radical party, however, could not originally accept membership of NATO. And when it did, partly for reasons of coalition building in parliament, the Socialist People's party, founded in 1958, took over the role as the defender of the antimilitarist tradition.

Norway also experienced defeat and occupation during World War II. But it had a government-in-exile in London recognized by the Allies. Leading politicians and large parts of the population soon came to see close cooperation with Britain and the United States as an essential element of postwar Norwegian foreign policy. This undoubtedly was a major reason for Norway's refusal in 1948–1949 of the Swedish proposal for a neutral Scandinavian Defense Community and its insistence on a westward-oriented defense arrangement.

Until 1814 Norway was under Danish rule, but as a result of the Napoleonic Wars, Norway was transferred from the Danish to the Swedish monarchy—as compensation for Sweden's loss of Finland to Russia—and the Swedish-Norwegian union was created. Norway did not emerge from this union as an independent country until 1905.

This relatively recent development, combined with Sweden's dominant economic position within the Nordic region, has no doubt contributed to past Norwegian skepticism toward very close and formal relations with Sweden. This was seen in the debates over Nordic economic integration in the 1950s and 1960s. It seems, however, as if these fears have subsided in later years, partly due to the changes following the large oil and gas discoveries on the Norwegian continental shelf.

Yet consciousness about newly gained independence may have been a factor in popular attitudes toward membership in the European Community. The term *union* in Norway carries with it connotations of the unhappy union with Sweden and implies closer and more formalized relations than envisaged by many who use the term in discussing the future of the European Community.

The most dramatic recent history with profound influence on domestic as well as foreign policy has been experienced by Finland. In 1809,

Finland passed from Sweden to Russia where it became a grand duchy until the revolution in 1917. Independence was followed by the bitter and cruel civil war of 1918 between the Left (supported by the Soviet Union) and the Right. The Right won and a strong anti-Communist wave swept the country during the 1920s and 1930s. The Communist party was forbidden in 1930 and fascist tendencies were on the rise. Although the Winter War of 1939–1940 for a time smoothed internal conflicts, the Continuation War of 1941–1944 and the bitter recriminations of the following war trials led to a reemergence of strong political antagonisms. Under the new republic the Communist party was legalized and certain fascist or pseudofascist organizations forbidden.

This historical experience created domestic political antagonisms of a strength unknown in the other Nordic countries. The loss of lives and land in the war and the strenuous terms of the peace definitively brought home the country's dependence on its big easterly neighbor as the paramount fact of Finnish politics with which politicians and the public had to come to terms.[35]

In 1918 Iceland, until then a Danish colony, gained home rule under the Danish monarch. In 1944, during the German occupation of Denmark, the country unilaterally declared itself an independent republic. It is thus the youngest independent country of the five. Though not without occasional problems, Danish-Icelandic relations have not suffered from the colonial relationship. Besides its recent independence, its most important recent historical experiences seem to be connected with the increasing difficulties of a small people to maintain widespread and real independence in a world increasingly characterized by strategic and economic interdependence. Hence, the continued political importance of the U.S. base at Keflavík, the issue of fishing limits, and the economy's sensitivity to external economic developments can be well understood.

Public Opinion and Foreign Policy

Several times in the preceding sections we have touched upon general foreign policy attitudes as well as attitudes on specific foreign policy issues. In this final section only a few general remarks about the nature of public opinion and its possible influence on foreign policy will be made.

It is commonplace to note that under normal circumstances the electorate does not take nearly as great an interest in foreign policy as it does in the major domestic issues. Several opinion polls have demonstrated this. There are, however, exceptions to this general phenomenon. The more directly external events and the consequences of foreign policy decisions make an impact on the daily lives of the citizens, the greater their interest in foreign policy issues. A general illustration of this has been the increasing public interest in and the politicization of foreign economic questions during the economic crisis of the 1970s.[36] A more specific illustration is the controversy over Common Market membership in Denmark and Norway. Both countries saw an unprecedented mobilization of the public in the prolonged debate and in the turnouts of 90 and 79 percent respectively in the two referenda—an altogether unique situation where the electorate directly decided a major question of foreign policy.

Yet, the less tangible but ideologically sensitive issues can also generate widespread public interest. Such issues were involved in the questions of Common Market membership as well. But maybe the most potent example in this category is the almost permanent role of the base issue in Icelandic politics. It is difficult, however, to generalize about this category of foreign policy issues and explain why some command public attention and others not.

Not surprisingly, the international climate influences public opinion on foreign policy. If, for example, we look at public support for Danish and Norwegian membership in NATO, we find that it increases in times of international tension such as the time of the Soviet invasion of Hungary in 1956 and of Czechoslovakia in 1968. By contrast the percentage of voters responding with a "don't know" increases during periods of détente.[37]

With the exception of the unique event of the referendum, the influence of public opinion on foreign policy is indirect and primarily directed through the political parties. But foreign policy issues are seldom central issues in election campaigns, and party preference is only to a limited degree determined by foreign policy attitudes.

In all the Nordic countries there are groups and political parties representing fundamentally different views from those that have prevailed in the post-World War II years. But the general picture is one of clear majorities supporting established policies. The main exceptions to this seem, once again, to be base policy in Iceland and the Common Market membership in Denmark. Public opinion polls on several occasions since entry into the EC have shown a majority against continued membership.

We have already mentioned the broad-based public support for the basic principles of Swedish foreign policy. In Finland, the so-called Paasikivi-Kekkonen line has gained increasing and overwhelming public support, particularly since 1962.[38] In Norway, support for NATO membership has been growing during the 1970s and early 1980s, whereas the number of supporters of EC membership has been declining since the referendum.[39]

Conclusion

The purpose of this chapter has been to describe in broad and general terms the governmental institutions engaged in foreign policymaking as well as the nongovernmental organizations and groups trying to influence the policymaking process.

The distinction between decision makers and external groups trying to influence policymaking has, however, been difficult to maintain. In fact, it can only be maintained on the basis of purely formal criteria. We have seen, for example, that the role of parliaments can not be dealt with satisfactorily without discussing party systems and internal policymaking within the political parties. Likewise, in the corporate pluralism of the Nordic political systems, it is misleading to view the major interest organizations as external to the decision-making machinery. They are a part of it.

By and large this chapter has so far only listed a number of actors or potential actors in the foreign policy process. Only occasionally has anything more specific been said about their influence in different types of decision situations. Such an analysis would require an in-depth study of a number of actual decisions in each of the five countries.

In the introduction the two main channels of policymaking, the democratic and the corporate, have been mentioned. Based on that distinction Arild Underdal has discussed the mobilization of domestic actors in the foreign policy–making process. He has proposed a typology based on the answers to the following question: "*Who* feel affected (responsible), *how much*, and in *what* way?"[40]

The first part of the question refers to what he calls "the subgroup concentration of issue salience, i.e., the extent to which one specific client group within the nation can be identified as being particularly affected by the decision in question." This dimension varies from collective goods (for example, national security) affecting the whole nation via issues that affect only a limited number of groups in the society to, at the other extreme, issues affecting only one group (for example, the producers of a certain product).

The second part of the question refers to the importance of the issue to the group(s) affected and the extent to which the prospective decision will affect the values involved. This determines how intensely the group feels about the issue. Finally, the third part refers to the extent to which affected groups are affected in the same way or, in other words, to the amount of agreement or disagreement over the content of the decision to be made.

Though the typology is crude and does not take into account that real world decisions can contain a number of different elements that affect different groups in different ways, it can still serve as a starting point for a discussion of group mobilization in the foreign policy process. The three dimensions determine where the decision is made and who is mobilized in an attempt to influence the process.

"As subgroup concentration of issue salience increases, the role of sector agencies and organizations tends to increase, while the role of the numerical-democratic channel tends to decline."[41] In other words, issues affecting only one or a few groups, e.g., producers of certain products, tend to be decided within the corporate channel. If the organization(s) in question has (have) a clear and united stand on the issue, the role of government agencies (for example, ministries of foreign affairs or of trade) tends to decline. If, however, the organizations concerned disagree over how the issue should be resolved, the role of government agencies as mediators between the divergent views and representatives of the "common interest" tends to increase.

If the issue is a "national" one, the role of sector agencies and organizations is much smaller. Where such issues are decided depends on whether or not they become politicized. Nonpoliticized national issues are the issues in which the relevant bureaucratic agencies have the largest "independent" role in decision making. "As disagreement over policy increases, parliaments and political parties are likely to play more active roles, at the expense of actors in the organizational-corporate channel."[42] Even in this situation, however, the major socioeconomic interest organizations will not be completely without influence on issues within their scope of interest. Disagreement tends to push decisions upward to the highest level in the decision-making structure while at the same time increasing the number of groups trying to influence the process. Disagreement and the increasing number of actors also tend to increase decision time.

The higher the level at which the decision is made, the broader the considerations on which the decision could be based. The substantial content of the decision thus depends on who makes it and who is mobilized in an attempt to influence it.

Finally, though not mentioned by Underdal, the time available for decision-making influences who can be mobilized. The ultimate example is the sudden and decisive crisis where far-reaching decisions must be made by a small group of decision makers at the highest level without much time for consultation with others. Yet, the decision makers will tend to anticipate the reactions of the more important domestic actors even if they are not actually consulted.

The answers to Underdal's question may help identify the locus of the decision-making process and the major actors. It also indicates something about the relative strength of the different actors. But, to pursue this latter aspect a little further we must also look at the resources available to the different actors. The ability of a domestic actor to participate in the decision-making process and to influence the outcome depends upon the resources (people, money) as well as intangible resources (legitimacy, prestige). An actor can have a legitimate interest in participating in the policymaking process. This, of course, is the case with those who are formally responsible for the decision or for certain aspects of it. But legitimate interests can also be based on generally accepted political criteria such as being affected by the consequences of the decision or representing those who are. This aspect was touched upon earlier in the chapter, with emphasis on the political legitimacy of the socioeconomic interest organizations in the decision-making processes in the Nordic countries.

Expertise is another resource. It is found in the relevant bureaucratic agencies and in the major interest organizations within their specific branches of the economy. The political parties are generally weaker on expertise. It is probably primarily represented by individuals with ministerial experience. We have also, at an earlier point, mentioned the limited staff support available to the parliaments that depend heavily upon the expertise supplied by the administration.

The basic resources are votes and money. The more economic resources an organization has at its disposal, the stronger it is able to participate in the policy process on a continuous basis. There is, for example, a positive correlation between size of interest organization staff and the scope and intensity of its contacts with government agencies. Money can, of course, also be used to propagate the organization's views to the public at large and in support of certain political parties.

Compared to the major interest organizations, most political parties are financially weak. Their major resource is voter support and their ability to mobilize voters when needed. Yet, there is no automatic correlation between votes and influence. The nature of the party system and the party's position in it, mainly its coalition potential, is an intervening factor. Small parties in the political center have often had far greater influence than larger parties on the extremes.

The factors discussed so far may help us to understand the nature of the decision-making process. They are important when exploring discrete events. Yet, we cannot satisfactorily explain the general patterns of Nordic foreign policies, or of any other countries' foreign policies, by domestic factors alone. At the outset of this chapter, it was emphasized that foreign policy is the result of external as well as internal factors.

In an attempt to systematize explanatory factors in foreign policy analysis, James N. Rosenau in his well-known "pre-theory"[43] claims that all the potential explanatory factors can be grouped into four (at first five) categories: the individual, governmental, societal, and systemic. According to the pretheory, the ranking of the variables in explanations of the foreign policies of small, industrialized, and democratic states, like the Nordic countries, is the following: (1) systemic, (2) societal, (3) governmental, and (4) individual. This would mean that systemic, or external, factors are the most important in explaining the foreign policies of the Nordic countries. Whether Rosenau's ranking of categories of explanatory variables is accepted or not, any explanation must combine external and internal factors. But how should such a combination be made?

In several contributions to the theoretical literature on foreign policy it seems to be an implicit assumption that internal and external factors can be studied independently of each other and then in the final analysis be added together in a comprehensive explanation. This seems, for example, to be the case when Rosenau in the pretheory discusses the "relative potency" of categories of variables.

This conception, however, has been criticized.[44] The influence of the different variables cannot be conceived independently, but can be perceived only through their interaction with other variables. According to this critique, explanatory variables should not be seen as being "in competition with one another in accounting for foreign policy behaviors but as combining to produce a more adequate explanation than any one variable or cluster of closely related variables could do alone."[45]

This point of view can be illustrated with two examples from issues already touched upon earlier in this chapter. One is the abortive negotiations for a Scandinavian Defense Community in 1948–1949 and the eventual decisions by Norway and Denmark to join NATO. Several domestic factors also mentioned earlier are relevant in explanation of these events, among them the different political attitudes rooted in historical experiences and the resources for an independent defense effort. External factors influencing the important decisions were the advent of the cold war and a bipolar international system, as well as the strategic location of each of the Nordic countries in relation to the two blocs, the coup in Czechoslovakia, the Soviet note of February 1948 to Finland, and U.S. and British attitudes toward a neutral Scandinavian Defense Community.

But why did the Scandinavian negotiations fail, and why did Norway and Denmark join NATO while Sweden stayed neutral? It is not possible to claim that these outcomes were primarily produced by certain external factors nor that they were primarily the product of certain internal factors. The explanation lies in the ways in which these external factors combined with the different internal factors in each of the Nordic countries.[46]

Likewise, the Common Market policies of the Nordic countries cannot be explained by either external or internal factors analyzed independently of each other. Economic structure and the pattern of exports do not alone explain different policies on membership in the European Community. Nor do external events, e.g., the evolution of the Community or the developments in Britain's relations with the Community, explain the differing policies. The explanation lies in the impact of these external events on the different economic structures in the Nordic countries and in the compatibility of the basic foreign policy doctrines of these countries with the goals and prospective development of the Community.[47]

A general chapter on domestic sources of foreign policy thus cannot conclude with any exact statement as to the explanatory power of each of these sources. This task must be left to the chapters on specific issue areas and specific foreign policy decisions.

Notes

1. Stein Rokkan, "Norway: Numerical Democracy and Corporate Pluralism," in Robert A. Dahl (ed.), *Political Opposition in Western Democracies* (New Haven, Conn.: Yale University Press, 1966), pp. 70–117.

2. For a theoretical discussion of the relative influence of different groups in the foreign policy–making process, see Arild Underdal, "Issues Determine Politics Determine Policies: The Case for a 'Rationalistic' Approach to the Study of Foreign Policy Decision-Making," *Cooperation and Conflict* 14, no. 1 (1979):1–9.

3. See Chapter 3, "Changing Strategic Perspectives in Northern Europe."

4. Donald E. Nuechterlein, *Iceland, Reluctant Ally* (Westport, Conn.: Greenwood Press, 1961), pp. 54–72.

5. Jorgen Gronnegard Christensen, "Da centraladministrationen blev International. En analyse af den administrative tilpasningsproces ved Danmarks tilslutning til EF," in Niels Amstrup and Ib Faurby (eds.), *Studier i dansk udenrigspolitik tilegnet Erling Bjol* (Arhus: Politica, 1978), pp. 75–118.

6. Maurice A. East, "The Organizational Impact of Interdependence on Foreign Policy-Making: The Case of Norway" (Paper presented at the International Studies Association Annual Meeting, Los Angeles, March 1980), pp. 34–35.

7. *Bistandets organisation*, SOU 1978:61. Stockholm 1978, pp. 9–84, 245–253.

8. E.g., Graham T. Allison, *Essence of Decision. Explaining the Cuban Missile Crisis* (Boston: Little, Brown, 1971).

9. Christensen, op.cit.

10. Ingemar Dorfer, *System 37 Viggen. Arms, Technology and the Domestica-*

70   *Ib Faurby*

tion of Glory (Oslo: Scandinavian University Books, 1973).

11. See *Yearbook of Finnish Foreign Policy 1974* (Helsinki: Finnish Institute of International Affairs 1975), pp. 54–63.

12. Dag Anckar, *Om riksdagsmännens utrikespolitiska debattaktiviteter*, Communications from the Institute for Social Research, Åbo Akademi, no. 46 (Åbo, n.d.), p. 7.

13. Ib Faurby, "Party System and Foreign Policy in Denmark," *Cooperation and Conflict* 14 (1979):159–170.

14. Ottar Hellevik, "Stortingets Utenrikspolitiske Spørrevirksomhet," *Tidsskrift for Samfunnsforskning* 6 (1965):91–112.

15. Eigil Jørgensen, "Offentligheden og udenrigspolitikken," in Lars Alfvegren et al. (eds.), *Verdenspolitik-Journalistik. Festskrift til Erik Reske-Nielsen* (Viby: Centrum, 1980), pp. 111–116.

16. Ingemar Lindblad et al., *Politik i Norden. En jämförande översikt*, 2d rev. ed. (Stockholm: Aldus/Bonnier, 1974), p. 149.

17. Svend Auken et al., "Denmark Joins Europe," *Journal of Common Market Studies* 14 (1975): 1–36.

18. Mogens N. Pedersen, "Consensus and Conflict in the Danish Folketing 1945–65," *Scandinavian Political Studies* 2 (1967): 143–166.

19. Knut Einar Eriksen, *DNA og NATO. Striden om norsk NATO-medlemskap innen regjeringspartiet 1948–49* (Oslo: Gyldendal Norsk Forlag, 1972), especially p. 243.

20. Jerome Garris, "Sweden's Debate on the Proliferation of Nuclear Weapons," *Cooperation and Conflict* 8 (1973):189–208.

21. Nikolaj Petersen and Jørgen Elklit, "Denmark Enters the European Communities," *Scandinavian Political Studies*, 8 (1973):198–213.

22. For comparative Nordic statistics see, *Yearbook of Nordic Statistics 1979* (Stockholm: Nordic Council, 1980).

23. Jacob A. Buksti, *Corporate Structures in Danish EC Policy: Patterns of Organizational Participation and Adaptation* (Paper presented at the European Consortium for Political Research [ECPR] workshops, Brussels, April 17–21, 1979), p. 3.

24. Lauri Karvonen, *Korporativa drag i Finlands utrikeshandelspolitik* (Paper presented at Fifth Nordic Political Science Conference, Bergen, August 27–30, 1978.)

25. Buksti, *op. cit.*

26. Erik Lund, "Privilegie-, parti- og populærpresse," in Einar Østergaard (ed.), *Pressen i Norden* (Oslo: Gyldendal Norsk Forlag, 1978), p. 64.

27. Bo Präntare, "Före demokratin—på kommersiella villkor," in Østergaard (ed.), *op. cit.*, pp. 48–49.

28. Lindblad et al., *op. cit.*, p. 81.

29. Ulla-Stina Westman, "Från Censur til Självcensur," in Østergaard (ed.), *op. cit.*, pp. 127–128.

30. Ibid., p. 128.

31. Karen Siune and Ole Borre, "Setting the Agenda for a Danish Election," *Journal of Communication* 25 (1975): 65–73.

32. Henry Valen, "Norway: 'No' to EEC," *Scandinavian Political Studies* 8 (1973):214–226.

33. Barbara G. Haskel, *The Scandinavian Option: Opportunities and Opportunity Costs in Postwar Scandinavian Foreign Policies* (Oslo: Universitetsforlaget, 1976), p. 20.

34. Lindblad et al., op. cit., p. 22.

35. For an English-language history of Finland, see D. G. Kirby, *Finland in the Twentieth Century. A History and an Interpretation* (London: Hurst & Co., 1979).

36. Faurby, op. cit., and Nils Andrén, "Den svenska utrikespolitikens former," mimeographed (Stockholm, 1978), p. 11.

37. Nikolaj Petersen, *Folket og udenrigspolitikken—med særligt henblik på Danmarks forhold til EF* (Copenhagen: Gyldendal, 1975), p. 50.

38. Yrjö Littunen, "The development of public opinion on foreign policy since World War II," *Yearbook of Finnish Foreign Policy 1977* (Helsinki: Finnish Institute of International Affairs, 1978), pp. 32–42.

39. Henry Valen, "Norsk utenrikspolitikk—sett med velgernes oyne," *Norsk Utenrikspolitisk Arbok 1977* (Oslo: Norsk Utenrikspolitisk Institutt, 1978), pp. 95–144.

40. Underdal, op. cit., p. 2.

41. Ibid., p. 4.

42. Ibid.

43. James N. Rosenau, "Pre-Theories and Theories of Foreign Policy," in R. Barry Farrell (ed.), *Approaches to Comparative and International Politics* (Evanston, Ill.: Northwestern University Press, 1966), pp. 27–92.

44. Kjell Goldmann, "The Foreign Sources of Foreign Policy: Causes, Conditions, or Input?" *European Journal of Political Research* 4 (1976):291–309.

45. Charles F. Hermann and Maurice A. East, Introduction to Maurice A. East et al. (eds.), *Why Nations Act. Theoretical Perspectives for Comparative Foreign Policy Studies* (Beverly Hills, Calif., and London: Sage Publications, 1978), pp. 18–19.

46. Nikolaj Petersen, "Danish and Norwegian Alliance Policies 1948-49: A Comparative Analysis," *Cooperation and Conflict* 14 (1979):193–210.

47. Arild Underdal, "Diverging Roads to Europa," *Cooperation and Conflict* 10 (1975): 65–76.

4
Changing Strategic Perspectives in Northern Europe

Nils Andrén

Background

Strategic perspectives presently relate primarily to the changing conditions for the security of the Nordic countries in the East-West context. The means available for the Nordic countries to respond are of various kinds. In a long-term perspective their security goals are often defined as making the environment, regional or global, more "peace prone," by helping to dissolve tensions, to increase the respect for international law, and to create more social and economic equality in the international system as a whole. In current policy these aims are translated into United Nations-related activities, arms control and disarmament policies, participation in the North-South dialogue, and development aid. In domestic political debates and diplomatic activities, these questions often play a far greater role than the political and military responses to short-range threats and challenges such as alliances or neutrality, aid and armaments.

Changing strategic perspectives also include new ideas concerning possible threats emerging in the international system as a result of technological and economic developments. These new threats reflect the paradox that in spite of the high level of armaments in most industrial societies, the probability of war between them is generally regarded as low. Other methods of aggression, especially those of an economic character, are brought into focus. The impact of the oil crisis on the economic well-being of the industrial societies has illustrated the current vulnerability of the North, especially if confronted with actions directed against them from resource-rich countries in the South.

For their immediate security concerns the Nordic countries still depend primarily on the political conditions in Europe, which are dominated by the East-West cleavage. Historically these five Nordic or Scandinavian countries (Denmark, Finland, Iceland, Norway, Sweden) have reacted to their international environment in different ways. The traditional pattern has been one of both conflict and cooperation, internally as well as with states outside the Nordic area, and of integration and disintegration.[1] Insistence on mutual independence has greatly influenced the forms of cooperation and integration that have developed among the Nordic states. These forms are reflected in the role of the Nordic Council as a forum for consultation and recommendations rather than for mutually binding decisions.[2]

As in the past, present efforts to bring the Nordic countries closer together have always been counterbalanced by the strong pull of extra-Nordic forces and by the strategic necessity imposed on the different Nordic countries by both their geopolitical situation and their historical traditions. Each country has had, and still retains, its own profile in these respects.

Geographically, Denmark consists of a peninsula with surrounding islands on the Baltic side, connected to the Federal Republic of Germany by its only land frontier. Finland has two land borders, the longest in the east with the Soviet Union and the shorter in the west with Sweden. Norway's long mountainous "back" is turned chiefly to Sweden and Finland, but a short part in the extreme north faces the Soviet Union—forming the only direct borderline in the whole of Europe between NATO and the main Warsaw Pact power. Sweden alone in the Nordic area is sheltered by its neighbors from direct land frontier contact with any present or recent great power. These geographical conditions have to a great extent influenced the international roles of the states concerned.

Two observations concerning the traditions and historical experiences of the Nordic countries are important in the present context. The first is that on the eve of World War II, all the states had adopted a policy of isolated neutrality. There were no explicit bonds of mutual security obligations among the Nordic nations. The second point is that World War II taught the five states different lessons. Denmark, Norway, and Finland had all, for obvious but not identical reasons, concluded that splendid isolation had not provided security. Sweden alone was encouraged by the historical experience to believe that isolated neutrality remained a practical security policy option for the future.

Five National Security Policies or One Nordic Balance?

The basic preoccupation for Nordic, as indeed for all European security policy, has for more than thirty years been the overwhelming presence of one single dominating power on the European continent—the

Soviet Union. The efforts to redress this imbalance have successively led to alliance building, the confrontation of the cold war, and the subsequent era of negotiations, usually referred to as détente. The East-West antagonism remains the predominant factor for European tension and insecurity.

Only during the last decade has the idea of its overwhelming significance been challenged. The concepts of national security and of possible external threats have taken on a broader meaning. The impact of the oil policies of the Organization of Petroleum Exporting Countries (OPEC) on the economic well-being of the industrialized countries have brought home the lesson of the great economic vulnerability of the North—and especially of the "North-West." Other factors have pointed in the same direction: the restless mood prevailing in many underdeveloped countries, the experiences of international terrorism, and the perception of the increasing vulnerability in an automated, computerized, and growingly nuclearized society.

The East-West dichotomy remains the crucial problem for Nordic military security. The Nordic responses to the cold war in 1948–1949 resulted in a set of national policies that are still pursued and that constitute a regional pattern often referred to as the Nordic balance.[3] The national, historical backgrounds provide the chief explanation for the countries' different roads toward protection of national security. However, their choices were also influenced by different interpretations of the urgency of a growing Soviet threat. The main characteristics of the Nordic pattern are well established.

Denmark and Norway are members of NATO but have, in peacetime, neither nuclear weapons nor allied troops on their territories. The only exception is some 200 U.S. troops on Greenland, a territory under Danish sovereignty, with wide self-government since 1979. However, both countries reserve the right to reverse their no-base policies by a unilateral decision. In addition, Norway has very small forces deployed in the area adjacent to the important and vulnerable Soviet naval base on the Kola peninsula.

Swedish security policy is based on the absence of alignments with other powers. The declared ambition of Sweden is to remain neutral in the case of a war in Europe.[4] This goal is supported by a defense establishment with low peacetime preparedness, but with great strength when mobilized.

The security policy of Finland is conducted within the framework of the Treaty of Friendship, Cooperation and Mutual Assistance, concluded with the Soviet Union in 1948.[5] Like Sweden, Finland has a large wartime defense establishment. More than Sweden, Finland rotates the training of the conscripts in order to maintain constantly a number of army units in preparedness in peacetime. Technologically, the Finnish defense is restricted both by the peace treaty signed after World War II and by the limitations of its economic and industrial resources.

With the exception of Greenland, Iceland is the only NATO-aligned Nordic territory with permanently stationed allied forces on its soil. This is in accordance with agreements between Iceland and the United States since 1951.[6] The U.S. force on the Keflavík base is today limited to about 4,000 troops.

One important characteristic of this Nordic security pattern is the relative absence of a direct confrontation between the power blocs. In practice, the Nordic area as a whole constitutes a kind of buffer zone between the blocs. As a result of the individual strategic policies pursued by the countries, this buffer is neither totally self-reliant nor wholly allied. It is certainly true that the Nordic countries chose their roles—or accepted them—primarily with regard to their own national interests. Nevertheless, the final result of these security policies may well, with only a little exaggeration, be characterized as an experiment in international détente by means of partly unilateral, partly bilateral, "confidence building measures" of various kinds.

They are based on a common wish to combine national security with regional détente between the power blocs. While the Treaty of Friendship, Cooperation and Mutual Assistance between Finland and the Soviet Union represents a bilateral undertaking, Sweden's policy of neutrality and Denmark's and Norway's decisions to restrict allied military presence are clearly unilateral undertakings. There is, however, an implicit bilateralism or multilateralism involved in these unilateral undertakings. They are framed in order to be accepted and recognized as valuable by one or more other parties.

In theoretical retrospect, the Nordic countries were in 1948–1949 confronted with three different options: to fall back on an isolated national policy of neutrality, to establish a broad Nordic solution of regional security (with or without superpower linkage), or to conclude some kind of alliance with the great powers. In practice, no country seriously considered more than two of these options.

Sweden and Norway were the two chief actors during the negotiations that preceded the final choices. Sweden adhered to its traditional belief in a strict form of neutrality. Even if it had not always been able to conduct such a policy in perfect accord with the tenets of international law, the policy had been sufficiently successful to avoid hostile aggression. The war taught another lesson. Swedish attempts to create arrangements of mutual protection with neighboring countries to reduce wartime destruction and great power influence had always been unsuccessful, too weak, or too late.

Confronted with the new development in Europe leading to the formation of mutually hostile blocs, Sweden feared the intrusion of great power influence in Scandinavia. This would increase tension in northern Europe and also create difficulties for the Swedish policy of neutrality. Hence, Sweden was anxious to make Denmark and Norway abstain from joining the emerging Atlantic security organization. As an alternative, Sweden proposed a defense alliance between Denmark, Norway, and Sweden. Such a Scandinavian solution was not a totally Nordic solution as both Finland and Iceland were excluded. However, in spite of Danish support it proved unrealistic. The Swedes insisted that a Scandinavian defense alliance should remain outside the alliance system of the major powers.[7]

The Norwegian political leadership finally settled for a different view. Norway had learned other lessons than had Sweden. According to the Norwegian interpretation of recent history, security could not be attained by neutrality, either isolated or on a Scandinavian basis. It would be necessary to participate in a much broader security arrangement.

From a Swedish point of view, the Scandinavian negotiations were wrecked by the Norwegian demands for some kind of military collaboration with the Western powers in the emerging Atlantic pact. In Norwegian eyes, they failed because of stubborn Swedish refusal to abandon the goal of uncompromising neutrality. The Norwegian-Swedish disagreement did in fact also deprive Denmark of the Scandinavian option.

The two wars recently fought, and lost, against the Soviet Union decided Finland's orientation. Its position necessitated close and trustful ties with the big eastern neighbor. It could no longer take advantage of the absence of, or of a balance between, major powers in the Baltic. Finland in reality lacked the freedom to choose any solution that did not include virtual external dependence on the Soviet Union. Its problem was to find an acceptable formula that made such dependence compatible with domestic liberty and, if possible, with a neutral image. So far, the 1948 Treaty of Friendship, Cooperation and Mutual Assistance has successfully served as such a formula.

For Iceland, only recently fully independent, the pressure of its important strategic position, in combination with very small national resources and a complete lack of any domestic defense preparations, made an allied, Atlantic position a political necessity.

In comparison with the situation before World War II the final result was security policy disintegration in northern Europe. The Nordic countries, traditionally striving for neutrality, had been brought closely into the security systems of the predominant powers in Europe. In fact, the alignments and conditions of dependence created by the war were preserved; Denmark, Norway and Iceland relied on the Atlantic powers, Finland sought the confidence and support of the strongest power on the European continent (now the Soviet Union, not Germany), and Sweden resumed its efforts to establish credibility as a neutral nation.

The stability of a system can be preserved and protected in various ways. A fundamental prerequisite for stability is the absence of strong external and internal challenges. Another important condition is that the members of the system believe in the usefulness of the system. It is obvious that this belief among the Nordic peoples is by and large deeprooted and based on clearly perceived national interests. For Norway and Denmark the "minimum conditions" of the base and nuclear restrictions provide a combination of high security with low provocation, internationally as well as domestically. For Finland, the role has offered a unique opportunity to retain national and political identity by avoiding complete economic and security integration into the Soviet system. Sweden can pursue its traditional neutrality policy for its own best interest, for its Nordic neighbors and, indeed, for both the superpowers.

The last point is important, since a fundamental prerequisite for the continuation of the Nordic pattern is its usefulness to the major powers. By their NATO memberships the three "West-Nordic" countries (Denmark, Iceland, and Norway) contribute to the common Western mutual insurance against major war, which might well include the Nordic area. The base and nuclear restrictions are formulated in a manner indicating a permanent possibility of removing them should the situation appear critical. Similarly, the Soviet-Finnish treaty serves as an instrument to secure Finnish cooperation in protection of the Soviet North-West flank. Finally, as long as Sweden remains not-aligned and strong enough to make credible its refusal to allow either side access to its territory for strategic advantage, neither bloc needs to be preoccupied with the longest border in Europe between East and West. For these reasons, the pattern of the Nordic balance is, it is hoped, protected by the positive appreciation by the states and blocs dominating the European scene. It is, in fact, an element of European détente, established long before this term became a household word in European and global politics. This function is maintained also after grave doubts have been cast on the reality of a more general, European or global détente.

As a consequence of the positive view held of the Nordic balance as a stable and beneficial regional pattern in northern Europe, this concept also holds strong normative elements. It may be regarded both as a description of an existing reality and as a prescription for a proper Nordic security policy. Few critical voices are raised, and even fewer are taken seriously. Given the present external conditions, the prevailing situation is understood to be in the best interest of all the parties concerned. The idea of a Scandinavian defense alliance is dead. In fact, fear of unfaithfulness to the role provided by the traditional strategic cast is often the motive behind sporadic neighborly criticism of pursued security policies.[8]

A question frequently raised in regional strategic analysis is to what extent the Nordic security pattern offers both the superpowers and, to some extent, the Nordic countries certain "redressing" options should the balance be rocked or threatened. If these options are realistic and effective, the pattern or the balance is not likely to be exposed to serious challenges. So far, the political climate in the Nordic area has not been exposed to threats that have undermined the belief in the viability of the Nordic balance as a stable "system." There has, however, been at least one clear instance of considerable strain. The so-called note crisis between Finland and the Soviet Union in 1961 has served as a point of departure for more sophisticated theorizing about the Nordic balance as an explanatory model—or even as a model with predictive qualities.

As an explanatory model the Nordic balance is supposed to explain both the presence and the behavior of the superpowers in northern Europe and, also, some security related aspects of the mutual relations of the Nordic countries. One basic starting point is the idea that the two superpowers have interests in the northern area of Europe that are, in some sense, of a similar character. We have already suggested a mutual interest in regional balance and stability. From this assumption it follows that every attempt of one party to disturb the existing balance would be met by compensating measures from the other party to restore the previous state.

The mutual recognition of interests can explain the superpower behavior in the area. According to the theory, the Soviet Union has demonstrated relative moderation during the postwar years. In the first place, this applies to relations with Finland but also to relations with the other countries as well. This moderation also fits into the explanatory model. It is a result of the Soviet respect for countermeasures, which NATO could take in order to compensate for a more aggressive attitude. In other words, the deterrent capacity of the Western powers, rather than genuinely defensive ambitions, is identified as the restricting factor. The main motive behind the Soviet attitude to the Nordic countries is accordingly assumed to be a wish to avoid, as far as possible, increasing NATO influence in the region and a change of the present Danish and Norwegian minimum conditions for NATO membership.

A similar argument is supposed to explain NATO's acceptance of the Danish and Norwegian base and nuclear policies. A low NATO profile helps to allay Soviet fears and preserve the "North flank" as a low-tension area.

Finally, it is obvious that the Nordic security pattern has evolved and has been accepted in order to preserve vital national interests in the countries concerned. For the Nordic countries, regard for each other may be considered as an important aspect of enlightened national self-interest. For example, concern for the delicate position of Finland is assumed to have contributed to the policies chosen by Sweden and Norway.

The historical instance referred to in support of the balance theory, the note crisis of 1961, may serve as an illustration. Referring to the prevailing situation in central Europe and to what it regarded as increased West German military activity in northern Europe, the Soviet Union proposed consultations with Finland in accordance with the 1948 treaty. After a number of Finnish diplomatic moves—stressing inter alia the expected negative reactions from the Scandinavian states—the Soviet Union finally abstained from pressing the demand for formal consultations.

This explanation may be correct. It supports the idea of the political significance of a Nordic balance. Much of the discussion related to Nordic-Soviet relations has been colored by this experience. However, looking at the situation after the sobering influence of almost two decades, the explanation may be less satisfactory. After all, when the Soviet Union agreed to drop the idea of formal consultations according to the treaty, it had probably gained all or most of what it had wished. It had not been able to obstruct the developments to which it objected. But it had made its case and the points had been clearly understood by all. In doing so, it had, in a very dramatic manner, created uneasiness among many of its smaller neighbors, not only in Finland but also in Denmark, Norway, and Sweden.

However, even with this reservation it is obvious that the origin and development of the note crisis may support the idea of some kind of connection between the security policies of the Nordic countries and a system of checks and balances preserving the equilibrium in northern Europe. At least, the theory may serve as an explanation of events under very special circumstances.

However stable the Nordic balance as a political pattern has appeared since the emergence of the present bloc cleavage of Europe, it is dangerous to regard it as an automatic safeguard for an assured stability. The present and the future strategic perspectives are closely related to actual and potential changes in the conditions of the original pattern.

Stability or Change

On the whole, the Nordic pattern of security policy receives solid support among the governments and peoples immediately concerned. It is also evident that the main international actors, i.e., the superpowers, regard this regional "subsystem" with considerable confidence. Both the normative and the explanatory model concepts tend to underline the importance of and even the necessity of the Nordic balance.

It would, however, be far too risky to be comforted by these calming ideas. Recent comments, both at home and abroad, may be regarded as a warning that the future—if not the present—Nordic balance is a matter of some concern and anxiety.[9] In actual fact, the recent historical phase of the postwar period, the era of détente, is marked by strong dynamics. The forces that may have upset détente itself affect not only the external, international environment, but also the very internal conditions of the Nordic countries. However, these observations should not obscure the fact that the process of European détente did mainly improve the climate for the Nordic Balance and facilitate contacts across the bloc cleavage.

Changes in the external and internal conditions for the traditional Nordic security pattern affect the roles of the Nordic countries in two different ways. From a Nordic point of view there are "centrifugal" as well as "centripetal" forces.[10] A strengthening of internal Nordic interactions may reduce the relative importance of Nordic interactions with Europe and the rest of the world. Such developments may of course be influenced by external, international conditions and by internal, Nordic conditions. Judging from previous experience, the centrifugal forces seem in a short-term perspective more likely to prevail than the centripetal. In other words, the attraction of European, Atlantic, and global systems is likely to be greater than that of the Nordic system. It is difficult to imagine centripetal forces that would be strong enough to drive the Nordic countries toward seeking security also by closer cooperation. A possible exception would be a situation of actual or impending bloc dissolution and European anarchy.

The superpower interest in northern Europe is related not only to global, East-West relations and to the regional balance in Europe and the North Atlantic, but, possibly, also to local, domestic conditions in northern Europe. This includes inter alia the principles and practical execution of the security policies of the different Nordic countries. As long as the international system is dominated by the superpower relations, the viability of the Nordic balance depends primarily on superpower reactions in these respects.[11]

Superpower Interests

The role of superpower relations for the security pattern in northern Europe may be judged on different assumptions. Here, we leave aside unrealistic expectations concerning détente as a panacea for permanent reconciliation and for future peace. It is a safe assumption that the global confrontation will continue, however, without major disturbances of the European peace. Yet, it is clear that the efforts toward détente in Europe have not precluded the dominating powers from pursuing their strategic interests in a tension-provoking manner in other regions and in other fields. To many observers, détente appears to be an alternative method of striving for goals that, previously, were pursued with means with far less pleasing names. Pessimistic, or simply realistic, this view seems to be confirmed by the tiny results reached so far during the "era of negotiations." It is clear that the political expectations surrounding détente are of a quite different character today than a few years ago. The persistent growth in Soviet and Warsaw Pact military power and the NATO response in increasing military appropriations, Soviet activities in Africa and in Asia, the modest achievements of the 1975 Conference on Security and Cooperation in Europe (CSCE) in 1975, and the abject failure of the review conferences in Belgrade and Madrid—stressing inter alia incompatible positions on human rights—are well-known facts reflecting this change.

Superpower nuclear naval strategy makes northern Europe significant in a global perspective. The role of the Arctic and the Norwegian seas for the nuclear strategy of both superpowers is often stressed and rarely underestimated. These waters constitute the major Soviet naval highway to the open seas. This fact adds to their importance in the West. Recent decisions to increase the importance of the Soviet Pacific naval presence are unlikely to change this situation in any significant respect.[12]

The deployment of nuclear submarines is in a gradual process of change. Missile ranges increase. Already the superpowers are able to deploy strategic submarines at a much longer distance from the target area than before. Hence, they can also remain closer to their own homeland. These changes are not likely to reduce superpower interest in the north and northeast Atlantic waters or in northern Europe. The home waters will retain their attraction to the opposite party, but now increasingly for submarine watching and hunting activities. The possible effects of the future roles assigned to cruise missiles in the strategic balance may also affect the significance of the Nordic region—allied or not. Expectations and apprehensions for future military consequences of these new developments have been expressed both in the United States and the Soviet Union.[13]

It seems still plausible, however, to believe that both superpowers retain a genuine concern for the stability of the Nordic region. The stability of the Nordic countries in their traditional external roles is likely to remain in the best interest of both powers as long as neither of them believes itself capable of possessing and protecting the area alone. From an Atlantic point of view, special attention is primarily focused on two of the Nordic countries, Iceland—the Atlantic outpost—and Norway.

The strategic changes that have taken place in the North Atlantic since the war may sometimes be exaggerated but are nevertheless very significant. As late as fifteen years ago this area was undisputed NATO waters. Today both sides operate with large forces in them. The Soviet strength in the Atlantic waters outside Scandinavia will have direct consequences for the security pattern in northern Europe if it erodes the belief that Norway can receive sufficient and timely help from its allies if exposed to a threat of war. The credibility of NATO in Norway depends on its ability to bring in rapid reinforcements across the sea, also in the face of hostile counteractions.[14] Hence, it might be fatal if Iceland would deprive NATO of important reconnaissance base facilities.

The "cod wars" between Iceland and Britain over fishing rights in waters unilaterally claimed by Iceland are now history, but they must have given Atlantic strategists ample food for thought. Iceland has for many years been a restless partner in NATO. The popular support for NATO's military presence on the island has sometimes appeared doubtful. Successful anti-NATO election platforms preserve the clouds of doubt. An Icelandic cancellation of the security treaties, followed by an actual withdrawal of U.S. forces, might create a critical strategic situation. To both sides, Iceland would appear as a dangerous vacuum in what is probably—in the East-West context—the most important of all maritime areas. NATO would have to find other means of surveying the Soviet outlets.[15]

In such a hypothetical situation the following question would arise: Would a Norwegian agreement to serve as a substitute for Iceland be regarded as a new Norwegian policy toward peacetime stationing of allied units on its territory? The possibility of this kind of contingency seems to be anticipated not only by statements in recent years underscoring that the present base policy is no obstacle to command, control and communication, or to navigation installations for the allied forces, but also by the recent agreement on pre-stocking in peacetime of U.S. military matériel in order to facilitate rapid assistance in an emergency.

European Factors

The most dynamic postwar development in Western Europe has taken place in the economic field. In this area, Western Europe has emerged as a virtual superpower. To some extent this has also affected the character of the strategic balance. The relative significance of the European powers has also changed. Since the war, victorious Britain has moved down from the top to close to the bottom, while defeated and battered West Germany has moved to the top. However, France and Britain remain the only European nuclear powers. For a long time all the Nordic countries have participated, in different ways, with considerable vigor and success in the process of European economic growth and integration. How dependent have they become on Western Europe as an economic system? What consequences can this have for their security policies and hence for their place in the present East-West system of confrontation and détente?

The economic importance of European trade for the Nordic countries is illustrated in Tables 4.1 and 4.2. Among the Nordic countries, Denmark has the strongest community of interest with Western Europe. It is the only Nordic member of the Common Market. It is also a member of the West European–Atlantic security system. However, alongside this firm commitment to the West European system, the old ideological orientation toward the regional concepts of Nordism or Scandinavianism remains probably firmer in Denmark than in any other Nordic country. In the competition between, on the one hand, economic and security interests and, on the other hand, idealistic, Scandinavian attitudes, the latter is unlikely, however, to have any major importance in the wider political context. At its best, it may help to preserve Danish and Nordic values and social and cultural loyalties in the face of the forces pulling the society closer to Europe, especially to the Federal Republic of Germany.

For its security, Finland has been attached to the East by recent history, by strategic importance, and by necessity as well as by formal obligations under the 1948 treaty with the Soviet Union. However, as indicated by the trade statistics, the Western states, bloc aligned and neutrals, still form Finland's most important trading partners. Clearly, this imbalance between trade and security orientation has sometimes been regarded as a potential political problem. However, Finland's

85

TABLE 4.1

NORDIC WORLD TRADE 1960-1977

A. Imports

% share from country/countries of origin

country	Year	EFTA	EEC	West Germany	France	Great Britain	USA	Soviet Union	Other Eastern countries
Norway	1960	37.3	32.9	19.4	3.2	15.0	8.4	1.3	1.8
	1965	41.9	29.2	15.8	4.4	12.1	7.0	1.3	1.8
	1970	44.5	24.8	14.4	2.9	12.3	7.3	0.8	1.4
	1974	24.5	41.9	14.4	3.1	10.0	8.1	0.9	1.9
	1977	24.9	45.3	14.9	4.3	12.1	6.1	0.9	2.6
Denmark	1960	30.2	38.9	22.0	4.4	14.6	9.8	1.6	3.0
	1965	36.3	35.6	21.2	3.7	13.3	8.5	1.2	2.8
	1970	41.2	33.2	18.9	4.4	13.9	7.5	0.8	2.5
	1974	25.1	45.5	18.5	3.8	10.9	6.1	1.3	3.0
	1977	24.6	47.6	19.6	4.2	10.0	5.7	2.1	2.3
Sweden	1960	24.3	39.8	21.4	3.9	13.0	12.6	2.2	2.0
	1965	32.5	37.5	21.6	4.2	14.7	9.5	1.7	2.5
	1970	37.8	35.9	18.9	4.1	13.8	8.7	2.2	2.5
	1974	17.4	53.6	18.9	4.0	11.1	6.6	2.5	2.8
	1977	16.2	50.8	18.7	3.9	10.7	7.1	2.4	3.3
Iceland	1960	31.2	22.2	15.4	0.5	3.3	13.7	13.8	9.2
	1965	38.1	21.6	12.4	1.2	13.9	12.9	8.8	7.1
	1970	42.6	27.4	14.8	2.6	14.3	8.2	7.2	3.7
	1974	20.2	44.8	12.1	2.1	10.8	7.9	9.5	3.9
	1977	20.6	47.5	10.2	3.1	11.0	0.3	9.0	3.3
Finland	1960	30.1	34.0	19.4	5.6	13.3	6.3	14.2	6.0
	1965	34.3	30.9	18.5	4.2	13.5	6.2	14.1	4.2
	1970	39.1	26.9	16.5	3.4	13.1	5.2	12.5	3.6
	1974	23.3	36.6	14.6	2.9	8.5	5.1	18.3	3.8
	1977	20.9	34.5	13.7	2.7	8.7	4.7	19.7	3.9

B. Exports

% share to country/countries of consumption

Year	EFTA	EEC	West Germany	France	Great Britain	USA	Soviet Union	Other Eastern countries
1960	43.5	25.7	13.7	2.6	22.6	6.8	1.5	2.9
1965	44.8	25.0	13.7	3.1	17.8	8.9	1.3	3.1
1970	46.5	29.7	17.9	3.6	17.9	5.9	1.0	1.5
1974	24.0	47.0	10.5	3.4	16.6	5.3	0.6	2.5
1977	18.2	54.6	8.5	3.1	29.5	4.1	0.9	3.4
1960	42.3	29.4	20.3	1.6	16.6	6.8	1.1	2.8
1965	46.6	29.3	17.3	3.0	22.3	6.8	1.4	2.9
1970	49.8	22.7	12.9	2.4	18.9	7.7	0.8	2.6
1974	29.4	42.8	12.8	3.4	17.1	5.7	0.6	3.0
1977	27.5	44.1	15.2	4.3	14.0	5.7	0.8	2.1
1960	34.4	31.7	15.2	3.9	16.0	6.4	1.5	2.8
1965	42.6	31.1	14.4	4.9	13.2	6.0	1.3	2.6
1970	44.6	27.6	11.8	5.0	12.5	6.0	1.9	3.0
1974	22.3	47.9	9.8	5.2	13.2	5.3	1.1	3.8
1977	22.9	46.1	10.1	5.0	10.9	5.4	1.4	3.6
1960	34.8	14.6	6.9	1.2	15.2	14.1	14.5	9.7
1965	41.6	19.9	8.3	1.4	20.5	16.5	5.2	6.3
1970	37.3	16.8	8.0	0.9	8.5	30.0	6.8	3.2
1974	22.7	29.5	8.8	0.9	8.5	22.1	7.6	5.0
1977	14.6	30.0	6.7	0.7	14.5	30.2	7.0	5.1
1960	33.7	28.0	11.6	4.7	23.8	4.9	14.1	4.7
1965	33.2	28.0	11.3	4.5	20.1	6.0	15.9	4.7
1970	43.3	23.2	10.5	3.8	17.4	4.7	12.3	3.4
1974	22.1	43.3	8.4	4.2	18.9	3.8	13.8	2.5
1977	24.0	36.2	10.0	3.3	11.8	4.4	19.4	2.8

Source: Andren: The Future of the Nordic Balance. Ministry of Defense, Stockholm 1977. - Yearbook of Nordic Statistics. Published annually by the Nordic Council and the Nordic Statistical Secretariat.

TABLE 4.2

INTRANORDIC TRADE 1960-1978

A. Imports

country	Year	Total import Mkr,Mmk	% Share from country/countries of origin					
			Nordic countries	Norway	Denmark	Sweden	Iceland	Finland
Norway	1960	10 438.5	21.3		4.1	15.9	0.3	1.0
	1965	15 755.1	27.3		5.5	21.0	0.1	0.9
	1970	26 442.5	28.8		6.2	20.1	0.1	2.4
	1974	46 555.7	26.8		5.7	18.9	0.2	2.1
	1978	60 169	30.0		5.8	19.4	0.1	3.7
Denmark	1960	12 427.7	15.0	3.3		9.5	0.1	2.1
	1965	19 417.3	19.9	3.8		13.2	0.4	2.5
	1970	32 334.5	23.1	3.9		16.0	0.3	2.9
	1974	60 137.6	21.2	4.4		13.8	0.2	2.8
	1978	81 405	19.8	4.0		13.4	0.1	2.4
Sweden	1960	15 006.4	9.7	3.8	4.3		0.1	1.4
	1965	22 643.8	14.1	5.4	6.3		0.2	2.2
	1970	36 251.0	18.8	5.8	7.7		0.1	5.1
	1974	69 993.4	19.7	6.9	7.3		0.1	5.5
	1978	92 717	18.9	5.3	7.4		0.1	6.1
Iceland	1960	3 339.1	24.0	5.8	11.5	4.0		2.6
	1965	5 901.6	22.9	6.2	9.1	5.3		2.3
	1970	13 644.6	26.7	5.3	13.6	5.1		2.8
	1974	52 554.7	27.7	8.4	9.5	7.0		2.8
	1978	83 923	30.1	8.1	12.3	7.8		1.9
Finland	1960	3 403.0	14.3	1.3	2.5	10.2	0.3	
	1965	5 265.1	17.8	1.7	2.9	12.9	0.3	
	1970	11 071.4	21.6	2.4	3.0	16.1	0.2	
	1974	25 675.8	22.0	3.0	2.9	16.0	0.1	
	1978	32 338	21.1	2.5	2.6	15.8	0.2	

B. Exports

Year	Total export Mkr,Mmk	% share to country/countries of consumption					
		Nordic countries	Norway	Denmark	Sweden	Iceland	Finland
1960	6 289.1	21.0		6.4	12.1	0.6	2.0
1965	10 304.3	25.3		7.2	15.7	0.5	1.9
1970	17 549.4	26.2		7.2	16.2	0.3	2.5
1974	34 731.7	29.3		8.1	17.5	0.7	3.0
1978	57 084	18.5		5.9	10.2	0.5	2.0
1960	10 158.7	16.0	4.5		9.0	0.7	1.8
1965	15 701.6	21.0	6.0		12.6	0.6	2.1
1970	24 672.0	27.0	9.2		16.9	0.6	2.3
1974	46 914.8	25.6	6.2		16.1	0.9	2.6
1978	65 308	21.0	6.4		12.2	0.6	1.8
1960	13 272.8	20.2	9.1	6.6		0.1	4.2
1965	20 541.1	25.9	11.7	9.0		0.1	5.0
1970	35 150.1	29.0	10.8	9.8		0.1	6.3
1974	70 390.6	26.2	10.4	8.5		0.2	7.1
1978	98 205	24.0	9.8	8.9		0.3	5.2
1960	2 541.5	19.0	6.4	3.4	6.2		3.0
1965	5 563.2	19.3	1.5	7.4	7.1		3.2
1970	12 915.0	17.9	1.7	7.8	6.7		1.8
1974	32 879.8	13.0	3.2	6.5	2.1		1.2
1978	176 286	8.1	1.7	2.1	1.9		2.6
1960	3 164.7	9.3	1.3	3.5	4.3	0.2	
1965	4 566.0	12.2	1.1	3.8	7.1	0.2	
1970	9 686.7	23.0	3.7	4.1	15.1	0.2	
1974	20 686.5	22.7	2.9	3.6	16.0	0.2	
1978	35 206	26.4	5.4	6.0	14.8	0.2	

Source: See Table 4.1

Eastern trade (larger than her EFTA trade) is, relatively speaking, larger than that of any European country outside the Warsaw Pact/ COMECON bloc. Finland has demonstrated its ambition to maintain a formal balance between the trade blocs. In 1973, it successively signed treaties with both the COMECON and the Common Market. This "equal treatment" is claimed to accord well with the principles of the Final Act of the Conference on Security and Cooperation in Europe (CSCE). An increasing number of major Soviet-Finnish industrial schemes is another sign of the economic and political importance of trade and industrial relations between Finland and the Soviet Union.

In a European economic context, Iceland, Norway, and Sweden maintain positions between the two extremes discussed above. Iceland remains a reluctant member of the Atlantic security system. Probably there is no other serious option. Like Norway and Sweden, it is not a member of the EEC but joined EFTA in 1970. Its foreign trade is almost completely dominated by the fishing industry. Iceland has a stronger Eastern trade orientation than that of the other Nordic countries with the exception of Finland.

Norway is probably the most enthusiastic Scandinavian member of NATO. Although outside the EEC, its increasing importance as an oil-exporting country and its policy of trading oil for industrial investments reinforce the economic ties to a number of EEC countries. Western Europe, including Norway, is likely to remain dependent on the protection of the United States for external security. No serious conflict between general economic and security policy is hence to be expected for Norway. However, other difficulties may be envisaged or are already present. The international energy crisis adds to the pressure on Norway to expand its North Sea oil production more intensively than is locally thought to be in the true interest of the country.

Norwegian economic interest in the Arctic waters is a factor of growing importance. This concern raises problems at the crossroads of economy and strategy. Spitzbergen (Svalbard) constitutes an important problem. Legally a Norwegian territory, it is by treaty demilitarized and open to other countries. Economically, it is in fact shared between Norway and the Soviet Union. Its great potential strategic importance, as well as the ongoing conflict between Norway and the signatories of the Spitzbergen treaty on the right to economic zones in the surrounding waters, add to the sensitivity of the Spitzbergen issue.

The provisional compromise with the Soviet Union on fishing rights in the Barents Sea may serve as an illustration. Both countries have incompatible claims, as they vindicate different principles. Détente seems to be a desirable condition for harmonious economic development in the area especially in view of Norway's new policy of drilling for oil closer to strategically sensitive waters, far north of the sixty-second parallel, which has until very recently set the limit. According to its defense minister (November 1978), Norway is "not served by being in a situation of confrontation with our largest neighbor." Regional détente was necessary, for "if we are unable to maintain détente, then other nations will soon feel forced to exert influence in our area." Genuine tension would result.

The relative significance of the EEC and EFTA is, by and large, the same for Sweden as for Norway. However, since Sweden is not aligned with NATO, the fundamental harmony between security policy and economic interests is missing. Under normal conditions this does not seem to constitute a major problem.[16] It underlines, however, the importance for Sweden of a lasting détente between East and West.

Hence, the conclusions are that Denmark may be expected to be drawn more closely toward Western Europe, that a similar development may take place in Norway, and that purely economic factors may push Sweden in the same direction. For Sweden, however, considerations concerning neutrality policy serve as an intermittent brake. For Finland, security policy obviously imposes stronger restrictions than it does for Sweden.

These various kinds of "contradictions" are the result of the gradual West European economic expansion and integration during the postwar period. Given the position of the Nordic countries between East and West, the extent to which these conflicting interests will remain reconcilable also in the future is a matter of vital importance to the countries concerned. The disquieting question is if such a reconciliation will be possible. Will in fact West European integration constitute a threat to the Nordic security pattern, upsetting the balance? This could well be the case if the Nordic countries, by their reactions to European economic development, altered the superpowers' perceptions of the stability of their currently "assigned" roles.

Nordic Factors

The absence of any major breakthrough in the efforts to find common Nordic approaches to central security and economic problems is a measure of the strength of the centrifugal forces, driving the Nordic countries toward finding solutions to their problems outside their own region. It is also a reflection of the fundamental unwillingness for bold and creative initiatives in inter-Nordic relations. Both these conditions have been decisive in important situations.

A central question in the previous discussion deals with the extent to which the Nordic countries in the future may be influenced by various kinds of forces in their environment. It is a plausible assumption that the present unequal balance between "inwardness" and "outwardness" will remain. Nordic cooperation is not likely to breed common Nordic solutions to the great problems of security and economy. The "cobweb integration" that for several decades has characterized Nordic relations has had little or no direct impact on Nordic external security policies.[17]

Nordic integration is a peacetime policy, with little influence on the normal national institutions and their powers or on the "emergency preparations" of the countries concerned. There are no signs indicating that the present Nordic security pattern will be upset by new forms and by higher ambitions for Nordic cooperation. However, with all its limitations as an integrative force, Nordic cooperation is important, ideologically as well as practically, as a stabilizing element in the Nordic region. As long as the present position of the Nordic countries between East and West depends on superpower confidence in the stability of the region, Nordic cooperation is—within limits—important both as a symbol and as a reality. As a regional stabilizer and mechanism for reducing friction and eliminating suspicion, it is clearly both a forerunner and an adjunct of détente and possibly even a survivor of this phase.

Finland is of course an important test case for the viability and efficiency of this mechanism. With considerable skill and success, it balances on a razor's edge, between democratic independence at home and trustworthiness abroad—especially in the East. Ever since 1939 Finland has enjoyed in the West a reputation that only recently may be fading. This change has partly to do with what in some quarters in the West is regarded, rightly or wrongly, as overcompliance with perceived or anticipated Soviet expectations (Finlandization). The old Kekkonen "plan" of 1963 for a nuclear-free zone—revived and modernized in President Kekkonen's Stockholm speech of May 1978—has always caused some irritation in the neighboring countries most immediately concerned, especially in Norway.[18]

The NATO decision in 1979 on the deployment of a new generation of medium-range—Eurostrategic—nuclear weapons has, however, revived interest in a Nordic nuclear-free zone both in Norway and in Sweden. The revival of the zone issue in Norway has caused consternation in NATO quarters. The conclusion drawn is that in order to be compatible with the obligations imposed by the NATO treaty on its members a zone can only be realized as part of an agreement in a wider European context. Such an agreement does not seem likely in a foreseeable future.

The situation around the Kekkonen plan underlines nevertheless that the Nordic balance is not a static system, but a continuous balancing act between different interests. The plan may be interpreted as an effort to emphasize the role "assigned" to Finland within the Nordic pattern. If realized, the plan could well have negative effects on the conditions for the Nordic balance. It might alter the conditions for the strategic balance between the superpowers in the Nordic area. However, the cautious or negative reactions of Finland's Nordic neighbors are also important elements in the dynamic regional pattern. As long as Norway and Sweden are unwilling or unable to accept the plan, Finland can without detriment to the Nordic balance or to its own strategic situation use the plan and similar initiatives as confidence-building measures in relation to its eastern neighbor. The paradox is that such a policy is not only to Finland's benefit but is also beneficial to its Nordic neighbors. As Kekkonen has repeatedly emphasized, a good relationship between Finland and the Soviet Union is an important, positive asset to all countries in the area.

The military strength of a country may consist of its own resources, of borrowed strength, or of a combination of both.[19] The logic behind not-alignment and neutrality is that Sweden cannot have access to borrowed strength as a peacetime dissuasion. It has to rely on its own efforts. Denmark and Norway build much of their security on borrowed strength. Their domestic defense resources are assigned specific tasks in the common allied defense of their own countries. However, it is the borrowed strength—the alliance membership—that determines the dissuasive effect of their own military defense. It has often been argued that a neutral, well-defended Sweden contributes to the credibility of the Norwegian defense. The only access for a direct overland attack is over Swedish territory. However, in the NATO scenario of a Soviet aggression it is a matter of mutual dependence. Hence, a Norwegian-Swedish security linkage exists. A strong Swedish defense provides increased Norwegian security if the aggressor finds it necessary to violate Swedish territory. Credible NATO relief capacity increases Norwegian security and reduces the risk for a northern war. This provides greater security for Sweden also, assuming that the target of the would-be attacker lies beyond Sweden.

For Finland's Eastern-oriented, confidence-building policy, it is important that Sweden is neither aligned nor otherwise directly protected by a foreign great power or alliance. As long as Sweden remains a credible, well-defended, not-aligned country, Finland (and the Soviet Union) should feel equally reassured in the face of Western aggression as Norway (and NATO) feels in the reversed scenario. For this reason, Swedish defense might well be of greater importance for Finland's security than its own defense. For the preservation of a genuinely Nordic role for Finland it is important that the Finnish defense is so strong that the Soviet Union does not raise demands for direct participation in it. Such an involvement already in peacetime would both reduce its independence and be regarded as a threatening omen for the future. The strong Finnish reaction to tentative Soviet suggestions concerning joint military exercises may be interpreted as an acute awareness of the danger.

The significance of Swedish defense as the most important internal Nordic military factor raises the question as to how strong this defense must be to fulfill its national and Nordic roles in a satisfactory manner. The answer is not easy. The Swedish defense organization is presently in a period of retrenchment and contraction. The reasons for this development are primarily increasingly pessimistic evaluations of its economic and technological potential. Sweden's defense resources will be less impressive in the future than they have been in the past. Still, the Swedish economic efforts to maintain the defense level are likely to remain on a par with or above comparable NATO efforts.

In the domestic debate, this economic reality is often accompanied by gloomy predictions, not only by professional soldiers and strategists, on the future capability of the defense organization. The perceived necessity of the changes has also led to serious, sometimes perhaps too pessimistic, estimates of the ability of a weaker Swedish defense to fulfill its future role within a "détente-promoting Nordic pattern" between East and West. The realities of the current situation and the future prospects are explored in the following section on defense and security.[20]

Domestic Factors

So far, we have looked upon the changing conditions for the Nordic countries in a predominantly international and strategic perspective. It is, however, a well-known—albeit not always recognized—fact that security policy, like other national policies, is often influenced by purely domestic factors. Sometimes these factors dominate, even to the detriment of a realistic understanding of the prevailing or potential situation.

It is reasonable to assume that domestic factors are allowed a wider scope of influence when there is a low degree of consensus on the national interest. In the Nordic countries security policy represents a political field in which the objective factors decided by the environment promote consensus. However, this is true in varying degrees.

In no Nordic country is there an absolute unanimity on the security policies pursued. However, in decisive situations, the heavy strategic factors have prevailed. This is certainly true of Finland, ever since it decided

in 1944, before the final German collapse, that its future survival depended on good relations with the old enemy of the past. Traditional
fears have sometimes been expressed, but have never seriously affected
the security policy itself. We have already observed that Finland has successfully managed to balance its international commitments between
sometimes conflicting forces represented by strategic necessity and
domestic pressures created by various economic interests.

Moving in a westward direction Sweden represents in many respects a
situation both similar to and different from that of Finland. During the
first decades after World War II, the national consensus on major security problems was very great. It was reflected in the attitude toward
neutrality policy and defense alike. In recent years it remains as firm as
ever in respect to neutrality as a basic principle, but it is weaker as to the
demands put on Sweden in order to make neutrality credible. Opinion
polls in Sweden rarely take up the fundamental question of neutrality or
not. The degree of consensus makes it an uninteresting question. This
may be surprising in view of the fact that since 1952 less than 40 percent
and normally between 20 percent and 30 percent of those polled do not
believe that Sweden will succeed in remaining neutral in a major European war. It is difficult to point to situations in which the government
had to yield to domestic pressures demanding major deviations from the
course plotted on the consensus chart. This is natural, as Sweden has on
the whole consistently followed a long-established tradition in pursuing
the policy of not-alignment between power blocs.

For Denmark and Norway the war and the postwar posture have
meant a dramatic break in the continuity. Before World War II and until
the German invasion in 1940, both had a neutral tradition. In spite of the
decisions to join NATO in 1949, both were split on the NATO issue. In
Norway, the gradual acceptance of the alliance has grown into a wide,
national consensus on the necessity of NATO. Opinion polls in recent
years indicate a steady majority support, sometimes exceeding 60 percent. Open objections are few; those who are indifferent or uncertain
constantly constitute about one-third of the respondents.

Denmark, which opted for NATO more by necessity than by inclination,
has always been more split, at least emotionally, on the merits of the
membership. The growth of NATO and of the role of the German
Federal Republic have led to NATO decisions that, at the time, were
regarded as very objectionable by many Danes. However, even if the
percentage in opinion polls supporting NATO has never exceeded 60 percent and has often been less than 50 percent, the outright opponents have
never held a majority. The lack of assurance or engagement in relation to

NATO among large groups is evidenced by the high percentage of "don't knows", which is at times even significantly larger than that of the supporters.[21]

Sometimes it is easy to ascertain that domestic political considerations have acted as restrictions on foreign policy or defense behavior. At other times it may seem plausible, but not quite certain. Often it is possible to point to parallel influences. Here the Common Market policies of the Nordic countries offer interesting examples. Let us again move from east to west. For Finland the problem was simple as membership in the EEC was never regarded as a possible option. When plans for a Nordic market became closely connected with ideas of a joint Nordic move into the EEC, Finland resolutely abandoned the scheme that had become incompatible with the conditions for its security policy. When Sweden had to make up its mind on the European issue, the official explanations clarify beyond doubt that security policy and not-alignment provided the motives for the choice to remain aloof. However, it is also clear that domestic opinion—especially, but not only, among the government party of the day (the Social Democrats)—was an important consideration.

In Norway the decisiveness of the domestic reaction was beyond doubt, as the people, in a national referendum, voted against the considered advice of the established leadership, both in politics and in economic life. Here, security considerations should have operated in the opposite direction, in support of EEC membership. Of the three NATO members among the Nordic countries, Iceland also decided not to join the EEC, although almost completely composed of NATO members (Ireland excepted). Denmark alone accepted its European economic interests as compatible with EEC membership.

These instances are not directly related to the basic security policies. Nuclear issues play and have played an important role in all the four major Nordic countries. In the late 1950s Sweden seemed to be moving into the role of a minor nuclear power, when strong movements both inside and outside the established party structure forced the politicians as well as the defense establishment to think twice on the issue, gradually leading to an almost universal acceptance of the present nonnuclear defense. Norway and Denmark have never had the nuclear option in this form. Their nuclear problem has been of a different kind. Domestic pressure, as much as security policy considerations to avoid unnecessary provocations against the Soviet Union, led both to decide against having nuclear weapons on their territories in peacetime. Domestic political considerations have also definitely been behind the recent rejection of or hesitant attitude toward the introduction of neutron bombs in Europe and toward the deployment of Eurostrategic weapons.

Defense and Security

In this section the defense policies and present military strengths of the four major Nordic countries are briefly surveyed.[22]

Denmark

For Denmark the alliance policy of 1949 has led to a stronger emphasis on military power than ever before in the present century. Once an economic and military power with a strong foothold on the European continent, Denmark suffered military disaster against Prussia and Austria in the 1860s. Since then, Denmark has relied more and more on the diplomatic adjustment necessary in view of its strategic position as a peninsula north of Germany and as a gatekeeper to the Baltic Sea. This policy served it well during World War I, but was of no avail when Germany in 1940 decided to take control of the Scandinavian Atlantic front.

We have noted that Denmark's security policy, in principle, has followed these traditional lines after World War II. This may have been more or less accidental, but is nevertheless a fact of history. However, in the bipolar, postwar world, adjustment to the situation on the European continent became possible only in the form of regular membership in a military alliance that put definite demands on Danish rearmament and contribution to the joint military resources. Adjustment to the situation south of the border meant cooperation with the relevant occupation powers—the United States and Britain. Only later Germany, in the form of the Federal Republic (FRG), became the main defense partner within the NATO alliance.

Denmark's position in a war is exposed in several respects. We have mentioned its gatekeeper location at the Baltic outlets. It is a flat country, easily accessible from the air and with convenient invasion beaches. Naval invasions face difficulties, however, because of the narrow and shallow straits. The Öresund and the Belts are both excellent for mine defense.

The present Danish defense, within the framework of NATO, is based on peacetime preparations primarily in collaboration with the FRG and the UK. Together with the FRG north of the Elbe, Denmark—excluding the Faroe islands and Greenland—forms a separate NATO command BALTAP (for Baltic approaches). In turn, this is part of Atlantic forces north (AFNORTH), which also includes Norway.

In the joint NATO defense, the wartime role of the Danish forces is to prevent attempts to acquire control of the Öresund and the Belts. Even if full control of the Baltic approaches demands an operation involving Norway, and perhaps also Sweden, Denmark holds a key position that is regarded as very vulnerable to a surprise attack. Like other NATO countries Denmark maintains standing forces as a permanent protection in peacetime.

There are three brigades on Jutland, two on Sealand, and forces on the island of Bornholm. In all, the Danish standby forces amount to some 20,000 men (8,000 of whom are conscripts). Mobilization of additional personnel is necessary to bring the brigades up to full strength. The reserves include a 5,000-man "augmentation force" subject to immediate recall, a 41,000-man field army reserve, a 24,000-man regional defense force, and 56,000—including 12,000 women—in the home guard. Naval units include 6 submarines, 10 frigates, and 16 fast-attack missile or torpedo craft and numerous smaller craft. The air force has 116 combat aircraft. Naval personnel numbers approximately 6,000 (1,500 conscripts), and the air force has approximately 7,000 personnel (about 1,000 conscripts). The Danish defense costs (1980) amount to 2.4 percent of the GNP, or U.S. $1,404 million. Per capita cost is $295.[23]

Norway

The defense problems of Norway are different from those of Denmark. The large territory is mainly mountainous and difficult to approach. A short history as a sovereign state, since 1905, has already produced at least three different attitudes to defense. In the beginning, a positive defense attitude supported the movement for separation from Sweden and national independence. Between the wars a radical disarmament effort leading up to the catastrophe of 1940 was pursued. Finally, during the postwar period a relatively strong defense within the NATO partnership has been adopted. Neutral or aligned, weak or strong, Norway, as an Atlantic state, has always depended on good relations with the sea powers, first Britain, subsequently also with the United States.

The main emphasis in the Norwegian defense is in the far north where NATO territory meets Soviet territory. The very proximity of the chief Soviet naval military installation on the Kola peninsula, to which we have already referred, justifies a cautious Norwegian attitude. In peacetime, the Norwegian territory next to the border (the Finnmark province) is closed to non-Norwegian forces. Similarly, the Norwegian military presence consists of only two battalions in this area.

Peace time, standby army forces total 18,000 men, of whom about 90 percent are conscripts. The mobilizable reserves are estimated to be 120,000 men, with a training period of 12 to 15 months. The war organization includes twelve brigades, with five earmarked for north Norway. A home guard (all services) consists of 85,000 men. The naval forces, including coastal artillery, has a peacetime strength of 9,000 men (5,000 conscripts). It includes inter alia 15 submarines, 7 frigates and corvettes, and 48 fast-attack craft. A coast guard established as part of the navy protects the vast new Norwegian sea territories. The air force, with a personnel strength of 10,000 (half of whom are conscripts), has 115 combat aircraft. The Norwegian defense costs (1980) amount to 2.9 percent of the GNP, or U.S. $1,570 million. Per capita cost is $383.[24]

Sweden

Sweden's traditional threat perceptions have always had an eastward orientation. Historically, this is easy to explain. The erstwhile Swedish Baltic empire of the seventeenth century was founded on eastward expansion and disintegrated in conflict with the rising Russian empire. Once Sweden had accepted its position as a minor European power, the tradition of neutrality developed slowly but steadily. During the twentieth century, Swedish defense policy exhibits some parallels with the corresponding Norwegian development. During World War I, Sweden was well armed and remained neutral, in spite of Russian fears and German expectations.

After the defeat of Russia and Germany, the Baltic suddenly became a military vacuum. This fact, in combination with premature expectations for a durable peace, led to a substantial reduction of the Swedish defense in 1925. However, already by 1936, the political signals from central Europe led to a gradual rearmament. The war reinforced the belief in the peacekeeping qualities of a strong defense, supported by a competent domestic arms industry. This attitude was shared by all major parties and remained undisputed until the mid-1960s. At that time, the memories of World War II had lost momentum among a majority of the electorate. Since then, the Swedish defense debate has focused on the problem of balancing resources and threat perceptions. It has been colored by fading war reminiscences and the more immediate impression of a stable European peace under the dark shadow of the terror balance and interbloc détente, as well as by perceptions of traditional and new threats.

For Norway and Denmark, NATO supplies the justification and role of their national defenses. Sweden, as a not-aligned state, has both to conceive its own doctrine and to build its own defense. On the whole, the official Swedish defense policy has been marked by more than a modicum of optimism as to the meaningfulness of combining a policy of neutrality and a conventional military defense for the protection of national security. The belief in the defense component is supported by the idea that the greatest danger for Sweden will arise in connection with a major conflict between the power blocs in Europe. It is assumed that an attack against Sweden can only be undertaken with a marginal part of a superpower's resources. Consequently, one claims that a Swedish defense posture attainable within the resources of the country—however small in an international context—may well serve as a peace preserver. Military access to Sweden would appear more costly than the value of the gains from taking possession of the country or some part of it. Nuclear war can never be ruled out as an impossibility. However, a sufficient number of conventional war scenarios can well be imagined to justify a conventional defense with minute chances of survival in a nuclear battle environment.

The policy of neutrality has had a number of corollaries. A national defense industry exists to provide the Swedish defense with enough weapons to ensure considerable independence of foreign sources. This also offers a clear national weapons "profile" related to prevailing physical conditions and doctrines of defense. Major domestically produced weapons systems include aircraft, tanks, guns, and warships.

Fully mobilized the army amounts to 28 brigades, 150 independent battalions, and some 500 independent company units. To this strength one may add some 100,000 men in the home guard plus other, noncombat, voluntary auxiliary units. The navy is currently phasing out its destroyers. There are 12 submarines, 3 mine-laying ships, and about 70 minor light combat crafts, including fast-attack crafts and minesweepers. The coastal artillery consists of 34 battalions. The air force currently has a strength of some 400 combat aircraft.

The minimum training period for the majority of the army conscripts is seven and a half months. The length varies with the individual assignments within the war organization. The maximum training period is fifteen months. In peacetime the army consists of about 45,000 men, including 36,000 conscripts in basic training. The navy has 10,000 (6,600 conscripts) and the air force 9,800 men (4,600 conscripts). Total defense expenditure in 1979 was U.S. $3,588 million. This corresponds to 3.2 percent of the GNP and amounts to $432 per head.[25]

Finland

Finland is the youngest of the four major Nordic states. Unlike Norway and Iceland it has not had a historic period of independence previous to 1917, when it achieved its statehood. The importance of a national defense dominated Finland's security policy during the years up to the end of World War II. The Winter War (1939–1940) underlined the importance and possibilities of national defense for a small state. During the Continuation War (1941–1944)—closely connected with the German attack on the Soviet Union—the importance of military power as an instrument of defense policy was also obvious. This was seen in the recovery of territories lost after the Winter War. Later in defeat, it enabled the Finns to oust the German allies in order to secure reasonable armistice conditions from the Soviet Union.

After World War II, the priorities among the instruments of national security changed. The old obsession with the necessity of defense against the Eastern neighbor became obsolete. The impossibility of providing security primarily by military means was recognized. In the terms of the Second Parliamentary Defense Commission (1976), "the most important instruments of security policy are foreign policy and defense policy and, in the broad sense, also foreign trade policy. Foreign policy ranks first in Finland's security policy. . . . National defense policy must be seen with the whole of security policy as a support to foreign policy and guarantor of its continuity in the event of a crisis affecting Finland." The position of defense policy as an adjunct to foreign policy is clearly nothing special for Finland. However, the way in which this self-evident proposition is presented is more conspicuous.

Finland's defense, after mobilization, consists of twenty brigades, some twenty-five small naval attack (surface) crafts, and sixty combat aircrafts. Peacetime army personnel of about 35,000 includes 24,000 conscripts. Navy personnel amounts to 2,500 (1,900 conscripts) and the air force 3,000 (2,000 conscripts) with forty-nine combat aircraft. Defense expenditure in 1979 was U.S. $656 million, corresponding to 1.5 percent of the GNP. Defense cost per head was $142.[26]

The Significance of Détente

Détente between the major blocs is a clear security interest for the Nordic countries—irrespective of their own relations to the blocs. Normal relations with a minimum of tension between East and West is a valuable political asset for countries located in an exposed borderline region. This holds true for all the Nordic states, but especially for Sweden who must maintain its neutral credibility under conditions marked by far-reaching economic integration with the Western industrial world.

Hence, a state of European détente is an important asset for security.

However, the illusion of détente may be a danger if it leads to an underestimation of the risks involved in the international situation. This dichotomy between hope and fear has marked the security policy discussions concerning détente in the Nordic countries as well as elsewhere in the world.

In a political sense the greatest contribution the Nordic countries can make toward promoting conditions favorable to détente is probably to continue to play their part in making the Nordic area a region of internal stability. Continued credible role fulfillments within the East-West balance in line with the pattern previously presented is hence regarded as very important.

The impact *of* détente here also includes the impact *on* détente. The question has sometimes been raised to what extent the Nordic region may be said to constitute a "bridge" between two fundamentally different, mutually suspicious social and political systems. A "bridge-building" political philosophy appeared in the 1940s and early 1950s both in Norwegian and in Swedish foreign policy debates. Later it has primarily been promoted by Finland.

The idea of bridge building is imprecise and can be given different interpretations. It may reflect a belief in the special role of a third, alternative system between capitalistic, politically democratic systems and socialist systems, without political but, according to some definitions, with economic democracy. States representing both socialist ambitions and political democracy might then be regarded as some kind of link between the two opposite systems. These ideas have on the whole been abandoned. Social democracy—always repugnant to the communist brand of socialism—appears more as an alternative to other competing models than as a bridge in any practical political sense.

Bridge building may also have a less ambitious and more realistic meaning. It may simply mean a readiness and an ability to provide good offices in situations when some form of contact between antagonistic blocs or assistance in critical situations is required. In this sense, the individual Nordic countries have, from time to time, been able to "build bridges" together with other states in similar situations. Neutrals, not only Austria and Burma, but also Sweden and pre-NATO Norway, have supplied the United Nations with acceptable candidates for the office of secretary-general. Right from the beginning, the North European states have contributed personnel to United Nations troops for peacekeeping operations. This role is a limited but important subject for joint consultations and cooperation between the defense establishments of the five countries. The Conference for Security and Cooperation in Europe

(CSCE) has started a dialogue in which the Nordic countries have taken great interest. Finland has taken a very active part in promoting it by hosting some of its meetings, including the concluding summit session, thus making the Final Act of 1975 the "Helsinki document."

In the context of this chapter, the first of the three "baskets," in which the issues on the CSCE were grouped, is of particular interest. This deals with military, confidence-building measures (CBMs), such as advance notification of military maneuvers in Europe where more than 25,000 troops are involved. The Nordic countries would like to extend the application of prenotification to include not only maneuvers with a smaller number of troops (10,000) but also maritime exercises. Instances of Warsaw Pact invasion training close to the Danish and Swedish coasts have been sources of uneasiness and irritation.

A "strategy of détente" should also consist of positive measures, creating a new community of interest. The second, economic basket of the CSCE has often been regarded as a major tool to this end. The hopes or expectations have been twofold: to improve the economic exchange between the countries concerned and to change the character of East-West relations; improving also the atmosphere for better exchange of people, information, and ideas as envisaged in the highly controversial "third basket." In the latter controversy, all the Nordic countries have, irrespective of bloc alignments, acted according to their principles as open, democratic societies.

All the Nordic countries take an interest in the disarmament question. However, as evidenced by their present defense effort, they do not hold expectations for rapid results as a viable substitute for traditional security policies. Disarmament and arms control negotiations are of special importance for the not-aligned countries. They offer not least a means of access to an international dialogue on central issues of security policy. Sweden has for a number of years been a very active participant in the global efforts to find solutions to complicated problems in arms control negotiations. Recently, Sweden has offered to host a European disarmament conference. It has also been able to base its contributions on solid domestic research on pertinent problems of military and nuclear technology. Finland's efforts have always been focused more on the European aspects of arms control.

The promotion of bilateral contacts for solving practical peacetime problems may also be referred to as a kind of bridge building. It is in the interest of the countries concerned, but is sometimes criticized by the major powers. An interesting instance is represented by the Norwegian policies in the Arctic area concerning Spitzbergen, the economic territories, and fisheries. These policies have been pursued in a manner unacceptable in part both to Norway's own allies and to the Soviet Union. Less ambitious schemes also related to the law and the use of the sea may be cited, such as agreements on fishing zones and antipollution measures in the Baltic.

It is obvious that these cases involve contributions by individual Nordic countries rather than by the region as a whole. In a purely regional sense, however, some kind of strategic bridge-building function may be represented by the very security pattern of the Nordic balance itself.

In judging the possibility for more important roles of this kind it is necessary to keep in mind that the Nordic security pattern reflects an adjustment to outside forces and that external developments remain the chief governing factors. Efforts promoting détente are, in a general way, always in the interest of borderline countries. To what extent they will be feasible remains always a difficult but important problem. Obviously, there are limits to such efforts. Bloc membership is one important restriction. The differences in ideological outlooks and attitudes to fundamental questions such as human rights are, in principle, beyond compromise. In practice, however, the Nordic countries have, by and large, favored a certain moderation in pressing issues that they fear could imperil the détente process itself.

It is sometimes claimed that a true neutral position between the blocs should also be followed by an effort to establish relations with each that are as symmetrical as possible. As a political principle this claim has never been accepted by the governments most immediately concerned. In fact, the Nordic trade balance in relation to the two blocs has always been very asymmetric. This point emerges already from recent and current trade statistics. Several reasons have contributed to this state of affairs. Bureaucratic difficulties and political inhibitions arising from contacts between open market economies and closed, totalitarian societies have, at least in earlier days, been a contributing factor. At times, East-West trade has also been obstructed by U.S. restrictions on strategic goods to Communist countries. The basic difficulty is, however, of a very different character. In the West, the Nordic countries have found markets for their products and have sought attractive imports. The East has had much less to offer. Hence, the low volume of Nordic-East trade exchange has so far reflected the realities of the marketplace.

The statistics available indicate no significant trend in the overall figures and in the East-West trade balance. The most important change is the increase in Finnish-Soviet trade. However, this is still far too small to affect the total balance sheet. The changes that have taken place in the trade with developing countries are by far more significant. They reflect primarily the impact of soaring oil prices. These changes indicate the reality of some new dimensions of security, which can partly be measured in terms of economic dependence and vulnerability. Generally, they can be covered by the fashionable caption of North-South.

Some Conclusions

This chapter is based on the assumption that the East-West conflict is the most important condition for the security of the Nordic countries and is likely to remain so for some time to come. This is said with an open mind to other dangers and possibilities, which already are raising additional problems for the Nordic countries as well as for most other industrial nations.

From this basic assumption it follows that five factors are of special importance for the Nordic security pattern:

1. The power balance between the superpowers dominating the European scene, a balance in which the elements are not only military power but also a continuing dialogue and ambition to avoid the utter destruction of war and to favor a wider community of interest (sometimes called détente)
2. The credibility of a reinforced NATO presence especially in Norway, in case of crisis and war, representing part of the military and political balance
3. Mutual confidence and respect for Finland's integrity in the Soviet-Finnish relations
4. The strength and credibility of the Swedish policy of neutrality and the Swedish defense
5. The internal stability of the Nordic region and of the individual Nordic states

For a long time, we have viewed these problems in an exclusively East-West context. The tensions between the two blocs still remain unabated. Détente as much as the cold war and other relationships serves as an instrument for both blocs not only to seek accommodation but also to unilaterally promote their own interests. The politics of détente, no matter how important to all states—especially to small nations—creates a world not only of opportunities but also of dangers.

It is of little doubt that the general focus on the East-West context contributed to a virtual neglect of important aspects of the North-South dimension. Hence, all the countries involved have been—if not taken by complete surprise—caught off guard and insufficiently prepared for the new developments in the countries holding the keys to the energy resources which are more vital than ever for the well-being of the industrial world. It is probably a conservative estimate that the future security of the Nordic region depends largely on how these developments will affect the traditional East-West system, politically as well as economically.

Notes

1. Karl W. Deutsch et al., *Political Community and the North Atlantic Area* (Princeton, N.J.: Princeton University Press, 1957).

2. The most comprehensive and up-to-date work on Nordic cooperation is Frantz Wendt, *Nordisk Råd 1952–1978. Struktur—arbejde—resultater* [The Nordic Council. Structure - work - results] (Stockholm: Nordiska Rådet, 1979), including a very comprehensive bibliography of relevant literature. See also Chapter 7 in this book.

3. For a discussion of the Nordic balance concept, see inter alia A. O. Brundtland, "Nordisk balance for og na," *Internasjonal politikk*, 1966, pp. 491–541; and J. J. Holst, *Norsk sikkerhetspolitikk i strategisk perspektiv* 1 (Oslo: Norwegian Institute of International Affairs [NUPI], 1967. Further articles contributed to *Cooperation and Conflict* are Brundtland's "The Nordic Balance—Past and Present" 2 (1966): 30–63; and Erik Moberg's "The 'Nordic Balance' Concept. A Critical Commentary", ibid., pp. 80–93. A recent survey of the question along the lines of this chapter is Nils Andrén (ed.), *The Future of the Nordic Balance* (Stockholm: Ministry of Defense, 1977). See also J. J. Holst (ed.), *Five Roads to Nordic Security* (Oslo: Universitetsforlaget, 1973), jointly published as *Cooperation and Conflict* 7 (1972), nos. 3–4, including a comprehensive bibliography.

4. As nonalignment today represents a special type of absence of alignments that does not apply to Sweden, and as the author rejects the term *neutral* for a country when there is no war (going on) to which the neutrality refers, the Swedish variety of abstaining from alliance allegiances is called *not-alignment* in this paper. A *policy of neutrality* in peacetime means a policy aiming at making neutrality possible in war. Not to be aligned is an important part of such a policy.

5. Finland and the Soviet Union "shall confer with each other if it is established that the threat of an armed attack," by Germany or any state allied with it, "is present." Article 2 in the 1948 Finnish-Soviet treaty.

6. "A country that is important militarily cannot be left entirely undefended. . . This is where Iceland's difficulties begin. It is obvious that she is incapable of maintaining adequate national defence". Gylfi Gislason, *The Problem of Being an Icelander*, Almenna bókafélagid, Reykjavik, 1973, p. 81.

7. The formation of the present Nordic security pattern has been described in many studies. Barbara Haskel has analyzed the reasons for the failure to reach a

Scandinavian solution leading to bloc extension into Scandinavia in *The Scandinavian Option* (Oslo: Universitetsforlaget, 1976). Among numerous studies and surveys in Scandinavian languages, Krister Wahlbäck's "Norden och blockuppdelningen 1948-49" [The Nordic countries and the power bloc formation], *Internationella Studier* (Stockholm) 5 (1976), is most useful. A number of papers in the Norwegian journal *Internasjonal politikk*, especially in 1977 by Knut E. Eriksen, Geir Lundestad, Helge Pharo, and Grethe Vaernø, discuss the problem in the fresh light of new material, especially in the U.S. State Department archives.

8. The criticism referred to has basically concerned Finland, Norway, and Sweden. For example, Norway has criticized Finland for being too accommodating toward the big eastern neighbor; in Finland criticism is sometimes voiced against Sweden for casting doubts on its own policy of neutrality, e.g., by joining the International Energy Agency or by trying to market the Viggen aircraft in NATO countries.

9. The future of the Nordic balance has become a matter of some concern also outside the Nordic countries, as evidenced by international symposia and studies concerning the subject as well as by Soviet analyses of the consequences of the changing situation.

10. See the discussion in Robert S. Jordan (ed.), *Europe and the Super-Powers* (Boston: Allyn and Bacon, 1971), pp. 194ff.

11. There is in fact no political debate concerning the viability of the present pattern, only occasional "academic" efforts to raise pertinent questions—normally, however, in support of the present situation as the best or the only politically possible solution. So, in Denmark, *Problemer omkring dansk sikkerhedspolitik* [Problems of Danish security policy] (Copenhagen: Ministry of Foreign Affairs, 1970), pp. 340ff.; in Norway, John Sanness, "Svensk mønster for norsk alliansefrihet?" [Swedish model for Norwegian not-alignment?] and "Alliansefrihet og Norges sikker-hetspolitiske situasjon" [Not-alignment and Norway's security policy situation], *Internasjonal Politikk*, 1977/74, pp. 593–612, and 1978/81, pp. 41–59; in Sweden, Nils Andrén and Jan Wickbom, "Ett nordiskt alternativ i sakerhetspolitiken" [A Nordic alternative in the security policy], *Försvar i Nutid* 6 (1975).

12. See J. K. Skogan, "Nordflåten: utvikling, status, utsikter" [The North Fleet: development, status, prospectives], *Internasjonal Politikk* (Oslo) 3B (1978), pp. 491ff.

13. Such apprehensions are reflected in the West in connection with the NATO decision to improve the Pershing system ("Pershing II") and to deploy nuclear cruise missiles, in the East in the strong Soviet reaction to this decision, in SALT II the three-year moratorium on the deployment on long-range land- and seabased cruise missiles.

14. The apprehensions concerning Norway are widespread on both sides of the Atlantic: "The Soviet Union has great advantage on land and sea in the area of Northern Norway, where it might be assumed by the Soviet Union that the West should accept Soviet expansion." Roger Hamburg, "Soviet Perspectives on Military Intervention," in Ellen P. Stern (ed.), *The Limits of Military Intervention*

(Beverly Hills, Calif., and London: Sage Publications 1977), p. 56.

15. Barry Buzan, *A Sea of Troubles. Sources of Dispute in the New Ocean Regime*, Adelphi Paper no. 143, International Institute for Strategic Studies (London, 1978), p. 23.

16. The decision in 1975 by the late Social Democratic government, which provoked an angry EEC reaction, to protect by some mild measure the Swedish footwear industry for reasons of national security (ensuring basic domestic emergency supply capacity), illustrates the awareness of this dilemma, but dealt only with a very marginal part of the problem.

17. See Nils Andrén, "Nordic Integration," *Cooperation and Conflict* 2 (1967):1–25.

18. In a speech delivered at the Swedish Institute of International Affairs on May 8. Printed in *Internationella Studier*, no. 3, 1978, pp. 126ff.

19. The terms *borrowed* and *own* strength are taken from N. Ørvik, "Avspenningen som politisk virkemiddel" [Détente as a political instrument], *Samtiden* (Oslo), fall 1974, pp. 402ff.

20. These attitudes are reflected in professional military journals, in defense journals, and in the defense debate in the major daily newspapers. A recent survey of a wide spectrum of views in the Swedish defense debate, representing eleven prominent security analysts, is the book *Elva åsikter om svensk säkerhetspolitik* (Eleven views on Swedish security policy). Centralforbundet Folk och Forsvar, Stockholm 1979.

21. Attitudinal data related to security policy and defense are polled in Denmark by the Danish Gallup Institute for the *Berlingske Tidende* newspaper (quoted by Niels Jørgen Haagerup in *A Brief Introduction to Danish Foreign Policy and Defence*, 2d ed. [Copenhagen: Information and Welfare Service of the Danish Defense 1980]. Norwegian data are collected and published in *Kontakt Bulletin* under the auspices of the Folk og Forsvar ("People and Defense") organization. Swedish data are published in annual investigations since 1952 of defense aititudes by the National Psychological Defense Planning Committee.

22. Basic data on the defense resources of the Nordic countries are included in *The Military Balance* published annually by the International Institute for Strategic Studies, London. For a survey of the defense problems and policies and of the defense establishments, see Einar Lyth, *Militärt forsvar i Norden* [Military defense in northern Europe] (Stockholm: Centralforbundet Folk och Forsvar, 1979).

23. The tasks of the Danish defense are inter alia analyzed in *Danmark mellem supermagterne* [Denmark between the superpowers] (Albertslund: Det danske forlag, 1976). The significance of Denmark's Baltic position is a major theme in *Øostersøen* [The Baltic], edited by Sikkerhedspolitisk studiegruppe ("Security Policy Study Group"). (Copenhagen: Schultz, 1979).

24. The Norwegian Defense Commission, appointed in 1974, reported in 1978 on the place and structure of the defense as a part of Norwegian security policy. *Forsvarskommisjonen av 1974* (Oslo-Bergen-Tromsø: Universitetsforlaget, 1978).

25. Recent Swedish defense studies include *Vår säkerhetspolitik* [Our defense policy] and *Säkerhetspolitiken och totalförsvaret* [The security policy and the

total defense], the first reports by the 1978 Commission on Defense (Stockholm, 1979, 1981); and the program and perspective plans of the supreme commander (ÖB), published with five-year intervals by the defense staff (in Swedish only).

26. Finland's defense problems have during the last decade been surveyed in reports by ad hoc defense commissions, the latest in 1981 (Report by the third parliamentary commission on the defense, Helsinki, 1981).

5
Nordic Policies Toward International Economic Cooperation

Carl-Einar Stålvant

In their international economic policies, the Nordic countries have followed a pattern similar to that in most other West European countries. They were confronted with the same kind of external challenge that the restructuring of the European economy brought about after World War II. At the same time, the East-West split manifested itself, further complicating the setting. A repeated series of changes in relations between the major trade powers have since then forced them to reconsider their external strategic options in the economic field. Gradually a multilevel interlocking set of institutions and arrangements has been built up.

In this process, all of the Nordic countries have been characterized by their special features. Their behavior stems partly from the characteristics of their economic structures and their natural resources. Partly, they are derived from overt political evaluations of the preconditions for and consequences of taking part in such international arrangements. Also, the particular goals and means pursued within each context have been important. A detailed analysis reveals considerable differences in methods and instruments that have been only marginally tempered by a general "Nordic" outlook on world events.

There are two possible ways to analyze Nordic external policies. One would be to concentrate on a single-country, comparative perspective. The other would be to focus on a systemic regional level. The separation of approaches is easier to declare than to follow as there are considerable tie-ins between them. Relations among the Nordic countries are to a certain extent penetrated by and influenced by external regional and global factors, shaping a complex and differentiated picture. Thus, both levels will be taken into account. Viewed from a single-country perspective, the Nordic orientation represents an ever-present force in the formulation of policy. A regional formulation, however, would conceive the character and intensity of Nordic policy in each of the countries as an independent factor determining an aggregate, regional state of affairs.

These shifts in levels of analysis are important for understanding the foreign policies of northern Europe. At the same time, such an approach reveals the Nordic evaluation of joint behavior as an instrumental or intrinsic value in the pursuit of international cooperation. Furthermore, the multilevel focus constitutes an essential dimension of the interplay between the major geographical and functional areas that provide the policy context for each of the Nordic countries.

We first turn to the historical record of these dimensions. After some initial considerations, the pattern found will be followed to the present. The last decennium will be analyzed in detail. The extension of the European Communities is regarded as an overriding political issue. It represented a shift in depth and scope of the relations between the Nordic countries and the European Community (EC). The discussion in the following section will therefore focus on developments before and in connection with the enlargement. The final part of the chapter aims at analyzing the changes that EC-Nordic relations have undergone as a consequence of the Danish entry into the Communities. The distinction between being a member of the EC and remaining outside of this organization is an important one. It defines the political setting and coalition possibilities for each country in the pursuit of their objectives.

However, one should be careful not to take too narrow a view of issues. Overriding international concerns such as increasing economic complexity and uncertainty, the energy crises, the coming of newly industrialized countries, and developments within the law-of-the-sea-orbit affect all the nations. Such developments condition ever-growing interdependent relationships necessary for the continued prosperity and welfare reforms of these states. At the same time, management of these issues becomes more problematic.

Major International Orientations

Studies of international cooperation often distinguish between two fundamental dimensions: geographical domain and functional scope. In studies of Scandinavian foreign policies it has become customary to discern four general geographical and three simple functional values. Combining these dimensions for each of the five Nordic countries would give a matrix of sixty possible positions. The usefulness of such a comprehensive taxonomy is very doubtful. Some entries would be empty, while the validity of other entries would be questionable. Yet, thinking along these lines could be useful as an organizing framework in order to localize recurrent political problems. It could help in analyzing the timing and nature of the strategic choices made.

With one important exception, foreign policy in northern Europe seems by and large shaped along four international orientations. Three of them are regional, the Nordic, European, and Atlantic level, and the fourth one is global.[1] Viewed from a specific country, they could be seen as concentric circles. The content of foreign policy could be grouped into three major categories: security, economic, and identitive or value-promotive objectives. Of course, not all nuances could be captured by the framework. For one, it is ahistorical in the sense that the genesis and growth of action parameters are by no means part of a linear, ordered process.[2] Secondly, it obscures some other policy considerations.

The most important deviant factor is the almost exclusive bilateral character of the Finnish-Soviet relationship. The Finnish posture is analysed in detail elsewhere in this volume as it is is most often thought to be a central security concern. Here, I will concentrate on the ramifications that the general modes and trends in Finnish-Soviet relations bear upon the other dimensions listed above. This kind of dependence on *one* major power in the immediate vicinity is of course not a singular, time-bound phenomenon. Striking parallels in the security field could be drawn with acquiescent Danish reactions to demands from Germany in the 1930s.

The reappearance of the German Federal Republic as Europe's preponderant economic power makes it a legitimate task to inquire into the effects of its economic might on neighboring countries, especially Denmark. However, these contrasting juxtapositions could be countered by the argument that economic spillovers due to geographical proximity are more easily restrained. In the Finnish case the differences in economic systems serve as a damper, and in the Danish case economic pressures can be alleviated through the collective machinery of the EC.[3] But the restraining mechanisms are quite different and embody different political consequences.

The Universal Dimensions

It is not an exaggeration to maintain that the Nordic countries are among the most fervent supporters of the United Nations. The somewhat idealistic notions that were prevalent earlier have been replaced by somewhat more gloomy, but realistic, appraisals of the organization's competence. In the aftermath of World War II, the organization was thought to serve as the main vehicle for the maintenance of peace and security. Both Norway and Denmark were among the signatories of the UN Charter at the San Francisco conference in 1945. Iceland and Sweden joined one year later. In Sweden, some misapprehensions were aired over the temporary exclusion. Sweden was not entitled to take part in the drafting of the Charter since it was not a member of the victorious alliance.

A striking parallelism developed in Scandinavian foreign policy up to 1948. Efforts were made both at home and in the United Nations to alleviate tendencies toward a split between the major powers and to emphasize "bridge building." Remnants of traditional neutralist positions coupled with a belief in collective security reappeared. These sentiments were also a stimulating factor in the Scandinavian defense alliance probings of 1948–1949.

Finland's position was delicate. As a former ally to Germany and being defeated in the war, its foreign policy was quite circumscribed. The creation of trustworthy relations with its eastern neighbor was the overriding priority. Reestablishing traditionally close contacts with the Scandinavian countries came second. Contacts in other directions were slow to develop. A formal breakthrough for active international participation did not occur until 1955, in rapidly improved cold war conditions. From this time, neutrality became a professed Finnish aim. The country joined the Nordic Council and the United Nations. The entries no doubt were conditioned by the very success in consolidation and cementing of good relations with the Soviet Union that the official Paasikivi line yielded. Nevertheless, the attitude demonstrated was very cautious.

On the request of the Finnish government it was agreed that foreign policy should not be on the agenda of the Nordic Council. In consequence with its endeavor to stay out of big-power conflicts—an aim formally recognized by the Soviet Union in the preamble to the Treaty of Friendship, Cooperation and Mutual Assistance—Finland played a passive role in the United Nations until 1963.[4] In voting, it lined up with the other Nordic countries 80 percent of the time, but abstained from taking part in divisive East-West issues.[5]

Over time, the role of the United Nations in the foreign policy orientations of all the countries has changed. Within economics and security it now mainly provides a forum for long-range international reforms and for monitoring global changes. Important missions given to individuals from these countries have enhanced their good reputations and consolidated their foreign postures. It can not be denied that the United Nations is primarily used as a forum to promote ideas avd values held by the Nordic peoples.

In the economic field a break with prewar patterns occurred. Instead of economic nationalism, global ideals and institutions flourished after the war. In the U.S. strategy, two layers of policy were worked out, successively. The distinction between separate global institutions in the economic and political fields was agreed upon already at the Bretton

Woods and Dumbarton Oaks conferences.[6] Separating policy substance in such a manner coincided with the traditional trading interests of the Nordic countries. The attempts to create free trade, the dismantling of trade barriers and the freeing of currency regulations were endorsed. All the Nordic countries signed the General Agreement on Tariffs and Trade (GATT) and joined the International Monetary Fund (IMF), the World Bank, and its affiliated institutions.

The establishment of an open international economy was of vital importance to the Swedish metal industry, which was heavily competitive after the war. It was also a traditional orientation for a shipping nation like Norway. At the same time, the impact of internationalization was circumscribed in this country by the *Gjenreising* policy adopted by the Labour government. This reconstruction policy implied a defensive Norwegian stand regarding any powers that could be delegated to any international authority. The Danish attitude was somewhat different. Although these global institutions did not affect the agricultural sector very much, they did contribute to a rapid diversification of the economy and to investments within the industrial sector. The Finnish situation stood apart. Its economy became increasingly isolated. The war debts to the Soviet Union meant a considerable sacrifice. In the long run, however, these deliveries contributed to a revitalization of the local metal industry. Only the traditional exports of paper, pulp, and wood-industry products found their normal outlets in the West within a few years after the war. The modernization and competitiveness of this sector, no doubt, was enhanced by the lending provided by international institutions. Foreign capital was directed to this sector and a dualism appeared in the Finnish economy creating two enclaves dependent upon different export markets.[7]

The Atlantic Dimension

The introduction of a specific Atlantic level in U.S. policy gradually superseding global aims left its impact also on the Nordic countries. Secretary of State Marshall's proposals for a European Recovery Program (ERP) were interpreted by the East European countries as an aggravating bloc-building move. ERP also met with some suspicion among the Nordic countries. For a while these countries supported the UN Economic Commission for Europe, the ECE. Norway was perhaps the most reluctant party, defending the priority of all-European efforts.[8] After the firm French-British invitation and the inception of the Paris talks in 1947, these sentiments gradually evaporated.

The walkout of the East-European countries led by Soviet Foreign Minister V. M. Molotov meant that these nations abstained from taking part in the ERP. Finland postponed its decision until all other nations had made their positions known. Bearing in mind the harsh Soviet reaction to the interest revealed by the Czechoslovakian government prior to the February coup, the issue was not raised. The Finnish attitude might serve as a first example of an anticipation policy coupled with a delaying "wait and see" strategy.[9] Caution prevailed also in the all-European field. Although still not a member of the United Nations, Finland joined the ECE as a nonvoting member in 1949.

The Finnish position differed from that taken by the other Nordic countries and also by other neutral nations. Criticism by the Soviet Union was bluntly rejected by these countries. U.S. aid was declared to be an economic matter directed at hunger and poverty and open to all European countries. The exclusion of political military aims paved the way for the construction of a somewhat pluralistic intergovernmental organization. In reality, it seems that the leading powers took great pains to extend the organization's work as widely as possible.

Although GATT defined the overall rules of trade diplomacy and the IMF defined the rules of monetary exchange, the principles formulated by those bodies were most effectively implemented by regional organizations. The global aim of nondiscrimination was intentionally eroded by Article 24 of GATT, exempting the formation of free-trade areas and customs unions. This fact formally facilitated the formation of the EC and EFTA. Trade liberalization and the introduction of convertible currencies were greatly facilitated by the ambitious OEEC program for the 1950s. Over 90 percent of trade was multilateral toward the end of the decade. The clearinghouse of the European Payment Union was also instrumental in the rapid growth in the European economies. The recovery sustained the U.S. lead in maintaining the regime and made it easier for the Nordic countries to ignore ambitious continental plans for economic and political coordination.

Once again, Finland had to keep up with the main currents by circumscribing and conditioning its participation. A basis for abandoning Finland's bilateral trade with Western Europe and for granting Finland preferential access to these countries was reached first with the "Helsinki Club" agreement of 1957. Gradually Finland expanded its activities in different OEEC/OECD organs. In 1969, the time was finally ripe for complete membership.

The European Dimension

Another mainstream dimension in postwar European relations has presented the Nordic countries with yet another option. Sometimes it has been considerably difficult to reconcile these impulses with other aims and orientations. The "pure" European initiatives and the transatlantic vision define a multilevel set of rules that stand in a complex, sometimes detrimental relationship to one other. In part, the problem originates from the open-ended nature of the European idea itself. In terms of functional coverage and geographical domain it has no precise limits. The political nature of the guiding goals is inherent in the process, i.e., a permanent redefinition of the relations among participating states toward an ever-growing-closer union. Ideas about the political machinery have been more definite than the goals to be fulfilled by these processes.

The Scandinavian countries joined the British in criticizing continental "federal" designs, favoring piecemeal functionalist proposals. They were ardent supporters of the British position almost every time European market politics was discussed. Their common views were for a time fostered by the United Kingdom–Scandinavia (UNISCAN) framework. This was mainly an attempt to facilitate payment transactions, but it also demonstrated the formation of a British-Scandinavian convergence.

The British-Scandinavian alliance was successful in defining the competences of the Council of Europe in 1949. Sweden even based its participation on the expressed understanding that matters of defense did not fall under the jurisdiction of the council. However, these restrictions were a blow to European expectations and programs. Later achievements such as the European Coal and Steel Community (ECSE), the European Defense Community, and the European Political Community had little impact on their stands. Also in this area one can note a deviant Finnish position. Participation was limited to technical matters within some suborgans of the Council of Europe. No specific policy was formulated toward the other integration efforts.

It was only the success of the six continental countries in relaunching Europe that forced the Nordic countries to reconsider their previous position. The construction of a "little Europe" around the core of Brussels profoundly affected the outsiders. Discrimination was felt in both agricultural and industrial trade.

There were inhibitions to a rapid conversion to the European bandwagon in all the Nordic countries. Their first instinct was to follow the British lead. This is easy to understand for several reasons. Britain was in all cases a dominant trade partner and the largest customer. Psychological and cultural ties had also grown since the war. Although none of the countries seriously considered any effort to accommodate themselves with the European Economic Community (EEC) without a simultaneous solution for Britain, there were slight differences in their attitudes.

Denmark had for a long time felt that its share in the international liberalization efforts was insufficient since agriculture was kept separate. The prospect of increased trade discrimination from the EC converted large parts of Danish opinion to the economic necessity of taking part in these schemes.

Norway's anglophile affinities were stronger. Although some leading politicians were inclined also to consider continental developments in favorable terms, the prevailing attitude was that its firm position in Atlantic cooperation schemes might be undermined. The prospect of developing close relations in a group partly dominated by Germany only fifteen years after the war was another restraining factor. In Finland and Sweden the idea of such overtures was even more alien.

For all of the Nordic countries, the indirect consequences of British policy considerations in the form of applications to the EEC in 1961 and 1967 repeatedly upset their positions. The repercussions of these developments forced the Nordic countries to search along several roads. Both Nordic and European options were considered for substantial as well as tactical reasons. Nordic discussions also served as a useful "diplomatic ploy"[10] to improve their joint standing. It is to this Nordic dimension that I now turn.

The Nordic Dimension

As a starting point one should note that the split in the Nordic security pattern is a fundamental political factor. Having arrived at such a "cemented" yet fragile political constellation as that connoted by the Nordic balance concept, issues of high politics and security policies are included in considerations of economic policy.

It is primarily within the economic and trade dimensions that a European versus Nordic orientation has posed a continuous dilemma to policymakers. Over the last twenty-five years a pattern between these orientations has evolved. Nordic solutions are only sought in a committed manner when no other options are available. Similarly, developments in exclusive Nordic efforts are conditioned by prior overarching and wider agreements covering more extensive areas.

Joint Scandinavian discussions in the 1940s to create a defense union collapsed as did the simultaneous effort to create a Nordic customs union between Denmark, Norway, and Sweden. It has been argued that the creation of the Nordic Council in 1952 was a psychological compensation to those circles that advocated the Nordic ideal. The council soon became the center for the propagation of Nordic schemes and proposals. Variations of the previous plan for economic cooperation were discussed for several years, from 1954 to 1957. The fact that Finland joined the council in 1955 led to the inclusion of this country in cooperation.

In 1956 a governmental committee composed of experts from all the Nordic countries recommended the pursuit of a Nordic common market. However, the proposal was mistimed in relation to the creation of the EEC, and the idea was overtaken by the wider free trade area negotiations pursued under the auspices of the OECD. When the Paris talks broke down, a new option crystallized in the form of the "outer seven." Finland participated as an observer during the negotiations for the Stockholm Convention establishing the EFTA. It was able to join the European Free Trade Area through the Finland-EFTA (FIN-EFTA) agreement of 1961. The terms allowed it to continue treating the Soviet Union as a most favored nation. Similar concessions to the Soviets were denied by the EFTA members, including the three neutrals.

The plans for Nordic economic cooperation were buried at a ministerial meeting in Kungälv, Sweden, in 1959. But three of the pillars, independently created, that would have been integrated into the more comprehensive policy structure survived. The achievements were a common labor market, a social security convention that extended the privileges of a country's own citizens to other Nordic residents, and an agreement to abolish passports and to rationalize border controls. As a later effort to codify and summarize the existing level of public cooperation, a comprehensive treaty, the so-called Helsinki treaty, was signed in 1962.

EFTA proved to be a success for all the Nordic countries, although it remained a second-best solution to the problems of European trade and economics. However, EFTA's effects on the Nordic countries were considerable and led to a domestication of the neighboring markets.

Through the back door of the organization, a de facto free trade area developed. The increase in intra-Nordic trade from 1959 to 1967 was more than 200 percent, in comparison to the 100 percent increase of exports and imports outside the region and on the average of each individual country. In 1961, intra-Nordic trade nearly matched the value of the region's trade with the EEC. The rapid growth in volume and value of regional trade could best be demonstrated by some data on trade profiles. These reveal the emergence of a veritable intra-Nordic economic interdependence. Most remarkable is the degree of change in the Finnish orientation toward its neighbors.

Given the extent of each nation's dependence on foreign trade as a percentage of GNP, these changes are important and had political consequences that influenced each country's effort to accommodate the EEC. The Nordic element increased in relative importance between the first negotiation effort in 1961 and the second round in 1967.

When Britain submitted its application for membership in the EC in 1961 and 1967, Denmark followed suit and Norway applied on both occasions after much hesitation. In 1961 Sweden applied for association and six years later it submitted a letter asking for an agreement to participate in the expansion of the EEC that did not jeopardize its neutrality. Finland had on these occasions not yet taken any official action. However, it had declared a positive attitude toward European economic integration, in order to take part in "the international division of labor."

TABLE 5.1

INTRA-NORDIC TRADE AS A PROPORTION OF TOTAL TRADE,
1960-70

(Percentage for each country)

Export	1960	1965	1970
Denmark	16	21	27
Finland	10	13	24
Norway	21	25	26
Sweden	20	26	27
Average	17	21	26
Import			
Denmark	15	20	23
Finland	15	19	23
Norway	21	27	29
Sweden	10	15	19
Average	15	20	23.5

Source: Wallensteen-Vesa—Vayrynen: The Nordic system. Structure
and change 1920-70 (Uppsala: Uppsala University, 1973) p. 24.

The standstill on the European situation that resulted from General de
Gaulle's second veto confirmed the pattern I have discussed. A new Nordic initiative was taken by the Danes only a short period after the
general's press conference on November 28, 1967. It called for an examination of the possibilities to expand Nordic economic cooperation.
The idea materialized in 1969 in the form of a proposal to create a Nordic
customs union. The proposal, generally known as the Nordic Economic
Union (NORDEK), was based on an understanding that each country's
sacrifices and obligations should be balanced by corresponding advantages and gains. This was reminiscent of the official Brussels formula of
"just return." Iceland did not participate in these deliberations.

Several aspects of the proposed treaty text resembled those found
within the Treaty of Rome. The suggested institutional setup, a council
of ministers, a permanent committee of government officials and a permanent, but independent, secretariat represented a bold innovation in
the style of intergovernmental collaboration among the Nordic countries. Decisions had to be adopted unanimously by the council, and no

supranational elements were imminent in the scheme. The draft treaty went beyond the creation of a customs union and a joint trade policy by calling for economic policies to be treated as a matter of common interest. Special policies in agriculture and fishing would have been established. A first reduction of tariffs would have occurred by January 1, 1972, and the transitional period should have come to an end only two years later.

Two clauses in the preamble to the treaty distinguished it from the open-ended commitment to an ever closer union that guides the European Common Market. High politics—security and foreign policy—was excluded from the joint endeavor. NORDEK was also to facilitate the four countries' participation in or cooperation with an enlarged European market. On the insistence of the Finns a special phrase was later included stating that the treaty might be suspended, should one of the Nordic countries gain entry into the EEC. Due to developments within the EC during the winter of 1969-1970 the Finnish position hardened. It was clear that Finland reserved the right to break off the negotiations should any other country start negotiations with the EEC before NORDEK came into force. In March 1970 the government in Helsinki announced that it would not ratify the treaty. A fortnight later Finland joined the others' efforts to find national accommodation with the EC and applied for a pure trade agreement.

The NORDEK scheme rapidly won acceptance by all governments and by several main interest organizations. In addition, it was endorsed by the public at large. This was due to a convergence of economic interests and developments within the EEC and in EFTA-EEC relations.

The Danes emphasized the importance of the agricultural questions. It was agreed that for each country's so-called additional need—above the level of self-sufficiency determined by security considerations—preferential treatment should be given to Danish exports. The Finnish representative agreed that a customs union would be the institutional framework required to create various agricultural arrangements. It would also have consolidated a framework for the growing cooperation between private enterprises. Norway adopted the most cautious attitude and maintained that it was not as easy to judge the immediate advantages for Norway. The fishery policy was naturally a question of great concern to Norwegian interests. Their hesitation was overcome by an agreement to create a common fishery policy to stabilize prices and to establish a special fishery fund. It was also decided that a certain amount of support should be earmarked from the general fund for structural changes in Norwegian fisheries.[11]

Several reasons seem to account for the support that Sweden gave the idea. The effects of a customs union were thought to be quite beneficial for smaller firms, whereas its economic influence on large and advanced processing industries was more uncertain or negligible. Symbolizing Nordic unity, NORDEK would have served as a means to balance and to countervail the centripetal forces present in the different solutions adopted by each country for security reasons. Significantly, it was hoped that it would provide the Nordic countries with a strong bargaining position versus third countries. The successful joint Nordic approach under one negotiator in the Kennedy round in 1966–1967 immediately came to mind. This objective appeared to be a reasonable one, given the prevailing lack of unanimous agreement among the member states of the EEC at that time on the meaning of the "political nature" of the Common Market and also on the political implications of full or associate membership.

Despite the fact that the four applications for membership to the EC and "the letter from Sweden" remained on the council's agenda, Swedish optimism was probably based on the likelihood that General de Gaulle would remain in power at least until 1972 and be able to influence developments in Brussels. Already in May 1967, when the general hinted at his "velvet veto," he had declared that a British entry, accompanied by other nations, would profoundly change the character of the Community, a development that would amount to actual destruction of the Community. The general then went on to ask by what other solutions and under what other conditions a British entry would be possible. Two other solutions were subsequently envisaged: a regime of associations, which was moreover provided for by the Treaty of Rome, and which would multiply and help economic relations; and a waiting game. The consistency in and development of the president's thinking was confirmed by the leaks caused by his talks with the British Ambassador Christopher Soames in early 1968. Evidently General de Gaulle suggested the creation of something entirely new, "an arrangement—an association" radically transforming the Common Market into a free trade area, but complemented by exchange agreements for agriculture.[12] An expanded EEC, where much of the political superstructure was less pronounced, was an attractive combination for Sweden's competitive economy and non-aligned foreign policy.

Also when the prospects for an agreement among the six members on the entry question became more favorable with the election of the new French president in 1969, the final result for the Nordic countries of this overture remained ambiguous. The new French foreign minister, Mr. Schumann, in his maiden speech to the Council of Ministers, ascribed a particular importance to the economic weight of the trade between the EEC and the Nordic countries. The subsequent support of France for parallel negotiations between candidates and noncandidates at the summit conference in the Hague on December 2, 1969, was endorsed by

Sweden.[13] Repeating this pledge in later Swedish efforts to influence the procedure of the enlargement negotiations, Sweden made an ambitious attempt to accommodate three different but interconnected objectives: NORDEK, EEC, and its traditional neutrality posture.

For Finland, it is likely that the sudden reversal of policy was motivated by the fact that actual membership negotiations with Norway and Denmark were soon overdue. It might thus find itself connected with the EEC through a group of countries, some of which were members of the EEC. This could give an impression of a gliding Western orientation. Should this not succeed (depending on how stiff the conditions adopted for a British entry would be), it would be connected through forms that were far from clearly and unambiguously defined, given the oscillating Swedish position. At the same time, one might perhaps interpret the Finnish maneuver as the introduction of two options to the Soviet Union. Given a certain Russian reluctance both to extended and to closer economic Nordic relations and to the ambitions of the EEC, it is by no means certain that a Nordic solution, once accepted, was more preferable to Moscow than a precisely delineated trade agreement with the enlarged EEC. In any case, it is a fact that Finland supported the NORDEK proposal on its intrinsic value, whereas Denmark did not downgrade its final aim so as not to be excluded as a member of an organization that at the same time encompassed Denmark's main trading partners, the United Kingdom and West Germany. NORDEK could not satisfy these dual aims. From April 1970, it was clear that each of the countries had to deal individually with the EC in trying to reach an agreement in accordance with its own aims. They fell into two categories: the applicants (Norway and Denmark) and the nonapplicants (Finland, Sweden, and Iceland). Before going into the substance of the solutions that were arrived at, a few words are given on the role of the Nordic issue in the talks.

The Nordic Countries Face the European Communities

In their opening statements to the Council of Ministers, all Nordic ministers called attention to inter-Nordic relations. Denmark and Norway made their declarations on the opening of the enlargement negotiations on June 30, 1970. Sweden headed the noncandidates on November 10 and Finland and Iceland appeared a fortnight later. What problems were identified and what wishes were advanced?

To elucidate this question it is vital to note what prior commitments were undertaken. The Nordic countries had agreed at several meetings between their prime ministers on the need to prevent a re-erection of tariff barriers. Recognizing the diverse forms of application for which they each had opted, a common position in this respect was impossible. Instead, they agreed to support each country's position to achieve the kind of solution that best served that country's interests. The position on tariffs, of course, was not a genuine Nordic undertaking, as it was subsumable under the wider interest of EFTA. The association committed itself to this purpose in 1961 and 1967. The position was reiterated in several EFTA communiqués in 1970 and 1971. In addition, the Nordic ministers had also agreed to safeguard and maintain other common Nordic institutional achievements: the labor market, the social security legislation that does not discriminate on a national basis, and the harmonization of civil law and agreements on educational matters.

The ministers differed in the emphasis and degree of elaboration that they attributed to the Nordic cause in their declarations. It was not clear what implications their arguments might entail. One might compare this situation to the problems that the British brought to the bargaining table. Their demands were explicit and backed by strong legal commitments in the case of New Zealand and Commonwealth sugar.

On a purely vocal level, the Danes raised the Nordic connection more often than did Norway. This can partly be attributed to domestic pressures. At the same time, Denmark found less obstacles to an EC entry and could have entered without any transition period. The Danish minister hoped that it would be possible also to find a formula for relations with the other Scandinavian countries, and he estimated that it was logical that the deepening of the European cooperation ought to be pursued on the widest extension possible. The pragmatic and comprehensive character of Nordic cooperation was underlined. The Danish government desired to continue to strengthen the Nordic relations for the future, a development that would serve the interests of the entire European Community.

The Norwegians remembered the "ancient and solid" traditions of Nordic cooperation. The Nordic market was mentioned as an important achievement. In both Norway and Denmark, new Labour governments in 1971 replaced the coalition of non-Socialist parties. The Norwegian minister mentioned the importance that was attached to free trade for the development of Nordic cooperation. But it was once again the Danes who raised the Nordic questions more as a matter of principle. Foreign Economic Minister Ivar Norgaard gave an exposition of the Danish conception of European political integration on November 9, 1971. He thought that Nordic cooperation should continue and develop after the entry and accords concluded with the nonmembers. No immediate reaction was given to the statement, but the president of the commission thought that an answer was required. In the evening, Italy's Foreign

Minister Aldo Moro indicated that the principles of the EEC did not allow its members to commit themselves to decisions taken in other regional groupings.

On the level of principle, his declaration was outright. Faced with the option of a Nordic decision on harmonization or coordination and a decision taken by the EEC, Denmark as a member must obey the latter.[14] The Danes later confirmed and accepted that also derived Community law owed priority to Nordic cooperation. In practice, few problems were encountered. Given the vague and uncommitting nature of Nordic common agreements, these links were found to be of a rather porous and fictitious kind in comparison with the legal character of European decisions. After all negotiations were completed, only one single point in the whole package of Nordic agreements was found irreconcilable with Community membership: The Nordic labor market allows favorable treatment to residents from other Nordic countries. The provision is contrary to the rule and principle of the Rome treaty concerning labor mobility. The practical consequences of eliminating the rule are small for the Nordic countries: after eighteen days a vacant post is free to be applied for by anybody. The Nordic governments agreed to discuss the matter in common and to accept the aforementioned consequences by solving the matter through "administrative practices."

The two neutral countries devoted certain parts of their statements to a Nordic perspective. The elements constituting the cohesion enjoyed by the group were spelled out in detail by the Swedish minister. In the Swedish view, many of the substantial problems involved in the deliberations were similar to all EFTA countries and especially to the Nordic group. Sweden therefore proposed that its own talks should be pursued parallel with those of Denmark and Norway. But its proposal met with resistance, as such a procedure would have blurred the distinction between different categories of applicants. Norway and Denmark also gave some support to the Swedish desire to establish a far-reaching agreement. Both delegations urged the Communities to accentuate the evolutionary character of the accords with the remaining EFTA members. The pledges, however, were not specific enough to jeopardize their own position as candidates by challenging Community doctrine.

The Finnish minister was more modest in his exposition than the Swedish minister had been and advanced no procedural proposals. However, special importance was attached to the industrial cooperation between the countries.

So far, I have only described one specific dimension of the talks. It reaffirms the previous contention of a close connection and a partial subordination of Nordic economic interests to wider European needs. Of

TABLE 5.2

CHRONOLOGY OF THE MAIN NORDIC DEPARTURES AND EVENTS
IN EC RELATIONS 1961-1978

Time	Affiliation	Remarks
Denmark		
1961	Application for membership	Transfer to international organization constitutionally accepted 1953
1967	2nd application for membership	Nordek course 1968-69
1970	Membership negotiations started	Downgrading of foreign political implications
1972 Jan	Signing of entry treaty	Parliament approval 141-32-2
1972 Oct	Entry affirmation by Danish people in referendum	57% in favor and 32% against entry
1973 Jan	Denmark becomes member of EC	
1973 July	1st Danish period as chair of the EC	Copenhagen report envisaged intensified foreign-policy consultation
1977 June 30	End of transition period	West European Free Trade Area completed, subject only to deferred timetables for sensitive products
1978 Jan 1	2nd Danish period as chair of the EC	
Iceland		
1962	"Discussions" with EEC-members concerning Icelandic interests	
1970 April 1	Iceland becomes member of EFTA	
1970 Nov 24	Iceland presents its case to the EC in exploratory rest- EFTA talks	
1972 July 22	Signing of Free Trade agreement with the EC	Agreement covers most Icelandic fishery products in addition to industrial goods
	Agreement (or rather par. 6) held in abeyance by both parties pending an acceptable solution of problems caused by Icelandic extension of fishery jurisdiction	
1972 Sept 1	Extension of Icelandic fishery borders to 50 miles	2nd Cod War with the British
1975 Oct 15	Extension of fishery jurisdiction to 200 miles	Bilateral agreements with Belgium and West Germany over fishing rights suspended as conflict is prolonged: 3rd Cod War with the UK
1976 July 1	Free Trade agreement - tariff concessions enter into force	British-Icelandic agreement on fisheries after good office mission by the Norwegian Government.

TABLE 5.2, continued

Time	Affiliation	Remarks
Finland		
1962	No formal commitment	
1967	No formal commitment	
1970 April 6	President announces Finland's intention to seek trade agreement with the EC	Declaration that NORDEK would not be signed by Finland
1971	Trade agreement for industrial products sought	Recognition of non-interference with existing treaties with other countries, no evolution, no harmonization
1972 June	Free trade agreement initialled but not signed by Finland	Ratification postponed several times
1972 Dec	Finnish treaty proposal to Comecon concerning cooperative arrangements	
1973 May	CMEA treaty signed	Bilateral trade agreements successively signed with other East European states than the USSR
1973 July	CMEA treaty entered into force	
1973 Oct 5	Free trade treaty with EC signed	Parliament approval 141-36-7
1974 Jan 1	EC agreement in force	
1975 Jan 1	Agreement with the Coal and Steel Community operative.	
Norway		
1962 April	Application for membership	113 of 150 MP's in favor. Application preceded by debate on constitutional amendment allowing transfers of limited powers to international organization
1967	Application for membership	Approved by 136-13. NORDEK negotiations 1968-69
1970	Membership negotiations started	Application reaffirmed, 132-17
		Change of government in March 1971 after Borten's resignation due to EC news leaks. Minority Labour Government formed
1972	Negotiations ended and signing of treaty	Difficult negotiations due to Norwegian demands on far-reaching concessions in fishery and agriculture
1972 Sept.	Referendum	53.5% reject membership
		Labour government resigns, succeeded by Christian People's Party Minority Government
1972 Autumn	Application for free trade agreement	

TABLE 5.2, continued

Time	Affiliation	Remarks
Norway (continued)		
1973 April	Free trade agreement initialled	Agreement approved unanimously by Parliament in May
1973 July 1	Free trade agreement in force, tariff cuts	
1975 Jan 1	ECSC agreement in force	
Sweden		
1962	Application for association	Neutrality reservations in coordination with Switzerland and Austria
1967	"Open" application	"Extensive, close and durable relations in form compatible with continued pursuit of Swedish neutrality"
1970	Reaffirmation of far-reaching Swedish goals	Autumn: EC adoption of far-reaching Davignon and Werner plans within the EC for a "deepening" of integration
1971 March	Membership ruled out by Swedish government: customs union proposed	Farreaching harmonization outlined
1971 Dec	Negotiations for a free trade agreement	Included "evolutionary clause"
1972	Free trade agreement reached	Ratified by parliament 298-15
1973	Free trade agreement operative	
1974	ECSC agreement also in force	

course, a number of other equally important considerations influenced the negotiation process and its result. I now turn to a narrative of the negotiations and an analysis of these influencing factors.

The European Dependence

It is self-evident that it is quite different for a group of nations to support the goals chosen by each other than to act in common as a bloc. The failure of NORDEK and the character of the negotiations with the EC enhanced the split between the countries. However, so far I have only touched upon the surface of the external politics to hold the impact of the domestic scenes and economic structures constant. In order to understand the final shape of the affiliations arrived at, these dimensions must also be touched upon. Table 5.2 summarizes the main features in the historical sequence of events from 1961 to 1978.

Table 5.2, summarizing the main formal developments in each country's relations, reveals considerable differences. The journeys to Brussels were not straight, marked by a change of itinerary and a reversal of appropriate end station in some cases. In 1976, all agreements had come into force. The result was that one country only, Denmark, joined the Communities. The others were all placed into the rest–EFTA camp. After the Norwegian people rejected EC membership, this country quickly resolved its relation by a free trade agreement shaped after that of the others. Apart from Iceland, relations were formally channeled into two agreements: one with the EC as an organization and one with EC and the member countries covering questions falling under the competence of the ECSC (European Coal and Steel Community).

However, there are contrasts both in the content and in the contextual conditions determining each accord. Indeed, there have been tendencies to overhomogenize the nature of their affiliations due to formal or structural attributes.[15] To account for variations one must go beyond one-factor explanations such as offered by small state theory and add country specific factors.[16]

Conditions for European Integration

Over the years quite an extensive body of knowledge into the prerequuisites, processes, and mechanisms of regional integration has been built up. Although there are considerable disagreements over theoretical designs and the content of the dependent variable, we would like to apply a shorthand device derived from such studies in order to reveal divergencies and parallels in the efforts of the Nordic countries to adjust themselves to European integration processes.

Such preconditions facilitating integration have been given a distinct formulation by Johan Galtung: "There are two bases of integration, similarity and interdependence."[17] In the West European setting it is customary to stress the importance of concurrent political as well as economic incentives to further an integrative outcome.[18]

Relationships and efforts of intensified cooperation that are confined to one sphere in the matrix of Figure 5.1 only are more rigid in the sense that they determine parameters for sectorial bonds, but assume other factors ceteris paribus. It is a common assertion that a complex interplay between economic and political factors facilitates integrative outcomes allowing relations to grow and change qualitatively. Expectations of rewards in both areas constitute an important ingredient.[19] We will consequently organize a discussion of how fears and expectations were distributed among the Nordic countries in their talks with the EC along

TABLE 5.3

MARKET POLICY NEGOTIATIONS 1967-1973

	1967	1968	1969	1970	1971	1972	1973
Year	1967	1968	1969	1970	1971	1972	1973
Month:	May	April	Dec.	June, Nov.	Dec.	Jan.	July
Event:	2nd British application	NORDEK negotiations	Hague meeting	Enlargement negotiations with Denmark, Norway	rest-EFTA negotiations with Iceland, Finland Sweden		EC-Norwegian free trade negotiations

FIGURE 5.1

INTEGRATIVE CONDITIONS

	positive conditions	negative conditions
political model	identity or communality of values	divergence of values
economic model	differences and complementarities of factor proportions	indifference or similarity in economic resources

the dimensions heuristically suggested above. For both the economic and political factors, one may make a distinction between an *external* and *internal* aspect.

The economic side of the coin is tapped by two indicators: (1) externally, a dependence perspective revealing intensities of interest to reach an accommodation; and (2) internally, a discussion of the adaptive structure—or homology—of each economy to an adoption of EC policies. The political dimension is manifested by declaratory positions taken in committing ways (1) externally, through overarching Europe concepts, and (2) internally by Community concepts, including ideas about the nature, elements, and future prospects of the EC and its relations to nonmembers.

Economic (Inter)Dependence

First some comments on common traits. As small states with open economies, all Nordic countries are much dependent on foreign trade. About one-fourth of their welfare is derived from international exchange. Their most important markets have been in Western Europe for a considerable time, especially in the United Kingdom. England's position was at its height in the latter part of the nineteenth century and has since diminished when measured in relative figures. Its position has been equaled on some occasions by Germany. In recent years Germany's position has been consolidated as the only country with which all the Nordic countries have a negative trade record, a deficiency balanced by surpluses elsewhere. The regional concentration is made evident in the trade tables included in Chapter 4. There are, of course, deviations. The most important deviant pattern is the extensive trade between Finland and Soviet Union. This oscillates between one-quarter and one-sixth of

TABLE 5.4

IMPORTANCE OF THE EC MARKET
(I970)

	Export to:					
Export from:	EC (6)		UK/Ireland		EC (10)	
	% Exp.	% GNP	% Exp.	% GNP	% Exp.	% GNP
Denmark	21.7	4.7	20.3	4.4	48.7	10.5
Finland	25.6	5.8	21.1	4.7	56.2	12.6
Iceland	17.3	4.8	15.4	4.3	41.3	11.4
Norway	30.9	6.6	19.7	4.2	57.7	12.3
Sweden (68)	29.5	5.7	13.5	2.6	64.3	12.4

Source: UN Statistical Yearbook, 1971. Adapted
from Underdal as cited in note 20.

foreign exchange. Nevertheless, it is clear that the combined strength of the two regional West European groupings, the EC and EFTA, amounts to 60 to 70 percent for each country.

The change from a Common Market of six to one of nine meant a dramatic increase in the importance of access to the EC market. It might come as a surprise that Denmark was the country that had the least to defend. But the figures in Tables 5.4 and 5.5 are static in the sense that they do not reveal what could be gained. In fact, Danish export losses in agriculture had been quite substantial since the inception of the EC, from 39 percent in 1960 to 29 percent in 1970. More than half of its trade with the EC was in this sector. There were strong pressures to halt the decline, because during the same period the relative importance of agriculture versus industry in its total trade profile was reversed.

It is no surprise then that the Danish farmer's organizations and their political spokesman, the Venstre party, have been the most ardent supporters of entry into the EC. They could point to, other things being equal, a gain of approximately 2 billion Danish kroner (approximately $320 million) by adhering to the common agricultural policy (CAP).

But dependence is a two-sided concept. How attractive partners were the Nordic countries measured in terms of their relative role in the EC economy? Together they only accounted for about 6 percent of the foreign trade of the six members before enlargement.[20] Of course, with the entry of the United Kingdom and Denmark the role of the Nordic countries as customers became much more pronounced. But trade is unevenly distributed as Sweden takes almost half of the regional share. Viewed on economic premises alone, the prospects for agreeing on far-

TABLE 5.5

IMPORTANCE OF THE NORDIC MARKETS
(1970)

Exports from:	Denmark	Finland	Iceland	Norway	Sweden
		Exports to (in per cent of GNP):			
Belgium/Lux	0.5	0.2	0.01	0.4	0.9
FRG	0.4	0.2	-----	0.3	0.7
France	0.1	0.1	-----	0.1	0.2
Italy (69)	0.1	0.06	-----	0.07	0.2
Netherlands	0.6	0.2	0.03	0.4	1.0

Source: See Table 5.4.

reaching solutions with Sweden would therefore seem rather bright, bearing in mind the more modest exchange with the other Nordic countries.

Internal Economic Consequences of Integration

The two candidates for membership, Norway and Denmark, differ sharply in their economic prerequisites for integration into the EC system, especially in the agricultural sector. The EEC's condition for opening negotiations was that all applicants accepted the Treaty of Rome, its political objectives, all subsequent decisions, and the guidelines drawn up for further and future developments. Problems of adaptation should be solved by transitional measures. Denmark declared a willingness to join the CAP virtually without any transition period. Norway, however, challenged Community dogma. The unfavorable natural conditions for agriculture were to be offset by considerable support to this sector from the government. A direct nondiscrimatory application of CAP would, according to an official study, result in a loss of income of 58 percent for Norwegian farmers. In the industrial sector, however, negotiations went smoothly.

The long-held Norwegian insistence on a permanent exemption of the agricultural sector and its efforts to influence EC fishery policy to a line more favorable to its own fishery structure were considerable obstacles to a smooth and quick conclusion of the negotiations. In fact it was the government's insistence on safeguards for its coastal population and a recognition of the "vital" importance of the fishery sector to the economy that delayed and almost upset the entire enlargement. The formula found for harmonizing the interests of both parties turned out to be insufficient for domestic reasons. The minister of fishery resigned. The conditions reached affected public opinion negatively. In the last resort it was probably the clear-cut opposition stemming from the agricultural and fishery communities that led to the realignment of forces that rejected Norwegian entry in the referendum of 1972.

Sweden had far-reaching ambitions concerning its participation in both of the principal arenas of EEC activity: the customs union and the CAP. When it became clear that Sweden did not contemplate membership, aspirations for participating in agriculture were abandoned. Consequently, negotiations concentrated on the possibility of reaching a special agreement in the form of a customs union with the EC. Sweden would then adjust its tariff to that of the EEC and cooperate with the Community in negotiations with third countries. Such a formula was found to be irreconcilable with the Community's view on its foreign ties. A sector-confined harmonization would upset the balance between rights and obligations that membership implied. Structural homology in the trade and industrial sectors was by itself an insufficient condition for an agreement. EC's counterproposal, a free trade area, was much more restricted. Sweden complained over the various exemptions and delays proposed by the EC in its concept of a free trade area. Prolonged transitional periods and indicative ceilings for certain products were directed at two of the sectors where Swedish competitive capacity was very strong—special steel and paper and pulp. Countermeasures were taken but only as a quid pro quo tactically motivated.

Finland used quite a different strategy. It emphasized modest ambitions and was satisfied with the free trade concept. The exclusion of agriculture did little harm. As its general attitude of the nature of the agreement was close to that of the EC, most efforts were directed at finding an "overall economic balance." For example, two-thirds of its exports were from the beginning on the exception list. But in Finland's case one might say that the special conditions for paper and pulp eased its efforts to receive exemptions from the EC regarding different "infant industries," which for a prolonged period might enjoy restricted international competition.

Iceland stands apart from the others as its economy is almost entirely made up of fish and fish-processed products. Membership was never contemplated. It was also not self-evident that Iceland would be a party to a free trade arrangement for industrial goods. However, the EC gave it a number of concessions and broke the otherwise uniform shape of the agreements concluded with other rest-EFTA countries. Its invocation was nevertheless pending on when and how agreements with some EC states on the extension of Iceland's fishing limits could be reached. This extraneous issue was solved in 1976.

Communality of Foreign Policy Values

In this brief overview of declarations I will concentrate on some broad aspects. It is no surprise that the two neutral countries offered a much broader conception of European politics than that of the applicants. In the former cases all-European efforts and the role of neutrality as an integral part in the total constellation was given much emphasis. It was thought to be in EC's interest not to change this state of affairs. Norway and Denmark assumed, however, that closer West European integration was a precondition for détente and the general improvement of political relations within the West as well as between East and West.

The EC did not only demand a pledge to the organization and its goals, but also to all decisions taken along its development and to the prospects that were inherent in the adoption of the Davignon plan for foreign policy consultation and the Werner plan for an economic and monetary union. These commitments were a precondition for joining. Of the two applicants, Norway was the most reluctant. Not until the shift of government in 1971 was a clear "European" statement delivered. Foreign Minister Andreas Cappelen emphasized the broader political aspects of the enlargement and also Norway's devotion to a democratic unification of Europe. Denmark had already declared its acceptance of the common goals although it deemphasized the military repercussions of the forthcoming Davignon procedures. Defense was thought to remain firmly in the NATO organization. This attitude evoked some disappointed reactions among federalists and devoted Europeans in Brussels, but they did not impede the formal issues under negotiation.

For the other Nordic countries, their status as nonapplicants went far to define what kind of ambitions they had in common with the Community. When Sweden eventually ruled out membership as a realistic alternative, its efforts to find a   unique accord sui generis came to nothing. A central theme for the EC was to defend the existing (and time-consuming) decision-making procedures and not to allow outsiders to interfere. Swedish proposals for a customs union and specific sectorial integration were rejected. Such a formula would not balance equal rights and obligations in contrast to those accepted by a member.

Finland concentrated on achieving a trade agreement in conformity with GATT rules. At several instances, both in presentations at home and for foreign audiences, efforts were made to view an accommodation with the EC as an adaptation to and fulfillment of previously accepted undertakings in the GATT, EFTA, and other organizations. The autonomy of both parties was to be ensured. Finally, it was acknowledged that an agreement should not interfere with other international treaties.

In sum, favorable conditions in the foreign policy field were not sufficient to guarantee membership for those nations that applied for it.
Neither was a certain degree of industrial homology sufficient for
Sweden to convince the counterpart about the mutual advantages flowing from special concessions. Entry to the EC presupposed expectations
of rewarding returns within both the political and economic sector. The
last proposition should be supplemented by an important corollary—such expectations should be fairly equally distributed among
political parties and interests organizations.

The integration policies of the Nordic countries have been formulated
in a complex web of relations among domestic power groups. Foreign interests are very often a rationalization of or a spillover from the particular partisan interests that they further. It is not difficult to discern a
pattern where the interest to reach an accommodation with the EC is proportional to the strength and self-confidence of the sectorial material interest lying behind it. The role played by the farmer's organizations and
the Center parties constitute the most divergent positions, with Norwegian and Danish politics at different poles. Similarly, the rural-urban
cleavage helped create a temporary alignment of interests between the
leading circles of Social Democrats and Conservatives in Sweden and
Norway.

Although the Finnish EC agreement took a longer time to reach, there
was nevertheless a straight conception of the foreign considerations involved. In contrast to Sweden, Finnish neutrality has been based on the
understanding and relation with *one* superpower. Different integration
impulses from Western Europe have been met with efforts to compensate
and expand Eastern relations at the same time. According to President
Kekkonen, "The greater the trust between Finland and the Soviet Union,
the larger the freedom of movement for Finland in relation to other
states."[21]

Domestic considerations certainly played a large role in delaying a Finnish agreement. But opposition to the accord was mostly based on fears
of repercussions in the relations with the Soviet Union, rather than on
economic premises. For this reason, EC policy was integrated into a
wider framework. As indicated in Table 5.6, the conception of a global
solution for its foreign trade dilemma contrasts with the course followed
by Sweden, who was confined to strict considerations of EC policies only.

Trends and Issues in EC-Nordic Relations Since 1973

The European Community influences the Nordic region in two ways:
by development of internal policies, thus strengthening the ties to Den-

TABLE 5.6

ELEMENTS IN FINNISH AND SWEDISH EEC-POLICIES
1969-73

Orientations	Finland		Sweden	
global	GATT		GATT	
regional	Agreements	EEC	Agreements	EEC
		ECSC		ECSC
	maintenance	EFTA		EFTA
	framework agreement	SEV		
	free trade agr	USSR		
	bilateral trade agr	other socialist countries		

mark; and by the evolution of its relations with the nonmember European nations. Thus, an active—and to some extent reciprocated—interest in establishing broad functional collaboration outside the scope of the free trade agreements has been displayed by both Norway and Sweden.

As a result of different solutions reached, the integration policies of the Nordic countries have become more fragmented at the same time as the limits for regional cooperation have been clarified. Denmark is bound by arrangements worked out within the EC and has to evaluate other options from that point of departure. For each country, policies are channeled into different "integration spheres." Rather stable constellations of actors and issues are discernable along the four dimensions that were introduced earlier.

The following observations may be somewhat cursory and selective. They nevertheless give some implications of the main trends and the important issues that have come to the forefront since the EC question was solved.

Purposes and processes of international economic cooperation are not solely determined by external parameters of course. In a discussion of prospects for Nordic cooperation it is tempting to overexploit the effect of the Danish entry into the EC. The fortunes and perils of domestic economic developments are also important. Somewhat hastily we may observe that since the oil crises, which coincided with the EC entry, the economic prospects in northern Europe have changed. Norway's newfound oil resources and relative economic success have bred a feeling of assertiveness and national self-confidence. In many ways Norway has replaced Sweden as a Scandinavian "model." Like Denmark, Sweden has in the last years of the decennium suffered from a stagnant economy, high inflation rates, and severe balance-of-payments problems. While these two countries, formally the core of the Nordic scene, have witnessed a relative recession, Finland's economic achievements have, by and large, been impressive.

When discussing effects of policy measures, counterfactual propositions are of course difficult to judge. Supporters of Danish EC entry arguing that Denmark's situation would have been much worse if it had chosen not to join the Norwegian promarketeers may be equally justified in reversing their stand on the advantages of joining. At least, nonmembership in conjunction with domestic economic growth has provided a good cover to the fissures opened during the Norwegian market campaign. It has given Norway an opportunity to develop a more selective, sometimes bilaterally oriented economic integration policy toward Europe. At the same time, its attractiveness as a partner has increased. Germany, Sweden, and occasionally France have sometimes found themselves in a situation of overbidding competing offers for industrial cooperation in exchange for Norwegian oil and gas.

In a similar vein, bilateral trade and industrial conditions pertain also to Finland. It is often argued that Finland's energy sensitivity is less severe than that of other countries. Almost two-thirds of its needs are supplied in long-term arrangements by the Soviet Union. In quite a different manner, Finland has also managed to counteract the mainstream of developments in the OECD area. A purposeful investment into the construction of special ships, such as atomic icebreakers, has resulted in back orders, while many other European shipyards have been forced to close down.

However, these are but a few general observations. It may be an open question as to what specific extent such economic factors retroact on the particular economic and political goals pursued along the Nordic, European, Atlantic, and global orientations. But the picture of relevant issues would be incomplete without taking such background factors into consideration.

New Paths In Nordic Cooperation

In 1971, the possibilities of a wider European solution resulted in a reactivation and strengthening of the Nordic apparatus extraneous to the ill-fated NORDEK proposal. The previously mentioned Helsinki treaty of 1962 was revised. Collaterally, a new and expanded cultural treaty was ratified. This treaty established a secretariat for cultural and educational questions in Copenhagen. Also, a common secretariat to serve the presidium of the Nordic Council was created in Stockholm. At the cabinet level firmer institutionalization of the division of labor was agreed upon. Each government nominated a special minister responsible for the coordination of Nordic affairs. Together they constitute a Nordic Council of Ministers, although other ministers responsible for their specific functions could meet in the council. However, these are all procedural achievements. The substantive achievements are not as clear-cut.

The evidence points in different directions. Declarations made in 1973 and 1974 affirmed that future Nordic cooperation should embrace all the Nordic countries. But a reversal of strategy has occurred. From broad designs the emphasis shifted to piecemeal, sectorially confined action programs, e.g., in industrial policy and traffic policy. Harmonization and mutual adaptation are managed in a more incremental and less visible way. There is also a common feeling that the pace of this cooperation process has slowed down and that its direction though manifold is indecisive. This is a reflection of both a lack of political will and economic resources.

It may be an open question as to who is the least willing member of the scheme and consequently the pacesetter. Critics often pinpoint Denmark as being unwilling to invest either manpower or new economic resources into the Nordic sphere. From the Danish side, however, the choice of "Nordic versus European" spheres has been regarded as a misunderstanding of the issue at stake. Foreign minister K. B. Andersen wrote in 1977 that

we have always maintained, and continue to do so, that our participation in the European Community and our cooperation with other Nordic countries are complementary, not contradictory. We are convinced that our share in the European construction is enriched by our continued participation in the traditional Nordic cooperation. Also we have had numerous assurances that others see it as an advantage both to the Nordic countries and to the EEC that the two groupings overlap in the position of Denmark.[22]

Partly for domestic reasons Denmark has described its own role as a bridge builder, trying to accommodate the two spheres.[23] The concept is much less popular today since other members of the two groupings have preferred to deal directly with each other, foregoing the Copenhagen liaison office.

Apart from the EC factor, there are also other externally motivated inhibitions influencing Nordic proposals. A Nordic Investment Bank, situated in Helsinki, began its operation on July 1, 1976. It possesses a basic capital of about $500 million and a lending capacity of just above $1 billion. It may invest in joint Nordic projects. However, one of the purposes of the bank that Finland supported the most fervently, i.e., pooling resources into projects outside the Nordic region such as in Eastern Europe, came to nothing. Opponents from the Norwegian Conservative party attached restraining conditions to the scope of operations by the bank.

If all-Nordic designs have reached a plateau, the same impression does not seem to hold true for bilateral relations. Cooperation has recently intensified in the Swedish-Norwegian and the Finnish-Swedish dyads.

Danish Membership

A few main elements in EC-Nordic relations in the aftermath of enlargement deserve a closer scrutiny. A paramount aspect is Denmark's role as an EC member. A second aspect pertains to developments in the Community's relations with the remaining four Nordic countries, especially outside the confines of the free trade accords. It has often been assumed that contacts between these nonmember countries were bound to intensify after Danish entry. The prediction has scarcely been confirmed by events, nevertheless there is an element of truth in it. The rest-EFTA organization serves as a substitute for a more "northern" clearinghouse in coordinating common attitudes toward the EC. Finally, I would like to set the individual countries and the EC in the context of fisheries policy. The intricacies of this issue have come to the forefront during the latter part of the 1970s.

Denmark has consistently sought the inclusion of agriculture into European market arrangements. Above all, the existence of the CAP pulled Denmark to pursue its membership line. During the EFTA period, Danish industry prospered and diversified its interest. Few difficulties were encountered in adapting Danish rules and procedures into the EC policy framework over the five-year transitional period. But there are some structural differences between the industrial and agricultural sectors. With both Germany and Britain within the EC, Denmark has achieved a secure and expanding market at guaranteed prices for its agricultural exports. The role of agriculture in the economy could be roughly indicated by the following figures. About one-third of the GNP is derived from the primary sector and two-thirds of this is geared for export. Some 70 percent of this production is exported to Denmark's main customers within the EC.

In the industrial sector, however, the roles of supplier and customer are reversed: 35 percent versus 45 percent of Danish exports and imports, respectively, is EC bound. To compensate, preferential and continued access to the EFTA markets (especially Swedish) has constituted an important aim. Many Danish firms operate as subsuppliers within a Nordic division of labor. Danish industry has shared the concern expressed by the EFTA countries about the rigidities of the EC's rules of origin. These rules have in some respects worked to the detriment of established commercial links and engagements.

Membership, in itself, has scarcely influenced the volume and composition of Danish trade. Drastically changed price relations with third countries, namely, the OPEC area, is probably much more important. This group of countries has expanded its share of Danish trade at the expense of EFTA relations. In Europe, a reorientation of Danish economic activity from Sweden and Britain to Germany has also occurred.[24]

Certainly, membership has been advantageous in other respects. It has given Denmark legitimate possibilities to influence developments in its vicinity that would have affected it anyway. The privileged access to information is reflected in the special EC missions that other Nordic countries have been allowed to establish close to the Danish Foreign Office. This arrangement has caused some disenchantment in Brussels. Although the Danish conception of the EC as a confederate system is sometimes met with disappointment among federalists, the Danish attitude to practical measures in European integration is more unconditional and active than that of several other countries. Often Denmark has supported the commission's proposals. Like the other small members, Denmark has realized that it is often small countries that gain from binding international cooperation and the observance of strict rules. During the seven years since entry, Denmark has chaired the EC twice. Although the task put considerable strain on the administrative capacity, it is thought that the Danes very quickly learned to master the Brussels apparatus.

A paradox in Danish EC policy is the discrepancy between official satisfaction and the attitudes of the Danish population. Indeed, since accession, a series of opinion polls have revealed a consistently falling level of public support for the EC. There is also a difference between Danish and British EC opposition. While the latter group, by and large, reacted to the first direct elections to the European Parliament by abstaining, the Danish countered by electing the largest delegation of anti-EC representatives.

Special Relations

The free trade framework agreed upon in 1973 remains the cornerstone of the EC's relations with the other Nordic countries. Despite turbulent international economic conditions, the program it outlined for the dismantling of tariff barriers has been fulfilled. Some incidents, such as a Swedish decision to adopt a temporary import duty on shoes in 1975, and an EC countermove on Swedish steel imports, do not alter the overall judgment. The trade arrangements have been supplemented with other measures whose net effect may be to involve these countries even more in the EC's sphere. Outsiders have been forced to accept the EC's rules about minimum prices within the steel industry and to accept certain market-sharing agreements in times of recession. In other respects, close collaboration has been sought by these countries themselves. Sweden and Norway both participate in the EC fusion research program (Joint European TOKAMAK, or JET) and the European Scientific and Technological Cooperation (COST) program. They are also observers to the EURONOM, dealing with nontariff barriers to trade. Sweden has also joined the European Patent Office in Munich.

In yet another area the EC has proved to be a rather artificial demarcation line for the handling of certain European economic and monetary problems. One of the organization's most ambitious programs, the Economic and Monetary Union, has repeatedly failed to function as an integrating framework. The "snake"—the narrow margin of fluctuation allowed for EC currencies in the wake of the breakdown of the Smithsonian agreements—soon developed into a D-mark zone. While certain large EC members such as France, Britain, and Italy only occasionally have accepted the disciplines of a limited float, Sweden and Norway joined in together with Austria and Switzerland on special conditions. Sweden now has left the arrangement, but Norway and Denmark remain.

The continued importance of the economic and political interdependence between the Nordic countries and the EC found an expression in the 1977 summit meeting of EFTA. On this occasion an initiative was taken that the two integration groupings, the EC and the EFTA, should work together for increased West European integration. The initiative was greeted with diplomatic responses on the part of the EC, but few concrete projects resulted. It is only very recently that the EC has shown a willingness to accommodate some long-held wishes of the countries who stay aloof from the Community network. The EC has proposed that in the future a regular annual meeting should be held at the ministerial level between representatives of the Community and Sweden and Norway, respectively. Such an agreed procedure for consultation has been sought by both governments. In yet another respect the developments on the EC scene have had repercussions in the Nordic area. The prospect of enlarging the Community with new members from southern Europe—Greece, Spain, and Portugal—has in certain quarters raised the problem of the future balance within the EC. Compensating moves to develop closer northern links have been proposed, especially from Danish and German spokesmen.

Fisheries

The rapid developments within the law-of-the-sea sphere have had great consequences for the internal and external policies of most north European and west Atlantic States. The North Sea, the Baltic, and large parts of the oceans have been carved up between different fishing zones proclaimed by adjacent coastal states.

The EC has encountered considerable difficulty in formulating a common fisheries policy. While an agreement to establish a 200-mile limit was reached in October 1976, discord has reigned on the principles of an internal EC fishery policy. The so-called EC sea is composed of what used to be British waters to 60 percent. Britain, as well as Ireland, wanted to secure a very broad exclusive national coastal belt exempting fishermen from other countries. The position has been especially harmful to Denmark. Much of the Danish catches have historically been caught in British waters.

The British, however, used to fish considerably in Norwegian, Icelandic, and Faroese waters. In this respect, there has been a reciprocal interest in securing access to old fishing areas. As a result, a series of agreements have been concluded with Norway, Sweden, the Faroe Islands, and other nations spelling out the conditions for fishing and allowable catches. The regime is very rigid and catches are put under strict surveillance. It seems that with the exception of the Icelandic fishery disputes, these questions have been regulated according to functional rules. Efforts to put pressure on prospective parties to fishing arrangements through the free trade agreements have been hinted at, but hardly fulfilled in practice. This may also be explained by the general uncertainty of sea affairs, where linkages often are drawn between disparate issues to the detriment perhaps of those pressing for change. These linkages easily escalate to include sensitive security issues.

Integration Dimensions and the Future

The decade of the 1970s has been a period of change and successively altered economic conditions for the Nordic countries. After a period of twenty years, the integration dilemmas were resolved. However, European solutions are not only conditioned by their own merits. Increasingly, extraneous impulses influence the course of events and the level of affluence enjoyed by the inhabitants of these countries. Competition from Japan and some newly industrialized countries (NIC) will be present to an even larger extent. The dependence, in some cases excessive, on Middle East oil makes northern Europe vulnerable to developments there. Over time, alternatives are likely to develop, but investments into new sources of energy are strained by the cost of present imports. These are economic challenges, in a long-term perspective.

As this paper has shown, Nordic integration policies are also shaped by security considerations. Here the prospects seem more alarming and short term. We know the ambitions and achievements of the earlier period, which was characterized by détente and economic growth. We also know that the solutions reached have been strong enough to cope with détente and stagnating economies. However, we do not know the options and dangers inherent in a combination of recession and receding détente.

In this respect, the European versus the Atlantic orientation of Norway and Denmark may become crucial. While Denmark has oriented itself toward the mainstream of general European foreign policy postures, Norway has become increasingly isolated from European diplomatic attention and access. Its defense arrangements have in recent years been shaped by a growing bilateral relationship with the United States. To the extent that European and U.S. policies with respect to the new tensions between the superpowers and toward world politics at large differ, repercussions will also be felt in the northern area.

Notes

This overview of international economic and integration policy in no way intends to cover the overall economic policies pursued by the Nordic countries. Balance-of-payments problems, inflation rates, monetary supply, and fiscal taxation policies all remain outside of the scope of this article. The focus is rather on the political setting and the structural environment in which such policies are borne out.

1. See, for instance, Niels Amstrup, *Dansk Udenrigpolitik* (Copenhagen: Gyldendal, 1975); Peter Hansen, "Adaptive Behavior of Small States: The Case of Denmark and the European Community," *Sage International Yearbook of Foreign Policy Studies*, vol. 2 (ed.) Patrick McGowan (Beverely Hills, Calif.: Sage, 1974); Sverre Lodgaard, "Norway and Eastern Europe," and Simone Alapaeus, "La politique étrangère et la Cooperation de la Finlande avec l'Europe," in Johan Galtung (ed.), *Cooperation in Europe* (Oslo: Universitetsforlaget, 1970); A. O. Brundtland, "Norwegian Foreign Policy," *Cooperation and Conflict*, no. 3 (1968); Carl-Einar Stalvant, "Sverige, avspanningen och den utrikespolitiska doktrinen," Research Report, no. 1, Department of Political Science, Stockholm University, 1977.

2. A well-documented study of the Nordic countries and the erratic process of European integration especially in the 1950s is Toivo Miljan, *The Reluctant Europeans* (London: Hurst & Co., 1977). However, the growth of the EC is sometimes analyzed from a deterministic and normative point of view.

3. These arguments could be further strengthened by maintaining that distance is out as a concurrence factor, offset by factors such as time and cost. One may wonder whether geopolitical argumentation based on core area concepts regain ground in worsened international situations, namely, continued negative détente and increased national parochialism in the early 1980s.

4. The Treaty of Friendship, Cooperation and Mutual Assistance was signed in Moscow on April 6, 1948.

5. See the two voting studies by J. Kalela and J. E. Lidstrom and C. Wiklund in *Cooperation and Conflict*, Nos. 3–4 (1967).

6. See "world order" analysis, e.g., Lars Anell, *Sweden In a New International Economic Order*, Secretariat for Future Studies, Stockholm, 1978.

7. Raimo Vayrynen, "Finland's Role in Western Policy Since the Second World War," *Cooperation and Conflict*, no. 2 (1977).

8. Helge Pharo, "Bridgebuilding and Reconstruction. Norway Faces the Marshall Plan," *Scandinavian Journal of History*, no. 1, 1976.

9. Harto Hakovirta, "Wait and See" (Paper delivered to the Fifth Nordic Conference of Political Scientists, Aarhus, 1975).

10. Barbara Haskel, *The Scandinavian Option* (Oslo: Universitetsforlaget, 1976), p. 94.

11. Claes Wiklund, "The Zig-Zag Course of the Nordek Negotiations," *Scandinavian Political Studies* 5 (1970).

12. Couve de Murville, *Une politique étrangère* (Librairie Plan, 1979); Harold Wilson, *The Labour Government* (London: Weidenfeld, Nicolson, 1971).

13. Agence Europe, December 2, 1969. The French reversed the London commitment of 1961 between the EFTA countries, urging the six not to accept British entry until the relations with the rest of the EFTA countries had been solved, in opposition to the British proposal first to enter and then wait a year for others to complete their negotiations.

14. Agence Europe, November 10, 1971.

15. Johan Galtung, *The European Community. A Superpower In the Making* (London: Allen & Unwin, 1973).

16. Hansen, op. cit.

17. Johan Galtung, "A Structural Theory of Integration," *Journal of Peace Research*, no. 4 (1968). There are varieties of this proposition; see Haskel, op. cit., pp. 31–32.

18. It does not seem worthwhile to discuss various approaches to the definition of the elusive concept of integration. One should be careful, however, not to adopt a usage close to EC politics, such as equating EC entry with criteria of integration. Rather we confine the term to an "open" usage stressing a search for new forms of international cooperation, an increase in the level and scope of collaboration, and a respect for goals declared by the parties themselves in joint negotiations.

The matrix is *heuristic*: the consequences flowing from absolute, comparative advantages are not always integrating and there might inhere more dynamics in specialization fostered by concurrence between economies than in monopolies of production factors. However there are built-in limits for "integrative logic" captured by this mode of reasoning.

19. Karl Deutsch, *The Analysis of International Relations* (Englewood Cliffs, N.J.: Prentice-Hall, 1968), p. 198.

20. Arild Underdal, "Diverging Roads To Europe," *Cooperation and Conflict,* Nos. 1–2 (1975).

21. *Economist,* June 25, 1977.

22. Ibid.

23. Niels Amstrup and Carsten Lehmann Sorensen, "Denmark—Bridge Between the Nordic Countries and the European Communities?" *Cooperation and Conflict,* Nos. 1–2, 1975.

24. Rolf Buschardt Christensen, "Denmark: Consequences of EC-Membership," *Scandinavian Political Studies* 3, no. 1 (1980).

6
Nordic Policies
Toward the Third World

Lars Rudebeck

Introduction

This study is about policies and activities of the five Nordic countries with regard to the countries of the Third World. The countries of the Third World are treated more or less the same as the formerly colonized or semicolonized countries of Asia, Africa, and South and Central America. They have emerged as a third force in world politics during the second half of this century. They are not predominantly socialist. In fact, most of them are clearly capitalist, often including important elements of precapitalist forms of production. Generally, they are not united among themselves. They do, however, share nationalist opposition to the colonialism and imperialism of capitalism. This is justification enough for using the term *Third World* to refer to the broad category into which they fall, despite all obvious differences. Mainly for its historical connotations, this term carries more meaning and is more straightforward than the euphemistic and confusing synonym *developing countries* used by the United Nations and the Organization for Economic Cooperation and Development (OECD).[1]

Among the external policies of political and economic actors in the Nordic countries, some are specifically directed at the Third World. Such policies may be strictly within the realm of action by the state itself, or they may be economic policies involving actors such as industrial and business corporations, banks, and trade unions. In this study I shall be dealing with the international aid policies (also called development cooperation) of the Nordic states, with some of their more important diplomatic activities, and with foreign trade and investments. There are

Work on this chapter was finished during the fall of 1979. Only minor additions have been made since then.

close connections between these four types of policies and activities, both with regard to their casual origin in the structure of society and with regard to actual policymaking. Together they represent the most important types of contemporary Third World policies.

I shall begin Nordic comparisons at the economic level of society and then move on to policies involving state action in a more direct sense.

Trade with the Third World

Foreign trade statistics are fair indicators of the degree and type of involvement of any country with the outside world. Like other small, industrialized, capitalist countries, the five Nordic countries take an active part in international trade. Their national economies are highly dependent upon exports. In 1975 their share of the world's total exports was as high as 4.5 percent, whereas their combined population was only a little over 0.5 percent of the world's total population. As a whole, the Nordic countries import more from Third World countries than they sell to them. This is due in particular to their need for oil, a few other raw materials, and food products such as coffee. During the 1970s, only Sweden has come close to balancing its trade with the Third World over a long period. In other words, Third World export markets are relatively more important for Sweden than for the other Nordic countries, at least in a quantitative sense. This is indicated by the fact that with only 37 percent of the Nordic countries' total population of about 22 million people, Sweden accounts, on an average, for close to half of the value of Nordic exports to the Third World. At the other extreme, Iceland with exactly 1 percent of the Nordic population contributes less than 0.5 percent of total Nordic Third World exports, an almost insignificant share. As shown in Table 6.1, Norway, Denmark, and Finland each have about one-fifth of the Nordic population. The Danish and Norwegian shares of Nordic exports to the Third World are roughly equal to their population shares, whereas Finland reaches a share of only one-tenth.

Table 6.2 shows how much of the Nordic countries' total exports reached the Third World during the first eight years of the 1970s. There were clear increases in all five countries during this period, both in absolute and relative terms. This trend developed as compensation was sought in the Third World for increasing oil prices and declining profits during the crisis of world capitalism. Sweden's dominant position was fortified, but Denmark and Norway come close in relative terms. In spite of a fourfold increase in absolute terms, the share of Finnish Third World exports remains quite limited. Iceland's 1977 figure is only half of that for Finland.

TABLE 6.1

EXPORTS OF NORDIC COUNTRIES TO THIRD WORLD
COUNTRIES 1970-1977

(Percentages of total Nordic third world exports)

Nation	%	(% pop)
Denmark	22	(23)
Finland	10	(21)
Iceland	0(.3)	(1)
Norway	20	(18)
Sweden	47	(37)
Total	100	(100)

Each country's percentage of the total Nordic population of 22 million is
shown within brackets.

Source: Yearbook of Nordic Statistics 1978, Nordic Council, Secretariat
of the Presidium, Stockholm, 1979, Table 117.

TABLE 6.2

NORDIC COUNTRIES' EXPORTS (FREE ON BOARD) TO
THIRD WORLD COUNTRIES

(In percentages of total exports and in million US $)

Year	Denmark		Finland		Iceland		Norway		Sweden	
	%	$	%	$	%	$	%	$	%	$
1970	10	320	7	151	2	2	8	207	9	610
1971	9	355	7	157	2	3	8	203	9	698
1972	10	448	6	172	3	5	10	339	10	906
1973	10	596	7	276	2	7	14	667	10	1,207
1974	11	820	8	454	3	10	13	816	11	1,799
1975	12	1,020	8	412	3	8	10	796	11	1,873
1976	11	992	7	463	3	11	12	939	14	2,565
1977	13	1,291	8	634	4	21	14	1,250	14	2,693

Source: Yearbook of Nordic Statistics 1978, Tables 104 and 117.

TABLE 6.3

FOREIGN TRADE RELATIONS BETWEEN NORDIC AND THIRD WORLD COUNTRIES

(Percentages for different types of goods 1977)

		food and related goods	mineral fuels, lubricants and related goods	manu-factured goods (except food)	other commod-ities and transactions	total %	total million US $
		%	%	%	%		
Denmark	imp	37	34	22	7	100	1,548
	exp	29	0	70	1	100	1,291
Finland	imp	41	43	10	6	100	866
	exp	6	0	69	25	100	634
Iceland	imp	38	26	32	4	100	31
	exp	79	--	15	6	100	21
Norway	imp	18	47	18	17	100	1,358
	exp	13	0	85	2	100	1,251
Sweden	imp	21	49	25	5	100	2,780
	exp	3	0	91	6	100	2,693
All Nordic countries	imp	27	44	22	7	100	6,583
	exp	11	0	82	7	100	5,890

Source: Yearbook of Nordic Statistics 1978, Tables 121 and 122.

It has already been pointed out that the Nordic countries have a negative balance of foreign trade with the countries of the Third World. Table 6.3 is an attempt to give a closer and more differentiated view of the structure of foreign trade relations between these two groups of countries. Figures for 1977 are used as illustrations.

Emerging from Table 6.3 is almost a caricature of the text book image of relations between developed and underdeveloped countries. Sweden's exports consist of 91 percent manufactured goods (67 percent is machinery and transport equipment). Finland's imports are 84 percent food (mainly coffee) and mineral fuels (oil). Only Iceland deviates strongly from this pattern. Its exports are 79 percent food stuffs (fish), and it actually buys more manufactured goods from the Third World than it sells there. The special figures for Iceland in the table reflect the fact that its economic structure is, in important respects, more like that

TABLE 6.4

BALANCE OF FOREIGN TRADE BETWEEN NORDIC
AND THIRD WORLD COUNTRIES AS PERCENT -
AGE OF EXPORTS AND IMPORTS, 1977

Nation	%
Denmark	− 9.1
Finland	−15.5
Iceland	−18.9
Norway	− 4.1
Sweden	− 1.6
All Nordic countries	− 5.6

Source: Yearbook of Nordic Statistics 1978, Tables 121 and 122.

of an underdeveloped country than that of an industrialized capitalist country. As shown later, Iceland was even a net receiver of development aid until as late as the end of 1976.

Although the dominant pattern remains that of the Nordic countries buying mainly oil and tropical food products from the Third World and selling high productivity specialized goods, it is worth noting that over one-fifth of Nordic imports from the Third World was actually manufactured goods. This reflects the fact that a relatively small number of capitalist Third World countries have begun to compete successfully on the world industrial market during the 1970s, mainly by efficient exploitation of disciplined, low-cost labor.

In addition to the Icelandic situation, one notes in Table 6.3 that Denmark's vocation as an agricultural country shows in a high share of manufactured food exports to the Third World. High shares of crude materials in Finland's exports, i.e., wood, and Norway's imports, i.e., alumina, are hidden under the lump heading of "other commodities and transactions." As far as Finland is concerned, this explains the relatively low share of manufactured goods in its exports. In Table 6.4, I have calculated the 1971 foreign trade balance for each country as a percentage of Third World exports and imports to illustrate the relative importance of the foreign trade deficit toward the Third World. The general pattern of the 1970s is clearly reflected in the table: a small deficit for Sweden (Sweden actually had positive balances in 1973 and 1975), a

TABLE 6.5

GEOGRAPHIC DISTRIBUTION OF NORDIC TRADE WITH THE
THIRD WORLD IN 1977

(Percentages)

Nation		Africa %	America %	Asia %	total %
Denmark	imp	13	28	59	100
	exp	28	30	42	100
Finland	imp	10	33	57	100
	exp	28	26	46	100
Iceland	imp	8	60	32	100
	exp	69	16	15	100
Norway	imp	16	30	54	100
	exp	42	28	30	100
Sweden	imp	16	24	60	100
	exp	31	24	45	100
All Nordic Countries	imp	14	28	58	100
	exp	32	26	42	100

Source: Yearbook of Nordic Statistics 1978, Tables 119 and 120.

fairly small one for Norway (even Norway had a small positive balance in 1973); Finland, Denmark, and Iceland all buy much more from the Third World than they sell there.

The geographic distribution of Nordic trade with the Third World is much more balanced than the pattern of investments, as we shall see in the following section. At the end of the 1970s, in particular, Nordic exports were quite evenly distributed among the three continents, whereas imports were dominated by Asia. This means that the role of Latin America in Nordic foreign trade has decreased since the 1950s and 1960s. The situation in 1977 is shown in Table 6.5.

In this section I have studied the size, the composition, and the geographical distribution of trade between Nordic and Third World countries. The emerging picture contains no great surprises. It is in fact quite similar to the general picture of trade relations between developed capitalist countries and the Third World. Sweden dominates in quantitative terms, although the Third World shares of Danish and Norwegian exports are about the same as Sweden's. Finland and, in particular, Iceland are less involved than the other three with Third World markets. There has been a rising trend for all five countries during the 1970s. A simultaneous increase in Nordic imports of manufactured goods from the Third World has not fundamentally upset the dominant pattern, which continues to be marked by an exchange of Nordic manufactured goods for oil and food products. The geographical distribution of Nordic trade over the three continents of the Third World is fairly even.

Investments in the Third World

Getting involved in production or business abroad by investing capital and committing personnel is a deeper type of involvement in a foreign society than just buying or selling. It affects society more directly and has more political implications both at home and in the recipient country. Statistics about Nordic investments in the Third World are therefore more valid indicators of Third World economic policies than foreign trade statistics alone. Unfortunately, investments statistics are more difficult to come by and are less reliable. Still, some pieces of information are available.

In principle, there are two different types of investment statistics, those presenting annual flows of capital and those indicating in some way the total amount of national resources invested in any given country at any given time. The former type is fairly easily available in various documents and statistical publications. The latter type of data, however, is necessary in order to have a valid picture of influence and dependency in international economic relations.

The officially registered annual flows of capital from the Nordic countries to the Third World are quite small. Sweden shows by far the largest flows, but it was not until 1977 that the net flow of private capital reached 1 percent (0.99) of the Swedish gross national product (GNP). This includes not only direct investments (actually only one-sixth of the registered flow), but also export credits and international lending by Swedish banks. Table 6.6 gives these kinds of data for the major part of the 1970s. Iceland is not included, since no flows of private capital from that country to the Third World have been registered.

TABLE 6.6

NET FLOWS OF PRIVATE CAPITAL FROM NORDIC
TO THIRD WORLD COUNTRIES

(Directly and through multilateral agencies)

Year	Denmark $ million	%	Finland $ million	%	Norway $ million	%	Sweden $ million	%
1970	29	0.57	17	0.16	30	0.26	112	0.36
1974	36	0.12	28	0.13	56	0.25	239	0.43
1975	67	0.19	42	0.16	94	0.34	187	0.27
1976	239	0.62	16	0.06	240	0.77	527	0.71
1977	101	0.24	25	0.09	249	0.70	774	0.99

Disbursements in million US dollars and as percentages of GNP

Source: Development Co-operation, 1978 Review, OECD, Paris, 1978,
Table A 6, p 194.

TABLE 6.7

PRIVATE DIRECT INVESTMENT FLOWS (NET) FROM
NORDIC TO THIRD WORLD COUNTRIES
(Million US dollars)

Year	Denmark	Finland	Norway	Sweden
1970	8	1	19	37
1971	25	1	11	40
1972	10	1	7	42
1973	16	-	14	22
1974	26	-	15	49
1975	30	3	17	82
1976	30	1	43	125
1977		2	16	126

Source: Development Co-operation, 1978 Review, OECD, Table VI-7,
p 118.

As already mentioned, published figures for private direct investments are even smaller, as shown in Table 6.7.

As interesting as Tables 6.6 and 6.7 may be for comparative purposes—they give convincing evidence of Sweden's dominant position among the Nordic countries—they tell us very little, however, about the actual "controlling influence"[3] of Nordic interests over production and economic policies in the Third World. They do not even indicate the real amount of annual investments, since Nordic transnational companies, like those of other countries, are able to borrow capital abroad or reinvest profits from companies they already control in other countries. In order to proceed, therefore, the second type of statistics mentioned above is required. Whatever is available of that kind, however, is incomplete and does not enable us to carry out any systematic comparisons of the Nordic countries. Four recent papers by Danish, Finnish, and Norwegian researchers attempt to draw some conclusions.

Basing an assessment upon various United Nations sources, Hans-Henrik Holm estimates that Sweden's total production abroad, as a share of total exports, is almost three times as large as that of Denmark and almost seven times as large as that of Norway.[4] This indicates the high degree of internationalization of the Swedish economy as compared with those of the other Nordic countries. Judging by Tables 6.6 and 6.7, we may assume that this Nordic difference applies also to production in the Third World separately as a part of the world economy.

The authors of one Finnish and two Norwegian papers draw together some information about the number and types of Nordic investments in different parts of the world.[5] They show that the types of investment made reflect the economic structures of the investing countries.

Swedish investments are primarily made in metal and electronic industries, followed by chemical, processing, and mining industries. Chemical and processing industries are found also among Danish and Norwegian interests in the Third World, to which we can add one Danish specialty, i.e., food industries, and one Norwegian specialty, i.e., shipping. The Norwegian and Finnish investors are furthermore represented within metallurgy, electronics, and construction. The Finns as well have a specialty of their own, namely paper mills.

As far as the geographical distribution is concerned, the cited authors show that Swedish investments are concentrated mainly in Latin America, in particular Brazil, whereas Norway and Denmark emphasize Brazil as well as a number of Asian countries. The few Finnish Third World investments seem to be more evenly distributed among the three continents of the Third World than those of the other Nordic countries.

Here, Nigeria is included among the main recipients together with Brazil and a few Asian countries.

It must be emphasized that the information given so far is quite meagerly documented. Using the *number* of investments or establishments, regardless of their combined size, as the basis for comparisons is of course particularly questionable in terms of validity. It would be much more interesting to compare the number of employees in establishments owned or controlled by Nordic interests in the Third World. This piece of information is available only for Sweden, however. It shows that Swedish industry employed 1.143 million people in 1974. Nineteen percent of these were employed abroad and a little over 4 percent (46,000 persons, 21 percent of those employed abroad) were employed in the Third World.[6] About 30,000 worked in Brazil alone.[7] There are, in fact, more Swedish employed industrial workers in the city of São Paulo than in any Swedish city except the two largest ones. Regrettably, Sweden is the only Nordic country on which we have some more detailed knowledge of investments in production and business in the Third World. Swedish involvement is also by far the most extensive, accounting for considerably more than half of all Nordic investments in the Third World. This difference between Sweden and the others has been growing during the 1970s.

Table 6.8 is based upon Birgitta Swedenborg's investigations of Swedish investments abroad. It shows that the Third World as a whole slightly increased its share of Swedish manufacturing abroad from 1960 to 1974. All of this increase was in Latin America, whereas Africa's and Asia's combined relative share actually declined. There was no absolute decline, however. Measured by total assets Swedish manufacturing abroad, in all parts of the world, increased by 15 percent *annually* during the period investigated. The absolute value of total Swedish manufacturing assets abroad reached about U.S. $6 billion in 1974, according to Swedenborg's findings. Measured by number of employees, the annual increase was 5 percent during the same period, from 147,800 in 1960 to 219,700 in 1974.[8] It should be remembered too that there was a surge of capital export from Sweden to the Third World in 1975–1977, as the crisis of world capitalism began to seriously affect the Swedish economy. This, of course, is not included in Swedenborg's research report, which ends in 1974. It is, however, indicated by Tables 6.6 and 6.7.

The geographical patterns are more or less the same, whether they are measured by number of employees or by total assets. As shown in Table 6.9, a similar pattern also emerges when measuring by permissions granted to invest Swedish capital abroad during the period 1970–1977.

Sweden's exports to the Third World, however, show quite a different

TABLE 6.8

GEOGRAPHICAL DISTRIBUTION OF NUMBER OF EMPLOYEES
AND TOTAL ASSETS OF SWEDISH MANUFACTURING
COMPANIES ABROAD

(Percentages)

Location	Number of employees			Total assets		
	1960	1970	1974	1960	1970	1974
Africa and Asia	10	8	7	4	2	2
Latin America	7	12	14	9	12	13
All Others	83	80	79	87	86	85
total %	100	100	100	100	100	100

Source: Birgitta Swedenborg, Den svenska industrins investeringar i utlandet 1970-1974 (Swedish industrial investments abroad 1970-1974), Research Report No 5, Industriens utredningsinstitut (Industrial investigation institute), Stockholm, 1976, Table 6, p l5.

TABLE 6.9

GEOGRAPHICAL DISTRIBUTION OF THIRD WORLD INVESTMENT
PERMISSIONS GRANTED BY SWEDEN'S NATIONAL BANK,
1970-1977, AND SWEDISH THIRD WORLD EXPORTS,
1977

(Percentages)

Location	investments %	exports %
Africa	5	31
Asia	15	45
America	80	24
(of which Brazil)	(52)	
total	100	100

Sources: Special table prepared for the author of this study by officials of Sweden's National Bank (Sveriges Riksbank) and same source as for Table 6.5.

geographical distribution. Here, Latin America holds a relatively much less important position, whereas the opposite is true of Africa and Asia. This difference between the patterns of trade and investments was pointed out earlier but is worth emphasizing also in this context, through inclusion of the Swedish trade pattern in Table 6.9.

The most striking figure of the table is perhaps the one within brackets, i.e., the investment figure for Brazil. During 1970–1977, 52 percent of all permissions to invest Swedish capital abroad concerned Brazil. As we have already seen, about 65 percent of all persons employed by Swedish subsidiary companies in the Third World are also employed in Brazil. These data confirm the outstanding position of Brazil as receiver of Swedish Third World investments. Still, Swedish investments in Brazil accounted for only 2.4 percent of all foreign investments in Brazil in 1976.[9] This last figure reminds us of the fact that Nordic, and in particular Swedish, involvement in the international and thus Third World economy is large in relation to its small population base, but naturally small in absolute terms.

Swedish interest in the Brazilian economy dates back to the nineteenth century, when trading agencies were founded by Swedish firms. Manufacturing in Brazil by Swedish companies began during the first two decades of the present century, but rapid expansion did not come about until after World War II.[10] Claes Brundenius has investigated Swedish manufacturing companies in Brazil and found that they are no different from other transnational companies. They produce at high social costs, use capital intensive technology that does not resolve the unemployment problem, create technological dependence, and contribute to balance-of-payments problems by importing from parent companies in Sweden.[11] In fact, Brazil's military dictatorship of the 1960s and 1970s, favoring a capitalist strategy of development, did create a particularly propitious climate for Swedish private investors as well as for those of other countries.

We have no reason to assume that Swedish or other Nordic companies apply other principles in other parts of the world than they do in Brazil. They export capital and they produce abroad in order to raise their profits. They use every means tolerated by the regime of the country in which they operate. In so doing they execute an important part of Nordic policies toward the Third World.

The sensitivity of Swedish transnational companies to changing political circumstances has been documented in the case of Chile.[12] During the presidential period of Salvador Allende, 1970–1973, when a socialist-oriented strategy of development was attempted in Chile, Swedish investments came to a standstill in spite of good political relations between the governments of Chile and Sweden. After the counter-revolutionary coup that brought General Pinochet to the presidency in 1973, political relations between the two countries deteriorated rapidly and drastically. All Swedish development aid was simply broken off. But investments resumed. This is a striking example of conflicting Third World policies originating in one and the same country.

Aid and Development Cooperation

Probably, aid policies come first to the minds of many people in connection with relations between developed and developing countries. It is true that such policies are important from a political point of view. Their functions are manifold. At the receiving end, development aid is sometimes beneficial and sometimes detrimental. It almost always creates some kind of dependence. At the other end, that of "donor countries," the major function of development aid may well be that of a collective tranquilizer. This role may be particularly important in the case of small countries such as the Nordic ones that lack important strategic or political interests in the third world. As will be evident later, there are of course also important economic interests involved in development cooperation.

Initially, it must be recognized that development aid is not by any means the most important type of Third World policy in a quantitative sense. Other flows of resources and capital are much more important when added together. Sweden, Norway, and Denmark are among the world's major donors of development aid in relation to their gross national products. Sweden is even number one among the developed capitalist countries. Still, the total amount of these three countries' development aid is only slightly larger than their officially registered annual flows of private capital to the Third World and less than a quarter of what they disbursed for imports from the third world in 1977. The net registered flow of private capital from all of the developed capitalist countries taken together was more than double that of their total amount of development aid in 1977.[13] With this in mind, I shall proceed to analyze the flow of official Nordic development assistance.

As shown in Table 6.10, the rate of increase of Nordic development assistance has been very high since the second half of the 1960s.[14] Growth has been rapid also in comparison with the 1950s, when everything started from zero (except in Iceland's special case, for which the first year was 1973). Sweden's aid/GNP ratio is the highest of all among the developed capitalist countries, as already pointed out; Norway comes third in 1977, surpassed only by the Netherlands; Denmark

TABLE 6.10

OFFICIAL DEVELOPMENT ASSISTANCE FROM NORDIC TO THIRD
WORLD COUNTRIES THROUGH 1979 (net)

(Directly and through multilateral agencies)

Year	Denmark $ mill. %		Finland $ mill. %		Iceland $ mill. %		Norway $ mill. %		Sweden $ mill. %	
1966-68 average	25	0.21	4	0.05	0.40	0.03	18	0.22	63	0.26
1970	59	0.38	7	0.07			37	0.32	117	0.38
1974	163	0.55	38	0.17	0.40	0.03	131	0.57	402	0.72
1975	205	0.58	48	0.18	0.53	0.04	134	0.66	566	0.82
1976	214	0.56	51	0.18	0.43	0.03	213	0.70	608	0.82
1977	258	0.60	49	0.17	1.03	0.06	295	0.82	779	0.99
1978	281	0.72	65	0.20	1.14	0.06	356	0.90	859	1.01
1979	398	0.70	78	0.21	1.02	0.05	436	1.00	1,017	1.01

in million US dollars and as percentages of GNP

Sources: For Denmark, Finland, Norway, and Sweden, 1966-1977,
Development Co-operation, 1978 Review, OECD, Table A 3,
p 191. For Iceland and for the years not covered by the OECD
publication, various national sources have been used. See note
14 at the end of the chapter for specification.

shares the fourth place with France. Almost all Nordic aid is in the form
of grants or credits on very easy terms. Only the members of the
Organization for Petroleum Exporting Countries (OPEC) surpass the
three mentioned Nordic countries with respect to official assistance. As a
group, these countries provided on an average over 2 percent of their
GNP as development aid during 1973-1977. The major donors—Saudi
Arabia, Kuwait, and the United Arab Emirates—actually provided over
5 percent.[15]

As I have already emphasized, the case of Iceland is very special in the
context of developed and developing countries. Iceland is not only a
great exporter of food and a net buyer of manufactured goods from the
Third World, but also a very minor donor of development aid (0.05 percent of GNP in 1979). Until very recently Iceland was even a net receiver
of development aid. During 1971-1976 it was granted a total of U.S. $ 1
million in regular assistance from the United Nations Development Programme (UNDP). Iceland was offered continued assistance, but declined
this offer in December 1976.[16]

There is abundant documentation available on the aid policies of the
Nordic countries, particularly in comparison with the scarce documenta-

tion on the equally important investment policies. Here, I shall consider the distribution of aid between bilateral and multilateral channels, this issue having received a great deal of attention in the internal Nordic debate on development cooperation. I shall then take a brief look at the geographical distribution of bilateral aid, which is in a sense also a political distribution. The section will be concluded with a brief discussion of the joint Nordic efforts in the field of development assistance.

The issue of bilateral versus multilateral aid—i.e., the issue of aid given directly from state to state versus aid given through the various branches of the United Nations or some other international organization—has been significant ever since the Nordic countries first became involved in development cooperation on a larger scale during the early 1960s. The sense of this significance, however, has shifted from the 1960s to the 1970s. During the 1960s two factors, one practical and one ideological, favored multilateral aid through the United Nations. At the practical level, the various state development administrations had not yet expanded to the extent that they did later. They simply did not have the administrative capacity to channel very much assistance. At the ideological level, there was a strong pro–United Nations sentiment in the Nordic countries, which favored multilateral assistance as the most proper and progressive (most altruistic) form. This has aptly been called "the multilateralist ethic" by Björn Beckman.[17]

Both of these factors changed during the 1970s. The state development administrations expanded and developed their own vested interests in development cooperation. Secondly, the total amount of aid increased and became more important in national politics and economics. Finally, views on the relative degree of progressiveness of bilateral versus multilateral aid began to be partly reversed.

The last mentioned problem deserves some comment here. It has two aspects. First, aid administrators began to raise some criticism against UN aid as being too bureaucratic and cumbersome. Second—and probably more important in the internal Nordic context—an intensive debate began, particularly in Sweden, on the selection of recipient countries. It was claimed by many, specifically from the more radical wing of the Social Democratic party then still in power, that Swedish aid ought to be channeled to countries with political regimes able to use the aid in accordance with the official goals of Swedish development aid. These objectives were, and are still, economic and social equalization, change of society in a democratic direction, and support for national and economic independence. These criteria, it was claimed, would in the long run rule out several traditional recipients of Swedish aid, such as imperial Ethiopia and Pakistan, while they would favor some, such as Tanzania

TABLE 6.11

THE SHARE OF MULTILATERAL AID IN NORDIC
DEVELOPMENT AID

(Percentages)

Year	Denmark %	Finland %	Norway %	Sweden %
1965	64	80	67	55
1968	45	83	53	42
1971	51	77	57	57
1973	46	51	54	43
1975	46	43	45	34
1977	45	43	44	34
1978	48	48	46	35
1979	48	48	----	33

Sources: For the years 1965-1975, Sveriges samarbete med
u-landerna, (Sweden's cooperation with the developing countries; report by the state commission on
development cooperation), SOU 1977:13, Stockholm,
1977, Table 7.4b, p 243. For the years not covered
by this source, various national sources have been used.
See note 18 for specification.

and possibly Zambia, and bring in new ones such as the Democratic
Republic of Vietnam, Chile, Cuba, the national liberation movements of
Portugal's (then) African colonies and of southern Africa. As Swedish
development cooperation—and to some extent also that of the other
Nordic countries, in particular Norway—became more politicized at the
donor's end, the selection of recipient countries naturally also became
more important, which ultimately favored bilateralism.

As shown in Table 6.11, this reorientation led to a noticeable decline in
the share of multilateral aid given by the Nordic countries.[18] The decline
has been particularly sharp in Sweden since the early 1970s. Here the
share of multilateral aid has gone down to one-third. Toward the end of
the 1970s, Denmark, Finland, and Norway seemed to settle slightly
below half. Iceland has not been included in Table 6.11 since almost all
of its aid is multilateral. The exception is a fishing assistance agreement
with Kenya involving expenses for the Icelandic government of some
U.S. $40,000 during the first year. This was signed on June 12th, 1979.

As the bilateral share of total aid has been growing, the selection of
aid-receiving countries has become more important. All of the Nordic
countries (except Iceland) give development aid to a great number of

TABLE 6.12

MAJOR RECIPIENTS OF BILATERAL NORDIC DEVELOPMENT AID

(Percentages of total bilateral aid)

Denmark 1974-1978		Finland 1978		Norway 1978		Sweden 1978	
Tanzania	21	Tanzania	31	Tanzania	16	Vietnam	20
Vietnam	12	Vietnam	21	India	11	Tanzania	16
India	9	Zambia	20	Bangladesh	8	India	14
Bangladesh	9			Kenya	7	Mozambique	6
Kenya	8			Pakistan	7	Bangladesh	6
Malawi	3			Vietnam	5	Zambia	5
Total %	62		72		54		67

Sources: Various national sources. See note 19 at the end of the chapter for specification.

countries. Norway has as many as thirty recipients, Sweden twenty, Denmark around fifteen, and Finland eleven. However, all of them concentrate the major part of their bilateral aid on a much smaller number of countries. Finland has even designated as few as three main recipients—Tanzania, Vietnam, and Zambia—which is why no other countries are included in the column for Finland in Table 6.12.[19] Denmark, Norway, and Sweden do not concentrate their aid quite as strictly as Finland. In the table, six recipients each are included to get above 50 percent of total aid for all four countries.

A distinct pattern emerges from Table 6.12, as from several others in this study. Vietnam, Tanzania, and India are clearly the main favorites of the Nordic states in their capacity as donors of development aid. Tanzania and India have had this role ever since the 1960s, whereas Vietnam is a newcomer of the 1970s. Besides Finland, Sweden has the greatest degree of concentration. The three countries mentioned received exactly half of all Swedish bilateral aid in 1978 (46 percent in 1979). Norway's aid is considerably more dispersed than that of the others.

The most striking difference between the geographical distribution of Nordic bilateral development assistance and the distribution of trade and investments is that Latin America is almost completely absent from the picture, whereas Africa and Asia get roughly half each. At the end of the 1970s Latin America received only a small percent of total Nordic aid, most of this being destined for Cuba. Norway also gives some aid to

Jamaica, and Finland to Peru, but the amounts are small in relative development cooperation, although Chile began to receive Swedish assistance during the brief period (1970–1973) of the popular front government of Salvador Allende. As mentioned earlier, this aid was cut off by the Swedish government after the military coup had brought an end to the Chilean experiment in Democratic Socialism.

After heavy criticism from the non-Socialist parties of the Swedish parliament in connection with Cuba's active military support for the threatened independent regime in Angola, Swedish aid to Cuba was cut down in 1976, but did not cease immediately. In 1978 and 1979 this aid was down to U.S. $6.7 million—1.5 and 1.3 percent respectively of total bilateral aid—after having reached a high point of close to $16 million in 1974. In contrast, Norwegian aid to Cuba was cut off completely in 1976, for the same reason that Swedish aid was gradually withdrawn. Sweden's Conservative party, successful in the 1979 election, has also asked for sizable reductions in aid to Vietnam, because of its intervention in Kampuchea and its refugee policies. As a consequence, the new center-right government did in fact, in October 1979, propose a certain reduction of the amount of this aid and, more importantly, that it be reduced to one-year, instead of long-term, agreements. This was later approved by the Swedish parliament. Similarly, and for the same reasons, the Danish government, made up at the time of Social Democrats and Liberals, decided in June 1979 that no new aid projects would be negotiated with Vietnam.

The main Nordic criteria for selection of bilateral aid recipients are poverty conditions and readiness within the recipient country to use the aid in such a way that poverty and social and economic inequalities are reduced. As indicated above, the latter criterion has sometimes been interpreted in political terms—mostly so in Sweden and least so in Denmark. This has caused some political controversy, particularly in Sweden where the official tendency to assist radical regimes has been the strongest—at least until the Social Democratic electoral defeat in 1976—and has thus also aroused the strongest right-wing opposition. This opposition scored some notable successes in Sweden and Denmark toward the end of the 1970s. However, regimes such as those of Vietnam, Angola, Mozambique, Guinea-Bissau, postimperial Ethiopia, and to some extent Cuba have still continued to receive bilateral aid from some or all of the four largest Nordic countries through the 1970s, even when Social Democrats have been out of governmental office. Part of the explanation is probably that aid to these countries, except Cuba, can be fully justified by the poverty requirement.

In concluding this section on aid policies, it might be worth pointing out that surprisingly little in quantitative terms has come of some ambitious intentions to organize concrete development assistance projects on a joint Nordic basis. As early as 1962, an agreement was signed between the governments of the five Nordic countries to this effect. Three additional agreements followed, the latest in 1973.[20] But at the end of the 1970s, there were only four active all-Nordic projects, two in Tanzania, one in Kenya, and one in Mozambique. They involved agricultural development and assistance in the field of consumers' and producers' cooperation. There was also a Danish-Finnish-Norwegian institute of management and administration training in Tanzania. These projects involved only small fractions of the development cooperation budgets of the Nordic countries, altogether slightly less than 0.3 percent in 1979.[21] There is, however, a great deal of ongoing mutual consultation and cooperation among the development administrations and foreign ministries of the five countries. In 1976, the Nordic Council of Ministers even created a special committee of civil servants to facilitate such cooperation.

Trade, Investments, and Aid

We have seen that Nordic investments in the Third World and bilateral aid have so far taken almost opposite roads. The Swedish economy is the most internationalized among those of the Nordic countries, but only a couple of tenths of 1 percent of all Swedish permits to invest abroad during the 1970s concerned the major recipients of Swedish aid.[22]

There is more overlap between trade and aid than there is between investments and aid. Nordic exports have long been selling on the Indian market, Tanzania is on its way to becoming a major African market for Nordic goods and know-how—the same is true of Angola for Sweden—and Nordic firms sign many contracts in the wake of large-scale industrial assistance to Vietnam. An interesting example of this tendency, although insignificant in quantitative terms, is provided by Guinea-Bissau. This small country receives more aid from Sweden than from any other country except Portugal.[23] This tendency for trade to follow aid is probably not related to the question of tied aid, although Denmark and Finland do use tied credits quite extensively (see below) as a form of development assistance. Instead, contacts established through aid—and not only by commercial consulting firms whose services are provided by aid donors[24]—often clear the way also for commercial agreements.

During the 1970s, the separation between aid and business that used to be a trademark of Nordic development cooperation with the Third World has become less distinct. There are several factors behind this change. One reason is that the character of Nordic development cooperation itself changed significantly, as the total amount of aid expanded rapidly. I have already noted the shift away from multilateral aid, despite the "multilateralist ethic" still upheld at the ideological level.

Bilateral aid has changed too. First, there has been a shift from separate projects to integrated country programs. These plans for the long-term use of aid are worked out in cooperation with the national authorities of the recipient countries. This change, in turn, has led to a noticeable increase in the share of industrial bilateral aid by the Nordic countries. In particular, Finland and Sweden provided between one-fourth and one-third of their assistance in the form of industrial aid in 1977 and 1978. Denmark's and Norway's shares of industrial bilateral aid reached around one-tenth in 1978.[25] As industry in the Nordic countries is mainly in the hands of private interests, this tendency has naturally led to a need for more coordination and cooperation between aid authorities and private business.

A second reason why the clear separation between aid and commercial interests has become more difficult to uphold is simply the growing importance of the expanding aid budgets in the national economies of the Nordic countries. The larger the aid programs, the more they will compete with other government activities, and the more they will also affect (or be thought to affect) employment opportunities and business interests. A third reason is the growing importance of Third World markets for Nordic exports during the economic crisis of the capitalist countries. A fourth reason is also related to the crisis of capitalism. The private companies have a growing need for various kinds of state support and subsidies in order to survive the ever harsher conditions of the world market. Such forms of state support include export credits, guarantees for credits and investments, and investment companies or funds financed either through the development cooperation budget or from some other public source.

It is interesting to note in this context that Denmark, with a relatively low degree of industrial concentration and integration and a high share of agricultural products in its exports, is also the Nordic country where the official inclination to separate aid and business has been least pronounced. Sweden, however, with the strongest and most highly developed export economy, has held on longest to the doctrine of separation.[26] Danish official pronouncements on development cooperation usually do not conceal that aid can also have beneficial economic effects at home. As early as 1967, a state Industrialization Fund for the Developing Countries was created in Denmark. The purpose of the fund is to help finance industrialization efforts in the Third World by Danish firms. This was over ten years before time was beginning to ripen for such a step in the other Nordic countries.

All of the Nordic countries have various systems of state credits and credit guarantees that naturally play an important role in facilitating exports. All these systems include specially favorable conditions for Third World countries. Furthermore, close to half of Denmark's and Finland's bilateral assistance is in the form of easy-term credits tied to purchases in the donor countries (80 percent tied in the case of Finland, close to 100 in Denmark). Denmark, Norway, and Sweden also have special investment guarantee systems. Some use of such guarantees has been made by Danish industry and also, more recently, by Norwegian industry. The Swedish system, however, has not been used at all. It is limited to the major recipients of development aid. This criterion makes it of no interest to Swedish private investors, who prefer to invest elsewhere.[27]

Special public companies or funds for Third World investments are a stronger and more direct form of linkage between state aid policies and private business interests. The Danish fund was just one in a series of such institutions set up before 1970 in Great Britain, the German Federal Republic, the United States, and the Netherlands. A combination of ideological barriers and limited interest by private industry prevented the idea from becoming public policy in the other Nordic countries, until the economic and political climate began to change in the seventies. Only on January 1, 1979, did a Swedish fund for industrial cooperation with developing countries (Swedfund) start its operations. The whole idea was opposed by the Social Democrats and the Communists in a close parliamentary vote.[28] An equivalent Finnish fund (Tekera) came into existence on April 1, 1979.[29]

Both funds are financed through the development cooperation budgets, and both are intended to facilitate the establishment of manufacturing industries in Third World countries. This will be done by engaging Finnish and Swedish industry in various kinds of joint ventures or similar kinds of cooperation. The targets of this new kind of development assistance will mainly, but not exclusively, be countries that at present receive Finnish or Swedish aid. A similar Norwegian fund was proposed as early as 1974. Due to the government's budgetary problems in the face of general economic difficulties and stagnating incomes from oil, no legislation had as yet come out of this by the middle of 1979.

These briefly summarized new tendencies of the 1970s obviously imply closer linkages than before between the aid, trade, and investment components of Nordic policies toward the Third World. At least in the short run, it does not seem likely that these tendencies will be able to divert the mainstreams of direct investment capital from Latin America or from the OPEC countries to the major recipients of bilateral aid. Nor does it seem very likely that the mainstreams of aid will be diverted to the present target countries of Nordic investors. It seems more likely that new forms of capital export, such as technology sales, consulting agreements and turnkey factories, rather than direct investments, will be fitted into new forms of development cooperation. It seems likely, too, that special, comprehensive cooperation agreements between states will provide the framework for such Third World policies.

Sweden has already signed such agreements with Algeria, Libya, Egypt, and Iran. They are all oil-producing countries, and the agreements were signed somewhat hastily in the wake of the crisis produced when the price of oil first began to rise sharply. So far, the concrete effects of these agreements have been quite modest. An exception is in Algeria where several big contracts have been signed by Swedish manufacturing and consulting firms, both in the fields of industry and agriculture.[30] Similar comprehensive agreements with other countries were proposed as an alternative by the Socialist opposition, when the Swedish parliament passed the law on Swedfund and provided for its financing.[31] In 1978, Norway signed such an agreement with Jamaica. This provided for development assistance from Norway, but also for extended economic relations between the two countries.[32] Norway had earlier signed agreements on extended economic and technological cooperation with Iran and Brazil, but without the development aid element.

Another type of Third World policy through which state action strongly influences commercial and other economic interests is related to market access and tariffs. All the Nordic countries have followed recommendations by the United Nations Conference on Trade and Development (UNCTAD) and introduced some kind of generalized system of preferences (GSP) for imports from the Third World. Since the most typical Third World imports are exempted from customs duties anyway, as Nordic tariffs generally are fairly low, and because the preferences in practice cover only a limited number of manufactured products from relatively few so-called newly industrializing countries, it would seem that the issue of Nordic tariffs on Third World goods had greater relevance for internal Nordic politics and labor market policies than for the Third World.

In 1977, 90 percent of all Third World imports into Sweden were actually free from tariffs (99 percent of imports from the least-developed countries). Products not included in the Swedish preference system are textiles, shoes and leather goods, and some agricultural products, e.g., sugar.[33] The Swedish and Norwegian tariff systems are very similar, whereas the Finnish list of exceptions to the preferences is somewhat longer and includes also such manufactured goods as automobiles, rubber products, and toys.[34] Denmark, as the only Nordic member of the European Economic Community (EEC), has had to adopt more protectionist policies than the other Nordic countries. According to a recent UNCTAD report cited by Helge Hveem, Denmark is the most restrictive of the four largest Nordic countries in its trade practices with the Third World.[35]

Several of the issues involved in the discussed linkages between aid, trade, and investments are heavily loaded with political implications. Some of these, as well as a few other political issues, will be briefly touched upon in the following section of the study, before I turn to a few concluding comparisons.

Political Issues

A study of Swedish Third World policies entitled *Solidarity or Imperialism* was published in 1977 by two Swedish economists, Kenneth Hermele and Karl-Anders Larsson.[36] By this pointed title, they wanted to draw attention to the double face of Third World policies. On the one hand, Sweden's economy is closely integrated into the capitalist world economy. To the extent that basic economic interests are at stake, Swedish Third World policies thus cannot be expected to differ much from those of other capitalist countries. On the other hand, it is a fact that Swedish aid policies have had a specific "progressive" profile. Aid has been given to politically radical regimes, to national liberation movements, and to the Democratic Republic of Vietnam at the height of war with the United States. In addition, aid has been given on favorable terms, largely without ties. The actual aid volume increased rapidly, reaching 1 percent of Sweden's gross national product in 1977. The doctrine of separation between aid and business seemed to prevail until the second half of the 1970s. The contour of this political profile was becoming more vague, but it had not yet dissolved by the end of the seventies.

It seems that political conditions in Sweden have had a specific and considerable role in shaping the aid component of Swedish Third World policies. Among the factors directly making for this specific political context, one can note the political strength of the Social Democratic party (in power almost without interruption from 1932 until 1976) and the labor union movement, neutrality in foreign politics, a strongly pro–United Nations multilateralist ideology, and the temporary political radicalization of the 1960s. Propping up this political and ideological structure, there was a strong, export-oriented economy with a vested interest in an open world market, seemingly able to manage its international relations without the state until the economic crisis reached Sweden with some delay around 1974. This strong economy had in fact evolved in close cooperation with the Social Democratic state, but a kind of mutual autonomy had been upheld and respected. In the field of Third World policies, this was manifested in the two doctrines of free trade and separation between aid and business.

There were also moments when the politicians "went too far." The most dramatic of these was in 1969, when the foreign minister at the Congress of the Social Democratic Party promised large-scale reconstruction aid to North Vietnam in the midst of war. Strong pressures from Swedish business and from the United States forced withdrawal of the promise within a week. Later, in 1970, part of the promised aid was conveyed to North Vietnam through the Red Cross.[37] These were moments of open conflict. On the whole, Swedish Third World policies appeared to work harmoniously enough until later in the seventies.

Third World policies grew important in the internal politics of the other Nordic countries a little later than they did in Sweden. As we have seen, Icelandic policies are at the same time the most specific and the most limited in quantitative terms. They do not seem to have any great significance in Icelandic internal politics.

Several recent papers by Norwegian researchers point at significant parallels between Norwegian and Swedish Third World policies—some of those parallels have already been indicated earlier in this chapter.[38] There is in particular a clear similarity in policies in the sense that aid policies in Norway also have a fairly progressive profile, whereas more basic economic policies are less idealistic.

Norway has, together with Sweden (and the Netherlands), played an active and important role in the group of "like-minded" countries. This group tries to bridge conflicts of interest between the developed capitalist countries and the countries of the Third World in the negotiations on a so-called new international economic order (NIEO). Denmark and Finland belong to the same group, but have been more passive. Iceland does not take part at all. Asbjorn Lovbraek has studied the positions of the Nordic countries in these negotiations. At the fifth round of UNC-TAD negotiations held in Manila in 1979, he found that Norway's positions on the various issues had on the average been closest to those of the Third World countries, while Denmark's had been the most distant. Sweden and Finland came in between. He notes at the same time growing internal inconsistencies in the positions of Norway and Sweden, in comparison with previous negotiations. This indicates growing difficulties for Norway and Sweden in the implementation of "international social democratic reformism," which is the term coined by Asbjorn Lovbraek and Arve Ofstad to denote the special Swedish-Norwegian (Nordic) type of Third-Worldism.[39]

In spite of the similarities mentioned, the political contexts of Norwegian and Swedish Third World policies do of course differ. The position of the Social Democratic party has long been less dominant in Norway than in Sweden before 1976. In fact, it is important to emphasize the nonpartisan sense in which international social democratic reformism should be interpreted. Center-right governments in Norway and Sweden may even represent this kind of international reformism better than Social Democratic governments do in Denmark, depending upon the national and international constellation of forces. One important difference between Norway and Sweden has to do precisely with international politics. Norway is a member of the Atlantic pact (NATO), whereas Sweden is neutral. This made it possible for Sweden, for instance, to come out earlier and more strongly than Norway in support of national liberation movements in Indochina and in Portugal's former African colonies. Norway's economic structure is quite different, too. The economic basis for more radical Third World policies was in fact not present until Norway's oil boom of the early 1970s. This has since proved to be quite a shaky basis. These and other factors contribute to explaining why Norway's special profile in Third World policies developed later and has on the whole been less pronounced than that of Sweden.

We have noted several times that Denmark's Third World policies are less "Nordic" than those of the other Nordic countries. Explanations in this case seem to be less specifically political and more easily reducible to economic and international political factors than in the cases of Sweden and Norway. Denmark has long suffered serious economic difficulties. It is a member of NATO as well as of the European Economic Community. Its aid and other Third World policies bear close resemblance to those of other countries in similar situations, although aid appropriations are unusually generous in international comparison. No dramatic political controversies have been aroused in Denmark over Third World policies, although aid to Socialist and Socialist-oriented countries has been criticized by the non-socialist parties, thus forcing even the Social Democrats to move cautiously in this respect.

Finland's position is curiously mixed. Its foreign trade and investment policies are naturally geared to national economic interests, whereas aid appropriations have so far been small in the Nordic context. Finland's bilateral aid, however, has a progressive profile with regard to the selection of recipient countries. It has also been suggested by the Finnish political scientist Esko Antola that Finland benefits as a "free rider" from being associated with the Third World image of Sweden and Norway.[40] The special Finnish kind of neutrality between East and West is, however, an autonomous factor that distinguishes Finland from other countries and probably contributes to making it appear more Third World oriented in a political sense than Denmark. For example, Finland, together with Sweden, was present among the invited guests at the sixth summit meeting of the movement of nonaligned countries, held in Havana in 1979. They have been guests also at earlier meetings.[41] Otherwise, the most characteristic feature of Finnish Third World policies is perhaps a certain caution.

Finally, Denmark, Finland, Norway, and Sweden all give humanitarian aid to the national liberation movements of southern Africa, as they did earlier to the liberation movements of the former Portuguese colonies in Africa. This assistance is financed through the development cooperation budgets. They also give diplomatic support in the United Nations, although sometimes cautiously, to resolutions condemning South Africa, trying to put various kinds of pressure on it to leave Namibia, to cease intervening in the affairs of neighboring countries, and to put an end to apartheid.[42] In 1979, the Swedish parliament passed a politically important law that explicitly prohibits new investments by Swedish companies in South Africa, while still allowing investments to maintain existing establishments at present level.[43] An administrative rule applied by the Norwegian government on exports of capital to South Africa has a similar effect.

It seems fair to conclude that a kind of Nordic profile in Third World policies emerged from the experiences of the 1960s and first half of the seventies. This profile has largely, but not exclusively, been marked by Swedish and Norwegian policies. It has manifested itself largely within the realm of aid policies and political manifestations. What about its future?

The second half of the 1970s has offered difficult conditions for international reformism of the Nordic type. The structural crisis of international capitalism has not loosened its grip over the living conditions of the peoples of the Third World nor over the national economies of the Nordic countries. The separation between aid and business is on its way out. "Industrial cooperation" is on the agenda. Labor unions and popularly based political parties watch with concern the restructuring of the international and national economies that is taking place. They fear that employment and capital will disappear to the Third World, where the working class is more vulnerable to exploitation than in the Nordic countries. Comprehensive agreements between the respective states as discussed in the preceding section offer a more innovative way of meeting the difficulties than publicly financed investment companies. What social classes and groups benefit from such agreements (at both ends), if they are attempted on a larger scale, will depend upon the political constellation of forces (at both ends) that contributes to shaping them.

Brief Analytical Summary

An attempt will now be made to bring out the structure and general findings of this comparative study in a schematic but clear manner and then to indicate very briefly a possible mode of explanation. Here the details and nuances of the preceding text will be sacrificed. No more than a table and a bare outline of an argument will be given. It is hoped that this will serve as a summary and possibly even as a small contribution to the search for causes of what happens.

The differences and similarities noted in Table 6.13 cannot be properly explained unless seen simultaneously in their socioeconomic structural context, in their international political context, and in the context of domestic political struggle and policymaking. As far as the present study is concerned, the three following broad types of independent variables could be used, in hierarchical order:

1. Concentration, centralization, and internationalization of the economy—hence strength and flexibility
2. Membership in international alliances and military pacts
3. Constellation of internal political forces

We have seen that Sweden ranks first among the Nordic countries on the first category of variables. It has also remained outside all military pacts as well as Western Europe's supranational economic community (EEC). This has at times given considerable space to internal political forces favoring a fairly radical international reformism in aid and diplomacy, while hardly preventing trade and investment policies from being closely geared to the needs of Sweden's capitalist economy.

Iceland is at the opposite extreme among the five Nordic countries. With a small population and a weak economic structure, resembling in

TABLE 6.13

SUMMARIZING PERSPECTIVE OF NORDIC THIRD WORLD POLICIES

	Denmark	Finland	Iceland	Norway	Sweden
Trade 1970's					
Exports as % of total exports	10-13 % and increasing	7-8 %	2-4 % and increasing	8-14 %, an uneven increase	9-14 %, a steady increase
Imports	Food, 1/5 manuf. goods, oil	Food (coffee), oil	Food, 1/3 manuf. goods	1/2 oil, food, manuf. goods, bauxite	1/2 oil, 1/4 manuf. goods, food
Exports	Manuf. goods, food	Manuf. goods, wood	Fish	Manuf. goods	Manuf. goods
Geographical distribution (dominant tendency)		F a i r l y e q u a l			
Investments					
Amount	Small	Very small	None	Small	Fairly large
Geographical distribution (dominant tendency)	Latin America, Asia	Fairly even		Latin America, Asia	Latin America
Aid					
% of GNP 1979	0.70	0.21	0.05	1.00	1.01
% multilateral aid 1978	48	48	97 (1979)	46	35
3 major recipients, % of total bilateral aid 1978	Tanzania 21 Vietnam 12 India 9 ̄42̄ (1974-78)	Tanzania 31 Vietnam 21 Zambia 20 ̄72̄	Kenya 100 (1979)	Tanzania 21 Inida 11 Bangla-desh 8 ̄40̄	Vietnam 20 Tanzania 16 India 14 ̄50̄
Ideology	OECD type	Cautious, non-aligned	Multi-lateralist	Inter-national reformism	Inter-national reformism
Controversy between major political actors	No great political controversy	No great political controversy	No great political controversy	Some political controversy	Political controversy at times
Relation state-business	State invest-ment fund since 1967	State invest-ment fund since 1979		Proposed state in-vestment fund, not decided by 1979	State invest-ment fund since 1979

important ways those of Third World countries, it has had very limited space for active Third World policies. Iceland is also a strategic link in the NATO system which puts some implicit restrictions on its freedom of action in international politics. Among the three other Nordic countries, Norway's situation is less vulnerable than that of Denmark; it is a member of NATO, but vigorous popular resistance kept it out of EEC. Space has thus existed for international reformism in the fields of aid and diplomacy.

Denmark has a weak and vulnerable economic structure, and it is firmly integrated in the Western world both economically (EEC) and politically (NATO). This has clearly marked its Third World policies. Political forces proposing alternatives have had little influence in policymaking—much less than in Norway at times.

Finland's economy is less internationalized than those of the other three larger Nordic countries. Its Third World orientation has therefore been more limited in a quantitative sense. As opposed to Swedish neutrality, Finnish neutrality also has an economic dimension, as around 20 percent of its foreign trade is with the socialist countries of Europe. This combination of national economic and international economic and political factors has created the conditions for cautious Third World policies. These borrow perhaps some of their Nordic image from Sweden and Norway and are not seriously contested by any major political groupings.

Nordic Third World policies thus illustrate the importance of trying to combine structural and political action-oriented approaches to explain politics. The relevant structural factors are in this case economic strength and international autonomy. These in turn determine the space available to internal political actors for shaping Third World policies through open confrontation of ideologies and interests. Viewing the Third World policies of the Nordic countries in this way helps us understand the differences and similarities charted in this study.

Notes

1. The concept of Third World countries, as used in this chapter, does not include European countries. Because of the statistical documents used, however, most of the tables do include some European "developing countries." Tables 6.1, 6.2, 6.3, and 6.4 are based on *Yearbook of Nordic Statistics 1978*, which counts Yugoslavia, Gibraltar, and Malta as developing countries. The 1977 imports of the Nordic countries from these three countries were 0.22 percent of total imports; the equivalent percentage for exports was 0.5. The resulting distortion of

the tables is thus negligible. Table 6.5 is based on the same source, but there I was able to eliminate the developing countries of Europe. Tables 6.6, 6.7, and 6.10 are based on OECD's *Development Co-operation, 1978 Review*, which counts not only the three mentioned countries but also Portugal, Turkey, Greece, and Spain as developing countries. This is a little more serious than the negligible distortions introduced by the Nordic yearbook, as Spain and Portugal in particular do receive Nordic investments that are bound to have distorted the figures of Tables 6.6 and 6.7 somewhat. Unfortunately, I have not been able to adjust the OECD statistics except for Finland, thanks to special information from the Bank of Finland. For the sake of comparison, Tables 6.6 and 6.7 still have not been adjusted at all. Table 6.10 has hardly been affected, as only Portugal among the mentioned European countries receives some Nordic development assistance (around U.S. $9.5 million from Sweden and some $5.3 million from Norway in 1978, or 1.1 percent of Sweden's and 1.5 percent of Norway's total development aid that year).

2. See note 1.

3. *Controlling influence* is the term actually used by specialists to denote an important goal of investors.

4. Holm, Hans-Henrik, *De skandinaviske lande og kravene om en ny ökonomisk verdensorden* [The Scandinavian countries and the demands for a new economic world order], Institute of Political Science, Aarhus University (Aarhus, February 1979), p. 27.

5. Nylund, Trygve, and Rosberg, Tiina, "Nordens u-landsrelationer: handel och investeringar" [Nordic countries' relations with developing countries: trade and investments], *Nordisk Forum* (Copenhagen), no. 24, 1979, pp. 17–40; Hveem, Helge, "Scandinavia and the NIEO. Obstacles to a New International Economic Order in the Area of Scandinavian Economic, Political, Social, and Cultural Structures and Processes," in Laszlo, Ervin, and Kurtzman, Joel, eds., *Europe and the New International Economic Order* (Oxford: Pergamon Press, 1979); Lovbraek, Asbjorn, and Ofstad, Arve, "The Role of Likeminded Countries in the North-South Contradiction: The Case of Norway's Policy Towards a New International Economic Order," *Cooperation and Conflict* (Oslo) (1979):121–132.

6. Swedenborg, Birgitta, *Den svenska industrins investeringar i utlandet 1970–1974* [Swedish industrial investments abroad 1970–1974], Research report no. 5, Industriens utredningsinstitut [Industrial investigation institute] (Stockholm, 1976), Table 4, p. 12; Table 6, p. 15.

7. Brundenius Claes, *Foreign Investment and Technology: The Case of Swedish Manufacturing Subsidiaries in Brazil*, Research Policy Program, University of Lund (Lund, 1978), Table 1, pp. 3ff. This table is a complete list of Swedish manufacturing subsidiaries in Brazil in 1976. An updated presentation of this material is also found in Brundenius, Claes "Svensk export—Made in Brazil," in Brundenius, Claes; Hermele, Kenneth; Palmberg, Mai; *Granslosa affarer—om svenska foretag i tredje varlden* [Business without limits—Swedish corporations in the Third World] (Stockholm: Liber, 1980), pp. 38–104.

8. Swedenborg, op. cit., Table 3, p. 10.

9. Brundenius, op. cit., Table 2A, p. 8.

10. Ibid., pp. 1ff.

11. Ibid., pp. 13ff.

12. Parra, Bosco, *Forbindelser mellan Sverige och Chile 1964-1976. Bilateralt bistand, produktiva investeringar och utrikeshandel* [Relations between Sweden and Chile 1964-1976. Bilateral assistance, productive investments, and foreign trade], Working Group for the Study of Development Strategies (AKUT) 6 (Uppsala: Uppsala University, 1979), pp. 9-11, 17-18.

13. *Development Co-operation, 1978 Review* (Paris: OECD), 1978, Table A3, p. 191; Table A6, p. 194.

14. Denmark: *Danmarks deltageise i det internationale udviklingssamarbejde, 1977/78 og 1978* [Denmark's participation in international development cooperation; annual report of the Danish development cooperation agency] (Copenhagen: Danish International Development Agency [DANIDA], 1979).

Finland: *Government's Budget Proposal for 1979*, main budget heading no. 24 (Helsinki, 1978), p. 137; *Kehitys yhteistyo* [Development cooperation], no. 4 (Helsinki: Development Cooperation Division of the Ministry for Foreign Affairs, 1978), p. 8.

Iceland: *Utanrikismal*, report for 1979 to the Icelandic Parliament/Althingi of the foreign minister (Reykjavík, 1979), p. 23.

Norway: *NORADs arsmelding og regnskap 1978* [annual report of the Norwegian development cooperation agency] Norwegian Agency for International Development [NORAD], (Oslo: 1979), p. 1; Letter from NORAD to the author, September 26, 1979, giving total aid appropriations for 1979 and its estimated share of GNP.

Sweden: *Bistand genom SIDA* [Aid through Swedish International Development Agency (SIDA)], report and planning document of the Swedish development cooperation agency) (Stockholm: SIDA, August 1978), p. 28; *Minutes of the Swedish Parliament (Riksdag)*, 1978/79, pp. 136, 169.

15. OECD, op. cit., pp. 21-22.

16. *Report from the Ministry for Foreign Affairs* (on the role of Iceland in future Nordic cooperation within the field of development aid), mimeographed (Reykjavik, May 1979).

17. Beckman, Bjorn (AKUT), *Aid and Foreign Investment: the Swedish Case*, Part 1, no. 7 (Uppsala: Uppsala University, 1978), p. 24.

18. Denmark: *Danmarks deltagelse 1979*, Table 7, p. 29.

Finland: *Fakta om Finlands bistand* [Facts about Finland's aid], Development Cooperation Division of the Ministry for Foreign Affairs, FINNIDA (Helsinki, 1978); *Kehitys yhteistyo*, no. 4, 1978, p. 8.

Norway: *NORADs arsmelding og regnskap 1978*, p. 1. Sweden: *Bistand genom SIDA*, 1978, p. 219.

19. Denmark: *Danmarks deltagelse 1979*, Table 9, p. 34. Finland: *Kehitys yhteistyo*, no. 4, 1978, p. 8. Norway: *NORADs arsmelding og regnskap 1978*, p. 3. Sweden: *Bistand genom SIDA*, 1978, p. 7.

20. *Nordisk samarbejde for u-landene* [Nordic cooperation for the developing

countries], Special report of the development aid authorities of the Nordic countries (Stockholm, 1974), p. 19. Detailed information is found in *Framtida nordiskt samarbete rorande utvecklingsbistandet* [Future Nordic cooperation on development aid], NU A. 1979:20, Secretariat of the Nordic Council of Ministers, Oslo, 1979.

21. *Yearbook of Nordic Statistics 1978*, Nordic Council, Secretariat of the Presidium (Stockholm, 1979), pp. 257–258; *Minutes of the Nordic Council*, Report on Nordic Cooperation, 28th sess., 1980, p. 62

22. *Sveriges utvecklingssamarbete pa industriomradet* [Sweden's industrial development cooperation], Report by the state commission on industrial development cooperation), SOU 1977:77 (Stockholm, 1977), p. 85.

23. Rudebeck, Lars, "Development and Class Struggle in Guinea-Bissau," *Monthly Review* (New York) 30, no. 8 (1979):22, 24.

24. Beckman, op. cit., pp. 17–19, gives concrete examples of the upsurge in consulting firms in Swedish development cooperation.

25. Denmark: *Danmarks deltagelse*, 1979, Table 8, p. 30; Table 13, p. 39. Finland: *Fakta om Finlands bistand*, 1978. Norway: *NORADs arsmelding og regnskap 1978*, p. 5. Sweden: *Bistand genom SIDA*, 1978, p. 271.

26. Rasmussen, Roland; Holst, Jan; Lauridsen, Laurids; Holm, Hans-Henrik; and Simonsen, Jakob, "Arbejdsdeling, u-landspolitik og faglig strategie: Denmarks og Sveriges u-landspolitik i lyset af en ny international arbejdsdeling og de heraf folgende faglige modstrategier" [Division of labor, developing country policies, and labor union strategy: Developing country policies of Denmark and Sweden in the light of a new international division of labor and resulting counterstrategies of labor] *Nordisk Forum* (Copenhagen), no. 24 (1979), pp. 80–101; Neerso, Peter, *Danmarks u-landspolitik i krisens og EF-medlemskabets tegn* [Denmark's developing country policies under the sign of economic crisis and EEC membership], Working paper no. 5, 1979, Institute no. 8, Roskilde University Center (Roskilde, 1979), gives several illustrations of close contacts between business interests and aid authorities in Denmark.

27. Denmark: *Industrialiseringsfonden for udviklingslandene* [Industrial fund for the developing countries], Special report of the executive committee of the fund] (Copenhagen, 1975), pp. 14–17: Industriradet [Danish industrial federation], *Industrien og u-landene* [Industry and the developing countries] (Copenhagen, 1977); *Udenrigsministeriets tidsskrift for udenrigsekonomi* [International economics journal of the Ministry for Foreign Affairs], Special issue on state loans to developing countries, (Copenhagen, February 1978); *Danmarks deltagelse*, 1979, pp. 51–55; 154–157.

Finland: Rosberg, Tiina, "Finlands ekonomiska relationer till utvecklingslanderna" [Finland's economic relations with the developing countries], *Rauhaan Tutkien* [Peace research] nos. 2–3 of Finnish Peace Research Association (1978), pp. 2–24.

Norway: Hveem, op. cit., i Eriksen, Tore Linne, "Norsk bistandspolitikk, staten og naeringslivet," [Norwegian aid policies, the state, and enterprise], *Internasjonal Politikk* (Oslo), no. 4 (1977), pp. 720–721; *NORADs arsmelding og regnskap 1978*, p. 174.

Sweden: Beckman, op. cit.

28. Beckman, Bjorn, "Aid and Foreign Investment: the Swedish Case," *Cooperation and Conflict* (Oslo) (1979):133–148, gives a detailed analysis of the whole issue of Swedfund; *Svensk Export*, no.2(1979), p. 21, a journal published by the semiprivate Swedish Export Council, reports about Swedfund's start.

29. Rosberg, Tiina, and Rytovuori, Helena, *The Evolving Schizophrenia of Finnish Development Cooperation Policies. A Fund for Industrial Cooperation,* mimeographed (Tampere: Political Science Institute, Tampere University, 1979). See also Myllymaki, Eeva-Liisa, and Rosberg, Tiina, "TEKERA-rapporten: nagra kommentarer" [The TEKERA report: Some comments], *Rauhaan Tutkien* [Peace research], nos. 2–3 of Finnish Peace Research Association (1978), pp. 53–60.

30. *Svensk Export*, no. 2 (1979), p. 22, reports a project worth close to U.S. $600 million for which a Swedish consulting firm has been given full responsibility by the Algerian government. The project is within the field of agricultural industry and rural construction.

31. *Minutes of the Swedish Parliament: Committee on Foreign Affairs,* 27 (1978/79): 80–84. Countries such as Vietnam, Mozambique, Angola, and Cuba were mentioned by the Communists, whereas the Social Democrats preferred not to be specific.

32. *NORAD's arsmelding og regnskap 1978*, pp. 132–134.

33. Hermele, Kenneth, and Larsson, Karl-Anders, *Solidaritet eller imperialism. Om Sverige, varldsordningen och tredje varlden* [Solidarity or imperialism. On Sweden, the world order, and the third world] (Stockholm: Liber, 1977), pp. 115–120, and *Sveriges samarbete med u-landerna* [Sweden's cooperation with the developing countries]; Report by the state commission on development cooperation), SOU 1977:13 and 1977:14, Stockholm 1977, pp. 180-184, give good summaries of the Swedish system of preferences and related issues.

34. Rosberg, op. cit., pp. 9–11, gives a good summary of the Finnish system. Lovbraek and Ofstad, op. cit., do the same with the Norwegian system. Hveem, op. cit., also provides information on the Danish and Norwegian systems.

35. UNCTAD, 1979, TD/229/supp 2, p. 26.

36. Hermele and Larsson, op. cit.

37. Rudebeck, Lars, "Ord och handling i regeringens Vietnam-politik" [Words and deeds in the government's Vietnam policies], *Tiden* (Stockhold) 62, no. 8 (1970):457–468, with an answer by the minister for foreign affairs on pp. 468–471. Humanitarian aid on a larger scale to North Vietnam had begun in 1968 (about U.S. $5 million.)

38. Hveem, op. cit., Lovbraek, Asbjorn, *De nordiske land pa UNCTAD V: Ideologi og praksis i statlig nordisk u-landspolitikk under forhandlingene om en ny okonomisk verdensordning* [The Nordic countries at UNCTAD V: Ideology and practice in Nordic developing country policies in the negotiations on a new economic world order], mimeographed (Oslo: Norwegian Foreign Policy Institute, 1979); Lovbraek and Ofstad, op. cit.; Ofstad, Arve, *Norsk u-landspolitikk pa 1970-tallet* [Norwegian developing country policies in the 1970s], mimeographed (paper prepared for the 5th Nordic Political Science Conference, Bergen, August 1978).

39. Lovbraek, op. cit., pp. 25–26 and 2 ff; Lovbraek and Ofstad, op. cit., pp. 2ff.

40. Antola, Esko, "The Developing Countries in the Finnish Foreign Policy," *Rauhaan Tutkien* [Peace research], nos. 2–3 of Finnish Peace Research Association (1978), p. 36; Antola, Esko, *The Evolution of the Official Development Policy of Finland,* mimeographed (Paper prepared for the 5th Nordic Political Science Conference, Bergen, August 1978), pp. 15–16.

41. The movement of nonaligned countries makes a formal distinction between *observers* (potential member countries and national liberation movements) and *guests.* Guests at the last two summit meetings were Austria, Finland, the Philippines, Portugal, Rumania, Sweden, and Switzerland.

42. Palmberg, Mai, "Present Imperialist Policies in Southern Africa: the Case for Scandinavian Disassociation," in Anglin, Douglas; Shaw, Timothy; and Widstrand, Carl, eds., *Canada, Scandinavia, and Southern Africa* (Uppsala: Scandinavian Institute of African Studies, 1978), pp. 124-149, reference here to pp. 144–146; Thunborg, Anders, "Nordic Policy Trends Towards Southern Africa," in ibid., pp. 111–123; and Leys, Roger, "Scandinavian Aid to the 'Victims of Apartheid,'" Appendix to "Scandinavian Development Assistance to Botswana, Lesotho and Swaziland," in ibid., pp. 47–68.

43. The law follows the proposals formulated in *Forbud mot investeringar i Sydafrika* [Prohibition of investments in South Africa], Report by the state commission on South Africa, SOU 1978:53, Stockholm, 1978. Also see Mai Palmberg, "Svenska foretag ut ur Sydafrika?" [Swedish corporations out of South Africa?], in Brundenius, Hermele, Palmberg, op. cit. pp. 105–205.

The Nordic Model of
Neighborly Cooperation

Bengt Sundelius

Although U.S. political scientists have explored the North European region less than other parts of Europe, several studies have been made of the Nordic political systems. Often, foreign observers have been struck by the relatively successful manner in which these countries have solved their political problems and worked for social and economic reform. Concepts, such as the politics of compromise, working multiparty systems, the politics of postindustrial change, co-optive politics, corporate pluralism, the middle way, and stable democracy, have been used to describe the Nordic political scene. The impression prevails that in comparison with many other regions these countries are characterized by a fairly successful method of handling major domestic social problems and developments.

In this chapter, I shall outline the political techniques used for managing regional relations and the motives and sources of these joint problem-solving processes. Whether these countries in their regional interactions have also been able to develop fairly successful management of joint social problems and changes is of primary interest. Possibly, the Nordic experiences can contribute to the increased understanding of international cooperation, just as these countries' domestic political activities have improved our knowledge of the process of democratic politics.

The Historical Context of Contemporary Nordic Relations

In a historical perspective, Nordic relations have been characterized as much by conflict and rivalry as by peaceful coexistence and cooperation.

In contrast to the other chapters in this volume, Chapter 7 does not use a comparative, national approach. It presents a systemic, regional perspective of neighborhood relations. The overview replaces a commissioned but not yet completed comparative study of Nordic neighborhood policies. Important dimensions of Nordic relations are also discussed in the contributions by Nils Andrén and Carl-Einar Stålvant.

Efforts during the Middle Ages to form one unified Nordic state failed at the hands of Swedish separatists. In its place, two distinct entities were gradually established. Denmark-Norway-Iceland made up one unit, which at first dominated the region, and Sweden-Finland formed another unified entity.

The traditional struggle for regional hegemony between Denmark and Sweden continued throughout the sixteenth, seventeenth, and eighteenth centuries. Numerous wars were fought, alliances were formed, and provinces were conquered and reconquered. This rivalry was further aggravated by the temporary power vacuum in northern and central Europe, as both Prussia and Russia were weakened by internal difficulties. Slowly these countries emerged as great powers in the region and came to dominate the political scene of the area at the expense of both Denmark and Sweden.

These two countries had gradually become consolidated domestically and at the end of the eighteenth century were fairly well-integrated political units. The political administrations, legal codes, educational systems, and church organizations had all developed somewhat separately in the two kingdoms and laid the foundation for later structural differences between East and West. At the beginning of the Napoleonic Wars the Nordic region was made up of two distinct state-units, dominated, respectively, by the Danish and Swedish political elites.

At the end of the Napoleonic Wars, some drastic changes in the political configuration of the Nordic region had taken place. The Swedish province of Finland was seized by Russia in 1809 and turned into a semiautonomous province until its independence in 1917. The shock in Sweden over the loss of one-third of its territory was great and resulted in a coup d'état and a new constitution, which remained intact until 1975. Norway was taken away from Denmark in 1814 and given to Sweden as compensation for the loss of Finland. However, Norway was never totally integrated as a part of Sweden, as Finland had been, but instead was attached in a union under the same monarch. The Norwegians had their own constitution, government, and central administration. Only in foreign policy did the Swedish government represent the Norwegians.

This Norwegian-Swedish union never penetrated from the political-constitutional level down to the economic-cultural-social levels. Instead, the two societies developed separately during the nineteenth century. As a result of growing cultural, social, and economic differences, the political conflicts increased through the century until in 1905 the union was finally dissolved. Thus, the Norwegian union with Sweden did not have the same fundamental impact on society as had the earlier association with Denmark. Denmark was stripped of much of its possessions in

1814 and kept only Iceland. That country remained a Danish colony until it received autonomy in 1918 and finally declared itself independent in 1944, at a time when Denmark was occupied by Germany.

It seems that the period between 1800 and the end of World War II can be described as an era of Nordic political disintegration, as the two traditional entities in the region were split into five separate nation-states. This development did not take place only on the constitutional level, but with the rise of nationalism, public sentiment favored such a division of the region into distinct national units. In fact, some resentment was voiced against the former governing elites in Denmark and Sweden. For example, a part of the Finnish majority in Finland wanted to rid the country of any Swedish influence, and some Norwegians tried to reestablish their national cultural and linguistic heritage. Even today, the memories of foreign domination are on the minds of many Norwegians and Finnish-speaking Finns.

Since 1814, the Nordic region has not experienced any internal military conflict. This fact contrasts sharply with the tradition of almost continuous wars prior to that time. At the same time the Nordic region, after the Napoleonic Wars, was split up into many smaller entities, these countries were united in a common destiny as small powers, vulnerable to great power interference. Since that time one can talk about the Nordic region as an area of peace, because violent solutions have been avoided whenever serious conflict has arisen. For example, Norway could peacefully secede from the union with Sweden in 1905; the Swedish-Finnish dispute over the rights to the Åland Islands was settled peacefully in 1921; and the conflicting Norwegian and Danish claims to eastern Greenland were adjudicated by the Permanent Court of International Justice in 1933.

The original reason why violent action was avoided in these situations was mainly the fear of great power intervention in the area. External dominance of the region was to be avoided even if it meant making sacrifices to the neighboring countries. Slowly, these separate decisions in favor of compromise solutions established a tradition of peaceful regional relations. For example, all the Scandinavian countries stayed neutral during World War I in spite of strong sympathies with the different parties to the war. Similarly, the military planning of today does not include options for attacks by any of the other Nordic countries. Thus, a "pluralistic security community" has slowly developed, where dependable expectations of peaceful settlements of regional disputes are found.[1] This condition has clearly been motivated by the common fear of potential great power involvement. It is interesting that this condition was not reached until the region was politically divided into several states, which were reduced to small power status.

At the same time as the Nordic region was split into several smaller units, the need for cooperation and joint activity among these units increased. For a time, the memories of the rivalries and domination inhibited such efforts. For example, the Norwegian resentment of the union with Sweden affected relations between those countries. Likewise, Iceland still is influenced by its recent independence from Danish rule.

Deliberate efforts toward Nordic cooperation first took place in the middle of the nineteenth century. During the time of liberalism and nationalism, and inspired by the movements for national unity in Germany and Italy, the period of Scandinavianism occurred. An ideology of Scandinavian unity developed among the intellectual elites in Denmark and Sweden. No doubt, the recent reduction of these countries to a very marginal postion in world politics influenced this desire to unite the countries into one larger, stronger Scandinavian state. Several Scandinavian conferences were held among students and other intellectuals to manifest the desire for further unity. Numerous speeches were made and pamphlets were written in favor of the movement, and the rhetoric of Scandinavianism flourished.

This movement toward a Scandinavian union was also supported by the Danish and Swedish kings, who saw in it a means to unite the region under their crown. For example, the Swedish king Oscar I participated in some of the meetings and in 1856 expressed the now famous words: "From now on, war between the Scandinavian brothers is impossible." In particular, the Danish monarch was eager for Scandinavian support in his effort to resist the emerging Prussian empire. However, at the time of the Prussian attack on Denmark in 1864, the Swedish government declined to send military support to the Danish front. This failure to live up to the rhetoric about Scandinavian unity and brotherhood made a deep and lasting impression on the supporters of Nordic cooperation. From that time on, the efforts to create alliances or develop a unified Scandinavian state were abandoned in favor of more low-key, pragmatic, and functional cooperation.

During the latter part of the nineteenth century, several practical measures aimed at furthering Nordic cooperation were taken. Conferences were held on a regular basis among representatives of various scientific, legal, and political groups. Joint committees were created to harmonize national laws. In 1875, a Scandinavian currency union was established, which lasted through World War I. Collaboration among many industrial, commercial, agricultural, and labor organizations appeared. However, it was not until World War I that the cooperation efforts again reached the government level. Faced with the external threat of war, the Scandinavian governments saw the advantages of a joint position and close regional cooperation. To symbolize the new developments, the three Scandinavian heads of state met officially for the first time in December 1914. During the war, the countries tried to present a common front of neutrality toward the belligerents in spite of having different sympathies toward the participants in the war. To compensate for the loss of foreign trade, the countries engaged in extensive barter trade, which greatly increased regional trade. In 1918, 30 percent of all foreign trade was with other Nordic countries. This was a significant increase from the prewar level of 12 to 13 percent.[2]

The regional cooperation achieved during the war was unprecedented, and hopes were expressed that it could be continued after the war was over. However, the governments made no serious efforts during the 1920s to continue Nordic governmental cooperation; instead the activities relapsed into the prewar pattern. As earlier, low-key, sectoral efforts were carried out in certain areas of low political significance. Only in the League of Nations did the Scandinavian governments cooperate extensively to increase their chances for influencing the decisions in that international organization.[3]

Since World War II, Nordic relations have been characterized by a gradual but steady increase in intergovernmental cooperation. Not only have joint policy projects and intensive governmental interactions been continued from the interwar period, but some significant institutions have been established to help channel these regional activities. This trend of increased Nordic cooperation is quite evident in spite of some major setbacks during the period. In fact, to many foreign observers the publicized failures seem to overshadow the many smaller, less dramatic and less well-known achievements. For example, in 1948-1949 negotiations to form a Scandinavian defense alliance failed; continuous efforts during the 1950s to create a Nordic economic market led to nothing; the intensive effort in 1968–1970 to establish a Nordic economic union (NORDEK) resulted in final collapse; and the hopes for a united front in the negotiations with the European Economic Community (EEC) in 1971–1973 were not fulfilled.[4]

History seems to indicate that the Nordic countries have failed dramatically when they have tried to undertake some major, conspicuous cooperation projects. In contrast, they have been quite successful in achieving incremental and low-key steps toward closer cooperation. For example, numerous joint government committees and organs have been established throughout the postwar period to help coordinate policy in various issue areas. As a result of these functional activities, Nordic public policy is to a great extent jointly planned, formulated, and executed. A regional parliamentary body, the Nordic

Council, was created in 1952 to serve as a forum for debate and initiative. Various Nordic funds have been established to finance joint cultural, industrial, and development projects. A Council of Ministers, with small, permanent secretariats, exists to facilitate regional coordination and planning.

One interesting point about all these aspects of Nordic cooperation during the postwar period is that they were created piece by piece. Although the major proposals for increased cooperation failed, much of the substance of these projects has been achieved through incremental developments. The major thrusts forward in the cooperation effort have also occurred at times when the region seemed to be threatened with further disintegration due to external developments. Thus, the driving force for Nordic cooperation today is perhaps not as much a desire to unite the region as a wish to keep it intact. For example, the recent expansion of the EEC to include Denmark has been combined with a significant structural strengthening of the Nordic cooperation process.[5] Today, the regional relations are so intense and diversified that one can more properly describe them as an extension of domestic policymaking rather than as foreign relations in a traditional sense.

The Nordic Pattern of Integration

Having traced the development of a Nordic pluralistic security community and briefly touched upon the growth of regional government collaboration during the twentieth century, I now turn to the dynamics of contemporary interactions. Of interest are the processes by which a situation characterized merely by the absence of violent conflict has been transformed into a pattern of intimate collaboration. An effort will be made to sketch in a summary fashion the Nordic strategy of regional integration. The brief review is based on a more comprehensive, empirical study and only highlights the broad outlines of this process.[6]

For the purposes of this study, integration is conceptualized as a process that reaches across the various national entities rather than links these with a higher, regional level of activity. The regional level is not seen as increasing in authority, salience, or capacity to act, to the extent that the national units lose those characteristics of statehood. The process of political integration is less one of centralization of regional authority and more one of finding collective and nationally acceptable solutions to pressing national problems.

Three dimensions of integration are used. Societal integration is defined as the process whereby the involved societies are becoming increasingly interconnected through growing transnational ties and networks. Both regional elite interactions and various forms of aggregate transactions are studied. One potential link between societal integration and political integration is found in the attitudinal setting in the region. The responses by the public authorities to the changing degrees of societal interconnectedness are partly dependent on the attitudinal ties within the region.

Where a favorable attitudinal setting is found, a foundation for constructive responses and mutually advantageous solutions exist. In contrast, societal integration that is combined with unfavorable attitudes toward regional cooperation can easily spur hostile reactions and increase conflict among the countries. Attitudinal integration is defined as the process whereby the peoples of a region develop increasingly favorable attitudes toward their regional partners and to joint management of regional problems. Such changes are evidenced in surveys indicating a strengthening of regional identity ties and the maintenance of a supportive attitudinal setting for the cooperation processes.

Political integration is defined as the process whereby the public authorities in the region increasingly manage national problems jointly. Three aspects are involved in political integration: the growth of collective public institutions, increased transgovernmental interactions, and increased joint public policy output.

I have now identified three conceptual types of integration and specified seven operational dimensions of the concept. The organizing framework is presented in summary form in Figure 7.1. Next, I shall outline the Nordic pattern of cooperation in terms of these types of integration. This will help identify the dynamics of the Nordic strategy as well as indicate in what areas it has proven to be most successful and in what areas it has shown less success.

The general impression of Nordic transaction flows during 1952–1972 is that of high regional rates combined with marked discontinuities between the region and the external areas.[7] For all types of transactions except trade, the Nordic flows were already very intensive in 1952 and significantly more intensive than the external exchanges. Except for a marked increase in regional trade during the 1960s, the Nordic societies have not experienced any drastic increase in mutual relevance during the period studied. Instead, high rates of mutual transfers have characterized the region for a considerable time. While the volumes of Nordic flows have grown, the proportion of regional transactions to total foreign exchanges has not increased substantially. It has sometimes even declined. On the whole, it might be more appropriate to describe these transaction flows as indicating stagnation rather than rapid societal integrations. The region was already in 1952 closely tied together by various flows and the changes since that time have not been significant, except for the trade data.

FIGURE 7.1   CONCEPTUAL FRAMEWORK

Basic Assumption: Integration is not seen as a process reaching vertically upward towards a 'higher' regional level above the nation-states, but outward, transcending across the nations in the region.

Types of Integration:	Societal Integration	Attitudinal Integration	Political Integration
Conceptual Definitions:	The process whereby the regional societies are becoming increasingly interconnected through growing transnational ties and networks.	The process whereby the people of the region develop increasingly favorable attitudes toward their regional partners and to joint management of regional problems.	The process whereby the public authorities in the region increasingly manage national problems through joint processes.
Operational Dimensions:	1. Increased transactions of goods, messages, and people. 2. Increased activity of non-governmental elites across the national boundaries in the region.	1. Strengthening of regional identity ties. 2. The maintenance of a supportive attitudinal setting for joint cooperation processes.	1. Growth of joint public institutions. 2. Increased trans-governmental interactions. 3. Increased joint public policy output.

The growth of transnational elite activities in the Nordic region has experienced a two-step development. First, contacts were initiated in an effort to manage common problems resulting from the high mutual relevance of the Nordic societies. Nordic nongovernmental organizations (NGOs) are generally older than other international NGOs and the greatest relative expansion of such transnational elite contacts took place prior to World War II. Only 62 percent of all now existing Nordic organizations were established during the postwar era, a period associated with a major surge of transnationalism.[8] The regional activities were at this time mainly responses to developments at the aggregate level of societal relations and cannot be characterized as aiming at influencing the joint government decision-making process.

In more recent years, the trans-Nordic contacts have been channeled into more structured, formal, and institutional means. An effort was made to create joint coordinating bodies that could ensure continuous exposure to regional considerations and serve as a spokesman for the national organizations in their dealings with the joint government institutions in the region. At this time, the transnational interactions intensified as contacts with the joint public organs became more important. The goal of influencing the joint government policymaking process also became one of the major ambitions of the trans-Nordic activities. As before, many aspects of these interest-group-oriented activities are targeted at the national administrations, but a second focus toward the joint institutions has also developed.

To determine the possibilities for joint management of the high level of mutual societal relevance in the region, the regional identity ties were explored. Although the data were very limited, they pointed to a continued positive evaluation of and identification with the other Nordic societies during the postwar period.[9] In fact, some limited evidence indicated the possibility of a growing affinity among the Nordic people during the period. Thus, the high level of mutual relevance among the Nordic societies was found to be combined with substantial identity ties among the Nordic people. This combination of ties among the Nordic societies could provide a basis for constructive and mutually beneficial management of common problems. At the same time as the high rates of regional transactions make for common tasks in need of solutions, the strong identity ties can facilitate such joint solutions.

The public views of the Nordic cooperation process were also explored. Data, although rather limited, indicated a generally positive and permissive attitude toward Nordic cooperation. This process seemed to possess certain symbolic and emotional values regarding neighborly friendliness and regional harmony. It appeared to be strongly supported as an idea by the people. Specific proposals for increased cooperation were also generally supported, although a substantial number of the respondents could not offer definite opinions on these more specific questions. The general impression is that the political elites of the region have a relatively free hand in implementing the vague notion of Nordic cooperation. At the same time, since no major opposition to this concept was found, we could not trace any strong support for specific, concrete measures of cooperation.

The first operational dimension of political integration explored was the growth of joint public institutions.[10] The main observation regarding this dimension was the great expansion of the institutional structure since the middle of the 1960s. Not only have the joint organs grown in quantitative terms since 1964, but the degree of institutionalization in terms of size of personnel, joint secretariats, financial resources available, and activity within these organs has also expanded drastically. In particular, the changes since 1970 are important. Since that time many new important structural features have been added to the regional cooperation process. For example, a joint secretariat for the Nordic Council, a Council of Ministers with two secretariats and numerous permanent committees of high officials, a Fund for Industrial Development, and a Nordic Investment Bank have been created in this relatively short period of time. Thus, this dimension of political integration has recently experienced considerable growth. This expansion of the joint public institutional structure has also induced a wave of increased trans-Nordic activity among various nongovernmental groups. Apparently, there is a link between the growth of joint public institutions and the development of more structured, centralized interactions among various nongovernmental elites in the region.

The growth of joint public policy was found to experience its greatest expansion before the recent structural changes in the region. Both the scope and intensity of joint policy grew significantly prior to 1970. Since that time, the region has mainly experienced a continued slow increase in scope, intensity, and salience of joint policy. In particular, the economic sector has expanded during the last fifteen years.

One interesting observation is that the policy dimension of political integration has developed prior to and presumably independently of institutional growth in the region. Thus, the results or outputs of the joint processes operating in the area already show significant changes prior to the institutionalization and formalization of these joint policymaking activities. This finding leads us to question why the political elites in the countries have undertaken a major structural reorganization of the joint activities, when significant policy results were achieved prior to this change.

The answer may rest in a fear that external developments during the last ten years, such as the growth of the EEC and the enlargement of that group, would undermine the results already reached in the Nordic region. A greater structural rigidity and formalization would, it is hoped, facilitate regional coordination and ensure that a regional perspective was maintained on all major issues. The goal was not so much to expand the cooperative ventures, but to make sure that the countries could hold on to what they had achieved when faced with a strong external challenge. To that end, new joint structures were established and several programs for new cooperation schemes were agreed on to help symbolize the continued importance of Nordic cooperation.

Transgovernmental interactions in the Nordic region were analyzed to determine if in fact the joint policy output in the region was the result of joint processes of consultation, coordination, and decision or if it was arrived at separately. We found an intensive network of both formal and informal interactions across the national administrations. In particular, the informal contacts seemed important to the joint policymaking process. The various joint institutions in the region were also part of this transgovernmental activity as their staffs played a crucial part as initiators and mediators of policy. In addition we examined the norms for interaction and decision among the political elites active in those transgovernmental interactions. Belief in compromise, consensual decision-making, rational choice, openness, and emphasis on politics as a means to reach practical and beneficial solutions to problems seemed to dominate the political cultures of the area. This normative structure seemed to give the Nordic cooperation process a unique style of joint policymaking. Here, informal interactions, pragmatic goals and methods, an incremental approach toward task expansion, and an emphasis on broad consensus behind decisions dominated the joint efforts.

We noted an increase in the frequency of transgovernmental interactions during the last ten years. Thus, the recent organizational strengthening of the joint cooperation process has been combined with more intensive activity within this new structure. We also found that the main actors in this regional policymaking process are the bureaucratic segments of the governments. The political leaders of each country have limited direct involvement in the process and are heavily dependent on their staffs for guidance.

It is interesting to compare the results achieved in each of the dimensions of integration discussed in this study. The first observation is that Nordic societal integration has not been very impressive during the last twenty-five years. In many respects, the transactional dimension has stagnated or even suffered some disintegration, while the transnational elite activities have only very recently experienced an expansion. However, the fact that the Nordic societies have not experienced a major process of integration during the last twenty-five years is mainly related to the very strong initial ties in the region.

In the three dimensions of political integration, the region has experienced a clear process of integration during the last twenty-five years. This is the case because of lower initial levels of joint management and because of a consistent effort to further increase these joint governmental activities. The growth of joint public policy has been the most impressive dimension of political integration. Here a continuous process of joint outputs have been maintained throughout the period, which has produced comparatively substantial results. The transgovernmental interactions among the public authorities in the region are also very important. In this dimension intensive political integration has been experienced.

The institutional dimension of political integration is far less impressive than the other two aspects of the process. For a long time, the Nordic region did not experience any growth in this dimension, but was characterized by stagnation. It is only during the last ten years that a considerable expansion can be noted. Since the latter part of the 1960s, a process of integration is obvious in this dimension as well. However, in comparison with other regional efforts the institutional results of this process are still modest.

Finally, we noted a continuous process of a more favorable attitudinal setting for the joint efforts. This dimension seems to have been keeping up with the changes in the other dimensions of political and societal integration during the time period. For example, we could point to the clear possibility of a strengthening of regional identity ties during the postwar period. However, we could not find any strong demands for or interest in greatly expanded governmental cooperation beyond the present levels. Thus, in these dimensions of integration it might be more appropriate to talk about a continuous acceptance of and vague support for the developments in the region rather than of a definite process of attitudinal integration.

The pattern of integration developing in the Nordic region is summarized in Figure 7.2. Initial high levels of mutual societal relevance combined with modest identity ties lead to transnational and transgovernmental elite activities. The transgovernmental interactions lead to joint policy results. A few joint public institutions are established to facilitate coordination and planning in various areas. Gradually, the growth of joint public policy increases the need for further transnational coordination of the major nongovernmental organizations in the region. The attitudinal base for further governmental cooperation and regional

FIGURE 7.2   NORDIC PATTERN OF INTEGRATION

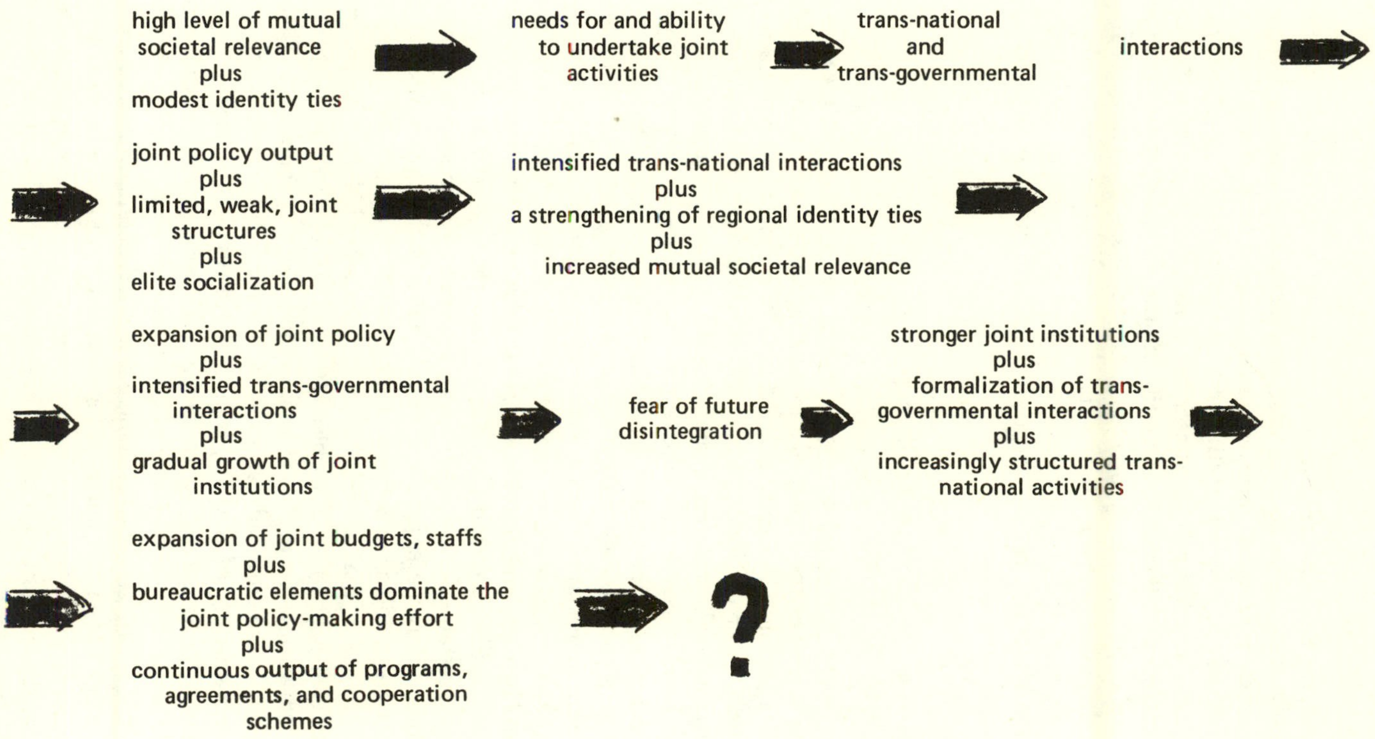

high level of mutual
societal relevance
plus
modest identity ties

needs for and ability
to undertake joint
activities

joint policy output
plus
limited, weak, joint
structures
plus
elite socialization

trans-national
and
trans-governmental
interactions

intensified trans-national interactions
plus
a strengthening of regional identity ties
plus
increased mutual societal relevance

expansion of joint policy
plus
intensified trans-governmental
interactions
plus
gradual growth of joint
institutions

fear of future
disintegration

stronger joint institutions
plus
formalization of trans-
governmental interactions
plus
increasingly structured transnational activities

expansion of joint budgets, staffs
plus
bureaucratic elements dominate the
joint policy-making effort
plus
continuous output of programs,
agreements, and cooperation
schemes

interactions

identity ties are strengthened and allow for increased cooperation. Finally, the considerable achievements made in joint policy and the intense transgovernmental interactions are coordinated, organized, and formalized through the creation of a new joint institutional structure in the region. In addition, the transnational activities of major groups are structurally strengthened to better fit with the new institutional features of the public policymaking process. Due to these structural changes, the policymaking process is now stabilized, institutionalized, and mainly the concern of the bureaucratic elements of government. The joint cooperation effort has become clearly established and given its own organizational foundation.

Motives and Sources Facilitating
Nordic Cooperation

Earlier I pointed to the prevalent desire to avoid great power interference in the region as a motivating factor behind the establishment of a pluralistic security community. This aspect still plays a role in the formulation of Nordic security policies. Through the dynamics of the so-called Nordic balance, characterized by mutual restraint and sensitivity in security postures, the superpower presence is far less pronounced in northern Europe than in other East-West borderline areas.[11]

It is also widely believed that the maintenance of a stable region, domestically and internationally, gives major external parties less reason to become involved in local affairs. By settling local disputes peacefully and by providing a stable and predictable economic and political setting, the Nordic governments help retain their positions as autonomous nation-states. Thus, the Nordic cooperation process is not only valued for its immediate, practical results, but it is also appreciated as a means toward reducing great power interests in the area.

It appears that a fundamental motive behind Nordic cooperation is of a defensive nature. The objective seems to be to help protect the nations from various forms of external domination or penetration. This dimension was mentioned earlier as a motive behind the recent structural strengthening of the cooperation processes. It is widely accepted that each Nordic country traditionally maintains strong cultural-economic-political links with major external areas. In many ways, the countries focus their international involvements in different directions giving room for centrifugal pressures on regional unity. Often, a favored solution to national problems, such as security or prosperity, has been the strengthening of such outside commitments even at the expense of Nordic solidarity.

Nordic cooperation schemes have sometimes offered alternate, often second-best solutions when broader international involvements proved beyond reach. In most cases, one or more of the Nordic governments have promoted such ventures in the face of major external challenges. Particularly strong attempts to maintain regional unity have been made when major international commitments by some of the governments would leave others in isolated and exposed positions. Nordic cooperation offers a defensive adjustment mechanism to serious political or economic external challenges that may undermine national autonomy and enhance foreign domination.

Nordic cooperation is seen as enhancing the national postures in another respect as well. Through regional collaboration and the presentation of a united front, the governments greatly strengthen their otherwise rather limited influence on the international environment. Living by the principle of "strength in numbers," the Nordic governments are often motivated to cooperate in order to increase their international influence. If such external efforts are to prove successful, internal agreement on policy is required. Thus, the external ramifications of disunity offer strong incentives for reaching mutually acceptable solutions on many issues. It is often said that the Nordic governments find it more difficult to settle internal disputes than to find common ground in international arenas.[12]

In addition to the externally oriented motives for Nordic cooperation, important local aspects are also included. It is realized that a number of domestic objectives cannot be reached without some form of joint effort. For example, the geographical proximity of the nations generates a number of common problems with transportation, migration, pollution, and social and judicial services. The Nordic countries have a long and strong record on finding joint solutions to such neighborhood issues.[13] These often low-key and informal arrangements may not be recognized as major political achievements in regional cooperation. However, the ramifications for the local populations are significant as various obstacles to regional mobility, interchanges, and equality have been removed. They provide an important public service to the people in the countries.

Nordic cooperation is also seen as a useful mechanism to overcome the limited national resources of the countries. A number of nationally desirable objectives are only possible with the addition of externally available resources. For a number of reasons, a pooling of Nordic resources may often seem more satisfactory than collaboration with other, more distant and significantly larger partners. This motive has stimulated Nordic efforts in the educational, scientific, communications, industrial, energy, and regional development fields. In other areas, such as security and trade, the Nordic region has not offered sufficiently large collective resources to satisfy the individual national needs. In these sectors, cooperation that extends beyond the Nordic region generally has offered the most promising solutions.

With intensified regional interactions and heightened national sensitivities to developments in the neighboring countries, an additional motive for cooperation has emerged. It is recognized that the Nordic economies are closely connected and that national economic policy often has implications for the other societies. A desire to avoid policy choices with negative effects on the regional partners is evident among the governments. Through a continuous dialogue aiming at policy coordination, government officials hope to foster regional stability and collective prosperity. Although national priorities often make it impossible to find one common policy posture, at least several undesirable alternatives can be avoided. Continuous contacts are maintained across most areas of public policy, including judicial, financial, fiscal, industrial, energy, and foreign policy.

We have pointed to several external and internal motives for pursuing Nordic cooperation. It is evident from this brief review that the Nordic governments have strong incentives to participate in regional collaboration. Valuable national objectives and benefits can be achieved through such collective efforts. However, the existence of political motives for cooperation can not alone explain the comparatively successful record of Nordic cooperation. It is also important to recognize a number of factors that facilitate the accomplishment of the desired results. The sources of Nordic cooperation can be found in the cultural heritage, social and political structures, and in prevalent values and norms. Possibly, these background conditions are unique to the Nordic setting and are not easily transferred to other areas.

With the growth of nationalism in Europe, a sense of a Nordic heritage developed in this region. We previously discussed the pan-Scandinavian movement of the mid-1800s. Also more recently one can note a sense of a Nordic identity among the peoples. Although this is less noted domestically, it becomes very evident in international dealings. The psychological distance to fellow Nordics is considerably shorter than to other foreign groups. As discussed earlier, several opinion polls indicate the affinity of the Nordic peoples relative to other nationalities.

Several factors reinforce this common feeling of belonging to a group set apart from others. The language similarities facilitate relaxed communications. The values, life-styles, and interests are often very similar. One is, in general, relatively well acquainted with these countries and their inhabitants. During the time period covered by the memories of the present generation, no serious antagonizing conflicts have been experienced. In addition, Nordic nationalism may serve as a substitute for traditional nationalism. Although the latter notion is somewhat discredited in these very internationally oriented societies, a belief in Nordic unity, strength, and even exclusiveness seems more in accord with the modern emphasis on international cooperation. In all, the Nordic region offers a focus for national identity that seems less alien and perhaps more comfortable than the larger international environment. This common perception may facilitate stable domestic support for intimate regional governmental collaboration.

In many respects, the Nordic societies and political systems have developed in parallel fashions. The common heritage of gradual, generally peaceful domestic change has not only affected the contemporary political cultures, but has also resulted in very similar national structures.[14] Government machineries, political parties, and interest groups are organized along similar lines and serve similar functions in society. The noted parallelism facilitates close interaction among political leaders, governmental officials, and interests groups. The widely recognized similarities with the other Nordic countries also encourage using these nations as initial reference points and as sources of inspiration for national action. The parallelism is also a primary factor behind extensive policy diffusion among the governments.

In addition, the parallel national structures may significantly facilitate the cooperation process.[15] It is easy to identify one's functional counterpart in the other countries. Participants in the cooperation effort generally face similar restraints and possibilities as they basically perform identical functions in society. All parties can without difficulty appreciate the details of policymaking in the other governments since they do not vary significantly from their own. Basic ideological beliefs and fundamental social and economic objectives are often shared across the state lines. It should be relatively easy to work together when so many of the national attributes are held in common or are very similar.

There are some notable exceptions to the dominant feature of Nordic parallelism. I previously pointed to the divergent external orientations as forces limiting regional cooperation. The economic structures of the countries also vary significantly. National resources, economic activity, and economic interests are different for the countries. Traditionally it has been more difficult to reach agreement in the economic sector than it has been in other policy areas. Recently, the national differences in this regard have tended to be somewhat reduced as all countries have experienced similar economic trends and pressures.

Today, the sharpest economic contrasts may not be between the nations but rather between the southern and northern parts of the region. A pattern of stable economic activity and presumed financial dominance persists in the south while the north experiences relative stagnation and demands for government subsidies. It is not clear how the anticipated Norwegian oil exploration north of the sixty-second parallel will affect this relationship between the regional periphery and center. Possibly, the potential infusion of substantial new resources in this area may stimulate new cooperation projects among the concerned governments.

The Nordic political systems are well known for their prevalent norms of consensus formation, compromise, and fact finding. It is widely felt that these dominant values have facilitated the development of stable, harmonious, high-performance polities. As could be expected, the norms influencing domestic developments are also crucial factors in the regional processes. The Nordic preference for consensus formation is manifested in an emphasis on national accommodation. Decisions are not made over the objections of any of the parties. Unanimity is the rule in the collective policymaking process. National sovereignty is recognized and respected as a vital political force. Proposals that would drastically violate the essential interests of any nation are not seriously considered. However, this emphasis on consensus formation does not necessarily result in obstructionism leading to immobilism.

The value placed on compromise is reflected in the emphasis on accommodation to others. Mutual sensitivity to each other's needs and interests are dominant features of the cooperation process. These norms give an assurance of not being disregarded or compromised. They also involve a responsibility to respond to the demands by the other participants. Possibly, the absence of a supranational pretense generates some confidence among the governments. These governments are aware that they can at any time refuse to support a policy or even withdraw from the proceedings. The existence of limited formal commitments and the strong preferences for cooperation may combine to facilitate mutually acceptable solutions.

The Nordic policymaking sequence proceeds from extensive and detailed investigations to lengthy deliberations and to final political decision. Often, this process takes several years. The value given to fact finding prior to making a political commitment is rooted in the domestic political cultures. This bias makes for an extremely slow, often tedious and cumbersome cooperation process. However, it also gives some assurance that all ramifications of a decision are fully explored and that all legitimate interests are considered. Perhaps, this lengthy process is a prerequisite for finding common ground on the many important policy issues covered by the regional cooperation efforts. An established sense of confidence in that no vital interests are overlooked or ignored may also facilitate more far-reaching commitments than hastier decisions would allow.

Together with the other sources discussed, the dominant norms for regional interactions may be crucial factors behind the generally successful record of contemporary Nordic cooperation. The governments in this area have managed to solve numerous national problems through joint actions. They have established a solid pattern of intimate collaboration covering a wide scope of public policy. It is an open question as to what extent the Nordic model for neighborhood cooperation can be applied to other regions experiencing similar needs for collective solutions to vital concerns.

Notes

1. Karl Deutsch, *Political Community and the North Atlantic Area* (Princeton, N.J.: Princeton University Press, 1957); Raymond Lindgren, *Norway-Sweden: Union, Disunion and Scandinavian Integration* (Princeton, N.J.: Princeton University Press, 1959).

2. These early developments are reviewed in Frantz Wendt, *The Nordic Council and Cooperation in Scandinavia* (Copenhagen: Munksgaard, 1959).

3. Shepard Jones, *The Scandinavian States and the League of Nations* (Princeton, N.J.: Princeton University Press, 1939).

4. These developments are reviewed in Claes Wiklund and Bengt Sundelius, "Nordic Cooperation in the Seventies: Trends and Patterns," *Scandinavian Political Studies*, n.s., no. 2(1979):99–120.

5. This is argued in Bengt Sundelius, "Nordic Cooperation: A Dead Issue?" *World Today* 33 (July 1977):275–82.

6. Bengt Sundelius, "Nordic Cooperation: A Dynamic Integration Process" (Ph.D. diss., University of Denver, 1976).

7. Supporting data are presented in Bengt Sundelius, *Managing Transnationalism in Northern Europe* (Boulder, Colo.: Westview Press, 1978), pp. 15–42.

8. Abraham Hallenstvedt, "Nordisk Foreningsliv: Omfang og Karakter" (Paper given at the Seminar on Nordic Organizations, Gothenbourg, Sweden, May 1974).

9. Supporting attitudinal data are found in Jacobsen-Rokkan-Vetti, *Kontakt og Samarbeid mellom de nordiske folk* (Oslo: Polhogda Stiftelsen, 1956); Bjorn Alstad, *Norske Meninger, I* (Oslo: Pax, 1972); Nordic Council, *Den nordiska allmanheten och det nordiska samarbetet 1973*, Nordisk Udredningsserie 4/73 (Stockholm: Nordic Council, 1973).

10. Supporting data on the three dimensions of political integration are presented in Sundelius, *Managing Transnationalism*, pp. 43–102.

11. Nils Andrén, *The Future of the Nordic Balance* (Stockholm: Swedish Research Institute of National Defense, 1977). Also see his contribution in this volume.

12. Nordic cooperation in international forums is reviewed in Ake Landqvist (ed.), *Norden pa varldsarenan* (Stockholm: Tema, 1968).

13. This is reviewed in Frantz Wendt, *Nordisk Rad 1952–1978* (Stockholm: Nordic Council, 1979).

14. Folmer Wisti (ed.), *Nordic Democracy* (Copenhagen: Danish Institute, 1981). Also see the contribution to this volume by Ib Faurby, who points to both similarities and important differences.

15. Compare Gunnar P. Nielsson, "The Parallel National Action Process: Scandinavian Experiences," in Paul Taylor and A.J.R. Groom (eds.), *International Organization: A Conceptual Approach* (London: Frances Pinter, 1977), pp. 270–316.

8
North European Foreign Policies in a Comparative Perspective

Bengt Sundelius

The literature on northern Europe generally points to the many similarities in the policies and national attributes of these countries. In an international perspective, the minor variations among the nations seem far less pronounced than their many common features. On most standard schemes of classification Denmark, Finland, Norway, and Sweden fall within the same category of nations.[1] For example, in the widely discussed Rosenau pretheory for foreign policy studies these countries belong to the same genotype of small, developed, open nations.[2]

According to the Rosenau approach, the external behavior of countries can be explained by an identifiable set of broadly defined background factors. In addition, the relative potency of each independent variable cluster should be the same for all nations within each group. Finally, the particular combination of influencing factors would generate largely similar external behaviors for all countries of this genotype. The implication of the Rosenau pretheory and of much of the international foreign policy literature is that North European foreign policies are very similar and can also be explained in terms of similar background conditions. In an international perspective, the countries covered in this study comprise most-similar systems.

A dichotomous classification of nations in terms of size, economic development, and degree of political accountability may be very useful for broad, global comparisons. Such an approach can give initial insights into the main patterns of foreign policy behavior. However, this orientation is not likely to provide more than a rather superficial knowledge. Both the explanatory variables and the dimensions of the external behavior analyzed tend to be defined in such general terms that little additional understanding is generated. The kind of general propositions formulated on the basis of such global investigations tend to be very vague or riddled with limiting qualifications.

Several analysts have pointed to the potential utility of using a generally applicable framework for comparison also within distinct nation types.[3] By using this approach, the impact of certain variables such as political accountability or economic development can be viewed as constant, across the cases, allowing a focus on other, salient factors. These remaining background factors can be more specifically defined and offer, it is hoped, a more differentiated and complete explanation of the external behavior. The description of foreign policy activities can also be more detailed, making for a clearer comprehension of the dependent variable and its main dimensions. Variations among countries that are easily obscured in the global context may also come to light adding substantially to such initial efforts. The approach would not only give a richer comprehension of the relationships under study, but also tend to offer a more accurate descriptive picture of the cases. Although the conclusions arrived at may be limited in scope, they would perhaps bear more resemblance to reality. As such, they would make for more reliable and relevant building blocks in an empirical theory of foreign policy.

The studies contained in this volume clearly indicate the need to look beyond global, cross-national comparison. Although the countries covered fall within the same nation type and manifest numerous similarities in attributes and policies, several major differences are found. Both in the areas of security policy and international economic policy, the nations behave quite differently in spite of the many similar background conditions.

Traditionally, particularistic analyses have accounted for these phenomena. It would be valuable if one also could map out these variations more systematically and try to offer explanations of them in terms of a generally applicable set of dimensions and factors. If one could successfully combine the insights of the area specialists with the theoretical consciousness of the Rosenau school, the North European case studies may contribute somewhat to the comparative study of foreign policy. In the following, a modest attempt is made in this direction.

The Dependent Variable

The foreign policies of the North European countries can be viewed within different time frames. In a long-term perspective, for example the postwar era, one can point to the particular patterns of foreign policy actions undertaken. To varying degrees the countries have manifested involvement in international affairs, promotion of international change, and emphasis on self-reliance and governmental autonomy. Taken together, different scores on such dimensions can give distinct national profiles of foreign policy behavior. Enduring patterns of external policy can be identified and related to various determining factors. Through cross-national comparison one may also be able to link the manifested behavior pattern to certain crucial background variables. Within this long-term perspective, explanations are most likely to be found in the more stable, enduring features conditioning the external postures.

It is conceivable that national behavior in discrete situations deviates considerably from the established long-term pattern. As long as such fluctuations are not consistently directed toward one end of a dimension, they may still, over time, reinforce the established national profile. However, the explanations given for the foreign policy behavior would tend to differ markedly depending on which time reference was used. Within such a short-term perspective, the analysis would include more volatile factors, which may prove instrumental in single events. In this comparative review I shall distinguish between the pattern of foreign policy and discrete foreign policy actions in situations.[4] The main focus here is on outlining and explaining the long-term pattern of North European foreign policies.

Contemporary foreign policies are multidimensional, extending across a wide spectrum of external relations. To give a full description of national involvements and actions, one would have to cover areas such as defense, trade, financial, scientific, cultural, educational, social, and diplomatic issues. In this volume, we have chosen to focus on four sectors of foreign policy that seem central to all countries covered. Comprehensive overviews of each foreign policy area have been given in the preceding chapters. The explanatory analysis in this chapter is limited to two sectors—security policy and international economic policy. It is in these areas that the differences are most apparent.

The previous chapters also indicate the usefulness of distinguishing among policy sectors in comparative analysis. While overall national behavior may appear closely similar, the sector analysis can reveal a number of significant differences among the nations. Similarly, vast differences in total foreign policy profiles may be reduced or concentrated in such more differentiated studies. Subsequently, widely held images of the patterns of national behavior within a specific nation type may be modified as a result of such analysis.

Ib Faurby stresses in Chapter 3 that any meaningful linkage between domestic background factors and external policy must be made within the context of specific issue areas. The mobilization of interest groups and government actors tends to vary between policy sectors and perceived potential policy effects. It is a fair assumption that contemporary foreign policy, covering a broad spectrum of issues, can most adequately be explained in terms of distinct policy types.[5]

In this study, a functional separation has been made to allow for different possible linkages for each policy sector. Subsequently, explanations given will not merely be for foreign policy as a general phenomenon but for more specific types of external behavior. Such a strategy may render results richer in substantive content than what a more general approach could offer.

An important prerequisite for comparative analysis is the identification of several dimensions of the dependent variable that can be compared across the cases. Uniform and comparable indicators of the potential variations in foreign policy should be established. This way one can determine which aspects of the foreign policy behaviors of the nations manifest uniformity and which show variance. Numerous dimensions could be conceived depending on the purposes of the study. As this analysis attempts a most similar systems comparison, it will focus on a few critical dimensions where significant differences have been noted.

It should be emphasized that a number of dimensions where no significant variations among the countries are found could be identified. For example, one could study the involvement in international relations, the extent of cooperation or conflict behavior, the adherence to international norms and rules, and the proportion of military-diplomatic-technical activity. When pursuing comparisons with nations of other genotypes, an inclusion of such dimensions would prove most rewarding.

A reading of the previous chapters of this book reveals that the North European nations differ in their foreign policy behaviors in several respects. For the purposes of this exploratory analysis, a focus on four basic aspects seems reasonable. These dimensions are chosen in the belief that they cover fundamental features of foreign policy, they are relevant for cross-national comparisons, and they illustrate particularly well the national variations among the North European countries. The selection of the four dimensions as well as the scoring of cases on these attributes are based on the previous chapters outlining the content of the foreign policies. However, this does not necessarily mean that the other contributors to this volume agree with my interpretation of their essays.

An important foreign policy dimension in the present context is that of relative degrees of self-reliance. To what extent does the nation manifest a policy of self-reliance versus reliance on external parties to achieve major national objectives? A posture of self-reliance would be indicated by reluctance to make commitments to other governments or international organizations. The opposite course would be found where nations were deeply engaged in international collective ventures or in working closely with another government.

Another basic foreign policy dimension concerns the tendency toward a multilateral or a bilateral approach toward international issues. Are ex-

TABLE 8.1

BASIC FOREIGN POLICY DIMENSIONS

Strategy:	Self-reliance				External Reliance			
Channel:	Bilat		Multilat		Bilat		Multilat	
Objective:	Change	Contin	Change	Contin	Change	Contin	Change	Contin
Style:	Inc Con	Inc Con	Inc Co	Inc Con	Inc Con	Inc Co	Inc Co	Inc Co
Case:								

ternal activities mainly focused on multilateral forums or on bilateral relationships? This difference would be indicated by the relative resource commitments and priorities given to the various channels for international interaction.

External policy can also be distinguished according to what extent it tends to promote international change or continuity. Is the foreign policy behavior characterized by activities geared toward changing the international environment or toward maintaining this external setting? The frequent sponsorship of or support for proposals aimed at international change versus declared defense of the present international order could be seen as indicators of these tendencies.

Finally, external policy can be characterized by consistency over time or by recurrent inconsistencies or fluctuations. Are policy stands mutually supportive or do they tend to contradict each other? A comparison of national positions within specific sectors would reveal potential inconsistencies in policy. While one state may show a coherent, clearly defined policy within a sector, another state may manifest inconsistencies and sudden fluctuations in positions.

The four dimensions of foreign policy are shown in Table 8.1, which also illustrates the many potential combinations. Even with these very basic categories, a great variety of national profiles are possible. It is important to emphasize that the dichotomized variables presented in the tables really should be viewed as end positions on the four discussed dimensions. Rather than making clear-cut choices between the categories, the analysis tries to point to dominant tendencies toward one or the other of the two extreme points. In contrast, the tables tend to exaggerate the distances among the cases and obscure the fact that in many instances only marginal differences in policy are experienced. Since the purpose of this analysis is to bring out variations among nations otherwise characterized by great similarities, this approach seems justifiable.

Bengt Sundelius

TABLE 8.2

NORTH EUROPEAN FOREIGN POLICY PATTERNS

A. National Profiles

Nation	Denmark			Finland			Norway			Sweden		
Sector	Sec	Econ	Aid	Sec	Econ	Aid	Sec	Econ	Aid	Sec	Econ	Aid
Reliance	E	E	E	S	S	E	E	S	S	S	S	S
Mult/bil	M	M	M	B	M	M	M	B	M	M	B	B
Change/cont	S	S	S	C	S	S	S	S	C	S	S	C
Consist/inc	C	C	C	C	C	C	C	I	C	C	I	C

B. National Patterns in Functional Sectors

Sector	Security Policy				Int. Econ. Policy				Aid Policy			
Nation	Den	Fin	Nor	Swe	Den	Fin	Nor	Swe	Den	Fin	Nor	Swe
Reliance	E	S	E	S	E	S	S	S	E	E	S	S
Mult/bilat	M	B	M	M	M	M	B	B	M	M	M	B
Change/cont	S	C	S	S	S	S	S	S	S	S	C	C
Consist/inc	C	C	C	C	C	C	I	I	C	C	C	C

Strategy: E=external reliance, S=self-reliance
Channel: M=multilateral approach, B=bilateral approach
Objective: S=support of continuity, C=support of change
Style: C=consistency, I=inconsistency

As outlined above, the North European nations show interesting variations on these four dimensions of foreign policy. In addition, the countries score differently across the three functional types of external policy covered here, i.e., security policy, international economic policy, and third world policy. Subsequently, it seems useful to combine the dimensions of foreign policy behavior with the types of policy discussed earlier. The matrix in Table 8.2 indicating national profiles illustrates only the differences in the pattern behavior of North European foreign policies and ignores the many basic similarities. In addition, it represents only a very crude approximation of the comprehensive and refined reviews given in Chapters 2 through 6.

The overall national profiles illustrated in Table 8.2A show some interesting variations. On the dimension of reliance, Denmark appears to differ most clearly from Sweden, whereas Finland and Norway have profiles closer to that of Sweden. Apparently, some explanation is necessary for the deviant Danish pattern of consistent external reliance. Similarly,

Denmark tends to rely more on multilateral approaches to international issues than do the other nations. Again, Sweden falls at the other extreme tending toward a bilateral focus.

All four countries pursue policies mainly in support of international continuity. Exceptions are found in Finnish security policy and Swedish, and possibly Norwegian, aid policy. Consistency over time is the standard across the groups, but two interesting exceptions are noted. Both Norway and Sweden have manifested inconsistencies in international economic policy.

Denmark and Sweden appear to be the furthest apart in most dimensions, whereas Finland and Norway fall in between these two. Notable deviations from the overall pattern were found for Denmark on reliance, Finland and Sweden on international continuity, and Norway and Sweden on policy consistency. In the following analysis, a search for some explanations for these differences will be undertaken. As could be expected, an overall analysis of the four national profiles along the four discussed dimensions results in greater similarities than differences.

To more clearly indicate the national variations it is helpful to focus on the distinct policy sectors. In Table 8.2B the material is regrouped to illustrate better the national profiles in the individual functional areas. Initially, one can see the basic regional split in the security area on the dimension of reliance. It is also interesting to note the great similarity in North European security policies in the other dimensions. Only Finland manifests a deviant profile, primarily focusing on a bilateral relationship and periodically pursuing a policy of international change on this issue.

In the area of international economic policy several notable differences are found. Denmark alone tends to rely mainly on external actors for attainment of national objectives. Denmark and Finland emphasize multilateral approaches to international economic issues, whereas Norway and Sweden tend toward bilateral relations. In addition, Norway and Sweden have patterns of inconsistency in this policy sector. Apparently, the differences in international economic policy are even more widespread than they are in the security sector.

The third world policies of the North European nations are generally perceived as very similar. This analysis would tend to support such a view of the present patterns. Some differences are found in the stronger Swedish and Norwegian support of international change, the greater Swedish tendency to rely on bilateral approaches, and the regional split on reliance. Whereas Denmark and Finland seem to rely on external guidance and support for their policy, Norway and particularly Sweden more clearly tie their behavior to internally formulated objectives and resources. Compared to the discussed variations in security and international economic policy, these differences appear less pronounced and are even more a question of degree. In an international perspective, the similarities outweigh the differences.

The reviews of the foreign policies of the North European nations have resulted in the identification of a number of differences among the cases. The study has underlined the importance of giving a multidimensional description of the dependent variable. It has also shown the utility of a detailed, comparative study of cases belonging to the same nation type. In several respects, these most similar systems manifest most different forms of external behavior. In the next section, an attempt is made to link the noted differences in the dependent variables with observed variations in possible determinants.

Some Independent Variables

One of the major problems of finding plausible explanations for foreign policy behavior is the great many potential independent variables. Numerous factors ranging from the idiosyncracies of individual leaders to the restraints imposed by the global international system can be seen as playing important determining roles. The literature on foreign policy is filled with attempts at reducing this endless list of possible factors to a theoretically justifiable set of background conditions. Even so, the complexity is sometimes overwhelming.[6]

The selection of cases in this study allows for a significant reduction in the number of background factors included. Since it is the purpose of this comparative analysis to explain major differences in foreign policy with the aid of significant differences in the independent variables, a number of possibilities can be omitted. Across a broad range of background factors the North European nations manifest great similarities. As indicated in the previous reviews, the values, cultures, social settings, political systems, governmental structures, and positions in the international system are quite similar. A most similar systems approach enables us to focus on a few remaining features, where significant variations are evident.

Presumably, the noted variations in the dependent variable can somehow be attributed to some notable differences in background conditions. In this analysis, the focus is on several national and domestic factors. It is assumed that the long-term impact of external and international system variables is basically similar for all the nations. The close geographical proximity of the cases and their similar external orientations would suggest such a simplifying assumption. This necessary but limiting condition should be kept in mind.

Many analysts have recognized the need to somehow weigh the

relative effect of single variables or combinations of variables.[7] It is argued that only through an assessment of their relative potency or through an understanding of the combined effect of the interaction of different types of background factors can one give meaningful explanations. Unfortunately, the frequent failure to isolate a few key variables has made it difficult to successfully assess such relative potencies. In a most similar systems analysis, this task would seem more promising as many possible influences are kept constant across the cases.

It is also often stated that different explanatory variables can best be linked to specific types of foreign policy behavior. Some broad factors do not account for all policy behavior, but each set of factors must be related to a specified dimension or particular sector of the external behavior. A multidimensional description of the dependent variable, as given above, would facilitate such a targeted explanatory analysis.

Although all the North European nations belong to the same global genotype of small, developed, open systems, differences in size are significant. As indicated in Table 8.3, in terms of land area, population and GNP, Sweden stands out as possessing considerably greater resources than the other three countries. In 1978, this nation alone accounted for 37 percent of the regional population and over 40 percent of the total economic output. In addition, the economic gap between Sweden and the others has gradually narrowed and was even greater during the first twenty years of the postwar era. It can be assumed that the significantly greater Swedish resources have had an impact on its external behavior. This factor alone could account for some of the noted differences in foreign policy.

For example, the clear Swedish preference for self-reliance, its stronger tendency toward a bilateral approach, and the limited promotion of international change could be explained by this factor. In contrast, Denmark, a nation possessing less resources, has opted for external reliance, a multilateral approach, and a promotion of international continuity. However, Norway and Finland with population and economic resources more at the level of Denmark than Sweden do not clearly follow this pattern. In both cases, strategies of self-reliance have been used and both multilateral and bilateral approaches are found.

Subsequently, the size factor may give a plausible explanation for the behavior of the larger unit, Sweden, but it cannot account for the differences among the smaller countries. Yet, it seems valuable to differentiate according to size also within a specified nation type as the differences may be substantial. In particular, such variations may be crucial factors behind policy differences toward regional or neighborhood issues.

In addition to the consistent size differential between Sweden and the

Bengt Sundelius

TABLE 8.3

INDICATORS OF NATIONAL SIZE

Indicator	Denmark	Finland	Norway	Sweden	Total
Land Area:					
Sq. Miles	17,028	130,119	125,181	173,665	445,993
Proportion	3.8 %	29.2 %	28.1%	38.9 %	100 %
Relative size	1:	7.6	7.4	10.2	26.2
Population:					
Mill. 1978	5.1	4.75	4.06	8.28	22.21
Proportion	23.0%	21.4%	18.3%	37.3%	100%
Relative size	1:	0.9	0.8	1.6	4.4
GNP 1967:					
Bil. $	12,156	8,692	8,411	24,132	53,391
Proportion	22.8%	16.3%	15.7%	45.2%	100%
Relative size	1:	0.7	0.7	2.0	4.4
GDP 1977:					
Bil. $	46,040	31,740	35,610	87,290	200,680
Proportion	22.9%	15.8%	17.8%	43.5%	100%
Relative size	1:	0.7	0.8	1.9	4.4

other countries, an outstanding feature of Table 8.3 is the great discrepancy between land area and the other Danish indicators of size. This country has the second largest population and substantially greater economic wealth than Finland or Norway. In contrast, Denmark has a tiny territory (exempting the vast Greenland possession) and, as indicated earlier by Ib Faurby, possesses very limited natural resources.

The apparent gap between population size and economic output (factors related to need and performance) on the one hand and territorial size and domestic resources (factors related to indigenous capabilities) on the other hand could account for the greater Danish commitment to international involvements. It would appear that the large and crowded population is sustained at a very high level of national wealth only through intensive exchanges with the international environment.

For both Finland and Norway, one finds a greater consistency between the various indicators of size. In these countries, economic performance and population size are more in proportion with the given territory and resources. Although all three countries have similar rates of trade to GNP (around 50 percent), this external linkage may be regarded as more essential for continued prosperity and stability in Denmark. Here, national awareness of the extreme "smallness" would be most apparent as it includes a very tangible and highly visible form of the concept.

The Danish case as compared to Finland and Norway suggests the usefulness of comparing different indicators of national size and resources to establish potential gaps between internally available capabilities and national performance. The apparent Danish discrepancy in this regard could help explain its strong preference for external reliance, multilateralism, and its support of international continuity. On this score, Finland and increasingly Norway come closer to the opposite Swedish pattern.

Among nations of similar overall size, discrepancies between different types of national resource attributes may prove to be an important determining factor for foreign policy. Status discrepancy has been used to explain the tendency toward national aggression.[8] Similarly, resource discrepancy could account for different orientations toward other forms of international involvements. Among Western, open, highly developed societies, rank disequilibrium may not foster external aggression as a means toward achieving congruity, but instead would stimulate participation in international collaboration. One could hypothesize that for this type of nation there is a positive relationship between experienced resource discrepancy and the tendency to engage in international collaborative undertakings.

For overachievers, like Denmark, active engagement in international cooperation schemes may be an important means by which to compensate for low rankings on ascribed size dimensions, such as territory or resources. In contrast, nations experiencing greater harmony between the given attributes and the achievement-oriented dimensions of size, such as GNP, have relatively less incentive to stress such involvements. They would be more likely to emphasize self-reliance over extensive external commitments. The combined effects of absolute, overall size and the extent to which the national economic performance and population is compatible with tangible domestic resources would seem to offer an intriguing set of background conditions for external behavior.

So far I have focused on the general pattern of North European foreign policy during the last thirty years. When analyzing specific sectors, such as security and international economic policy, one needs to move beyond the very general determinant of size and also consider other factors. If not, the inconsistent Swedish and Norwegian policies toward the EC versus the clear Danish and Finnish positions on the same issue could not be understood. Similarly, the opposite Norwegian and Swedish security preferences in contrast to the more flexible Danish position in 1948 remain to be explained.

Although all four North European nations are characterized by high levels of development and affluence, their economic structures vary considerably. In this respect, the differences may outweigh the similarities. As indicated by Ib Faurby in Chapter 3, the agricultural sector is most important in Denmark, fishing and now oil are crucial in Norway, the metal industry is dominant in Sweden, and forestry is vital to Finland. Each country has its own economic sector of specialization. Obviously, the external economic needs of the nations differ. Assuming a rational decision-making process, one could calculate what external policies would prove most beneficial to insure continued prosperity and, in this way, attribute foreign economic policy to some overriding national economic interest. Certainly, differences in behavior could be related to significant national differences in this respect.[9]

In addition, and perhaps even more interesting, the relative political weight of various economic groups differs between the countries. Economic interest groups perceive different potential benefits and probable costs of possible foreign policies and will try to affect these choices. Here, the strategic position and political impact of various economic groups seem more important than their absolute importance to the national economy. Ib Faurby previously reviewed the relative political salience of different economic sectors in the national policymaking processes. He pointed to the size and objective value of various groups to the national economy. He also emphasized traditional ties between special interests and major parties as well as the disproportional political roles of certain occupational groups.

In some cases, cross-cutting political demands will be made by various concerned groups. Such situations can easily result in prolonged policy disputes that at times lead to inconsistencies in national policy postures. For example, both Sweden and Norway suffered from drawn out internal debates on the merits of membership in the European Community. In these exchanges, strong arguments were made on both sides of the issue as crucial economic interests were seen to be affected by the outcome. One side did not have a clear-cut advantage but a difficult political choice was required. In contrast, the situations in Denmark and Finland were less complex. Leading economic groups in Denmark favored EC membership while pro-EC groups in Finland did not push the issue. The result was less uncertainty about the outcome and also a more consistent national policy on the issue.

Apparently, the economic structure of a nation is an important background factor for foreign economic policy. Among developed, open systems, such as the North European countries, the extent to which different economic sectors can participate in and influence the political debates relevant to their interests would appear to be a crucial factor. The outcome may be determined more by the relative political weight of different sectors than by the economic structure itself. One could also suggest that in situations where opposing political demands by strategically located groups concerned with foreign economic policy are made, a likely result is not only internal policy disputes but also inconsistencies and fluctuations in official policy.

The different national policies toward the European Community can be understood in this context. Possibly, the minor variations in policies toward the Third World can also be explained in this way. In particular, this would be the case for the different attitudes toward international economic change resulting from the creation of a new international economic order.

According to some public policy analysts, the formulation of government policy can be seen as a continuous learning process. In considering future policies, the experiences of previous efforts are dominant influencing factors.[10] In the absence of pronounced policy failures, previous strategies generally are continued in more or less a modified form. Due to governmental inertia, continuity is the norm in public policy. One of the significant features of North European foreign policies is the great continuity throughout the postwar era and even preceding that period.

If stability in foreign policy behavior is the norm, it is interesting to focus on those cases where fundamental alterations in policy have taken place. The Danish and Norwegian decisions to join the NATO alliance in 1948–1949 offer such a deviant case of drastic policy reformulation. In comparison, Sweden did not alter from its traditional posture of nonalignment.

A major influencing factor behind these different policy choices can be found in the linkage with past policies. The national interpretations of the merits of prior behavior differed significantly. Although Sweden came out of the war without direct involvement, Denmark and particularly Norway paid a high price for the previous neutrality stands. Similarly, Finland undertook a major foreign policy shift as a result of the war experiences.

However, a national recognition of previous policy failure could not by itself explain the radical shifts in behavior. If past actions were inadequate, limited adjustments may serve to correct these deficiencies. Through incremental change the optimal strategy would gradually be found. In this fashion, continual marginal alterations in policy would be experienced. For example, Denmark originally opted for such a limited change in national security policy by supporting a neutral, Scandinavian defense alliance. Also, Sweden envisioned potential marginal adjustments to its neutrality tradition.

The more drastic Norwegian choice seems to have been motivated by a recognition of policy failure in combination with an image of again facing a very similar threat. Through an analogy with the past, Norway was given an opportunity to address the prewar situation once more. Based on the experience of a previous failure, the choice this time was to meet the threat in a radically different fashion to ensure success. When faced with a situation or a threat identified and understood in terms of previous experiences, a repetition of past policy or a radical shift may seem more appropriate than incremental change. In situations involving high stakes, such as a major national security decision, a clutching to the familiar, successful position or a drastic departure from this unsuccessful experience can appear less risky than marginal adjustments to established policy.

Similar conditions prevailed in the Finnish postwar choice of accommodation with the Soviet Union. Here, the major external party and its leadership had not even changed. Thus, the opportunities to present a different and hopefully more successful posture seemed unique. In contrast, Danish security did not appear as severely threatened as in the prewar situation. Marginal adjustments of traditional policy would conceivably be sufficient to ensure success. Finally, Sweden saw little reason to alter its successful posture since the security situation certainly had not changed for the worse.

The emphasis on a linkage with the past points to the importance of inertia and preference for continuity as influencing factors on foreign policy. Assuming excessive policy failure has not been experienced, future actions can be understood in these terms. The North European security policies since 1949 would support this point. A major objective for all governments seems to be to continue and even to protect their stakes in their present regional security roles.

In cases of perceived failure to achieve national objectives with previous policy, marginal adjustments are likely. In addition, radical alterations in foreign policy can be attributed to previous policy failure in combination with images of facing identical, high-risk situations. The North European cases underscore such analogies with the past rather than stressing national images of facing radically different, new situations requiring fundamental policy changes. The motivation may be more to avoid policy failure within the context of a previously known situation than to create a new policy appropriate for a yet unexperienced condition. As a result the choice would tend toward a drastic revision of previous policy. Possibly, such shifts are more common in the security than in the economic sector, where it would be less tempting to make such simplifying analogies with past situations.

The factors of inertia, relative success, and historical analogy appear to be crucial forces behind North European security policies. It seems policy choices can be understood less in terms of the objective features of the present situation, but more in the context of a continuous learning experience, where past activities and situations are basic motivating factors. In all, the historical linkages of the nations vary and these traditions contribute to significant differences in their external choices in discrete situations.

No claim can be made that the independent variables used here explain North European foreign policies in general. This study has focused only on the major differences in external behavior and tried to account for these by pointing to significant differences in background factors. Along a number of dimensions, external behavior as well as possible independent variables show little if any variation. For example, all countries are characterized by cooperative behavior, active participation in international affairs, emphasis on diplomatic rather than military exchanges, and a high proportion of verbal activity.

The sources of these common behavior characteristics must be sought in the numerous factors that were regarded as constant in this analysis. Among others, one could focus on the positions in the international system, the direction of major external ties, the common cultural, social, and political settings, the advanced level of economic development, and the shared political beliefs and values.

To account for the potential influence of such variables, one would need to undertake a different kind of comparative analysis. Possibly, a most different systems analysis would be helpful in this regard. Here, a few commonalities would be studied in the context of a mass of diversity. Hence, similarities in external behavior would be explained by isolated similarities in determining factors. Possibly, the crucial sources of the many common features of North European foreign policy could be identified this way. A valuable supplement to this study would result from such an investigation.

Concluding Propositions

This comparative study suggests that the external behavior of the North European nations differ along several dimensions: (1) Although three countries manifest some strategies of self-reliance, one seems to prefer reliance on external actors. These differences are found both in the security and international economic policy sectors. (2) Most countries emphasize a multilateral approach to the international issues discussed but in a few cases bilateral approaches are used. (3) Although all nations seem to promote continuity in their international environments, most also indicate a limited interest in international change. This pattern is noted both in the security and aid sectors. (4) Consistency in foreign policy during the last thirty years is the norm, but in two cases international economic policy is characterized by inconsistency. (5) With the exception of some major policy shifts in the security sphere during the 1940s, the foreign policies are characterized by great continuity in all sectors of external behavior.

Four background factors stand out as potential determining conditions for the noted variations in external behavior: (1) The significant difference in overall size between Sweden and the other three nations is noted. (2) The countries experience different degrees of discrepancy between various types of size attributes. This observation indicates variations in the gap between national achievement and visible, ascribed capabilities. (3) The economic structures and the relative political weight of particular economic sectors vary considerably among societies. (4) National interpretations of the relative success of previous policies in combination with prevailing images of present situations make for different linkages with the past.

This essay concludes with five explanatory propositions generated from the study. The assertions are based on the reviews of North European foreign policies in this volume and the subsequent most similar case analysis in this chapter. They represent a primitive effort to move beyond descriptive analysis of particular countries toward also offering empirically founded theoretical propositions of more general relevance. As such, the statements are open for retesting by other methods and in other empirical settings. It is hoped that the suggested relationships can find their place in the broader search for global patterns.

Among nations characterized in a global perspective as small, developed, and open, the following statements are plausible ceteris paribus:

1. The greater the overall size, the greater the tendency is toward national self-reliance in security and international economic policy.
2. Among nations of similar overall size, the more the society experiences a discrepancy between different attributes of size, such as population and economic output (achieved) and territory and natural resources (ascribed), the less likely the nation is to opt for a policy of self-reliance.
3. The less the agreement among major domestic economic sectors of political significance, the greater the probability of inconsistencies is in official foreign economic policy.
4. Unless a clearly negative national interpretation of previous policy success is experienced, continuity in foreign policy is the norm.
5. Radical shifts in security policy are most likely when a clear

negative national interpretation of previous policy is combined with a leadership image of again facing an identical, high-risk external situation.

Notes

1. Iceland is excluded from this analysis because of its many fundamentally different national attributes. As indicated in the previous surveys, it is questionable if that country could be included in a most similar systems analysis with the other North European nations. Although sharing the cultural, social, and political traditions of Scandinavia, its tiny size, one-sided economic structure, and isolated geographical location make for some vast differences.

2. James Rosenau, "Pre-theories and theories of foreign policy," in R. B. Farrell (ed.), *Approaches to Comparative and International Politics* (Evanston, Ill.: Northwestern University Press, 1966), pp. 27–92.

3. Note James Harf et al., "Systemic and External Attributes in Foreign Policy Analysis," p. 246, and David Moore, "National Attributes and Nation Typologies: A Look at the Rosenau Genotypes," p. 264, in James Rosenau (ed.), *Comparing Foreign Policies* (Beverly Hills, Calif.: Sage, 1974) and James Rosenau, "The Adaptation of Small States," in ibid. *The Study of Political Adaptation* (London: Frances Pinter, 1981), Chapter 6.

4. Compare the discussion of pattern and discrete foreign policy behavior in Maurice East et al. (ed.), *Why Nations Act* (Beverly Hills, Calif.: Sage, 1978), p. 196.

5. Compare the discussion of this question in William Potter, "Issue area and foreign policy analysis," *International Organization* 34, no. 3 (summer 1980):405–428.

6. For example, note the frameworks suggested in Stephen Andriole et al., "A Framework for the Comparative Analysis of Foreign Policy Behavior," *International Studies Quarterly* 19, no. 2 (June 1975):160–198; and in Maurice East et al. (ed.), op. cit., Chapter 10.

7. This point is stressed by, among others, James Rosenau, op. cit.; M. East et al., op. cit.; D. Moore "Governmental and Societal Influences on Foreign Policy in Open and Closed Nations," pp. 171–200, and James Harf et al., op. cit., in James Rosenau (ed.), op. cit. An empirical assessment of the relative potency of different clusters of independent variables is presented in Jonathan Wilkenfeld et al., *Foreign Policy Behavior* (Beverly Hills, Calif.: Sage, 1980).

8. See Johan Galtung, "A Structural Theory of Aggression," *Journal of Peace Research* 2, (1964):95–119.

9. A number of studies have explained the different Scandinavian approaches to the European Community in these terms. Among others see Arild Underdal, "Diverging Roads to Europe," *Cooperation and Conflict* 10, Nos. 1–2 (1975):65–76.

10. Compare the discussion of prior behavior in M. East et al., (eds.), op. cit., Ch. 8.

For Further Reading

The studies on contemporary North European foreign relations cited below by no means comprise a complete bibliography on the subject. This listing merely enables interested readers to proceed beyond the introductory overviews in this volume. The selection is limited to major English-language publications and a few significant studies in other languages. More comprehensive listings can be found in a number of recent bibliographies as given below:

A Bibliography on International Relations: Literature Published in Denmark, Finland, Norway and Sweden 1945–1960. Stockholm: Swedish Institute of International Affairs, 1973.

Books, Articles, Reports Concerning Nordic Cooperation. Nordisk Udredningsserie 1975:3. Stockholm: Nordic Council, 1975.

Sven Groennings. *Scandinavia in Social Science Literature: An English-Language Bibliography.* Bloomington: Indiana University Press, 1970.

Nils Orvik. *Norwegian Foreign Policy: A Bibliography, 1905–1965.* Oslo: Universitetsforlaget, 1968.

Scandinavian Political Studies. Vol. 12 (1977). Oslo: Universitetsforlaget, 1978.

Several English-language periodicals are devoted to the study of North European affairs including foreign relations. A primary source is the quarterly *Cooperation and Conflict (CoCo)*, published by the Nordic Cooperation Committee for International Politics since 1965. The Nordic Political Science Associations sponsor *Scandinavian Political Studies*, formerly a yearbook but since 1978 a quarterly. *Scandinavian Review* and *Scandinavian Studies* are the two major U.S. journals in the field. However, both titles are only to a very limited extent devoted to foreign policy issues.

Some major Scandinavian-language journals are also important. *Internasjonal Politikk* is published by the Norwegian Institute of International

Affairs, *Internationella Studier* by the Swedish Institute of International Affairs and *Ulkopolitiikka* by the Finnish Institute of International Affairs. The Danish journal *Okonomi og Politik* is also valuable. Finally, *Nordisk Kontakt*, sponsored by the Nordic Council since 1956, gives timely and comprehensive reviews of the political activities in the five countries.

The Norwegian Institute of International Affairs also publishes valuable articles and documentation in the annual *Norsk Utenrikspolitisk Arbok*. The Finnish counterpart is the *Yearbook of Finnish Foreign Policy*, whereas the Danish Institute of International Affairs publishes the annual *Dansk Udenrigspolitisk Arbog*. The Swedish Ministry of Foreign Affairs annually puts out the official *Documents on Swedish Foreign Policy*. *International Studies in the Nordic Countries*, a biannual newsletter published by the Nordic Cooperation Committee for International Politics, is the best source to follow current research, workshops, conferences, and publications in the field.

General Overviews

Amstrup, Niels. *Dansk udenrigspolitik*. Copenhagen: Gyldendal, 1975.

Amstrup, Niels, and Ib Faurby (eds.). *Studier i dansk udenrigspolitik—tilegnet Erling Bjol*. Arhus: Politica, 1978. Bibl.

Andrén, Nils. *Power-Balance and Non-alignment: A Perspective on Swedish Foreign Policy*. Stockholm: Almqvist and Wiksell, 1967.

Barnes, Ian R. "Swedish Foreign Policy: A Response to Geopolitical Factors." *CoCo*, Vol. 9, No. 4 (1974):243–262.

Essays on Finnish Foreign Policy. Helsinki: Finnish Political Science Association, 1969.

Henningsen, Sven. "The Foreign Policy of Denmark," In *Foreign Policies in a World of Change*, ed. Joseph E. Black and Kenneth W. Thompson. New York: Harper and Row, 1963.

Jacobson, Max. *Finnish Neutrality*. London: Hugh Evelyn, 1968.

Jervas, Gunnar (ed.). *Utrikespolitik i Norr*. Lund: Studentlitteratur, 1973.

Karvonen, Lauri, and Raimo Vayrynen. *Finlands utrikespolitik: Riktlinjer och framtidsperspektiv*. Helsinki: Finnish Institute of International Affairs, 1978.

Tagil, Sven, et al. *Sweden in the World Society*. New York: Pergamon Press, 1980.

Security Policy

Andrén, Nils. *The Future of the Nordic Balance*. Stockholm: Swedish Research Institute of National Defense, 1977. Bibl.

Brodin, K., C. Lange, and K. Goldmann. "The Policy of Neutrality: Official Doctrines of Finland and Sweden." *CoCo*, Vol. 3, No. 1 (1968):18–51.

Brundtland, A. O. "The Nordic Balance—Past and Present." *CoCo*, Vol. 2, No. 2 (1966):30–63.

Einhorn, Eric S. *National Security and Domestic Politics in Post-War Denmark. Some Principal Issues 1945–1961.* Odense: Odense University Press, 1975.

Gilberg, Trond, et al. "USSR and Northern Europe." *Problems of Communism,* Vol. 30, No. 2 (March-April 1981):1–24.

Grondal, Benedikt. *Iceland from Neutrality to NATO Membership.* Oslo: Universitetsforlaget, 1971.

Hart, Jeffrey A. *The Anglo-Icelandic Cod War of 1972-73. A Case Study of a Fishery Dispute.* Berkeley: Institute of International Studies, University of California, 1976.

Holst, Johan Jorgen (ed.). *Five Roads to Nordic Security.* Oslo: Universitetsforlaget, 1973. Bibl.

Maude, George. *The Finnish Dilemma: Neutrality in the Shadow of Power.* London: Oxford University Press, 1976.

Meyer, Kenneth. *North Atlantic Security: The Forgotten Flank?* The Washington Papers, No. 62, Beverly Hills, Calif.: Sage, 1979.

Moberg, Erik. "The 'Nordic Balance' Concept: A Critical Commentary." *CoCo,* Vol. 3, No. 3 (1968):210–214.

Nuechterlein, Donald E. *Iceland, Reluctant Ally.* Westport, Conn.: Greenwood Press, 1961.

Quester, George H. "Sweden and the Nuclear Non-Proliferation Treaty." *CoCo,* Vol. 5, No. 1 (1970):52–64.

Skodvin, Magne. *Norden eller Nato? Utenriksdepartementet og alliansespors-malet 1947–1949.* Oslo: Universitetsforlaget, 1971.

Sollie, Finn, et al. *The Challenge of New Territories.* Oslo: Universitetsforlaget, 1974.

Ulstein, Egil. *Nordic Security.* Adelphi Papers, No. 81. London: International Institute for Strategic Studies, 1971.

Vayrynen, Raimo. *Conflicts in Finnish-Soviet Relations: Three Comparative Case Studies.* Tampere: Tampere University, 1972.

Vloyantes, John P. *Silk Glove Hegemony: Finnish-Soviet Relations 1944–1974.* Kent, Ohio: Kent State University Press, 1975.

Wahlbäck, Krister. *Norden och blockuppdelningen 1948–49.* Stockholm: Swedish Institute of International Affairs, 1973.

International Economic Policy

Allen, Hilary. *Norway and Europe in the 1970s.* Oslo: Universitetsforlaget, 1979.

Amstrup, Niels and Carsten L. Sorensen. "Denmark—Bridge Between the Nordic Countries and the European Communities?" *CoCo,* Vol. 10, Nos. 1–2 (1975):25–32.

Archer, Clive T. "Britain and Scandinavia: Their Relations Within EFTA." *CoCo,* Vol. 11, No. 1 (1976):1–24.

Bergqvist, Mats. "Sweden and the EEC: A Study of Four Schools of Thought and

Their Views on Swedish Common Market Policy in 1961–1962." *CoCo*, Vol. 5, No. 1 (1971):39–55.

Hancock, Donald. "Sweden, Scandinavia and the EEC." *International Affairs*, Vol. 48, No. 3 (July 1972):424–437.

———. "Swedish Elites and the EEC: Models of the Future." *CoCo*, Vol. 9, No. 4 (1974):225–243.

———. (ed.). "Scandinavia and the European Community." Special issue of *Scandinavian Studies*, Vol. 46, No. 4 (1974).

Hansen, Peter. "Adaptive Behavior of Small States: The Case of Denmark and the European Community." In *Sage International Yearbook of Foreign Policy Studies*, Vol. 2, ed. Patrick McGowan, pp. 143–174. Beverly Hills, Calif.: Sage, 1974.

Knudsen, Olav. "Foreign Investment and Multinational Corporations in the Nordic Countries." *CoCo*, Vol. 15, No. 4 (1980):209–216.

Leslie, Peter. "Interest Groups and Political Integration: The 1972 EEC Decisions in Norway and Denmark." *American Political Science Review*, Vol. 69, No. 1 (March 1975):68–75.

Miljan, Toivo. *The Reluctant Europeans. The Attitudes of the Nordic Countries Towards European Integration*. London: C. Hurst and Co., 1977.

Orvik, Nils (ed.). *Fears and Expectations: Norwegian Attitudes Toward European Integration*. Oslo: Universitetsforlaget, 1972.

Saeter, M., and I. Smart (eds.). *The Political Implications of North Sea Oil and Gas*. Oslo: Universitetsforlaget, 1975.

"Scandinavian and Western European Economic Integration." Special issue of *CoCo*, Vol. 4, No. 1 (1969):1–72.

Scandinavian Political Studies. Vol. 8 (1973). Special issue on Nordic relations with the European Community.

Sorensen, Carsten Lehman. "Danish Elite Attitudes Towards European Integration." *CoCo*, Vol. 9, No. 4 (1976):259–278.

———. *Danmark og Ef i 1970erne*. Kobenhavn: Borgen, 1978.

Underdal, Arild. "Diverging Roads to Europe." *CoCo*, Vol. 10, Nos. 1–2 (1975): 65–76.

Waite, John. "The Swedish Paradox: EEC and Neutrality." *Journal of Common Market Studies*, Vol. 12, No. 3 (1974):319–336.

Third World Policy

Anglin, David, et al (eds.). *Canada, Scandinavia and Southern Africa*. Uppsala: Scandinavian Institute of African Studies, 1978.

Barnes, Ian. "The Changing Nature of the Swedish Aid Relationship During the Social Democratic Period of Government." *CoCo*, Vol. 15, No. 3 (1980):141–150.

Brundenius, Claes. *Foreign Investment and Technology: The Case of Swedish Manufacturing Subsidiaries in Brazil*. Lund: Research Policy Program, University of Lund, 1978.

Eriksen, Tore Linne. "Norsk bistandspolitikk, staten og naeringslivet." *Internasjonal Politikk*, No. 4, (1977):711–736.

Hermele, Kenneth, and Karl-Anders Larsson, *Solidaritet eller imperialism. Om Sverige, varldsordningen och tredje varlden*. Stockholm: Liber, 1977.

Hveem, Helge. *En ny okonomisk verdensorden og Norge*. Oslo: Universitetsforlaget, 1977.

_____. "Scandinavia and the NIEO. Obstacles to a New International Economic Order in the Area of Scandinavian Economic, Political, Social, and Cultural Structures and Processes." In *Europe and the New International Economic Order*, ed. Ervin Laszlo and Joel Kurtzman. Oxford: Pergamon Press, 1979.

Jorgensen, Klaus. *Hjaelp fra Danmark, En studie i dansk u-landspolitik 1960–71*. Odense: Odense University Press, 1977.

"Nordic Aid to Underdeveloped Countries." Special issue of *CoCo*, Vol. 5, No. 2 (1970).

"The Nordic Countries and the New International Economic Order." Special issue of *CoCo*, Vol. 14, Nos. 2–3 (1979).

"The Nordic Countries and the Third World." Special issue of *Nordisk Forum* (Copenhagen), No. 24 (1979).

Rudebeck, Lars. "Ord och handling i regeringens Vietnam-politik." *Tiden* (Stockholm), Vol. 62, No. 8 (1970):457–468. With a reply by the minister for foreign affairs on pp. 468–471.

Stokke, Olav. *Norsk utviklingsbistand*. Uppsala: Scandinavian Institute of African Studies, 1975.

_____. *Sveriges utvecklingsbistand och bistandspolitik*. Uppsala: Scandinavian Institute of African Studies, 1978.

Neighborhood Policy

Anderson, Stanley V. *The Nordic Council: A Study in Scandinavian Regionalism*. Seattle: University of Washington Press, 1967. Bibl.

Andrén, Nils. "Nordic Integration: Aspects and Problems." *CoCo*, Vol. 2, No. 1 (1967):1–25.

Dickermann, Robert. "Transgovernmental Challenge and Response in Scandinavia and North America." *International Organization*, Vol. 30, No. 2 (1976):213–240.

Haskel, Barbara G. "Disparities, Strategies and Opportunity Costs: The Example of Scandinavian Economic Market Negotiations." *International Studies Quarterly*, Vol. 18, No. 1 (1974):3–30.

_____. *The Scandinavian Option: Opportunities and Opportunity Costs in Postwar Scandinavian Foreign Policies*. Oslo: Universitetsforlaget, 1976.

Kalela, Jaakko. "The Nordic Group in the General Assembly." *CoCo*, Vol. 2, Nos. 3–4 (1967):158–170.

Karvonen, Lauri. "Semi-Domestic Politics: Policy Diffusion from Sweden to Finland." *CoCo*, Vol. 16, No. 2 (1981):91–108.

Landquist, Ake (ed.). *Norden pa varldsarenan.* Stockholm: Tema, 1968.

Lindgren, Raymond. *Norway-Sweden: Union, Disunion and Scandinavian Integration.* Princeton: Princeton University Press, 1959.

Lindstrom, J. E., and Claes Wiklund. "The Nordic Countries in the General Assembly and Its Two Political Committees." *CoCo,* Vol. 2, Nos. 3–4 (1967):171–187.

Lyche, Ingeborg. *Nordic Cultural Cooperation.* Oslo: Universitetsforlaget, 1974.

Nielsson, Gunnar P. "The Nordic and Continental European Dimensions in Scandinavian Integration: Nordek as a Case Study." *CoCo,* Vol. 6, Nos. 3–4 (1971):173–181.

————. "The Parallel National Action Process: Scandinavian Experiences." In *International Organization: A Conceptual Approach,* ed. Paul Taylor and A.J.R. Groom. London: Frances Pinter, 1977, pp. 270–316.

Orvik, Nils. "Nordic Cooperation and High Politics." *International Organization,* Vol. 28, No. 1 (1974):61–88.

Petersen, Nikolaj. "The Popular Basis of Nordic Cooperation: A Danish Case Study." *Acta Sociologica,* Vol. 20, No. 3 (1977):263–285.

Solem, Erik. *The Nordic Council and Scandinavian Integration.* New York: Praeger, 1977.

Sundelius, Bengt. *Managing Transnationalism in Northern Europe.* Boulder, Colo.: Westview Press, 1978.

Sundelius, Bengt, and Claes Wiklund. "The Nordic Community: The Ugly Duckling of Regional Cooperation." *Journal of Common Market Studies,* Vol. 18, No. 1 (1979):59–75.

Ueland, Grete K. "The Nordek Debate: An Analysis of the Attitudes of Nordic Elites Toward the Relationship Between Nordek and the EC." *CoCo,* Vol. 10, Nos. 1–2 (1975):1–20.

Wallensteen, Peter, et al. *The Nordic System: Structure and Change 1920–1970.* Uppsala: Department of Peace and Conflict Research, Uppsala University, 1973.

Wendt, Frantz. *The Nordic Council and Cooperation in Scandinavia.* Copenhagen Munksgaard, 1959.

————. *Cooperation in the Nordic Countries.* Stockholm: Almqvist & Wiksell International, 1981. (Bibl.).

Wiklund, Claes. "The Zig-Zag Course of the Nordek Negotiations." *Scandinavian Political Studies,* Vol. 5 (1970):307–336.

Sources of Foreign Policy

Anckar, Dag. "Party Strategy and Foreign Policy: The Case of Finland,1955–63." *CoCo,* Vol. 8, No. 1 (1973):1–18.

Auken, S., et al. "Denmark Joins Europe: Patterns of Adaptation in the Danish Political and Administrative Process as a Result of Membership of the European Communities." *Journal of Common Market Studies,* Vol. 14, No. 1 (1975):1–36.

Birnbaum, Karl. "The Formation of Swedish Foreign Policy." *CoCo*, Vol. 1, No. 1 (1965):6–31.

Bjol, Erling. "Foreign Policy-Making in Denmark." *CoCo*, Vol. 1, No. 2 (1965): 1–17.

Bruun, Hans Henrik. "Miraculous Mandarins? Investigating the Functions and Influence of Bureaucracy in Foreign Policy." *Scandinavian Political Studies*, Vol. 11 (1976):113–129.

Burgess, Philip. *Elite Images and Foreign Policy Outcomes*. Columbus: Ohio State University Press, 1968.

Christophensen, Jens. "The Making of Foreign Policy in Norway." *CoCo*, Vol. 4, No. 1 (1968):52–74.

Dorfer, Ingemar. *System 37 Viggen*. Oslo: Universitetsforlaget, 1973.

East, Maurice. "The Organizational Impact of Interdependence on Foreign Policy-Making: The Case of Norway." In *Sage International Yearbook of Foreign Policy Studies*, Vol. 6, ed. Charles Kegley and Patrick McGowan. Beverly Hills, Calif.: Sage, 1981.

Eggertsson, Thrainn. "Determinants of Icelandic Foreign Relations." *CoCo*, Vol. 10, Nos. 1–2 (1975):91–99.

Faurby, Ib. "Foreign Policy Making in Scandinavia." In *Foreign Policy Making in Western Europe*, ed. William Wallace and W. E. Paterson. New York: Praeger, 1978.

Hart, Thomas G. *The Cognitive World of Swedish Security Elites*. Stockholm: Esselte, 1976.

Hveem, Helge. *International Relations and World Images: A Study of Norwegian Foreign Policy Elites*. Oslo: Universitetsforlaget, 1972.

Orvik, Nils. *Departmental Decision-Making*. Oslo: Universitetsforlaget, 1972.

The Contributors

Nils Andrén is professor and, since 1970, head of the Division for International Security Studies, Swedish National Defense Research Institute. He has served as director of the Institute for English-speaking Students at the University of Stockholm and has held academic positions at the Universities of Gothenburg, Stockholm, and Copenhagen. He has been vice-president of the Swedish Institute of International Affairs since 1965 and a member of the Executive Council of the International Institute for Strategic Studies since 1975. He has published numerous works in English, as well as in other languages, on international and strategic issues.

Ib Faurby is associate professor of international relations at the Institute of Political Science, University of Aarhus, Denmark, and was a Fulbright scholar at the School of International Relations, University of Southern California in 1976. His main areas of interest are comparative foreign policy and Danish foreign policy. He has published articles on foreign policy analysis and textbooks on Chinese politics, and he coedited a study on Danish foreign policy. Presently he is director of the Secretariat, Danish Commission on Security and Disarmament Affairs.

Lars Rudebeck is associate professor of political science at the University of Uppsala, Sweden, and a founding member of the Working Group for the Study of Development Strategies (AKUT). He has published several books and articles, both in English and Swedish, on the politics of social transformation in the Third World. His most recent major book in English is *Guinea-Bissau: A Study of Political Mobilization* (Uppsala: Scandinavian Institute of African Studies, 1974).

Carl-Einar Stålvant is director of studies and lecturer in the Department of Political Science, University of Stockholm, Sweden, and has served as research secretary of the Nordic Cooperation Committee for International Politics. He has been a visiting fellow at the University of Sussex and has published several studies in English on European politics, integration, and foreign policy in *Cooperation and Conflict*, *Scandinavian Political Studies*, and *Scandinavian Studies*.

Bengt Sundelius is associate professor of international studies at Bradley University and a visiting research associate of the Swedish Institute of International Affairs, Stockholm. He has published *Managing Transnationalism in Northern Europe* (Boulder: Westview Press, 1978) as well as articles on European affairs in *Cooperation and Conflict*, *Journal of Common Market Studies*, *Scandinavian Political Studies*, *West European Politics*, and *World Today*.

Krister Wahlbäck is associate professor of political science at the University of Stockholm. Since 1976, he has been a policy-planning analyst at the Swedish Ministry for Foreign Affairs. He has been a visiting fellow at Harvard University, University of California (Berkeley), and Johns Hopkins University, School of Advanced International Studies (SAIS), and has authored several studies on the international relations of northern Europe, on French politics, and on the doctrine of neutrality.

Abbreviations

AFNorth	Atlantic Forces, Northern Europe
AKUT	Working Group for the Study of Development Strategies
BALTAP	Baltic Approaches
CAP	common agricultural policy
CBM	confidence-building maneuvers
CMEA	Council for Mutual Economic Assistance
CoCo	*Cooperation and Conflict*
COMECON	CMEA
COPA	Comité des Organisations Professionelles Agricoles de la CEE
COST	European Scientific and Technological Cooperation
CSCE	Conference on Security and Cooperation in Europe
DANIDA	Danish International Development Agency
EC	European Community or European Communities
ECE	Economic Commission for Europe
ECPR	European Consortium for Political Research
ECSC	European Coal and Steel Community
EEC	European Economic Community
EFTA	European Free Trade Association
ERP	European Recovery Program
FIN-EFTA	Finland-European Free Trade Association
GATT	General Agreement on Tariffs and Trade
GSP	Generalized System of Preferences
IMF	International Monetary Fund
JET	Joint European TOKAMAK
NATO	North Atlantic Treaty Organization
NGO	nongovernmental organization
NIC	newly industrialized countries
NORAID	Norwegian Agency for International Development
NORDEK	Nordic Economic Community

NUPI	Norwegian Institute of International Affairs
ÖB	supreme commander
OECD	Organization for Economic Cooperation and Development
OEEC	Organization for European Economic Cooperation
OPEC	Organization of Petroleum Exporting Countries
SAIS	School of Advanced International Studies (Johns Hopkins University)
SEV	Russian abbreviation for CMEA
SIDA	Swedish International Development Agency
UNCTAD	United Nations Conference on Trade and Development
UNDP	United Nations Development Program
UNISCAN	United Kingdom and Scandinavia

Index

AFNorth. *See* Atlantic Forces, Northern Europe
Africa. *See* Third World; *individual countries*
Agrarian parties, 45, 49. *See also* Centre party (Finland)
Åland Islands, 11, 23, 60, 179
Alexander I (czar of Russia), 20
Algeria, 164
Allardt, Erik, 3
Allende, Salvador, 154, 160
Anckar, Dag, 43
Andersen, K. B., 135
Angola, 160, 161
Antola, Esko, 168
Arms control. *See* Nordic region, and arms control
Arms industry. *See* Sweden, arms industry
Asia. *See* Third World; *individual countries*
Atlantic Forces, Northern Europe (AFNorth), 94
Austria, 138

Balkans, 9–10, 11, 12–13
BALTAP. *See* Baltic Approaches
Baltic Approaches (BALTAP), 94
Beckman, Björn, 157
Belts (straits), 94, 95
Bilateral
    aid, 157, 162. *See also individual*

countries, and development assistance
    approach, 200–201, 202(table), 211
Bipolar international system, 68
Bolshevik revolution, 10, 20–21
Bornholm (island) (Denmark), 95
Bourgeois political parties, 45, 47
Brazil, 151, 152, 154, 164
Bretton Woods Conference (1944), 110–111
Brundenius, Claes, 154

Campaign for Nuclear Disarmament, 54–55
CAP. *See* Common agricultural policy
Cappelen, Andreas, 131
CBMs. *See* Confidence-building measures
Centre parties, 45, 46, 47, 49, 132
Centre party (Finland), 46, 48(table)
Centre party (Norway), 45, 48(table), 54
Centre party (Sweden), 45, 48(Table), 54
Chile, 154–155, 158
Christian People's party (Norway), 45, 48(table)
Cod wars, 51, 83
Cold war (1947), 24, 68, 75
COMECON. *See* Council for Mutual Economic Assistance

Acknowledgments

I hereby gratefully acknowledge the help and stimulation of many students, friends, and colleagues. In my university department, successive heads, Tom Boag, John Waldron, and Klaus Minde, have supported me; Paul Harris has been friend, discussant, and proofreader; Felix Letemendia has backed me up as potential literary executor. Don Ross of Cincinnati has been my mentor and guide over many years in many ways, including teaching me how to do research. Will Seeman helped germinate this book when we worked together, as I mention in the Introduction. In London in 1976 and 1977 I first met Dr. James Tanner, who has since kindly helped me with drafts reviewing his work; Dr. John Bowlby, whom I had admired from a distance, also became a friend and guide, most specifically on scientific models and attachment theory, and a facilitator of this book; Dr. Barbel Inhelder kindly received me in Geneva to discuss applications of Piagetian theory to psychiatry. Dr. George Engel, whose writings I had long esteemed, has entertained and corresponded with me in recent years.

I acknowledge indebtedness to Dr. Margaret Emery, Editor-in-Chief, and to Mr. Martin Azarian, President, International Universities Press, for encouragement and hospitality. The illustrations in this volume are the work of Mr. Andrew Pedersen of the Department of Medical Illustration at Queen's University, whose cheerful collaboration I greatly appreciate. The intricate task of indexing the book has been undertaken

ix

by Christine M. Jacobs, who taught me a great deal in the process.

Finally, a special word of gratitude to my wife and partner of many years, Edith Pritchard Powles, whose encouragement through multiform vicissitudes has kept this book progressing over time. Not only has she converted reams of my hand-written notes into legible typescripts, but latterly she has set herself the daunting tasks of mastering the word processor and producing the manuscript itself. I am enormously in her debt.

Table of Illustrations

Introduction

Origins and Aims of this Book

Two dozen years ago, I was chatting during a coffee break with the late Dr. William Seeman. We were teammates on a research project investigating mental health in industrial settings in Cincinnati, under the direction of Dr. Donald Ross, and I had come to value and warm to Will Seeman for his gentle humor and flow of interesting ideas. He told me then that he had compiled a list of books needing to be written to fill vacant ecological niches in the literature. One which he envisioned was a treatise on the basic sciences underlying clinical psychiatry. We jokingly agreed that I might "lift" this idea from his list, to have it then simmer in my mind over some years. Would that I had attacked the work immediately, when the science of psychiatry was a more comfortably manageable field! I accomplished considerable preparatory reading and thinking on sabbatical in 1976 and 1977, but it was not until formal retirement was nearing that I had the time for the work of writing, in a field that had now been expanding exponentially.

How to organize a guidebook on the many models, issues, and complex research findings of the science of psychiatry today? My guiding orientation has been to offer a work substantive enough, yet readable and clinically relevant enough, that it will help postgraduate and undergraduate students of psychiatry: residents, candidates for board examinations, medical students, and their teachers. I also hope that students and critics of psychiatry from other disciplines (neurology, child development, psychology, social work, occupational therapy, nursing, and perhaps even the philosophy of science) may find this volume informative. I have tried to write with the minimum possible technical jargon, though this is at times difficult if one is to avoid lengthy definitions and explications.

Organization and Orientation of this Book

In organizing this volume, major questions arose of selection of content and manner of organization. There have been many excellent monographs on the science of psychiatry, most of them covering a restricted subject area in depth. Two other books, to my knowledge, address the broad field of basic science for psychiatry: they are encyclopedic, multiauthor texts, which are not organized by a clear theoretical (e.g., developmental) model, or by any apparent principle of clinical relevance. This present work by one author has the strength, I believe, of an integrative overview and a relatively consistent perspective and style. I have tried to make it readable, since I confess that for me the monographs I have consulted are sometimes ponderous, cold, dull, and tedious in their scholarship, or tend to information overload. My references are to a relatively restricted number of key sources, which the reader may pursue, rather than being an exhaustive loading of the text with learned citations. The priorities which organized my work might be stated as follows:

1. *Clinical relevance* for the mental health worker, including some attempt at making the text comprehensible to clinicians of more than one discipline.
2. *A biopsychosocial or whole-person* view of human personality and its decompensations, avoiding the pitfalls of a narrow commitment to any one biological, learning, psychoanalytic, or social model.
3. *A consistent focus on "hard," scientifically derived* formulations to the exclusion of the clinically derived. Where scientific

enquiry has been lacking in some areas, I so indicate, and fall back on the best "soft" investigations available.

4. *Sexual dimorphism in the human species*: There is now a barely beginning science of sex differences. Since we can no longer afford, scientifically or ethically, to "homogenize" together the findings for the two sexes, or, worse still, take the findings for males as the definitive standard for females too, I have attempted to digest available researches on sex differences.

5. *A "review of reviews" approach*, seeking to present review articles, chapters, and books which are suitable for further detailed study.

6. *A "great names" approach*, seeking to present significant or dominant figures for a given research area, with enough indication of their "career line" to stimulate further reading.

7. *A relatively non-time-bound approach*, rather than a state-of-the-art presentation, which would be outdated the day it is published. With this also a historical approach to the development of certain concepts and themes, since understanding their development may be heuristic, and also because some old work is still very good work.

8. *Organizing perspectives* of my own construction, as orienting or coordinating devices. These perspectives are not necessarily original, but I find that I can no longer properly cite many of their sources (my teachers, other authors) which contribute to them. I am not a believer in "scientific detachment" except as something to be rigorously adhered to during an actual investigation. I am an admirer of scientists of commitment, who take clear positions, decide to attack important problems, and are prepared to change their minds upon evidence. Therefore, I present my own positions and biases, I hope clearly, and I beg the reader to distinguish these from the findings and positions of the scientists whom I review.

Problems of Selection of Material

One major dilemma to be faced is the problem of selection of content areas, of inclusion and exclusion. Quite practically, what will have to be *left out* of a book of manageable size, which purports to be an orienting digest and not an encyclopedia? I have already set forth some of the priorities governing my selection, and clearly much of my selection is personally motivated. I present some scientists who are not yet assimilated into psychiatry as they deserve, but whose contributions will in time, I believe, be found to be indispensable: Piaget, Tanner, Bowlby, for example. There are subjects on the borderline of clinical relevance: the extraordinary complexities of neuroanatomy and neurochemistry, of communication and linguistics, and of human sexuality, for example. I have had to choose to simplify or even omit consideration of a number of these. Fortunately, good review articles, monographs, and encyclopedias exist to remedy this problem of selection.

Plan of This Book

This volume is organized into two major sections, each underlain and structured by a major model. The first section is structured around a developmental–structural model, going back originally to Hughlings Jackson: human personality grows, is "built," over time into successively more complex and effective "structures," and illness and injury impair these structures with the reemergence of earlier, less sophisticated, structures and functions. Five chapters trace five "streams" of human growth and development: the body and the brain, intelligence and cognition, the developmental life cycle, object relations and attachment, and moral judgment.

In the second section I deal with the science of clinical problems. The model here is a homeostatic–dynamic one, dating back to Claude Bernard: human personality is an intricate, self-regulating machine, constantly maintaining intactness, differentiation, and balance within its own boundaries, as it maintains interdependent relations with the external world. Several levels or styles of homeostasis, both under normal conditions and under conditions of stress and decompensation, give us useful headings for chapters on the science of psychiatric disorders. Thus five chapters are organized not around clinical syndromes, but around groupings of them: psychiatric normality, tensional or "fight–flight" states, depressive or "conservation–withdrawal" states, psychotic or "disintegration" states, and the process of dying. In addition, I interpose a chapter on brain syndromes and brain systems, since brain damage strikes at the root mechanisms of human homeostasis.

Section I

*Human Growth
and
Development*

1

A Developmental–Structural Model Underlying Psychiatric Formulations: Implications and Corollaries

Introduction

Overview

The first half of this book examines issues of human growth and personality development. The present initial chapter expounds a major theoretical model implicit in, and organizing, many aspects of psychiatric history taking and clinical conceptualization. This I am terming the *Developmental–Structural Model*. Each subsequent chapter will then deal with one sector or "stream" of human growth and development, and the work of major researchers and exponents in that sector or stream.

The developmental–structural model views the human being as an exceedingly complex edifice, built progressively over time, from a genetic blueprint, the genotype, which is then

3

realized by further genetic programming and by familial, cultural, and accidental experiences into a functioning building, the phenotype, which possesses more or less strength, beauty, and effectiveness, and which is subject over time to stress, breakdown, and self-repair.

In reconstructing this model, I shall first examine briefly the nature of conceptual models in science, medicine, and psychiatry, then attempt to paint the principal image or metaphor involved. Next, three principles relating the developmental elements of human personality will be summarized: structure, epigenesis, and emergence. Structure deals with the evident existence of organizations within the body and the mind. Epigenesis, or the epigenetic principle, acknowledges that of necessity human development evolves by the building of newer structures or functions over older ones, and that although the older seem to disappear they are in fact assimilated as building blocks for the newer. Emergence clarifies the hierarchical relationship between organizations of matter at the physical, chemical, biological, psychological, and social levels, and the methods of properly studying these.

After this will follow several clinically relevant implications and corollaries of the model, principally the nature of weaknesses (fixations) and breakdowns (regressions) in the edifice. I shall give space and attention to the definition and criteria of the constructs of fixation and regression, and some critique of their usefulness and limitations. According to the developmental–structural model, psychiatric disorders display regression; that is, a breakdown of more mature or newer structures and functions, and the reappearance of more primitive, older ones. Fixations and regressions may involve the total (adult) life cycle: thus a developmental dimension is highly relevant to both diagnosis and treatment planning.

Finally, I shall examine conceptually the nature of growth and development. This includes an account of methods of recording and depicting the developmental flow, and of dividing the vast complexities of growth and development into manageable sectors or developmental streams. The five streams which appear out of this discussion are associated with certain key investigators, whose work I shall attempt to summarize in the five subsequent chapters.

Models, Metaphors, and Principles

Models in Science, Medicine, and Psychiatry

Theoretical models in science are "analogical (and idealized) representations of things, processes, etc. and more recently of formal systems" (Harré, 1983a, p. 397). A "homeomorphic" model has the same source as its subject: an example of Harré is a doll, which draws on the source "baby" to depict the subject "baby." Black (1962) terms this the "scale model," which reproduces selected features of the original thing either by reduction or magnification. Such models are useful for examining details or functions of a relatively well-known entity; testing, for example, the wind resistance of an airplane, or obtaining a more accurate picture of the microscopic structures of a mosquito (Black, 1962).

Paramorphic (Harré, 1983a,b) or analog (Black, 1962) models draw on something, as source, which differs from the subject, and have a metaphorical quality. They involve a change of medium, and are a "symbolic representation of some real or imaginary original . . ." (Black, 1962, p. 222). Although this involves distortion, such a model may be helpful in imagining and picturing less well-understood matters. Darwin (Harré, 1983a,b) used the metaphor (source) of domestic selective breeding of plants or animals to understand the unobservable processes of natural selection (subject). Harré and Black both point out that it is not the phenomena of nature, in themselves, which models seek to explain, but the mechanisms underlying these (Harré), the "structure or web of relationships" (Black).

A paramorphic or analog model is therefore an idealized explanatory depiction of complex, inadequately understood phenomena, based on an analogy with some known and understood thing or process; that is, containing a metaphor or simile. It is heuristic, in that it stimulates creative thinking; and, most practically, it must be useful in generating clear hypotheses for exploratory testing. This of course means that a model is much larger or more embracing than a hypothesis. One final property is that models must usually be capable of some mathematical expression.

I need hardly remind the critical reader that many important models have been the *truth* of their times, only to be unseated by new minds, new methods, and new data, often amid cultural ferment and intellectual resistance. Embedded in the collective preconscious, accepted as the only possible explanatory metaphor, were such constructs as the flat earth, surrounded by ocean and overarched by heaven; or the geocentric view, in which quite sophisticated mathematical formulas accounted for the orbits of sun and planets about the earth. Today it is accepted truth that great ice sheets once covered the land and shaped our present landscapes; that the plates of the earth's crust are, or are like, great rafts (metaphor, simile) drifting about on an ocean of semiplastic mantle, separating, colliding, closing and opening up oceans or raising mountain ranges. Black (1962) applies the term *archetype* to such "metaphysical systems," "world hypotheses," or "systematic repertoires of ideas . . . which . . . describe, by *analogical extension,* some domain to which those ideas do not immediately and literally apply" (p. 241). An archetype may be found in the work of an individual scientist. Black examines the work of Kurt Lewin, pioneer of group dynamics, who disclaimed the use of models, yet who employed many key words and expressions clearly drawn from the domain of physics: "visible symptoms of a massive archetype awaiting to be reconstructed by a sufficiently patient critic" (p. 241).

In this chapter and in chapter 7 I shall endeavor to realize or reconstruct certain aspects of two just such "hidden conceptual models in clinical psychiatry." This quotation is the title of a thought-provoking paper by Lazare (1973) who examines four common theoretical models or archetypes of causation in psychiatry: the medical, the psychologic, the behavioral, and the social. He depicts these as mutually exclusive, and basically reductionistic in nature, since they suggest that cause is "nothing but" the espoused single factor or set of variables. The models Lazare presents have as metaphor the nineteenth-century concept of the specific infectious disease agent; *"the cause"* of schizophrenia, pictured as a discrete or unitary disease entity, is a construct based on such a metaphor.

By contrast, the work of the great clinician–researcher, George Engel, has long stood for a holistic or integrative view of causation in psychiatry, and in fact for illness in general. His biopsychosocial model (Engel, 1977, 1980) calls for invoking all available data, interacting from various levels of emergence (see below), in picturing the etiology of illness and the therapeutic attack upon it. This model of causation sees illness as multidetermined, an interaction between a complex organism and a complex environment.

The two models I attempt to reconstruct are not models of causality, but rather models of the whole human personality and its various vicissitudes. Both are holistic and integrative, avoiding the reductionist trap. Both are capable of mathematical expression, though this area is presently undeveloped for the most part, and I shall pay greatest attention to the metaphorical or analogical aspects.

Historical and Architectural Metaphors for Personality

Why do psychiatrists, in their clinical training and management of patients, study personality development, and investigate and record lengthy personal histories? Adolf Meyer laid the groundwork for such an emphasis, making a kind of art form of it (see Diethelm, 1936; Billings, 1939). Why do psychiatry texts speak at length about personality development and "structure"? Why is our technical language filled with epithets such as strong, rigid, brittle, resilient, flexible; weak, shaky, fragile, vulnerable; build up, wear down, stressed; breakdown, shattered, fall apart; superficial, deep, accessible, inaccessible? This is just the kind of list of key words and expressions which Black requires if one is to reconstruct an archetype, and the following will be my attempt at just such a reconstruction.

Human personality is a most elegant and complex edifice, erected and articulated over historical time, which, at the point

of clinical examination, we usually confront in a state of disre-
pair. It has been built from an ancient and evolving blueprint
(genotype) by many builders amid many environmental and
cultural influences to its final form (phenotype), and it is now in
a period of malfunction (clinical disorder). We take a systematic
personal history because the course of construction gives us
important leads, and we do a cross sectional or mental status
examination to assess the present state, including structural
damage. We want to know what were the strengths and vulnerabilities in the phenotype, and in what ways the edifice is failing
and in need of repair.

The best, strongest, most competent buildings (persons)
have firm, resilient, effective structures at all levels, contributed
to by sound genes, competent child-rearing figures, and environmental good fortune. Weak and shaky foundations leave
their mark in precarious functioning despite later attempts at
good construction. It is the outer, newer, more accessible structures which tend to be eroded, damaged, and impaired by excessive wear and tear or by sudden catastrophe. When this
happens, deeper, older structures become exposed, and function at the interface with the world, usually in an inferior
fashion.

This theoretical model or archetype is analogical and paramorphic: its subject is human development; its source, the construction industry.

A Note on the Principle of Structure

Structure has been a term so taken for granted by psychologists
of the past 150 years that I have been unable to locate accounts
of its origin and meaning. Today we find structure a rather
static construct: probably, terms such as *system* and *organization*
would be preferred. Here one might consult Miller (1983, pp.
38–39) in her section on information processing.

However, the metaphor of structure is firmly embedded
in our clinical traditions: for example, see the epithets I have
listed above. The exponents of most developmental streams
appear to be structuralists also, in that they stress in some form

organizational arrangements in the personality. Bowlby employs the term *behavioral system* (Bowlby, 1969, pp. 37–174; 1980, pp. 44–47). Freud's (1923) structural theory was his proposed method of picturing an organization of the psychic apparatus into id, ego, and superego; and therefore it has been codified. Piaget constantly uses the term *structure*, without ever defining it: for him it can mean almost everything from a primitive action schema to a sophisticated mathematical flow chart or truth table which the possessor of fully developed hypothetico–deductive intelligence pursues. Piaget (1968) authored a small, dense treatise on Structuralism, contrasting this approach in science to Atomism and strict Empiricism. These latter treat all data as of equal rank and importance, whereas Structuralism seeks the organizations underlying the data and through which data are meaningfully and hierarchically related. Structuralism probes for a map of parts within a whole, for relationships and interactions within parts, between parts, and between parts and the whole, and for the development over time of such relationships and interactions. Thus, Piaget asserts (p. 8) Structuralism provides a preferable alternative in science to the approaches of "Emergent Totalities" (see below for discussion of Emergence) and of "Atomist Association." His various chapters examine the whole range of science, from mathematical and physical to psychological and social, including linguistics. Interestingly, Wundt, the pioneer of the experimental approach to psychology, developed a corpus of "structural" psychology, yet in fact seems to have been not a structuralist but rather an empiricist in his basic views (see Murray, 1983). Most recently, it appears that many behavior therapists have had to yield up their empiricist position in favor of seeking and dealing with cognitive structures underlying behavior.

Mathematical Expressions; the Epigenetic Principle

The mathematical expressions of this model are best carried out in graphic form. For personality *structure* (which we examine at a particular point) the form would be that of multidimensional architectural plans, topologically organized around a general and invariant principle of layering. Human personality is successively "laid down" upon ancient and primordial (essentially biological) foundations. The more ancient formations are overlain and hidden by successively more recent, sophisticated, socialized superstructures. A kind of archaeological or geological cast therefore enters our metaphor: depth psychology embarks on an archaeological dig or prospector's drilling, sampling "down" from the "surface," the "accessible," "conscious" layers, to "deeper," "inaccessible," "preconscious," "unconscious," "primitive" ones.

This layered arrangement of personality architecture is the subject of the epigenetic principle, according to which the more ancient and primitive seems to have disappeared during development, but in actual fact has been assimilated as a necessary foundation or building block for later formations, which amplify and differentiate its original functions. Thus, the relatively older is not lost, but "buried" and living. It may reemerge if later formations are injured (see the Jacksonian principles in the section on the "Evolution of the Construct of Regression" below) and, further, it can be explored inferentially by techniques such as free association and dream analysis. The more ancient is always "deeper," and what is deeper is always the more ancient: the same reciprocal relationship holds for the more superficial and the more recent.

For personality *development,* which is a continuous process, mathematical expression would best be carried out in the form of curves or graphs of various functions or structures. Their vertical axis represents progressive achievement of size, power, differentiation, and sophistication: the horizontal axis, biographical time. I know of no actual attempt to depict personality functions in such mathematical form. Bodily growth and measured intelligence are regularly displayed in graphic form (see chapter 2, including Figures 2.1 and 2.2, and chapter 3); and one can wrestle with the attempt to fit equations to such empirically derived curves (Marubini, 1978).

The Principle of Emergence

To resume the depiction of personality structure, we should note clearly that the edifice (the human person) is by no means a random assemblage of materials. It is not, as humorously and reductionistically suggested, merely a collection of oxygen, carbon, nitrogen, phosphorus, calcium, and so on, worth a few dollars. Its building units are molecules, DNA, proteins, semiprecious minerals, lipids, enzymes, and so on; and it is the specific *relationships* between them, the design or architectural arrangement of the edifice, which is able to make of it a wholly *unique* person, not merely a clone of any other human, certainly not any primate, let alone any member of the animal kingdom with whom it shares many fundamental features.

Our architectural metaphor is further realized and illuminated by the important principle of emergence (Novikoff, 1945; Hoskins, 1946). This principle states that, as matter is organized into structures of increasing complexity, something new emerges, whose properties cannot be predicted by understanding (however completely) the behavior of the underlying, component structures. The emergent whole is not only "larger than," but now different from, the sum of its parts. These authors warn us that we must use tools of analysis which are appropriate to the understanding of each level of emergence in its own right. The following represents a sequence of these emergences, and the sciences which have grown up to deal with them, as schematically depicted in Figure 1.1.

At the most basic level are fundamental particles and forces, the province of physics, which is still pushing back the limits of what indeed is basic or fundamental. As particles combine into atoms, molecules, and substances, under the influence of fundamental forces, something new emerges, which can only be understood through the study of chemistry. As molecules and substances are combined in the intricate organizations of cells, organs, organ systems, and organisms, we see a qualitative shift into life itself. Here biology (with its many branches, e.g., genetics, physiology, biochemistry, anatomy, and physical anthropology) is the valid approach to somatic phenomena; that is, phenomena of the body.

Another qualitative shift appears as we view mind or personality. Certain organisms, among which the human species is preeminent, display complex behaviors, with the ability to

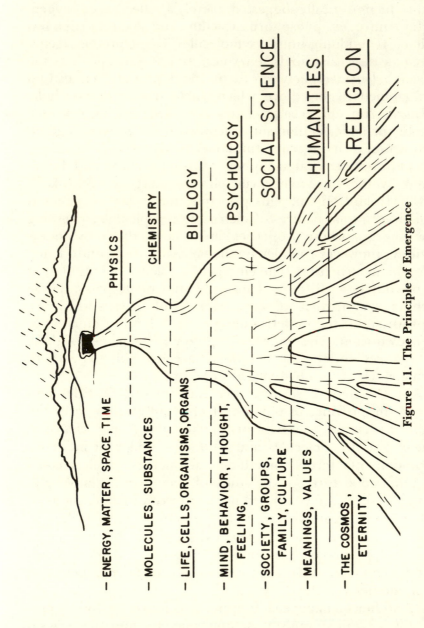

PHYSICS
— ENERGY, MATTER, SPACE, TIME

CHEMISTRY
— MOLECULES, SUBSTANCES

BIOLOGY
— LIFE, CELLS, ORGANISMS, ORGANS

PSYCHOLOGY
— MIND, BEHAVIOR, THOUGHT, FEELING,

SOCIAL SCIENCE
— SOCIETY, GROUPS, FAMILY, CULTURE

HUMANITIES
— MEANINGS, VALUES

RELIGION
— THE COSMOS, ETERNITY

Figure 1.1. The Principle of Emergence

Each successive level of organization of matter creates a new emergent, whose properties are not predictable from knowledge of previous emergents; thus, a new and appropriate science or group of sciences becomes necessary for its understanding.

move, to feel, and to reflect. Life (i.e., cells, organs, organ systems) gives birth, so to speak, to a new kind of emergence, whose organization and laws require a new group of sciences if it is to be confronted and understood properly. In fact, mind or personality is not something concealed inside, and limited by, the body. It transcends, is larger than, the body. As Hofling (1975) put it, mind is the whole person in action. Generally, it is mind which contacts other minds, communicates, forms social organizations, influences and adapts to the environment. Understanding physics contributes not at all to understanding mind; chemistry may assist a little, biology considerably more. That is, understanding of a more proximate emergence will assist us more than even thorough understanding of a more remote one, when attempting to understand or predict the phenomena of a given level of emergence. But we need an autonomous group of sciences, the psychological, to deal with the emergence of mind or personality.

Here we must draw attention to and define the scientific fallacy of reductionism, which is the mistaken attempt at explaining higher and more complex emergences as "nothing but" simpler, more basic ones; for example, as noted earlier, that the human body is nothing but a few pounds of carbon, nitrogen, oxygen, hydrogen, calcium, worth but a few dollars; or that complex altruistic or belligerent behavior is nothing but human selfishness, a confounding of social and psychological emergences. Thirty years of biochemical and genetic research into the mechanisms of depression has brought us few definitive answers, only more questions, in part because the preoccupation with the high technology of molecular biology has been to an extent merely reductionist.

Before we complete this subject, several further emergences must be considered. Humans are supremely social beings, whose social bonds and cultural organizations have been crucial in mastering a bewildering variety of ecological niches, more than any other animal species, by far. The field of psychiatry simply cannot comprehend the human condition, and its disorders, without accounting for the emergence of society, using appropriate social science: group dynamics for small, face-to-face groups; ethology, social and cultural anthropology, and sociology for larger aggregations; communication theory, economics and politics, and geography.

As we pass on to even higher emergences, we begin to leave the province of science, and enter the territory of the humanities: history, literature, philosophy, theology, and the arts, which wrestle with the transcendent issues of human existence and the meaning of life and the cosmos.

To sum up: human beings, with their psychological and social existence, are more than the sum of their physical and biological parts. However well we may understand those parts, using the appropriate sciences, we cannot with this understanding either comprehend or predict human behavior and its disorders. We have to study phenomena at the level of emergence to which these properly belong: in the case of the human condition, these are principally the biological, the psychological, and the social, to be illuminated with the appropriate scientific disciplines. We need to be clear as to which level we are examining, and tidy when we attempt to synthesize concepts from differing levels. Some understanding from levels above and below these three (i.e., from the physical sciences and the humanities) may assist us partially in our quest.

Growth, Development, Fixation, and Regression

Growth and Development

Growth and *development* are overlapping but not synonymous terms. The idea of *growth* represents quantitative increase: expansion in mass, power, in the size of cells or organs or limbs, and in the number of cells or their processes.

The idea of *development* implies, in addition, qualitative rearrangement, improvement in sophistication of function. Blasi (1976) proposes that the crucial features of human development are unvarying sequence, lawful order, relatively enduring change, and organization, within the individual. Piaget and Inhelder (1966) and Flavell (1963) stress the invariant succession of stages in development as something that is not only found empirically but is logically necessary, since the functions of subsequent stages can only be founded on the earlier, the epigenetic principle. Werner (as reviewed by Baldwin [1967]), most thoroughgoing of developmentalists, stated that for a biological process to be a developmental one it must follow the orthogentic principle: progression from a global, general, undifferentiated, rigid yet unstable, condition, to a condition which is differentiated, articulated, hierarchically organized, flexible yet stable. Werner's principles bring to mind those enunciated by Herbert Spencer for biology in general and by Hughlings Jackson for the human nervous system in particular (see J. H. Jackson [1887a,b], S. W. Jackson [1969]).

Piaget's depiction of the conditions and the process of cognitive development has been particularly lucid (Gruber and Vonèche, 1977), seeing it as a continuing interaction between a brain ready for experience and a surrounding milieu offering that experience. Such a depiction may be usefully extrapolated to both physical development (Knobloch and Pasamanick, 1974) and to affective–motivational development (Bowlby, 1969, 1982). At birth, the central nervous system (CNS) is not a tabula rasa: it is preprogrammed to take advantage of age-appropriate experience. It is also programmed to an active outreaching for experience—Piaget's concept of knowledge as the acting of the knower upon the known. This nervous system cannot be made to capitalize on experience for which it is unready: no amount of skillful teaching will result in an infant's learning to walk or to talk. When ready, its assimilation of and accommodation to new experience seems almost effortless. Once one set of experiences has been successfully mastered, the nervous system is enriched (doubtless through the setting up of new synaptic networks) and becomes ready to deal with yet more challenging experience. Lack of age-appropriate experience results in developmental delay, possibly in a long-persisting defect. Both genius and nonspecific mental retardation may be hypothesized to be instances of optimum or pathological development in such a framework.

This interactional view of development saves us from one-sided, reductionist perspectives; for example, that all behavior is learned, or that adult personality is wholly genetically determined. Nature and nurture are in constant dialectic.

For human personality, growth *plus* these organizational and interactional principles equals development. Since somatic growth and the growth of measured intelligence both level off in adolescence, we may practically consider that human development, in the *quantitative* sense, is a ladder culminating with the closure of the epiphyses, fertile sexual functioning, maturation of the tools of intelligence, and the solidification of identity and vocation at the end of the adolescent years.

For quantitative purposes, therefore, we are occupied with reciprocal concepts of growth, development, fixation, and regression measured on a scale from birth to late adolescence, even when we use such a scale in monitoring fully adult patients. It remains, of course, to wrestle with the important progressions and tasks of the adult portion of the life cycle (see chapter 4) and with methods of estimating defects (fixations) and breakdowns (regressions) in these.

Fixation

An important corollary of the present model, with its epigenetic and Jacksonian principles, is that personality can "be built" with both strengths and weaknesses. Strength means that humans, like edifices, are designed to meet expectable conditions under which they live and work; the metaphor is of extra bracing or resilience or protection against high winds, floods, fires, or earthquakes. Weakness or vulnerability means a structure giving way under everyday, expectable conditions. There appear to be relatively few people who are endowed with strengths which hold under exceptionally stressful conditions, and a few who are unusually weak or vulnerable. Generally speaking, stress for humans is an individual matter, usually an interpersonal event which is meaningful and specific vis-à-vis an identifiable point of vulnerability in a particular personality structure. Only in war and rare civilian catastrophes do we have overwhelming stress which results in the decompensation of many persons.

Defects in the development and structure of a human personality are termed *fixations*. The developments that are built upon them are incomplete and weak, and they predispose to subsequent malfunctions and breakdowns even if for some time the defect has been compensated for by homeostatic mechanisms. Such resultant malfunction is often due to a stressor which is (as above) specific to the fixation and therefore activates the "point of fixation." Fixations can in many cases be located by psychotherapeutic exploration, and some of them can be repaired or resolved by psychotherapeutic work. It must be assumed that poverty and social disorganization (e.g., in slavery and in the inner city today) are particularly prone to lead to fixations and deformities in personality.

Mathematical representation of a fixation would appear in the form of an indicated zone of fracture or instability in an architectural drawing; its depiction on a developmental curve would show a point where the curve departs from its previous normal gradient and assumes a flatter form, below the expected slope.

Fixation is an important construct for the historical analysis of a patient's development, and in that part of diagnostic formulation termed *genetic* or *psychogenetic diagnosis*. The construct is psychoanalytic in origin. Alexander and Ross (1961) state simply that " 'Fixation' designates the tendency to retain previously successful behavior patterns" (p. 9). Brenner (1955) suggests likewise that "no really strong libidinal cathexis is ever completely abandoned," but he states further that, "The use of the word 'fixation' ordinarily indicates or implies psychopathology" (p. 28). Freud (1917, Lectures XVIII and XXII) indicates a judgment of abnormality when he explains that some parts of a libidinal function will be permanently *arrested* at these early stages, the result being that with ongoing general development there results a certain area of inhibited development.

Clearly, we need to distinguish between two processes here. First, in normal or healthy development, the products and residues of earlier developmental stages or tasks remain, though hidden, as building blocks and underpinnings for subsequent construction. They can be inferred or demonstrated by appropriate techniques. They may be "exposed" or "released" by damage to or removal of overlying structures. They are logically necessary for more mature developments (Jackson, Werner, Piaget; see "Growth and Development" above). This is in fact the crux of the epigenetic principle.

But, second, there is a class of pathological *and* pathogenic developmental happenings which leave weaknesses or vulnerabilities in the structure. As underpinnings for later construction, such developmental happenings are unsound. They actually predispose to disorder as "receptor sites" for specific noxae, and as points to which regression may well take place. These fixations have been classically believed (Levine, 1961, pp. 222–223) to stem from two kinds of developmental experience: trauma (unmanageable stress) including separation and rejection during an important developmental epoch, and overindulgence or seduction in an age-appropriate need satisfaction.

The key difference between normal residues and abnormal fixations appears to lie in the latter containing unfinished business, whereas the former constitute a satisfactory resolution and completion of a developmental task. A fixation tends to produce a self-reinforcing developmental lag, for which therapy is necessary to permit "catching up."

The biological concept of "critical periods" in development (Tanner, 1978) would seem to be very closely related to the psychological concept of fixation. It is not clear how specifically this concept applies to human children and to the more complex issues of psychological development. It apparently does apply to more circumscribed functions such as the acquisition of binocular vision.

A condition rarely of concern to the clinician is precocity, the "opposite" of fixation. Some persons are found to be advanced in development, that is, they are on a developmental curve steeper than normal. I mention this chiefly for the sake of logical completeness rather than clinical relevance.

Regression

The decompensation of a human personality is viewed in the light of our present model as regression. Although regression describes only some phenomena of psychiatric disorder, it is

empirically true that ill people of all kinds exhibit some reversion to less mature modes of personality functioning. In the
architectural analogy, edifices suffer deterioration or collapse.
They never disintegrate and disappear totally, even when in a
state of ruin. They remain recognizable as edifices, impaired,
damaged, even dangerous. Damage usually starts in outer,
more recent and superficial structures (the analogy for neuroses) while inner and foundational parts remain intact and
sound. Sometimes the foundation or framework founders (a
perilous state of affairs) even while the visible superficies may
be left apparently undamaged (the analogy for psychoses). The
relation of this architectural metaphor to the Jacksonian principles will become more evident below in the next section.

Regression is defined as a "return to a former or earlier
state" or "return to earlier, especially to infantile, patterns of
thought and behavior, a characteristic of many mental disorders . . ." (Taylor, 1988, p. 1444), and as a "return to an earlier
level of adaptation as from an adult to an infantile level . . ."
(Becker, 1986, p. 2458). Regression is a second important corollary of the developmental–structural model, so we shall examine it here in some detail, using an essentially descriptive approach.

In such a descriptive light, regression simply happens: in
both normal and disordered life we revert, quite unwittingly
(i.e., in an ego syntonic or unconscious way), to younger ways
of experiencing and behaving. Regression does not *cause* psychiatric or psychosomatic illness; it is a part of them, accounting
only for certain symptoms. Its stylistic aspects may be very useful as a monitoring device in following the progress or deterioration of a given case of illness (Powles, 1973). Two illustrations
of this: In an attack of ulcerative colitis, we usually find a reversion to somewhat helpless, childlike styles of functioning; however, the diarrhea and bleeding have no normal counterpart in
earlier life, that is, are not regressive. In an attack of paranoid
schizophrenia, the accusing or menacing hallucinations have no
normal counterpart in early life (though see chapter 6 on
Freud's interest in the auditive aspects of the superego). However, a person in this condition is usually panicky, in the manner
of a frightened child, and concrete and egocentric in mode of

thinking—styles which are normal at an earlier age and thus regressive.

We have both normal or adaptive forms of regression, and pathological or clinical ones. In the following list of properties or criteria of regression, I stress pathological features, but include adaptive regression for comparison:

1. There is an onset, sudden or slow, of experiencing and behaving in an altered mode; regression is a change or discontinuity in a person's life, with time relations unlike those of the learning of new behavior.

2. This altered mode is ego syntonic or unconscious; the subject is not aware of changes in motivation and behavior.

3. In clinical regressions there is almost always discomfort or dysphoria; the adaptive regressions of daily life are neutral or pleasurable in feeling tone.

4. There is a duration persistent enough to be a measurable shift in personal function; adaptive regressions are cyclical or rhythmical, and self-limited.

5. Clinical observation reveals that several elements of personal function (e.g., style of conceptualizing, drive state, object relationships, moral judgment) have shifted measurably from more to less mature, developmentally speaking.

6. There is a recovery or restitution, sudden or slow, often correlated with some interpersonal–psychotherapeutic or pharmacologic intervention, to more comfortable and identifiably more "normal" (i.e., age-appropriate) functioning; again, the time scale does not fit a learning curve.

7. Mathematically represented, regression is a discontinuity in one or more of the individual's developmental curves, represented by a sag, then a recovery to the premorbid developmental curve. Some regressions do not recover; that is, they become fixations, with a lasting flattening of the developmental curve. Such a picture ensues from some childhood disturbances; it represents intractable chronicity in the adult.

Case Example: Mrs. U.P. An intelligent twenty-five-year-old surgical nurse received painful but not life-threatening head and neck injuries in a rear-end car accident; 5 months later, while still under treatment for severe neck pain and stiffness, a psychiatric consultation was requested. The patient was despondent, but in behavior lively and restless. Her thinking was in style concrete and egocentric, in content a florid preoccupation with early sexual traumas. She was repulsed by her husband's sexual advances and severe marital conflict had developed. Soon after this consultation she made a serious suicidal attempt with sedative drugs, and after intensive care she was transferred to a psychiatric ward.

As a member of this community she quickly acquired a reputation for being capricious, negativistic, the center of attention; her gorgeous auburn hair, good looks and figure, and prominent neck brace seemed constantly to attract compassionate and amorous advances from the men. She decided to leave her husband and go off with a male patient, with whom she attended a weekend healing retreat. The morning after returning to the ward (after 2 weeks of supportive care and exploratory psychotherapy) she reported to her nurse a "sudden snap" in her neck, and an "awful grinding sensation." She immediately lost all her pain and regained a full range of motion.

But further, she had also changed suddenly and strikingly into a modest, cooperative, empathic human being, an altruistic ward community member, no longer disruptive and attention-getting, now helpful to staff and patients. Her thinking became abstract, "decentered" or governed by universal rather than egocentric and capricious norms, no longer focused on childhood sexual trauma. She shortly returned to work and to an improved marital and sexual relationship.

Evolution of the Construct of Regression

S. W. Jackson (1969) offers a definitive review of the history of Freud's concepts of regression; I summarize his presentation. John Hughlings Jackson, the seminal pioneer of British neurology, worked at a time when the whole scientific milieu had become excited and stimulated by Darwin and the evolutionary model. Jackson's key principles (J. H. Jackson, 1887a,b) were in fact modeled upon the evolutionary thinking of Herbert Spencer (see S. W. Jackson [1969]). These were that the central nervous system is organized hierarchically, with phylogenetically more recent "higher" centers (frontal lobes, forebrain) dominating more primitive "lower" centers (brain stem, cerebellum, cord); and that disease or injury of a higher center will "release" functions of a lower center which it previously had controlled and inhibited. J. H. Jackson (following Spencer) gave the alternative names *dis-evolution* and *dissolution* to such a happening, implying that the phylogenetic and ontogenetic evolution of the central nervous system is undone or reversed.

Sigmund Freud admired Jackson, and endorsed and extrapolated the "Jacksonian principles." In an early monograph, "On Aphasia" (Freud, 1891), and writing in a neurological frame of reference, Freud both coined the term *agnosia* and propounded a principle of functional retrogression (Rückbildung) to account for a speech disturbance more profound than anatomic injury alone would explain. Later, he built a psychological construct of "regression" in successive editions of *The Interpretation of Dreams* (Freud, 1900; see especially his 1930 revisions). Regression has three aspects: topical, temporal, and formal. The topical or topographic aspect deals with the reversal of normal sequences such as stimulus–response (sensorimotor) or conscious–preconscious–unconscious, as these are observed in dreaming. The temporal aspect deals with the anachronism of regressions. The formal aspect deals with the stylistic changes involved in regressions. Our concern here will be mostly with pathological temporal regression and with the stylistics of formal regression.

Problems with the Construct of Regression

The term *regression* appears recently to have fallen into some disrepute, as its meaning has become diffuse and rendered pejorative in the lingua franca of popular psychology. If the construct is to be useful clinically, and if it is to be submitted to further needed research, the following qualifications would seem to apply:

1. Distinction needs to be made between the *process* of regressing, the flow or movement against the developmental curve (topical aspect), and the developmental level reached in regression (temporal, formal aspects) with its thematic and stylistic colorings. One might call this latter the *regression age* as contrasted with the patient's chronological age or premorbid developmental age level.

2. More precise estimates need to be made as to where the patient has reached in regression. I have located no definitive research establishing whether regression is a segmental process (whether some personality functions can be immature while others remain mature) or whether of necessity all functions regress. Classically and clinically regression has been seen as a rather pervasive process (Fenichel, 1945; A. Freud, 1965). The developmental streams outlined below may provide us with some more operational criteria for estimating the "regression age" of different personality functions. Piaget's concept of décalage (Flavell, 1963; Gruber and Vonèche, 1977) of different functions suggests that regression may be an uneven process too.

Analysis of the above case vignette, for example, suggests that this young woman's inner world and preoccupations were at about age seven to eight (a point of traumatic fixation); her cognitive style at about age five to six; her object relations generally at an oedipal age; and her social behavior at early adolescence or puberty, twelve to thirteen years. Her onset, her dysphoria, her shift in functioning, her lack of awareness of regression, and her abrupt remission following therapeutic intervention, match well with criteria outlined in the section on "Regression" above.

3. Stringent testing of the construct would require that a stylistic shift from a more mature to a less mature position be demonstrated by independent observers and standardized measures; that the premorbid developmental position and the "regression age" be established using more than one set of developmental norms or streams; that the change be found to be pervasive in the sense of involving several different personality

functions; that the processes of regression and recovery be observed to show some lawful order by traversing known developmental streams in a predicted direction and sequence; and that the timing and cause–effect relations of the regression be shown not to follow the curve of systematic learning of new behaviors.

The Study and Analysis of Development

Developmental Curves

The data of *growth* are quantitative for the most part, and can practically, usefully, and often elegantly be displayed on graphs or smoothed curves against some age or time scale. The ingenuity of the investigator seems the only limit to what kind of data and what kind of curve can be displayed (see chapter 2). It is to be hoped, therefore, that the softer data of *development* might be also dealt with in a similar, quasi-quantitative manner.

One useful clinical approach is to view patients against idealized or schematic curves. For example, a clinical illness, somatic or psychological, can be pictured as a temporary downward departure *(regression)* from a life curve. A *fixation* can be pictured as a falling off of a developmental curve, at a point in life, to a slope below the normal gradient and which persists at this flattened gradient; observation will then show whether the curve rises toward its expected normal if therapeutic intervention is successful. It is often possible to monitor untreated problems, particularly in young patients, and to find that they resolve spontaneously; that is, catch up with the expected developmental curve. In the case of Mrs. U. P. above several developmental curves would show a distinct dip to the regression ages which I have suggested. Her rebound to an approximately normal position on her developmental curves was a surprisingly abrupt one. What would have been the fate of these curves if she had gone on into chronicity?

Developmental Streams

Although human growth and development is an indivisible, global, integrated process, we may do it better scientific justice by viewing it from several manageable and intelligible vantage points. Anna Freud (1963, 1965) has proposed the idea of "developmental lines": stepwise progression from dependency to emotional self-reliance and adult object relationships (8 steps); from suckling to rational eating (6 steps); from wetting and soiling to bladder and bowel control (4 steps); from irresponsibility to responsibility in body management (3 steps); from egocentricity to companionship (4 steps); from the body to the toy and from play to work (6 steps). Gesell and his successors (Knobloch and Pasamanick, 1974) have selected five "fields of behavior" for their scales: adaptive behavior, gross motor behavior, fine motor behavior, language behavior, and personal–social behavior.

In somewhat the same way, I shall propose a conceptual division of human growth and development into five streams. Each stream is broad and inclusive enough to portray adequately the complexity and richness of the human condition. There are enough distinctive features in each stream, including their investigation and exposition by different leading workers, to make of each an intelligible field of discourse, even though there may be overlap and cross-connection between them. Five streams are few enough that we can keep an account of such interconnections; for example, language as both a cognitive operation and a vehicle of interpersonal relating, or egocentricity in both cognitive and social frameworks.

These proposed five developmental streams are briefly summarized as follows, then a chapter will be devoted to each of them; where possible, differential development of the two sexes will be reviewed.

Somatic Development: Body and Brain. Growth of the body generally, in its parts and proportions, and particularly the central nervous and sexual systems, is the tangible and quantifiable aspect of this stream. In fact, growth and development are virtually synonymous as we watch the *soma* mature. Progressive biological change in bodily organs and systems (biological level of emergence) forms the substrate for many psychosocial developments (psychological and social levels), which will be reviewed under the other developmental streams.

The principal investigators and exponents of this stream have been pediatricians: Tanner (1978, 1981), Gesell and his followers (Knobloch and Pasamanick, 1974), Illingworth (1980) for example. Anthropologists such as Boas (chapter 10 in Tanner, 1981) and Young (1971), for example, have also contributed to study of this stream.

At this point an important caveat should be noted. We must avoid the fallacy that adults become children during regressions. It is not *growth* which is reversed, though it may be slowed or halted in growing children. Rather, it is functions and behaviors which regress, and development which is undone. In dealing with this stream it might be wiser to resort to the Jacksonian terms *dis-evolution* or *dissolution*, as more appropriate to a biological frame of reference, than to regression, a psychological construct.

Intellectual and Cognitive Development. This stream represents the ontogenesis of that key evolutionary achievement of humans, the intellect. Measured intelligence, with its associated constructs of mental age and intelligence quotient, traces the quantitative or growth aspects. Qualitatively, the study of cognitive style traces development from primitive, sensorimotor precursors of thought, through capricious, egocentric, concrete forms of reasoning and knowing, to the emergence of fully adult hypotheticodeductive reasoning, judgment, and wisdom. Study of this developmental stream includes the study of failures and defects in the development of intelligence; and also what I believe to be a new and profitable study of the disturbances and distortions of judgment in the psychiatric disorders.

Although the field of ego psychology within psychoanalysis (Freud, 1923; Hartmann, 1958; A. Freud, 1965) has made important qualitative contributions, it is psychologists who are the investigators and exponents of this stream. Binet and Wechsler (Wechsler, 1958), Piaget (Piaget and Inhelder, 1966; Gruber and Vonèche, 1977), and Luria (1932) provide a quasi-quantitative framework which should be particularly useful for our clinical purposes.

Another caveat: Piaget has warned us to avoid the key fallacy that children (and by extrapolation, emotionally ill adults) think like normal adults: they do not. We shall later (chapters 3, 6) comment upon some of the cognitive and moral judgments of persons suffering from psychoneurosis, depression, elation, and psychosis, in illustration of this proposition.

Developmental Tasks and the Life Cycle. In the life cycle, each stage has its overriding priorities which maximize the chances of survival and which also are stepping stones in the continued personal development and social integration of the individual. Nowhere do we get a clearer illustration of the epigenetic principle: only by succeeding in the developmental task of establishing personal trust and security, through successful caregiving and attachment, can the child go on to establish successful neuromuscular and ego autonomy, then socialization, then procreation, and so on. The exponents of this stream are psychoanalysts; for example, Sigmund Freud (1938, Lecture XXXI), who progressively elucidated psychosexual development; his successors Abraham (1924) and Fenichel (1945), who systematized his discoveries; Bowlby (1969), who has criticized and probably revolutionized psychoanalytic theory; and Erikson (1976), who is a social scientist as well and who has extended our view of human developmental tasks all the way through to old age and death. The data of this stream are probably the "softest" or least quantitative of all the streams: the challenge is to make them operational as clinical measuring norms.

The Object Concept and Attachment. Here we have dual contributions by psychoanalysts and basic scientists: Bowlby, a most important contributor to this area, is both. The work of Piaget and the Geneva group (Flavell, 1963; Piaget and Inhelder, 1966; Gruber and Vonèche, 1977) delineates the child's progress in objectification of the self and other objects, and how successful development places the self firmly as one in a world of relating and interacting objects; degrees of "egocentrism" and "decentration" can now be estimated along a developmental scale. Bowlby (1969, 1980, 1988), combining the tools of clinical psychoanalysis, child observation, ethology, and control theory, has developed a complex picture of attachment and its disruptions, of the development of object constancy and specificity, of the place of attachment and its actualizing mechanisms in human evolution and in the life cycle, as well as in psychiatric disorders.

For a clinical measuring tool, it would be hoped that a combination of Piaget's and Bowlby's strongly observational work will provide a quasi-quantitative base.

Language as communication probably belongs in this stream, as a vehicle of object relationship and socialization, though language as thinking also comes under intellectual and cognitive development in stream 3.

Development of Value and Moral Judgment. Disturbances in moral judgment are found throughout the psychiatric disorders: neurotic guilt, depressive self-recriminations and hallucinations, and the expansive amorality of mania represent some examples. Both psychoanalysis and psychology have provided exponents of this stream. The group of functions termed the *superego* was proposed in Freud's structural theory (Freud, 1923) and systematized in evolving psychoanalytic theory (Fenichel, 1945). Piaget conducted a study on evolving moral judgment and the sense of law in children playing a street game (Piaget et al., 1932). More recently, Kohlberg (1981; see also Mischel, 1971) has provided a transcultural base for measuring the development of moral judgment. Gilligan (1982) has offered a foundation for research on the thorny question of the sexual dimorphism of moral judgment, in her comparative studies of the development of moral judgment in women and men.

Bibliographic Notes: Key Readings

As I shall do for each chapter, I recommend certain references as basic or definitive: these are asterisked in the reference list. All are intriguing and thought provoking, and most are a pleasure to read. The real problem has been how to narrow the selection down. Young (1971) an anatomist, presents a true "anthropology," a scientific survey of the human condition ranging from physical to evolutionary to cultural issues, and in the kind of integrative framework we badly need today. Hoskins (1946), a psychiatrist, and Novikoff (1945), a philosopher of science, present the important principle of emergence. Sigmund Freud (1923) and John Bowlby (1969,1980) present seminal versions of the view of structures or systems in the human psyche; Freud as the originator of psychoanalysis, Bowlby as its most constructive critic and enricher. J. Hughlings Jackson (1887a,b) should be read on his principles of evolution and dissolution (or "dis-evolution") of the nervous system, the "Jacksonian principles." His namesake, Stanley W. Jackson (1969), a psychoanalyst, gives the clearest summary I know of Freud's thinking on regression. Baldwin (1967) and Patricia Miller (1983) give reviews of developmental theories with critical comments; they are recommended as good monographs and overviews, Miller's being particularly lucid and compact as well as recent. Piaget and Inhelder (1966) give a readable overview of Piagetian theory. Finally, Anna Freud (1963, 1965), who in many ways carried on her father's work, should be consulted for the construct of developmental lines.

References

Abraham, K. (1924), *Selected Papers on Psychoanalysis*. New York: Basic Books, 1949.

Alexander, F., & Ross, H., eds. (1961), *The Impact of Freudian Psychiatry*. Chicago: University of Chicago Press.

*Baldwin, A. L. (1967), *Theories of Child Development*. New York: John Wiley.

Becker, E. L., ed. (1986), *International Dictionary of Medicine and Biology*, Vol. 3. New York: John Wiley.

Billings, E. G. (1939), *Handbook of Elementary Psychobiology and Psychiatry*. New York: Macmillan.

Black, M. (1962), *Models and Metaphors: Studies in Language and Philosophy*. Ithaca, NY: Cornell University Press.

Blasi, A. (1976), The concept of development in personality theory. In: *Ego Development: Conceptions and Theories*, ed. J. Loevinger and A. Blasi. San Francisco: Jossey-Bass, chap. 3, pp. 29–53.

Bowlby, J. (1969), *Attachment and Loss, Vol. 1: Attachment,* 2nd ed. London: Hogarth Press, 1982.

——— (1980), *Attachment and Loss, Vol. 3: Loss: Sadness and Depression*. London: Hogarth Press.

——— (1988), Developmental psychiatry comes of age. *Amer. J. Psychiat.*, 145:1–10.

Brenner, C. (1955), *Elementary Textbook of Psychoanalysis*. New York: International Universities Press.

Diethelm, O. (1936), *Treatment in Psychiatry*, 2nd ed. Springfield, IL: Charles C Thomas, 1950.

Engel, G. L. (1977), The need for a new medical model: A challenge for biomedicine. *Science*, 196:129–136.

———— (1980), The clinical application of the biopsychosocial model. *Amer. J. Psychiat.*, 137:535–544.

Erikson, E. H. (1976), Reflections on Dr. Borg's life cycle. *Daedalus*, Spring: 1–28.

Fenichel, O. (1945), *The Psychoanalytic Theory of Neurosis*. New York: W. W. Norton.

Flavell, J. H. (1963), *The Developmental Psychology of Jean Piaget*. Princeton, NJ: Van Nostrand.

*Freud, A. (1963), The concept of developmental lines. *The Psychoanalytic Study of the Child*, 18:245–265. New York: International Universities Press.

*———— (1965), *Normality and Pathology in Childhood: Assessments of Development*. New York: International Universities Press.

Freud, S. (1891), *On Aphasia: A Critical Study*. London: Imago, 1953.

———— (1900), The Interpretation of Dreams. *Standard Edition*, 5:539–549. London: Hogarth Press, 1953.

———— (1917), Introductory Lectures on Psycho-analysis. *Standard Edition*, 16:273–357. London: Hogarth Press, 1963.

*———— (1923), The ego and the id. *Standard Edition*, 19:12–66. London: Hogarth Press, 1961.

———— (1938), New Introductory Lectures on Psycho-Analysis. *Standard Edition*, 22:5–182. London: Hogarth Press, 1964.

Gilligan, C. (1982), *In a Different Voice: Psychological Theory and Women's Development*. Cambridge, MA: Harvard University Press.

Gruber, H. E., & Vonèche, J. J. (1977), *The Essential Piaget*. New York: Basic Books.

Harré, R. (1983a), Models: Role in theories. In: *Encyclopedic Dictionary of Psychology*, ed. R. Harré & R. Lamb. Cambridge, MA: MIT Press.

———— (1983b), History and philosophy of science in the pedagogical process. In: *Science Under Scrutiny*, ed. R. W. Home. Dordrecht: D. Reidel.

Hartmann, H. (1958), *Ego Psychology and the Problem of Adaptation*. New York: International Universities Press.

Hofling, C. K. (1975), *Textbook of Psychiatry for Medical Practice*, 3rd ed. Philadelphia: J. B. Lippincott.

*Hoskins, R. G. (1946), *The Biology of Schizophrenia*. New York: W. W. Norton.

Illingworth, R. S. (1980), *Development of the Infant and Young Child, Normal and Abnormal*. Edinburgh: Churchill Livingstone.

*Jackson, J. H. (1887a), Evolution and dissolution of the nervous system (Croonian Lecture, 1884). In: *Selected Writings*, ed J. Taylor, A. Holmes, & F. M. R. Walshe. London: Staples, 1958.

*———— (1887b), Remarks on evolution and dissolution of the nervous system. In: *Selected Writings* ed. J. Taylor, A. Holmes, & F. M. R. Walshe. London: Staples, 1958.

*Jackson, S. W. (1969), The history of Freud's concepts of regression. *J. Amer. Psychoanal. Assn.*, 17:743–784.

Knobloch, H. & Pasamanick, B., eds., (1974), *Gesell and Amatruda's Developmental Diagnosis*, 3rd ed. New York: Harper & Row.

Kohlberg, L. (1981), *Essays on Moral Development*, Vol. 1. San Francisco: Harper & Row.

Lazare, A. (1973), Hidden conceptual models in clinical psychiatry. *New Eng. J. Med.*, 288:345–351.

Levine, M. (1961), Principles of psychiatric treatment. In: *The Impact of Freudian Psychiatry*, ed. F. Alexander & H. Ross. Chicago: University of Chicago Press.

Loevinger, J. (1976), *Ego Development: Conceptions and Theories*. San Francisco: Jossey-Bass.

Luria, A. R. (1932), *Cognitive Development: Its Cultural and Social Foundations*. Cambridge, MA: Harvard University Press, 1976.

Marubini, E. (1978), Mathematical handling of long-term longitudinal data. In: *Human Growth*, Vol. 1, ed. F. Falkner & J. Tanner. London: Plenum Press.

*Miller, P. H. (1983), *Theories of Developmental Psychology*. San Francisco: W. H. Freeman.

Mischel, T., ed. (1971), *Cognitive Development and Epistemology*. New York: Academic Press.

Murray, D. J. (1983), *A History of Western Psychology*. Englewood Cliffs, NJ: Prentice-Hall.

*Novikoff, A. B. (1945), The concept of integrative levels and biology. *Science*, 101:209–211.

Piaget, J. (1968) *Structuralism (Le Structuralisme)*, trans. & ed. C. Maschler. New York: Basic Books, 1970.

———— Baechler, N., Feldweg, A. M., Lambercier, M., Martinez-Mont., L., Maso, N., Piaget, Y. J., & Rambert, M. (1932), *The Moral Development of the Child*. London: Routledge & Kegan Paul.

*———— Inhelder, B. (1966), *The Psychology of the Child*. London: Routledge & Kegan Paul, 1969.

Powles, W. E. (1973), Regression as a monitoring device in clinical psychiatry. *Samiksa: J. Ind. Psycho-Anal. Soc.*, 27:1–12.

Tanner, J. M. (1978), *Fetus into Man: Physical Growth from Conception to Maturity*. Cambridge, MA: Harvard University Press.

———— (1981), *A History of the Study of Human Growth*. Cambridge, MA: Cambridge University Press.

Taylor, E. J., ed. (1988), *Dorland's Illustrated Medical Dictionary*, 27th ed. Philadelphia: W. B. Saunders.

Wechsler, D. (1958), *Measurement and Appraisal of Adult Intelligence*, 4th ed. Baltimore: Williams & Wilkins.

*Young, J. Z. (1971), *An Introduction to the Study of Man*. Oxford: Oxford University Press.

---

*Recommended readings.

2

A First Developmental Stream: Growth of the Body and the Brain; Human Sexual Dimorphism

Introduction

Overview

This stream concerns the steady increase, from conception to adulthood, in the size and strength of body parts and of the whole soma. But study in this stream is not only of size and strength, but of organization and differentiation; of changes in shape and proportion, in macroscopic and microscopic structure, and in evolving function; that is, study of both growth and development. We are occupied here for the most part at the biological level of emergence, and with appropriate methods of recording and analyzing living, but basically bodily structures and processes. The subject matter of this chapter forms the biological substrate of two higher emergences: psychological and social development, which are considered in subsequent chapters.

Bodily growth is continuous, smooth, and resilient. It cannot be broken down into discrete stages, though the spectacular growth velocities of prenatal life and of the early adolescent period make of these periods the nearest thing to arbitrarily definable stages. Growth may be slowed, even arrested, by insults such as malnutrition, serious illness, or hormonal disturbance, but it will almost always catch up when the insult is relieved, to reach a position decreed by genetic programming.

In this first stream, *growth* and *development* are so intertwined that it is always difficult to be sure which is the more appropriate term. We are certainly speaking of development when we view the proliferation and unbelievably complex organization of neuronal processes and synapses within the brain, or the onset of reproductive maturity. And we must remind ourselves that these are influenced, for better and for worse, by the interaction between genetic programming and a favorable or a hostile environment.

Human sexual dimorphism, which is only moderate in degree, is established at conception. Girls are developmentally advanced over boys from before birth, and they complete their growth about 2 years earlier than boys. In addition to the qualitative or absolute differences of the genitalia, relative or proportional differences develop in various body dimensions. The increasing evidence that the female brain differs from the male will be reviewed.

Finally, some examples will be given of clinical problems to which the data of this stream might be applied with advantage.

Mathematical and Statistical Representations

The data of bodily growth, being analog measures of continuous processes, are particularly aptly displayed in curves. Various ingenious applications of curves or graphs are found in Tanner's publications (1978a,b; Tanner and Whitehouse, 1982) and are further explicated by Falkner (1966, pp. 16–20) and in their most esoteric form by Marubini and Milani (1986). The following are examples of commonly used curves.

Distance and velocity curves carry out different tasks. Body height, for example, can simply be plotted at succeeding ages.

This is a distance curve, showing cumulative distance covered at various points in a voyage. In a velocity curve, the rate of change is plotted at succeeding ages. It plots the speed of growth, just as the speed of a vehicle can be plotted at various points on a voyage.

It may be of interest to plot the actual size of various limbs, organs, or body segments at various ages (distance curves). However, it may be more useful to plot at various ages what percentage of the total body each part contributes. Or, it may be useful to plot the rate of growth of such parts at various ages (velocity curves). The growth of both body height and weight shows a sharp acceleration at adolescence, and a sharp deceleration on achieving adult size. Distance curves for postnatal growth have mostly the same form, whether for height, weight, body dimensions, muscle or fatty tissue (skin-fold thickness), with two exceptions. These are for lymphoid tissue, which reaches a peak at 10 to 12 years, then declines sharply; and for the brain, which grows steeply in early childhood, the curve flattening out smoothly in late childhood and adolescence when most other parts go into the adolescent growth spurt (see Figures 2.1, 2.2).

Curves can be plotted in which absolute chronological age is not the scale of time (abscissa). Tanner (1978a,b; Tanner and Whitehouse, 1982) notes that real or chronological time is only one, not particularly useful, form of time against which to plot a number of developmental data. "Developmental time," that is, some way of standardizing individual growth against its own time scale, provides another, and in some ways more valid framework. For this two methods can be used, one of which is retrospective, measuring events that have occurred against a time scale whose reference is to a point such as the peak of the adolescent growth spurt, or the onset of menstruation. A curve such as this can be surprising and useful. The other method is the use of standardized norms as the scale of developmental time; for example, the developmental scale of "bone age," the known sequences of patterns of ossification. Tanner believes that bone age comes closest to a developmental time scale or

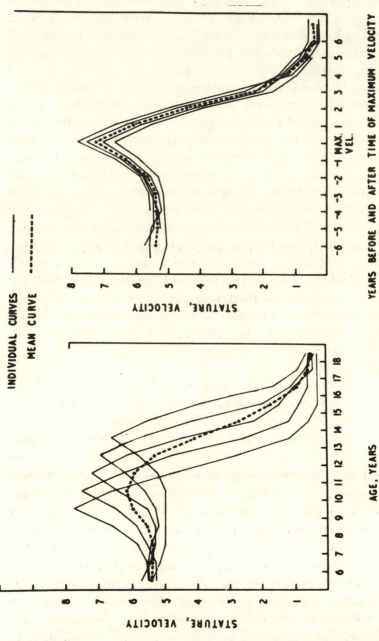

Figure 2.1. The Adolescent Growth Spurt

The striking acceleration of growth velocity starting just before puberty is best displayed by plotting individual growth velocity curves. Tanner shows that averaging them takes away much of their character, whereas placing the curves on a common scale, of years before and after the peak of the spurt, displays the mean curve to advantage. Reproduced, by permission of International Universities Press, from J. M. Tanner, *Education and Physical Growth*, 2nd edition, 1978.

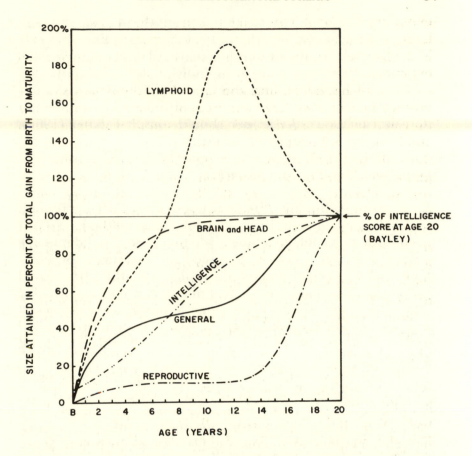

Figure 2.2. Growth of Bodily Parts and Intelligence

From Tanner's *Education and Physical Growth* two graphs have been combined. First, these show how different are the growth curves for different parts of the body. Second, the curve of growth of measured intelligence has been added to show that it comes closest in form to that of brain growth. Reproduced, by permission of International Universities Press, from J. M. Tanner, *Education and Physical Growth*, 2nd edition, 1978.

scale of "real age"; he has produced detailed radiological norms for its measurement.

There are a number of other statistical devices for producing curves from data, comparing individuals, assessing the significance of individual variations, and establishing norms. A few will now be mentioned. For a more comprehensive treatment of statistical methods, the reader should consult Falkner (1966), and Falkner and Tanner (1978a,b,c).

Survey and Measurement Approaches

There are two broadly different approaches to the collection of developmental data. In the cross-sectional method, a cohort of children is assembled at one given time, and divided into age groups; each age group is examined and measured for whatever data are being sought; these data can then be treated statistically. The method is useful in establishing standards for various peer groups at a given point in historical time. Successive cross-sectional surveys over the years will show up so-called secular changes; for example, changes in the relative age of puberty.

But the cross-sectional method has two quite serious disadvantages. Since the subjects in the various age groups are different children, the method cannot be relied upon to tell what happens as children grow from one age to another. Individual histories or curves are not obtained, and false conclusions about growth may be reached. Further, the method tends seriously to bleach out the significance of individual differences in growth rate. Working with such age groups one will obtain a very flat, "averaged," curve of the adolescent growth spurt, for example, which gives a colorless and misleading picture of growth at adolescence (see Figure 2.1).

In the longitudinal approach, children are recruited into the study at an early age, and examined and measured individually at regular intervals. Data can then be plotted and curves constructed for each individual, as well as for the spread of data in defined peer groups. Comparisons can be made based on developmental age rather than chronological age, and attempts at prediction made which can be followed up subsequently. Such an approach highlights individual differences. It does not bleach or level out by averaging growth curves of developmentally slow and developmentally advanced individuals of the same age; further, it makes possible intelligent comparison of different individuals' growth rates. The method requires enormous and persistent work over many years, and is vulnerable to the dropping out of probands through loss of motivation or migration.

Falkner (1966) has proposed a "mixed" approach in which individuals may enter and leave the study over variable periods. This avoids some of the obstacles and discouragements of the pure longitudinal study, and can provide much useful data if statistically processed in a sophisticated manner.

Growth Gradients

The body and its parts do not grow evenly, so curves for growth of various parts are of significance (see Figure 2.2). For example, the growth curves for lymphoid tissue and for the head and brain have a very different shape from those for height and weight. Thus, there appear to be certain principles which can be applied to the differential organization of human bodily growth.

The concept of "growth gradients" deals with the fact that the growth of certain parts will be ahead of the growth of other parts. Two such general gradients can be observed: Generally, structures toward the head end (the head, upper trunk, and upper limbs) grow and develop in function ahead of the lower trunk and lower limbs: a craniocaudal gradient. In addition, the distal aspects of limbs develop in advance of the proximal: the hand is ahead of the forearm and the forearm ahead of the arm.

For the central nervous system (CNS), the gradient is "caudocranial": the cord, medulla, brain stem, cerebellum, and cerebral hemispheres develop in that order.

The study of the organizing principles and organizing mechanisms of somatic growth and development is not yet well advanced, though clearly genetic programs must be assumed to be dominant in such organizational guidance.

It is difficult here not to abandon science altogether, and to be lost in contemplation over the organization of form and function, even in such a structure as the lowly fingernail. How does it take its form? How does it remain defined and organized over a lifetime, though its component cells have turned over thousands of times? Such amazement turns to awe if we shift attention to the myriad working cells of the brain, and their even more myriad processes and synapses. How is it possible that the genetic code which guides their growth and correct arrangement can be contained within the microscopic confines of the ovum and spermatozoon?

Bodily Growth

The following is essentially a summary and paraphrase of Tanner (1978a,b), with contributions from other sources indicated as appropriate.

The Embryonic Period: 4–10 Weeks Postmenstrual

The embryonic period occupies the time from 2 to 8 weeks after fertilization (4–10 weeks "postmenstrual"; see below) when a recognizably human form is attained in the 3-cm-long fetus. The embryo does not grow rapidly at this stage. Differentiation of tissues (histogenesis) and body parts (morphogenesis) are the tasks of this early period. About 50 percent of embryos are aborted, usually without the mother's awareness, due to genetic abnormalities and failure of nutrition by the maternal endometrium.

Prenatal age is usually reckoned from the first day of the last menstrual period (postmenstrual age) despite the obvious difficulties and irregularities of such measurement. Fertilization is arbitrarily reckoned as occurring 2 weeks after the onset of the last menstrual period. Therefore postfertilization age will be 2 weeks less than postmenstrual age. Unless otherwise noted, ages will be given here as postmenstrual.

The Fetal Period: 10–40 Weeks Postmenstrual

The first great growth spurt is in fetal life, where growth in length is reaching its peak velocity at about 20 weeks. There are serious gaps in the study of prenatal growth. Obviously, longitudinal studies of living individual fetuses were impossible before the advent of ultrasound monitoring. Firm modern data exist on abortuses of 10 to 18 weeks, and on premature babies of 28 weeks onward, so that interpolation is necessary for the growth curve between 18 and 28 weeks.

The growth spurt of the fetus is related to cell multiplication; growth in size of cells accounts for considerable further growth. From about 30 weeks the velocity of growth drops off sharply, by which time probably few or no new nerve and muscle cells appear; from 30 to 40 weeks of (postmenstrual) age the fetus stores something like 400 grams of fat, a huge energy reserve. Growth in body weight reaches a later peak than growth in length, at about 34 weeks. Thereafter it slows down as the uterus becomes relatively crowded for the fetus. One evidence for this interpretation is that the growth of twins slows down earlier than for singletons, and one twin is often smaller; another is that small babies characteristically grow rapidly in their first postnatal 6 months in a "catch-up" fashion.

Poor maternal nutrition has its greatest effect in the last few prenatal weeks, whereas in previous weeks the fetus is "protected" in growth at the mother's expense. Hence it may take several generations for a population to respond fully to changes in nutrition.

Birth length does not correlate at all well (correlation coefficient 0.3) with adult height, though by 2 years of age the correlation is high (0.8). Small mothers give birth to small babies (one of the reassuring prognostic facts for the obstetrician) but the child's ultimate size will be determined too by the father's size. Tanner reports the crucial experiment of crossing a Shire horse with a Shetland pony: both crosses were employed, Shire sire with Shetland dam, and Shetland sire with Shire dam. The offspring were about the size expected for the dam, at birth, but both foals eventually grew to the same size, about halfway between that of their respective parents.

Although "prematurity" is now a dubious concept, a real distinction can be made between babies who are smaller than average because of low postmenstrual age and those who are apparently chronologically mature, yet small in size. The prognosis for survival, and for later capacities such as intelligence, is much poorer for the small child born after a normal-length gestation.

Postnatal Growth

Evidently (Tanner, 1978a) genetic templates govern the rates of postnatal growth of various body parts; this influence determines differences in body proportions in different races of humankind. Thus, different individuals will predictably mature at different rates, attain different sizes, and develop different bodily and facial shapes and proportions. Nature and nurture interact to fulfill the genetic template, to which both parents contribute equally (Tanner, 1978a, p. 123). Children within a family, given the same care, develop differently. Social hardships, such as wartime conditions in Holland and Germany, can be shown (Tanner, 1978a, p. 132) to set back the growth of children, and also to give way, when better times come, to an impressive "catch-up" period of growth. There are developmental gradients between races. Given equivalent nutrition, African and Asian children are developmentally advanced as compared with European ones. Urban children are usually larger, and they mature more rapidly than rural children, including earlier menarche (Tanner, 1978a, p. 144). This is best explained by the harder physical work required of rural children coupled with a less bountiful diet.

Secular trends (trends in a population over decades or a century or more) indicate that children in west European countries (and North America and Australia) and in Japan have increased steadily in height and in speed of growth. The age of menarche for western Europeans has shown an astonishing change from over 16 years in 1860 to about 13 years in 1960 to 1970. That is, earlier maturation is a major secular trend, though this rapid change currently appears to be slowing down.

A Note on Dentition

Dentition is not a particularly useful developmental marker. The subject is not mentioned in textbooks of developmental pediatrics such as Knobloch and Pasamanick (1974), Holt (1977), and Illingworth (1980). Tanner (1978a) offers only a few comments, such as that girls generally erupt their permanent teeth earlier than boys, and that dentition correlates very poorly with other indices of growth and development. Demirjian (1986) presents a detailed and technical review of dentition updating Tanner's (1962) careful treatment of the subject. Demirjian finds various studies to have shown that the eruption, or, more correctly, the "clinical emergence" of the teeth is little influenced by secular trends or by favorable or unfavorable environmental and nutritional conditions; that clinical emergence correlates very poorly with other measures of growth; and that clinical emergence clearly is determined by genetic, including racial, programs.

Demirjian's review assigns greater significance to the *radiological* study of the maturation, formation, and calcification of teeth, which can be related with standardized norms and from which a dental age score can be calculated reliably. However, these ratings again correlate very poorly with the other indices of growth.

All authors agree that the clinical emergence of the 20 deciduous teeth occurs between 6 and 30 months in both sexes; that the last of these teeth are finally discarded by 12 to 14 years; and that the 32 permanent teeth emerge commencing at 6 years and finishing at 10 to 12 years, except for the third molar ("wisdom tooth") which emerges with great variability between 14 and 20 years. Tanner notes that girls erupt their permanent canines some 11 months earlier than boys, and their first molars 2 months earlier.

It would seem appropriate, then, to neglect the timing of dentition as significantly correlated with normal growth and development in a useful fashion.

Neurobehavioral Milestones of Development in Childhood

In the search for normative milestones of bodily development, Gesell's neurobehavioral framework appears particularly relevant to clinical psychiatry. Charts summarizing Gesell's norms are presented in Knobloch and Pasamanick (1974). Gesell's schema, however, takes us only as far as about age 5; further, he omits examination for specific immature reflexes.

Developmental pediatricians such as Holt (1977), Illingworth (1980), and Tanner (1978a,b; Tanner and Whitehouse, 1982) may be drawn upon to complete our ladder of developmental milestones; Tanner's (1962) work on adolescence is unsurpassed.

At birth the normal baby behaves little differently from the baby lacking a cerebral cortex (Tanner, 1978a). However, the normal newborn baby's competences soon prove to be variegated (Illingworth, 1980, chapter 4): sight, hearing, even the sense of smell for the mother's body come into play quickly. Between 48 and 70 "primitive reflexes" have been described for the newborn, many of which disappear by 1 to 3 months. Stated differently, manifold reflexes can be elicited almost everywhere over the newborn's body, but soon the cortex begins to take over and to control and inhibit random rhythmic and reflex activity, starting from upper limbs and trunk. However, primitive reflexes necessary for survival, such as sucking, rooting, and palmar grasp, persist.

Gesell's neurobehavioral schema (Knobloch and Pasamanick, 1974) may be summarized as follows:

By 4 weeks of life the baby has control of his eye muscles, though he cannot support his own head; the tonic neck reflexes are present. By 16 weeks he can balance and support his own head steadily, and is competent at following a moving object with his eyes. By 28 weeks he can grasp and manipulate objects somewhat crudely and can sit leaning forward on his hands. By 40 weeks the child can sit upright, unsupported; can creep and poke at things, and can hold his own bottle. By 52 weeks (1 year) he can stand by himself, walk with help, and "cruise," that is, move, standing up, along a rail or wall which he uses for support. By 78 weeks (1½ years) the toddler walks without falling, can seat himself, is using words and phrases, and will scribble spontaneously if given writing materials. By 24 months (2 years) the child is capable of bowel and bladder control and can run well. By 36 months (3 years) he can stand on one foot and speak in sentences. By 48 months (4 years) the child can walk down stairs, one foot to a step, stand on one foot for at least 4 seconds, throw overhand, and dress and undress with supervision. Social and psychological behaviors are now becoming major test items. By 60 months (5 years) he can skip on alternate feet, stand on one foot for more than 8 seconds, and dress and undress alone. By 72 months (6 years) the child can jump from a 1-foot height and land on his toes, stand on alternate feet with eyes closed, throw competently, and tie shoe laces. He knows right from left, and social and psychological test items are of great importance in evaluation.

The Phenomena of Adolescence

Apart from steady growth, specific milestones have not been detailed for latency age. The next series of observable milestones comes with the whole process of puberty and adolescence, where growth takes a spurt and then ceases, and reproductive maturity is established. Tanner (1962, 1978a,b), the leading exponent on adolescent growth and development, uses the terms *puberty* and *adolescence* interchangeably; he notes that puberty originally meant the appearance of pubic hair.

The adolescent growth spurt takes place in most girls between 10 and 12 years, with broad limits of 8 to 14 years; and in most boys between 12 and 14 years, with broad limits of 10 to 16 years. Height ("distance achieved" and "velocity") curves are the most expressive of this period of rapid growth: peak velocity in girls is at 10 to 12 years and in boys 12 to 14 years. Peak velocity in weight gain comes rather later for girls, at 11 to 13 years (broad limits of 7 to 15 years), and at 12 to 14 (broad limits of 9 to 16½) for boys. Girls are not only temporarily taller than boys, due to their earlier growth spurt, but they have already been 2 years advanced over boys in skeletal age when adolescence arrives, findings for which Tanner advances some tentative evolutionary explanations.

The chief implications of understanding adolescent growth patterns lie in their individual variability and the influence this has on prediction. Thus, one can predict that a child with an accelerated developmental rate, resulting in an early growth spurt and puberty, will ultimately reach only the same adult size as a child showing slower development. Adult size reached will correlate with the size of the child's parents and with the child's own size in earlier childhood. Girls who have early puberty will stop growing earlier, despite their temporary "advantage" over boys or later-developing girls. The boy with a later growth spurt may be reassured that he will ultimately be a good-sized man (his size correlating with that of his parents and his own early childhood).

A striking demonstration of individual variations is in photographs shown by Tanner (1962) of three boys, all chronologically aged 14, but at very different stages of adolescence: one is a child, the second a teenager, the third a grown man; all ultimately reached normal manhood. Adults may in later years retain unresolved problems related to their size and sexual development during adolescence. Some will be convinced that they were underdeveloped and still are. Others wrestle with the problems of precocity, large size and physical power, and earlier sexual development than their peers.

Spectacular as is the burst of growth in body size at adolescence, two other rapid changes are as important, if not more so: changes in *shape*, the definitive divergence or dimorphism of the two sexes; and endocrine changes with the possession of new, powerful, sexual urges. The changes in body proportion are documented in great detail by Tanner (1962; Tanner and Whitehouse, 1982) whose indices and norms can be consulted. These include changes in skeletal proportions, such as relative broadening of shoulders in boys and of hips in girls, and changes in trunk to leg length. They include quantifiable changes in fatty subcutaneous tissue. Most particularly, they include quantifiable development of the secondary sexual characteristics: breasts, pubic hair, and menarche in girls; penis, testes, and pubic hair in boys. Norms for these can be consulted in Tanner (1962; Tanner and Whitehouse, 1982).

With the end of adolescence (18 years of age for practical purposes) bone maturity is reached, bodily growth has ceased, and sexual and reproductive maturity has been attained. We are now at the end of the "ladder" of growth and development against which many clinical regressions are to be measured. The basic machinery and tools of intelligence, motivation, socialization, and procreation are established.

Growth of the Brain

Postnatal growth curves for the brain are quite different in form from those for other organs or limbs or for the body as a whole. The rapid growth of early childhood levels off smoothly until it reaches an asymptote in adolescence. There is no adolescent spurt or peak in growth velocity (see Figure 2.2).

The Prehistoric Growth Spurt in Brain Size

Two great growth spurts have, however, preceded postnatal life. The first one occurred in the prehistory of our kind, in a setting of phylogenetic evolutionary and geologic time. The primates, to which our species belongs, have specialized in brain development: it is their single distinguishing feature. Our own distant ancestors took this specialization a quantum step further, and participated in a "spectacular increase in brain size in the 1 million years between 1.3 and 0.3 million years ago . . . even more astonishing because it does not involve a superficial structure but an organ as elaborate as the central nervous system" (p. 384) ". . . [which equally astoundingly] came to a sudden halt some 100 thousand to 200 thousand years ago" (p. 386) (Mayr, 1970). Young (1971) offers parallel comments. An interesting account of 230,000 years of the evolution of *Homo erectus* (Peking man) at Zhoukoudian near Beijing (Peking) is offered by Wu and Lin (1983). Here the fossil record shows progressive brain size increase, over the considerable segment of human evolution represented by these years, from some 900 cc to 1140 cc; it shows too some evidence of the cultural developments that paralleled brain growth.

Passingham (1982, chapters 1 and 4) reviews research on human brain size. This has grown from 500 cc in *Australopithecus* of 3 million years ago, through *Homo erectus* of 1.5 million years ago with a brain capacity of 800 cc, to *Homo sapiens neanderthalis* (Neanderthal man), and modern man *(Homo sapiens sapiens)* with their 1400 to 1500 cc brains. Passingham points out that, whatever ratios and quotients one may calculate, the human brain is, first, like other primate brains, and second, quite outstanding and unique among them. Brain size in itself does not support the weight of this argument, for there are animals with brains four (elephant) and five (whale) times the size of their human counterpart (see also discussions in Mayr [1970]; Young [1971]). A calculation first needs to be made relating the brain to total body size (the "encephalization quotient"); a prediction next needs to be made as to what size of brain will be expected in a given sized body; then finally it must be established where a given encephalization quotient, such as the human's, stands in relation to that of other creatures.

The human brain, by this calculation, is 3.1 times the size predicted for a nonhuman primate of human weight. Another ratio proposed by Passingham is that between the weight of the medulla, the oldest part of the brain, and the total brain. By this ratio the gap between the brain of the human and our closest relative, the chimpanzee, is greater than the gap between a chimpanzee's brain and a shrew's (a most primitive probable ancestor). From every aspect the finding is that the human brain *is* a primate brain, and that its remarkable size stems from development of "newer" brain structures (neocortex particularly) and not merely from proportional magnification of the whole ape brain.

While the attainment of this brain size in a very short period of evolutionary time, and the curiously sudden halting of the "growth spurt," cannot be explained by fossil evidence, the explanatory conjectures made in terms of evolutionary selection pressures are summarized by Mayr (1970): a sharp change in ecological habitat as the land dried and savannahs and deserts appeared; a consequent change from casual consumption of small game along with a vegetable diet to hunting big game as a systematic occupation; the necessity for tool making and social organization and cooperation, leading to speech; a breeding structure of small polygamous groups in which a dominant male could particularly well pass on traits of success; a new kind of parental care needing and permitting lengthy childhood. Passingham (1982) points out that there is no real evolutionary problem with the upright posture and grasping hand of man: tree-dwelling primates live in an upright position, and grasp rather than claw (as cats or squirrels) their way about. However, the anatomy of bipedal locomotion is another matter. Lovejoy (1988) summarizes evidence that human bipedality and its anatomical specializations were well established 3 million years ago; in fact the pelvis of *Australopithecus* was a more efficient one for upright walking than that of *Homo sapiens,* who has had to provide a wider pelvis with a larger birth canal as brain size grew. Lovejoy conjectures that this may have been a definitive step in the first truly human evolution, "among the first anatomical characteristics to mark the ascent to cognitive life" (p. 125). Lovejoy relates bipedality to the rise of the nuclear family and lasting monogamy, in a society where males "provisioned" the family by hunting and carrying high-energy food (in the form of game) home over long distances. One should note that this argument, differing in important respects from Mayr's, deals with evolutionary developments preceding the explosive growth of the human brain by 1 or 2 million years.

With the halting of evolutionary growth in brain size, human evolution currently concerns social and cultural rather than biological issues. We shall see in due course whether this social evolution, based on the remarkable brain we possess, will lead to our annihilating ourselves with environmental destruction and pollution or from nuclear holocaust, or not!

Intrauterine and Postnatal Growth Spurts

The "second" growth spurt of the brain is in the prenatal period of the individual fetus. The 10^{12} (or 1 million million) neurons have all made their appearance between 10 and 18 weeks postmenstrual, though like other immature cells they are mostly nucleus, with little cytoplasm or processes developed. No further neurons will appear during the lifetime of the individual. Growth of the brain is rapid up to 32 weeks where growth velocity is maximal, just as general bodily growth is slowing down due to uterine crowding. The neurons have filled out and are developing their complex processes. Glial cells have made their appearance and probably go on multiplying up to 2 years postnatally, when brain growth is at something like 10 percent of the 32-week prenatal velocity. By 1 year postnatally, the growth rate of the brain has already slowed down to 25 percent of that in the late prenatal period.

At birth the baby's brain is nearer adult weight than any other organ except possibly the eye. Passingham (1982) notes, however, that compared to other mammals it weighs a much smaller proportion of its adult weight. The whole brain of the newborn infant is about 25 percent of adult weight, at 1 year about 50 percent, at 2 years 75 percent, at 5 years 90 percent, and at 10 years 95 percent: this is the smooth growth curve so different from other bodily dimensions. This third growth spurt of early childhood, and the gradients of development of various areas of the brain, correlate well with what we now know of the origins and development of intelligence, as we shall see in the next chapter (see Figure 2.2).

Growth of the Neocortex

The growth of the neocortex, being the crucial feature of humankind among primates, deserves our particular interest. A primitive cortex is identifiable at 8 weeks (postmenstrual) and clearly visible with its basic cell layers by 26 weeks. The "primary" areas of cortex (see Figure 8.2, chapter 8) are the first to differentiate and develop. These in order of organization are: the primary motor area (precentral gyrus), the primary sensory area (postcentral gyrus), the primary visual area (calcarine fissure in occipital cortex), and the primary auditory area (superior temporal gyrus). The primary motor area for the arms and upper trunk appears histologically by 1 month after birth to be in a mature working state. The primary sensory area for the corresponding body parts follows shortly. Only by 2 years after birth do the motor and sensory areas for the legs appear to have caught up in their microscopic structure.

After these primary motor and sensory areas organize histologically, the "silent" or association areas of the brain, frontal, parietal, temporal, develop by a kind of radiation from the primary areas. The "visual analyzer" system seems to organize much earlier than the auditory, suggesting that visual competence comes early in the human baby, as well as reinforcing the construct that humans, like other primates, are visual creatures (Passingham, 1982, pp. 36–48). The reticular activating system, so closely related to awareness and thinking, is not completely myelinated until puberty. Tanner (1978a) relates many, or most, of these brain developments to what we now know of the progressive development of intelligence (see chapter 3).

Physiologically the brain has attained a mature state by the 32nd intrauterine week; changes occurring thereafter will proceed whether the baby is born prematurely or remains in utero.

We shall not here pursue the questions of lateralization and lateral dominance, because they are not of great clinical relevance. Right- or left-handedness is a rather specific feature of humans (Passingham, 1982, p. 95). The reader may pursue the subject further through Tanner (1978a,b), and Wexler (1980).

Human Sexual Dimorphism

Our social evolution currently involves much ferment concerning the social, political, and economic rights of women within the industrial or capitalist system. It thus seems important to investigate, as far as the data will take us at the moment, which components of female and male physique and personality are granted by nature and which are formed by life experience—the nature–nurture equation. In this chapter I shall focus mostly on nature, that is, on the product of the phylogenetic and of hereditary programming, and on the biological level of emergence; but we must heed Tanner's caveat, that the further

we proceed along the course of human growth and development, the more we must invoke nurture, including such determinants as nutrition, physical circumstances, parental care, and
social teaching.

How and why are girls and boys somatically different? The
term *sexual dimorphism* refers to differences in physical size and
form between the sexes. When apparent differences are lacking, for example, in the Canada Goose or Spotted Hyena (which
was once popularly supposed to be hermaphroditic, since even
the external genitalia of males and females look alike) the term
monomorphism applies. Sea lions are extremely dimorphic, the
grotesquely huge males sometimes crushing their mates and
offspring in their incessant fighting with other males. Generally
(Wilson, 1975), sexual dimorphism correlates with sexual competition among males and with polygamy or a "harem" system;
and monomorphism with cooperative, gregarious living, and
monogamy. Our nearer evolutionary relatives show both patterns. The gorilla is highly dimorphic and polygamous; the
gibbon is monomorphic and monogamous. Ninety-one percent
of birds are monogamous for the breeding season, and a number for life, such as the Canada Goose.

We humans seem to be intermediate in the animal kingdom, in being only moderately dimorphic. Our males are only
8 percent taller than our females, on average, and our females
are capable of all physical tasks. We are generally gregarious
and cooperative (we are the supremely social beings) and generally monogamous, though some societies are highly competitive
and some permit polygamy; in our own society males not infrequently joust with other males for female attention, and stray
into polygamy.

Dimorphism Is Established at Conception

I draw again heavily on Tanner (1978, a,b). Sexual dimorphism
commences at the very moment of conception: it is to be remembered that every cell in a female body is female, and every
cell in a male body is male, neurons, sex cells, and all. I shall
summarize here some very basic information, which the sophisticated reader may well gloss over. The maternal gametocyte,

being female, contains two X chromosomes, and it splits into two ova, each normally containing one X chromosome. The paternal gametocyte, being male, contains one X and one Y chromosome, so that on splitting, half the spermatozoa contain an X and half a Y. On fertilization, ovum and sperm combine so that each cell descending from this union contains either two X chromosomes, the female karyotype or genetic code (expressed XX) or an X and a Y, the male state (expressed XY). Abnormal splits and combinations can occur, though practically all embryos from such unions are not viable and are aborted early; few abnormal females and males survive, usually mentally retarded with sex chromosome counts such as XXX or XO (one too many and too few X chromosomes, both abnormal females) or XXY or XYY (abnormal males).

We need to remind ourselves that the basic or fundamental body form is the female's, as determined by the karyotype containing only X chromosomes. The Y chromosome, which commands the production of androgenic hormones, performs a variation upon this basic body type, and the modification becomes a male body.

Up to 9 weeks postmenstrual only chromosome examination will reveal the sex of the embryo: an undifferentiated gonad and external genital can be identified. The Y chromosome directs the undifferentiated gonad to become a testis, by 9 weeks, and at 11 weeks the testis has Leydig cells which are secreting testosterone, driven by chorionic gonadotrophin from the placenta. This testosterone then organizes the external genitalia as scrotum and penis, by 15 weeks recognizable in their complete form. Simultaneously the Sertoli cells in the new testis secrete the hormone which "erases" the female structures in the undifferentiated internal genitalia. Testosterone hereafter has a pervasive organizing influence upon the whole body as well as genital tract and brain.

The female internal genitalia, in the absence of testosterone, assume their "basic" or female form a week or two later than in the male. The Mullerian system and the external genitalia proceed to develop automatically, while the Wolffian system which is potentially male simply does not develop.

These important differences in the genitalia are what make up the absolute or qualitative differences between the sexes, as noted below.

Females Are Advanced Developmentally

The fundamental or basic female condition, apart from the slightly later differentiation of the genitalia, is one of developmental advance over its male counterpart; that is, testosterone in some way retards development. During the great fetal growth spurt of 20 to 30 weeks postmenstrual, the female fetus is already 3 weeks advanced compared to the male. At birth, though averaging 150 gm smaller than the male, the female is 4 to 6 weeks advanced in skeletal development. This lead continues through childhood. Girls reach 50 percent of adult height at age 1.75 years: boys only by 2.0 years. Though girls remain slightly smaller than boys, they reach puberty about 2 years earlier (10—12 years old), then surpass boys in size during their pubertal growth spurt; the boys overtake them in size during their pubertal growth spurt (12–14 years old).

Absolute and Relative Differences

Differentiation or dimorphism of the genitalia is, in normal children, an absolute or *qualitative* matter: the genitalia are *either* female or male. This usually very reliable dimorphism is the focus of attention of obstetrical staff and parents in declaring the baby's gender immediately upon its birth. A few babies are born with improperly developed or ambiguous external genitalia.

There are other, relative or *quantitative* differences in proportion between the sexes, which can be discerned prenatally but which are evident particularly after puberty (Tanner, 1962). The difference between biacromial and biiliac measurement reliably differentiates (in 90% of cases) women from men. Growth in height during puberty is mainly in the trunk, so that boys end up taller due to the extra 2 years their legs have had to lengthen. The growth spurt in the male larynx (a testosterone effect) brings a deepening of the voice. The beard, heavier body hair, and the outline of the pubic hair are also testosterone effects; baldness, very uncommon in women, is genetically sex-linked. Girls and women have a smoother distribution of body fat. Other less well-known differences include the ratio between length of arm to forearm (arm longer in women, forearm in men); carrying angle at elbow and knee (more acute in women); digital formula (index finger longer than ring finger in women, the reverse in men); and left- and right-handedness (women tend to be more marked in their preference for use of the right or left hand than men).

Dimorphism of the Human Brain

We can no longer speak simply of *the* human brain: rather, we have to learn to speak of the female brain or the male brain, such is the present knowledge of their relative differences in structure and function. These differences fall under the quantitative, not the absolute or qualitative heading; or, to put it another way, there are both overriding similarities and some differences of function and organization between women's and men's brains, with their implications for some innate affective and cognitive patterning. Although the human brain is grossly symmetrical, and there are no visible dissimilarities between female and male brain, we know now of *functional* asymmetries, both between halves of the brain and between the sexes.

Tanner notes the following paradox: it is testosterone which organizes the male brain, including the hypothalamus; testosterone, however, acts on the brain by first being transformed into an estrogen, estradiol; estradiol does not pass the blood–brain barrier and, hence, though circulating in females, does not influence the brain.

The male brain diverges from the female as soon as the new testis starts its secretion of testosterone (11 weeks postmenstrual). A number of psychomotor, cognitive, and affective–motivational or temperamental differences between girls and boys are summarized by Restak (1977, pp. 196–206); it must be assumed that the earlier these are found in life, the more likely it is that they are innate rather than acquired by the operant conditioning of early childhood. Their sum total is suggestive but so far we do not have the evidence to confirm a structural basis for them (see further in chapter 3).

The brain has one visible asymmetry in most persons; this is shared with the higher primates (Wexler, 1980). The planum temporale, the flat surface revealed on the upper surface of the temporal lobe when the brain is cut horizontally, is larger on the left side; the Sylvian fissure too is longer on that side (Passingham, 1978, p. 94). This correlates with the location of verbal centers in the left hemisphere of most persons, both left- and right-handed; uncommonly the verbal center is in the right hemisphere, probably resulting from some left-sided injury in early childhood and a transfer of verbal functions to the right (Penfield and Roberts, 1959; see also chapter 8).

Let me briefly summarize some of the differences found between the sexes which appear indicative of differential brain structure and function; I draw on Restak (1977), Tanner (1978a,b), and Inglis and Lawson (1984); see also chapter 3.

1. The female brain is a cycling one, compared to the steady state of the male. The female hypothalamus drives the familiar monthly cycle through the pituitary and ovaries.
2. The female brain also organizes puberty 2 years earlier than in the male. This precocity is found in many other animals, and raises unresolved questions about evolutionary advantages.
3. The male brain (i.e., hypothalamus) appears to be the base for more aggressive personality traits.
4. Lateral dominance is more pronounced in the female, whose right- or left-handedness is more specialized than in the male.
5. Girls are more expert in fine motor coordination, and boys in larger body movements.
6. Boys have a much higher incidence of stuttering and of learning disabilities than girls. Restak (1977) believes that this correlates with girls' superior verbal fluency and fine motor coordination, and Inglis and Lawson (1984) believe that it represents clear evidence of differential specialization in hemispheric verbal organization between the two sexes.

We shall return to this whole subject in the discussions of intellectual and cognitive development (chapter 3) and on states of brain injury (chapter 8).

Clinical and Research Implications

Based upon this developmental stream, a few examples may be suggested of problems encountered clinically, and which require research clarification. I shall marshal these under the two headings of fixations (injuries and defects in growth and development) and of regressions (breakdowns and reversions in established developmental functions). There are in fact very limited possibilities for regression in the dimension of somatic growth: the body and brain do not shrink to youthful size, the teeth do not recede, the male voice does not become treble. However, the soft tissues can assume immature proportions, and certainly more mature functions (e.g., reproductive ones) may regress. It is therefore development, rather than growth, which may regress. I would suggest that a developmental perspective may aid in further investigation of psychosomatics, the complex interplay of psychosocial variables and the soma in general medical illness.

Fixations

The "continuum of reproductive casualty" (Knobloch and Pasamanick, 1974, pp. 130–132 and 242–252) is a thought-provoking and heuristic construct. It pictures and implies a continuity between (1) chromosomal and embryonic disasters which are lethal in very early intrauterine life; (2) events during pregnancy culminating in abortion, stillbirth, and neonatal death; and (3) various injuries to the fetus from anoxia, toxemia, and dystocia. All of these result in general developmental defects, and all involve the central nervous system. The continuum of syndromes ranges from early to late death, through pervasive conditions such as cerebral palsy, autism, and mental retardation, to less general and disabling handicaps such as strabismus, hearing impairments, tics, behavioral and learning disabilities, and school accidents.

It is true, of course, that potentially disabling early developmental insults (and even some late ones) can be overcome, or greatly compensated for, by the time adult life is reached, such is the wonderful resiliency of the youthful body, including the brain, especially when abetted by a favorable milieu and good morale and motivation. We cannot yet tell whether some cases of potential autism or mental retardation were prevented by favorable circumstances in infancy. We do know that these pervasive developmental problems remain as a serious challenge to both clinical practice and research.

Regressions

Certain patients, usually elderly, will display during serious mental illness those primitive reflexes which can be elicited in profusion in young infants: palmar grasp, palmomental, snout, glabellar tap, and so on. These reflexes then disappear following successful treatment (Burra, Powles, Riopelle, and Ferguson, 1978). This clearly profoundly regressive phenomenon merits further careful research, though it is difficult to quantitate. It should, further, be possible to examine the seriously mentally ill (i.e., sufferers from functional psychoses) against the neurobehavioral norms of Gesell (see above), thus, to establish the kind of "regression age" discussed in chapter 1.

I select anorexia nervosa as exemplary for the study of psychosomatic interactions in a developmental light. The syndrome is considered a good paradigm for psychophysiological disorders (Garfinkel and Garner, 1982). Its incidence and prevalence have been steeply on the rise in Western European (including North American) society, and like many other psychophysiological disorders it is a serious and life-threatening condition. It is not normal at any age to flout the self-preservative urge by starving oneself. However, an examination of anorexia nervosa patients also suggests other truly regressive phenomena: cognitive and motivational style in particular. Cognitively, there are virtually delusional distortions of body image and bodily dimensions, compatible with preoperational intelligence; these in part impel the self-starvation (Garfinkel and Garner, 1982). These patients usually are locked into struggles for control and autonomy of the self, age-appropriate to the late anal period. Further, and this widespread clinical impression is confirmed by systematic observation and analysis (Garfinkel and Garner, 1982), the self-starvation achieves as a result a prepubertal body silhouette and the cessation of female reproductive functioning. Thus we have a grouping of regressions along cognitive and somatic developmental streams, and in terms of the life cycle, regression from adolescent or adult developmental tasks to those of early childhood; all of these are quantifiable using appropriate scales of development.

Bibliographic Notes: Key Readings

The principal exponents of this stream have been developmentally oriented pediatricians, of whom Tanner is the most impressive and definitive. As with Bowlby and Piaget, I find that his detailed, prolific work is not well known in North America. Every clinician should possess a copy of his readable, yet information-packed, digests of human somatic development, either or both *Fetus into Man* (1978a) and *Education and Physical Growth* (2nd edition, 1978b). His *Atlas of Children's Growth*, with Whitehouse (Tanner and Whitehouse, 1982), his classic on *Growth at Adolescence* (1962), and his "History of the Study of Human Growth" (1981) are also highly recommended.

For a far-ranging presentation on the human condition, with special reference to our primate status, Passingham (1982) is most stimulating reading. Should the reader wish to range even further into the realm of biological processes and principles and physical anthropology, Mayr (1978) and Young (1971) are remarkable general resources.

Restak's (1977, pp. 196–206) compact summary of sex differences in the human, though now somewhat dated, is a good guide. Inglis and Lawson (1984) offer a relatively nonjargonistic review guide to the dimorphism of the female and male brains, and Wexler's review (1980) of cerebral lateralization is detailed, yet clear.

For those requiring an encyclopedic source, the two compendia of Falkner (1966) and Falkner and Tanner (1978a,b,c, 3 volumes) contain chapters by many experts, including much relatively non-time-bound material.

References

Burra, P., Powles, W. E., Riopelle, R. J., & Ferguson, M. (1980), Atypical psychosis with reversible primitive reflexes: A case report. *Can. J. Psychiat.*, 125:74–77.

Demirjian, A. (1986), Dentition. In: *Human Growth: A Comprehensive Treatise*, ed. J. M. Tanner & F. T. Falkner, 2nd ed., Vol. 2. New York: Plenum Press, chap. 12, pp. 269–298.

Falkner, F. T. (1966), General considerations in human development. In: *Human Development, by 29 Authorities*, ed. F. F. Falkner. Philadelphia: W. B. Saunders, chap. 10, pp. 10–39.

———— Tanner, J. M., eds. (1978a), *Human Growth: A Comprehensive Treatise*, 2nd ed., *Vol. 1: Developmental Biology, Prenatal Growth*. New York: Plenum Press, 1986.

———— ———— eds. (1978b), *Human Growth: A Comprehensive Treatise*, 2nd ed., *Vol. 2: Postnatal Growth, Neurobiology*. New York: Plenum Press, 1986.

———— ———— eds. (1978c), *Human Growth: a Comprehensive Treatise*, 2nd ed., *Vol. 3: Methodology, Ecological, Genetic, and Nutritional Effects on Growth*. New York: Plenum Press, 1986.

Garfinkel, P. E., & Garner, D. M. (1982), *Anorexia Nervosa: A Multidimensional Perspective*. New York: Brunner/Mazel.

Holt, K. S. (1977), *Developmental Paediatrics*. London: Butterworth.

Illingworth, R. S. (1980), *The Development of the Infant and Young Child: Normal and Abnormal*, 7th ed. Edinburgh: Churchill Livingstone.

*Inglis, J., & Lawson, J. S. (1984), Sex differences and the brain. *Queen's Quarter.*, 91:37–54.

Knobloch, H., & Pasamanick, B., eds. (1974), *Gesell and Amatruda's Developmental Diagnosis*, 3rd ed. Hagerstown, MD: Harper & Row.

Lovejoy, C. O. (1988), Evolution of human walking. *Scient. Amer.*, 259:118–125.

Marubini, E., & Milani, S. (1986), Approaches to the analysis of longitudinal data. In: *Human Growth: A Comprehensive Treatise*, ed. J. M. Tanner & F. T. Falkner, Vol. 1, New York: Plenum Press, chap. 4, pp. 79–94.

*Mayr, E. (1970), *Populations, Species, and Evolution*. Cambridge, MA: Harvard University Press.

*Passingham, R. E. (1982), *The Human Primate*. Oxford: W. H. Freeman.

Penfield,W., & Roberts, L. (1959), *Speech and Brain-Mechanisms*. Princeton, NJ: Princeton University Press.

*Restak, R. M. (1977), *The Brain: The Last Frontier*. Garden City, NY: Doubleday.

*Tanner, J. M. (1962), *Growth at Adolescence*, 2nd ed. Oxford: Blackwell.

*———— (1978a), *Fetus into Man: Physical Growth from Conception to Maturity*. Cambridge, MA: Harvard University Press

*———— (1978b), *Education and Physical Growth,* 2nd ed. New York: International Universities Press.

*———— (1981), *A History of the Study of Human Growth.* Cambridge, UK: Cambridge University Press.

*———— Whitehouse, R. H. (1982), *Atlas of Children's Growth: Normal Variation and Growth Disorders.* London: Academic Press.

*Wexler, B. E. (1980), Cerebral laterality and psychiatry. *Amer. J. Psychiat.,* 137:279–291.

Wilson, E. O. (1975), *Sociobiology: The New Synthesis.* Cambridge, MA: Belknap Press/Harvard University Press.

Wu, R., & Lin, S. (1983), Peking man. *Scient. Amer.,* 248:86–94.

*Young, J. Z. (1971), *An Introduction to the Study of Man.* Oxford: Oxford University Press.

---

*Recommended readings.

3

A Second Developmental Stream: Measured Intelligence and Cognitive Development; Intellectual and Motivational Sex Differences

Introduction

Overview

Intellectual functioning, as it is relevant to clinical psychiatry, can be approached in two main ways, both highly developmental in character.

"Measured Intelligence" is the ability to solve problems of various grades of difficulty, a power or potential which can be estimated and reported quasi-quantitatively, using standardized measures. Measured intelligence grows along a time curve which generally resembles the curve for the growth of head and brain during childhood (Figure 2.2, chapter 2). Thus, while the brain is still growing, measured intelligence represents a function of age. Once the brain ceases growth the curve of

63

intellectual growth also reaches an asymptote, and new statistical methods are required in reporting measured intelligence. The formulas of mental age and intelligence quotient express in numbers what a person (child or adult) can master in comparison with norms for his or her chronological age.

Clinically, measured intelligence in a testable patient tells us very little of that person's mental health. There is a low correlation between intelligence quotient and success in the life cycle, or failure and delinquency. Further, in testable ill subjects, measured intelligence is depressed only a little by problems in attention and concentration, and formal testing offers us little differential information about the current disorder. It is only in states of brain damage (see chapter 8) that certain intellectual functions are measurably lost. Therefore, since the clinical relevance of measured intelligence is relatively sparse, I shall confine treatment of the vast literature on the subject to historical notes on two pioneer exponents, Alfred Binet and David Wechsler, and their contributions.

The other main approach to intellectual functioning is the cognitive, the examination of style of knowing (*cognoscere* = to know), remembering, estimating, judging, reasoning. For clinical purposes we use this approach when we speak of judgment, insight, depressive cognitions, and so on; that is, how the patient formulates external and internal experience or "reality," not merely the patient's answers or conclusions, but the method of registering information and processing it. Qualitative shifts in judgment, insight, or "reality testing" occur in all grades of psychiatric disorder. It is not true that reality testing is impaired only in the psychoses. In these disorders we do indeed locate clear, gross evidences of egocentric or autistic interpretations of reality, usually in a concrete and delusional mode. In paranoid, depressive, and euphoric disorders we find a narrowed, stereotyped range of interpretations of reality, again with a somewhat concrete and idiosyncratic quality. And in the neuroses, where it has been classically taught that reality testing is intact, we can locate more subtle but identifiable misjudgments; for example, regarding the body and its malfunction, or regarding the motives and moral responsibilities of the self and others. As for cognitive alterations in states of brain damage, these will be further examined in chapter 8.

The only unified major body of research and theory for this cognitive domain, as developed by Jean Piaget, has been surprisingly neglected in British and North American psychiatry.

Piaget operates almost wholly at a psychological level of emergence. He implies that cognitive development parallels the growth of brain complexity, and he clearly assumes that the material and social milieu have an active role in an interplay with the developing brain. Nonetheless, unlike Luria (1932), a close contemporary, Piaget pays scant attention to social processes in stimulating cognitive development.

Piaget's principal themes are fairly well known: cognitive intelligence emerges from the total egocentrism of the baby via motor activity, or at least the actional aspects of experience; it traverses nonverbal, nonrepresentational stages having a strongly concrete and egocentric character; symbolic representation and socialization interact toward a final product which is highly sophisticated, objective, and capable of abstraction, speculation, and hypotheticodeductive thought.

Our challenge is to use Piaget's frame of reference in constructing a quasi-quantitative measuring instrument for examining psychiatric patients. I offer a few examples of such a possibility. We already use clinical tests of abstraction and classification, for instance; I believe Piaget's work adds considerable interpretive depth here. Such constructs as "projective space," with its relationship to interpersonal egocentricity, appear fruitful for clinical application.

Finally, we need to enquire into what is known of sex differences in intellectual function. Here we draw on three sources: problems in the construction of general intelligence tests; large-scale surveys of studies on sex differences; and findings derived from examination of brain-injured women and men. In the standardization of intelligence tests, certain subtests have to be rejected, or balanced up by others, since generally females are favored in verbal problem-solving tasks, and males in arithmetical ones. Although these differences are not large, they are significant. This is confirmed in the classical survey of Maccoby and Jacklin who, despite their great interest in social learning, have to conclude that innate differences are important. I look to Eagly (1987), also a social psychologist, for an updating of methods of analysis of sex differences, mostly in the area of temperament and style, as well as in the intellectual. She demonstrates a method combining the new "meta-analysis" with a sharpened focus on real-life social role behavior. These authors deal with temperamental and motivational sex differences, which are difficult to separate from the intellectual; therefore I include this group of variables here, somewhat arbitrarily.

Finally, work stemming from examination of brain-injured adults and of children with learning disorders by Inglis, Ruckman, Lawson, MacLean, and Monga (1982), Inglis and Lawson (1984) and colleagues strongly suggests that the two cerebral hemispheres function differently in the two sexes.

Measured Intelligence

Orientation

Binet (Binet and Simon, 1916, p. 182) urged us to desist from endless debate over what intelligence is, and to proceed forthwith in attempts to measure it.

That is to say, intelligence *is* what is measured by standard test items of increasing difficulty. Measured intelligence has a fundamental relation to growth and development. Binet, who fairly may be called its discoverer, proceeded from a developmental basis, as did his followers: the gradient of intellectual development in children was the fundamental instrument or yardstick. Later on, Wechsler, attempting to deal with adult intellectual capacity, when a growth gradient no longer exists, resorted to an actuarial and normative approach to individual differences in adult populations.

Alfred Binet: Discoverer of Intellectual Measurement

Since we have long taken for granted the concept that measured intelligence is a function of development, I elect here to reexamine Binet's discoveries in this field. Then we can consider more briefly the work of Wechsler, the pioneering exponent of the actuarial approach to adult intelligence. The following biographical note is drawn from sections in Sattler (1974) and Matarazzo (1972). Alfred Binet (1857–1911) was a kind of gentleman adventurer in the psychological realm. Independently wealthy, son of a physician, he rejected medicine for the study of law, took a doctorate in biology, and after somewhat erratic incursions into hypnosis and abnormal psychology, became in 1895 Director of the Laboratory of Physiological Psychology of the Ecole Pratique des Hautes Etudes in Paris. Thereafter, he remained a clinical and educational psychologist. By the turn of the century he was groping with assessment of global functions such as memory, attention, and imagination, having become convinced that in global functions, rather than molecular ones such as reaction time, lay the key to individual human differences.

Thanks to what seems to have been Binet's temperamental traits of gregariousness and leadership in his working milieu, he was constantly becoming aware of and incorporating ideas from colleagues and collaborators. One of these was Theodore Simon, a physician who had done anthropometric studies on retarded boys, and who became Binet's lieutenant and successor. Challenges in the educational system led Binet and Simon to methods of assessing grades of subnormal intelligence, which up to that time had been classified by soft and rather subjective criteria. He made a submisssion to the Ministry of Public Instruction, whereupon he was appointed to a commission to carry out his own suggestions; namely, that systematic methods be developed for grading the mentally retarded in the school system, and for offering special instruction to the educable among them. I present here the three versions of the Binet–Simon scales as they illustrate steps in the evolution of Binet's concepts of measured intelligence and its relation to chronological development.

The First Scale. In 1905, indebted to Blin and Damaye (Binet and Simon, 1916, pp. 10, 28–36), Binet published a first assessment scale, a list of 30 question topics or psychomotor tasks, of increasing sophistication and difficulty (Binet and Simon, 1916, pp. 37–181). The intent here was still one of qualitatively separating out three grades of mental retardation, but the underlying theoretical framework was clearly one of relating this to normal intellectual development and capacities at ages up to 11 years.

The Second Scale. In 1908, after much observation and testing, a revision was published. Here the norms and age levels are presented even more clearly. The emphasis is still on grading the retarded. A new concept, mental age, first makes its appearance (Binet and Simon, 1916, pp. 270–272), though somewhat implicitly.

The Third Scale: Mental Age. Just before his untimely death in 1911 (and we are left with many questions around Binet's potential greatness had he survived into old age as Piaget did) a third revision appeared. This time a much clearer quantitative aspect was introduced. Five questions, topics, or tasks, are given for each of eight age levels (6, 7, 8, 9, 10, 12, 15, and adult). A quasi-quantitative score or mental age is computed by adding all the questions or tasks passed successfully, so that a degree of refinement (which Binet carefully repudiates!) to one-fifth of a year in mental age becomes possible. Thus it becomes feasible to state measured intelligence as a mental age for mathematical comparison with chronological age. Normal and gifted children in school, and army recruits, now became a much more general focus of attention, though identifying the retarded was still the key requirement.

The Intelligence Quotient and Binet's Methods. What Binet would have thought of the Intelligence Quotient (I.Q.) proposed by Stern in 1912 (cited in Matarazzo [1972, pp. 95, 119]) is open to question. This construct was the numerical value obtained in dividing the mental age by the chronological age and multiplying by 100. Binet, it seems certain, would have deplored and fought the glorification of the I.Q., for he was always at pains to point out that measured intelligence (mental age) was an artificial construct; and that although it should be estimated or tested for with great care, formal testing was but one way of studying intelligence. The three methods he believed should always be combined were the medical, the pedagogical, and the psychological, in that order (Binet and Simon, 1916, p. 40) though he explicates these in reverse order (Binet and Simon, 1916, pp. 70–90). The medical method includes careful physical examination, as applicable particularly to the retarded. The pedagogical method refers to actual classroom performance. The psychological refers to formal testing toward a measured intelligence or mental age. Not only does Binet emphasize this assessment tripod, he carefully notes the influence of social conditions on variations of intelligence (Luria, 1932).

The Further Course of Intelligence Testing

Thus, though Binet is the originator of intellectual measurement and of the construct of mental age, and indirectly of the intelligence quotient, he remained a patient and devoted clinician, interested in the whole person and a balanced, thorough, multifactorial assessment of that person, an approach to measured intelligence which is still of fundamental importance to the clinical psychologist and the practicing psychiatrist. In contrast we may note a later tendency to exalt the I.Q. as if it were an objective fact (as height or weight are), to classify the individual inflexibly as a point on a statistical curve, and to base important clinical or educational decisions on I.Q. alone. Such a tendency has been an unfortunate outcome of two necessary and useful endeavors: research in the academic setting on large human populations, and the need for group tests to sort out individual abilities under the pressures of wartime.

Shortly after Binet's third revision and his death, a spate of research on measured intelligence began to pour forth. Two world wars added impetus to such research, and provided a trove of data for further research. Research issues over the next 30 years included such questions as: Is measured intelligence learned or innate (the nature–nurture controversy)? Do different races have different intelligence levels? How do education and social conditions influence intelligence? Is intelligence a global, integrated function or an aggregate of special capacities, or both? Does intelligence remain stable or decline through life? As I have noted, the literature is vast, and because of its limited clinical relevance, we shall not pursue it further, except for the issue of differences in intellectual capacity and cognitive style as between women and men, which we examine below.

David Wechsler and Adult Intelligence

We pass to the 1930s when the present-day methodology of intellectual appraisal was being worked out, and, because of his dominant position, to the work of David Wechsler (see Matarazzo, [1972], pp. 72–76, for biographical sketch; and Wechsler [1958]). For many years the chief psychologist at Bellevue Hospital in New York, Wechsler perceived the limitations of the developmental approach to intelligence, especially in the testing of adults whose intellectual capacities had reached an asymptote years previously. Wechsler pointed out that the usual computation for the intelligence quotient, which is

> Intelligence Quotient (I.Q.) = Mental Age (M.A.) divided by Chronological Age (C.A.)

should really read

> I.Q. = Attained or Actual Test Score divided by Expected Mean Score for Age

In other words, mental and chronological age are just two scores expressed in a notation of age units which have no intrinsic value of their own. Also, because of the problems of coping with a growth curve for intelligence that is anything but linear (see Figure 2.2, chapter 2) Wechsler struck out on a new approach. By 1939, when he published the Wechsler–Bellevue Intelligence Scale, he had adopted a thoroughly statistical or actuarial system; I.Q. 100 was to be the arbitrarily established mean score. Fifty percent of the population was to fall in the average range I.Q. 90–110, by placing 90 and 110 at the two points one probable error from the mean. By repeated trials, testing large samples of subjects, and varying the subtests employed, Wechsler standardized an instrument that would indeed "measure" where any individual falls in relation to his age peers. That is, although he retained the intelligence quotient as a practical short-hand statement of intellectual capacity, I.Q.s would be assigned by a formula of scores and their deviation from the mean-for-age; that is, deviation scores or deviation quotients. Such an approach obviates fictions required by Binet's original developmental method; for example, a mental age of 20 obtained by a 15-year-old, when the average mental age for 20-year-olds is 15; or the necessity of assigning an arbitrary chronological age of 16 in a 45-year-old, since, up to Wechsler's time, various arbitrary chronological ages from 14 to 18 had been used to compute the I.Q.s of adults.

A major point raised again and again by Matarazzo is this: Wechsler, like Binet before him, was a patient clinician, dealing in depth with individual cases as well as researching cohorts. Wechsler, as Binet, stressed that measured intelligence is only a part of clinical assessment, having an imperfect correlation with how well an individual performs in real life, where "nonintellective factors" are significant contributors. In fact, intellectual measurement tells us almost nothing about why one person does well in life, and another is a derelict; or conversely (as noted above) why rather severely disabled people can do relatively well on testing. We therefore have to examine an entirely different approach to functioning intelligence which may be revealed in major part in the work of Jean Piaget.

"Cognitive Style" in Relation to Growth and Development: Jean Piaget

Orientation

Piaget's roving and precocious genius (his principal education was as a biologist) was captured for his life work when Simon (Binet's collaborator) engaged him in the study of intelligence in Paris schoolchildren (Miller, 1983, p. 32). He was soon deep into an infatuation with the thought processes of these children; their incorrect answers to test questions intrigued him, and his clinical method was born. For 60 years, through 40 books and hundreds of papers, assisted by many students and collaborators of whom his senior colleague and successor, Bärbel Inhelder, deserves particular note, Piaget explored every conceivable permutation of the questions, How do children know? and How does intelligence unfold? Technically, his work is "genetic epistemology": genetic, because highly developmental in orientation; epistemology, because it involves that branch of philosophy dealing with the nature of knowledge. Piaget has called his work "a sort of embryology of intelligence" (quoted in Miller, 1983, p. 33). While any attempt at a brief summary of Piaget's gigantic corpus of ideas is a risky one, nevertheless, we must try to capture some essence of his approach, his findings, and his formulations.

Piaget's Methods

How did Piaget go about his work? He observed a few babies and very small children over a period of years and in microscopic detail, starting with his own three children. He left the field of 2 to 4 years of age least tilled of all his work. With children able to communicate in words (i.e., 4 years upward) he developed a clinical method of interviewing his young subjects in semistandardized fashion, while at the same time setting them tests or experiments of infinitely ingenious variety. His interest was always to find out how children think, reason, and know, not merely how they performed the experiment or what end result they generated. This clinical method, because it was flexible and shifted from one child to another, and because it probed subjective experience, has been criticized as soft or unscientific. It is difficult to know how Piaget might have studied thought processes otherwise. He has also been criticized for intermingling theory and observation in his reporting. Clearly, the critical reader must decide upon the validity of his major propositions. It may be of help to recall the components in Piaget's many-faceted genius. He was, first and perhaps foremost, a biologist: biological principles keep reappearing throughout his work. He immersed himself in clinical and educational psychology under Binet, and like Binet eschewed the narrowly controlled testing approach: he considered himself a "psychologue." His central interest became the development of knowledge and reasoning in children: thus, he combined psychology and philosophy in an era when these two disciplines were still separating. But if anyone doubts his scientific modernity, his use of Boolean algebra and his daunting mathematical models of thinking should be reassuring.

Piaget and his students examined, and conducted investigations upon, all the categories of knowledge recognized by epistemologists: space, time, movement, causality; quantity, mathematics; play, language, logic, and morality (an area overlapping with ethics). In addition, Piaget carried out "minors" of great interest, on perception, memory, and will (Piaget, 1961; Gruber and Vonèche, 1977; Miller, 1983, p. 67). Affective and motivational elements are not widely reported in his work, though he certainly does not exclude these as valid components of experience, or indeed of cognitive functioning; for example, the consistent urge to explore. He clearly does not deal with the influences of social and familial variables: he appears to ignore the superior intellectual conditions under which his own children (as subjects of observation) grew up; or the social class and gender of the boys whom he studied for their development of moral and legal judgment (see chapter 6). Such elements in Piaget's work probably require a corrective such as the work of his contemporary Luria (1932). This author, who managed successfully to resist reductionist Pavlovian psychology, has pictured very convincingly the influence of postrevolutionary changes in the U.S.S.R. upon modes of thinking in rural people. Working in rural villages of Uzbekistan and Kirghizia in the 1920s, Luria correlated changes in the economy, the elimination of illiteracy, an expansion in world view, and a decline in traditional Muslim influence, with a measurable shift from concrete, graphic modes of cognition to abstract, verbal, and logical ones, in young adults.

Piaget's Basic Findings and Principles

First, intelligence is neither solely determined by learning nor innately and genetically programmed: intelligence evolves in an evolving interaction between the developing child and the environment, as the brain reaches readiness for increasingly complex and integrated experience, and as the child is driven by a constant urge to reach out and explore (see discussion in chapter 1). Knowledge is an activity or process, not a state: the acting of the knower upon the known. Not surprisingly, Piaget concludes that intelligence arises from and grows upon a foundation of motor activity, in a way which no other investigator has stressed. Related to this is one of the most plausible explanations of play in the life of children: play is the beginning of thinking. Though Piaget did not say this, to my knowledge, he may well have related these concepts to the function of the frontal lobes which are an outgrowth of our motor brain.

Second, the development of intelligence is a progression from the simplest, crudest, most concrete sensorimotor activity in the small baby, through various intermediate stages and periods, to the capacity for wholly reflective, hypotheticodeductive, abstract thinking in the adolescent and adult. Piaget was a strong developmentalist and structuralist. His developmental principles are strongly congruent with Werner's (see Baldwin, 1968, as noted in chapter 2): progression from the crude, simple, undifferentiated, to the complex, sophisticated, differentiated but integrated. His structural principles are emphatic: extremely simple organizations or schemas in infancy give way (the epigenetic principle) to increasingly complex and embracing ones through childhood, exemplified in his difficult logico-mathematical models.

Third, there are key processes or "invariants" in cognitive development. They are common to all living beings: Piaget, as noted, was consistently a biologist. The two major invariants are organization and adaptation. Organization evolves, pervading and guiding all growth through all stages and periods. Organization is the inward aspect of development. Adaptation is the outward aspect, the interface in interaction with the environment. We should know now that Piaget would see adaptation, not as passive, but as active and dynamic, striving for equilibrium without and within. Adaptation, and the growth in childhood of which it is a formative ingredient, appears in two forms: assimilation and accommodation. Assimilation, a concept applicable physiologically to nutrition and metabolism, is the processing, "digestion," breaking down, and absorption of experience, fitting it to the templates of previous experience (schemes, structures). When a rabbit eats cabbage, the cabbage becomes rabbit, not vice versa—"that's assimilation," joked Piaget (Miller, 1983, p. 72). Assimilation consistently fits facts to the self, bends or distorts experience. When the strain of assimilation is too great, the organism must yield to the data of experience and fit, bend, or change itself, create some new adaptive device, alter its templates to new circumstances: this is accommodation. Growth proceeds in thousands of daily assimilations and accommodations. At the high points of development there is dynamic equilibrium between the two (see Figure 3.1).

Fourth, although cognitive development is a continuous movement, there are important qualitative epochs and plateaux of achievement in the process. Piaget does not claim that there are any abrupt discontinuities in the developmental pathway. What he does suggest is that development is not a linear or plane curve, but a kind of three-dimensional spiral whose track comes back repeatedly to points of previous achievement, but each time at a higher level. The child reaches certain points of competence or autonomy (the high point of equilibration noted in the last paragraph) then destabilizes again as his own internal growing resources and external life experience force new adaptations. A new cycle of struggle and growth ensues, ending in a new, but more sophisticated mastery and equilibrium. I attempt to depict this developmental spiral in Figure 3.1.

These cycles in the spiral are the developmental periods which Piaget has outlined. In contrast to the thousands of day-by-day assimilations and accommodations by which we grow in molecular fashion, these major periods extend over years. A brief sketch of them will now follow: the reader must consult the cited works for proper detail and further exposition.

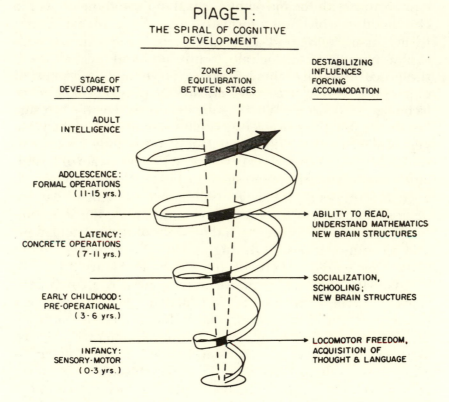

Figure 3.1. Piaget: the Spiral of Cognitive Development

Cognitive development, according to Piaget, is best viewed, not as a simple linear progression, but as a spiral which keeps coming back to a point of equilibration (between assimilation and accommodation) as each stage is completed. Internal and external influences, suggested here, force new accommodations as the next stage commences.

Periods in the Spiral of Cognitive Development

Infancy: Sensorimotor Intelligence

Infancy, from birth to about 2 years, is termed the *sensorimotor period,* or period of sensorimotor intelligence, for the reason that it precedes the development of true thought and language, that is, the ability to deal with symbols and images. The new-born operates with a multitude of reflexes (see chapter 2) which are perfected by repetition but rather quickly give over into more organized, purposive activity. The very young baby is believed to have no sense of awareness, no consciousness of either self or the outside world: the solipsistic position (see chapter 5). She probably begins to experience her universe as a kind of moving picture going on about her (Bruner, 1968), since visual competence is advanced in babies. By 4 months a baby is coordinating visual experience with motor competence so that she can bring her thumb to her mouth to suck success-fully. Rhythmic, stereotyped activity is beginning to give way to intent and purpose. By 8 months the baby can do simple things intentionally to her environment. She shows recognition of fa-miliar objects by making a kind of motor sign or signal. Her "thinking" consists of running through familiar motor patterns (such as a repertoire of grasping, sucking) or through sensory ones (a repertoire of looking, hearing). Now she begins to com-bine her schemas to produce and prolong events of interest to her, or to produce new and novel events.

Although the baby "recognizes" familiar objects and people at 8 months, she cannot cope actively with their disappearance: she whimpers if important objects disappear, loses interest if unimportant ones disappear, and that is all. She does not, ap-parently, remember them mentally, and she does not search for them. After 12 months the baby begins actively to experi-ment with a large variety of objects, new and old. She identifies specific parent figures and she searches stereotypically for lost objects and persons, evidently remembering their whereabouts in some fashion. This stage would appear to coincide with the beginning of object constancy, attachment, and separation anxi-ety as described by Bowlby (1969; see also chapter 5). The terms *memory* or *remember* are a misnomer in such a context. The baby's mental structures are sensorimotor ones: organized collections of sensations and motor patterns of both personal and external actions: things to suck, things that roll, things that taste cold, things that make one smile and kick. Piaget's term for these is *schemes* or *schemata,* a central but never explicitly defined construct.

The sensorimotor period is divided by Piaget into half a dozen rapidly evolving "stages," each with a conceptual title. We shall not enumerate these here. They are full of interesting developments and complexities which Miller (1983) summarizes briefly and well, and Piaget (Piaget and Inhelder, 1966), Baldwin (1968), and Flavell (1963) describe in additional detail.

By 18 months the guidance schemata, still very concrete and sensorimotor in nature, are becoming increasingly ingenious; for example, there is simple tool-using, such as pulling on a string or cloth to bring objects closer; simple and repeated experiments on the trajectories of moving and falling objects; tracing the position of things that are out of view. A kind of motor "thinking-out-loud," rather than crude trial and error, is pursued in solving problems, and is a precursor of thought and speech. Mimicry can recall objects not in the immediate present, or suggest even a few simple ideas; this is the beginning of representation.

By 2 years a baby has completed the first round and ascent in the spiral of knowledge and mastery, and achieved the first equilibrium: a clear framework of space and causality, a clear view of the continued existence and position of objects out of view, an ability to function in a predictable world, obeying lawful interactions, peopled by identifiable and interacting objects including the self. This toddler lacks one very important faculty, but she does not yet know how much she is missing: the ability to symbolize and communicate, or speech and thought. In her developmental spiral she is now in a new egocentrism: the unawareness of how little she knows compared to older children and adults. A new ability to communicate becomes the stress which disequilibrates the achievement of the sensorimotor spiral and leads to the next period (this disequilibration is represented in some of the phenomena of the "terrible twos").

Early Childhood: Preoperational Intelligence

Early childhood, from about 2 to about 7 years of life, is termed the *preoperational period* or period of preoperational intelligence. What does "preoperational" mean? and what is an "operation"? By "operation" Piaget means an action upon a problem of a systematic, logical, thoughtful kind, based upon a well-organized mental frame of reference or "structure," such as a multiplication table, a taxonomic system of classification, or an inductive-deductive flow chart. The preoperational period is the long and transitional period of preparation which intervenes between sensorimotor and operational intelligence. It leads from the very concrete acting upon the world of the infant (note again that Piaget regards sensation as an acting upon things) to the logical analysis and synthesis (within the child's mind) of the latency and teenage youngster. We shall return to the concepts of operation and structure with the two subsequent periods.

The bridge into the preoperational period, and also the destabilizing force which stimulates and drives it, is the acquisition of representational thought. Piaget (with others) terms this the *semiotic function;* that is, having to do with signaling. It is the process, the activity, of representing concrete things, situations, and ultimately complex and abstract concepts, within the mind and interpersonally by signs and symbols, or signifiers. Piaget defines signs as arbitrary labels which carry no intrinsic hint of the signified; for example, "desk," "algebra," "relativity," a red flag or light meaning "stop." Symbols contain a hint or allusion: "hum," "yodel," a gesture for flying or shooting, a road sign for a curve. (There is a fundamental inconsistency in the literature on the definition of these two terms, but for the present I shall follow Piaget's terminology.)

Piaget, unlike some other theorists, concludes that thought precedes speech: the ability to think precedes the ability to talk, and we cannot teach concepts such as "more," "taller," or "same" by teaching the words (Miller, 1983, p. 55). He places the acquisition of semiotic functions in this order: mimicry, symbolic play, drawing, speech, and mental imagery. These unfold rather quickly in the transition from sensorimotor to preoperational. Piaget considers that mimicry is the sensorimotor achievement which precedes the others, which are early developments of a preoperational kind. Like other stagings or sequences, Piaget considers that mimicry has to come before play, play before drawing, drawing before speech, and speech before the ability to form and retain truly mental images. Until about age 4 even mental images are very simple and static.

The child enters the preoperational period with the new egocentrism noted above: unable to recognize the views and superior knowledge of others, using speech in essentially a noncommunicative way. The beginning of thinking is at first rigid and static, able to focus only on fixed states, single features of a situation, unable to retrace sequences backward to beginnings (a lack of "reversibility"). Reasoning is semilogical or prelogical, full of capricious jumps and conclusions, mystical, inconsistent, anthropomorphic, intuitive, impulsive. These qualities are what seem to give Piaget's mini-interviews with his young subjects their delightful quality.

The preoperational child has very limited social *cognition*. He is confused between natural and human events and concerning the identity of persons whose appearance has changed. In moral judgment, his focus is on externals. By the end of the period the child is able to think in functions (i.e., that x varies as y), regulations (tentative compensations for the previously rigid fixation on states) and identities (things or people are the same despite changing appearances).

Let me give some brief examples to illustrate the above abstractions. A preoperational girl can find her way expertly to and from school; but when asked to explain how she does it (categories of space, logic) she responds with a charming series of nonsequiturs which can only thoroughly confuse the asker. Invited to draw and then explain the working of a bicycle, (causality, logic) a little boy gives a mixture of a listing of its parts with quite mystical explanations of what makes the whole machine operate. Asked to depict what others could see, from different angles, of a model of three mountains, a child keeps reporting her own fixed view of the mountains, or she presents seriously distorted views from other angles (egocentrism in regard to projective space).

The preoperational child thus flounders at first with the newfound skills of mental representation and language. But his egocentrism spares the little one the pain of insight into just how much he is floundering. Next he progressively organizes and integrates these new skills with his previous excellent psychomotor expertise. His egocentrism steadily melts away: as he interacts with older peers and adults, he learns to appreciate their points of view and thus (assimilation–accommodation) his general learning is facilitated and enriched. A focus on the self, with a narrowly personal viewpoint (which coincides with limited, "rigid," "centered," views and perspectives on people, things, and events) gives way to the ability to focus on multiple and shifting aspects of a situation, processes rather than states. His organization of spatial percepts progressively becomes more mature: he becomes able to draw graphically with some perspective, and to represent states of motion. In general, the acquisition of geometric and geographic perspective parallels the ability to take the mental perspectives or viewpoints of other people, as distinct from the child's own: the beginning of empathy and altruism (see further discussion of "projective space," pp. 88–90, and in chapter 5).

Latency: Concrete Operations

The latency period of about 7 to 11 years is termed the *period of concrete operations* or of concrete–operational intelligence. It is the period within which thinking progressively becomes systematic, dynamic, fluid, and conceptual, although this new logical intelligence remains anchored to real or concretely imagined situations. Truly abstract, theoretical, hypothetical thinking comes only in the final developmental period of formal operations.

A central or crucial achievement in concrete operational thinking is the example of "conservation." The child becomes able to recognize that the identity and quality of a substance remains the same despite its position, dimensions, and shape. For example (Miller, 1983, p. 59) the experimenter puts out two identical beakers containing identical amounts of water; then, pours the water from one into a tall, slim beaker. The preoperational or "nonconserving" child firmly believes the amount of water is increased, centering only on the dimension of increased height. The concrete–operational child, following several operations simultaneously, recognizes that it is the *same* water in the *same* amount. Another Piagetian principle applies to conservation: conservation of different properties (volume, mass, length, number) is achieved at different ages. This phenomenon Piaget calls "décalage" or staggering: it applies to a number of phenomena in the developmental streams, an unevenness between the age of completion of different apparently closely related abilities. Miller notes that Piaget never appears to have researched the phenomenon of "décalage" in itself.

In analyzing problems in a systematic and dynamic way, the latency-age child is using a number of operations, hesitantly and inconsistently at first, firmly and consistently later. Such operations are illustrated in the conservation task: addition–subtraction, compensation, identity, reversibility. Other operations include multiplication, division, substitution, reciprocity (if Mr. S. is Jim's uncle, what relation does Jim have to him?), classification (taxonomy, principles of inclusion), seriation (rank-ordering). Since classification is a centrally important component of logical operations, we should note the formidable logicomathematical models of classification which Piaget devised and which systematize his formulation of latency-age intelligence. These eight or nine "groupings" have intimidating titles such as "Bi-univocal multiplication of classes": any explication of these models will not be attempted here; the reader may further consult Flavell (1963, pp. 168–187), Baldwin (1968, pp. 251–262), Miller (1983, p. 83), and their critiques. In effect, fully developed concrete–operational intelligence has developed exceedingly intricate, yet automatic, computational, and classificatory abilities.

Besides classification (in which we shall be interested clinically) the latency-age child develops other operations which include new kinds of social reasoning. Moral judgments come to be made based on the subject's personal intentions and a framework of a universal and dispassionate justice (see chapter 6).

At the end of the period of concrete operations the child has progressed (Miller, 1983, p. 62) from understanding the world by action schemata, then to understanding it by mental and communicational representations, finally to understanding it by internalized, organized structures or operations: a lawful world appraised by logical thought, a new equilibrium. But, so far, these operations deal with "what is" rather than what "could be." The latency-age child sees the nonpresent or abstract as a very special instance of the present or concrete: the adolescent later comes to see the present and the concrete as special instances of the possible. Further, the operational groupings of the latency-age child exist in some isolation from each other. There is yet to be created the kind of integrated grid which allows a smooth access to all parts of the cognitive system.

Adolescence: Formal Operations

The pubertal period of about 11 to 15 years is termed the *period of formal operations* or of formal operational intelligence. In this period the adolescent becomes able to float free of real and concrete situations and problems and to indulge in abstract speculation and inductive–deductive hypothetical reasoning. We have already considered the meaning of "operation." The term *formal* I would illustrate by the system of algebra where, within agreed rules of procedure, one can conduct purely formal manipulations of abstract (x, y, z) and even wholly imaginary quantities (surds), or rather manipulations of *symbols* for these, pursuing whatever direction logic takes, performing an infinitude of procedures and possibilities. At any time one can insert real quantities, concrete numbers, using the abstract and formal system to solve actual practical problems. But the system stands on its own as a formal and abstract one. It is not in itself tied down to reality, and it may therefore be of great heuristic value.

This is something like what adolescents achieve in the final development of their intelligence, whereafter the basic machinery of problem solving does not develop further. Internalized thinking now becomes autonomous. The adolescent thinks in propositions, and in propositions about propositions, thinks about thinking, logically manipulates symbols and meanings, searching the "truth tables" which now come to make up a coordinated, yet richly complex and flexible system of information retrieval and logical comparison. Piaget has produced logicomathematical models (see Baldwin [1968, pp. 275–287]; Flavell [1963, pp. 211–222]) to illustrate adolescent operational thinking: the lattice, the 4-group, and eight schemes of formal operations.

The social repercussions of adolescence are in part, Piaget finds, a direct outcome of this new cognitive expertise. There is a new egocentrism in early adolescence: a kind of intoxication with thinking for thinking's sake, an impatience with the cold reality which places obstacles and limitations in the way of abstract speculation. There is an idealism born of the ability to reach soaringly beyond the here-and-now, an interest in pondering and theorizing about the self and the meaning of life, and an active, enquiring, challenging outreach into a new network of social structures. We leave the adolescent entering the world of adult thought with the machinery of thought basically perfected, though his actual fund of knowledge and experience will continue to multiply vastly. He faces adult life with an ability to take part in the scientific method, marshalling and working through evidence, testing it by designed and systematic trials (as opposed to trial and error), and drawing logical conclusions.

Many of our patients do not have these abilities. Either they have never developed them (Piaget does not deal with fixations, arrests, or relative failures of cognitive development) or they have lost them in the process of falling ill (regression). We proceed to look at some of these possibilities.

Clinical Correlations

"Cognitive Style": Hysteroid, Paranoid, Depressive

I first draw attention to the brilliant collection of clinical essays by Shapiro (1965) which is surely destined to be a classic. For many years I was uncomfortable (and no doubt rejecting) with a class of patients, those whose ongoing personality functioning was in the "hysteroid" or "hysterical" mode. Mrs. U. P. of chapter 1 is a typical example of this class. I considered these patients to be unreflective, unpredictable, flippant, capricious, dishonest; melodramatic in manner and fantasy, shallow in feeling, and inconsistent and corrupt in motivation; manipulative of me and of my feelings. Even the quieter, gentler, shyer, more inhibited members of this class were difficult to deal with. Our therapeutic contracts (or what I had believed to be contractual agreements) often proved unreliable, with the abrupt disclaimer, "I never said that!" cutting off all discussion.

Shapiro, then Piaget, were the first to help me in becoming interested in, rather than impatiently rejecting of, this cognitive style. To summarize Shapiro's thesis, the hysteric registers information in sweeping, impulsive, intuitive, impressionistic strokes; stores and retains knowledge in just as vague, mystic ways; and retrieves, uses, and communicates it as impressionistically and melodramatically. Hence, history taking and psychotherapeutic transactions tend to elicit colorful but imprecisely organized communications and conceptions whose content and structure are amorphous. Such a cognitive style seems clearly related to the consistent finding in the Rorschach test that hysterics respond with exclamations or shudders to colored cards, but neglect form as a determinant.

It progressively occurred to me that what Shapiro's and my own patients were doing, and what Rorschach workers were reporting, was strikingly akin to Piaget's description of the thinking of preoperational, prelogical, preconceptual children; and with this my patience and my curiosity grew progressively. It seems correct to view the cognitive style of the hysteric as preoperational. Such patients are relatively mature and competent people, but they do not conceptualize and communicate reality with precision, nor reflect well upon their own inner experience. They either lack (fixation) or have lost (regression) the stable structures and logical operations which would give them cognitive precision and the ability to reflect. Just as psychoanalytic thought conceives that they are conflicted and fixated at, or regressed to, a phallic or oedipal level, so Piagetian thought seems to place them at a similar developmental age, though for quite different reasons.

One might similarly consider the cognitive style of the paranoid (Shapiro, 1965, chapter 3) and the depressed (Beck, 1967; Beck, Rush, Shaw, and Emery, 1979), and reflect on how these rather rigid, stenosed, egocentric, assimilative ways of thinking meet Piagetian criteria. We shall discuss these states further in the second half of this book.

Piagetian method and theory has, unfortunately, not been applied widely to the cognitive problems of psychiatrically disordered adults. It would seem to offer a highly sophisticated framework for more precise identification of fixations and regressions, and for monitoring the progress or relapse of our patients. Some pioneering attempts are reported by collaborators of Piaget (Inhelder, Chipman, and Zwingman, 1976), and by Donati Lucchin, Rebosio, and Rovere (1968). These are certainly suggestive that mentally retarded, senile, and psychotic patients show various nonadult modes of cognition.

I shall content myself in the following with some general examples of clinical correlations and suggestions for future research endeavors.

Abstraction and Classification

In clinical examination, particularly of our more disabled or ill patients, we observe, test, and record for a number of cognitive functions: memory, orientation, personal identity, abstraction, classification, interpretation, judgment, insight. So far we have tended, I believe, to register our findings in such crude polarities as "abstracts well," "very concrete," "lacking in social judgment," or "poor insight." With Piagetian concepts as our framework, we may be able qualitatively and perhaps quantitatively to do far better than this. For example, in reporting the interpretation of common proverbs, we have two Piagetian dimensions to measure: abstraction–concreteness and egocentrism–decentration. To the proverb "People in glass houses shouldn't throw stones," a patient may respond, "Well, if you throw the stone it will break the glass," a very concrete response, but not palpably egocentric or autistic in interpretation. Formulation of this would indicate concreteness in the early preoperational mode, but objectivity in the late preoperational mode. The response to this same proverb may be bizarre and idiosyncratic, yet quite well abstracted: "It means when you do a person a good turn, they'll hurt you back": egocentrism of a preoperational kind, together with abstraction of a formal operational kind. That is to say, that the two dimensions do not have to show equal levels of cognitive maturation; there may be a décalage.

Piaget has paid considerable attention to classification, which becomes a competent function in the period of concrete operations. Baldwin (1968, pp. 262–268) describes a typical clinical testing for classification, using an assortment of objects with various shapes, colors, and consistencies. He gives the criteria of a proper classification as nine in number. These include the principles of parsimony (the best classifications employ a minimum number of taxonomic dimensions) and elegance (logical and esthetic appeal and attractiveness) and the requirement that all objects must be included. Children's classifications ascend by age through some five stages. The youngest children (age about 4) make "graphic collections," arrangements which are not classifications at all, but pretty arrangements, a sort of attractive collective object. Children at about ages 5 to 6 produce three kinds of "nongraphic collections": clustering similar-looking objects while leaving some objects out; many small collections but including all the objects; and a clustering with some orientation toward a real classification, for example by color. Finally (ages 6 to 8) there is true taxonomic or hierarchical classification, from somewhat tenuous and crude to clear and sophisticated. The challenge for the examiner is in making sure (by Piaget's clinical interviewing method) whether the arrangement was guided by a logical cognitive organization or by some prelogical, intuitive process. Piaget's guidance on the subject of classification is a very good supplement to methods already used by clinicians, especially with psychotic and brain-damaged patients.

Case Example. Mr. E. S., a 36-year-old artist of some competence, was admitted in a disturbed and resistive state with auditory hallucinations and grandiose preoccupations. He had a long history of recurrent, rather atypical manic episodes. After initial neuroleptic and supportive management, he was offered a classification test using 20 small pieces of medical and clerical equipment. He arranged these into an elegant and attractive overall pattern, with some emphasis on the color black. He could give absolutely no account of his ideas for this arrangement: "they just look nice that way." This arrangement appeared to meet the criteria for a "graphic collection" at about age 4.

Space and Egocentrism

The development of the child's knowledge of space has been broken down into a number of categories (Laurendeau and Pinard, 1970; Gruber and Vonèche, 1977) of which two appear to be of particular clinical interest. It is relatively easy to persuade patients to undertake pencil-and-paper drawings. From this, a relatively simple method of estimating cognitive regression or fixation takes advantage of the developmental progression of the category of geometric space. Piaget found that children's coordinates of space are not fully developed until 8 to 9 years of age, by which time the ability to draw realistically will be completed, including some ability to draw in perspective and to indicate movement and distance. If one asks children of 2½ to 3 years to draw, they merely scribble. Soon (ages 3 to 4) they show a "topological" capacity; that is, they indicate correct relationships between parts of a figure, while the whole (e.g., a human face) may be grossly inaccurate. "Euclidean" shapes (squares, triangles, rhomboids, circles) only become possible later: the square about age 4, the triangle at 5, the rhomboid at 6. If one has patients attempt such drawings, one can assign an approximate developmental age to their productions. In this instance, we do not need to know the inner reasoning process, merely the ability to represent correctly.

But of more intriguing conceptual and clinical interest, I believe, is the category of projective space (Espace Projectif) and its relationship to grades of interpersonal egocentrism.

Some years ago I asked Dr. Bärbel Inhelder's advice on studying psychiatric patients with Piagetian methods. I had thought that perhaps studying their sense of time, in particular with depressed persons, might be fruitful; however, Dr. Inhelder reported that time was on all counts a very unreliable epistemological category to quantify, and suggested instead that I focus on projective space. The assumption here is that persons who are out of touch with the thoughts and feelings of others, self-absorbed, unable to be empathetic and altruistic (i.e., fixated or regressed in various degrees of egocentricity or autism) will also in various degrees show immaturity in managing projective space. Such an assumption would seem to be eminently testable, using standardized clinical ratings against test results.

Practically, the reader should consult the sources for proper explication of projective space (Laurendeau and Pinard, 1970, pp. 310–403; Gruber and Vonèche, 1977, pp. 621–626) and of examining for it using the three mountains test. This test employs a board or table on which are three model mountains differing in size and color. The child or patient is invited to examine this panorama carefully, walking about the table and viewing the mountains from all directions; then to take a seat in one fixed position. From here the subject has to imagine the view a photographer might see from various other positions around the table, and either to draw them, or to select pictures on cards offered by the clinician.

This test draws on integrated operations including spatial coordinates, mental imagery, perspective, and reciprocity (right–left, before–behind, higher–lower); since these are developed progressively during childhood, children of different ages show a relatively poor or good expertise in deploying them. Psychiatric patients may be expected to have lost these developments to a degree. At the youngest age at which the test can be applied (4 years) there is "complete egocentrism": the child keeps repeating the same view, that from her own position, no matter from where around the table she is imagining that she is looking. By 7 years, the child makes errors, but of a systematic kind: the imagined view may be correct but totally reversed in mirror-image, or reversed in a near-to-far dimension. Only by 9 to 10 years does she consistently give a correct picture by imagining the view from any angle. It is at this latter age that a child becomes able also to draw indicating distance and perspective.

Case Example. Mrs. C. B., age 30, was a skilled technician, with multiple psychosomatic difficulties, marital disruption, and violent personal crises with suicidal attempts. She had assaulted a previous psychotherapist with a knife when she learned that his wife was having a baby and he would be leaving town. Blonde one visit and brunette the next, she had a kind of overwhelming heartiness that belied most precarious self-esteem. She fulfilled well all the criteria I have enumerated above for hysteroid personalities; her cognitive style was perfectly as described by Shapiro; her psychosexual history was appalling; her clinical diagnosis has been borderline personality disorder; and she has made progressive developmental headway during treatment. When offered the three mountains test early in our contact, this intelligent woman was completely unable to visualize any perspective except that from where she sat, as appropriate to age 4 or a position of "complete egocentrism." She struggled repeatedly, since she knew her views must be incorrect, to produce something different, but could not.

Sex Differences, Intellectual and Motivational

General Tests of Intelligence

What, if any, is the evidence that girls and boys develop differentially in intellectual and motivational styles and capacities? We start with the fact that, in the construction of tests for measured intelligence, certain subtests have to be rejected because they clearly favor one sex over the other. One example of this was the discarding of a "cube analysis" test during the construction of the first Wechsler–Bellevue Scale (Matarazzo, 1972, p. 195). Maccoby (1966a) summarizes: "Most widely used tests of general intelligence have been standardized to minimize or eliminate sex differences" (p. 25). When this has been done, the two sexes do not differ with regard to global measured intelligence (Matarazzo, 1972, pp. 352–356). However, examining subtest performance, using a properly large sample, females are found to score higher on three, and males on five subtests in the Wechsler adult intelligence tests; though the differences are small, they are significant, and have suggested a greater expertise of females on verbal tasks, and of males on arithmetical ones. Wechsler at one point attempted a masculinity–femininity score subtest analysis, but the validity of this attempt has not been empirically borne out.

Maccoby and Jacklin: A Classical Study

I turn to the classical work of Maccoby and Jacklin (1974), not for final answers in this swiftly evolving field, but for an exemplary methodology. Both these authors are professed feminists, and both are clearly competent scientists. A developmental emphasis continues in this volume: Maccoby (1966b) had already edited a developmentally oriented compendium on sex differences. The 1974 work is a massive review of hundreds of studies, and includes extensive tables and a 233-page bibliography of abstracts.

The analysis pursued by Maccoby and Jacklin is rigorous and their conclusions are cautious. Their first principle is to get the facts straight, before proceeding to analysis and explanation; that is, to be as clear as possible regarding what various studies have empirically found. From this, it emerges that (1) a large number of studies are poorly designed for the purpose; (2) a majority show empirically no difference between the sexes; and (3) there are additional problems with researchers and journals, who have failed to publish positive findings because they are unexpected or unpopular, and negative findings because they are negative.

After proper registration of data or findings, analysis and interpretation proceed. The following major groups of explanatory variables are seen by Maccoby and Jacklin as undoubtedly *interacting*, rather than acting in a simple, linear fashion. I paraphrase them as follows:

1. *Biological factors,* variables which are evolutionary, cut across species and across cultures, including genetic, metabolic, and nutritional ones.
2. *Imitation* (or identification), the observation of, and modeling of the self upon a *same-sexed* parent or other environmental figure.
3. *Self-socialization,* the formation of a gender-appropriate self-concept, followed by the self-guidance of the child's own behaviors toward such a concept.
4. *Approval and disapproval,* the receipt of direct reward and punishment from adults for gender-appropriate or gender-inappropriate behaviors; also self-regulations based on covert study of adults' reactions.

Clearly, in assigning weight to explanatory variables, Maccoby and Jacklin stress the psychosocial, the effects of social learning. They do not dismiss biological variables: these they see as inclining children toward certain kinds of temperament and social learning. But they honestly admit a lack of biological expertise: hence they do not attempt to account for such processes as genetic programming of girls' and boys' brains, or differential hormonal effects on the brain during the prenatal period.

First, to the facts or findings, I follow Maccoby's and Jacklin's own schema of reporting. I include motivational aspects in this discussion of intellectual and cognitive differences, as difficult to separate out without impairing the total picture:

1. Unfounded beliefs or "myths" about sex differences, which are clearly unsupported by this survey. Findings: contrary to previous impressions, girls and boys are equally affected by heredity and environment, are equally sociable and suggestible, are equally competent in auditory and visual modes, and equal in self-esteem (see below for one specific exception), motivation to achieve, and in rote-learning versus analytic–cognitive competence.

2. Differences fairly clearly established, that is, a small but significant lack of overlap when populations of females and males are compared; this is essentially the type of relative or proportional difference between the sexes noted in chapter

2. Findings: It is fairly well established that males are more aggressive than females, in all cultures examined, in verbal, actional, and fantasy modes, from the earliest age at which social play commences (ages 2 to 2½); and this despite their consistently receiving more punishment for such behavior than females. While both sexes at most ages are equal in self-esteem, young women of college age (18 to 22) showed lower self-esteem and sense of control over their own life than their male peers. Populations of girls and boys have equal verbal, visual–spatial, and mathematical abilities during childhood; but from preadolescence onward there is increasing divergence. Girls develop greater verbal ability (differences amounting to 0.25 standard deviation); boys develop greater visual–spatial ability (about 0.4 S.D.), and, with considerable variation among studies, somewhat greater mathematical ability even when they have not taken mathematical courses. Two further design problems revealed themselves in the studies which were reviewed. Most are on white middle-class Americans; and age cohorts are inadequately represented.

3. Open or ambiguous questions requiring further, better designed studies: sex differences or lack of these in tactile sensitivity, activity level, competitiveness, dominance, compliance, timidity, and "nurturing" or "maternal" propensities. Age cohorts need particularly to be studied here, for there may be real shifts during development, and gradations in age in part help solve the nature–nurture equation (the younger, the more likely that prenatal biological variables are determinants; the older, the higher the likelihood of social learning).

In seeking causes for the differences found, Maccoby and Jacklin are, as noted, insistent on an interactional view of the variables. Some of these authors' causal explanations came as a surprise to themselves, and may be surprising to the reader. For example, they discovered little or no evidence that children observe, study, and carefully imitate the same-sexed parent: rather, children learn social roles and skills from both parents equally, and sometimes appear to ignore important sex-role behavior in the same-sexed parent. Though gender identity and sex-typing are established early, children do not seem to focus on a sex-role concept as their learning goal, and there is a huge overlap between the ways in which girls and boys conduct their lives. The data also indicated that the two sexes are treated by caregivers remarkably similarly as children (the differential handling of aggression is noted above) and that it is highly unlikely that differences in parental or pedagogical management direct the cognitive development of girls and boys differentially. One other unexpected explanatory variable was the possibility of a sex-linked recessive gene influencing superior visual–spatial performance.

Before leaving this study, it would be wise to make it explicit that the authors were *not* studying *sexual* attitudes and behavior; this was a study on cognitive and affective–motivational differences of a general kind as between males and females.

The Newer Methods of Eagly

Eagly (1987), an admirer as well as a critic of Maccoby and Jacklin, presents an updating of methods since 1974. Eagly's work is on social behavior and its temperamental and affective–motivational aspects; she is not studying intellectual and cognitive differences between the sexes. I select it primarily because of its methodological interest, but also because it answers some of the questions left open by Maccoby and Jacklin. Eagly's criticism of work up to and including Maccoby and Jacklin (1974) is that it is carried out in a "narrative" or "box-score" style; that is, the studies which are analyzed are examined descriptively, with the skill of the examiners responsible for adequate assessment and comparison between studies. This approach, through its sheer breadth, may make uneven judgments, or it may miss the significance of small, borderline, or null differences.

Eagly's two principal contributions are the use of the newer "meta-analysis" and a new sharpened approach to hypothesis construction. In meta-analysis the results of scrutinized studies (in scores, means, and standard deviations) are expressed as a "d-metric" in standard deviation units; this can then be compared with the d-metrics elicited from other studies. D-metrics of about 0.20 are considered small effect sizes; of about 0.50 to be medium effect sizes, indicating a degree of difference which ordinary observers are likely to discern; and of about 0.80 to be large effect sizes.

Eagly constructs hypotheses for testing which are based on a framework of naturalistic, ethological, observation of social roles in real society. One of her principal criticisms of previous studies is that they have been carried out in a highly artificial, short-term, laboratory or field setting; the subject and other participants are strangers to each other; therefore sex differences, which in real life are based on ongoing role relationships, may be badly bleached out, leaving the participants only the role of "experimental subject" to be played out. Why not, Eagly proposes, study real-life role interactions such as between male doctors and female nurses, or male bosses and female secretaries, with their corresponding complementary behaviors and the elements of hierarchy and power usually built into such ongoing role interactions?

Out of pilot studies using this social-role or "structural" approach, Eagly selects the construct of "communion" to represent a characteristic quality of female sex roles and role behaviors. Communion involves a subjective sense of belonging to the people to whom a woman relates daily; being a part of the lives of others, being impelled to help those who are close, serving, ministering, conscious of the needy and the oppressed; somewhat apprehensive of relating to strangers. The construct of "agency" she likewise identifies in male role transactions (the adjectives are "communal" and "agentic"). Agency involves a sense of taking charge, leading, directing, protecting the weak, rescuing the stranger in trouble; the ancient virtues of heroism and chivalry appear to be subsumed under agency. In constructing research hypotheses Eagly posits that female roles will be strongly tinged with communion, and male roles with agency. Women will tend to nurture those close to them, and to fear interactions with strangers. Men will easily enter the heroic role, particularly when that role is reinforced by an audience, and will take relish in helping even strangers who are in difficulty.

Based on hypotheses derived from these constructs, Eagly conducted two meta-analytic surveys: one on helping behavior and one on aggression ("behavior intended to inflict harm or injury") in adults. In the helping behavior survey it was predicted that adult men in laboratory and field experiments would show more helping behavior than women, since the situation and the experimenters' confederates are strange, and there are no ongoing personal roles and ties involved. The prediction was borne out clearly, with a combined d-metric of 0.34 (about one-third of a standard deviation unit) representing differential behavior between the sexes. The hypothetical model was calculated as explaining about 70 percent of the found differences.

In the meta-analytic survey of studies on aggression, much variation between individuals and experimental groups was discovered. An overall d-metric of 0.29 distinguished the male from the female cohorts, and in the direction predicted; that is, males tend to show more aggression than females. In this survey the hypothetical model accounted for only about 40 percent of the found difference. Clearly the evidence for greater aggression in adult males does not emerge here as strongly as in the instance of helping behavior. Studies on children, Eagly reports, have regularly found boys to exhibit more aggression than girls (d-metric of 0.50). This implies that developmental processes are involved, including a shift from aggressive behavior in juvenile males to protective behavior in adult males. This possibility seems to be strengthened by the observation (in the Helping Behavior Survey) of a significantly higher number of helping gestures by men toward women; whereas women tended to help both sexes equally. Clearly, the effects of experimental design and setting seem particularly crucial in aggression studies.

Eagly's meta-analyses in the social-role framework appear also to have clarified some of the categories left as ambiguous by Maccoby and Jacklin. Eagly found women to show scores higher than men for "influenceability," nonverbal behavior, ability to decode nonverbal behavior, skill in discussion and negotiation, and social–emotional orientation; and men to show scores higher than women in the overall category of task orientation.

Evidence from Studies on Brain Injury

I refer once more to work by colleagues at my own university on the differential effects of unilateral brain damage on the two sexes (Inglis and Lawson, 1981, 1982, 1984; Inglis, Ruckman, Lawson, MacLean, and Mongo, 1982) and on learning disabilities in children (Lawson and Inglis, 1985; Tittemore, Lawson, and Inglis, 1985; Bellemare, Inglis, and Lawson, 1986). Inglis and Lawson became interested in findings published by McGlone (1977, 1978); they then explored and reanalyzed the literature and examined several cohorts of stroke patients themselves. McGlone had found unilaterally brain damaged men to show a quite specific drop in either verbal or performance (visual, spatial, tactile) abilities dependent upon whether left or right brain lesions existed. Women, she reported, showed relatively little decrement in either verbal or performance abilities with lesions of either hemisphere. McGlone interpreted this to mean a great hemispheric specialization in men's, and a kind of nonspecific versatility in women's brains. On their first literature review, Inglis and Lawson (1981) were actually able to predict the number of women included in the various studies from the overall scores obtained; that is, on the basis that the higher the number of women, the less specific an overall effect of unilateral injury would emerge. When they tested their own cohort of stroke patients carefully, Inglis et al. (1982) found that:

1. Men with right hemispheric damage showed a sharp drop in performance abilities.
2. Men with left hemispheric damage showed a sharp drop in verbal abilities, with both clearly aphasic and relatively nonaphasic subjects showing much the same effect.
3. Women with left hemispheric damage resembled their male peers in a verbal deficit.
4. However, women with left hemispheric damage showed a significant loss in performance abilities, as had the men with right hemispheric damage; that is, injury to

the left brain produced significant depression of *both* performance and verbal scores in women.

5. Women with right hemispheric damage showed a lesser impairment in both verbal and performance capacities.

A sophisticated meta-analysis (Inglis and Lawson, 1982) of 16 studies (which included 899 patients with a variety of unilateral lesions) showed, somewhat to their surprise, the same results, and to these the authors give the same interpretation as to their own study. The adult male brain is clearly specialized as to the lateralization of verbal and visuospatial functions; but the female brain, rather than being unspecialized, relies heavily on the left hemisphere in dealing with the solution of visual, spatial, and tactile problems, or, in the authors' terms, relies upon verbal strategies in doing nonverbal tasks; both verbal and performance functions suffer rather globally when the verbal hemisphere is impaired.

What about children? This same group of investigators reminds us that, from midlatency onward, girls show increasing superiority in verbal abilities; and that learning disabilities (highly dependent on verbal mediation) in the presence of normal intelligence, are almost entirely confined to boys (sex ratio 5:1), as is stuttering. Girls who show learning disabilities are much more likely to have globally depressed intelligence. Inglis and Lawson have been able to connect left-brain problems very clearly (in a psychological rather than a neurological context) with learning disabilities in schoolchildren, and they propose the same interpretation for the sex differences as they do for brain-damaged adults. The male brain is clearly specialized as to lateralization, hence verbal incapacities due to left-brain developmental difficulties can exist in the presence of a good nonverbal intelligence. For girls the case is different: left-brain incapacity impairs a wide array of functions, since even "nonverbal" functions are regularly mediated by "verbal" strategies.

Sex Differences, in Summary

Studies to date suggest that the intellectual performances of boys and girls diverge steadily after midlatency, though the differences never become large. Girls become more expert in verbal problem solving, boys in mathematical and visuospatial. Boys are consistently more aggressive across all cultures studied than girls, despite consistently receiving punishment for aggressive behaviors. As adults, men are "agentic" and somewhat less aggressive (though still more so than women by a relatively small difference) and more chivalric and protective; women operate under a broad mandate of "communion," a caring for others close and known to them. These themes will be reflected in the discussion of differential moral development in chapter 6. Somewhat surprisingly, the influence of teaching, social learning, and punishment fails to account well for these sex differences, intellectual and temperamental.

Learning disorders and consistent stuttering develop in boys from midlatency onward, and these are uncommon in otherwise normal girls (sex ratio 5:1). Brain-injured adults show a differential pattern: hemispheric injury correlates well with depression of verbal scores (left) and visual–spatial–tactile scores (right) in men; however, injury to either hemisphere depresses visual–spatial–tactile scores in women. This suggests a clear division of labor between the hemispheres in men; and a marked tendency in women to use the left hemisphere, or "verbal strategies," in solving nonverbal problems. Such a view also accounts for learning disorders, which are highly verbal in mediation, in boys of normal intelligence, and the uncommonness of these in otherwise normal girls. Left-brain problems in boys will produce a relatively circumscribed learning disorder, but are likely to produce general intellectual impairment in girls.

Bibliographic Notes: Key Readings

The history of measurement of intelligence and the vast literature of this field are well covered by Matarazzo (1972): he reviews the work of Binet and Wechsler; his book is an updating of Wechsler's own textbook (Wechsler, 1958). Binet's own reports are of great interest and should be read either in the original or its English translation (Binet and Simon, 1916). Sattler (1974) offers stimulating comments on Binet and the development of his approaches.

Piaget is difficult to read. He wrote in French in a turgid style, introducing many new terms which he rarely defined, and the language of the English translations reflects this problem; two shorter volumes give direct access to his thinking (Piaget and Inhelder, 1966; Piaget, 1967). Gruber and Vonèche (1977) have compiled an encyclopedic collection of Piaget's writings with editorial comments, which must be considered the definitive sourcebook today. Flavell (1963) and Baldwin (1968) give expositions of Piaget which are in sufficient technical detail to give a clear flavor of his work. A particularly compact and lucid exposition of Piaget is that of Miller (1983); being recent as well as clear, I recommend it to the beginning student of Piaget.

Shapiro's (1965) rather old but classic collection of clinical essays on cognitive style in various psychiatric disorders should be carefully read by every clinician. On the subject of sex differences in intellectual and cognitive performance, another classic authored by Maccoby and Jacklin (1974) sums up historical and methodological issues and actual findings in a rapidly evolving field. Inglis and Lawson (1984) give a relatively nontechnical review of sex differences and the differential results of brain injury.

References

*Baldwin, A. L. (1968), *Theories of Child Development.* New York: John Wiley.
Bayley, N. (1966), Mental measurement. In: *Human Development, By 29 Authorities,* ed. F. Falkner. Philadelphia: W. B. Saunders.
Beck, A. T. (1967), *Depression: Causes and Treatment.* Philadelphia: University of Pennsylvania Press.
———— Rush, A. J., Shaw, B. F., & Emery, G. (1979), *Cognitive Therapy of Depression.* New York: Guilford Press.
Bellemere, F. G., Inglis, J., & Lawson, J. S. (1986), Learning disability indices derived from a principal components analysis of WISC-R: A study of learning disabled and normal boys. *Can. J. Beh. Sci.,* 18:86–91.
*Binet, A., & Simon, T. (1916), *The Development of Intelligence in Children.* New York: Arno Press, 1973.
Bowlby, J. (1969), *Attachment and Loss, Vol. 1: Attachment.* London: Hogarth Press, 1982.

Bruner, J. S. (1968), *Processes of Cognitive Growth: Infancy.* Worcester, MA: Clark University Press.

Donati, A., Lucchin, A., Rebosio, L., & Rovere, C. (1968), 1. Investigation of operational regression in a group of schizophrenics. 2. Investigation of the conservation of length. *Riv. Sper. Freniatr.,* 92:79–127.

Eagly, A. H. (1987), *Sex Differences in Social Behavior: A Social-Role Integration.* Hillsdale, NJ: Lawrence Erlbaum.

*Flavell, J. H. (1963), *The Developmental Psychology of Jean Piaget.* Princeton, NJ: Van Nostrand.

—— (1971), Comments on Beilin's "The development of physical concepts." In: *Cognitive Development and Epistemology,* ed. T. Miscvhel. New York: Academic Press.

*Gruber, H. E., & Vonèche, J. J. (1977), *The Essential Piaget.* New York: Basic Books.

Inglis, J., & Lawson, J. S. (1981), Sex differences in the effects of unilateral brain damage on intelligence. *Sci.,* 212:693–695.

—— —— (1982), Meta-analysis of sex differences in the effects of unilateral brain damage on intelligence tests results. *Can. J. Psychol.,* 36:670–683.

—— —— (1984), Sex, intelligence and the brain. *Queen's Quart.,* 91:37–54.

—— —— (1985), The cross-cultural validity of the learning disability index: A reanalysis of Mishra's data. *J. Clin. Psychol.,* 41:680–685.

—— Ruckman, M., Lawson, J. S., MacLean, A. W., & Monga, T. N. (1982), Sex differences in the cognitive effects of unilateral brain damage. *Cortex,* 18:257–276.

Inhelder, B., Chipman, H. H., & Zwingman, C., eds. (1976), *Piaget and his School: A Reader in Developmental Psychology.* Berlin: Springer-Verlag.

Laurendeau, M., & Pinard, A. (1970), *The Development of the Concept of Space in the Child.* New York: International Universities Press.

Lawson, J. S., & Inglis, J. (1985), Learning disabilities and intelligence tests results: A model based on a principal components analysis of the WISC-R. *Brit. J. Psychol.,* 76:35–48.

Luria, A. R. (1932), *Cognitive Development: Its Cultural and Social Foundations.* Cambridge, MA: Harvard University Press, 1976.

Maccoby, E. E. (1966a), Sex differences in intellectual functioning. In: *The Development of Sex Differences.* Stanford, CA: Stanford University Press.

—— ed. (1966b), *The Development of Sex Differences.* Stanford, CA: Stanford University Press.

*—— Jacklin, C. N. (1974), *The Psychology of Sex Differences.* Stanford, CA: Stanford University Press.

*Matarazzo, J. D. (1972), *Wechsler's Measurement and Appraisal of Adult Intelligence,* 5th ed. Baltimore: Williams & Wilkins.

McGlone, J. (1977), Sex differences in the cerebral organization of verbal functions in patients with unilateral brain lesions. *Brain,* 100:775–793.

—— (1978), Sex differences in functional brain asymmetry. *Cortex,* 14:122–128.

*Miller, P. H. (1983), *Theories of Developmental Psychology.* San Francisco: W. H. Freeman.

Piaget, J. (1961), *The Mechanisms of Perception.* London: Routledge & Kegan Paul.

*———— (1967), *Six Psychological Studies*. New York: Random House.
———— Inhelder, B. (1966), *The Psychology of the Child*. London: Routledge & Kegan Paul.
*Sattler, J. M. (1974), The development of the Stanford-Binet. In: *Assessment of Children's Intelligence*. Philadelphia: W.B. Saunders, pp. 87–106.
*Shapiro, D. (1965), *Neurotic Styles*. New York: Basic Books.
Tittemore, J. A., Lawson, J. S., & Inglis, J. (1985), Validation of a learning disability index (LDI) derived from a principal components analysis of the WISC-R. *J. Lern. Dis.*, 18:449–454.
Wechsler, D. (1958), *The Measurement and Appraisal of Adult Intelligence*. Baltimore: Williams & Wilkins.

---

*Recommended readings.

4

A Third Developmental Stream: The Life Cycle and Developmental Tasks

Introduction

Overview

The raison d'etre for this chapter is well expressed by Colarusso and Nemiroff (1987): the need for greater precision in delineating the life cycle and its developmental tasks, so that such improved understanding will increase the relevance of a developmental perspective in clinical diagnosis and treatment planning. It is clear that in diagnostic and therapeutic formulation we must always bear in mind these questions:

Is this patient coping successfully (i.e., normally) or unsuccessfully (i.e., pathologically) with the developmental tasks appropriate to his or her age?
What templates may we turn to in order to be specific about age-appropriate tasks?

Is such a person developmentally arrested (fixated), or thrown back (regressed) to tasks of an earlier age?

How do we attack therapeutically in a manner relevant to the developmental task being grappled with?

In this chapter the attempt is to marshall what has been outlined, by pioneering exponents, of the life cycle and the developmental tasks along its way, a developmental stream whose data so far are among the more descriptive or "soft" of our various streams. Reasons for this relatively soft or imprecise state may become evident below. Much of the data are clinically derived, retrospective and subjective, something of a generalization from single-case studies (clinical, anthropological, or historical). Much more attention appears to have been paid to men's than women's life cycles. The adult portion of the life cycle has only relatively recently come under scrutiny, possibly for defensive reasons (Colarusso and Nemiroff, 1987); though the field is by no means a new one (e.g., van Gennep, 1908) it is late in entering the purview of psychiatry, and late too in attaining some operational and quasi-quantitative status (Vaillant, 1977; Gilligan, 1982).

What is the life cycle, and what are developmental tasks? We may conceive of the life cycle as a relatively invariant, epigenetically arranged, sequence of adaptational stages and tasks, each lasting several years, through which humans, of all peoples and in all generations, pass from birth to death. The cyclical nature of life is one defining property of the human condition: death is as normal a part of it as is birth, and it is small wonder that speculations and doctrines of immortality and reincarnation arise in response to our eternal circling through the world. Shakespeare gave us seven ages of man; Erikson presents us with eight (Erikson, 1950, chapter 7), adding to Shakespeare's renaissance catalogue the crucially modern epoch of adolescence. Our traversing of the life cycle takes us from the helplessness of the newborn, through increasingly active and autonomous development of childhood, into the prolonged preparation of adolescence and its sequels of productive adult life and the wisdom and involution of old age.

Developmental tasks are those personal undertakings between the evolving individual and the social milieu, which have a specific and critical cast at each stage of the life cycle. Chronological stages have rather variable time limits, the more variable as life goes on: tasks have a more precisely identifiable character, and, at least in adult life, should be considered the "markers" on which we focus (Colarusso and Nemiroff, 1987). Success in each stepwise task is a requirement for progression along the life cycle. Such success in task achievement should not, however, be seen as a rigid, all or nothing accomplishment. Rather, Erikson (1950, 1959) points out, relative success is always a dynamic balance between ego strengths developed, and their obverse, weaknesses or failures. He epitomizes developmental tasks as building "ego qualities which emerge from critical periods of development—[as the]—ego, at a given stage, is strong enough to integrate the timetable of the organism with the structure of social institutions" (1959, p. 246). The dynamic balance between success and failure in a developmental task determines a person's preparedness to face the biological and social demands of what comes next.

Developmental tasks are epigenetic by definition. They correlate with drive states or instinctual unfoldings appropriate to any given age, and with the familial and social expectations for persons of each given age or stage. The immediate community is usually highly aware of members who, through psychiatric disorder or developmental difficulty, are deviating from the expected social roles and responsibilities for their chronological age.

Our first review will be of exponents of the "classical" psychoanalytic view of epigenetic development; by "classical" I mean prior to the major impact of ego psychology in the 1930s. Classical theory, difficult to test, verify, or refute, because of its sweeping, metapsychological quality, was much focused on drive and instinct patterns, and on the epigenesis of the procreative instinct groupings. Freud was also, however, very much interested in the parallels between procreative and social or ethical maturation, as seen in his construct of "genitality." Psychoanalytic theory, whatever its drawbacks, must be respected because of the unique source of its data: the intimate, confiding, patient–doctor relationship in psychoanalytic therapy. Freud's findings and concepts were systematized by his followers; for example, Abraham and Fenichel. He himself never settled into satisfaction or closure, particularly on issues of feminine developmental tasks.

Erikson, an artist and social scientist as well as a psychoanalyst, participated in the now flourishing ego psychology movement. He was the first and, so far, outstanding theorist of the life cycle from birth to death. He pictured developmental tasks very much as interactions between nature (biological preparedness) and nurture (the immediate community). His data were drawn from a remarkable range of sources, clinical, anthropological, and historical–biographical. His constructs are somewhat more testable than Freud's, and he lets us see him at work more, I think, than either Freud or Piaget. His writings, as with these two authors, combine a philosophical and literary quality with observational science, and like them he was a brilliant observer and questioner, of great honesty and integrity. Thus, his corpus of ideas is extremely valuable, both at the "bedside" in clinical work, and as a source of scientific hypotheses for further replication and testing.

We shall finally look at two contemporary exponents, one working chiefly with male subjects, and one a pioneer on the specifics of the female ego and its development. Vaillant and his colleagues have been following a prospective cohort of well-endowed American men for over 50 years now. They have confirmed most of Erikson's schema and made some alterations to it, in an operational and quasi-quantitative approach. Gilligan, whose prime interest was to research moral or ethical judgment in girls and women, has also let us see some important development issues, from which vantage point it becomes necessary to question certain Eriksonian formulations.

Classical Psychoanalytic Formulations

Freud, Instincts, and Psychosexual Development

Freud was the originator of this developmental stream. In fact, he was the first great developmentalist and one of the towering psychological theory builders of our time (Baldwin, 1968; Miller, 1983). In harmony with the hope of his day for a biologically based psychiatry, calling into use new models of the reflex arc and of hydraulics and electromagnetism, attempting to create a scientific psychology in which the crucial themes of human motivation and conflict would play a part, forced by his own compulsive honesty to recognize sexual problems where Victorian prudery would keep them hidden (Freud, 1905, 1915), he outlined an epigenetic theory of the emergence, development, and integration of the sexual instinct or instincts. Freud never attempted closure as to how many or precisely what kind of instincts there were (Freud, 1915, 1923), believing apparently that only man-made constructs could impose order here. He used practical, clinical, rather global groupings: "the sexual instincts," the instincts of self-preservation or "ego instincts"; somewhat speculatively a grouping into instincts favoring construction and conservation, preservation of the individual and the species, versus a grouping favoring destruction and disintegration, whether of the self (e.g., in suicide), of other individuals, of society, or of the species (1923, p. 135).

The developmental stream which Freud outlined for the sexual instincts is the one which concerns us here. For a critique of his ideas regarding the conservation of energy of libido, see Baldwin (1968) and Miller (1983); Freud certainly described libido as if it were a hydraulic force within a closed system, as well as an electromagnetic force attaching to and affecting objects.

The following summary brings together the lucid reviews of Baldwin (1968) and Miller (1983); publications of Freud himself at various periods (1905, 1915, 1923, 1933); and the systematizations of two followers (Abraham, 1924; Fenichel, 1945).

Freud (1905) outraged members of the scientific and lay communities by insisting that human sexuality did not begin with puberty, but had precursors onward from infancy: adult sexuality was a bringing together of "component instincts" appearing epigenetically through several phases of childhood. Each of these (Freud, 1915, 1923) obey the criteria of an instinct, with its physiologic origin in an organ or body area, its aim, content, and object, and its affective tones of tension (unpleasant) and discharge or satisfaction (pleasant). *Libido* was his term for the psychological representation of the instinctual tension or energy in all the sexual instincts, component or integrated (Freud, 1905, p. 553). Freud's contemporaries, and moderns too, have difficulty with his extension of sexuality into the instinctual processes of infancy. Nonetheless, Freud's evidence for this should be examined fairly. His arguments can be marshalled as follows: the sexual instincts are expressed in adults in a wide variety of behaviors and sexual objects ("normal" and "deviant"); the behaviors making up the sexual act contain elements which appear directly derived from dominant infantile interests, in the mouth, skin, anus, and so on; and disturbances in normal development of children result in both neuroses and disorders of adult sexual behavior; therefore, he concludes, some prominent developmental priorities of children are incomplete expressions of a growing and finally integrated sexual drive.

Abraham's Schema

Using Abraham's orderly table of the "development of the libido" (1924), we shall simplify Freud's presentation of the epigenetic sexual developmental tasks of children. Each task or stage is divided into two parts, early and late, for empirical clinical reasons.

Early Oral. The newborn infant is helpless, passive, dependent upon care and nourishment by others for its survival. It constantly uses its mouth, both for suckling but also for what Bowlby (1969) would term "non-nutritive sucking" and exploring. Indeed, interest and pleasure seem to center on the mouth area (origin of this component instinct) and to dominate the child's activity. The infant's basic instinctual aim is to survive by nursing; it gradually, from a totally objectless position, begins to have as a main object of instinctual satisfaction the breast or bottle, then the mother as a person. The main modes of this phase are helplessness, dependency, passivity, the need for intake ("oral-receptive"); because the phase is relatively objectless and conflict-free the baby's feelings are "preambivalent."

Late Oral. Later in its first year of life as it becomes more active, and particularly as teeth begin to erupt, the baby begins to use the mouth more actively and aggressively, biting and chewing as well as sucking, inflicting pain or injury when annoyed, as well as inadvertently. The mouth remains a principal locus of interest and activity, and for testing of new experiences. Now the baby recognizes principal objects such as the mother-as-a-whole, and reacts to them as both gratifying and frustrating. The main modes become activity, exploration; a drive to attack, either in anger or exploration, with the mouth. Feelings now are "ambivalent" since the baby is capable of both love and hate toward the same object. Some origins of sadism reside in unresolved conflicts in this developmental phase, which has variously been termed *oral-aggressive* and *oral-sadistic.*

Early Anal. In the second year of life the child's interest and drive turns to excretory functions and areas (in Freud's model the influence of culture, e.g., in toilet-training practices, and the conflicts engendered by these, was acknowledged but not given a major place). Defecation, feces, and soiling; pleasure in stimulation of the anal area; instinctual tension from a full rectum, rapidly and pleasurably relieved by uncontrolled emptying; these are the central priorities. The bladder and urethra, with their tensional and pleasurable sensations, such as warm urine in the diaper, are included too, but somewhat tentatively, in the Freudian schema. The mode here is of soiling, of disorder and lack of control as pleasurable, of impulsivity, rapid discharge of tension; anger in association with the act of defecation and soiling relates to struggle with the parents for control. Ambivalence is considered to be at its height in this "anal-expulsive" or "anal-sadistic" phase of development.

Late Anal. By the end of the second year of life a most important and fundamental shift has occurred, one which is crucial to adult mental health and to civilized human living; the normally developing child has crossed a crucial watershed. Early anal priorities are typified by a glorying in excretion, a satisfaction and pleasure in excretory products, a lack of restraint and control, an impulsive release in response to instinctual tension: values which are, to the adult, filth, mess, chaos. Now the child must make a 180-degree reversal in its priorities. It learns to manage, then enjoy, sphincter (and overall muscular) competence and control. It learns to view its precious, pleasant excreta as dirty, worthless, disgusting, and to defer excretion to appropriate times and places. With this muscular competence there is a broad acquisition of a sense of competence and self-sufficiency of the person, what Erikson (1976) would term *autonomy*. The main modes or priorities have become self-control, order, independence, and pride in the achievement of cleanliness. A prototypical mental mechanism, reaction formation (the ability to reverse a cognitive judgment and its associated feeling into the opposite) is acquired, with strong potential for good or ill in further personality structuring. From anal-expulsive and anal-sadistic the child has moved to anal-retentive.

Early Genital. I have deliberately used the impersonal neuter pronoun for children thus far. To this point (around 2 years of age) small girls and boys have pursued a common pathway with little of gender differences in their priorities. They are simply small persons. (Again, Freud pays relatively little attention to parenting and culture and its influence on gender role.) In this phase gender becomes a paramount preoccupation and a source of major conflict; and a two-track developmental divergence between girls and boys has its origin. The term *pregenital* applies to the first two stages, where the sexual instincts are at first indistinguishable from the survival instincts (Freud, 1905, p. 597; 1915, p. 69; 1922, pp. 131–135).

The preoccupations of young children are not with abstract gender: they are with a concrete organ, the phallus. Because of the preoccupation, this stage is often called the phallic phase. Freud inferred that both little girls and little boys become fascinated with the penis as their first awareness of gender differences. He never became completely confident of his ground in conceptualizing female development, but for boys he was sure that a juvenile pride in the penis and the pressures from sensations in that erotogenic zone were the first formative experiences in this stage; from this follows an anxiety in seeing that little girls displayed no such organ, as if they must have lost it (the castration complex); then follow juvenile theories about why this might be. A truly complex "complex" (often misunderstood) is gradually worked out by little boys as a crucial part of their gender development and ultimate ethical maturity. This Oedipus complex Freud named after the legendary Greek king who *unwittingly* killed his father and married his mother, then blinded himself in atonement. In Freud's formulation, phallic sensations in the little boy become linked up with early, inchoate, sexual fantasies toward his primordial object, his mother. He comes to believe that his father will punish him by injuring or amputating his precious phallus, based on the mental mechanism of projection of his own rivalrous and hostile impulses, and on the primitive ethical principle of retaliation. If all proceeds well, this intricate triangular conflict (the first major triangular situation he has had to manage) resolves with a decision that he will *join* or identify with his father as a male and renounce his mother as a sexual object. Alternative, pathogenic solutions fall into two classes; "oedipal victory," various modes of actually vanquishing his father and possessing his mother; or various versions of submitting masochistically to his father. Following this resolution comes latency and the solidification of the superego or of mature ethical judgment.

For the girl's development the reader would be wise to follow Freud's own tentative formulations, doubts, and uncertainties (Freud, 1905, 1933). In short, he felt that clinical material did not give a firm basis for retrospective judgment; he was sure that the girl's development was lengthier and more intricate, since she had somehow to transfer her libidinal attachment from her mother to the opposite sex; he rather tentatively invoked a triangular conflict (the Electra complex) in which a girl hates her mother for not providing her with a phallus, yearns for her father to provide her with one, perhaps by impregnating her; she ultimately resolves the conflict by a healthy identification with her mother and the search for a sexual object like her father, but outside the family. Freud had an impression

that the woman's superego was different from the man's because of this more tortuous and lengthier series of developments, which is interrupted much more by latency than in the
case of the boy, and which is only finalized at puberty.

Latency Period. Freud (1905, pp. 176–179) borrowed the term
sexual latency period from his friend Fliess, as a title for the remarkable moratorium on active sexual conflict which intervenes from
about 6 years of age to puberty. He emphasized (1905, p. 177;
1923, p. 246) that its developmental task is the building up of
ethical restraints which control and divert the sexual instincts. (We
shall focus more fully on this in chapter 6.)

Late Genital. At puberty a great surge of sexual interests
reappears. At this time, if all proceeds well, all the previous
"component instincts" become integrated together by, and subordinated to, a strong genital procreative drive. There are most
important interpersonal developments. The triangular (Oedipus or Electra) complex reappears in greater or lesser degree;
greater, Freud was inclined to believe, in the case of girls, who
in many normal instances might never completely resolve it.
Transient substitutes for incestuous sexual objects appear in
adolescent crushes. Finally a mature, nonincestuous, sexual object choice and attachment is made. Freud chose to picture the
earlier genital phase as "phallic," preoccupied with a primitive,
egocentric, grandiose penis cult, with anxieties about the presence of, absence of, or damage to the penis, with pleasure in
the penis and clitoris as an end in itself, and with an incestuous
quality to sexual objects which are transitional and not far from
the self. Thus "phallic" for Freud meant immature, egocentric,
primitive. He valued and praised "genitality," attainment of
which he conceptualized in two ways: the primacy of the genital
drive and of procreative activity; and ethical maturity, with
selection of and relatedness to a nonincestuous mate involving
empathy, faithfulness, and consideration toward the object as
person with all his or her individuality, needs, and feelings. Loving becomes unambivalent. Abraham terms the stage "Post-
ambivalent," a condition which few of us have attained ideally!

Erikson's Neo-Freudian Formulations

Why Is Erikson Important?

Erik Homberger Erikson is the most important neo-Freudian for our present purposes. His writings are literary, eminently readable, evocative paintings and reflections of his work with younger and older patients, visits to other cultures, and meetings (real or imaginary) with historical figures. His constructs are perhaps even more "soft" and philosophical than Freud's, "Platonic" as Vaillant and Milofsky (1980) would have it. We must pay them serious attention for a number of reasons:

First, Erikson well satisfies criteria of honesty and integrity; somewhat more than Freud and Piaget, he lets us see him at work, so that we may sift our own impressions. Second, he is the first and as yet dominant developmentalist to provide a conceptual framework for the whole life cycle from birth to death. For Erikson, humans unfold and continue to seek meaning at all life stages, whereas for Freud personality was basically formed by about 5 years of age, and for Piaget by 16 or so. Third, while accepting the Freudian psychobiologic and psychosexual schema, Erikson elaborates personality development as a vital interaction between nature and nurture, chronology and social experience, between the individual with his biological endowment and the culture of the mother–child dyad, the family, and of later social groupings. Fourth, he teaches from a multimodal data base: play therapy with children, psychoanalysis with adolescents and adults, visits to different societies and cultures, and the literature of great historical and fictional figures. Finally, if one can master his rich ideas, they are both highly heuristic in terms of generating research hypotheses, and clinically applicable to real patients.

Erikson's Schema

Erikson's concepts of stages and developmental tasks will now be summarized. I again turn to Miller (1983) for an excellent distillation, to several works of Erikson himself (1950, 1976) and to the readable, Erikson-based paperback of Lowe (1972).

Colarusso and Nemiroff (1981) provide us with useful correlative chapters and tables and bibliographic suggestions.

Erikson's description of life stages and developmental tasks gives them a colorful, dramatic quality, like acts in a play, and emphasizes the appearance and resolution of typical turbulent crises. This is perhaps because he studies disturbed people and the stormy characters of history and literature. Vaillant and Milofsky (1980), who steady us by empirically validating Erikson's schemata, emphasize the smoothness of development, the gradual evolution of stages, and a relative absence of crisis. This is perhaps because they study in depth the adaptation of numbers of "normal" men; as their team has come to know their subjects very well, we can certainly not accuse them of producing superficial work.

Here we shall try to give but a little idea of Erikson's color and drama. For each stage he paints, we shall, following Miller (1983), take it for granted that Erikson subscribes to, and finds useful, Freud's psychosexual developments. Mainly we shall indicate how he goes beyond Freud; and he does, of course, go completely beyond Freud, beginning with adolescence.

Stage 1. The infant's challenge (to about 1 year of age) is to develop a sense of basic trust in his mother (thence by extension to the wider world and to himself), as reliable, likely to meet his needs, predictable, constant. Failure in this task produces degrees of basic mistrust, a kind of paranoid anxiety. Naturally the healthy infant must develop some objective index of suspicion for real dangers, and ultimately a judgment of his objective enemies and ill-wishers. But, as in other stages to come, a favorable balance in favor of basic trust should be the algebraic outcome. The social modality for this stage is that of getting, taking in (incorporation based on the stage's biological orality) including taking in by the senses, and learning to give in return. If this stage is completed satisfactorily, with its strong and imperative drives being met and harmonized through good parenting, the child can pass on to confront with confidence what comes next. Hope is the affect accompanying the child who has mastered this stage. With unsatisfactory parenting, the child remains insecure, suspicious, unready for the next developmental tasks, ready for abiding problems.

Stage 2. In the second and third years of life nature brings neuromuscular competences in locomotion, speech, and sphincter control. The developmental challenge is in attaining autonomy. Developing mobility and independence correlates with a peak in separation anxiety (see also chapter 5) and with conflict and struggle in relation to the will of parents and others. Will develops in those children whose wise parents neither subjugate nor indulge them. Failures in self-control bring shame and doubt which temporarily at least damage self-esteem. Rules, law and order, become important social preoccupations: the child either masters them or they master him. The social modality, in line with biological anality, is that of holding on and letting go.

Stage 3. In the fourth and fifth years the child, who is now solidly a person, begins to wrestle with his admired and feared parents who keep intruding in his life. He too feels intrusive in his new maturity. The social modality is making, and "making like" or playing, taking the initiative, forming and carrying out goals, competing. The child's life fills the space of his basic family but now reaches out to ideal prototypes or heroes who provide a guide to his social order. None of this neglects the basic Freudian phallic and oedipal turmoils and crises. Successful outcomes leave a positive balance of initiative over guilt; guilt is over intrusive sexual fantasies and secret behaviors, a guilt which may forever force the child to feel he must be *making* (or making up), doing, competing, to be of worth. Out of the conflict and crisis of this epoch comes the sense of purpose.

Stage 4. From about 6 years of age to puberty, turmoil and crisis give way to a period of calm as sexual fantasy and activity subside (Freud's "latency"). This is the base for a new "industrial age" (Miller, 1983, p. 169). Learning to work, the pursuit of knowledge and skill, fascination with school, technology, the world of peers, occupy and impel the child whose previous tasks of basic trust, autonomy, and initiative have been mastered. Competence, mastery, energy, in short, industry are polarized against inferiority, the feeling of inadequacy, failure, of being good for nothing. The child's social world expands into the neighborhood and the school. The social modality is now not merely of making but of making things and making them together. If humans are working animals, and tend to make things or to make work when there is nothing to do, this stage surely makes or breaks: any clinician can produce case vignettes of sad young women and men who do not know how to work, take no reward from working, have never developed study or work habits; or of retired men who could work at one thing, their trade, and nothing else. The sense of competence emerges from a successful stage 4, with its favorable balance between industry and inferiority.

Stage 5. From about 12 to 20 years of age is the turbulent period of adolescence. Freud carried his developmental schema only to the early phase of adolescence, where the Oedipus/Electra complex is revived and resolved, ethical maturity is consolidated, and genitality is established. Thus, with Erikson we are now breaking new ground. Erikson (1950, p. 92) comments on Freud's rather utopian views of genitality, as expecting a great deal of the adolescent and even the mature adult. Erikson views the central developmental task of adolescence as the attainment of solid identity: a confident answer to the question "Who am I?" This is a difficult construct to make operational for research purposes or for clinical assessment, one of those "Platonic" (Vaillant and Milofsky, 1980) statements which are so thought-provoking, yet mystical too. Vocational certainty is one measurable aspect of identity. For Erikson, identity is a lifelong developmental priority, expressed in unique form at each stage of the life cycle, always in need of consolidation, always in some danger of dissolution: but during adolescence it becomes the paramount concern and source of conflict and crisis. New, internal pressures from the pubertal body and its urges, and demands from the external social body for vocational clarification, force the adolescent to pull together his or her previous, more partial identities into a working whole. If this task ends in failure, the person suffers some permanent impairment in the form of identity diffusion or confusion, and becomes unable to be himself or herself, either when alone, or in interaction with others.

To be oneself, to be able to share being oneself, is the social modality emerging from this stage. If all proceeds well (see also Sullivan [1953]) the adolescent emerges into early adulthood an integrated personality, sure of the self, being, identity, gender, and vocation. This young person has achieved fidelity to himself, his ideals, and goals, and fidelity to others also. He can thus trust and share himself intimately with another. If his adolescence has failed in its central developmental task, or if the epigenetic foundation from previous stages makes adolescence incomplete, he cannot be himself and share himself, for he really does not know who he is and where he is going: he simply "can't get it all together." The reader will note here that I have lapsed into the masculine pronoun. This is partly to avoid grammatical clumsiness, for "he" is meant to embrace persons of both sexes. But it is also to hint at the doubt raised by Gilligan (1982) regarding the appropriateness of Erikson's formulation and staging for adolescent girls and women (pp. 121–123).

Stage 6. The young adult (age 20 to 35) who carries a solid identity can now risk "losing himself in another." Only with a good sense of identity can intimacy and solidarity with another, or with oneself, be achieved. This life stage carries the task of serious courtship, engagement, and marriage (by whatever current titles, we might add, these endeavors are known). The young adult who does not achieve intimacy goes onward in a series of cool, formal, emotionally rather empty personal relationships. Isolation is the polarity when a major achievement of intimacy has not been possible, while love is the quality of an achieved intimacy. The social modality is that of psychosexual genitality, to lose and find oneself in another.

Stage 7. Middle adulthood (roughly 35 to 65 years of age) is entitled by Erikson the period of *generativity versus self-absorption*. Both terms require some explication. In the most concrete sense generativity means an interest and satisfaction in producing: both in the procreative sense, and in the social field of work, the individual is and feels productive. But more, there is a sense of caring, of being able to care and care for: care is the accomplishment of this period. Caring for children, one's own or those of others; selfless devotion (not merely duty-bound or masochistic self-sacrifice) to a cause or enterprise; leadership in the workplace or in community endeavor; an interest in establishing and guiding the next generation. When generativity fails to predominate, its polar opposite is self-absorption or stagnation; varying proportions of the two appear in any given individual. The self-absorbed or stagnating person lives a sterile, introspective life, uninterested in giving, producing, caring for, and leading.

Stage 8. Late adulthood, or old age (roughly 65 years upward) marks the final episode in our life cycle. Here the polarity Erikson delineates is integrity versus despair, and the final accomplishment is wisdom. Integrity means holding fast, despite failing strength and health and the loss of intimates and surroundings, to a sense of worth and accomplishment, a sense of being part of history and a participant in accumulated human culture, looking back on a life reasonably well lived, and contemplating not being with some equanimity. The social modality, Erikson believes, is given as "to be through having been and to face not being." The sad obverse of integrity is the sense of regret for a life not well lived, disgust for oneself, and a fear of death, subsumed as despair. Erikson (1976) gives a moving commentary on a fictional presentation of old age in the film "Wild Strawberries" (Bergman, 1957) written when he himself was 74.

Contemporary Studies of the Life Cycle

The Grant Study

In 1937 a philanthropist and a student health physician combined their resources and launched an important prospective study of healthy male college sophomores (Vaillant, 1977). In this remarkable project, the Grant Study, 268 young men have been systematically followed to the threshold of old age (and in some cases, to their death) and regularly examined through interviews, physical examinations, and various standardized tests. In a series of publications (Vaillant and Milofsky, 1980) it has been possible to report on a number of aspects of the lives of these men: their passage through stages in the life cycle, their evolving mental health and interpersonal relationships, their success or relative failure in life and health, and the relationship of these to the adaptive mechanisms they use. In the earlier days of the Grant Study the work of Anna Freud, Harry Stack Sullivan, and Erik Erikson was barely beginning to be known: later, the concepts of these investigators were gradually assimilated.

Therefore the publications of Vaillant and his colleagues have accomplished two things for us: a quasi-quantitative validation and enrichment of the Eriksonian schema; and a quasi-quantitative approach to the dynamics of male mental health (see further in chapter 9). The study has its realistic limitations. It is confined to male Americans from a privileged class of society, who were in fact selected for their apparent normality and likelihood to succeed (though some in fact turned out to be unsuccessful personalities).

It is, further, confined to those stages and tasks in the life cycle beyond late adolescence. Despite these limitations, the breadth, depth, and prospective nature of the Grant Study afford us a remarkable data pool and the opportunity to examine much more empirically the Freudian and neo-Freudian/Eriksonian formulations.

The Grant Study up to 1976 is presented in a consolidated fashion by Vaillant (1977), including the design, participants, follow-up examinations, and conceptual conclusions; it combines skillful biographic narrative and objective analytic science in lovingly presented, engaging style. One in the series of ongoing papers (Vaillant and Milofsky, 1980) not only tests the Eriksonian model empirically, but is able to compare the Grant Study cohort with a sizable cohort (392 subjects) of men from the underprivileged, crime-ridden inner city.

In general these detailed reports confirm Erikson's delineation of developmental stages and tasks in the adult phases of the male life cycle. This empirical confirmation applies not only to the relatively privileged men but to the inner-city ones. Some modifications and additions are, however, strongly suggested by the empirical studies. First, Vaillant and colleagues find the adult male life cycle to be much more a smooth spiral than a staircase of discrete steps; further they fail to find the degrees and colors of turmoil and crisis filling the developmental stages as depicted by Erikson (they do not attempt to "explain" Erikson here). Clearly, his materials were drawn not only from clinical work with disturbed children and adults, but from study of some of the high-powered and conflicted geniuses of history. The epigenetic principle is solidly confirmed: the developmental stages and tasks must evidently proceed in a required order, and subsequent ones cannot be successfully managed without resolution of the preceding ones. Empirically, Erikson's stages cannot be precisely attached to the chronologic age ranges: even in the cohort of normal to superior men, many are found to be lagging years behind Erikson's expectations. This is confirmed by Colarusso and Nemiroff (1987) who agree with Vaillant that the focus on "development task" is preferable to the focus on "developmental stage."

In general (see further in chapter 9) the Grant Study team perceive mental health as correlated with successful and "joyful" coping with developmental tasks; but mental health is by no means a unitary nor painless phenomenon, but rather an exceedingly complex, variegated, dynamic struggle with conflict, trouble, and distress.

Vaillant and Milofsky (1980) report that, empirically, two stages (they term them *Substages 6A* and *7A*) require to be added to Erikson's schema. Erikson offers little detail on the fourth decade of life. Here Vaillant and colleagues find a kind of second round of the latency task of industry, a consolidation of the man's life-work in a kind of senior apprenticeship, a passage from journeyman to master craftsman. This Vaillant and Milofsky conceptualize as Substage 6A, career consolidation, occupying the period of approximately 35 to 40 years of age. The data requiring insertion of a formulation of such a substage included Erikson's own life history. A remarkable epigenetic finding for this substage is that it is almost always based upon a good marriage, and the achievement of intimacy as defined by 10 years in a stable intimate relationship. Isolation is antithetical to career consolidation, as is self-absorption.

A second substage which these authors find necessary to interpolate is 7A: keeping the meaning. This developmental task of late midlife concerns cherishing and passing on to younger hands the knowledge and values that sustain us. It is to be distinguished from mere stubborn insistence (rigidity) on old ways for their own sake.

Despite the limitations of the Grant Study, it continues to deserve very respectful attention (Colarusso and Nemiroff, 1981). Its conclusions can be considered as hypotheses for testing and replication. Most broadly, these fall into three clusters: mental health correlates with successful developmental maturation and the use of mature adaptive mechanisms; mental ill-health correlates with failure or retardation in developmental tasks; and fortunate or adverse circumstances can facilitate or halt progression through the life cycle at any stage. We shall return to these themes in discussing defense mechanisms (chapter 7) and psychiatric normality (chapter 9).

Toward a Developmental Psychology of Women

It is difficult to escape the impression that the groundbreaking exponents of the life cycle operated under the sway of a pervasive but ego-syntonic male bias, and this despite their evident honesty, integrity, observational skills, and soulsearching. Freud agonized repeatedly to the end of his life about what he regarded as the unfathomable mystery of female development, though he felt considerable certainty about the male (Freud, 1933, pp. 112–135). The pioneer investigators were men. They were men in a historical context of male dominance and leadership. Their observations favored male subjects in both quantity and quality. They tended to assume that findings from male subjects could safely, and reliably, be extrapolated to women. Worst of all, their bias hinted that where comparisons had to be made, the male was the norm and the female was defined by comparison as "less than," "more than," "weaker than," "stronger than," the male.

The feminist movement has brought a sharp corrective to such thinking in the behavioral sciences. Its influence has been in consciousness-raising, warning us to watch our language as an indicator of bias, and to design and interpret research so that women and men shall not be amorphously lumped together, so that women shall be seen in a frame of reference appropriate to their being, not merely as offshoots from the normative male line.

Jean Baker Miller has written a highly regarded and widely read position statement, "Toward a New Psychology of Women" (Miller, 1987). Miller's clarion call cannot be ignored: it is high time to focus our understanding on the unique strengths, values, and vulnerabilities of the female psyche without eternal, often pejorative, comparison with the male. It may be, she muses, that even constructs such as ego and superego do not properly apply to women. This is because the characteristic relational mode of women is through others to surrounding reality, which, in our industrial society, women have lacked the power to shape for themselves. "Affiliation" rather than self-enhancement is the woman's skill, and she is *"outside the ongoing action."* The only regret I can express regarding Miller's powerful manifesto is that it takes relatively little account of the dominant economic values and the sociopolitical power relationships inherent in the capitalist culture in which we live.

Eagly (1987) and Maccoby and Jacklin (1974) are scientists operating within the feminist movement, and Eagly certainly approaches a degree of socioeconomic analysis in her structural sex-role theory. I refer the reader back to the findings of these authors, in chapter 3, pp. 90–96. These have generally developmental implications, though developmental tasks and stages in the life cycle are not specifically enumerated. Eagly, for example, proposes the construct of "communion" as embracing many social roles in girls and women. Both publications look seriously at differences in aggression between the sexes, and Eagly in particular teases out in her meta-analyses the interesting finding that male aggression diminishes during maturation in favor of a protective or heroic social behavior.

It seems clear that prospective and observational studies are needed, in which cohorts of girls and women will be followed in their own right, in order to clarify just what their specific developmental tasks and sequences are. Ideally, these need to include a clear comparison with the life cycle of boys and men. Further, they should be based on an interactional model involving nature (i.e., genetic programming, brain differences, and neurohormonal influences) and nurture (familial and scholastic shaping, and the role and power relationship of the socioeconomic world).

Gilligan's Pioneering Framework

A highly promising framework for further hypothesis testing in observational and comparative studies emerges in the important book *In a Different Voice* by Carol Gilligan (1982). The title indicates the pervasively different outlook on life, the self, and interpersonal relationships from which girls and women speak. This life view forces us into a new look at developmental tasks, and a revision of such schemas as Erikson's and Kohlberg's (see chapter 6 for Gilligan's contributions to the theory of moral development).

Gilligan, while working principally on the subject of the consolidation of mature moral judgment in young women, touches on the problems of earlier developmental tasks somewhat as follows. In early childhood, the consolidation of gender identity and personal autonomy are almost synonymous tasks. The little girl takes on this task with the sense of being a part in a continuum of maternal generations, the experiencing of being one with one's mother, in a state of *empathy* with her in her feminine and mothering role. Thus for the little girl, ego boundaries are not a major issue: previous researchers have seen her as having ego boundaries "less clear than" the little boy. Boys, in consolidating a clear gender identity, must separate themselves sharply from their mothers, and in completing this task must establish clear ego boundaries, together with an ongoing sense of distinctive maleness in their relationships.

In middle childhood, the social group of peers becomes an important formative influence; with Piaget, Gilligan sees the forum of games children play as a useful research device. Here, girls play less competitive games of shorter duration than boys do. Any disruption in the game tends to terminate it, since the *continuance of relationships* takes precedence over the continuation of the game. Girls care little for rules and principles. Eagly's construct of communion comes very close to the personal and interpersonal ethos described by Gilligan as pervading young girls' lives: preserving the nexus of relationships; avoiding being at the top or at the fringes of any social pyramid; and following a caring, empathic stance. These are the dominant values at this developmental stage. By contrast, boys play competitive games and play at them longer, in the process taking satisfaction from both competition and conflict resolution via an interest in the codification of rules and principles, and in legal wranglings. The latency boy strives to win and glories in rising to the top of the social pyramid, a position the girl finds lonely and threatening. The boy's ethos fits him well for the capitalist world and the ladder of corporate success.

By adolescence, girls and boys arrive at their developmental tasks very differently prepared. For the girl, the achievement of intimacy is a higher priority than the consolidation of identity: this finding forces a reversal in the epigenetic order of Erikson's stage 6 (intimacy) and stage 5 (identity) in the case of the young woman. Gilligan suggests that for adolescent girls the consolidation of intimacy precedes the final achievement of personal identity. The girl emerges into adulthood with a strong ability to care and care for, a serious reservation regarding the costs of public social success, and a general devaluation of achievement motivation in favor of empathy and attachment. A preponderance of expressive over instrumental capacities appears to be her repertory. By contrast, the adolescent boy has long ago completed the task of separation from his mother, is preoccupied with instrumental tasks and achievement motivation, and must come back to working on intimacy *after* his personal identity is safely consolidated; attachment and intimacy are threatening until he is quite sure of who he is and where he is going.

Research and Clinical Implications

The Challenge

Colarusso and Nemiroff (1987) issue a clear challenge for the clarification and pursuit of this developmental stream: solidify and make operational our knowledge of the life cycle and our criteria for developmental tasks; and increase our consciousness of the value of diagnostic formulation and treatment planning as oriented by this stream. These authors give case material showing how useful an awareness and knowledge of developmental tasks can be.

The challenges for further *research* on this developmental stream appear to be:

1. To take the somewhat soft ("Platonic") findings and formulations of Erikson and to submit them to further replication studies.
2. In this task, to replicate studies on limited cohorts (Vaillant, 1977; Gilligan, 1982) where an operational and empirical approach has been pursued.
3. Thereby to rework and consolidate templates of an operational and quasi-quantitative type for the life cycle and its developmental tasks, such as can be applied to clinical case material.
4. To establish more reliably differences between the sexes in the sequencing and properties of their developmental tasks.

The challenges to *clinical* work appear to be:

1. To raise awareness of the developmental approach in diagnosis and treatment planning, as crucially useful.
2. To carry, in clinical work, adequate operational templates on the developmental stages and tasks of women and men, so that diagnosis and treatment planning can be truly guided by these.

In practical terms, the clinician needs to address such questions as: Where does this patient now stand in her life cycle? What is the central developmental task with which she is now wrestling? Is it appropriate, or inappropriate, to her chronological age? Has she slipped back (regressed) to this developmental task after previously having attained a more mature level? Is she arrested (fixated) on the unsuccessful completion of a task without ever having gone beyond this position? Does she need therapeutic assistance, or will she proceed adequately if left to her own resources (a question frequently of importance with younger patients)? How do we focus treatment efforts on the task with which this patient is struggling? I offer a clinical vignette, of a somewhat discouraging color, in illustration of these points.

Case Example

Mr. D. Q., aged 29, came to psychiatric attention for a third time, referred by the Emergency Department. Three days earlier he had inflicted two parallel incisions on the back of his left forearm, requiring 26 sutures. A tall, not unattractive young man, he was poorly and drably dressed; his warm brown eyes were tired and sunken, his voice was dull and flat. He could give very little account of his problem, his feelings, or his motives. He would vaguely like to "know why he does it." He denied suicidal motivation at present, though he admitted to feeling suicidal at some previous times. His cutting, which he had done before, seemed to give relief from vague tensions; to him it was painless, as was the suturing. His head felt clearer after doing it. He showed no clear symptoms or signs of a definable psychiatric disorder.

D. was alienated from his family, unemployed, but too proud to apply for public welfare (he may also have been afraid to apply for fear of being caught cheating). He was mildly ashamed of living in a dependent relation with a young woman whom he had met 5 months ago on the psychiatric ward. She boarded him and gave him cigarette money from her grant as a rehabilitation candidate; they lived in a basement room in her mother's house, and received help from her mother. Although sexually intimate, they spent much time bickering, and he was afraid he might blow up and injure her cat. He constantly dreaded the prospect of being thrown out by his girl friend.

In this quasi-independent, quasi-marital, alexithymic state, what developmental tasks are represented? Practically, D. had not emancipated himself from a family, and had little sense of vocation or of his own thoughts, feelings, and motives. He said he hated being unemployed: but he was listless and unmotivated to seek work. He would take a test soon for a cab driver's license, vaguely looked forward to driving a taxi, but confidently predicted that he would either fail the test or quickly become bored with the job itself. Confidentially, he stated, he might like to be a policeman or a prison guard, so that he could rough up the bums that frequent the parks, or the prison inmates; but he might like too to be just a bum himself. These ambitions resemble those of a 6-year-old.

The initial impression was that D. had not completed any developmental task above that of autonomy; even here, he appeared to suffer shame and doubt. His gender identity was solidly masculine. He was of average intelligence, and he had completed high school. Yet he never appeared to have attained an interest in industry (Erikson's stage 4) or shown initiative or intrusiveness (stage 3); he lacked even a competent street wisdom, and lived in a state of nervous inferiority. He was uninterested in ethical debate, felt a little ashamed at depending on a woman, justified his position shallowly, and had no impelling value system to guide him. His fleeting and juvenile vocational interests and his lack of awareness of his thoughts, feelings, and motives strongly suggested identity diffusion (stage 5): there was no evidence that he had functioned well at any higher level, though he apparently had an indolent, quarrelsome heterosexual life, with his third or fourth girl friend.

The problem for treatment planning was motivational: he had achieved neither initiative, industry, nor identity. Any kind of goal-setting or contracted therapy would seemingly not work, and he had, in fact, rapidly drifted away from proffered assistance twice before. Vocational rehabilitation programs were available. Perhaps in some more regimented society he could be forced to adhere to such a program, with incarceration and operant conditioning applied to help him pick up his long-abandoned developmental tasks. D. Q. failed to keep his second appointment, and a third offered him. We discovered at this only interview, where he was accompanied by his girl friend, that she "suffers (his and her term) from *Münchausen's syndrome*," and has "had to have several [surgical] operations because of it."

This clinical illustration returns us to the concerns expressed at the head of the chapter, particularly to the challenge of Colarusso and Nemiroff (1987) that we use the data of the life cycle as a focusing instrument in diagnosis and treatment planning. The developmental–structural model views clinical data in the perspective of fixations and regressions. Today we can apply this perspective using what is known of the whole life cycle. Is this patient engaged in the developmental tasks appropriate to his or her age? If not, how much fixation is represented, and how much regression, for regression is generally the first thing to be attacked in treatment? And how can we help the patient most effectively by remedial means geared to those very developmental tasks at which the patient is fixated, or to which the patient has regressed?

Bibliographic Notes: Key Readings

It is surprising that the pioneer observer and theorist of the life cycle, the anthropologist van Gennep (1908), has had to be rescued from obscurity by a reissue of his very interesting book *The Rites of Passage*. A number of useful compendia can be recommended for reasonably up-to-date papers, many of them directly related to the life cycle: Sze (1975) on various aspects of the life cycle, Howells (1981) on middle age, and Wolman's (1982) encyclopedic handbook.

Miller (1983) provides compact and lucid capsule views and critiques of Freud and Erikson, while Baldwin (1968) focuses in a challenging way on Freud. Freud speaks for himself in early (1905) and late (1933) writings. It is difficult to find one systematic presentation by him of his developmental ideas, a task which Abraham (1924) and Fenichel (1945) undertook. Erikson (1950) leads us through his many sources of data and presents (chapter 7) a summary and "epigenetic diagram" of the "Eight Ages of Man." Erikson (1959) gives more extended treatment to developmental stages and tasks, and to the important and difficult construct of identity, as well as including epigenetic tables. In his own old age he wrote an empathic commentary on the tasks of old age in a fictional film (Erikson,

1976). Lowe (1972) gives us a very readable summary of Eriksonian theory.

References

*Abraham, K. (1924), A short study of the development of the libido, viewed in the light of mental disorders. In: *Selected Writings of Karl Abraham.* New York: Basic Books, 1953.

*Baldwin, A. L. (1968), *Theories of Child Development.* New York: John Wiley.

Bergman, I. (1957), *Wild Strawberries* (Smultronstället). Film Script and direction by Ingmar Bergman. Stockholm: Svensk Filmindustri.

Bowlby, J. (1969), *Attachment and Loss, Vol. 2: Attachment,* 2nd ed. London: Hogarth Press, 1982.

Colarusso, C. A., & Nemiroff, R. A. (1981), *Adult Development: A New Dimension in Psychodynamic Theory and Practice.* New York: Plenum Press.

———— ———— (1987), Clinical implications of adult developmental theory. *Amer. J. Psychiat.,* 144:1263–1270.

Eagly, A. H. (1987), *Sex Differences in Social Behavior: A Social-Role Integration.* Hillsdale, NJ: Lawrence Erlbaum.

*Erikson, E. H. (1950), *Childhood and Society,* 2nd ed. New York: W. W. Norton, 1963.

*———— (1959), Identity and the Life Cycle. *Psychological Issues,* Vol. 1, Monograph 1. New York: International Universities Press.

*———— (1976), Reflections on Dr. Borg's life cycle. *Daedalus,* Spring:1–28.

Fenichel, O. (1945), *The Psychoanalytic Theory of Neurosis.* New York: W. W. Norton.

*Freud, S. (1905), Three essays on the theory of sexuality. *Standard Edition,* 7:135–243. London: Hogarth Press, 1953.

———— (1915), Instincts and their vicissitudes. *Standard Edition,* 14:117–140. London: Hogarth Press, 1957.

———— (1923), Two encyclopaedia articles. *Standard Edition,* 18:235–259. London: Hogarth Press, 1955.

*———— (1933), New Introductory Lectures on Psycho-Analysis. *Standard Edition,* 22. London: 1964.

Gilligan, C. (1982), *In a Different Voice: Psychological Theory and Women's Development.* Cambridge, MA: Harvard University Press.

*Howells, J. G., ed. (1981), *Modern Perspectives in the Psychiatry of Middle Age.* New York: Brunner/Mazel.

*Lowe, G. R. (1972), *The Growth of Personality: From Infancy to Old Age.* Harmondsworth, Middlesex, UK: Penguin Books.

Maccoby, E. E., & Jacklin, C. N. (1974), *The Psychology of Sex Differences.* Stanford, CA: Stanford University Press.

*Miller, J. B. (1987), *Toward a New Psychology of Women,* 2nd ed. Boston: Beacon Press.

*Miller, P. H. (1983), *Theories of Developmental Psychology.* San Francisco: W. H. Freeman.

Sullivan, H. S. (1953), *The Interpersonal Theory of Psychiatry.* New York: W. W. Norton.

*Sze, W. C., ed. (1975), *Human Life Cycle*. New York: Jason Aronson.
*Vaillant, G. (1977), *Adaptation to Life*. Boston: Little, Brown.
———— Milofsky, E. (1980), Natural history of male psychological health, IX: Empirical evidence for Erikson's model of the life cycle. *Amer. J. Psychiat.*, 137:1348–1359.
*van Gennep, A. (1908), *The Rites of Passage*. Chicago: University of Chicago Press, 1960.
Wolman, B., ed. (1982), *Handbook of Developmental Psychology*. Englewood Cliffs, NJ: Prentice-Hall.

*Recommended readings.

5

A Fourth Developmental Stream: The Object Concept and Human Attachment

Introduction

Overview

Our human relationships mirror our inner psychological organization, and vice versa. Inner organizations of thought, feeling, and memory (representation) constantly express themselves in our interactions with other people: from these interactions it is possible to infer and to reconstruct the inner organizations. Thus, "outer" and "inner" aspects of human psychology are everlastingly complementary. Good mental health is reflected in good social and sexual functioning (Erikson, 1963; Vaillant, 1977) and all psychiatric phenomena may in fact be depicted as "interpersonal," even the dreams we have in our solitary state of sleeping (Sullivan, 1953). Therefore, though Knobloch and Knobloch have criticized the distinction between outer and inner experience as a false dichotomy, this

131

perhaps serves also to reinforce the reciprocity between them, in our "assumptive world" (Knobloch and Knobloch, 1979, pp. 38–41).

The essence of human existence is in our social nature. As individuals, we are neither solitary nor symbiotic, but autonomous and interdependent, with our mental health following upon and reflecting the state of our object relations. In psychoanalysis, the term *object* technically connotes the person or thing which is necessary to actualize or consummate the expression of a drive; the more or less specific target for the satisfaction of an instinctual need (Freud, 1915). Such an object may, because regularly available and reliable, become important and distinct to the subject (cathected) in a specific fashion. In fact, the relationship thus developed may acquire the qualities of an instinctually motivated system, the so-called "secondary drive" phenomenon (see pp. 141–144). According to such a formulation, attachment of the baby to its mother develops because the mother is the object which consummates the baby's instinctual need for milk.

I shall here use the terms *subject* and *object* in the broader, more everyday sense. In this usage, subject indicates the self, and object what is nonself but acted upon by the self. The awareness and representation of the self is a gradual and important developmental achievement, which, like other developmental achievements, can be degraded or lost. Likewise, awareness and representation of objects are developmentally built, and may be partially or largely lost in later life.

In this chapter, I shall trace research on two principal aspects of object relations. The first is the cognitive, intensively explored in the work of Piaget and his students. The somewhat cool and formal-sounding constructs of "object concept" and "object permanence" form the backbone of developmental theory here. Piaget teaches us how the young child gradually emerges from total subjectivity and self-absorption (the "solipsistic" condition), through growing awareness of self and surrounding objects and their durability and reliable existence, to an objective understanding of a world of lawfully interacting objects including the self. Such constructs are closely paralleled by the child's development of awareness and competence in dealing with *space*. Sophistication in understanding both the object world and space can, of course, be degraded or lost during a psychiatric disorder, an implication of great importance to the clinician.

A second aspect is the affective–motivational: the study of the motivational systems, with their accompanying range of emotions, which appear to link humans to each other. Here the outstanding researcher has been Bowlby, with his steady pursuit, in the light of modern scientific models, of the way in which small children *attach* to their caregivers, the behaviors and mechanisms included; the aims and functions of attachment in the evolutionary world; the gradual development of attachment toward its adult forms in courtship, marriage, and caregiving; the quasi-quantitative measurement of attachment; and the implications of attachment theory for developmental psychology and psychopathology, and for the conduct of psychotherapy.

A third aspect, the communicative, will be deferred for discussion in chapter 7.

Cognitive Aspects: The Object Concept, Object Permanence

Piaget's "Solipsistic" State

Piaget (Gruber and Vonèche, 1977, pp. 198–204) conceives of the very young infant as existing in a state of *"solipsism,"* a state difficult for rational adults to imagine. The basis for this conception is that children are found to be increasingly egocentric, the younger their age: therefore, by extrapolation, we may imagine a condition of *absolute* egocentrism in the newborn.

Let us try to follow Piaget's picture of this inaccessible and imponderable state. The infant is wholly alone (*solus* = alone; *ipse* = self), absorbed in a kind of total subjectivity, and also quite unaware of any distinction between self and nonself. The infant simply experiences. Experience impinges both from within her body, in sensations such as taste, pain, proprioception; or from seeing or touching her body; for example, seeing her hands move or touching her face; or from the behavior of wholly independent external objects and scenes. All, internal and external, keeps forming a kind of moving panorama, a "waking dream" or multimodel cinema. All is taken for granted, and there is no ego state or consciousness as such, shedding the light of focused awareness. Only gradually, as the infant operates upon her world by both sensory and motor means, by constant assimilations and accommodations and by the first emerging primitive intentionality (the "primary circular reaction") does it gradually dawn on her that certain parts of this waking dream are more connected with the actions of the self than are others: a blurred distinction arises between things that simply happen and things that one can make happen with some regularity. The first traces of *memory* develop in attempts to make interesting things happen again, often in a most primitive and bizarre manner. With this, the first vague boundaries congeal between self or subject and acted-upon objects; even such objects as the hand, foot, or thumb may be parts of what adults call the self.

Magical Thinking and New Learning

Since in young babies "there is total continuity between internal and external experience" (Gruber and Vonèche, 1977, p. 205), and since every experience is both physical (taste, color, shape, etc.) and subjective (pleasant, painful, frightening, frustrating, etc.) we must assume also that things and experiences actually possess, for the baby, these properties as intrinsic. This is to say that a thumb, for example, becomes known as an intrinsically pleasant thing or experience. Or, a strange face is experienced as an intrinsically frightening thing. A kind of magical and animistic thinking (i.e., in sensorimotor terms, not thought as adults think) emerges: the baby's own efforts and the behaviors of objects around her are joined, continuous, are one and the same thing. But experiments (assimilations) and the resistance of real objects to these experiments gradually convince her otherwise (accommodations). Slowly the baby realizes (i.e., accommodates to) the fact that indiscriminate wishful action does not always produce desired results: objects in many cases obey other laws than the baby's magical gestures.

Although we shall never, probably, see clearly into the young baby's mind, it would seem important to try to infer and judge what a baby's experiencing is like. Partly this is an intellectual corrective to our tendency to project adult ways of thinking on young children. But practically and clinically, it may be helpful to assume that patients suffering psychotic breakdown actually experience in this way: self and other have become blurred together, animistic and magical ways pervade thinking, primitive sensorimotor sequences take over from rational thinking, and objects are endowed with intrinsic properties of good and evil, joy and terror, and obedience to magical gestures.

Evolution of an "Object Concept" and "Object Permanence"

At about 7 to 8 months of age, still basically solipsistic and animistic, the baby begins to *imitate* as a method of prolonging interesting experiences. This slender beginning of thought is also the beginning of differentiating individual objects and attributing continuing existence to them: object permanence. It becomes possible to study with some confidence the baby's behaviors vis-à-vis objects. Some of Piaget's most ingenious, engaging, and amusing experiments and observations cover this transitional period. At first, when a familiar toy is hidden or a familiar person leaves the field of view, these objects seem simply to evaporate from the baby's sensorimotor world, perhaps with some whimpering of frustration, but certainly with no effort to search for or to regain the lost object. By 9 months the baby begins to search, but wildly, clumsily, and incorrectly. This suggests that there is now a recognition of the object as enduring, permanent, existing somewhere despite its disappearance.

By 15 to 18 months a new sophistication and skill has emerged. At 19 months little Jacqueline Piaget could successfully find a coin that had been hidden, then moved several times in her sight without her actually viewing the coin itself. Evidently she could trace a pattern of successive displacements in some spatial grid: through its concealment and shifts it remained the coin she wanted. With this kind of representation the child also becomes capable of regarding her own body as an enduring object (Gruber and Vonèche, 1977, p. 269). Her schemata have become flexible, adaptable, capable of combinations into a framework of space–time. And with this comes a knowledge of enduring objects (including the self) moving and interacting in space and time. The remainder of childhood is spent in refinement and elaboration of an increasingly sophisticated, lawful, conceptualization of the universe of objects and their interaction; although Piaget does not use any clear term for the obverse of "egocentrism," the term *objectivity* would seem to describe the adult condition.

In Summary. Attempting to summarize these cognitive themes of Piaget, we can say that, like other spheres of knowledge, the knowledge of objects, and the ability to deal with them in thought, progresses as other streams do: from animism and absolute concretism into abstraction, classification, conceptualization; and from solipsism and absolute egocentrism into objectivity, relationism, public consensus, and validation. Through thousands of assimilations and accommodations the infant and child moves steadily forward, sometimes with a gentle leap or a bound. He or she forms a knowledge and a state of expertise regarding a universe of interacting objects, separate, distinct, obeying predictable principles of space, time, motion, cause and effect, of which universe the child is one defined participating object. Of the categories of knowledge involved, space and time (motion) and causality appear to be paramount (Gruber and Vonèche, 1977, p. 198, 272). In thinking therefore of the growth of object relatedness, I believe we should also rely heavily on the study of how children learn about space, particularly the category of "projective space." The reader is referred back to the discussion in chapter 3 and to the replication of Piaget's work done by Laurendeau and Pinard (1970) as well as to the digest by Gruber and Vonèche (1977). I believe that, for our neurotic patients, an examination of their thinking as compared to middle and late childhood, using drawings and the three mountains test, will operationalize Piaget's object concepts. As for psychotic patients, whose regression is more severe, we will need to examine them with a view to the earlier developments of solipsism, concretism, animism, and magical thinking. This area requires considerably more operational delineation.

Affective–Motivational Aspects: Attachment Theory

Bowlby and the "New Science"

Attachment theory, as presented extensively in John Bowlby's trilogy (1969, 1973, 1980), provides us with a principal scientific base in understanding the development of human relatedness and the influences therefrom in personality structure and psychopathology. Piaget, although there was an entertaining, joyous quality to his clinical interactions with children, leaves us somewhat detached, cool views of the cognitive aspect of object relations. Bowlby, introducing the affective–motivational aspects, tells us (1969) that "No form of behaviour is accompanied by stronger feeling than is attachment behavior—love —joy —anxiety—sorrow—anger" (p. 209).

Bowlby has tended, I believe, to be reduced in stature by those who have not read his work at first hand. He is indeed centrally concerned with how little children relate to their mothers and how they suffer distress in separation from them. He has studied this in depth, but he offers us much more. Attachment theory is a rather comprehensive and cohesive scientific schema which attends to a number of dimensions. It deals with an important sector or stream in personality development, and predicts outcomes in adult mental health or ill-health. It provides a new and useful model for the nature and conduct of psychotherapy. It is a heuristic schema, capable of generating testable hypotheses. In the broadest sense, it is a critique and a corrective of both psychoanalytic and learning theories of child development, as it employs contributions from the newer sciences.

These newer sciences are ethology and its relatives, analytic biology and sociobiology, and the theory of systems, particularly information and guidance systems, all of which Bowlby appears to have introduced in a pioneering role into Great Britain and into personality theory. The ethological approach stresses several methods or frameworks. Its experimental subjects are observed in their natural habitat (for children, the home or institution) as contrasted with "unnatural" settings such as the artificial conditions of laboratory, zoo, or psychotherapeutic or psychoanalytic consulting room. Not that Bowlby discredits or abandons psychoanalysis. He builds upon psychoanalysis as "the most serviceable and the most used of any present-day theory of psychopathology" (1969, p. xv). He believes, and many would agree, that Freud would commend his efforts to replace some of the nineteenth-century models involved in psychoanalytic theory, which are now scientifically *passé* and discredited, and to substitute for them a series of models drawn from contemporary science.

Ethology and related approaches stress, in addition to naturalistic observation, an evolutionary approach across living species: biologic, psychologic, and social patterns are viewed as adaptive and homeostatic, with functions which, if successful, perpetuate the species, or more specifically the genes involved in such successful function. Attachment theory stresses biologic adaptation as its basis. This forces us to consider the whole nature of instinctual behavior as a product of behavioral systems brought into play, and terminated, by appropriate conditions, and which are built up of more behavioral units. Attachment is one major behavioral system, distinct from, though often interlocking or competing with, other great systems such as those for feeding, sex, and agggression.

This brings us to Bowlby's consideration of information and guidance systems. The processing of information, both environmental (outward) and organismic (inward); the progressive setting up of templates, plans, and maps of information about the self and the environment and of courses of action that have been tested; these interlock with the innate guidance systems which regulate behavior (see also Miller, Galanter, and

Pribram [1960]). Various organizations of action make up behavioral systems (see also Piaget's sequences, chapter 3). These
range from simple, virtually reflex actions in the newborn,
through behaviors which come to have a relation to intention
or purpose, but which are linked as chains (one behavior leading to another as stimulus to response, but a chain which can
be interrupted at any link by distractions or failures) to behaviors which are dominated and organized by a plan and an overall "set-goal." Examples of the latter are maintaining optimal
distance from a predator, or proximity to a parent, seizing prey,
or copulating successfully. This set-goal (or more precisely, the
estimated discrepancy from the set-goal) is what constantly
monitors and guides behavior.

The models for "instinctual" and goal-directed behavior
(Bowlby, 1969, pp. 37–174) and for systems of memory and
mental mechanisms (Bowlby, 1980, pp. 44–47) are two contemporary viewpoints which deserve careful scrutiny. Bowlby's introduction of such scientific models into psychoanalysis and
psychiatry is one of the many contributions he has made.

An Introduction to Attachment Theory

To represent the complexities of attachment theory is an intimidating task but one which we cannot evade. Bowlby's main
corpus is contained in the three volumes of a trilogy on *Attachment and Loss*. Volume 1, *Attachment* (1969), has been revised
and expanded in a second edition. It presents the conceptual
bases and the integration of findings from multiple sources
which together formulate the nature and ontogenesis of attachment. Volume 2, *Separation: Anxiety and Anger* (1973), traces
the ramifications of the pathogen, separation, through normal
personality development and emotionality, and through personality maldevelopment and emotional disorder. Volume 3,
Loss, Sadness and Depression (1980), delves even further into
models of psychopathology and in particular into the implications of despair and detachment.

The young human child, like other primates, and indeed
many other warm-blooded creatures, is constantly impelled by
two great behavioral systems (Bowlby strongly advises against

use of the term *instinct* as simplistic and rigid). One system motivates and guides exploring, learning, and practicing, with curiosity as a dominant affect; the other promotes and regulates security, keeping proximity to a source of security, and seeking reassurance, with love and fear as dominant affects. The two are complementary, competing, alternating in the life of the child. The child's mother (we shall use the term as Bowlby does in shorthand for "principal, central, preferred caregiver") is the complementary protagonist in interaction with the child, and the object for enactment of the ongoing attachment behavioral system. If the relationship with her is secure and untroubled ("secure attachment"); if she is sensitive in responding to the child's needs and signals; if she is readily available on demand; if she interacts actively with the child at a pace monitored by the child's rather than merely her own needs, then, the child alternates actively between contact with her and his daily task of exploring and learning. He grows in behavioral repertoires. His excursions away from his mother became further and more prolonged. His world expands. He develops an internal sense of security, rightness, and *basic trust* (Erikson's term, which I have interpolated here).

If the relationship is precarious and insecure ("insecure attachment"); if there have been unresolved separations; if the mother is herself insecure and inexperienced, strained, parsimonious of attention, or overly intrusive in sharing herself with her child; then the relationship is more turbulent, uncomfortable, tentative, conditional, anxious. The child does not venture as far or explore as confidently, and may cling, whine, avoid, or torment his mother. His world and his behavioral repertoire do not expand as prosperously. He retains some pervasive sense of apprehension and mistrust, in self as well as in people and things.

In the more secure attachments, as in less secure ones, any threat to the mother–child system (activating stimulus) puts into train a series of actions whose set goal is to reestablish close proximity. Attachment behaviors come into action, exploring–learning behaviors cease. Attachment behaviors may be calm and joyful ones such as smiling, cooing, babbling, calling, caressing, when all is well. When stress or threat supervenes, they are uncomfortable and distressed ones: crying, following, clinging, demanding to be picked up. Attachment is the consistent propensity to seek proximity to a preferred caregiver. Attachment behavior is the repertoire of goal-directed and goal-corrected actions for increasing and assuring proximity. (Bowlby permits use of the term *instinctive behavior* though he finds the term *instinct* unsuitable). When the set goal of proximity is attained, then the more urgent and anxious attachment behaviors diminish and terminate; pleasurable ones, as above, ensue; exploratory learning behaviors are likely to resume. For securely attached children, the "terminating condition" of proximity is likely to halt active attachment behavior quickly. With less securely attached children, such behavior is likely to be more prolonged.

In ordinary day-to-day living, a child's exploratory activities will be punctuated only briefly by small bursts of attachment behavior. Under *organismic* conditions of fatigue, illness, hunger, or pain; or under *environmental* conditions such as unfamiliar surroundings, the presence of strangers, darkness, bright light, loud noises, or the disappearance of the mother; then attachment behavior with its affects is likely to appear in its full gamut and strength.

Function and Aim of Attachment: A Behavioral System

This leads us to consider the function, aim, and success of attachment and attachment behavior. Why does it occur? The aim of attachment behavior is clear: it is to restore proximity to a preferred and trusted caregiver. Its eliciting and terminating conditions suggest this, but they also hint at something of its function; just what does it accomplish, and how may its success be measured?

There is suggestive to convincing evidence that attachment behaviors are innate or instinctive (Bowlby 1969, second edition, p. 38) and not conditioned or learned (the "secondary drive" theory). Instinctive behaviors have these properties:

1. They occur among many species. Attachment behaviors are observed in our closest and more distant primate

relatives, and also among remotely related mammals such as ungulates (foals, lambs) and even ground-dwelling birds (ducklings, goslings).

2. The pattern is predictable within a species, or within one sex of the species.
3. The complex series of behaviors runs a predictable course.
4. The behaviors have consequences for the preservation of the individual or of the species; more strictly, for the preservation and propagation of the genes mediating the behavior.
5. Certain behaviors emerge despite an absence of the opportunity for real learning, or despite punishment for them.

Attachment behaviors meet these general criteria for instinctive patterns. But what is the evidence that they tend to preserve individual and species? This becomes much more vivid when Bowlby examines the environment in which our original adaptation probably occurred. This "environment of evolutionary adaptedness," in response to which the genetic programming of our present brains and constitutions developed (see chapter 2) 100,000 to 200,000 years ago, was likely an open savannah where small cooperative human groups lived as hunter–gatherers. The males roved and hunted big game together. The females stayed close to home with their young, forming a kind of nucleus community with the young whose childhood, with increasing brain size, had become increasingly lengthy. A protected home base gave shelter and defense against dangerous predators, of which Bowlby is particularly impressed with the significance of the leopard (see his citations for evidence [1969, p. 62]). Attachment behavior has meaning as a vital survival device in such an environment: staying close to, or within easy signaling distance of, mother; fear of the dark, of loud noises, even of too bright or open daylight spaces; avoidance of strange creatures, of exposure, falling, or drowning.

Two implications emerge from such a picture. Success of a behavioral trait involves study of a *population*, not merely of the individual (Bowlby, 1969, p. 128). And, puzzling behaviors such as attachment or altruism have meaning when they can be seen to aid success of a breeding population or, indeed, actual propagation of genes mediating attachment or altruism.

Having examined the general evidence that attachment is an instinctive behavioral pattern, let us look at one psychoanalytic model which Bowlby wishes to replace, a model also shared by behaviorists—the secondary drive theory. It is the construct that dependency and attachment are learned or conditioned patterns, conditioned principally through feeding (fulfilling of a "primary drive"). The baby becomes attached to the mother as a secondary object through the satisfaction and reward of the breast or bottle.

The likelihood that attachment is an autonomous behavioral system, or primary drive in itself, is suggested first by its survival value, as the above evolutionary view suggests: this argument is certainly correct for other animal species. There are additional items of evidence, the sum total of which is convincing:

Feeding in itself does not reinforce attachment (i.e., increase the preferential specificity of the caregiver and prolong and intensify attachment behaviors toward her), but abundant social interaction does. An interesting example is that of children raised in Israeli Kibbutzim, who do not become attached meaningfully to (and do not later recall with specificity and warmth) the nursery worker who fed and toileted them; but they do become attached to the parents with whom they have joyful interaction during evenings and weekends (Bowlby, 1969, pp. 314–317).

Punishment actually reinforces attachment behaviors, including separation anxiety, in other species and in our own, contrary to the predictions of learning theory (Bowlby, 1969, pp. 213–215; 1973, pp. 231–232).

A most interesting observation of Bowlby's is that the attachment behavioral system belongs to a class of behavioral systems which watchfully and dynamically maintain a steady state: in this case, optimal proximity to the mother. Such systems are highly unlikely to be learned or conditioned by reward and punishment, since they do not pleasurably consummate an immediate organismic need such as hunger. An intriguing example of such systems is that of alarm behavior in ungulates, which maintains steady optimal distance from a predator (Bowlby [1969, p. 72]; see also Ratner's model in chapters 7 and 10). Attachment involves a proximity-keeping and safety-regulating system (1969, p. 374).

Ontogenesis of Attachment

How does attachment develop and unfold? A synthesis, marshalled by Bowlby from many observations and reports, may be summarized as follows.

The first sign of attachment to a specific, preferred, caregiving figure appears at 4 to 6 months of age; the baby starts to smile when his mother appears, and particularly at her face in full view, and begins to stop smiling on seeing other faces. Up to this point, smiling has been elicited by any human face, even a crude drawing of one. Even at 3 months (Bowlby, 1969, p. 199) there is some evidence of a baby's perceptually discriminating its mother, but of course there is as yet no proximity-seeking behavior. The latter begins to be manifested clearly around 6 months of age (and henceforth we must keep recalling that *there is considerable individual variation* in all attachment phenomena), the baby crying and crawling in attempts to regain proximity. Around 9 months, clinging to mother is especially evident, and fear of strange figures begins to develop, though the infant will still follow his father or other familiar adults (p. 223).

By 18 months an intense primary attachment to the mother (see discussion of specificity and preference below) can be demonstrated, though in most families attachment to other figures develops too. Attachment behaviors are strong, though not particularly efficient, up to 3 years, the latter age often representing a peak in intensity of attachment. The baby plays a very active part in initiating social interaction, and exerts a powerful behavior-shaping influence upon her caretakers. From 3 years on, attachment behaviors are steadily less urgent and less frequent, but more competent (Bowlby, 1969, p. 244). A particularly interesting finding, noted also by Piaget, is that up to at least 3 years a child cannot successfully follow, or walk by the side of, a moving adult: the child simply becomes lost and help-less, and has to be carried or dragged! This is apparently due to a lack of competence in carrying out goal-corrected, proximity-maintaining behavior vis-à-vis a moving target.

Very early attachment behaviors seem to have no content or aim: they are simply primary behaviors of displeasure on separation. By the end of the first year the baby appears to have some plan or purpose involved in its proximity-seeking, and thereafter becoming increasingly sophisticated in initiating social interaction and using social skills to fulfill her security needs (Bowlby, 1969, p. 351).

Between 2 and 3 years of age small children are most reluc-tant to go alone into an unfamiliar situation (Bowlby, 1969, p. 205). By 4 to 5 years of age they will enter a strange test setting cheerfully.

Attachment continues as a dominant behavioral strand in the organization of latency-age behavior (Bowlby, 1969, p. 206). Attachment behaviors by this time are subtle and sophisticated. Mother no longer *appears* to be the dominant center of a child's life, but she probably is. Most children in our culture are not allowed to go far from home unattended. With great individual variation, attachment to parents gradually gives way in adoles-cence to an interest in adults other than one's parents, a strong interaction with peers, and a sexual attraction to age-mates (Bowlby, 1969, p. 207). Bowlby believes that for most people a degree of attachment (i.e., to the primary, preferred parent as well as to family members) continues in attenuated form throughout life, especially the daughter–mother bond, and perhaps in the form of attachment to institutions and causes.

Attachment Beyond Childhood

Although the studies of Bowlby do not take us solidly beyond childhood, it seems clear that in the human life cycle a progres-sive revision or reversal of the primordial interpersonal bond takes place: from the highly asymmetrical, helpless, unskilled position of the infant (Bowlby rejects the term *dependency* as too rigid and judgmental) through greater give-and-take in early childhood and latency, to the "breaking" of the asymmetrical bond in adolescence in favor of a symmetrical interdependence of peers in sexual and marital intimacy. Finally there is a move toward the role of parent and caregiver to the helpless infant and growing child, a new and reversed asymmetry for the now "older, wiser, stronger" adult vis-à-vis the youngling.

The semantics of the term *attachment* are therefore understandably in some state of flux. Bowlby prefers to reserve the term for the behavioral propensity (and the system mediating that propensity) of the child to seek proximity and safety with a specific and preferred caregiver. We shall restrict the term therefore to that usage. We shall not debate here just how to denote propensities which fairly evidently grow out of and along with attachment: the sustained and specific interest of an affective–motivational kind in a peer or playmate, a sexual partner, a spouse, one's own children; there are eight possible types of relationship depicted by Knobloch and Knobloch (1979) in their "group schema." These problems are discussed by Bowlby (1969, p. 229) and his colleagues and successors (e.g., chapters by Ainsworth, Hinde, and Weiss in Parkes and Stevenson-Hinde [1982]).

Can we achieve clearer resolution on what happens with attachment as children grow into adults? Weiss (1982), after carefully redefining attachment, addresses the question. Surveys which he reports from Harvard University have revealed bonds that meet the criteria of attachment in (1) well-functioning and even dysfunctional marriages and committed nonmarital relationships; (2) between some single parents and an elder child; (3) between male buddies under conditions of stress; and (4) occasionally between single women and peers or parents. Generally in adults peer relationships are felt to be of unique importance. Attachment behaviors are not dominant (and highly competitive) in relation to other systems in such adult relationships, and separations are much better tolerated than in children. A pilot study reported by Weiss included recently separated spouses and recently moved spouses whose marriage was intact. Subjects in both groups reported on the phenomenon of "loneliness," an experience that could not be allayed by new friends or even an intense new sexual relationship. Weiss has come to believe that loneliness ("separation distress without an object") is an important developmental acquisition as people grow toward adulthood.

Adolescence is a period when quite clear attachment behaviors (the seeking out of a parent, a sense of security when near parents, a sense of distress when parents are inaccessible, and homesickness) alternate with periods of clear relinquishment of parent figures. The task of emancipation, so long recognized as crucial to successful adolescent development, is not, according to Weiss (cited in Parkes and Stevenson-Hinde, 1982, pp. 176–177) a smooth and gradual one. Rather, the adolescent experiences gradually increasing periods of *interruption* of attachment. Finally, the "interruption [becomes] the steady state" that "gives way to brief resurgences of attachment." That is, attachment does not fade smoothly. Rather, it is entirely absent for longer and longer intervals, usually to be replaced by a relationship with a unique and preferred peer in which again all the earmarks of attachment can be observed: comfort, security, and pleasure in the other's company, separation distress if the relationship is rifted. A group may assume this role of significant other, and the group must be intact. Interestingly, Weiss has observed firm evidence that attachment to these new objects is sudden and strong, with a certain all-or-nothing quality.

Weiss is inclined to the hypothesis that a single perceptual–emotional system carries over from childhood, finding a new object, rather than the alternative hypothesis that a new and different attachment system develops for adulthood.

The Measurement of Attachment: Ainsworth

Obviously it is desirable to measure or quantify an observable phenomenon such as attachment behavior. For example, Weiss' comment on the all-or-nothing quality of adolescent attachment is a quantitative statement.

Ainsworth and her colleagues have developed a standardized and quasi-quantitative method for assessing the strength and quality of attachment in toddlers, the "Strange Situation" technique (Ainsworth, Bell, and Stayton, 1974; Ainsworth,

1982; Bowlby, 1969, p. 336). The young child is placed in a series of episodes in a controlled and observed setting, using various permutations of being alone, alone with mother, alone with a stranger, and in the presence of both. This permits study of the child's alternating play–exploration behaviors and attachment behaviors, in relation to the variables of a strange setting, the preferred caregiver, and a friendly but strange adult. Not only have some unpredicted and interesting behaviors been discovered, but it has become clear that these laboratory findings can be generalized to the home and to subsequent personality development (Bowlby, 1969, p. 361; Ainsworth, 1982, p. 9; and see pp. 151–154 below).

Ainsworth and her colleagues have found that these small children fall into three rather distinct groupings. The majority (about two-thirds) assigned to group B are found to be securely attached. These children cry little at home, they show less anxiety in everyday separations, they greet their mothers positively after an absence, and they are content to be put down after being held. They initiate being picked up, are soothed by bodily contact, and are glad to be held. Their mothers show all the indices of sensitive responsiveness to their child's signals, and an evident enjoyment of close social and bodily contact with them. In the laboratory situation, the children explore actively when mother is present, are upset and stop exploring when she leaves, and show keen interest and a desire to interact closely with her when she returns. Group A (about one-fifth) were termed both "anxiously attached" and "avoidant": they avoided proximity, interaction, and contact with their mother, some persistently, after being reunited with her; during the standardized separation periods they showed little or no distress. The mothers of these children were found to be somewhat rejecting, hostile, rather compulsive, and wooden in expression, with an aversion to close bodily contact. Group C (about one-eighth) were termed "anxiously attached" and "ambivalent": they were anxious even before an episode of separation from their mother, then very upset by separation; upon reunion they sought close bodily contact, but then fought off contact when it was offered, a curious mixture of contact-seeking and angry resistant behaviors. The mothers of these children were not rejecting, and seemed to enjoy bodily contact, but they were highly insensitive to their child's signals and needs.

Factor analysis clearly identified a security–anxiety dimension (Parkes and Stevenson-Hinde, 1982, p. 16). Groups A and C showed more general distress in everyday home situations, cried more in greeting their mothers after an absence, and responded more negatively in regard to physical contact. The other principal dimension identified involves bodily contact. The group A children seem to wish, but have come to avoid, close contact through fear of actual rebuff. The group C children likewise wish contact, but respond automatically with anger because this need has been frustrated by their mother's insensitivity to their signals.

This is one example of attempting to quantify and classify attachment. A second example deals with the question of the exclusiveness or preferential quality of attachment. Bowlby's own review of the matter (Bowlby, 1969, pp. 303–308) points to the general conclusion that most or all children, by 2 years of age, have attached themselves to "a most preferred" caregiver, most usually their natural mother, but in some cases a father or grandparent. To this figure they will turn as a first priority when hungry, distressed, frightened, injured, or sick. However, for most children there are other attachment figures and these to some extent can be ranked in order of preference by observation of distressed children. These degrees of preference can be measured or inferred by the amount of protest upon separation, as well as seeing to whom a distressed child will turn if more than one figure is available. These relationships shade off in quality into other kinds of bonds, properly not to be termed attachment; for example, a lateral or peer relationship as with a playmate. Playmates are usually sought when a child is in good spirits. A child's mother can fill the role of playmate.

Thus, although a plurality of attachment figures is the rule by 2 years of age, these figures do not all possess the same valence. The role of principal attachment figure is gained by the person who shares the most extensive social interaction with the child. This, for familial reasons, and quite possibly hormonal variables as well, is most likely to be the woman who gave birth to the child. But, the role can certainly be filled by someone else close to the child.

One other quasi-quantitative finding is important (Bowlby, 1969, p. 308): children who show an early and strong interest in a principal figure also develop interest and attachment toward others. The infant who remains attached to only one principal figure is likely to show relatively weaker evidences of attachment. A multiplicity of attachment figures does not "diffuse" nor render nonspecific the nature of a child's attachments; specificity and hierarchical preference remain significantly correlated. The bias of a child toward an important and specific attachment is termed by Bowlby "monotrophy" (1969, p. 309). Ainsworth (1982) updates the whole matter of specificity and possible hierarchies in preferential attachment.

Clinical Correlations of Attachment Theory

General Comments: Models for Emotion

We may consider the clinical applications of Bowlby's work under three headings: the principal human emotions; the natural history of personality development and psychopathology; and the structure of psychotherapy.

One can, for example, create new hypotheses for clinical testing, as does de Lozier (Parkes and Stevenson-Hinde, 1982, p. 111) in viewing *passages* from one life stage to another in the light of attachment theory and the security-base–exploration–learning interaction. One can consistently examine clinical material, as to both present and recent happenings, and remote or contributing life events, in the light of attachment and separation.

In addition to the security–exploration interaction we have the well-known sequence of protest, despair, and detachment which follows enforced separation (Bowlby, 1973, pp. 24, 34, 46–47) as a source for clinical formulation. Protest, the phase of active and vigorous distress, of clear-cut attachment behavior, and of strong affect of the general type fight–flight, is highly relevant to problems of separation anxiety and anxiety disorders (see chapter 10). Despair, a phase of greater quietude, with cessation of active attachment behavior, and affect of the general type of sadness or despondency (see the consideration of "Conservation–Withdrawal" in chapter 11) follows on, and is highly relevant to clinical depression and depression proneness. Finally, if the separation is continued, detachment, a failure to respond to the reappearance of the lost attachment figure, with apathetic or bland affect, has much relevance for the constructs of defense and the contribution of defense mechanisms to clinical syndromes and character formation. The affective–motivational aspects of attachment span the gamut of emotions, from peace, love, and joy to fear, panic, and rage.

A Model for Normal Development and Psychopathology

Bowlby relies here considerably on Ainsworth's studies (Bowlby, 1969, pp. 333–340, 362–364; Ainsworth, 1982). The organization of childhood behaviors shows considerable stability: the child who is securely attached at 1 year of age is likely at 5 years of age to be friendly, secure, and cooperative, self-directed, curious, and sociable, in comparison with insecurely attached children. Bowlby (1982, p. 364), citing a study by Arend finds that around age 5 (1) securely attached children show good "ego resilience" and are "moderately controlled"; (2) anxiously attached and avoidant children are now lower in ego resilience and "overly controlled"; while (3) anxiously attached and resistent children are lower in ego resilience but "undercontrolled." In more general clinical terminology, we might paraphrase this as follows: the attachment behavior of very young children in the laboratory can be generalized safely to their behavior outside the laboratory, and to behavior in later the years; so that by around 5 years we have a picture likely to persist in personality structure. The securely attached (group B) become children with good social confidence and a repertoire of relational techniques; their emotionality is expressed in warm and appropriate ways. The anxiously attached and avoidant (group A) become constricted in social repertoire and emotionality, tending to perseverate in adaptive strategies. The anxiously attached and resistant (group C) are constricted in social or adaptive skills, but turbulent and inconsistent in emotionality. Paraphrasing further, we might say that group B seem to become "normal" human beings, group A become compulsive and schizoid characters, and group C become hysteroid and impulsive ones.

What happens to children who undergo traumatic separations? This question still requires considerable careful research, preferably of a prospective type. However, Bowlby's writings clearly indicate a trend, which I shall attempt to synopsize in my own terms with a great deal of oversimplification (see Volumes 2 and 3 of *Attachment and Loss*). Using the protest–despair–detachment formulation:

Children who are separated, once or several times, from an important or primary attachment figure, and whose attachment behavior does not pass beyond protest, will tend to be anxiously attached as children, and prone to anxiety and the psychoneuroses as adults. Their basic trust is moderately stable but can be shaken, and residuals of separation anxiety can be revived by later external stress, intrapsychic conflict, and actual separation experience, as further noted in chapter 10.

Children whose separations go on to the development of despair, particularly if this experience is repeated or prolonged, will tend to be sensitive, easily hurt and rejected children, and as adults will be depression prone to various degrees. My impressions here should be seen in the light of several studies noted in chapter 14.

Children whose separations go on to the phase of detachment, including those who develop detachment as a defense against the repeated and traumatic threat of abandonment or parental suicide, such as occurs in the turbulent setting of poor, isolated, and single-parent homes (Bowlby, 1973, pp. 263–274, 1984; De Lozier, 1982) will develop varying degrees of emotional coldness and aloofness from interpersonal or social interaction. These developments we may call compulsive, schizoid, paranoid, or psychopathic configurations, with all their complex character defenses. Persons with these character structures are the most difficult to help by psychotherapeutic endeavor.

A Model for Psychotherapy

Bowlby in two thought-provoking papers (1977, 1978) suggests that psychotherapy can be understood as a reenactment of the security–exploration paradigm. An insecure or troubled person gradually attaches himself to a new primary attachment figure, the therapist, from whose encouraging and supporting presence he becomes able progressively to explore, more and more courageously and extensively, the world of his present, past, and intrapsychic self. Bowlby proposes that an awareness of concepts of attachment and separation provides the therapist with some new tools, that is, in seeing psychopathology as the resultant of pathogenic attachments and separations, and in dealing with lacunae in memory and history as the result of *parental injunctions* to keep ugly family secrets hidden (Bowlby, 1979).

Guided by this model, the therapist is advised to spend much time reviewing relationships, key objects or people, attachments, and separations; and to avoid or minimize the exploration of primitive fantasy. As one might expect, this is analogous to what needs to be done in the psychotherapy of actual grief, to which Bowlby devotes a considerable section of the papers: the reviewing of *all aspects* of the important affectional bond which has been ruptured.

For the psychotherapist, there are four tasks which continually interweave:

To provide for the patient a *secure base* from which to explore the self and the significant others with whom the patient has had affectional bonds;

To provide companionship in that exploration of self and of relationships, including exploration of the relationship with the therapist;

To point out the way in which the patient seems to construe the relationship with the therapist, and its possible inappropriateness;

To help the patient view real-life situations in which he is involved, in the perspective of actual attachment experiences of childhood.

Clearly, as Bowlby points out, we are dealing here in a new light with the fundamental processes of support, exploration ("free association," not labeled as such by Bowlby), transference, and interpretation, the analysis and reconstruction of the past, and (again not labeled as such by Bowlby) the repetition–compulsion or stereotyped replication in the present of relationships and solutions based on the past. The model for these processes is that of the little child bravely and cheerfully exploring new experiences from the vantage and secure base of his mother's presence; or less securely, clinging, being afraid to explore, constricting his life-space, developing slowly and restrictedly. One might picture psychotherapy as an interaction of two mutually reinforcing cycles: the struggle to attain closeness and security with the therapist; and the resultant gradual expansion of, and confidence in knowledge of self and others. The model also informs us as to why some patients are difficult or even impossible to treat psychotherapeutically.

Thus, Bowlby's model of psychotherapy stresses the exploration of the real self and of real relationships, and putting trust in the patient's historical recollections as valid for the psychotherapeutic endeavor.

Summary of Attachment Theory

1. Attachment theory is based on psychoanalytic theory which it attempts to reorient and update through contemporary models in behavioral science: ethology and analytical biology, with their emphasis on naturalistic observation and an evolutionary perspective; and the theory of information and control systems.

2. Attachment is the widespread and consistent propensity of young creatures to seek out and maintain proximity with a preferred, older, stronger, caregiving figure. It is mediated by a well-defined, autonomous attachment behavioral system, distinct from and often competing with other behavioral systems for feeding, for curiosity and exploration, for sex and reproduction, and for aggression.

3. Attachment behaviors are the cluster of behaviors activated or elicited under conditions of separation or threatened separation from the preferred caregiver. These eliciting conditions call into action, in young humans, crying, calling, clinging, and crawling or running, together with affective distress. These might well be thought of as separation behaviors, and they are equivalent to "protest" (noted below). Eliciting conditions include not only separation, but fear, hunger, cold, fatigue, pain, illness, loud noises, darkness, bright light, and the presence of strangers. The conditions terminating attachment behaviors are a satisfactory closeness to, and reciprocal responsive actions on the part of, the caregiver.

4. Attachment behaviors become identifiable from 4 to 6 months of age, when evidence also begins to appear that a baby can identify specific faces in the environment. There are gentle and pleasurable behaviors such as eye contact, smiling, cooing, and babbling. Strange faces, pain, fear, and separation bring the more unpleasant, urgent and protesting behaviors noted above. Alarm in the presence of strangers builds rapidly and clearly in the second half of the first year, as does the specificity and intensity of attachment to the mother (shorthand for preferred caregiver).

5. The attachment behavioral system reaches a peak of intensity at about 3 years of age, when a little child is mobile and highly vulnerable. This, with much other evidence, suggests that its function is best understood in an evolutionary perspective as safety maintaining. Ground-dwelling birds, ungulates, and primates observed in nature show an intense attachment of infant to mother. In the savannah environment in which our genetic programs and the human brain probably evolved, our young must have survived, and thus passed along the genes for their survival, by attachment behavior which protected them from hunger, cold, exposure, drowning, and particularly from large predators.

6. The attachment behavioral system has all the earmarks of being innate or instinctive and not a propensity that has been conditioned or learned via other unconditioned need-satisfactions (the "secondary drive theory") such as feeding. It is found transculturally and indeed across many animal species;

it is not reinforced by feeding, and is reinforced by social inter-action including, paradoxically, punishment. It has the aim of dynamically maintaining a steady state, that of optimum prox-imity to a preferred caregiver. It competes with and periodically supplants other systems: a curious baby, if frightened, stops exploring to return to her mother; hungry baby, if frightened, stops feeding to cling.

7. Attachment can be to several preferred persons, and a hierarchy of preference can be demonstrated. Attachment behavior must be distinguished from more symmetrical rela-tionships to playmates and peers. The strongest attachments are shown by children who have a hierarchy of preferred fig-ures; attachment to only one figure is usually demonstrably weaker in nature, and occurs in children whose attachment behavior develops late.

8. A secure intense attachment leads to exploration, learn-ing, and personality growth. Insecure attachments lead to some restriction in personality growth and social repertoires. If a child is separated from its parents, but provided good substitute care, he or she will reattach to the parents upon reunion; but if such is not provided, subsequent attachment developments will be delayed and problematic. Small children tend to show intense, preferential attachments for substitute caregivers, given good conditions. They do not diffuse their relationships without peril to their development.

9. When young children are separated from the preferred caregiver over longer periods, a characteristic sequence of be-haviors is observed, each lasting from hours to weeks. The initial phase, termed *protest,* involves active, sometimes frantic, and prolonged attachment behavior. In the second phase, de-spair, a kind of resignation sets in, with an affect of apathy and despondency. In the third phase, detachment, the characteristic affect is an emotional blandness together with a failure to show any interest in the preferred caregiver when she reappears.

10. In late childhood, attachment remains an active deter-minant even though peers and social groups begin to have much importance. Attachment to a parent probably never ex-tinguishes totally during an adult's lifetime. During adoles-cence, peer bonding and the potential for marital intimacy be-come important developmental tasks. Later, the adult shows the reciprocal behavioral system of parenting and caregiving.

11. From a clinical perspective, attachment theory provides several important models: for the systems of emotion and memory; for the pathogenic influence of unmanageable separation in subsequent psychopathology; and for the process of psychotherapy and the tasks of the psychotherapist.

Bibliographic Notes: Key Readings

There is a large literature on object relations within psychoanalytic theory. Like other psychoanalytic formulations, the constructs are retrospectively and clinically derived, and difficult to test, verify, or refute experimentally. I therefore elect to bypass this literature, and to focus instead on studies which are observational and prospective, chiefly the important studies initiated by Piaget and Bowlby, and now pursued by their students and colleagues. A somewhat unique volume, pioneering modern models of motivation and complex human behaviors, is that of Miller, Galanter, and Pribram (1960): I recommend it highly, and somewhat arbitrarily include it here.

Gruber and Vonèche (1977) compile major extracts from Piaget's writings on the development of object concept and object permanence, together with their editorial comments. This is a good introduction. Laurendeau and Pinard (1970) conducted a major replication of Piaget's experiments on the development of cognitive space, and their section on projective space should be particularly consulted. The reader should also refer back to chapter 2 and the appropriate references.

Bowlby's (1969, 1973, 1980) impressive trilogy on attachment should be studied by anyone who requires a good understanding of attachment theory, with its scientific models and its developmental and clinical implications. Volume 1, in its second edition (Bowlby, 1969), will provide the firmest basis if the reader is limited to one book. Clinical and therapeutic implications of attachment theory can be well sampled in two further papers by Bowlby (1977, 1984) on the nature of psychotherapy and of family violence.

Bowlby has generally left the field of attachment at late childhood and early adolescence, posing a number of questions regarding the later fate of the attachment behavioral system. His followers are now pursuing such questions. An important collection of papers is that edited by Parkes and Stevenson-Hinde (1982), including contributions by Ainsworth, De Lozier, Hinde, and Weiss. At the time of going to press, an important compendium (Parkes, Stevenson-Hinde, and Marris, 1991) had just been published, summarizing and extending attachment theory and its implications. Its chapters include tributes to John Bowlby on his eightieth birthday, while the whole is a monument to his passing.

References

Ainsworth, M. D. S. (1982), Attachment: Retrospect and prospect. In: *The Place of Attachment in Human Behavior,* ed. C. M. Parkes & J. Stevenson-Hinde. New York: Basic Books.
—————— Bell, S. M., & Stayton, D. J. (1974), Infant–mother attachment and social development: Socialization as a product of reciprocal responsiveness to signals. In: *The Integration of a Child into a Social World,* ed. M. P. M. Richards. London: Cambridge University Press.
*Bowlby, J. (1969), *Attachment and Loss, Vol. 1: Attachment,* 2nd ed. London: Hogarth Press, 1982.
*—————— (1973), *Attachment and Loss,* Vol. 2. London: Hogarth Press.
*—————— (1977), The making and breaking of affectional bonds: II. Some principles of psychotherapy. *Brit. J. Psychiat.,* 130:421–431.
—————— (1978), Attachment theory and its therapeutic implications. In: *Adolescent Psychiatry,* Vol. 6, ed. P. L. Giovacchini & S. C. Feinstein. Chicago: University of Chicago Press.
—————— (1979), On knowing what you are not supposed to know and feeling what you are not supposed to feel.*Can. J. Psychiat.,* 25:403–408.
*—————— (1980), *Attachment and Loss, Vol. 3: Loss: Sadness and Depression.* London: Hogarth Press.
*—————— (1984), Violence in the family as a disorder of the attachment and caregiving systems. *Amer. J. Psychoanal.,* 44:9–27.
De Lozier, P. P. (1982), Attachment theory and child abuse. In: *The Place of Attachment in Human Behavior,* ed. C. M. Parkes & J. Stevenson-Hinde. New York: Basic Books.
Erikson, E. H. (1963), *Childhood and Society,* 2nd ed. New York: W. W. Norton.
Freud, S. (1915), Instincts and their vicissitudes. *Standard Edition,* 14:117–140. London: Hogarth Press, 1957.
*Gruber, H. E., & Vonèche, J. J., eds. (1977), *The Essential Piaget.* New York: Basic Books.
Knobloch, F., & Knobloch, J. (1979), *Integrated Psychotherapy.* New York: Jason Aronson.
Laurendeau, M., & Pinard, A. (1970), *The Development of the Concept of Space in the Child.* New York: International Universities Press.

*Miller, G. A., Galanter, E., & Pribram, K. H. (1960), *Plans and the Structure of Behavior*. New York: Henry Holt.
*Parkes, C. M., & Stevenson-Hinde, J., eds. (1982), *The Place of Attachment in Human Behavior*. New York: Basic Books.
————— ————— Marris, P., eds. (1991), *Attachment across the Life Cycle*. London: Routledge & Kegan Paul.
Sullivan, H. S. (1953), *The Interpersonal Theory of Psychiatry*. New York: W. W. Norton.
Vaillant, G. (1977), *Adaptation to Life*. Boston: Little, Brown.
Weiss, R. (1982), Attachment in adult life. In: *The Place of Attachment in Human Behavior,* ed. C. M. Parkes & J. Stevenson-Hinde. New York: Basic Books.

---

*Recommended readings.

6

A Fifth Developmental Stream: Sequences in the Development of Moral Judgment; Sex Differences

Introduction

Overview

It is some years since I became uneasy and dissatisfied with the clinical precept that severely depressed patients experience and express severe guilt. A closer look at their ostensible moral judgments is instructive. First, we can be confident, following Freud, that the stereotyped and exaggerated self-criticisms are, in disguise, accusations against someone else. Both the verbal professions and the auditory hallucinations which may accompany them have a kind of melodramatic quality, however muted and subdued they may be. If one tries to enter the patient's experience, it does not feel like a mature moral judgment of guilt, but rather a kind of pleading, groveling, terror, some masochistic self-prostration or self-immolation before a wrathful and primitive Zeus or Yahweh. The moral judgment expressed is not truly the taking of responsibility for a real wrong committed, with regret and a wish to make restitution; it is, rather, a fending off of retribution, an exaggerated but false admission of guilt in order to stave off capricious, unjust, and savage punishment. Thus, the superego process of moral judgment is a primitive and regressive one. It must relate to some early state of moral development in which the true mode is a fear of retribution, retaliation, and direct physical punishment by an unpredictable and terrifying parent. We might call this "depressive" or "psychotic" guilt, but I do not even think that *guilt* is a correct term for it. In some psychoses, this "guilt" can be totally projected as fear of external punishment. Further, in certain character disorders and in the euphoric states, we may find an apparent total absence of moral concern or guilt.

We find disturbances of moral judgment of a more subtle kind in less severe depressions, and indeed in most neuroses and character disorders: what might be called the whole phenomenon of "neurotic guilt." In general, this consists of an indolent, haunting sense of wrongdoing, or rather of fear that one be found out somehow to have sinned, a constantly unresolved apprehension of judgment, an inability to clear the slate and feel forgiven, and in many cases a reciprocal tendency to keep repeating those very acts by which one ends up feeling so haunted.

We are therefore concerned with the question of whether psychotic and neurotic "guilt" can be found to compare with the style of moral judgment of normal children, at various stages of development.

The dimensions of a fully developed morality (Carroll and Rest, 1982) include: recognition, sensitivity, empathy for the welfare of others and the community; moral judgment, based on ideal norms; an accounting for social values and influences in planning moral action; and the execution and implementation of a moral decision in action.

In this chapter I shall review four principal sources on the development of moral judgment: psychoanalytic theory as conceived originally by Freud and as updated by modern child psychoanalysts of an observational and ego psychological bent; rather early work by Piaget on the nature of rulemaking, justice, and the social contract; and two modern exponents who started from Piagetian bases and have respectively clarified for us the development of moral judgment in the two sexes, Kohlberg and Gilligan.

In the psychoanalytic tradition, the superego is an organization of special functions within the general system of the ego, which initially solidifies ("precipitates") during latency, and further matures in adolescence. The superego contains both a facilitating guidance system and a punitive limit-setting one. Freud began to conceptualize the superego after pondering the nature of accusatory hallucinations in depressive and schizophrenic psychoses. More recently, child analysts have achieved some agreement on the steps, or precursors, leading toward the formation of the autonomous superego, as summed up in a paper of Holder (1982). Psychoanalytic theory gives us a developmental ladder reaching from about 1 to 7 years of age. Much unresolved debate in the psychoanalytic literature has centered upon the differences between women's and men's superegos; here, prospective studies are clearly needed.

In exploring categories of knowledge and cognitive development, Piaget (Piaget, Baechler, Feldweg, Lambercier, Martinez-Mont, Maso, V. J. Piaget, and Rambert, 1932) relatively early became interested in the development of the sense of obligation and of the progression of moral judgment from heteronomy (outer-directed) to autonomy (inner-directed). His principal research subjects were boys from 2 to 13 years of age playing a traditional street game of marbles, and girls of the same years playing a special version of hide-and-seek. With them he was able to discover how the practice of rules is advanced in time (a décalage) over the consciousness and conceptualization of rules. We summarize developments along the ladder of both these processes.

Kohlberg (1981a,b), founding his research on Piagetian theory, studied how subjects grapple with and attempt to resolve moral dilemmas. His work has the particular interest that it extends across many human cultures. He finds (apparently based on masculine thinking as the norm) a series of six devel-opmental levels, extending "upward" from the "preconven-tional," or highly personal and concrete, to the "postconven-tional," or abstract, universal, and transcendent in moral judgments. Because evidently the Kohlbergian tasks require hypothetical thinking (i.e., formal operations), the develop-mental ladder he constructs extends from about 10 to about 20 years of age.

Gilligan (1982), who started working from a base of Kohl-berg's methods, discovered that women do not fit his schema at all well. Accordingly, based on several distinctly different studies, she has evolved for women a tentative developmental ladder of moral judgment which seems to accord well with material we have already noted in chapter 3 as conceived by Maccoby and Jacklin and by Eagly. Her schema suggests that moral development in girls and women builds from a sense of aloneness and survival to a dominant sense of rightness highly related to concern for the welfare of others, in reciprocity with fairness to the self. Persons, not principles, appear to anchor feminine morality.

Finally, I attempt to formulate questions which need to be kept in mind when examining patients. These have to do with their style of moral judgment and the developmental age it appears to represent.

Psychoanalytic Studies: The Superego

The Nature of the Superego

There has been a complex theory of the superego in psychoana-lytic literature, which deals with chronological ages earlier than have been investigated by other research approaches. Since it is partly based on direct observation rather than merely retro-spective reconstructions, let us look at this "soft" but important research. In particular we may compare the initial formulations of Freud with recent contributions by child psychoanalysts.

The superego is an organization of functions (Gillman, 1982), a system (Brickman, 1983), a "group of compromise formations" based on mastery of successive conflicts (Brenner 1982), a "mass of contradictions," a "conglomeration of many identifications" (Arlow, 1982). It was originally defined by Freud as a special part of the ego, a "precipitate" within the ego of major identifications with idealized and feared parents and their judgments (Freud, 1933, Lecture XXXI). For a classical statement on the superego, see Fenichel (1945, pp. 102–110). The superego performs the functions of a guidance system, with two major aspects: a collection of ideal behaviors which are goal directing and positive, and a collection of critical, punitive judgments vis-à-vis failure to attain these ideal values, which are negative. We might well consider this dual system against Bowlby's explication of a "goal-corrected" behavioral system (Bowlby, 1969, pp. 8–9). However, by definition, the superego does not deal with everyday behaviors and skills, but with values, acquired from the parents and later reinforced by the wider society (Freud, 1914).

Freud began in 1914 focusing systematically on these judgmental functions in a study of the schizophrenic psychoses (paraphrenias) and in 1917 in a study of severe depressions (melancholia). He noted (Freud, 1914) that delusions of being observed, and auditory hallucinations commenting upon a patient's behavior, both suggest regressive externalization of an internal monitoring system. Interestingly, he commented on the verbal or "auditive" nature of the system (Freud, 1914, 1923) as being related to the many verbal instructions, comments, criticisms, or tongue-lashings which a child receives, the memories of which he accumulates (see chapter 8 on memory systems). In the severe depressions Freud (1917) noted the regressive savagery of the self-criticisms and self-revilings. Both sets of clinical findings pointed to an inner establishment having two qualities. One, an "ego ideal," is a set of standards of admiration and excellence: a mixture of idealized views of the parents and of later objects of emulation, and of memories of one's own early "perfection." The other is a "conscience" (1914) or "superego" (1923) which watches over the ego in the light of these standards. In his reformulation of personality in the structural theory into id, ego, and superego Freud did not separate ego ideal and superego (1923). Subsequently, several major theorists continued to insist on the continuity between the two (Fenichel, 1945; Arlow, 1982). Although there are many problems of terminology (Guerrero, 1982; Brenner, 1982) general psychoanalytic usage seems to have continued in the concepts of a positive system of goals and ideals (ego ideal) and a warning, inhibitory, punitive and generally negative system (superego). Brickman (1983) considers the superego a system of which the ego ideal is a part, the superego system in turn being part of the ego system as a whole.

Classically, the superego has been conceived and described as developing and solidifying ("precipitate") out of the complicated triangular conflicts of the oedipal period (age about 5 to 7) and their successful mastery and resolution in a gender-appropriate fashion, a virtually untestable psychoanalytic formulation which I shall not pursue further, though I have deep respect for its mysteries. What concerns us here is the question of "superego precursors"; what style of moral judgments children make *before* they have a proper or autonomous superego. Fenichel (1945) reviews this question in his methodical fashion.

Holder (1982) puts forward a view, apparently feeling support for it, that, analogous to the continuous longitudinal development of ego functions, we might regard the superego as longitudinally developed, from its feeblest, frailest, most incomplete anlagen in infancy. What Freud purports to say is that a superego which can function independently, and when alone (i.e., can function autonomously without the auxiliary help of parents or other disciplinarians), makes its appearance as an "heir" to the parents of the oedipal period.

Of great interest is that, from very different approaches, both Freud and Piaget propose that essentially mature moral judgment takes shape and emerges in the same age period, namely latency (see below for Piaget).

Holder and Others: Superego Development

Let us try to scan the development of the superego, whether viewed as a continuum (Holder, 1982) or as a series of precursors (Fenichel, 1945). Kennedy and Yorke (1982) and Brickman (1983) picture the process as essentially a progression from conflict with the external world and external controls, to inner conflict and inner controls. The infant, protected by good parenting, is helped to manage external frustrations, limitations, and dangers. This combination of protection and manageable frustration lays the foundation for the development of inner controls. The "no-experience," as Brickman (1983) points out, relates to the verbal or "auditive" nature of much of superego functioning; he considers congenital deaf mutes and finds, however, that their superego development can be normal.

The toddler's early ego begins to classify experience. With this, an ability grows to delay, inhibit, and modify gratifications, a kind of early superego function (Holder, 1982) which lacks any true autonomy since it requires an external caregiver to maintain it. Repeated curbings and prohibitions lead from a fear of punishment or injury to a fear of loss of parental approval or love, against which, however feebly, the child begins to monitor conforming behaviors. But the child still fears the real parent who will discover or observe wrongdoing: hence, the fear of being found out, not a bad conscience, is the operative influence (Holder, 1982, p. 265). The period of toilet training is a paradigmatic illustration of moral development in the very young (Gillman, 1982; Kennedy and Yorke, 1982; Brickman, 1983). In this acquisition of *sphincter morality* (a term of Ferenczi cited by Gillman) the child must come to believe, to have a personal ideal, that cleanliness and control are good; he must identify with the parents against his own soiling impulses.

Summing up, and using Holder's discussion as a basis, we may trace superego development (or the superego's "precursors") in the following qualitative steps:

1a. The fear of punishment: up to 1 year (all ages given are approximate)

1b. The fear of punishment *if* one is discovered: up to 2 years.

2. The fear of authority *if* one is discovered, and a partial identification with this authority (sphincter morality): 3 years.

3. The fear of loss of parental approval and love *if* one is discovered: 3 to 4 years.

4. The fear *of being discovered* and found out (*shame*): 4 to 5 years.
5. The fear of one's own conscience or superego ("conscience anxiety," "moral anxiety," or guilt): 5 to 7 years and up.

The affect of crude fear is associated with the first two of these steps, and fantasies of retaliation or punishment in kind persist through the oedipal period, as "castration anxiety." Separation anxiety is the painful affect of stage 3. Shame, that rather unique human emotion with its connotations of being caught, exposed, and ostracized, and its physiological accompaniment of blushing (see chapter 7, pp. 229–237) accompanies stage 4. Only finally, as the monitoring functions become solidly internalized and operate autonomously in the absence of any controlling, approving, or disapproving external figures, do we find the subtle and complex "emotion" (see chapter 7, pp. 229–237) of guilt. When wrongdoing is contemplated or temptation presents, the well-functioning superego generates a pulse of "signal" or "superego" anxiety, the warning of disapproval from the monitoring system. Such a signal motivates right behavior in normal people, and right behavior generates a pulse of pleasurable, relieved satisfaction from the ego ideal, as reward and reinforcer. If wrong is carried out, tension between ego ideal and ego (as monitored by the critical and disapproving agency of superego) generates guilt, a kind of complex, appalled anxiety with lowering of self-esteem, which can be allayed by restitution and expiation, and which provides a negative reinforcer for the future.

A Note on the Female Superego

Although there has been repeated attention given to the "dimorphism" between the woman's and the man's superego (Jacobson, 1976; Bernstein, 1983; Casgrain, 1983) it has never been solidly demonstrated how women's and men's superegos, consciences, and moral judgment and reasoning develop along different paths. Freud thought so, basing his ideas partly on intuitively sensing a difference in the cognitive modes of the two sexes, and partly on enumerating the greater number of steps in the pathway which the woman traverses toward self-differentiation, object relationships, and personal autonomy. His general conclusion, for which he has understandably been berated by feminists, seems to have been that the feminine superego is "weaker," somehow less clear, logical, and assertive, than the male's. Jacobson (1976) reflects a "classical" psychoanalytic position, relating the superego to the female castration complex. Women are capable of becoming just as depressed as men, and their superegos may be very harsh in the process, as Bernstein, a psychoanalyst, points out (1983). Interestingly, she notes that the symbol of impartial justice is a blindfolded *woman* holding a pair of scales, and that in Freud's era women were the keepers of morality. Bernstein concludes on clinical grounds that women's superegos are more flexible than men's, and that this flexibility may be due to a greater range of conflict about mandates. I have been unable to locate any prospective psychoanalytic studies which determine *how* female and male superegos may indeed come to be different.

Gilligan (1982), a woman educational psychologist and a follower of Kohlberg's methodology, provides us (see below) with the one systematic observational study I have found. This, in conjunction with what we know of the developmental dimorphism of female and male brains and cognitive styles, may help in answering the question.

Piaget: Obligation, Rules, and Justice

Piaget's Cognitive Approach

We have already, in chapter 3, reviewed the basic principles evolved by Piaget; I shall summarize the essence of these here, thereby laying the ground for understanding his findings on the development of moral sense and judgment. The general progressions of cognitive development: from motor to intellectual; from concrete, random, unintegrated, particular, rigid, to abstract, organized, integrated, embracing, fluid; from egocentric, idiosyncratic, subjective, to universal, socialized, objective.

In the case of moral development, we might particularly remind ourselves of what Piaget calls Claparède's law of "prise de conscience," or conscious realization (Piaget et al., 1932) based on the repeated observation that conscious thought consistently lags behind actual practice. This will apply not only to the *décalage* or staggering in time between the age at which Piaget's children obeyed rules and that at which they later conceptualized them. It will apply also to the fascinating reworking of moral judgment studied by Kohlberg in adolescents and adults (see below).

Piaget's research on moral development is quite old now (Piaget et al., 1932) though it has been somewhat updated (Piaget and Inhelder, 1966; Gruber and Vonèche, 1977, chapters 16 and 17). Nonetheless I believe going back to origins is the valid way to proceed here. Later critics of Piaget's main formulations have the onus of producing some new, and all-embracing theory if they are to replace him.

Piaget's subjects were boys living in poorer districts of Geneva and girls apparently of more favored circumstances; he reminds us to consider his very loose age norms in comparisons between less and more favored children. The situation used in the study was another of Piaget's ethological operations: participating in, observing, and asking questions about a traditional game of marbles as played by boys of 2 to 5 to 12 to 13 and the game of hide-and-seek by girls of like age. Some of the dimensions of this research cohort have been considered defects by later critics: differences in socioeconomic groups, Genevans, no parents involved. The interest of the study, however, lies in these very limitations. It is a study *within* two tight subcultures of children; these microcosms transmit children's traditions from elder to younger; and within the subcultures, contemporary shaping of a social contract can be studied.

Children lose interest in and "graduate" from these games at puberty, an end point for the moral developments illustrated. Meanwhile they carry on the evolution and codification of rules, and teach their juniors. Somewhere in the process the crucial sense of *obligation*, the hallmark or keystone of morality, can begin to be observed. How did the rules, with all their complexity and their variations between villages, districts, and schoolyards, evolve? It was a children's task, not that of adults. How do rules become codified? How do the younger children pick them up, and more important, how do they develop the moral sense of obligation which binds them to the social contract? How well do they practice and conceptualize rules? What do rules mean, and do?

The Sense of Obligation, Heteronomy, and Autonomy

We shall begin with some general concepts. First, the key sense of obligation: in English usage the irreducible principle or feeling of "ought to." Where does this sentiment originate in psychological terms?

The sense of obligation emerges, Piaget believes, from the "unilateral respect" a child feels for its protecting, controlling, and enforcing parent (Piaget and Inhelder, 1966). This respect for the parent is a compound of affection (love, fondness, admiration) and fear (awe, apprehension of power, punishment, or pain). Respect can later become dissociated into such ambivalent feelings as affection, hostility, sympathy, or jealousy. It is when respect becomes attached to parental commands which have an indefinite time span ("Don't tell lies" etc.) that we have the foundations of the sense of duty and obligation. The child's world is full of regularities, or natural law: the cycles of time, household routines, causes and effects. But there is a real difference between the sense of regularity and order and the sense of obligation and duty. "Don't touch the hot stove" can mean two things: simply cause and effect, "if you do, you get burned"; or, a moral judgment associated with a moral feeling, a command of indefinite duration, "one ought not to touch hot stoves." This corresponds to ego versus superego functioning in psychoanalytic terms.

This sense of unilateral respect for a more powerful parent gradually gives way to a collection of internal controls (Piaget and Inhelder, 1966). At about 7 to 8 years of age (and here we note the important concordance with the psychoanalytic view of superego consolidation at this age) there is a definitive transition. Prior to this age, moral judgment is based on "heteronomy," the rule or law of the other, of external authority. Now it becomes based on "autonomy," the self is the director, law is in one's own hands, the regulation is internal and is carried on by the self regardless of external circumstances. At this age too, a sense of objective justice becomes consolidated (this is the age when "concrete operations" become established). Heteronomy is a morality of obedience, dependent on the presence of the person who gives the orders of indeterminate time span. With heteronomy there is a curious preoperational cognitive structure termed by Piaget "moral realism"; the concrete *size* of a transgression, rather than its moral *quality,* dominates. For example, saying a dog is as big as a cow is a much more serious wrongdoing then bringing home a falsified school report card. With this "moral realism" goes a quality of "objective responsibility": a person is to be judged by the concrete letter of the law, by external standards, not by personal motives or the current relationship with others.

After 7 to 8 years, cognitive progress in abstraction and flexibility of thinking, together with the learning of social cooperation, leads to a concept of justice based on mutual respect, a reciprocal concern for the rights and needs of self and others, an ability to be concerned with social contract, a willingness to fit law to human relations, and a trust in and interchange with peers. In the preoperational, heteronomous period, rules are not only external, but traditional, sacred, inviolable, unchallengeable, seen as ultimately graven in stone by God, the ultimate rule-giver. Yet at this very time the child has a rather vague, rudimentary idea of the actual wording of the rules! In the operational, autonomous period, one becomes able to apprehend and codify the rules in explicit detail. Yet, one is also liberated from the burden of law by the prevalence of justice over obedience, and by the sense that rules are agreements among peers, who respect each other and will change the rules if good and necessary. This is one of the fascinating features revealed in studying the game of marbles: despite the awe in which little boys hold its rules, it was in fact an invention of boys who have handed it down over the generations under the protection of mutual respect.

Now we come to the actual developments studied by Piaget and his collaborators (Piaget et al., 1932; Gruber and Vonèche,

1977, pp. 163–191). There are two progressions, with an ex-pectable "décalage" between them: progression as seen in the practice of rules, and progression as seen in the consciousness of rules.

The Practice of Rules

The practice of rules centers around the question, What are the rules as children practice them? The design of the investiga-tion was the Piagetian clinical method: to have the children play a game with the investigator or with each other, have them explain the rules as they go along, as if the investigator were a complete newcomer to the game, and to keep asking naive-sounding but ingenious and penetrating questions about *mean-ing*. Piaget warns yet again of the great individual variations of age level and time of emergence of different functions; the ages below are stated more rigidly than he indicates, in the context of a highly continuous developmental process.

1. Before ages 2 to 5 the rules are not rules of a game: they are "motor and individual" experiments directed at acquiring motor skill and investigating just what can be done with the game: There is no real social interaction, no competition, in fact no real game.

2. Between 2 and 5 and 7 and 8 is an "egocentric" period, where the children really play alone, even if in company with another; rules of the game are rudimentary and are abused constantly, yet this is the very time when children stand concep-tually in awe of these very rules as God-given, and expect divine retribution if they are broken. "Winning" is simply managing to play well, without an interactional social contract.

3. From 7 to 8 to 11 to 12 comes a period of "incipient cooperation." There is a contending, a genuine trying to win within the rules; the children are playing with and against each other, but the rules are vague, inconsistent, shifting, capricious.

4. Finally, for the short preadolescent period after 11 to 12 until they stop playing the game, ensues a period of "codifi-cation of rules," when the boys in particular become expert "legal authorities," able to demonstrate and explain all the points of law, including variations of the rules they have run

across in different contexts. With this codification also comes an ability to modify the rules, to invent and try new rules. Piaget and his collaborators noted a general tendency for the girls to show less interest in rule development, rule explication, and playing strictly by the rule, than with the boys; but like the problem of décalage, did not investigate this difference in itself.

The Consciousness of Rules

As to the consciousness of rules, the key questions asked the children are, Can rules be changed? Have rules always been the same as they are today? and How did rules begin? In this context, three general periods in the developmental continuum can be discerned:

1. Up to about 6 years a "motor rule" prevails: a purely personal, individual set of rituals without any obedience to the concept of a structured game. There are no coercive rules because activity is motor, not introspective or obligatory.

2. At about 6 to 10 years of age, as the child becomes aware of rules set by others and tries to imitate these, his practice is egocentric but he regards the rules as sacred and untouchable. He fights innovation. His unilateral respect has a mystical quality, yet his awareness of the content of rules is flawed and vague. Egocentrism correlates with external constraint, in this phase of "moral realism."

3. After age 10 there is another transformation: autonomy supervenes, rules become the product of group decision-making and earn respect in that they are recognized as emerging from consensus. Experiment is allowable. Rules are not eternal, in fact (the children may say) the games were probably invented by kids who were fooling around with pebbles or hiding for good reason. The community sets its rules within which good competition can occur, favoring skill rather than chance, and minimizing bickering and friction.

With all this, there is an emerging concept of justice. At first (up to about age 6) injustice or unfairness is doing what is forbidden (breaking a plate, telling lies, stealing). Later (up to 8) it is what goes against the rules. Justice up to age 8 is subordinated to adult authority. After 7 to 8, especially between 8 and

11, justice is that which ensures equality (getting equal pieces of cake, getting equal rewards for the same work). And finally, equality or social justice has the criterion of fairness or equity; questions of bias, for example in favor of better-dressed, stronger, cleverer children, can be raised. Here, equality or reciprocity are not seen in terms of absolute identity, but in terms of relativity. This ethical maturity should, I note once again, be compared with Freud's construct of the autonomous superego and ego ideal, including the age at which the super-ego is consolidated.

Kohlberg's Studies of Moral Dilemmas

Kohlberg's Methods

The studies of Lawrence Kohlberg (1981a,b) are of great interest and deserve to be better known, for several reasons: Although they are North American in origin, they have been carried out also in transnational and transcultural settings, and hence have a certain universal human significance; they appear to be relevant to our clinical field; they have a practical or applied importance in fields such as education and criminology (Muson, 1979; Kohlberg, 1981b); they are scientific studies, and not clinical observations with theoretical generalization.

Kohlberg's studies can be criticized for their shortcomings. For example, they appear to be predominantly derived from male subjects; we shall see below how a female investigator applies Kohlberg's approach to female moral dilemmas. They are not prospective cohort studies (following subjects along as they develop), but age-stratified surveys (assembling cohorts of the same age for subjects; see chapter 2 for methods of developmental assessment). There is the perennial problem of a general lack of correlation between moral *judgment* and moral *behavior*; Kohlberg is well aware of this problem (Kohlberg, 1981b) and in fact he worked at some length in both educational and reform settings.

Kohlberg designed a most ingenious research structure based on Piagetian principles. Unlike Piaget, whose team investigated how little boys practice and learn to respect and understand the rules of a juvenile game, Kohlberg had his subjects wrestle conceptually with moral dilemmas. That is, he presented his probands with a series of stories in which a conflict between motives, an interweaving of greater and lesser good or evil, is involved. Each subject had then to deliberate and deliver a verdict, with commentary, on how the dilemma should have been handled; for example, whether the protagonist should be punished, or not, and how, and for what reasons. The most famous of Kohlberg's stories (modified culturally and translated into many languages) involves a poor young man, Heinz, who decides to commit burglary upon a heartless and self-righteous pharmacist, in order to save the life of someone dear to him. What shall be done with Heinz?

Clearly, these stories and the process of dealing with them require considerable verbal and conceptual imagination, or more precisely in Piaget's terms, hypotheticodeductive reasoning of a formal operational order. It should come as no surprise then that Kohlberg's ladder of moral reasoning spans the developmental range of preadolescence and adolescence. This represents one of those, perhaps surprising, "décalages" or temporal staggerings with which Piaget became so familiar, though, as Miller (1983) notes, he never devoted serious research to why they occur. Piaget's ladder of development of moral judgment, using a social or operational game and extracting its rules, extends from about ages 2 to 5 to about ages 10 to 12. Kohlberg's extends from about age 10 to about age 20. Clearly, the two procedures measure different variables. It would be best for our purposes, I believe, if we regard Kohlberg's studies as representing a higher or later "spiral" in the development of moral judgment, based on hypothetical and conflicted verbal presentations. This indicates a caveat to clinicians: that their estimates of a patient's developmental age for moral judgment will differ considerably, dependent upon whether Piagetian or Kohlbergian tests are applied.

Developmental Findings: Kohlberg's Levels and Stages

An important generalization emerges from Kohlberg's study of a large sample of races and cultures. The reader is referred to the paper "From is to ought—" (Kohlberg, 1971) as well as others in the collection of Kohlberg's publications (1981a,b). The detailed *content* and statement of *outcome* for the moral dilemmas does, of course, vary from culture to culture. But the progression in process, style, and maturity of moral judgment correlates well with chronological age across all cultures studied. This developmental sequence for moral judgment strongly resembles what we might call Piaget's law of cognitive maturation: from egocentric to objective, from concrete to abstract, from rigid and fixed to flexible, reversible, reciprocal, functional. Thus, although cultural relativism applies to the manifest content or the solution of moral dilemmas, the developmental spiral for increasing maturity of moral judgment appears to be consistent and universal across cultures.

The process of moral maturation is a continuous one, so that again I need to remind the reader that stages and levels are somewhat arbitrarily imposed upon it. In this context, Kohlberg finds that the development of moral reasoning proceeds through three ascending levels, each level embracing two substages.

The preconventional level represents the least mature and the most personal, most egocentric and concrete, style of reasoning: what is good or bad is determined by immediate consequences, physical or power relations, and pleasure–punishments–favor colorings.

The conventional level is an intermediate one, in which good and bad are defined by reference to rules set by the social group, with such norms having intrinsic value regardless of immediate consequences or personal motivation; the family, the social group, the nation, sets the rules.

The postconventional level relates morality to values and principles which are efficacious and applicable in a manner transcending, or independent of, the authority of other persons, the social group, or the individual's loyalty to the group.

I summarize Kohlberg's schema more fully as follows:

1. *Preconventional*: thinking and judgment relates to concrete and immediate consequences, power relationships, and pleasure–pain or profit–loss equations.

a. *Punishment and obedience*: physical consequences and not any human value determine goodness–badness; one avoids punishment and defers to power; there is no principle of respect for the underlying social order of substage d.

b. *Instrumental–relativist*: what is good is what satisfies one's own needs, and occasionally someone else's; human relations are seen in "market" terms, as the exchange of favors (you scratch my back, I'll scratch yours); fairness is always a very concrete and pragmatic matter not based on values such as loyalty, gratitude, or justice.

2. *Conventional*: maintaining the expectations (as perceived) of family, group, community, as intrinsically necessary and valuable; conformity, loyalty, order, as values.

c. *Interpersonal concordance*: being nice, a good guy, pleasing and helping others; a stereotyped image (as "natural") of what the majority does and wants; some incipient concern for intent. A model based on the family.

d. *Law and order*: importance given to authority, clear and fixed rules, maintaining social stability; values now are duty, respect for authority and for social order, for its own sake. A model based on the community.

3. *Postconventional*: an autonomous, principled level, where values are seen as transcending the authority of persons or tangible groups and the individual's personal identification with these groups or persons.

e. *Social contract*: the individual participates in rights and standards agreed to by the whole society; personal values are relative, with a need for procedural rules to achieve consensus, such consensus being expressed in laws which, as contrasted with the rigidity of the "law-and-order" of substage d, may be changed; agreements and contracts, however, are binding. A "constitutional" model based on the *nation*.

f. *Universal ethical principles*: gradations of good and evil, and choices between them, are monitored by conscience through self-determined ethical principles which are logically comprehensive, consistent, and universally applicable (justice, reciprocity, equality, dignity, for example); the Golden Rule applies rather than the Ten Commandments which would apply to substage d. A *transnational,* universal mode of personal virtue.

Moral Judgment in Girls and Women

The Problem

I remind the reader of the major concern which has been expressed already in chapter 3. This is that investigators have principally been men, holding an ego-syntonic male bias, often employing male subjects, or failing to differentiate systematically between male and female subjects, and thence reporting views of psychological development as valid for all humans; and this despite repeated uneasy expressions to the effect that women must be different from men, but because of mysterious and unfathomable qualities cannot be clearly differentiated from men. Hence, at best, research findings have aggregated together, averaged, or homogenized findings from men and women. At worst, female development has been pictured to be an eccentric, exceptional, or inferior reflection of its male counterpart; that is, women's psychological positions and achievements have been stated as exceptions to, or imperfect or negative versions of, the male. In the present context, the female superego, even when studied by female investigators (Jacobson, 1976), is reported to be consolidated later than the male's, thanks to a more intricate development stream. This structure or system is less strong, precise, firm, objective, or principled than the male counterpart, in contrast with which it is soft, indulgent, or unreliable; epithets whose pejorative tone is inescapable. Only relatively recently (Gilligan, 1982; Casgrain, 1983; J. B. Miller, 1987) have we been issued a sharp challenge to this model of the male sex as the norm. Feminist scientists now insist, and quite rightly, that we seek to observe,

describe, and measure the steps and themes in female development in their own right.

Psychoanalytic views of female moral development, essentially clinically based, have been briefly reviewed above; women
authors have been specifically noted. A scholarly clinical essay
by Casgrain (1983), a male analyst, adds little that is new but
does begin to emphasize that the female superego deserves an
independent formulation. Jean Baker Miller (1987), a woman
analyst, ponders whether the construct "superego" even applies
to women, as she attempts to construct a specific female psychology. Rather than pursue findings from the couch, however,
it would seem important to examine somewhat "harder" research and directions in which it leads. Piaget et al. (1932), as
noted above, commented on a difference between older girls'
interest in rules and that of boys, but apparently did not pursue
these differences investigatively.

Gilligan's Pioneering Studies

Gilligan's (1982) pioneering work combines both proper research and conceptual and philosophical formulation. A former student of Kohlberg's, she commences with a cogent critique of findings using male subjects, and then proceeds to erect
a developmental progression and framework of moral values
unique to the female, based directly upon the legitimacy of
studying the female in her own right. Gilligan's treatise is upon
moral development and moral judgment. But it does touch on
a number of other developmental issues. Let me attempt to
capture the essence of its spirit and its conceptualizations.

First, on what kind of studies and data does Gilligan base
her reflections and tentative formulations? Her studies were
three in number. In the College Student Study, 25 female college seniors who had in their sophomore year completed a
course on moral and political choice, together with 16 dropouts
from this course, were interviewed and tested, and again followed up 5 years later. In the Abortion Decision Study, 29
diverse and unselected women, aged 15 to 33, were examined at
a point of quintessentially feminine moral crisis, namely when
candidates for therapeutic abortion, 21 of them being followed

up a year later. Finally, hypotheses generated in the first two studies were systematically tested in the Rights and Responsibilities Study: cohorts of eight females and eight males, carefully matched, at each of nine points in the life cycle (ages 6 to 60) and totaling 144 subjects, were studied systematically, focusing on the dimensions of identity and moral choice. Here, Gilligan's research method might best be described as a combination of Piagetian clinical interviewing with a flexible extension of Kohlberg's moral dilemma framework.

What does Gilligan find? It is true, she concludes, that if women are scored using Kohlberg's actual tests and norms, it emerges that the most mature achieve only a low to midrange moral maturity position. Normal mature women offer resolution to moral dilemmas on a basis of acting in the interest of others (and, at times, of the self), on meeting the needs of others in a concrete, practical, direct way, with rightness and fairness judged in a very personal framework; that is, at Kohlberg's substage b, the instrumental–relativist, preconventional level. They may stress in their judgments a dimension of kindness and consideration, of caring for and meeting the expectations of others, conserving and maintaining personal and social ties as an end in itself, an unquestioning personal loyalty and desire to please others; that is, at substage c, the interpersonal concordance, conventional level.

Such mature women do not appear much concerned with, nor particularly swayed by conceptions of law and order (substage d), nor of social contract (substage e), nor by transcendent, overriding moral principles (substage f). Thus, viewed within a male universe, female moral judgment never reaches maturity, remaining imperfectly developed, empirical, personal, sentimental; in short, defective, immature, and soft!

However, when we move away from the stylistic and structural framework based upon male norms; when we step back some distance and look and listen again for what women have to say in their own right; then we receive new messages. This "different voice," the title of Gilligan's treatise, is the confrontation of new themes: a *thematic* as opposed to a stylistic and structural dimension. From an early developmental age, the girl's, subsequently the woman's, view of personal identity and of human relationships differs radically from the boy's and the man's.

The girl sees her own identity as being defined by her network of human relationships: she lives, it appears clearly, in belonging, giving, and taking; attachment is the measure of her being. She commences her life at one with her mother, one link in the generations of females who came before and who will go on after her. As she becomes socialized, she plays noncompetitively, with small regard for rules and their careful codification (see notes on Piaget, above). She has security and fulfillment in closeness, in caring and helping. She prefers to live at the heart of a nexus of connections, fearing to be on the edge, isolated, or at the top, envied but alone. She achieves intimacy *before* identity, contrary to Erikson's and Vaillant's progression for males (see chapter 4). Danger lies in having people at a distance, in the fracture of relatedness. Her morality, as she grows and as it develops, is therefore a morality of caring and doing good for others, of protecting and avoiding hurting, of conserving human ties between herself and others, and between others. Lofty and abstract principles and disembodied social rules are for her distant, cold, uncaring things, providing no real moral motivation. We should note here the strong concordance with Eagly's concepts and the construct of communion, as reviewed in chapter 3.

By contrast, the boy child and later the man see their identity in separation and separateness; they live for competing and achieving. The boy plays competitively, keenly concerned with the facilitating value of rules and social structures. He fears intimacy as coercive and constricting. Danger lies in having people too close, mobilizing his fear and aggression. He strives for the top of his social pyramid, fearing being caught in the middle of a web of connections. He must achieve identity first before he can work on intimacy. His morality therefore progressively becomes a morality of distancing and abstraction, which he uses as his most powerful tool for engineering difficult moral choices. These concepts show a strong concordance with those elucidated by Stoller (1985) in studying the rare syndrome of the totally effeminate male. Such a man never escaped the close enmeshment and empathy with his mother which is so characteristic of normal development in girls.

Developmental Stages or Levels in Female Morality

In the nature–nurture equation, we must take note of female and male brains, which evolve differently: Gilligan appears to ignore this variable (see chapters 2 and 3 above). Gilligan (1982, p. 67) notes that girls are brought up in a world where, generally, men have power and make the decisions. Thus, they are uneasy with, and unused to, both the freedom or right to make bold decisions, and the sense of firm responsibility or power to stick by those decisions. Hence, female moral decision making eventuates in a diffident, sensitive, equivocal quality. Coupled with the consistent theme of *caring for* others, feminine morality thus may have a passive-appearing, wait-and-see or laisser-faire quality, in which preserving relationships, amid the vicissitudes of things that *happen to* us, is the dominant coloring.

Gilligan further suggests that there are indeed three stages in the development of human female moral judgment (1982, chapter 3). It would be hoped that these stages can be further investigated by a method analogous to Kohlberg's. Gilligan finds Kohlberg's moral dilemma stories to be rather abstract, and otherworldly, and uninteresting to women.

1. In the first level or stage, morality is a matter of survival. This quality emerged particularly clearly in the moral crisis of the abortion decision study. The self is experienced as alone, without connection. The action to be contemplated is judged in a purely expedient way, as conducive, or not, to survival, for what else is possible at such a juncture? There is no debate about rightness or wrongness, nor any distinction between "will" or "must" and "should" or "should not." Morality is simply a pragmatic concern, with survival as the substantive issue. One must, or will if necessary, steal or kill to survive, and one will expect others to do likewise. There is no social connectedness or participation, nor shared norms.

In transition to the next level or stage, self-doubts regarding selfishness and irresponsibility begin to creep in; here the beginnings of participation in a group or society, with its shared norms, appear.

2. In the second level or stage the "conventional feminine voice emerges with great clarity" (Gilligan, 1982, p. 79): care

for and protect others; do no hurt; sacrifice yourself if necessary. This stance always presumes the existence of a significant other. The basic moral dilemma here may be couched as a conflict between self-assertion, which may hurt the other, and dependency on or deference to the other, which may stifle or hurt the self. A concept of goodness rather than survival is at the heart of this stage.

In transition to the final third stage, this goodness begins to be objectified and questioned in some way, as to its relatedness to truth and honesty.

3. The final level or stage has as its central concern the themes of fairness and honesty to self and others: the direct facing of reality with all its complexity and conflict; the enumeration of pros and cons; the acknowledgment of both the reality of conflict and the absence of ideal solutions; the recognition and acceptance of the self and one's own needs in the equation, in an objective and unselfish way. All these, with *caring* as the ultimate touchstone or most adequate guide, mark the mature woman's morality. This is in considerable contrast with the disembodied and relatively impersonal principles relied upon by the mature man. Morality for the woman appears always to be anchored in a concern for persons, not principles.

Gilligan's schema promises a rich and fruitful basis for continuing hypothesis-raising and hypothesis-testing, on the road to the clarification of the sexual dimorphism of moral development.

Clinical Applications

Though the work reported above clearly has promising, even exciting, heuristic value for our clinical assessments, still, considerable caution and circumspection appear necessary in applying it to an examination of our patients' moral judgments.

The reasons, I submit, are twofold: each of our four major exponents uses a different method, and between the age ranges they report there is a truly major décalage. We may even be confronted with a comparison between apples and oranges if we try to integrate their findings. The psychoanalysts, for example, attempt to delineate a ladder of development of an autonomous conscience or superego. They do this principally by observing real children in play therapy, and troubled adults in a retrospective reconstruction of their lives. Their framework is clinical and affective–motivational. Piaget's team, some of whose findings accord remarkably with the psychoanalysts', uses a considerably different approach. They study the practice and the codification of rules as street urchins play a traditional game. A social psychology framework, dealing with cognitive issues in the achievement of the sense of social justice, is their perspective. Kohlberg presents hypothetical moral dilemmas for attempted resolution, and produces a ladder of increasingly mature style of judgment, valid across a number of cultures. The exercise is hypothetical and verbal, that is, highly conceptual, and apparently much more valid for men than women. Gilligan responds to the male bias inherent across many of these studies by directly observing women in moral crisis, as well as young women interested in ethics, and cohorts of women and men at points along the life cycle. Her approach stresses moral judgment in real life situations.

The décalages which emerge, as between age ranges reported in these several studies, are formidable: from about 1 to 7 years in psychoanalytic investigations to about 10 to 20 years in Kohlberg's surveys. Piaget's team itself gives us two age ranges, for practice and for conceptualization of rules, with a substantial décalage between them: about 2 to 12 for practice and 6 to 13 for conceptualization. Kohlberg commenced with age-stratified cohorts between 10 and 20 years of age, then went on to examine moral judgments in many ages across many cultures. He does not anchor his maturational levels in moral reasoning to distinct chronological norms. Even less does Gilligan suggest any direct correlation between chronological age and level of moral judgment. Although the descriptive stylistics emerging from her life-cycle study are suggestive, she makes no clear attempt to reconcile the egocentric, concrete, survival ethics of women in crisis with what may be normal for young, unsocialized children.

Nonetheless, I do not believe these differences of method, nor the décalages in findings, lead to any complete impasse. The analogy, in fact, should probably be to comparing grapefruit, oranges, and tangerines (i.e., related species) as more apposite than comparing apples and oranges. Therefore, how might we tentatively proceed with clinical applications? I propose that the following suggestions be regarded as hypotheses for careful examination and testing.

If the patient appears on other clinical grounds to be seriously regressed (i.e., psychotic or very profoundly depressed), the first resort in estimating moral judgment should be to psychoanalytic criteria for superego development; that is, superego precursors (see pp. 166–168). This frame of reference relates to early chronological ages, therefore to severe regression. Also, being in a rather clinical and qualitative mode, it may be adaptable to the utterances of patients too disorganized to be interviewed systematically. The following ladder of criteria is suggested:

The patient is crudely afraid of punishment by some external authority figure: regression age suggested, 1 year.

He or she fears punishment if discovered: 2 years.

Fears punishment if discovered, but identifies partially with the punishing authority figure as right (sphincter morality): 3 years.

The fear (note that *fear* is the affect in all these levels) is of loss of love and approval if discovered in wrongdoing (separation anxiety): 3 to 4 years.

The fear of being discovered is itself central, and the risk of ostracism and ridicule; a new affect, *shame*, enters the picture: 4–5 years.

Moral or conscience anxiety, the fear of doing wrong itself, or remorse after an identifiable wrongdoing, is what is experienced; the affect is *guilt* (see chapter 7 for discussion of shame and guilt as emotions): 5 to 7 years.

Less disturbed and regressed patients may well show qualities of moral judgment at the three higher levels in this framework. With such (neurotic or character-disordered) persons, it becomes appropriate to move into a higher age range of assessment, using Piaget's, Kohlberg's, or Gilligan's criteria.

For example, we might ask the patient to play a well-known game, and assess whether (1) he or she can play correctly and (2) give a coherent account of the rules of the game. Piaget's three key questions need to be asked: Can rules be changed? Have rules always been the same? How did rules begin? From the Piagetian criteria, the following concerns emerge; the age ranges are broad zones:

The patient does not play any recognized or coherent game, but *plays with* the materials in a pleasurable or harassed way: age 2 to 5 years (practice of rules). There is no expressed sense of rules as obligatory or coercive: 2 to 6 years (consciousness).

Play is solitary, self-absorbed, abusing the recognized rules, but somewhat organized and coherent: 5 to 8 years (practice).

The patient expresses a strong, rigid sense of being bound by rules given by a historic external authority, but rules whose content is vague (heteronomy, moral realism): 6 to 10 years (consciousness).

There is a degree of social cooperation, of playing with another person, contending within rules which are binding but vague (incipient cooperation, moral realism): 7 to 11 years (practice).

The game is played according to detailed rules which can be expounded clearly and logically; these rules were set by people, are for people's benefit (mutual respect, autonomy) and can be changed by mutual consent (justice, equity): 11 years and upward (practice): 10 years and upward (consciousness).

In applying Kohlberg's work, we are offering highly cognitive, hypothetical propositions without any benefit of a concrete situation such as a game. Within a rough age span of 10 to 20 years, we are to judge which of six substages the patient's moral judgment represents, using standardized stories depicting moral dilemmas. This may be somewhat beyond the reach of the bedside clinician, though I believe very useful in research on psychiatric populations. It may be that we can estimate the patient's style of moral judgment while conversing about many of the elements of his or her history and mental status examination (e.g., tests of social judgment). From this we may be able to note quite well the patient's style: preconventional, concrete, egocentric, hedonistic; conventional, tied to law and order in the context of familial or civic circles; or postconventional, objective, reciprocal, tied to transcendent and transnational views of personal morality. Reference to Kohlberg's actual templates (see pp. 177–179) can add precision to our estimates. I have noted that Kohlberg's hypothetical moral dilemmas are best applied to male patients.

In applying Gilligan's work, the same more general approach may suffice; that is, listening for instances of moral judgment in the clinical examination, then pursuing the reasoning involved by the "Piagetian clinical method." It should be relatively easy to establish Gilligan's first level, of survival morality; the higher levels will require, I think, a careful resort back to Gilligan's descriptions (see pp. 183–184). I believe, despite the newness and softness of Gilligan's constructs, that we should be attempting assiduously to test them with our women patients.

Bibliographic Notes: Key Readings

There is a limited literature on this developmental stream: its exponents are psychoanalysts and psychologists. I divide recommended readings into three groupings.

Freud proposed his structural theory of personality in "The Ego and the Id" (Freud, 1923), including the place and function of the superego; he updated his constructs 10 years later (Freud, 1933). It is important to read these contributions. I also recommend two papers (Holder, 1982; Kennedy and Yorke, 1982) in an international colloquium on the superego published in *The Psychoanalytic Study of the Child*. These studies present a modern, more observational and prospective psychoanalytic point of vantage.

Piaget's (Piaget et al., 1932) classical work focuses on the development of the sentiments of obligation and justice, and the practice and understanding of rules. Though drawn from a somewhat special population of street urchins playing marbles, it is seminal. Gruber and Vonèche (1977, chapters 16 and

17) present a digest of this work, and of a later summary by Piaget and Inhelder.

Contemporary psychologists, including particularly Kohlberg and Gilligan, have modified and extended Piaget's approach. A collection of Kohlberg's papers (1981b) and two compendia edited by Lickona (1976a,b) offer good summaries of Kohlberg's constructs, as well as critiques of his and Piaget's work, and papers by Lickona and other authorities. The reader might read any one of these three to advantage. Gilligan (1982) is the pioneering worker who has done prospective and observational work on moral development in girls and women, and has begun to set up norms for feminine as compared with masculine moral judgment.

References

Arlow, J. A. (1982), Problems of the superego concept. *The Psychoanalytic Study of the Child*, 37:229–244. New Haven, CT: Yale University Press.

Bernstein, D. (1983), The female superego: A different perspective. *Internat. J. Psycho-Anal.*, 64:187–201.

Bowlby, J. (1969), *Attachment and Loss, Vol. 1: Attachment,* 2nd ed. London: Hogarth Press, 1982.

Brenner, C. (1982), The concept of the superego: A reformulation. *Psychoanal. Quart.*, 51:501–523.

Brickman, A. S. (1983), Pre-oedipal development of the superego. *Internat. J. Psycho-Anal.*, 64:83–92.

Carroll, J. L., & Rest, J. R. (1982), Moral development. In: *Handbook of Developmental Psychology*, ed. B. B. Wolman, G. Stricker, S. J. Ellman, P. Keith-Spiegel, & D. S. Palermo. Englewood Cliffs, NJ: Prentice-Hall.

Casgrain, N. (1983), On the vicissitudes of female sexuality. *Internat. J. Psycho-Anal.*, 64:169–186.

Fenichel, O. (1945), *The Psychoanalytic Theory of Neurosis.* New York: W. W. Norton.

Freud, S. (1914), On narcissism: An introduction. *Standard Edition*, 14:73–102. London: Hogarth Press, 1957.

——— (1917), Mourning and melancholia. *Standard Edition*, 14:243–258. London: Hogarth Press, 1957.

*——— (1923), The ego and the id. *Standard Edition*, 19:12–59. London: Hogarth Press, 1961.

——— (1933), New Introductory Lectures on Psycho-Analysis. *Standard Edition*, 22. London: Hogarth Press, 1964.

*Gilligan, C. (1982), *In a Different Voice: Psychological Theory and Women's Development.* Cambridge, MA: Harvard University Press.

Gillman, R. D. (1982), Preoedipal and early oedipal components of the super-
ego. *The Psychoanalytic Study of the Child*, 37:273–281. New Haven, CT:
Yale University Press.
*Gruber, H. E., & Vonèche, J. J., eds. (1977), *The Essential Piaget*. New York:
Basic Books.
Guerrero, A. C. G. (1982), The superego concept, Part I: Historical review,
object relations approach. *Psychoanal. Rev.*, 68:321–342.
*Holder, A. (1982), Preoedipal contributions to the development of the su-
perego. *The Psychoanalytic Study of the Child*, 37:245–272. New Haven,
CT: Yale University Press.
Jacobson, E. (1976), Ways of female superego formation and the female
castration conflict. *Psychoanal. Quart.*, 45:525–538.
*Kennedy, H., & Yorke, C. (1982), Steps from outer to inner conflict viewed
as superego precursors. *The Psychoanalytic Study of the Child*, 37:221–228.
New Haven, CT: Yale University Press.
Kohlberg, L. (1971), From "is" to "ought": How to commit the naturalistic
fallacy and get away with it in the study of moral development. In:
Cognitive Development and Epistemology, ed. T. Mischel. New York: Aca-
demic Press.
*——— (1981a), *Essays on Moral Development*, Vol. 1. San Francisco: Harper
& Row.
——— (1981b), *The Meaning and Measurement of Moral Development*. Worcester,
MA: Clark University Press.
*Lickona, T., ed. (1976a), *Moral Stages and Moralization: The Cognitive–Develop-
mental Approach*. New York: Holt, Rinehart, Winston.
*——— ed. (1976b), *Moral Development and Behavior: Theory, Research, and
Social Issues*. New York: Holt, Rinehart, Winston.
Miller, J. B. (1987), *Toward a New Psychology of Women*, 2nd ed. Boston: Beacon
Press.
Miller, P. H. (1983), *Theories of Developmental Psychology*. San Francisco: W. H.
Freeman.
Muson, H. (1979), Moral thinking: Can it be taught? *Psychol. Today*, 12:48–68,
92.
*Piaget, J., Baechler, N., Feldweg, A. M., Lambercier, M., Martinez-Mont, L.,
Maso, N., Piaget, V. J., & Rambert, M. (1932), *The Moral Judgment of the
Child*. London: Routledge & Kegan Paul, 1965.
——— Inhelder, B. (1966), *The Psychology of the Child*. London: Routledge &
Kegan Paul, 1969.
Stoller, R. J. (1985), *Presentations of Gender*. New Haven, CT: Yale University
Press.

*Recommended readings.

Section II

*Human Adaptation
and Homeostasis*

7

A Homeostatic–Dynamic Model Underlying Psychiatric Formulations: Variations, Levels, and Variables in Human Homeostasis

Introduction

Overview

It is the aim of this chapter to examine a second major model or archetype underlying psychiatric thought and practice. This model views human beings as exceedingly complex machines, in never-ceasing action, possessing intricate moving parts which mesh with each other in a hierarchy of definable modes, ranging from normal to highly pathological. Unlike inanimate machines, human beings are open systems highly interdependent with each other and with other systems; further, they are self-repairing and self-reproducing.

In chapter 1 we considered the nature of models, how they are metaphorical in essence, should be capable of mathematical expression, and explain, predict, and expand knowledge, that

193

is, they are heuristic. They explain complex phenomena, particularly in terms of the unseen relationships between them; and they offer a predictive launching pad for new hypotheses to be tested. The model of human beings examined in chapter 1 was a somewhat static one, using the metaphor of the edifice. Now we shall deal with a much more dynamic, active model, concerning the maintenance of internal equilibrium in the face of external change. I shall neglect its mathematical expressions, in vector and factor analysis and in equations such as are used to predict dynamic relationships, as in the solar system. I shall use this space to develop some implications and extensions of the model, based on recent research. The suggestion stemming from these is that psychiatric disorders fall under a relatively simple hierarchy of homeostatic abnormalities (Foulds and Bedford, 1975), and in themselves represent pathological homeostatic states, as suggested by the curiously stubborn autonomy and momentum which so many of them show, an autonomy which resists both environmental and therapeutic forces.

The data of clinical psychiatry have to be referred to a framework of the *whole person*, as contrasted with the analysis of cells, organs, and organ systems in other medical disciplines. This is not a metaphysical statement, it is a pragmatic one. It simply does not make sense to report that "Mary's auditory system is disordered and is experiencing hallucinations." Rather, we are forced by the widespread ramifications of this experience to report that "Mary (the whole person) is hallucinating": her vocal apparatus, her emotions, and her behavior are all involved. *Personal illness*—Foulds' and Bedford's (1975; see also Foulds, Caine, Adams, and Owen, 1965) term for psychiatric disorders—requires a global, skillful, descriptive approach; classification has to be of syndromes, patterns of whole-person dysfunction, which we artificially cluster along continuous and multidimensional spectra. The causes of these syndromes are usually multiple and interacting, no one alone being sufficient to produce or explain decompensation. Often such causes are already in the past and out of our reach and control. Psychiatric therapeutics are therefore customarily directed at the maintaining or perpetuating mechanisms which give the syndrome its autonomy and stability, with the goal of restoration to premorbid functioning.

The metaphor central to this model may, I suggest, be painted by reference to the automobile, with its many makes and styles, its wide geographical distribution, and its modes of normal and abnormal functioning.

The homeostatic–dynamic model has been shaped over the past century by great physiologists, culminating in Walter B. Cannon (see Cannon, 1932). The model is based on the depiction of an unceasing effort to maintain dynamic equilibrium in an inner, fluid, *milieu intérieur*, in response to equally constant needs to adapt to an outer, gaseous *milieu extérieur*. Cannon developed the construct of a homeostatic shift under stress into fight–flight. To this, the more recent work of George Engel (1962a) added another homeostatic shift, conceptualized as "conservation–withdrawal"; Engel (see chapter 1) has updated the original physiologic model in his biopsychosocial approach, which requires attention to the three levels of emergence in which we operate. From the work of a number of others, Selye, Ratner, Foulds and Bedford, and certain recent clinicians, emerges a kind of ladder of homeostatic modes, ranging from normality to death, to which we can fit most of the recognized psychiatric syndromes. This ladder, I submit, has five steps: psychiatric normality, fight–flight, conservation–withdrawal, disintegration, and death; each step has pharmacologic correlates. Psychiatric diagnosis and treatment, in the light of the present model, has the task of discerning and shifting these in a more favorable direction.

In addition to a synthesis bringing together the properties and clinical relevance of this ladder of homeostatic modes, it seems appropriate to consider some broad issues or variables in homeostasis which are too inclusive to be dealt with in subsequent chapters. I therefore devote a section to behavioral systems, motivation, and conflict, and one to mental mechanisms or defense mechanisms, important in human homeostasis but rarely dealt with in a scientific fashion. I also devote a section to the science of emotions and moods, their number and nature. We will find here that emotions have been well researched, and their number and mechanisms are rather clearly known.

However, moods, which are clinically highly relevant, have not been adequately studied, and we are left uncertain at this time regarding their status and the laws and mechanisms which govern them. Human communication and human sexuality, both important and large fields in their own right, and important correlates of human well-being and dysfunction, are briefly treated in two final sections. I leave the major group of variables related to brain injury and brain disease to chapter 8, and more specific homeostatic issues to later chapters, which will deal with the steps in the homeostatic ladder.

The Model

Nature of Psychiatric Disorders

Psychiatry deals with disturbances, distresses, and disabilities such as can only be attributed to the functioning of the whole person (Hofling, 1975). The term *behavior* has been used in a somewhat reductionistic attempt to picture such whole-person events. In fact, the matter is so close to our consciousness that the English language, or even our lexicon of scientific terms, appears to contain no satisfactory words for whole-person experiencing, functioning, and behaving. We are literally forced to report that "Mary is hearing voices again": with this we attempt to capture not only the experiencing of auditory hallucinosis, but the terror Mary is suffering, with its subjective and visible components, her avoidant behavior, the subvocal speech which can be recorded from her larynx, and the social disruption which is going on. We cannot meaningfully report, as other disciplines can, merely that her auditory system is deranged, or her autonomic nervous system, or that her social role enactment is perturbed. The nature of psychiatric decompensation thus requires a global, descriptive examination of the whole person, and a classification of the global findings against a nosological system of templates for various syndromes which are recognized patterns of whole-person dysfunction. Other disciplines are required to deal with discrete organs or organ systems, by contrast: each discipline, against some overall medical model, pursues its own organ system in depth. Our syndromes are meaningful clusterings of highly complex human phenomena, useful for our therapeutic purposes, but basically artificial combinations of phenomena which extend along continuous spectra, and which are without natural boundaries.

Only a very few psychiatric syndromes are defined and classified by specific etiology. That is, they are compatible with the infectious disease model involving a specific pathogen. But even with this model causation is by no means simple (Halliday, 1943): variables of immunity and resistance can be crucial, a suitable vector may be present or absent; and less specific factors such as good general health or family and community support systems are particularly influential with psychiatric cases.

The causes which launch most psychiatric disorders ("precipitating" or "formative" causes) are usually multiple, interactional, and cumulative: no one variable is of itself sufficient or necessary to cause decompensation. Further, such causes are most often in the past, and beyond our reach and control, by the time the patient has arrived under our care. Therapy in psychiatry most usually attacks the mechanisms (Halliday's "mechanismic cause"; "perpetuating," "maintaining" causes) which keep the syndrome going autonomously, rather than the original causes. Quite simply, we primarily attack the syndrome rather than its causes. The more threatening that syndrome is, the more intensive, multifactorial, and economically costly must be the therapeutic attack, if we are to return the patient to premorbid function and obviate chronicity, disability, or even death. Usually, return to premorbid function is a legitimate goal. But in some cases we must also attempt reconstructive work aimed at particular vulnerabilities or social deficits ("predisposing," "contributing" causes).

Coherent research has apparently not addressed three problems implied above: the steps in the natural history of psychiatric disorders, both at onset and during recovery; the distinction between breakdown or decompensation and chronic maladjustment (personality disorder); and the autonomy and momentum of most disorders. Let me take the last first, the curious and self-evident fact that, once launched, most psychiatric disorders maintain a relatively fixed pattern, resistive to shifts in the environment and to therapeutic interventions. Such syndromes appear to have a kind of stubborn autonomy and momentum of their own, a kind of timetable which will eventually arrive at "spontaneous" remission, a timetable which therapeutic intervention aims to accelerate. This phenomenon of autonomy is one source of the somewhat confused concept of the "endogenous." It suggests strongly that many or most psychiatric disorders are states of dynamic equilibrium, self-maintaining modes of homeostasis, though the quality of the homeostasis is inferior and disabling. We shall return later to this thesis.

I shall not attempt here to deal with the distinction between chronic maladjustment (or personality disorder) and psychiatric decompensation, except to stress that it needs conceptual clarification. What is of greater clinical relevance, I believe, is the necessity to research the steps in the natural history of psychiatric decompensation and remission. Before our syndromes assume their "stable" form and autonomy, there have usually been a series of more or less distinct "prodromes," states of dysphoria and shifts in homeostatic style; these we often fail to delineate clearly in our own history taking. Similarly, during the recovery process we can, if we choose, monitor the interesting shifts in homeostatic style which I shall term *metadromes* in analogy with *prodromes*. Most clinicians intuitively perceive these, and assess whether they are favorable indices of restitution, or indications of relapse. But I know of no systematic study of them. Do they follow some lawful order? Can they be classified? Do most disorders show the same, or the same order of prodromes and metadromes? What are the psychophysiological shifts, and the mechanisms within them, during the succession of prodromes and metadromes? Again, we shall return to this subject below.

In earlier chapters we followed the evolution of the human phenotype in light of a developmental–structural model. Now we attempt to clarify a model or archetype, not of the building of an edifice, but of the functioning of an infinitely intricate machine, whose running order can assume many forms, some adaptive, some maladaptive. Movement, process, action, harmony, balance, adaptation, dominate this model. The machine has to be seen also as an open system (von Bertalanffy, 1968, pp. 120–125, 141–154), interdependent with other systems, particularly with other humans, for nurture, energy sources, waste disposal, personal satisfactions, reproduction of the species: a machine which is a unit or subsystem in larger systems. The human being is neither independent (as solitary animals are much of the time), nor symbiotic (as are colonial animals) but simultaneously autonomous and interdependent.

How may we picture this? What metaphor is most appropriate? I venture the following short essay on the automobile, a machine familiar to all readers of this book: in what follows, "automobile" stands in every instance for "human being."

A Metaphor or Archetype: The Automobile

The modern automobile has evolved from ancestors which bear it only faint resemblance, though their parts and functions are clearly replicated in today's phenotype. Originally designed as diurnal, it now functions quite well nocturnally. The automobile is found in a wider range of ecological niches than any other machine in history: it appears worldwide, from the frigid luminous night of the Arctic, to the burning noonday sands of the Sahara; from mountain valleys in the Alps, to lush Amazonian rain forests; from pastoral countrysides to urban rush hours. It has not only adapted to, but greatly influenced, the various milieux it has invaded. The modern automobile comes in a great variety of models, stylings, sizes, ages, and states of soundness; every car is basically the same machine, whose superficial variations are accommodations to environmental pressures. Though each individual car is a member of a recognized class, it is also a unique and recognizable entity: there is no other exactly its match.

All cars possess essentially the same complex subsystems, which must be in harmonic balance with each other. Cars never truly fall apart, though a few are destroyed in savage accidents. Most are laid to rest in their whole form, having ceased to function: their parts then corrode, decay, and become an amorphous jumble. "Breakdown" in actuality means a variety of classifiable dysfunctional modes, not collapse: cars become rusted, difficult to start; they emit steam, smoke, bangs, squeals, or stutters; they do not stop or steer properly, and can be a public menace. These modes of dysfunction can be precisely ranked as to the degree of threat and the costliness of repair. No careful owner allows such a dysfunctional mode to persist, though usually the car can function so for considerable periods. The goal of most owners is that of "normal" operation: a waterproof body, easy starting, smooth running, controls which are efficient, a reserve of fuel, and power for emergency demands.

Human personality never truly breaks down and stops operating: that would be death, where all systems cease working, and the physical boundaries and operating gradients between them decompose. When we speak of "breakdown" we mean that the organism (i.e., the whole, not merely one organ system) has shifted into a dysfunctional mode. Human personality functions in a variety of modes, from several "normal" ones, which best subserve homeostasis and adaptation, through a variety of pathological ones, ranging from mildly uncomfortable and hardly incapacitating to severely distressing and dramatically interfering with living. These might truly be called variants in homeostasis, since, as we noted above, many of them present with a stubborn persistence and a resistance to environmental shifts and therapeutic endeavors; we seek the mechanisms involved in and responsible for such a "steady state."

If we are to meet the requirement that an archetype or model can be reconstructed from epithets current in scientific or clinical discourse, here are a few rather informal examples from psychiatry: balanced, well organized, well adjusted, maladjusted, compensation, unbalanced, unsound of mind, disorganization, friction, sand in the gears, burnt out, disordered, run down, nervous breakdown, nervous wreck.

Architects of the Model: Cannon and Fight–Flight

I largely follow the great physiologist Walter B. Cannon in his account of the origin of his integrative concepts (Cannon, 1932) on human homeostasis. The precursors of our present model date at least from the classical Greeks, with their rather metaphysical ideas of harmony and balance, between organs, between body and soul, between humors, and of the derangement of harmony and balance in illness. Medical theories among contemporary nonliterate societies appear also to make use of cognate constructs. Cannon credits great European physiologists of the nineteenth century in the development of the modern view, in which there are two themes. First, that our bodies are made up of exceptionally unstable chemicals, which will degrade quickly if not immediately and constantly provided with nutrients and oxygen and efficient scavenging service, and that highly dynamic activity underlies apparently steady or calm bodily states. Second, that we do not live in a *gaseous* world as might appear, but we live, separated from the world by the horny layer of our skin and the mucous membranes, in an interior environment (in French, *milieu interne* or *intérieur*) which is aqueous and which envelops all our tissues and cells. Regulating this *milieu intérieur* and keeping it in dynamic equilibrium then permits the organism the freedom to make its way in adapting to the *milieu extérieur,* the world which surrounds us, with other animate and inanimate objects. Our model, evidently, is the creation of great physiologists. Cannon (1932) introduced the term *homeostasis* in the second edition of his second seminal work, *The Wisdom of the Body* (the title he adopted from Starling's Harveian Oration of 1923). *Homeostasis,* he thought, would be a better term than *equilibrium* (with its limited and rather linear connotations) for the dynamic regulation and balancing which constantly goes on in the body in order to maintain steady states and to respond to stress or changing conditions. I note that Cannon spoke years ago of "closed" and "open" systems: *equilibrium,* he considered, was a term more applicable to closed systems, while the human organism is a conspicuously open system.

Cannon not only developed the whole modern concept of homeostasis: he had in his first seminal work (Cannon, 1915) dealt with the responses of the organism to acute stress, to abrupt shifts in demands upon it, and to life-threatening situations such as hemorrhage and shock, as well as to pain and hunger and to strong emotions such as fear and anger. Cannon's contributions included the then new construct of two divisions of the peripheral nervous system: the somatic nerves which help cope with the external world, and the autonomic system which copes with the *milieu intérieur*; the latter again being subdivided into the parasympathetic, the regulator of vegetative and anabolic functions, and the sympathicoadrenal, the coordinator of homeostatic response to emergency. Cannon outlined the major homeostatic shifts which are embodied today under the construct of fight–flight; that is, the organismic preparation for either doing battle or making an effective escape. He showed experimentally how various responses (cardiovascular, respiratory, muscular, metabolic, hematologic) could be produced by stimulation of intact sympathetic–adrenal pathways, or could be prevented from responding by injury; and he discovered that the affects of fear and anger, as well as a characteristic alerting stance of the organism, were part of the physiologic shift into fight–flight. Fear and anger would themselves produce all the phenomena of fight–flight, as would other states such as pain. All the phenomena of fight–flight were found to be compatible with maximizing the chances of survival in a situation of danger and emergency, including preparation for being wounded.

Further Contributions: Engel and Conservation–Withdrawal

George L. Engel, whose career as a clinician–theorist has enriched us with many new insights into the relation between psychosocial processes and pathophysiology, consolidated Cannon's findings as fight–flight, a human homeostatic shift of high clinical relevance (Engel, 1962a,b). He also discovered, or perhaps more correctly, rediscovered another important mode of response to emergency and stress: this he called at first *depression–withdrawal*, until it became clear that it actually protected against depression; later the term became *conservation–withdrawal*, though for a short while these terms were reversed as *withdrawal–conservation*. This response came to his attention during intensive study of the now famous baby Monica, admitted for treatment of esophageal atresia, and whose gastric functions could be directly observed. Through her gastrostomy, (1956) noted that little Monica, when overstimulated, or when a stranger entered her field, would rather suddenly become limp and unresponsive for a period of time; this might give way to sleep, or to a return to activity and alertness, dependent upon environmental conditions. Clearly the response was adaptive, defending against flooding by stimuli or the unbearable impact of strangers in the absence of a familiar figure. It had also some clear resemblances to acute depression. With his colleague Schmale, Engel has broadened the study of this response, and its relation to depression (Schmale and Engel, 1975). Engel and Schmale (1972) believe that this response had been discovered several times before, but, because of its specifically unobtrusive nature, had been forgotten in the literature. In any case, this homeostatic mode contrasts markedly with fight–flight: it is withdrawing rather than actively coping; it is atonic, rather than alert and tense; its function appears to be the conservation of energy and resources through inhibition of activity, rather than providing a base for vigorous activity; but, like fight–flight, it is a protective response against further distress and injury.

A Construct of Disintegration: Summary of Homeostatic Modes

Clinical syndromes occur which display the above two homeostatic patterns: the anxiety–tensional states are good examples of prolonged fight–flight; the neurasthenias and depressive states show prolonged conservation–withdrawal. What of the psychoses, with their disarticulations of thought, perception, and affect? Are they examples of some pervasive homeostatic mode, or merely failures of proper homeostasis? From Cannon's criteria, we can say that psychoses permit life to go on, hence are in some sense homeostatic, though their homeostasis is a precarious and often life-threatening one. It is clear too that certain functional psychoses have just that stubborn autonomy and momentum I have alluded to above, so that in this sense they are steady states with some built-in stabilizing mechanisms. I suggest that this very maladaptive, yet autonomous state of being be considered a homeostatic mode in its own right. From Lehmann (1961) and from Foulds and Bedford (1975), as well as others, I adopt the term *disintegration* as a tentative label for the type of seriously maladaptive homeostasis manifested in the psychoses.

The model of human homeostasis first put forward by Bernard, considerably amplified by Cannon, added to by Engel, and more recently (see below) extended, might be summed up thus far: The human organism is an intricate machine which, by constant dynamic activity within, maintains highly labile parts in a steady state, and is thus free to adapt to the vagaries of the environment. Further, this intricate machine operates in several clearly different modes: normality, or day-to-day activity; fight–flight; conservation–withdrawal; disintegration; and death, which is the cessation of dynamic homeostasis. To this we may add one further overall finding. An examination of Lehmann's (1961) schema of the then new psychotropic drugs suggests that each of the altered states of homeostasis has pharmacologic correlates: the stimulants and sedatives with fight–flight; drugs which produce or relieve depression, with conservation–withdrawal; and drugs which induce or remit psychoses, with disintegration.

A Hierarchy of Homeostatic Modes

Evidence from Animal Studies: Ratner, Selye, and Stress Sequences

The question now arises as to how, if at all, these homeostatic modes relate to each other, in terms of their survival functions, or relative success in preserving well-being and life itself, the psychophysiological pictures they demonstrate, and the successive order in which they may be utilized in coping with real-life stresses? There is a paucity of convincing research addressed to these questions, but let us survey some studies which extend the model further in this regard.

Ratner (1967) and Adler (1979) have evolved an animal model of adaptation to urgent conditions; for example, pursuit and capture by a predator or handling by an experimenter. This suggests a somewhat consistent sequence of behaviors:

1. A potential predator appears at some distance, attracting attention by its movements. Response: the subject enters an alerted state and freezes (fight–flight).

2. The threatening stimulus approaches in "psychological space," a nonmetric measurement of "defensive distance." Response: subject moves away, or bolts (fight–flight).
3. The defensive distance closes to zero; predator (or experimenter) is inescapable. Response: subject struggles or fights (fight–flight).
4. Closure at zero continues, that is, subject has been completely cornered, seized, and held by predator (or experimenter). Response: subject becomes immobile and unresponsive (conservation–withdrawal).

Selye's general adaptation syndrome is of interest to us here because it includes both animal and human responses, as well as a consistent sequence of reactions to stress. He summarized his ideas in two papers (Selye, 1980, 1982) as follows. For some years Selye had pondered the general syndrome of being ill, with its lassitude, anorexia, and weight loss; while testing a possible new hormone by injecting rats (it was not effective as a hormone but turned out to be a nonspecific toxin), he found that the animals exhibited a characteristic sequence, later termed the general adaptation syndrome. A huge range of other stressors, provided they were both strange and hostile, were found to have similar effects. In humans, stress was found to ensue regularly on strong emotional arousal; this could in some cases be intensely pleasurable; but unconscious persons could also suffer stress when subjected to surgery or trauma. Selye, clearly, defines stress as the reaction of the organism, rather than the environmental conditions. His general adaptation syndrome consists of three stages; not all animals or people go through the three, for an organism may perish during each stage. The sequence in experimental rats is as follows:

1. *Alarm Reaction.* A "shock phase," atonic in nature, is soon followed by a rebound "countershock phase," mediated at first by sympatheticoadrenergic mechanisms (as described by Cannon), with cardiovascular shifts, release of glucose, and speeding of blood coagulation; shortly, the hypothalamus drives the

pituitary to secrete ACTH, which in turn leads to adrenocortical activity and swelling of the adrenal cortex; lymphoid tissues shrink, and bleeding ulcers appear in the stomach and upper bowel. The adrenal steroids have two effects: syntoxic, promoting adaptation and calm in relation to the insult; and catatoxic, promoting inflammatory response and an active attack on the foreign stimulus.

2. *Adaptation or Resistance.* If the animal survives and the stressor persists, symptoms diminish or disappear, and anabolic activities resume; the organism appears to settle down for some time, and will recover if the stress stimulus is terminated here.

3. *Exhaustion.* If the stress situation continues, sooner or later the animal becomes depleted, and will die; the adrenal cortex atrophies, and defenses collapse. Even here, if the stressor is lifted in time, the animal will recover after a period of rest, though it may be left with "scars."

This model includes responses or stages highly compatible with the constructs of fight–flight and conservation–withdrawal. Further, it suggests that these stages occur in orderly sequence, as the process of exhaustion follows acute mobilization. I find no evidence that Selye has given credit to Cannon's and Engel's constructs, in the sense of integrating them with his own. In the two compendia in which the Selye papers appear, there are no clear references to fight–flight or conservation–withdrawal.

Evidence from Human Patients: Foulds and Bedford

I shall cite two sets of studies suggesting that there may be a lawful sequence of homeostatic events, styles, or modes seen in the natural history of psychiatric illness in humans. But first, I note a general impression shared by many clinicians (Menninger, Mayman, and Pruyser, 1963) that psychiatric disorders can be grouped and ranked hierarchically. Luborsky's (1965, 1974) Health–Sickness Rating Scale had considerable empirical and analytic work behind its ranking of personality functioning from "an ideal state of complete functioning integration" down to a "condition which, if unattended, would quickly result in the patient's death"; positions along the scale include "mild neurosis/addictions," "clearly neurotic," "severe neurosis and compensated psychosis," and "clearcut psychosis requiring hospital care."

The first set of studies, of stages in the development and remission of schizophrenic psychosis, are, except for Donlon and Blacker (1973) and Docherty, van Kammen, Siris, and Marder (1978), descriptions of apparently unrelated clinical events (DeAlarcon and Carney, 1969; Hoedemaker, 1970; Roth, 1970; Stern, Pillsburg, and Sonnenburg, 1972; Rada and Donlon, 1975; McGlashan and Carpenter, 1976; Jeffries, 1977), but if we cumulate the findings the following integrated schema is clearly suggested:

1. Normal functioning gives way to vaguely tensional symptoms, restlessness, insomnia (fight–flight);
2. Restlessness gives way to anergic or vaguely depressive symptoms, loss of drive, discouragement, sluggishness (conservation–withdrawal);
3. Specific psychotic symptoms appear (disintegration);
4. With restitution, an often rather intractable postschizophrenic depression, rather nebulous in content but sometimes suicidal, develops; a number of explanations have been offered for it, but here I particularly note its conservation–withdrawal quality. It appears that chronic schizophrenics may continue to function at this level.
5. Tensional or anxiety symptoms have been reported as remission progresses (fight–flight);
6. Finally, normal function returns; this is, of course, the target for clinical efforts (normality).

The second set of studies by Foulds and colleagues (Foulds, Caine, Adams, and Owen, 1965; Foulds and Bedford, 1975) are of particular interest, and I wonder why they have not been better known and replicated. These workers found that psychiatric symptoms can be statistically grouped and ranked into four classes: that a syndrome of more severe symptoms can include symptoms from a less severe class, but not vice versa; that, as patients fall ill, they first develop symptoms of the mildest class, then symptoms from ascendingly severe classes; that, during recovery, the most severe symptoms disappear first, then symptoms in descending order of severity, the least severe persisting the longest; the diagnosis is based on the most severe symptom class found in the current illness. The symptom classes in this hierarchy are:

1. Nonpersonal illness (psychiatric normality);
2. Dysthymic states (pure mood states of anxiety, dejection, and elation);
3. Neurotic symptoms (relatively ego-alien psychological and somatic preoccupations);
4. Integrated delusions (well-organized, logically consistent, ego-syntonic, tenacious and unarguable cognitions of contrition, grandeur, and persecution);
5. Delusions of disintegration, having a bizarre, logically inconsistent, disorganized form.

Synthesis and Elaboration: The Nature of Homeostatic Levels

Summary of Accepted Issues

I believe that most clinicians and researchers would agree on the following statement of a rather robust model of the human being as an intricate machine. This machine operates in interdependence with its environment, particularly with other humans. It does so in a variety of adaptive styles: the normal alterations of activity and repose, and responses to stressful conditions. A host of homeostatic mechanisms, coordinated by the central and peripheral nervous systems and the pituitary–endocrine axis, is constantly at work to maintain the intactness of the organism and to forestall swift degradation of our very unstable components. These preserve the *milieu intérieur* so that we have freedom to cope with the *milieu extérieur*. Under conditions of stress and overload, the human organism (like other animals) shifts into a state of fight–flight, preparatory for emergency self-preservation, or into conservation–withdrawal, an abandoning of active, tonic adaptation in favor of passivity and disengagement. There is some agreement that these two homeostatic styles are relevant to clinical syndromes. What is not clear is whether these styles, together with several others which might be defined, have a hierarchic or lawful relationship, or are relatively inconsistent in mobilization. We shall now proceed to a hypothetical extension of the model, which posits such a lawful relationship, based on research evidence gathered from both animals and humans and summarized above.

A Scheme Requiring Research and Clarification

Evidence from laboratory studies (Ratner, 1967; Adler, 1979; Selye, 1980, 1982) is suggestive that animals and humans under stress exhibit both behavioral and pathophysiologic changes which follow a lawful sequence, from alerting and emergency action to passivity, depletion, and death. Evidence from clinical studies (Foulds et al., 1965; Donlon and Blacker, 1973; Foulds and Bedford, 1975; Docherty et al., 1978) suggest a rather similar sequence during the onset (prodromes) of psychiatric illness, and a reverse retracing of the steps in this sequence (metadrones) during recovery; the steps have the same stylistic qualities observed in animal studies.

I believe therefore that our model may be logically completed in the following hypothetical fashion. Much research and clarification will be required as to whether this is both valid, explanatory, and predictive.

Issues Requiring Research and Clarification

1. A style or homeostatic mode of "disintegration," embracing psychotic symptoms and processes, can be added to fight–flight and conservation–withdrawal; psychoses, though severe disruptions, and often life-threatening, have a built-in autonomy which in some sense makes them homeostatic processes, though in a highly maladaptive way.

2. The several homeostatic modes can be ranked hierarchically, in terms of the relative disruptions of personality functioning occurring in them, and as to their power to aid survival,

as follows: psychiatric normality, fight–flight, conservation–withdrawal, and disintegration.

3. Each mode has pharmacologic correlates.

4. These four homeostatic modes will be found to follow
each other in a lawful sequence, as observed over the natural
course of psychiatric illnesses. A "better" mode, one more conducive to survival, will shift to a "worse" one when the organism
becomes exhausted, or is unable to cope at that level for other
reasons; for example, a deficit of defensive repertoire, or a
biological vulnerability. In the natural course of such illnesses,
prodromes and metadromes (sequelae or stages in recovery)
traverse the hierarchy lawfully in opposite directions.

Modes or Levels of Homeostasis and Their Pharmacologic Correlates

Let me review this postulated hierarchy of homeostatic modes
and their essential properties, including their pharmacologic
correlates. Empirically, there are no abrupt discontinuities between modes, but transitions, which may present a blurred picture: phenomena of one mode may coexist with phenomena
of another; for example, psychological qualities of one mode
accompanying biological processes characteristic of the next. A
prominent example would be the agitated depressions which
appear to be transitional between fight–flight and conservation–withdrawal. These disorders combine the cognitive components of depression (conservation–withdrawal) and of psychosis (disintegration) with the biological or physiological
substrate of fight–flight, and are, in practice, often treated with
a mixture of approaches, sedative, antidepressant, and antipsychotic. The styles of and transitions between these homeostatic
modes are depicted in Figure 7.1.

We do not have research which illuminates these transitions; some useful new hypotheses might emerge if they were
carefully examined. For example, biological changes as a tensional and hypercatecholaminergic prodrome (fight–flight)
shade to those of an atonic, hypocatecholaminergic one (conservation–withdrawal or clinical depression). I review the succession of modes in the hierarchy as a series of homeostatic levels.

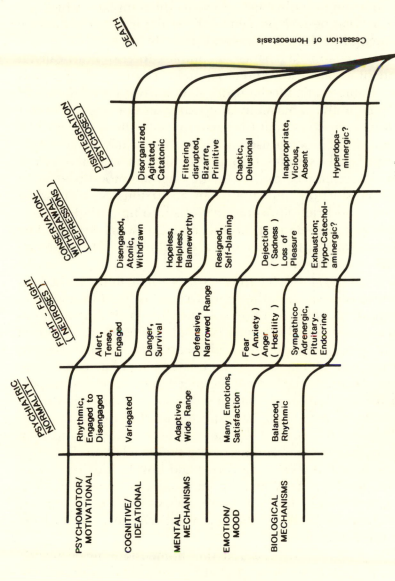

Figure 7.1. Homeostatic Levels and Their Styles

This chart suggests the stylistic components of an assumed hierarchy of homeostatic modes. During onset and remission of psychiatric disorders, the patient passes from one mode to the next. Generally, each disorder stabilizes in a given mode, including death.

1. *Psychiatric Normality* (see chapter 9), the nonpersonal illness of Foulds and Bedford. This level has been little researched, though it obviously presents the templates which are goals for treatment. Normality can be depicted as normative (ideal mental health), or statistical (how the majority of people adapt), or dynamic (a balance of complex forces). Practically, it is a state of great variety and rhythm, in activity, feeling, repertoire of homeostatic mechanisms. The individual is "on track" developmentally, in harmony or creative tension with his or her subculture, self-consistent (in harmony with the usual self, not changed, the self being used as control), and having generally stabilized bodily systems (though physical illness or developmental defect may be present). The ongoing mood is of some general satisfaction, punctuated by incursions of all possible emotions, and brief, appropriate shifts into fight–flight (emergencies) and conservation–withdrawal (personal losses). The abilities to work, play, and love are hallmarks. There are no pharmacologic correlates.

2. *Fight–flight* (see chapter 10). Normal fight–flight lasts minutes to hours: when the subject remains fixed in this state, we speak of an abnormal homeostatic shift, including a pathological mood state. This level is typified by a tense, alert stance, with all systems, biopsychosocial, geared to self-defense and self-preservation. There is general narrowing of activities, cognitive preoccupations, and coping mechanisms, to those appropriate for a situation of danger. The individual feels threatened, and acts defensively: a respected teacher insisted that we first diagnose this state of *defensiveness* before identifying what actual defense mechanisms are being deployed. The characteristic affects of this level are anxious and hostile: fear of various degrees, timidity, "state" anxiety, panic attacks; anger of various grades, irritability, hostility, rage attacks. We have, on the whole, clinically neglected the important reciprocal relation between these two affects.

The *psychiatric syndromes* at this homeostatic level include most of the psychoneuroses, but also a number of psychophysiological syndromes, and well-organized tensional disorders such as paranoia; it is hard to know where to fit in mania, but some of its features belong here. Vague, shifting prodromes to other syndromes pass through this level: during recovery we are alert to mark when depressed people become irritable, and apathetic ones frightened. Physiologically, the organism is in a state of preparedness for battle or swift escape: the metabolic functions are "powered up" through sympathicoadrenergic and pituitary–adrenocortical activity.

The *pharmacologic correlates* of this level are the stimulant/alerting or sympathomimetic drugs, and the sedative–hypnotic ones, which increase or diminish alerting (Lehmann, 1961).

3. *Conservation–withdrawal* (see chapters 12–14). The shift into this level is from tensional, alert, engaged, powered up, to withdrawn, atonic, inhibited, unseen, and disengaged: the organismic strategy is to conserve energies and strive to avoid attention, to foster survival by the risky posture of feigning death, to allow healing of wounds and restitution of depleted resources by immobility. In this gamble for survival the organism is clearly vulnerable to further mauling and death; it is the setting for much human illness (Schmale and Engel, 1975) and suicide, and is thus inferior in the scale of survival efficiency.

The psychiatric syndromes at this level are the neurasthenias (anergic states without painful affect) and depressions (with painful affect); more serious conditions such as the schizophrenias have prodromes and metadromes at this level. There has been much debate over whether grief, which shares both the painful affect and the autonomy or persistence of depression, should be considered a disease (Engel, 1961).

At this level, the psyche remains organized and symptoms tend to be logically consistent, but there is a further constriction of mental activity to cognitive themes of helplessness and hopelessness and to stereotyped defense mechanisms such as introjection of blame. The characteristic affect is dejection or despondency: there is no clear dejection in the neurasthenic states, but dejection is evident to extremely severe in depressions. The huge quantum of biological research on the depressions (perhaps more properly on conservation–withdrawal, though it is usually not labeled as such) of recent decades has as yet not rendered up a firm explanation of the essence of this level; clearly, disturbances in neurotransmitters and brain systems for alerting, mood, and motivation are important per-petuating mechanisms which have to be attacked.

The pharmacologic correlates of this level are those drugs and hormones which, albeit somewhat inconsistently, foster the de-velopment of neurasthenic and depressive states; and the anti-depressant drugs and convulsive therapy, which are effective in remitting the more severe depressions.

4. *Disintegration* (see chapter 15). This is a term which I adapt and adopt from Lehmann (1961) and Foulds and Bed-ford (1975), to encompass the syndromes in which mental life becomes disorganized in a disarticulation of perceptual, con-ceptual, motivational, and affective systems. Of these the schizo-phrenias are prototypical, and toxic deliria can also be included here. *Disintegration* and *psychosis* are equivalent terms, as used in this discussion. In the onset of psychoses, prodromes of fight–flight and then conservation–withdrawal are common; metadromes retrace the same levels. Disintegration does not seem to be a normal adaptive pattern, so that it can be consid-ered always pathological; it does, however, show in many cases just the stubborn momentum and autonomy which make it a homeostatic mode, however antithetical to survival (Luborsky, 1974) or however maladaptive.

The key features of this mode or level are hallucinosis and logical inconsistency: bizarre thinking, inappropriateness of af-fect (disarticulation, exaggeration, or absence), absurdity, chaos, make of most psychoses a severe discontinuity in the life of the individual and a severe break with the mores of the subculture. The pathophysiology of disintegration or psychosis is even less well elucidated than that of depression, despite decades of research effort.

Pharmacologic correlates of this level are the psychedelic, hal-lucinogenic, or psychotomimetic drugs, which produce model disarticulations of perception, affect, and motivation, and the antipsychotic or neuroleptic drugs, which aid in reintegration (Lehmann, 1961).

5. *A Note on Death.* I have been unable to find any homeo-static level intervening between disintegration and death itself. Further, most accounts of the experience of nearly dying report

phenomena which are compatible with disintegration: dream-like hallucinations, often very pleasant but sometimes terrifying, feelings of disembodiment, the experience of looking at the self from outside, and so on. Before the advent of the antipsychotic drugs we regularly encountered deaths in acute and chronic psychoses, for which no pathologic findings were explanatory; this suggests again how antithetical disintegration is to survival, but also hints at the sequential relationship to dying.

General Variables in Human Homeostasis

In leaving our review of the homeostatic–dynamic model, I shall address a few broad groupings of variables which partake in homeostatic–adaptive operations and which are of clinical importance. These groupings are broad enough that they fall under our present overview of human homeostasis: in later chapters we shall address more specific processes such as brain injury (chapter 8) and sleep and dreaming (chapter 13). The present groupings represent an interplay of independent variables (those which contribute to homeostatic operations) and dependent ones (those which accompany or result from such operations):

1. *Behavioral Systems, Drive, and Conflict.* These are the motivational aspects of homeostasis. Stress for humans is most frequently the experience of intrapsychic and interpersonal conflict.
2. *Mental Mechanisms.* I prefer this term to *defense mechanisms* as it embraces also nondefensive, adaptive, efforts in the regulation of intrapsychic and interpersonal conflict.
3. *Emotions and Moods.* Emotions have been well explored and understood, but science appears to have neglected the clinically important area of moods and pathological mood states.
4. *Human Communication.* This is important both as a vehicle of cognitive life and as the meeting of minds in social

interaction; we shall limit this very large subject to brief discussion.

5. *Human Sexuality*. This unites biological, psychological, and social issues so intimately and is an excellent barometer of human homeostasis–adaptation; again brief discussion only will be possible.

6. *Information Processing and Injury to the Central Nervous System*. Normal homeostasis becomes difficult or impossible when the central regulator and coordinator, the brain, is injured. This major group of variables will be dealt with in chapter 8.

Variables in Homeostasis: Behavioral Systems, Drive, and Conflict

Behavioral Systems

Human adaptation is active, outreaching, organizing. There are basic motivational patterns which propel this activity, for which learning theory and reflexology give a poor account. We need to review the nature of such behavioral systems, the motivational units of human homeostasis and adaptation.

Bowlby (1969) is critical of the constructs of instinct and drive, since they have become too reified and rigid to be of use in clinical science. For a modern perspective we turn to his review and analysis of the contributions of ethology and of the theory of information and guidance systems (see also chapter 5).

Human infants, like other primates and lower animals, are born with genetically coded behavioral systems, which are relatively independent of each other, and indeed can compete with each other. In humans, these systems are actualized and elaborated by social learning. They range in quality from highly "environmentally stable" (i.e., elicited by stimuli from the *milieu intérieur* and little or not at all by environmental events) to highly "environmentally labile" (i.e., responding to eliciting conditions in the *milieu extérieur* but otherwise lying latent). Such behavioral systems include patterns for feeding, attachment and security, curiosity and learning, self-defense, and procreation. When one system is activated, others may well be inhibited; a feeding creature suddenly stops feeding to scan the environment for possible danger and take necessary action. It is in this sense that behavioral systems are competitive with each other. Systems can "contaminate" each other: the aggression system enters into care-giving or procreation, for example (Bowlby, 1984), in instances of family violence.

Elicitation of Behavioral Systems

Even in lower animals learning is involved in the adult development of behavioral systems; learning is a dominant contributor in humans, as is well known for the sexual or procreative system and its lengthy and complex development (Freud, 1905). Bowlby's examples of anxious versus secure attachment (Bowlby, 1969) include very distinct components of learning in the attachment system. For humans, our complex abilities in cognitive evaluation make the distinction between "environmentally stable" and "environmentally labile" often a difficult one. A particularly vexatious instance would seem to be the lengthy theoretical controversies regarding human aggression. Clinicians such as Freud (1936), M. Klein (as reviewed by Segal, 1973) and Menninger (1938) have seen human aggression to be rather environmentally stable, a kind of perpetually boiling volcano which will regularly erupt, injuring the self or others, relatively regardless of external provocation (the death instinct). Social psychologists have consistently pictured human aggression as a predictable response to frustration, the "Frustration–Aggression Hypothesis" (Dollard, Miller, Doob, Mowrer and Sears, 1939; Berkowitz, 1969). What may account for such divergent and apparently irreconcilable views on human aggression surely resides in the complex variables of human cognitive evaluation: certain persons consistently interpret their environment as ungiving, menacing, and frustrating of their needs; others misinterpret intrapsychic conflict as external thwarting, through a combination of lack of self-awareness and the mechanism of externalization or projection. Such persons clearly live much of their lives in fight–flight. A balanced and clarifying view of the vicissitudes of human aggression is presented by Storr (1968) and Carthy and Ebling (1964), a view which successfully resolves the above theoretical antithesis.

Some obvious examples of differences in environmental lability come easily to mind. A most urgent, relatively environmentally stable system is that of breathing, regulated by internal sensors and capable of conscious inhibition for only very brief periods. The need to eat or to sleep are dictated by internal sensors also, though learning to defer these needs and to meet them in a socially desirable manner is important in human life. Disorders of the eating behavioral system are currently on the increase, apparently related to social learning and contamination from other behavioral systems.

The procreative behavioral system in humans is quite unlike the seasonal drive of other animals. In women it has a monthly (menstrual) cyclical pattern, in men it has a relatively steady pattern. In both sexes, this system is intermediate in environmental lability: there is a cyclical or steady pressure from the *milieu intérieur*, but environmental eliciting conditions are important in both arousing or inhibiting sexual desire. This system has a lengthy, complex, developmental history in which learning has a crucial shaping effect; it becomes contaminated and perverted in certain individuals as a result. Sexual deviations have all the earmarks of an innate behavioral system.

Behavioral systems, once elicited and in motion, have a quality of motivational "pressure" which is relieved on the achievement of the appropriate set-goal (Bowlby, 1969) with a sense of relief or of pleasure. They have arisen in humans (and other animals) as necessary for the survival of the species, as advantageous in an "environment of evolutionary adaptedness" in our prehistory, thus presenting some problems in our present urban societies. For humans, with their lengthy childhood, complex social organization, and dominant learning and cognitive apparatus, there is always the risk of behavioral systems being actualized as a *forme fruste* of amorphous or distorted quality in adult life.

Bowlby (1969, 1980) and Miller, Galanter, and Pribram, (1960) should be consulted for further detail on modern views regarding behavioral and motivational systems.

Frustration and Conflict

While *frustration* signifies the thwarting, by an external agency, of one's real or perceived needs, the term *conflict* properly designates the process of internal "friction" within the human machine when two or more behavioral systems compete. Conflict and intrapsychic struggle are an important ingredient of human discomfort and of the homeostatic process: normality generally represents skill in conflict resolution, versus the ineptness of neurotic operations. Conflict has been an important psychoanalytic construct: struggle between major behavioral systems, the id (physiological tensions, instinctual pressures), the standards and ideals of the superego (internalized familial and social prohibitions and commands) and the coping attempts, reality considerations, and effector capabilities of the ego. This "trinitarian" approach (Freud, 1923) has the merits of reflecting biological, psychological, and social levels of emergence. Other formulations basically agree: conflicts are pictured as between approach–avoidance, different priorities of approach or avoidance, and so on. A moral dilemma approach has already been noted in the work of Kohlberg (see chapter 6).

Normality consists in finding solutions to motivational problems which satisfy id, ego, and superego; that is, give instinctual satisfaction in a socially acceptable manner, with a resolution of tension and discomfort. "Neurotic" solutions are incomplete resolutions, leaving residual discomforts (shame, guilt, irritation, etc.) as modulated by pathogenic defense mechanisms.

Variables in Homeostasis: Mental Mechanisms

Psychological Homeostatic Mechanisms

A defense mechanism, as defined in the *Longman Dictionary of Psychology and Psychiatry* (Goldenson, 1984), is "a reaction pattern, usually unconscious . . . protecting the individual from anxiety, guilt, unacceptable impulses, internal conflicts . . . a common, normal means of coping . . . but excessive use of any mechanism . . . is considered pathological" (p. 205). The same dictionary credits Harry Stack Sullivan as introducing the term *dynamism* for essentially this same construct, thus suggesting an active, adaptive process (p. 240). I shall use the broader term *mental mechanisms* to embrace both the adaptive and constructive and the defensive and maladaptive varieties and deployments of such reaction patterns. In general (Vaillant, 1971, 1976) there is a continuum of mental mechanisms ranging from adaptive, developmentally mature, and conscious, to defensive, developmentally immature, unconscious, and pathogenic.

Mental mechanisms are clearly efforts at maintaining homeostasis, both in normal and in other modes. By definition, they function at the psychological level of emergence. Sigmund Freud (1926) and Anna Freud (1936) were the originator and the systematizer, respectively, of the construct of defense mechanisms, as specific strategies of the ego to modulate, resolve, or control intrapsychic conflict and to avoid or minimize *angst* (a term for distress more suggestive of pain or anguish than the usual English translation "anxiety"). Sigmund Freud's original notes on the various mechanisms are listed by Kline (1981), a useful reference source. Mental mechanisms, whether adaptive or defensive, control psychological experience and action as a whole (Siegal, 1969; Vaillant, 1971, 1976; Leigh and Reiser, 1982). The clinical distinction between the adaptive and the defensive is an important one, as Vaillant repeatedly suggests: I have commented before that making this distinction may be a higher priority than being able to "label" the specific mechanism a patient deploys. Vaillant (1976) suggests that identifying mental mechanisms is an important part of clinical diagnosis, supplementing the nosological diagnosis and illuminating variables such as severity and prognosis.

Anna Freud (1936) placed repression as the primary and central defense mechanism, one which, however, can only be inferred since it cannot be observed directly when it is in operation. She conceived the other mechanisms as actualizing and upholding repression. Sigmund Freud (Kline, 1981) earlier described repression as central, as virtually coterminous with the construct of defense itself; he stressed (Freud, 1926) how invisibly it operates, indeed the more successfullly, the more invisibly. In his later writings Freud saw repression as a much more specific mechanism, controlling "information flow," and deployed prominently in the hysterias (Kline, 1981). Freud selected the term *sublimation* for the most adaptive defense mechanism or group of mechanisms, also for its invisibility under scrutiny. His metaphor was the invisible passage of certain chemicals directly from solid to gaseous phase.

Gleser and Ihilevich (1969) grouped the mental mechanisms into five principal defensive patterns. "Turning against object (TAO)" includes all operations which deal with conflict by confronting an external frustrating object, including identification with an aggressor. Under "Projection (PRO)" are transactions which justify attack by attributing all undesired properties to the external object. "Principalization (PRN)" deals with conflict by resort to an overriding principle, thus excluding emotional response. "Turning against self (TAS)" encompasses all modes of coping with conflict by attacking the self. "Reversal (REV)" subsumes defensive operations which produce neutral or positive feeling in relation to frustrating objects. The work of these authors is further reviewed below.

I shall give considerable weight to the detailed empirical work of Vaillant, whose data are drawn from the men in the Grant Study, and two of whose papers (1971, 1976) and summarizing book (1977) pay specific attention to mental mechanisms. Vaillant (1971) described the function of ego mechanisms as being to "keep affects within bearable limits—restore psychological 'homeostasis' . . . by postponing or deflecting sudden increases in biological drives—obtain 'time-out' to master changes in self-image [and]—handle unresolvable conflict with important people, living or dead" (p. 107). Vaillant draws 18 mental mechanisms from the writings of Anna Freud and some subsequent psychoanalytic theorists. He presents evidence for ranking these mechanisms in a continuum by their developmental maturity and by their empirically found success in coping with living. A series of empirical ratings and statistical calculations reveal remarkable correlations between personal health (mental and physical) and personal and social success and the developmental level of mental mechanisms habitually deployed.

Vaillant classifies mental mechanisms under four developmental levels (see also chapter 9, pp. 301–304). "Psychotic mechanisms" are used normally before age 5, and include delusional projection and psychotic denial of external reality. "Immature mechanisms" are common between ages 3 and 15, and include projection, schizoid fantasy, hypochondriasis, passive–aggressive behavior, and acting out. "Neurotic defenses," common from 3 onward, include intellectualization, repression, displacement, reaction formation, and dissociation or neurotic denial. "Mature mechanisms," common from age 12 onward ("virtues" in the popular view), include altruism, humor, suppression (postponement), anticipation, and sublimation.

Leigh and Reiser (1982) approach mental mechanisms from the modern perspective of general systems theory. They agree with classical views that defense mechanisms reduce anxiety by modifying the fundamental units of the personality system: input (perception), processing (mediation), and output (execution). Mechanisms which alter input include constriction of awareness, denial, projection, introjection, and displacement. The mechanisms which influence processing are repression, rationalization, intellectualization, fantasy, isolation, and reaction formation. Modifying output are acting out, undoing, nonspecific activity, counterphobic maneuvers, and sublimation. All three segments in the personality system are involved in the pervasive operations of regression and identification.

Scientific Support for Mental Mechanisms: Kline's Work

Despite the clinical relevance and diagnostic importance of these psychological homeostatic mechanisms, research studies on them are few and far between. I have noted three classification schemas above. An early example of an attempt by controlled means to confirm the operation of projection is that of Bellak (1944) who gave volunteer subjects the Thematic Apperception Test (TAT), scolded them undeservedly during the testing, then looked for an increase of aggression projected into subsequent picture cards. The hypothesis was upheld that unexpressed resentment would be thus projected.

Paul Kline (1981) has assembled an important book reviewing psychoanalytic theory and, as far as is possible, putting it to scientific test by reviewing various psychological research studies. This volume can be consulted on a great variety of psychoanalytic issues. Our present concern will be to see how the psychoanalytic construct of defense mechanisms fares when scientifically scrutinized. Kline's approach is to make operational, in clear hypotheses, a range of psychoanalytic constructs; then to search out scientifically creditable studies which will confirm, fail to confirm, or clearly refute, these hypotheses.

Kline finds in fact that there is not one body of psychoanalytic theory, but a collection of theories; further, that psychoanalytic theory operates at four levels of abstraction (see below) several of which are testable, and thus fall within the province of science; and finally, that though this cumbrous assembly of theories has been neither wholly supported nor wholly falsified, as yet there has arisen no superior body of theory which has replaced it.

Kline's criteria of a science are threefold. First, there must be reportable observations, gathered under *controlled* conditions: psychoanalysis fails this test, for its data are retrospective, relying upon the memories of both patient and analyst. Second, there must be constructs which are *operational* in wording: psychoanalysis fares poorly here, as many of its constructs are vague and sweeping (but see below). Third, there must be hypotheses which are *testable*: psychoanalysis again does rather badly on this criterion. Therefore, psychoanalysis as a whole cannot be called a proper science.

However, when the actual propositions of psychoanalysis are ranked, some more hopeful prospect emerges. Kline finds four groupings: First, the "empirical proposition," such as that around age 4 boys regard their fathers as rivals: this type of proposition is testable. So, with some difficulties in methodology, is the second, the "specific psychoanalytic proposition"; for example, that the outcome of the Oedipus situation determines character and psychopathology. The third and fourth groupings, the "general psychoanalytic proposition" and the "metapsychological proposition," cannot be tested because of their sweeping and abstract quality; simply, they cannot be reworded or broken down into operational, testable form. Most of Kline's book proceeds with an examination of researches which will illuminate the empirical and the specific psychoanalytic propositions.

Mental mechanisms or the mechanisms of defense are the subject of Kline's chapter 8 (pp. 195–262). Kline first lists the principal mechanisms outlined by Sigmund Freud, and gives references to where and when Freud described them. He then takes up various areas of defense, and specific defense mechanisms, formulating hypotheses by which they can be tested, and reviewing studies such as will confirm or refute these hypotheses; that is, lend support, or otherwise, to the constructs of the various mechanisms. Kline is stringently critical of researches published: he often finds their methods or relevance deficient; he rejects projective tests in general (e.g., the Rorschach, and the Thematic Apperception Test which Bellak used) as valid measuring instruments. He shows great interest in newer methods such as Percept–genetics and the Defense Mechanism Inventory, to which I shall refer further.

Kline's review and arguments are quite intricate, so that I shall present them only in overall terms. He devotes considerable space to *repression*, noting that the term has several meanings. As a central or general defensive maneuver, it includes both holding in check information that has never reached consciousness ("primal repression," chiefly of instinctual impulses) and returning to unconsciousness what was once more accessible ("repression proper" or "after-repression," which may also be used to control affects). As a more specific or focal defense mechanism, it is found in the hysterias, this being Freud's later definition of repression. The various forms of repression are rather well supported by the studies Kline reviews. The new approach of percept–genetics, which investigates the organization of percepts by tachistoscopic methods, also supports the existence of a number of other mechanisms, particularly isolation, projection, denial, and reaction formation. The mechanism of displacement, Kline considers, has long (since about 1930) been solidly confirmed by studies in social psychology and ethology, at least for displacement of aggression. The mechanism of identification with the aggressor likewise is generally supported by one major study of Jews holding anti-Semitic attitudes. It is somewhat disappointing, Kline appears to ·suggest, that a number of quite vivid and clinically well-recognized mechanisms have neither been clearly supported, nor clearly refuted, by controlled studies. Here there are palpably difficult problems of method. Defense mechanisms are internal, unconscious, having to be inferred, not accessible directly by self-report or even laboratory observation; real-life situations are necessary to evoke them, and even careful designs to study them are often marred by irrelevance.

The Defense Mechanism Inventory (DMI) developed by Gleser and Ihilevich (1969), specifically to identify the operation of mental mechanisms, is considered by Kline to be a very promising instrument. These authors' five groupings or principal patterns of defense have been noted above: turning against object (hostility out), projection, principalization, turning against self (hostility in), and reversal. Gleser, collaborating with Gottschalk and others, has had long experience in developing standardized and quantitative content analysis of verbal samples, particularly for latent emotion and mood (Gottschalk, Winget, Gleser, and Springer, 1966). In the present context Gleser and Ihilevich present with considerable technical detail the development of the DMI. In form, it consists of 10 brief stories, in both female and male versions, depicting five types of social conflict; each story is followed by four clarifying questions; then the subject draws, from five proffered choices, the responses closest to and most distant from his or her own response. Scores are then calculated from these responses (which are coupled to the five defensive operations noted above) and the strengths of various defenses indicated.

Studies with the DMI confirm a number of the defense mechanisms outlined by Freud, but Kline is cautious and critical of these findings, on the grounds that the DMI has not been satisfactorily validated. Gleser and Sacks (1973) present a validation study of the DMI carried out on a sizable group of university students of both sexes, but this does not satisfy Kline. However, a short time after the publication of Kline's book (1981), Cooper and Kline (1982) published their own validation study of the DMI with an optimistic outcome. The DMI was here compared with a well-known and reputable personality inventory, the 16 PF. Cooper and Kline now express approval of Gleser's happy "marriage of psychoanalysis and psychometrics" and it will be of interest to see whether the instrument lives up to its considerable promise.

Nature of Mental Mechanisms: Summary and Synthesis

Mental mechanisms are homeostatic efforts operating and identifiable at a psychological level of emergence; their function is to preserve equilibrium by preventing or reducing tension in the *milieu intérieur,* by modulating intrapsychic conflict. In the Piagetian sense, they balance assimilation and accommodation to the *milieu extérieur.* In pathological instances, they neglect or distort external considerations, that is, are highly assimilative, and fail to produce tranquility within (i.e., produce symptoms).

The two central mechanisms, repression and sublimation, are also the most invisible: these must be inferred. Freud's earlier formulations depicted repression as a broad, general defensive mode; Anna Freud suggested that it is actually an abstraction, a resultant of other more specific mechanisms. Sigmund Freud's later position viewed repression as a much more specific shutting off of information, a view consonant with present models of information processing. Vaillant suggests that sublimation too may be an abstraction, brought about by more specific, healthy, developmentally mature mechanisms. Mental mechanisms operate across a spectrum from healthy to very pathological; for example, projection and introjection are necessary in the faculty of empathy (Aring, 1958), yet they also partake in paranoid and depressive psychoses. Dissociation and constriction of experience aid us in focusing attention and concentrating: they also contribute to obsessive–compulsive and amnestic syndromes.

The scientific status of mental mechanisms has been partially upheld in the reviews of Kline, but much work with experimental design and research instruments needs to be done. Generally, repression, displacement, isolation, projection, denial, and reaction formation have been confirmed, and no mental mechanism appears to have been falsified firmly.

How do mental or defense mechanisms operate? Bowlby (1980; and see chapter 4) and Kline (1981) favor an information-processing model. Bowlby reviews the current neurophysiological understanding of sensory processing. Here, a multiply staged but exceedingly rapid sequence involves early reception, sampling, evaluation, selective attention, and magnification of the relevant, and inhibition and exclusion of the irrelevant; this goes on within milliseconds and outside of conscious awareness. A finite number of information channels take part in this sequence. Some of the steps in the sequence have now been clearly identified, along with the mechanisms for them. Such a model suggests that the various types of repression, and, by extrapolation, other mechanisms, are actualized by an information processing and selective attention and exclusion system. It appears to be the breakdown of such selective tuning mechanisms which permit sensory overload, in one major view of the pathogenesis of schizophrenia (McGhie, 1969; see chapter 15).

Thus I believe it might be possible to classify defense mechanisms according to a principle of information processing; such a schema should be testable:

1. *Mechanisms which reduce, exclude, or reverse perceptions:* constriction of awareness, dissociation, isolation, reaction formation, repression (both of impulses and of feelings).
2. *Mechanisms which ignore internal conflict* by focusing on *external events*: externalization–attribution–projection, displacement (of feeling), identification with the aggressor.
3. *Mechanisms which ignore external frustration* by focusing on the *internal*: introjection, incorporation.
4. *Mechanisms which divert from conflict, yet symbolize it:* somatization, hypochondriasis, conversion, denial, acting out, regression.

For the more normal or adaptive deployment of mental mechanisms, see further discussion in chapter 9.

Variables in Homeostasis: Emotions and Moods

Studies of Emotion

There is essentially firm agreement between researchers on the number and nature of the human emotions. I shall therefore review this subject matter in a summarizing manner, rather than by comparing various *differing* approaches to emotion. The emotions are relatively discrete patterns of whole-person experiencing and behaving, with apparent natural boundaries, so that classification is relatively easy and satisfactory. The real problem, for clinicians, is the paucity of research on mood states, and how they resemble and differ from passing emotions; for it is mood states, particularly their pathological versions, which interest the clinician. At this time we cannot safely or reliably extrapolate from the science of emotion to the clinical understanding of mood.

Darwin (1872) studied the emotions of humans and animals from direct observation and from a multitude of anecdotal reports. His viewpoint was, naturally, evolutionary. How do emotions occur across the animal kingdom? What do they mean, and how can they be related trans-specifically? What do their expressions signify, both as external communications, and as relics of evolutionary events encoded in the nervous system; for example, what does a smile signify in these two ways? Darwin's book remains a rich gold mine for understanding and hypothesis raising. Izard's (1977) differential emotions theory classifies the emotions mainly by the differing facial expressions (affect); Izard and Buechler have also summarized his work (1980). Plutchik's (1980a) psychoevolutionary synthesis, with some attention to facial expressions, relies on the cognitive analysis of environmental situations for the principal meaning of emotions; in addition he summarizes his own approach as well as reviewing the state of research in emotions (1980b). An interesting device of Plutchik is the "circumplex" of emotions, a continuous circle on which the emotions can be arranged like the circle of the colors. Argyle (1975) is a student of social behavior, thus of emotions as social signifiers: his classification is by facial expression. Tompkins (1980) classifies emotions broadly into positive and negative (see my synthesis below).

Although there is significantly broad agreement on the number and nature of emotions, and this in the face of study and classification from rather different perspectives, it is interesting to note the few discrepancies or omissions from classification. Darwin (1872) devotes considerable space to the emotion of shame, with its unique human psychophysiological expression in blushing. Izard (1977) includes both guilt and shame as valid emotions, each with its facial expression. Tompkins (1980) includes shame, but not guilt. Neither Plutchik (1980a) nor Argyle (1975) include guilt and shame as valid emotions; this is remarkable considering Argyle's strong social orientation. I shall attempt to reconcile these views below.

The Properties of an Emotion

Since there is essential agreement, I offer the following synthesis of the properties and components of a human emotion:

1. An emotion is a global biopsychosocial, experiential, existential, motivational shift in the relatively steady state of the individual, of relatively short duration (minutes, hours), and which has meaning for both subject and onlooker.

2. An emotion is a feeling, a subjective cluster of musculoskeletal and visceral sensations, invariably reportable as either positive (pleasant) or negative (unpleasant). To some extent, it is possible to generate such a feeling by producing the facial expression or mimicking other musculoskeletal components (the James–Lange theory of emotion, Cannon [1932]). Individuals who cannot clearly identify what emotion they are feeling can usually report whether they feel "good" or "bad."

3. An emotion is an affect or expression, an objective, observable, describable, measurable cluster of facial expression, posture, gesture, gait, voice, and physiological changes (e.g., pupillary dilation, trembling, sweating, blushing). Facial expression has been considered the most reliable and specific criterion of an emotion by most workers.

4. An emotion is a social signal or communication, the affect arousing responses in onlookers which may be understanding, sympathetic (generating the same emotion, sadness,

anger, etc.), resentful, or otherwise motivational (a wish to re-spond or assist, to resist or reject, etc.). In transcultural studies, emotions, as depicted in photographs of the face, are well un-derstood by members of foreign societies, if only in "as if" terms (e.g., "this man looks as if he just lost his best friend").

5. An emotion is part of a cognitive–motivational sequence. A central issue in research (Izard, 1977; Plutchik, 1980a) has been that of identifying specific cognitive appraisals of an envi-ronmental situation or event which lead to specific emotions, which in turn are motivators for appropriate and specific ac-tion. Emotion is thus a key part of many motivational or behav-ioral systems (see for example discussion on attachment, pp. 137–157). We speak clinically of "appropriate" and "inappro-priate" emotional response, in this precise context. Cognitive therapy (Beck, Rush, Shaw, and Emery, 1979) has been much occupied with revision of cognitive appraisals contributing to depressive mood in particular; but here we come up against a methodological problem, that of whether pathological moods are caused by cognitions, or cause them.

6. An emotion is a cluster of physiologic events in the brain (limbic system, hypothalamus, basal ganglia) and the periphery (autonomic nervous system, endocrine glands, muscles, vis-cera). The specific physiological cluster associated with each emotion is experienced as the *feeling* in that emotion (no. 2 above).

7. An emotion is an evolutionary relic: the involuntary pat-terns of facial muscle tone, posture, and gesture of emotion are universal, therefore clearly innate and genetically pro-grammed, probably in the basal ganglia. They appear in their patterning (Darwin, 1872; Plutchik, 1980a,b) to be stereotyped traces or symbolic but abortive relics of actions our ancestors once took under various socially charged situations. Thus, the smile is presumed to be an abortive, checked, or denied snarl or threat to bite; generalized patterns of muscle tension and typical postures might have once been threats of physical assault or gestures of abject submission; the tears of sadness once had the function of washing out sand or dust someone had flung in our ancestors' eyes; and so on.

Classification of the Human Emotions

The following classification represents my own synthesis from the authors above, the ordering being most indebted to Tompkins (1980), with his division into "positive" and "negative" emotions. Agreement among these authors, despite their different approaches, is high, suggesting that we are indeed dealing with discrete natural phenomena: I shall comment on the uncertainties regarding shame and guilt as we come to these. I omit the subjective feeling clusters in emotion, as these are dealt with very thinly in the research literature.

Each emotion is defined by the cognitive–motivational sequence of which it is a part (Plutchik [1980a,b] in particular), by the facial expression (Argyle [1975], Izard [1977] in particular), and by the physiological response (Heilman and Satz [1983], Cannon [1915, 1932], Engel [1956, 1961, 1962a,b]) associated with it. I give synonyms for various grades of the emotion in parenthesis.

Positive Emotions

1. *Interest/Anticipation/Excitement* (curiosity, inquisitiveness, engrossment). Cognitive appraisal: something novel. Action ensuing: explore the novel situation or object. Facial expression: open-eyed, mildly smiling. Physiological response: mild to moderate alerting.

2. *Enjoyment/Joy/Ecstasy* (satisfaction, pleasure, happiness, mirth, elation). Cognitive appraisal: success, profit, triumph, being loved. Action ensuing: relax, enjoy, celebrate. Facial expression: broad smiling, laughter. Physiology: poorly studied.

3. *Surprise/Startle* (astonishment, amazement, shock, recoil, stun). Cognitive appraisal: something totally unexpected: friend or foe? Action ensuing: orienting or startle reflex, bringing all senses into play. Facial expression: eyes wide, whites showing, eyebrows raised, mouth open and rounded ("Oh!"). Physiology: burst of sympathicoadrenal activity (fight–flight).

Negative Emotions

4. *Anxiety/Fear/Terror* (uneasiness, apprehension, worry, dread, horror, panic). Cognitive appraisal: adversary or environmental danger, large and overpowering. Action ensuing: flight, rapid and efficient escape. Facial expression: eyebrows raised and pinched, lips tensed, drawn out and down, pupils and nostrils dilated (beads of sweat, hair standing up). Physiology: partial to full fight–flight.

5. *Hostility/Anger/Rage* (Dissatisfaction, resentment, malice, wrath, fury). Cognitive appraisal: adversary or physical obstacle frustrating progress or fulfillment, of a size and power to be grappled with; being cornered by dangerous foe. Action ensuing: active attack and struggle. Facial expression: scowling, frowning, menacing eyes and brows, tense, snarling mouth, pupils and nostrils dilated. Physiology: partial to full fight–flight.

6. *Contempt/Scorn* (disrespect, disdain, arrogance, derision). Cognitive appraisal: adversary or physical obstacle which is inferior or insignificant. Action ensuing: ignore it or step on or over it. Facial expression: supercilious, chin raised, eyes half-closed, mouth bowed downward. Physiology: poorly studied.

7. *Disgust/Revulsion/Loathing* (distaste, abhorrence, repulsion). Cognitive appraisal: filthy, noisome, putrid or poisonous substance or object. Action ensuing: back away, or, if touched, tasted, or ingested, vomit. Facial expression: nauseated, eyes squeezed almost shut, mouth drawn down, platysma muscle in neck tensed. Physiology: spectrum from anorexia through nausea to vomiting.

8. *Sadness/Distress/Anguish* (discouragement, dejection, despondency, heartsickness, despair). Cognitive appraisal: failure, abandonment, loss of something or someone of value, perceived as irremediable. Action ensuing: withdrawal, constriction of posture and activity, weeping. Facial expression: brows and eyes peaked up as in pain ("pain muscle"), face appears lengthened, nose narrowed, mouth drawn downward, tears. Physiology: partial to full conservation–withdrawal.

9. *Shyness/Shame/Humiliation* (abashment, embarrassment, mortification). Cognitive appraisal: caught by other(s) in disgraceful act or state. Action ensuing: hiding, self-concealment,

covering of face. Facial expression: face (and whole figure) averted, glance sidelong, with mild to furious blushing. Physiology: vasodilation of face and neck a specific but not consistent response.

Note: Despite the descriptive specificity and visibility of this emotion in its *acute* expression, and strong evidence for shame in other social animals, it is omitted from some classifications (see discussion above and chapter 6).

10. *Guilt* (rue, regret, contrition, remorse). Cognitive appraisal: as judged by the self alone, some wrong has been done, or injury to another. Action ensuing: self-abasement, penance, efforts at restitution. Facial expression (not clearly agreed upon): rather nonspecific, midway between fear and sadness. Physiology: not well studied.

Note: As mentioned above, there is disagreement about including guilt as an actual emotion. My impression is that *acute* (normal) guilt partakes of properties of fight–flight, with "conscience anxiety" (i.e., dread and fear) the main emotion felt. More *protracted* ("neurotic") shame and guilt, where cognitive appraisal views the wrongdoing alternatingly as potentially remediable and as irremediable and hopeless, will generate feelings of dread and struggle (fight–flight) alternating with dejection and despondency (conservation–withdrawal); where resignation is complete, dejection should dominate. It seems best to regard guilt as a *cognitive* complex, and not an emotion proper, of considerable variety in content and feeling. Chronic or neurotic shame might best be regarded in the same way.

Emotions, Moods, Traits, and Their Pathological Analogs

We now come to an area poorly defined by research: the understanding of the clinically important phenomena of moods and mood states. Grief, the protracted analog of acute sadness, is a prototype for mood states; but its psychophysiologic aspects have not been greatly clarified.

A mood appears to be a long drawn-out (days to months) emotion, which is suggestive of a cognitive appraisal and which certainly has behavioral correlates. The *Longman Dictionary of Psychology and Psychiatry* (Goldenson, 1984) merely defines mood as "a mild, usually transient, feeling tone such as euphoria or irritability." *The Encyclopedic Dictionary of Psychology* (Harré and Lamb, 1983) has no entry for mood or mood disorder.

A trait is a relatively lifelong propensity to repeat a certain response, in this case an emotion: timidity, joviality, irritability, belligerence, or melancholy may be seen as such traits. More correctly, from our review of emotions above, a trait must be a tendency to repeat a given cognitive appraisal, leading on to a certain emotional response.

It is possible (and indeed the clinical field is occupied with the actual occurrence of such possibilities) to have *abnormal or perverse* emotions and moods. "Inappropriate affect," the wrong emotion for a given situation, is seen in certain schizophrenic states. I shall use the term *pathological emotion* to mean what happens in certain neurological conditions when an emotion erupts violently on small stimulation, or inappropriately, for example, crying while telling a joke (I am indebted to Dr. Marshall Folstein for advising me on this definition). The term could be applied correctly, I believe, to the apparently sourceless outbursts of terror in panic disorders, and of rage in certain aggressive personalities.

A *pathological mood,* or mood disorder, appears to be a mood which flouts the recognized rules of emotionality, in the following ways; again, these criteria should be compared with a normal mood state such as grief.

1. *Persistence.* A mood would continue for months or years after a relatively clear onset; such mood states have been termed *autonomous* and *endogenous* in that they are clearly not responses to the current environment, which influences them little if at all; they are *states,* for example, anxiety states.

2. *Inappropriateness or Perversity.* The difficulty, to the clinician, of establishing just why these states appear, and remain so stable; what moods mean in normal living does not seem to apply, though psychodynamic study may be partially explanatory.

3. *Dominance.* Such mood states appear to dominate thinking and living, rather than being *resultants* of current life experience. Thus, the cognitive–motivational sequence for emotions and for more normal moods does not appear to prevail in

pathological mood states: cognitive appraisals and ensuing actions appear to follow from the prevailing mood state, a point which has not received clear research attention.

4. *Homeostatic Style or Level.* It would seem that pathological mood states are only part of a larger picture, a more global homeostatic shift involving physiological changes and perpetuating mechanisms of both psychosocial and biological kind; that is, pathological moods are one major symptomatic aspect of global psychiatric disorder.

Pathologic Mood States: How Many?

If mood states are classified as analogs of the identified emotions, how many become possible? It is immediately clear that several emotions cannot be prolonged as mood states, since they are momentary and are functions of novelty. Thus, interest/anticipation and startle/surprise must, a priori, soon give way to cognitive appraisals which will yield neutral feeling or a variety of emotions: enjoyment, fear, anger, contempt, disgust, or sadness. As for shame and guilt (as emotions), I have already suggested that if these are prolonged, they must consist of cognitive complexes and not be emotions proper. As such they may, indeed do, contribute to neuroses and depressions, that is, to mood states of anxiety and hostility, or of sadness/distress/anguish.

Empirically, contempt/scorn does not appear to correspond closely with any pathologic mood states encountered clinically. It may make its appearance episodically in grandiose and euphoric (i.e., manic) disorders. There is one autonomous disorder (possibly two) related to disgust/revulsion/loathing: this is the relatively uncommon condition of persistent psychogenic vomiting, where the cognitive content is repressed, but the psychophysiological pattern is *as if* the patient has seen, smelled, ingested, or had forced into her (usually the patient is female) mouth or stomach some noisome substance or object. It may be that such a dynamic operates in certain instances of anorexia nervosa also.

This leaves us with four possibilities, which are, in fact, empirically found in recognized clinical disorders. I have chosen to classify them as follows, not by Tompkins's schema of "positive" and "negative," but by reference to concepts of survival and well-being.

Pathologic Mood States Related to Survival. These two mood states share a pathophysiology which is highly similar, alerting, tensional, fitting the organism for both effective escape and effective struggle; that is, fight–flight. I believe that clinicians have not been sufficiently aware of their similarities. These mood states, as noted above, are symptomatic parts of a greater homeostatic whole.

1. Anxiety spectrum, analogous to the emotion of anxiety/fear/terror. Various continuous states of brooding uneasiness, worry, ranging through frank fear to terror and panic; both "state" anxiety and episodic outbursts of dread and horror. The total psychobiologic style is that of fight–flight. Various psychologic and physiologic perpetuating mechanisms are present in varying degrees. Cognitive preoccupations are of danger and disaster, internal (somatic) and external. The empirically related clinical conditions are the generalized anxiety disorders, phobic and panic disorders, and paranoid disorders. This spectrum will be the subject of chapter 10.

2. Hostility spectrum, analogous to the emotion of hostility/anger/rage. Various continuing states of irritability, simmering anger, feelings of destructive rage, and misanthropic to homicidal preoccupations. Empirically, I do not believe clinicians have recognized this spectrum consistently, possibly because its subjects are encountered by legal and penal authorities rather than by psychiatrists. I shall comment further in chapter 10 on the nosological possibility of "hostility neurosis." The total psychobiologic picture is of fight–flight.

Pathologic Mood States Related to Well-Being. The bipolar mood states of elation or euphoria, and dejection or despondency, may be seen as disturbances of the fundamental sense of well-being. One is pleasant, energy-giving, felt as desirable: the other painful, energy-sapping, and undesirable.

3. Elation or euphoria spectrum, analogous to normal enjoyment/joy/ecstasy. Like its normal counterpart, the physiology

of this state is poorly understood. Various states of cheerfulness, alerting, inappropriate heartiness, range on through exhausting and fatal hyperactivity. Cognitive preoccupations are optimistic, expansive, grandiose; the mental mechanism of denial is prominent. The empirically related clinical conditions are the hypomanias, manias, and elated schizo-affective disorders. Chapter 11 will include brief review of research on this spectrum.

4. Dejection or despondency spectrum, analogous to normal sadness/distress/anguish. A range of dejected, dysthymic states from mildly to psychotically and suicidally disturbed; anergia, anhedonia, aboulia, psychomotor withdrawal and retardation of various degrees are central. The painful dysphoria or dysthymia is difficult to describe, but experienced as unpleasant to excruciating. The physiology of the global homeostatic shift, of which the mood state is a part, appears to be that of depletion and exhaustion (conservation–withdrawal). Cognitive preoccupations are pessimistic, nihilistic, and self-blaming; the mental mechanisms of giving up and introjection of blame are specific or central. This spectrum will be further discussed in chapters 12—14. The relevant clinical conditions are the depressive disorders and neurasthenias.

Variables in Homeostasis: Human Communication

Nature of Communication

This large area of research tends to be technical, even esoteric, and rather beyond the comprehension of the clinician. We shall therefore touch on it but briefly. Communication is almost coterminous with cognitive processes (see chapter 3); it is also the linkage and the transmitting medium for much of human relatedness and for the structure and function of social groupings (chapter 5); and psychiatric disorders almost always include a component of problem or breakdown in human communication. Communication, as adaptive mechanism, makes needs known, motivates others, records history and human

ideas, transmits culture, makes blind trial-and-error unnecessary, and actualizes the social "emergence" of humans. It becomes ineffective or garbled in certain states of brain injury,
and in cases of psychosis; incoherence, circumstantiality,
blocking, and other distortions occur throughout the spectrum
of psychiatric disorders. I fear that we have relatively few bridges between the communicational disturbances recognized by
clinicians and research-derived theories of communication and
language.

Broadly, we can divide communication into two fields, verbal or syntactic, and nonverbal or bodily. All communication
involves two or more persons: a sender and a receiver. Both
are required if there is transmission, both sent and received. If
there is no sender, of course there is no message. But lacking
a receiver, then there is *no* communication; impairment of communication may be the problem of either sender or receiver,
but the system of sender, message, and receiver is what constitutes communication, intact or disordered.

Messages consist of "signifiers": signs and symbols. Though
there is marked inconsistency in usage, here I shall use "sign"
to mean a signifier that has some resemblance to the object
denoted, and "symbol" to mean a purely arbitrary signifier.
Piaget (see chapter 3) follows the opposite connotations. Signs,
such as a road sign for an approaching curve, actually depict
their object. Certain Chinese and Japanese characters are styl-
ized pictures (e.g., of sun, moon, person, water, numbers).
Some English words are *signs*: "buzz," "bark" (of a dog), "hiss."
Symbols have no clear connection with what they arbitrarily
denote: "red," "house," "love," "algebra," "Xmas," "piety." Intelligent animals such as gorillas and chimpanzees can be taught
to communicate with a limited range of both signs and symbols,
though their brain does not permit them to speak or write
intelligibly. Parrots and mynahs can mimic speech skillfully,
but do not comprehend it. It seems that verbal and syntactic
communication is a quintessentially human evolutionary
achievement (Passingham, 1982, pp. 192–241).

Nonverbal and Verbal Communication

Nonverbal communication (NVC) is something we share with
our animal relatives in the language of bodily signs, though we

have developed it over and beyond body language; road signs, clothing, musical expression, for example. Bodily communication (Argyle, 1975) is mostly out of awareness, not consciously transmitted nor consciously received, yet wielding considerable motivational influence. It consists of sounds, smells, postures, gestures, expressions, clothing, and a whole variety of more synthetic devices (Argyle, 1975; Ruesch and Kees, 1956). Nonverbal communications contain signs and symbols, but they tend to communicate *diffuse states,* and they are, at least on the human scene, vulnerable to misinterpretation: there is a vagueness, an imprecision about them. While a receiver concludes that "This person is being seductive," the sender's state and intentions may be something quite different, for example.

For competent and extensive treatment of nonverbal communication the reader is referred to Ruesch and Kees (1956), still an interesting and provocative treatise; to Argyle (1975), probably a classic on the subject; and to Weitz's (1979) compendium of seminal papers.

Verbal communication, or language or syntactical communication, appears to be uniquely human. It involves spoken or written signs and symbols, arranged in grammatical order (syntax) for recognizable transmission and reception. Our most precise and unequivocal communications are verbal: parsimonious, tidy statements in correct order, with skillful selection of words for maximum effect, punctuated and reinforced (if spoken) by "paralanguage," or nonverbal signals of pitch, accent, facial expression, gesture.

Bickerton (1983) reviews the development of creole languages, with a striking example from recent history in Hawaii, dating from only 1898. Creole languages, he notes, despite their isolation from each other, their wide distribution in the world, and their parentage in half-a-dozen different "established" colonial languages, possess a most remarkable similarity to each other in grammatical structure. Bickerton presents evidence that, when slaves and indentured laborers were transported from very different homes and language groups, the first generation (the immigrants themselves) learned to speak a "pidgin" to each other, and to their colonial masters, in an otherwise polyglot babel of tongues. This rudimentary language, the only common language available, is extremely simple whenever found and therefore restricted in expressiveness. Further, pidgin varies from one speaker to another, depending on their languages of origin; for example, in word order and verb placement. The evidence suggests that the children of the original immigrants then developed the creole languages. These are much richer and more flexible in expression. They are, unlike pidgins, uniform between different speakers. They are also, despite their derivation from English, French, Portuguese, and so on, amazingly similar in grammatical structure, whether spoken in Hawaii, Mauritius, or Angola, or other sites, many of them oceanic islands. This grammatical structure and word order is that of children age 2 to 4 starting to speak "established" languages anywhere in the world. Thus, Bickerton argues, the brains of children are programmed to start speaking in creole grammar, and if we were left unmolested by our parents and teachers, we might well all grow up speaking a creole language!

Verbal or syntactic language is an outward manifestation of, and close parallel to, thinking. Cognitive development passes through a phase (see chapter 3) when representational thinking takes over from sensorimotor activity, and the acquisition of language is a step in this transition. Thereafter, it is difficult to say that we think without using language. Our vocabulary and our ability to use abstract language parallels our developing intelligence and conceptual abilities. Thus, language is most closely intertwined with cognitive ability and activity. Proper syntactical language breaks down with brain injury and functional psychiatric disorder. For an introduction to theory and research on the development of syntactical language the reader might consult Ryan (1974, chapter 10); and, for more extensive reviews, Molfese, Molfese, and Carrell (1982) and Whitehurst (1982). Rieber (1976) has assembled a compendium including biological and psychological bases of language, with several chapters on language disturbances.

Variables in Homeostasis: Human Sexuality

Homeostatic and Developmental Issues Intertwined

If there is one area of human functioning quintessentially representing the trinitarian emergences of biological, psychological, and interpersonal or social, it must be sex. Successful sexual functioning is a barometer of mental health or normality (Freud, 1936, 1938; Erikson, 1950, p. 92). It is inhibited or impaired in fight–flight, conservation–withdrawal, and disintegration. The literature of sexology is vast, and highly clinically derived; reviews of a clearly scientific quality are in the minority (three will be mentioned below for reference). Developmental and dynamic–homeostatic issues are rather thoroughly intertwined in this area.

The main developmental–structural issues are two: the first concerns the emergence and consolidation of gender identity (the subjective cognitive structure and affective–motivational position) and gender role (the public, socially expressed reciprocal of identity). These appear to be firmly established very early in life, probably by the end of the second year (Ounsted and Taylor, 1972; Money and Wiedeking, 1980; Stoller, 1985) and thereafter relatively difficult to modify.

The second concerns the lengthy and complex, epigenetically phased, evolution of ultimate sexual performance, appropriate to gender and age, and its reciprocal, the vicissitudes of and developmental deviations from normality (see chapter 4). Both these concerns are of importance as they raise questions of development, the nature–nurture equation, the fabric of society, and human reproductive success. Homosexuality epitomizes these two issues, and the confusion of voices in facing them. Is it due to birth, fashion, nature, or nurture? Is it syndrome, life-style, political statement, even disease, or merely acquired behavioral pattern? What are its defined limits? Is it universal to the human race, even to the animal kingdom? Empirically, it is unknown to some societies, and no ethological studies of animals have revealed the practice of anal or oral intercourse or mutual masturbation. It appears principally to be a feature of advanced urban civilizations.

Modern Sex Researches

For this very large area, which I shall not attempt to cover further, the reader may wish to turn to three treatises which I shall cite in historical order. In some ways the most interesting, containing as it does much factual information, along with humor, color, and polemics, is the journalistic volume of Brecher (1969); he reviews the lives and works of Henry Havelock Ellis, Richard von Krafft-Ebing, Alfred Charles Kinsey, William H. Masters, and Virginia E. Johnson.

Beach (1977) edited a small compendium *Human Sexuality in Four Perspectives* which I believe to be an excellent orienting work. Ford and Beach had already published in 1951 one of the best of early modern treatises on sexual behavior across the human and animal kingdoms. Beach's "four perspectives" (each but the last presented in three chapters by competent authorities) are the developmental, the sociological, the physiological, and the ethological/evolutionary.

Finally, the major compendium, edited by Wolman and Money (1980), the *Handbook of Human Sexuality* may be consulted as a source book. It is divided into three parts: Section 1, on the life cycle and human sexuality; Section 2 on "Sex and Society"; and Section 3 on "Sexual Disorders and their Treatment." There is a strong scientific–evaluative emphasis, even in the considerably clinical sections.

Bibliographic Notes: Key Readings

Out of the huge literature relevant to the homeostatic–dynamic model and related issues, I select the following as particularly good guides to further study.

On fundamental questions of the nature of psychiatric data and the scientific method, the paper by Wallace (1988), a philosopher of science, will give a good entrée. Halliday's (1943) classic on causation, from his background as epidemiologist and psychosomaticist, remains sprightly and stimulating reading. The seminal work of Cannon (1932), which includes Bernard's earlier constructs, is required reading as central to the homeostatic–dynamic model and the fight–flight homeostatic mode. A relatively early paper of Engel (1962a) delineates his construct of conservation–withdrawal, as well as including fight–flight; the later paper of Engel and Schmale (1972) continues the development of the conservation–withdrawal construct. Selye's brief statements, published shortly before his death, summarize the general adaptation syndrome in animals as applicable to stress in humans (1980, 1982).

The evidence for conceiving a hierarchy of homeostatic modes in the natural history of psychiatric disorder can be briefly scanned by reference to Donlon and Blacker (1973), Luborsky (1974), Foulds and Bedford (1975), and Docherty, Van Kammen, Siris, and Marder (1978); and for the pharmacologic correlates of the several homeostatic modes, Lehmann (1961).

Neurobehavioral scientists Miller, Galanter, and Pribram (1960) collaborated in a classic that ushered in modern approaches to human motivational systems; Bowlby (1980) updated the nature of information processing, defense, and decision-making systems. Sigmund Freud (1926) proposed a central theoretical construct in psychoanalysis and psychiatry: intrapsychic conflict and defense operations to control distress. Anna Freud (1936), a pioneer in the emerging field of ego psychology, systematized the study of defense mechanisms. Both Freuds must be read at first hand. Kline's (1981) remarkable critique of psychoanalytic constructs reviews scientific studies confirming, failing to confirm, or rejecting psychoanalytic formulations; the work is exemplary in its treatment of psychoanalysis vis-à-vis the criteria of science, and is an excellent "argument settler."

Darwin's (1872) monograph on the emotions remains a keystone in the descriptive and comparative study of emotions. The reader may choose between two monographs, Izard (1977) and Plutchik (1980a), and a good compendium, Plutchik and Kellerman (1980), for comprehensive modern reviews of the number and nature of human emotions. Heilman and Satz (1983) are a source for the psychophysiology of emotion. I am unable to locate a good orienting work dealing with moods and their relationship to emotions.

The area of communication is a rather highly technical one and, for clinicians, esoteric. As an introduction to this area, I suggest Passingham (1982, pp. 192–241) and Argyle (1975), a classic on body language.

Human sexuality is likewise a large and technical field. Two references may be helpful here: Brecher (1969), a science reporter, provides, along with good humor and satire, an excellent factual account of pioneers in sex research. The encyclopedic compendium of Wolman and Money (1980) is an excellent reference source for key themes and recognized authorities.

References

Adler, N. T. (1979), On the physiological organization of social behavior: Sex and aggression. In: *Handbook of Behavioral Neurobiology*, ed. P. Marler & J. G. Vandenburgh. New York: Plenum Press, pp. 29–71.

*Argyle, M. (1975), *Bodily Communication*. New York: International Universities Press.

Aring, C. D. (1958), Sympathy and empathy. *J. Amer. Med. Assn.*, 167:448–452.

Beach, F. A., ed. (1977), *Human Sexuality in Four Perspectives*. Baltimore: Johns Hopkins University Press.

Beck, A. T., Rush, A. J., Shaw, B. F., & Emery, G. (1979), *Cognitive Therapy of Depression*. New York: Guilford Press.

Bellak, L. (1944), An experimental investigation and study of the concept of projection. *Psychiat.*, 7:353–370.

Berkowitz, L., ed. (1969), *Roots of Aggression*. New York: Atherton Press.

Bickerton, D. (1983), Creole languages. *Sci. Amer.*, 249:116–122.

Bowlby, J. (1969), *Attachment and Loss, Vol. 1: Attachment*, 2nd ed. London: Hogarth Press, 1982.

*——— (1980), An information processing approach to defense. In: *Attachment and Loss*, Vol. 3. London: Hogarth Press.

——— (1984), Violence in the family as a disorder of the attachment and caregiving system. *Amer. J. Psychoanal.*, 44:9–27.

*Brecher, E. M. (1969), *The Sex Researchers*. Boston: Little, Brown.

Cannon, W. B. (1915), *Bodily Changes in Pain, Hunger, Fear, and Rage*, 2nd ed. College Park, MD: McGrath, 1970.

*——— (1932), *The Wisdom of the Body*, 2nd ed. New York: W. W. Norton, 1963.

Carthy, J. D., & Ebling, F. J. (1964), *The Natural History of Aggression*. London: Academic Press.

Cooper, C., & Kline, P. (1982), A validation of the defense mechanism inventory. *Brit. J. Med. Psychol.*, 55:209–214.

*Darwin, C. (1872), *Expression of the Emotions in Man and Animals*. Chicago: University of Chicago Press, 1965.

DeAlarcon, R., & Carney, M. W. P. (1969), Severe depressive mood changes following slow-release intramuscular fluphenazine injection. *Brit. Med. J.*, 3:564–567.

*Docherty, J. P., van Kammen, D. P., Siris, S. G., & Marder, S. R. (1978), Stages of onset of schizophrenic psychosis. *Amer. J. Psychiat.*, 135:420–426.

Dollard, J., Miller, N. E., Doob, L. W., Mowrer, O. H., & Sears, R. R. (1939), *Frustration and Aggression.* New Haven, CT: Yale University Press.

*Donlon, P. J., & Blacker, K. H. (1973), Stages of schizophrenic decompensation and reintegration. *J. Nerv. & Ment. Dis.*, 157:200–209.

Engel, G. L. (1956), Spontaneous and experimentally induced depressions in an infant with a gastric fistula: A contribution to the problem of depression. *J. Amer. Psychoanal. Assn.*, 4:428–452.

—— (1961), Is grief a disease? *Psychosom. Med.*, 23: 18–22.

*—— (1962a), Anxiety and depression–withdrawal: The primary affects of unpleasure. *Internat. J. Psycho-Anal.*, 43:89–97.

—— (1962b), *Psychological Development in Health and Disease.* Philadelphia: W. B. Saunders.

*—— Schmale, A. H. (1972), Conservation–withdrawal: A primary regulatory process for organismic homeostasis. In: *Physiology, Emotion, and Psychosomatic Illness,* Ciba Foundation Symposium 8 (New Series). Amsterdam: Associated Scientific Publications.

Erikson, E. H. (1950), *Childhood and Society,* 2nd ed. New York: W. W. Norton, 1963.

Ford, C. S., & Beach, F. A. (1951), *Patterns of Sexual Behavior.* New York: Harper & Brothers.

*Foulds, G. A., & Bedford, A. (1975), Hierarchy of classes of personal illness. *Psychol. Med.*, 5:181–192.

—— Caine, T. M., Adams, A., & Owen, A. (1965), *Personality and Personal Illness.* London: Tavistock Publications.

*Freud, A. (1936), *The Ego and the Mechanisms of Defense.* New York: International Universities Press, 1966.

Freud, S. (1905), Three essays on the theory of sexuality. *Standard Edition,* 7: 135–243. London: Hogarth Press, 1953.

—— (1923), The ego and the id. *Standard Edition,* 19:3–66. London: Hogarth Press, 1961.

*—— (1926), Inhibitions, symptoms, and anxiety. *Standard Edition,* 20: 87–172. London: Hogarth Press, 1959.

—— (1936), New Introductory Lectures in Psycho-Analysis. *Standard Edition,* 22:5–182. London: Hogarth Press, 1964.

—— (1938), An outline of psychoanalysis. *Standard Edition,* 23:144–207. London: Hogarth Press, 1964.

Gleser, G. S., & Ihilevitch, D. (1969), An objective instrument for measuring defense mechanisms. *J. Consult. Clin. Psychol.*, 33:51–60.

—— Sacks, M. (1973), Ego defenses and reactions to stress: A validation study of the DMI. *J. Consult. Clin. Psychol.*, 40:181–187.

Goldenson, R. M., ed. (1984), *Longman's Dictionary of Psychology and Psychiatry.* New York: Longman.

Gottschalk, L. A., Winget, C. M., Gleser, G. C., & Springer, K. J. (1966), The measurement of emotional changes during a psychiatric interview: A working model toward quantifying the psychoanalytic concept of affect. In: *Methods of Research in Psychiatry*, ed. L. A. Gottschalk & A. H. Auerbach. New York: Appleton-Century-Crofts.

*Halliday, J. L. (1943), Principles of aetiology. *Brit. J. Med. Psychol.*, 19: 367–380.

Harré, R., & Lamb, R., eds. (1983), *The Encyclopedic Dictionary of Psychology*. Cambridge, MA: MIT Press.

*Heilman, K. M., & Satz, P., eds. (1983), *Neuropsychology of Human Emotion*. New York: Guilford Press.

Hoedemaker, F. S. (1970), Psychotic episodes and postpsychotic depression in young adults. *Amer. J. Psychiat.*, 127:606–610.

Hofling, C. K. (1975), *Textbook of Psychiatry for Medical Practice*, 3rd ed. Philadelphia: J. B. Lippincott.

*Izard, C. E. (1977), *Human Emotions*. New York: Plenum Press.

———— Buechler, S. (1980), Aspects of consciousness and personality in terms of differential emotions theory. In: *Emotion: Theory, Research, and Experience, Vol. 1.: Theories of Emotion*, ed. R. Plutchik & H. Kellerman. New York: Academic Press.

Jeffries, J. J. (1977), The trauma of being psychotic: A neglected element in the management of chronic schizophrenia? *Can. J. Psychiat.*, 22: 199–206.

*Kline, P. (1981), *Fact and Fantasy in Freudian Theory*. London: Methuen.

*Lehmann, H. E. (1961), New drugs in psychiatric therapy. *Can. Med. Assn. J.*, 85:1145–1151.

Leigh, H., & Reiser, M. F. (1982), A general systems taxonomy for psychological defence mechanisms. *J. Psychosom. Res.*, 26:77–81.

Luborsky, L. (1965), Clinicians' judgments of mental health: A proposed scale. *Arch. Gen. Psychiat.*, 7:407–417.

*———— (1974), Factors influencing clinicians' judgments of mental health. *Arch. Gen. Psychiat.*, 31:292–299.

McGhie, A. (1969), *Pathology of Attention*. Harmondsworth, Middlesex: Penguin Books.

McGlashan, T. G. H., & Carpenter, W. T. (1976), An investigation of the post-psychotic depressive syndrome. *Amer. J. Psychiat.*, 133:1–19.

Menninger, K. (1938), *Man Against Himself*. New York: Harcourt, Brace, & World.

———— Mayman, M., & Pruyser, P. (1963), *The Vital Balance*. New York: Viking Press.

Miller, G. A., Galanter, E., & Pribram, K. H. (1960), *Plans and the Structure of Behavior*. New York: Henry Holt.

Molfese, D. L., Molfese, V. J., & Carrell, P. L. (1982), Early language development. In: *Handbook of Developmental Psychology*, ed. B. B. Wolman, G. Stricker, S. J. Ellman, P. Keith-Spiegel, & D. S. Palermo. Englewood Cliffs, NJ: Prentice-Hall.

Money, J., & Wiedeking, C. (1980), Gender identity/role: Normal differentiation and its transpositions. In: *Handbook of Human Sexuality*, ed. B. B. Wolman & J. Money. Englewood Cliffs, NJ: Prentice-Hall.

Ounsted, C., & Taylor, D., eds. (1972), *Gender Differences: Their Ontogeny and Significance*. Edinburgh: Churchill Livingstone.

*Passingham, R. E. (1982), *The Human Primate*. Oxford: W. H. Freeman.

*Plutchik, R. (1980a), *Emotions: A Psychoevolutionary Synthesis*. New York: Harper & Row.

———— (1980b), A general psychoevolutionary theory of emotion. In: *Emotion: Theory, Research, and Experience, Vol. 1: Theories of Emotion*, ed. R. Plutchik & H. Kellerman. New York: Academic Press.

———— Kellerman, H. (1980), *Emotion: Theory, Research, and Experience*, Vol. 1. New York: Academic Press.

Rada, R. T., & Donlon, P. J. (1975), Depression and the acute schizophrenic process. *Psychosom.*, 16:116–119.

Ratner, S. G. (1967), Comparative aspects of hypnosis. In: *Handbook of Clinical and Experimental Hypnosis*, ed. J. E. Gordon. New York: Macmillan.

Rieber, R. W., ed. (1976), *The Neuropsychology of Language*. New York: Plenum Press.

Roth, S. (1970), The seemingly ubiquitous depression following acute schizophrenic episodes: A neglected area of clinical discussion. *Amer. J. Psychiat.*, 127:51–58.

Ruesch, J., & Kees, W. (1956), *Nonverbal Communication: Notes on the Visual Perception of Human Relations*. Berkeley: University of California Press.

Ryan, J. (1974), Early language development: A communicational analysis. In: *The Integration of a Child into a Social World*, ed. M. P. M. Richards. London: Cambridge University Press.

Schmale, A. H., & Engel, G. L. (1975), The role of conservation–withdrawal in depressive reactions. In: *Depression and Human Existence*, ed. E. J. Anthony & T. Benedek. Boston: Little, Brown.

Segal, H. (1973), *Introduction to the Work of Melanie Klein*. London: Hogarth Press.

*Selye, H. (1980), The stress concept today. In: *Handbook on Stress and Anxiety*, ed. I. L. Kutash & L. B. Schlesinger. San Francisco: Jossey-Bass.

———— (1982), History and present status of the stress concept. In: *Handbook of Stress: Theoretical and Clinical Aspects*, ed. L. Goldberger & S. Breznitz. New York: Free Press.

Siegal, R. S. (1969), What are defense mechanisms? *J. Amer. Psychoanal. Assn.*, 17:785–807.

Stern, M. J., Pillsburg, J. A., & Sonnenburg, S. M. (1972), Postpsychotic depression in schizophrenics. *Comprehen. Psychiat.*, 3:591–598.

Stoller, R. J. (1985), *Presentations of Gender*. New Haven, CT: Yale University Press.

Storr, A. (1968), *Human Aggression*. New York: Atheneum.

Tompkins, S. S. (1980), Affect as amplification: Some modifications in theory. In: *Emotion: Theory, Research, and Experience, Vol. 1: Theories of Emotion*, ed. R. Plutchik & H. Kellerman. New York: Academic Press.

Vaillant, G. E. (1971), Theoretical hierarchy of adaptive ego mechanisms: A 30-year follow-up of 30 men selected for psychological health. *Arch. Gen. Psychiat.*, 24:107–118.

———— (1976), Natural history of male psychological health: V. The relation of choice of ego mechanisms of defense to adult adjustment. *Arch. Gen. Psychiat.*, 33:535–545.

———— (1977), *Adaptation to Life*. Boston: Little, Brown.

von Bertalanffy, L. (1968), *General System Theory*. New York: George Braziler.

*Wallace, E. R. (1988), What is "truth"? Some philosophical contributions to psychiatric issues. *Amer. J. Psychiat.*, 145:137–147.

Weitz, S., ed. (1979), *Nonverbal Communication.* New York: Oxford University Press.

Whitehurst, G. J. (1982), Language development. In: *Handbook of Developmental Psychology,* ed. B. B. Wolman, G. Stricker, S. J. Ellman, P. Keith-Spiegel, & D. S. Palermo. Englewood Cliffs, NJ: Prentice-Hall.

*Wolman, B. B., & Money, J. W., eds. (1980), *Handbook of Human Sexuality.* Englewood Cliffs, NJ: Prentice-Hall.

---

*Recommended readings.

8

Information Processing, Memory, and Brain Damage: Brain Syndromes and Brain Systems

Introduction

Overview

Of the major groupings of variables affecting human homeostasis, brain dysfunctions hold a rather special place: they strike at the central coordinating mechanisms of human adaptation. Nevertheless, it remains a diagnostic challenge for clinicians, evidently one which needs reiteration in every generation, that we must be on the alert to seek and recognize them (Lipowski, 1984). Why is it that we must be repeatedly adjured to keep our neuropsychologic antennae tuned and searching? Why are brain syndromes consistently missed or ignored? Partly this is because they are not highly self-evident unless or until they are blatantly severe. They must be probed and examined for in an active search. Many of them are half-concealed behind the disturbances of homeostasis to which they contribute, disturbances which interest and attract attention: a schizopheniform psychosis, a paranoid state, an indolent depression, a drift into delinquency; in fact, the whole gamut of pathologic homeostatic styles. Perhaps too, the analysis of the psychodynamics of homeostasis is more appealing than facing the reality of brain damage with its often poor prognosis. Or, clinical skill may be more attracted to finding and interpreting intriguing localizing signs than to consideration of the global brain syndrome of which they are a part.

There is, essentially, *one* brain syndrome, a global difficulty with information processing, including the registration of recent memories and orientation of the self in space and time. The common features of the brain syndrome far outweigh differences between patients and their particular versions of the syndrome (Baddeley, 1986; Lishman, 1978). This fact allows us to deal fairly in the present chapter with the general and shared features of brain dysfunctions, without being intimidated and overloaded in attempting to cover all the problems and pathological entities which can occur. Brain damage or disease *anywhere* brings on, to some degree, the brain syndrome of global cognitive deficit, of difficulty in retaining information for processing, problem solving, decision making, orientation in space and time, and the filing of it for future reference. Recent memory difficulties are a pathognomonic feature. Older memories are, by contrast, spared. Ribot's law states (Lishman, 1971) that the older a memory is, the more indelible it will remain.

There is a clear continuum from neurological to neuropsychological syndromes. The former are likely to be associated with localized lesions, producing localizing signs (amnesia, agnosia, apraxia, hemianopia, etc.) with a mild background brain syndrome. The latter result from more widespread brain damage, with a global cognitive deficit and little in the way of localizing signs. But, as Lishman (1978) cautions us, it is only surgically or experimentally placed lesions which are truly localized: most usually, there is a mixture of local and more widespread damage. The amount of brain damage can be estimated quantitatively from the extent of loss of memory and the amount of temporal and spatial disorientation.

The field of brain disorders is rife with semantic difficulties and inconsistencies: it appears impossible that different workers will discipline themselves to adherence with an original logical terminology such as that found in the first edition of *The Diagnostic and Statistical Manual of Mental Disorders* (DSM-I) (American Psychiatric Association, 1952). Hence I feel the need to define my own terms clearly: *organic, functional; brain syndrome, acute brain syndrome, chronic brain syndrome, dementia;* also, the nature of syndrome versus disease, and the reliability of the associations between brain syndrome and actual brain damage.

The large research-oriented literature emerges from the work of three types of investigators (with considerable overlapping): clinician–theorists who observe and conceptualize what nature does in injury and disease (e.g., Nielsen, 1941; Bleuler, 1951; Wells, 1971; Katzman, 1979; Lipowski, 1984); clinician–theorists who also make certain things happen, as neurosurgeons or laboratory assessors (Papez, 1937; Penfield and Roberts, 1959; Scoville and Milner, 1957; Sperry, 1985); and basic scientists who conduct controlled experiments, mostly with animals (Lashley, 1929; Moruzzi and Magoun, 1949; MacLean, 1973; Mishkin and Appenzeller, 1987).

Today's psychiatrist can no longer also be expected to be a specialist in neuroanatomy. It would therefore appear that an understanding of brain systems is the most clinically relevant level of discourse at which we should operate. I review the systems concerned with information processing, climbing in the process from brain stem to cerebral cortex. The reticular activating systems of Magoun may be the most important part of the brain (Restak, 1979) as it regulates consciousness and modulates attention. Papez's (1937) visceral brain was discovered to subserve subjective emotion and emotional behavior; it was included by MacLean (1973) as the limbic system in his functional geography of the "triune brain," our concentric three brains of evolutionary origin. The limbic system interlocks crucially with centers organizing sensory experience and memory registration, particularly in the amygdala and hippocampus and in the basal forebrain. Lishman (1971, 1978) conjectures that mechanisms of psychogenic amnesia may lie in this interlocking. Localization of function in the neocortex (Nielsen,

1951) and the "meaning" of these evolutionary divisions (Penfield and Roberts, 1959) give us a functional map which is relatively easily remembered. Finally, hemispheric specialization, and the "life" of each hemisphere in the "split brain" (Sperry, 1985), show that the whole brain is more than merely the sum of its parts. I conclude the section on brain systems with a brief review of what is known of the "anatomy of memory" (Mishkin and Appenzeller, 1987): four systems for cognitive memory, one for motor or habitual memory.

As we move to the neuropsychology of memory, our bridge from neuroanatomy and neurophysiology is the question: why does any brain injury, anywhere, tend to cause the brain syndrome? Baddeley (1986), in dealing with this question, concludes that information *processing* systems are "modular," that is, relatively isolated and shielded in the brain, hence relatively safe from injury; however, information *storage* systems are widespread and diffuse, hence accessible and vulnerable to injury anywhere. Tulving (1984) is perhaps the outstanding theorist of memory. He has divided memory into two categories: episodic memory, for discrete facts and experiences, is what has been studied classically as memory; semantic memory, for relationships, processes, and meanings, obeys rather different rules. Motor or habitual memory (Butters and Cermak, 1980) obeys different rules again. Short-term memory, or retention, aided by rehearsal, has a surprisingly finite capacity (G. A. Miller, 1956) which is disrupted in brain disorders. Long-term memory is a filing system of essentially infinite capacity, requiring sophisticated retrieval methods. There is now believed to be a continuous gradation between these two, rather than the concrete steps formerly postulated.

I briefly review neuropsychological assessment through formal tests and rating scales, with its attendant problems. The neuropsychologist cannot be expected to be the sole or responsible diagnostician for brain damage and cerebral localization, but he can, through standardized measures and a sophisticated collection of norms, provide helpful, sometimes crucial, information.

Finally, I offer notes on three paradigmatic diseases, each producing the brain syndrome. I select Korsakoff's syndrome, partly because it displays very specific memory deficits in otherwise well-preserved personalities; but also because Butters and Cermak (1980) provide us with a model schema for the analysis of a brain disease and its neuropsychological manifestations. Alzheimer's disease is exemplary as a cruel and as yet undefeated foe of the elderly; however, despite its close correlation with advancing age, it is now known to be a distinct pathologic entity; here our focus will be on models for investigation of its etiology (Wurtman, 1985; Katzman, 1983, 1985; Reisberg, 1983). Chronic brain syndrome as a manifestation of depression (pseudodementia) is presented because of the semantic confusion it engenders, but also because it is one of the conditions correct diagnosis of which leads to successful remission.

Clinical and Semantic Challenges

The Challenge of Clinical Diagnosis

Mr. W. Y., a 54-year-old teacher, was admitted to the mental hospital where I served my very first psychiatric rotation; he had an acute, rapidly worsening, classical obsessive–compulsive neurosis of 2 months' duration. He was distressed, and knew something was wrong with his mind, but was nonetheless virtually incapacitated, as well as an increasing torment to his wife. He was troubled with constant, stereotyped, ego alien "bad thoughts," and occupied with constant tidying and rearranging rituals which left him frantic and without relief. He was pleasant and cooperative when engaged and distracted. Only rather careful clinical examination was able to reveal that he was disoriented by 2 hours in time of day and by 2 weeks in calendar date; he was quite unable to locate his ward and describe how he had come to the physician's office. His chronic brain syndrome was found to be due to cerebral syphilis. He made an excellent remission from both obsessive–compulsive neurosis and brain syndrome following the arsenic and malarial fever therapy in use at the time (Powles, 1944) and he returned to home and work.

Mrs. Y. G. was not as fortunate. A 48-year-old homemaker, an intelligent and creative person, she had become progressively dull, forgetful, and disorganized over 6 months. This confusional state was noticed by her family, but apparently because of the insidious onset any crisis point was long deferred. Mrs. G. presented with a classical pure chronic brain syndrome without personality disruption. Her premorbid personality with its mature defenses, as well as a supportive family, had kept her stabilized in normal homeostasis. Refined clinical examination soon revealed a finger agnosia and other signs of disturbed body image: hence our initial diagnosis favored a localized remediable condition such as subdural hematoma. Later, laboratory tests confirmed a diagnosis of cerebral syphilis. The case had a tragic outcome. Despite several courses of aggressive modern treatment, Mrs. G. remained demented and incapacitated, dependent on nursing home care.

The challenge to clinicians, both in psychiatry and at the front lines in other medical fields, is to be on the alert to discern brain syndromes, ideally in their earliest phases. Only an alert clinician can put forward an early presumptive diagnosis of brain tissue damage. Next, our duty is to consult tables of differential diagnosis (Lishman, 1978, p. 130; also Wells, 1971; Bird, Bartolucci, Garnett, and Cleghorn, 1985; Ropper, 1979; Weinberger, 1984) in search of possible causes for the brain syndrome. Next, we must enlist collaboration of colleagues from a wide variety of specialties in the effort to identify a precise pathology and causal factors. Finally, we must see to it that effective treatment is arranged as quickly as possible. There is a general theme, currently, that brain syndromes are no longer psychiatric illnesses: I personally believe that there is no better conductor and coordinator of their management than a good neuropsychiatrist, even if he or she is highly dependent on help from other specialists.

Problems of Terminology

The chronic brain syndrome will be the paradigm for this chapter. This is the cluster of cognitive impairments so typically associated with structural damage to brain tissue (deficits in information processing, problem solving, new learning, recent memory, and orientation) which the first *Diagnostic and Statistical Manual of Mental Disorders* (American Psychiatric Association, 1952) outlined.

1. This syndrome can be of any degree of severity, from mild, subtle, and unobtrusive, to pervasive, disorganizing, and visible to the most untutored observer;
2. It can appear in pure form, without homeostatic disruption and personality change;
3. It is more frequently concealed behind the minor to major homeostatic disruptions to which it is a contributing or precipitating cause;
4. It is titled "chronic" because it is frequently of gradual and insidious onset; this gradual onset makes it less likely to provoke homeostatic disruption than acute brain syndrome (delirium) which is of sudden onset;
5. It is typically the outcome of brain tissue damage, thus may call for a guarded prognosis and the label of "dementia" (e.g., in Alzheimer's disease, or Korsakoff's syndrome);
6. It may, however, be the result of functional derangements in the brain, which can be remedied if the cause is properly identified (e.g., subdural hematoma, hepatic encephalopathy, normal-pressure hydrocephalus, depression).

Terminology for this area of psychiatry presents many problems. Wells (1971) and Benson and Blumer (1975) note how difficult it has been to achieve and maintain consensus on terms for organic brain impairments. In the early 1980s, publications such as the DSM-III (1980), Strayhorn's excellent psychiatric text (1982), and Lipowski's review (1984) began to stretch the construct "organic" to such limits that it has been losing precise meaning. Perhaps this is an inevitable outcome of the North American libertarian ideal (Powles, 1968) that writers reserve the privilege of making words mean what they want, rather than submitting to the collective discipline of adhering to original definitions.

The first *Diagnostic and Statistical Manual of Mental Disorders* (1952) followed a consistent taxonomy. The most fundamental division was into disorders associated with brain tissue damage ("organic") and those associated with intact brain tissue ("functional"). All organic disorders were defined as showing a common syndrome of cognitive impairments, and also shallowness and lability of emotion. To this basic syndrome could be added qualifiers, both as to symptom picture and etiology, in further classification. The second edition (DSM-II, 1968) abandoned this fundamental division in favor of a major partition into psychoses, neuroses, and personality disorders. Within the psychoses was a section for "psychoses associated with organic brain syndromes," and immediately after this a somewhat awkwardly placed rubric for "non-psychotic organic brain syndromes." The third edition (DSM-III, 1980) appears to have dispensed with clear classificatory logic: the small "organic" section appears to be a collection, rather than a classification, of loosely related disorders, some not even associated with brain tissue damage. As with Strayhorn (1982) and Lipowski (1984) "organic" appears now to include disease elsewhere in the body, with an intact brain, in some instances. The DSM-III-R (1987), an interim revision of the third edition, returns to clearer logical principles, such as grouping the organic disorders on a basis of type and extent of cognitive impairment, and differentiating "syndromes" whose causes are unknown from "disorders" whose causes are suspected or known. "Organic" is defined more clearly as "psychological or behavioral abnormality associated with transient or permanent dysfunction of the brain." Lishman's monumental textbook (1978) exhibits a disciplined adherence to nomenclature and taxonomy as developed over many years; his principal headings somewhat resemble those of DSM-I (1952) and he furnishes synonyms for his own preferred terms.

Glossary of Definitions

Because of the semantic drift and diffusion in the literature, I offer a brief glossary of terms as I shall use them. I follow the logic and definitions of DSM-I (1952). In contemporary form, these definitions are based on Lishman's definitive text (1978).

1. *Organic* versus *functional*. This important and fundamental distinction is between psychiatric disorders which include the brain syndrome suggestive of brain tissue damage, and those whose signs suggest a structurally intact cerebrum.

2. *Brain syndrome*. Any psychiatric syndrome which includes the cognitive deficits characteristic of brain tissue damage.

3. *Chronic brain syndrome*. I retain this useful descriptive term from DSM-I. It is the paradigmatic syndrome specified above, typically, but not exclusively, associated with brain tissue damage of gradual onset and advancing severity. One criterion included in DSM-I and DSM-II (1968) has had to be abandoned as unreliable: shallowness and lability of emotionality, which does not accurately differentiate organic from functional disorders (Lawson, Rodenburg, and Dykes, 1968). Chronic organic brain syndrome (COBS) is a popular tautological synonym. *Amnestic syndrome* is not quite a synonym: the term implies a brain syndrome with particularly prominent disorder of memory; it may in fact include functional and psychogenic amnesias. Lishman's preferred term is *chronic organic reactions*. He gives the synonyms of chronic brain syndrome; chronic confusional state; chronic organic psychosis; chronic psycho-organic syndrome.

4. *Dementia*. I attempt to avoid this term, with its confusion of meanings. Most precisely, it indicates an acquired syndrome of cognitive deficits and poor prognosis, as contrasted with amentia, a congenital cognitive deficit state (Katzman, 1979). The term *dementia praecox* referred to the schizophrenic deficit state. Dementia is a syndrome, not a disease.

5. *Syndrome*. A consistently associated cluster of signs and symptoms, the pathological substrate and the causal factors for which have not been clarified. For example, strictly speaking, the schizophrenias and obsessive–compulsive disorder remain syndromes; and this applies generally to all the functional psychoses and neuroses.

6. *Disease*. A syndrome for which pathologic mechanisms and, ideally, causal factors have been established. An example is Alzheimer's disease: the pathology has been long known;

the causes are still being sought. Properly, it is my view that Korsakoff's syndrome should be termed *Korsakoff's disease* since its pathology and the causal factors in a majority of cases have been clarified (Butters and Cermak, 1980).

7. *Acute brain syndrome.* The term is synonymous with *delirium* and there are no real semantic confusions involved. I shall leave this syndrome to chapter 15, for, because of its usually rapid onset and toxic and metabolic causal factors, it is associated with severe homeostatic disruption (disintegration). One way to understand it is as a state intermediate between organic and functional disorders: it is not usually associated with *structural* brain damage; it is often reversible; it almost always includes phenomena of disintegration; and it is amenable to antipsychotic treatment (Wise, 1987). However, not all cases are reversible. A prominent example is Wernicke's syndrome, which not infrequently progresses onward into Korsakoff's (chronic brain) syndrome (Butters and Cermak, 1980). Lishman's preferred term is *acute organic reaction* and he gives synonyms of acute brain syndrome; acute confusional state; acute organic psychosis; acute psycho-organic syndrome.

8. *Associations and correlations.* The chronic brain syndrome is typically associated with brain tissue damage and irreversible changes, but the correlation is by no means perfect. The acute brain syndrome is typically associated with toxic and metabolic derangement, but again, it may be caused by structural damage (e.g., Wernicke's). This reminds us that associations and correlations in psychiatry (and, for that matter, many areas of general medicine) are very rarely perfect or 100 percent. *Always* and *never* are terms to be used with caution, as they usually turn out to mean "most of the time" and "rarely."

9. *The Jacksonian Principles.* Syndromes arising in cases of brain damage and dysfunction clearly follow the Jacksonian principles of dissolution or disevolution (see chapter 1). Jason Brown (1977) draws attention to the "new regressive organization" assumed by the brain in states of injury. Lishman (1978) points out that truly focal lesions are artifacts of surgery; any brain lesion in clinical practice involves surrounding tissues and interrupts other systems (see pp. 264–268).

The Organization of the Brain

Rather than details of neuroanatomy, the psychiatrist must master some understanding of *systems* within the brain, and it is such systems that I take as the basis for the following section; particularly systems closely connected with the processing of information and the organization of learning and memory. The lower brain stem and spinal cord can be safely left to the attention of neurologists and physiologists, I believe. My review will begin with the upper brain stem and work upward and outward toward the neocortex, our most recent evolutionary achievement and the most human development in our primate brain (Passingham, 1982).

Upper Brainstem: Magoun's Reticular Activating System

Restak (1979, chapter 3) proposes that the most important part of the human brain is the midbrain reticular activating system, which monitors consciousness, focuses awareness, and regulates the sleep–waking cycle. Lishman (1971) and Butters and Cermak (1980) alert us to the remarkable influence of small lesions of the upper brain stem in impairing memory and attention. This general region of the upper brainstem and diencephalon is a bottleneck of crucial tracts taking part in consciousness and information processing: it is *not* damage to the cerebral cortex, however extensive, which impairs attention and causes unconsciousness (Lashley, 1929; Penfield and Roberts, 1959).

Over a number of years it had gradually occurred to neuroanatomists that the brainstem reticular formation must be a functional system of some ascending or afferent kind (Brazier, 1980): yet this dense network (reticulum) or series of relays of uniform cells, with most extensive and rich connections, would surely not be just one more sensory apparatus, though it interweaves intricately with the major sensory pathways. In 1949 two arresting papers appeared (Moruzzi and Magoun; Lindsley, Bowden, and Magoun) which established that it was indeed an important system, and elucidated its functions. Using anesthetized cats, Magoun's team discovered that:

1. Stimulation of the ascending reticular formation, carefully avoiding influencing the major sensory tracts, would consistently produce electroencephalographic changes in the *cerebral cortex,* such as are typical of waking and alerted states; that is, fast, low-voltage patterns.

2. Transection of the brain stem in ascending steps resulted, when the level of the anterior midbrain was reached, in persistent electrographic changes in the cerebral cortex such as are typical of drowsiness, sleep, and anesthesia; that is, slow, high-voltage patterns. These cats remained persistently asleep after anesthesia had passed off.

3. Lesions made in the tegmentum and in the subthalamus and hypothalamus likewise produced the latter persistent effects.

Thus, activity in the anterior brain stem is required for the maintenance of alerting, the arousal reaction, and normal wakefulness: "maintained influence of the ascending brain stem activating system underlies wakefulness, while absence of this influence precipitates sleep" (Lindsley, Bowden, and Magoun, 1949, p. 485).

This remarkable system for which the label of "Reticular Activating System" was soon adopted (Starzl, Taylor, and Magoun, 1951) "almost certainly serves as the substrate for the rest-activity cycle . . . [of] sleep and wakefulness, and the enormous range of conscious states which mediate our interactions with the world around us"; it modulates such interactions, and focuses attention on the "consciousness of what" (Scheibel, 1980, pp. 58–59).

Moore (1980) notes that the "cell bodies of virtually all monoamine neurons are located within the brain stem reticular formation," a point which will be of some relevance in considering fight–flight and conservation–withdrawal and the anxiety and depressive disorders (chapters 10, 12, 13).

Papez's "Visceral Brain" and MacLean's "Triune Brain"

Proceeding upward and forward to the diencephalon, the group of structures between the two cerebral hemispheres, we find a system only relatively recently found to correlate with

human emotionality and with memory. Papez (1937) and Mac-
Lean (1952, 1973) describe how Broca had in 1878 conceived
of a great "limbic lobe" surrounding the corpus callosum and
hypothalamus, and how for many years this had been believed
to be the rhinencephalon or smell brain, due to its proximity
to olfactory structures. However, Papez (1937) struck a mortal
blow at this belief. In a closely reasoned paper he reviewed
complex evidence pointing to a "harmonious mechanism which
may elaborate the functions of central emotion [the subjective
experience of emotion] as well as participate in emotional expression" (p. 743). The basic interrelated structures in this system were found to be the hypothalamus, anterior thalamic nuclei, the gyrus cinguli, and the hippocampus, and their
connecting elements. Papez found no evidence to support an
olfactory function for this system, at least in humans, whose
olfactory system is grossly underdeveloped compared with that
of other animals.

The construct of a "visceral brain" subserving emotional
experience and motivation was further elaborated by Olds and
Milner (1954) who discovered in rats that stimulation of the
septal area, or forward limit of the hypothalamus, produced
"reward effects" indistinguishable from the effects of conventional, primary rewards such as feeding: rats stimulated in this
area developed learning curves identical to those following conventional rewards.

Further, rats with electrodes implanted in the septal area,
and given operant control over the switch activating these electrodes, would spend much time delivering stimulation to their
own septal area for, apparently, the generation of sheer pleasure. Though Olds and Milner were careful to avoid the terms
reward center or pleasure center, these came to be popular terms
for their discovery.

Paul D. MacLean, a versatile and integrative neurophysiol-
ogist, has built for us the intriguing construct of the "triune"
human brain. He drew together Broca's "great limbic lobe" and
Papez's "visceral brain" into a "limbic system" (MacLean, 1952).
He persuasively suggested that our brain is built up of three,
concentric, distinct brains of three phylogenetic ages, each distinct in its architecture and neurochemistry (MacLean, 1949,

1952, 1973), each with "its own memory, motor, and other functions" (1973, p. 8), and each remarkably autonomous or isolated in relationship with the others. Valzelli's (1981) original drawings show this triune brain well. MacLean outlines the triune brain as follows:

Our oldest, "reptilian brain" is buried inside the other two, which successively surround it. For reptiles, this constitutes most of the brain, essentially consisting of the basal ganglia, whose genetically programmed repertoires are stereotyped, repetitive, and blindly instinctive in quality. MacLean conjectures that highly repetitive and stereotyped human activities, even highly articulated social ones, come from this brain, "hidebound by precedent." Some investigators conjecture today that obsessive–compulsive disorder has its biological substrate in a derangement of stereotyped security patterns encoded in the basal ganglia (see chapter 10).

On the medial aspect of the cerebral hemispheres, in a roughly circular pattern around the diencephalon, lies the "paleomammalian brain," the limbic system. This represents the first respectable cortex of the primitive mammals. MacLean carried Papez's ideas considerably further. He viewed the hypothalamus as the "head ganglion" of the autonomic nervous system. He mapped the limbic system by meticulously exploring (in squirrel monkeys particularly, by stimulating and placing lesions) the ring or circle of structures, in which he found distinct localization of functions: the lower and forward areas are related to feelings and behaviors of self-defense and self-preservation; the upper and forward areas subserve sociability and preservation of the species. The limbic system is portrayed schematically in Figure 8.1. Its relation to memory will be included later.

While both reptilian (basal ganglia) and paleomammalian (limbic system) brains are "conscious and wide awake," both are "hopelessly inarticulate" (MacLean, 1973, p. 18). It is the neocortex, the neomammalian brain, wrapped about the outside of the others, as Valzelli's (1981) clever three-dimensional drawings show, which thrives on change and challenge, and which is capable of communication. I would recall Passingham's (1982) striking analysis comparing the development of this

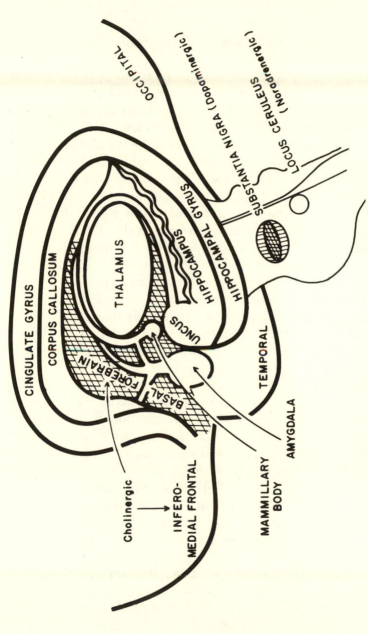

Figure 8.1. Systems of Emotion and Memory (Simplified)

A schematic view of the principal structures in the limbic system or paleomammalian brain, suggesting the close association between systems for emotion and for memory.

quintessentially human brain to that of even our near evolutionary primate relatives.

Cortical Localization: The Schemata of Nielsen and Penfield

Throughout this chapter we have to face two apparently conflicting themes or principles: that neuropsychological functions
can be anatomically localized, and that the brain operates as a
whole in global brain syndromes. The fact is that there is a
continuum with two poles. At one pole is the theme or principle
that functions or dysfunctions have an anatomical localization;
and that there are indeed focal, describable, and definable
symptoms such as paralysis, hemianopia, aphasia, apraxia, agnosia, and so on. These are much easier to define and describe
than is the more global brain syndrome (Wells, 1977); they are
"neurological," that is to say, defined at a biological level of
emergence. At the other pole is the theme or principle that
injury anywhere to the cerebral cortex or its important connections will injure or impair the brain as a whole, and will to
some extent reduce adaptive or cognitive capacity: the more
extensive the injury, the more global the impairment. This is
Lashley's law of mass action (Lashley, 1929), which operates
at the psychological level of emergence. Clearly, small, highly
localized lesions will chiefly cause a precise "neurological" type
of symptomatology, and wider-spread damage will likely be
manifested in a "psychological" syndrome; but we have already
noted that small lesions in a "bottleneck" such as the upper
brain stem or diencephalon will cause major disturbances of
attention and information processing, and that in clinical practice there are few if any precisely localized lesions.

Jason Brown (1977) provides a synthesis between these
apparently conflicting themes, indicating the complex resultants of even a small focal injury as follows:

Imagine a lesion at B, resulting in a focal paralysis. B subserves a function in the linkage A-B-C: damage at B will therefore either *remove* function B, or *block* function A, or disinhibit
function C, or produce any combination of these. (A like set of
possibilities arises for stimulation at B.) But also, a lesion at B
disturbs the patient's whole "cognitive space," resulting in a

new, regressive level of global organization. Here the whole brain is trying to do its best under injured and deprived circumstances.

This section will proceed to examine the subject of localization in the neocortex or neomammalian brain; the reader is to retain a background awareness of the brain's functioning as a whole.

Nielsen, a medical neurologist of extensive experience, provided us with a conceptual mapping based on the experiments of nature in disease and injury to the brain (Nielsen, 1941). There are four well-identified "primary" motor and sensory cortical areas, where lesions and stimulation have long been known to produce crude but precisely localized effects. Concentric with these are "secondary" and "tertiary" areas which mediate increasingly more integrated functions. Finally, the large silent or association areas lying beyond and between these continents of known function can be assumed, a priori, to integrate and mesh the functions of the more precisely known areas, and in fact empirically are found to do so.

The four primary areas are:

1. *Motor:* the precentral gyrus in the frontal lobe (Brodmann's area 4);
2. *Somesthetic:* the postcentral gyrus in the parietal lobe (Brodmann 2 and 3);
3. *Visual:* the cortex on both lips of the calcarine fissure in the occipital lobe (Brodmann 17);
4. *Auditory:* Heschl's transverse gyrus, at the top of the temporal lobe.

Localization in the somesthetic and motor areas is accurately depicted if one imagines Penfield's amusing homunculus, head down, large space devoted to tongue, thumb; buttocks at the top and hind limbs hanging over into the medial side of the cerebral hemisphere.

Localization in the primary visual cortex is accurately related to the opposite visual half-field (same-side half-retina); stimulation produces dots or flashes of light, a lesion produces a sharply defined blind spot or scotoma. For taste and smell no

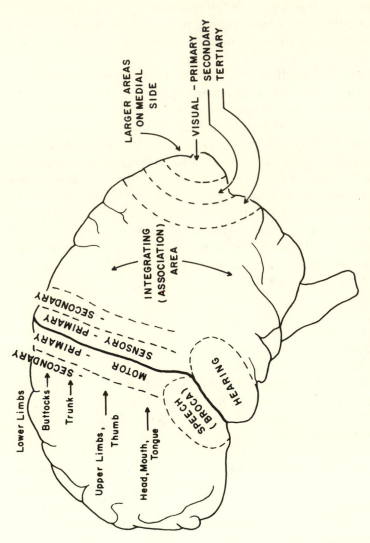

Figure 8.2. Cortical Localization

A schematic view of the principal motor and sensory "platforms" with their primary, secondary, and tertiary organizations; the "silent" or association areas lie between them, integrating their functions.

precise cortical localization is possible. There is rather vague localization for hearing; both ears evidently project to both cortical areas, and the localization of hearing in a spatial sense is performed by differential timing of the arrival of sound vibrations to the two ears.

The secondary areas border or surround the primary ones, and in turn are bordered or surrounded by the tertiary. For motor and somesthetic functions, the secondary area runs along the primary; no clear tertiary area has been identified. Secondary visual areas subserve a more integrated patterning, form engrams, produce with stimulation more patterned responses, and appear necessary for recognition; the tertiary areas appear necessary for formulating patterned images and for retention of visual memories. Similarly, the rather vague auditory secondary areas are necessary for retention of sound memories. The concentric nature of the visual cortex and its cytoarchitecture clearly indicate the stepwise processing so characteristic of the human brain; a like functioning must be assumed for other sensory areas.

The great association area for linguistic functions lies, as we might expect a priori, between the motor and somesthetic areas for the face, throat, and tongue, and the areas for hearing; that is, Broca's area. The parietal lobe, by this schema, should and does integrate auditory, visual, and somesthetic processes. The frontal lobe should be, and is in fact, an offshoot and higher development of motor processes.

Penfield pioneered the direct exploration of the cerebral cortex, using as his main tool the stimulation of areas of exposed cortex during the search for epileptogenic scars. His collaborators included the patients, who were under local anesthesia, and who could report the effects of this systematic exploration by stimulation as it proceeded. Penfield and Roberts (1959) produced a small classic which both describes these methods and goes on to conceptualize the results of cerebral exploration and localization of function. On the whole, Nielsen's schemata are confirmed here. For the auditory cortex, Penfield's group found no clear outline, nor any distinct separation, for the primary, secondary, and tertiary areas. They did find that stimulation around the upper and middle temporal gyri (a "silent" or association area) produced complicated, for-ward-flowing "dreams" (as the patients called them) or patterns of multisensory experience. Their findings for Broca's area, in which they had a particular interest, and where Broca had early recognized the effect of injuries in producing aphasias and dysphasias, will be reported briefly below in the discussion of hemispheric specialization.

Penfield's integrative schemata are of interest, and may be compared with Magoun's (Moruzzi and Magoun, 1949; Starzl, Taylor, and Magoun, 1951) and MacLean's (1973) formula-tions. Penfield and Roberts (1959, p. 23) regard each functional subdivision of the cortex as an "outward growth" and a projec-tion of subcortical gray matter nuclei of more ancient and fun-damental origin; for example, the geniculate bodies for vision and hearing. The cerebral hemispheres, they believe (p. 17) appear to have been built up around the activities of distance receptors (sight, hearing) as contrasted with subcortical struc-tures which are more important in lower animals (smell, taste) as centers for more visceral sensation. Consciousness accompa-nies activity in the "higher brain stem system," and "disappears with interruption of function in the centrencephalic system" (they do not apear to credit Magoun's discoveries by name) and the integration of various sensory modalities is carried out in the upper brain stem (pp. 20–22). An interesting view of the primary motor and sensory cortical areas is that they are "plat-forms," "transmitting strips" (apparently the analogy is to rail-road stations and airports), where messages arrive from the subcortex and are assembled, addressed, and sent out again (pp. 25–26, 29); these cortical areas are much larger than the more primitive subcortical nuclei which supply them.

Hemispheric Specialization: Sperry and the Split Brain

Not only are cortical areas specialized in function: each hemi-sphere carries an economic division of labor in the brain (Wex-ler, 1980); or, put in Sperry's (1985) terms each half of the brain has a life, an existence, a particular style of its own. This had been partially recognized for many years. Left- and right-handedness, and the differential effects of brain injury on linguistic functions, had pointed to distinct asymmetries. Penfield's studies (Penfield and Roberts, 1959) strongly suggested that centers for language function are in the left brain, even in left-handed people. If they are found to be located in the right brain, that is frequently due to a transfer following left-brain injury in early life: such transfer cannot take place after childhood.

Sperry's remarkable studies of the split brain (Sperry, 1985) earned him a Nobel prize in 1981. These were investigations of a series of patients who had to undergo division of the corpus callosum, the huge commissure of fibers joining the two cerebral hemispheres, usually for the relief of intractable seizure disorder. Sperry's ingenious experiments investigating the ongoing style and "life" of the two split half-brains have been continued by his many collaborators and students.

These studies confirm (see also Rieber [1976]) that indeed, in almost all humans, whether right- or left-handed, the left brain is "wired" for verbal and linguistic programming. Fromkin (1985) points out the innate propensity of the left brain for *language,* a better term than *"speech,"* which is merely the concrete sensorimotor expression of exceedingly complicated cognitive structures. The right hemisphere, Sperry (1985) states, "is unable to express itself either in speech or writing" (p. 11) and is wired for nonverbal, visual, and spatial operations. Rausch (1985) notes that it can recognize stimuli but it has no way of communicating this, and that unilateral temporal lobectomy produces differential results: left lobectomy impairs verbal-related memory; right lobectomy impairs "memory for material not easily verbalized, presented either visually or auditorily" (p. 247).

Sperry's philosophical reflections on the life of the two split-brain halves, and on the experiences of the split-brain subjects, make interesting reading. The brain, in effect, is an emergent, a whole which is more than the sum of its two halves when these two are joined and in an integrative whole-brain state. It is when the brain is split, by abolishing the massive interconnections of the corpus callosum, and the two hemispheres have to operate independently, that we see both the differential functioning of the hemispheres *and* the resulting defects in whole-brain processing (Jason Brown's "regressive functioning").

The Anatomy of Memory

I had selected this title, for a brief review of current knowledge of brain systems subserving memory, before the appearance of the excellent review article of Mishkin and Appenzeller (1987). I shall credit the title to them, and shall follow their paper in outline. References in this section will be to their paper unless otherwise indicated.

First, it is clear that a generally intact brain is necessary for integrated, optimal, cognitive processing, including the workings of the various aspects of memory. I have already pointed out that brain syndromes occupy a continuum with two poles. At one pole are syndromes of focal brain damage: pure aphasia, amnesia, and so on, but with some blunting of overall cognitive adaptive efficiency, the new regressive organization of Jason Brown (1977). At the other pole, widespread brain damage is associated with the "brain syndrome" proper of global cognitive impairment (Lashley, 1929; Bleuler, 1951; Blessed, Tomlinson, and Roth, 1968; Lipowski, 1975; Wells, 1978; McHugh and Folstein, 1979; Iversen, 1983; Squire and Zola-Morgan, 1983). Thus, all brain injuries are associated with small to extensive problems with memory, or more broadly, with relatively insignificant to very serious impairments in cognitive processing, new learning, orientation in space and time, and memory.

Lesions in some brain areas have a more specific and disproportionate effect on memory itself. Both animal experiments (Mishkin and Appenzeller, 1987), and careful study of human disorders (Scoville and Milner, 1957) have identified areas or systems which, if damaged, take part in anterograde (from the time of damage onward) deficits in new learning and the registration, association, and recall of memories. While heeding Baddeley's (1986) caution against the possible unsoundness of attributing too much power to lesions in small anatomic localities such as the mammillary bodies in Korsakoff's syndrome, let us proceed with the schema of five memory systems in the brain as developed by Mishkin and Appenzeller.

Memories most usually originate as sense impressions, these authors point out. In their own work they have particularly investigated recognition based on visual memory, but they believe it is safe to assume the same general organization of memory for other senses and for the common combination of memories in several sensory modalities.

The striking report of Scoville and Milner (1957) first drew attention to the hippocampus and amygdala as necessary for successful storage of sensory experiences. These structures are parts of the limbic system or at least very closely related to it (Figure 8.1); Mishkin and Appenzeller repeatedly draw attention to this relationship. Scoville and Milner studied a human case, the young man, H. M., whose experience has been quoted in many treatises on memory, and whom Milner later followed over many years. This patient had both temporal lobes removed for intractable seizure disorder. On recovering from his operation H. M. demonstrated a striking, global, amnestic state. Three years later his seizure disorder was improved, his personality was preserved, his technical skills were intact, and his Wechsler Intelligence Quotient had improved from 104 to 112, quite possibly because heavy medication could be discontinued. But his Wechsler Memory Quotient was only 68: H. M. continued to live in a world where every day, in fact every minute, was a new experience, immediately forgotten, and unrelated to any ongoing stream of awareness. He could retain new learning for only a few minutes by virtue of "rehearsal" (see below) and lost it again with the slightest distraction. His memories from times previous to his surgery were preserved, thus this was an anterograde amnesia.

A first memory-consolidation system has thus been identified: bilateral injury to hippocampus and amygdala are necessary in humans to produce anterograde amnesia. But (see also Lishman [1971]) clearly these structures are not the repository of memories, since when they are injured, memories registered prior to the injury are preserved: it is only *new* experience and learning that are impaired. Iversen (1983) also combines human and animal evidence to conclude that damage to amygdala and hippocampus (i.e., a combination of limbic and temporal structures) is crucial to the pure amnestic syndrome. An acute amnestic syndrome of very pure form appears to result from malfunction of the posterior choroidal artery supplying the amygdala (Lishman, 1971; Iversen, 1983). The Kluver–Bucy syndrome results from ablation of the amygdala in monkeys: lack of fear, and stereotyped, repeated, bizarre examination of familiar objects, suggesting a loss of associational memory, including a loss of emotional association.

A second circuit or system can be injured in conditions such as Korsakoff's syndrome, in this instance in the diencephalon: thalamus, hypothalamus, and mammillary bodies. These latter have clear connections with hippocampus and amygdala. Butters and Cermak (1980) believe that connections between mammillary bodies and dorsomedial (possibly also ventromedial) nucleus of the thalamus are crucially injured in Korsakoff's syndrome.

A third circuit or system includes the ventromedial frontal lobe cortex: injury and ablation here seriously impair new learning and memory. Finally, a fourth circuit or system, particularly related to the memory of spatial relationships, and responsible for spatial disorientation when injured, extends between amygdala–hippocampus and upper parietal lobe. These two systems are interconnected. Failure of the latter may well explain why spatial disorientation is an early feature of Alzheimer's disease (Katzman, 1983; Morris and Kopelman, 1986) in which senile plaques appear early in the hippocampus. The acetylcholine-producing neurons of the basal forebrain supply, via their many ramifications, acetylcholine to the cortex and limbic system, a function which relates clearly to the consolidation of memories: in some way this organizes synaptic networks around the sensory areas of the cortex (sites where memories can be recalled by stimulation or abolished by ablation). Evidence for this acetylcholine system includes results of experiments using physostigmine as a stimulant and scopolamine as a blocker, as well as the pathologic events in Alzheimer's disease (see also Katzman [1983]; Kopelman [1986]) in which acetylcholine production is reduced.

These four memory systems subserve memory in its sensory and cognitive, or informational, aspects. A fifth memory system subserves a distinctly different type of memory; motor or habitual memory. This is the type of remembering involved in habits, the learning, retention, and recall of psychomotor patterns. It is nonsensory and noncognitive. Brain-damaged people (Butters and Cermak, 1980) can learn new motor skills, provided that no verbal or ideational activity interferes with the task; that is, the learning must be strictly divorced from verbal mediation. Such people also retain old motor skills. Not surprisingly, the substrate for the collection and retention of motor memories is in the basal ganglia. We have already noted MacLean's (1952, 1973) view of the "reptilian brain," consisting mainly of the basal ganglia, where reside habit and stereotyped motor activity; and we shall return to this category of memory briefly below, pp. 275–276.

To sum up what is known of the anatomy of memory, I paraphrase Mishkin's and Appenzeller's schema as follows:

1. Sensory experiences activate the various sensory cortical areas (Penfield's "platforms") which then communicate with the hippocampal system.
2. The hippocampus and amygdala send return signals to the cortical sensory and association areas where, with the help of acetylcholine neurons in the basal forebrain, memories are registered or consolidated; such encoding is not into the hippocampal system itself.
3. Circuits through hippocampal system, diencephalic system, and inferior frontal lobe organize memory encoding.
4. The amygdala, a complicated group of nuclei, is the great crossroads where sensory experiences in multiple modalities are integrated.
5. Nonsensory, noncognitive, motor or habit memories are not dependent upon these systems, but upon intactness of the basal ganglia.

The Neuropsychology of Information Processing

Memory Systems and Information Processing

An editorial by Baddeley (1986) offers a good bridge between the anatomy of memory and the psychology of memory. His paper "Modularity, Mass-Action, and Memory" reexamines the polarity I have noted above: what is the relative importance, he asks, of the several brain systems for memory, "modular" in nature, as against the operation of the whole brain in the mass action principle of Lashley? Baddeley suggests that the "modular" systems should be well enough separated and shielded in the brain that a discrete brain injury should not affect memory as a whole. Yet, empirically, the commonest result of any brain injury, wherever located, is a general memory deficit (Baddeley's term is *amnesic syndrome*). Further, Baddeley and many others (e.g., Bleuler [1951]) find that the similarities between the amnesic syndromes of different patients with different lesions far outweigh their differences. He therefore concludes that:

1. Systems for processing information into memory are modular in nature and distribution (e.g., systems for integrating sensory experiences, for placing information in short-term and long-term holding pools).
2. Memory storage systems are much more broadly based and diffuse, thus accessible and vulnerable to brain injury anywhere, in accordance with Lashley's law.

As we proceed into the neuropsychology of memory, it becomes clear that memory can only be arbitrarily separated from information processing in general: memory is one group of processes, one link in the chain, of dealing with information. Memory and learning are reciprocal functions. Memory is the condition of *having learned,* whether facts, understandings (see below on episodic and semantic memory) or psychomotor habits. It is new learning which is impaired in amnestic states, and information processing which is impaired in temporal and spatial disorientation. Amnestic states represent the failure of new learning just as memory represents the success of new learning.

Successful memory storage depends on a chain of events: raw sensory intake (primary and secondary cortical areas), the organization of percepts (tertiary cortical area, amygdala–hippocampus) and their storage (basal forebrain acetylcholine system, tertiary and association cortical areas). Memory also depends on attention and focusing (reticular activating system) and on selective motivation (limbic system). Lishman (1971) offers a plausible explanation of the mechanisms in psychogenic amnesia in the close association of emotion and memory functions in the limbic system; Bowlby's (1980) information-processing approach to defense may also be relevant here.

These chains of events involving memory deal with information either as discrete units of experience or as cognitive conceptual organizations. There is further the system of motor, habitual, memory (basal ganglia). Short-term memory is a temporary holding pool, aided by rehearsal, for problem-solving and decision making (its mechanisms presently appear not to be established). Long-term memory (tertiary and association areas) is a vast filing system, whose effective utilization requires sophisticated retrieval machinery.

Categories of Memory: Episodic and Semantic

Different types of memory are tapped by different tests, and may be differentially impaired; old, long-term memory is preserved in brain damage, while new learning, short-term memory, and encoding are impaired. For the most part, neuropsychological studies have dealt with memory in its informational aspects, rather than with motor habit memory, and this cognitive aspect will be our chief focus.

Tulving (Tulving and Donaldson, 1972, chapter 10), giving credit to a graduate student, Quillian, introduced a major conceptual division of "episodic" versus "semantic" memory, which appears to have become accepted by researchers (Baddeley, 1986). The methods of classical memory research had relied on retrieving concrete "bits" of information, and this approach had in fact defined the nature of "memory." However, Tulving draws attention to a kind of memory dealing with *meaning*: the setting up of cognitive structures for language, referents, as

Tulving put it, for "rules, formulas, and algorithms" (p. 386). This type of memory integrates and melds, rather than merely storing concrete experiences, and the rules of its behavior are different from those discovered from classic approaches to memory. For example, this type of memory is much less prone to modification, distortion, and decay over time.

Tulving termed this newly described category of memory *semantic memory*. He named the other, classically studied category *episodic memory*. It is the category of concrete memories of "episodes" in one's life, a register of the properties of concrete experiences and inputs. Such memories are sensory, very much embedded in an ongoing calendar of time and space, and with highly personal and subjective references. What happened? When? Where? Before, or after, this and that? Such memories are rote ones, and they are much more subject to retrospective modification, transformation, and loss of information (Tulving and Donaldson, 1972, pp. 385–386).

When we ask a patient to repeat back a story by rote, we are tapping into episodic memory. If we ask for the story much later, what the subject gives is the *meanings* of the story as the subject recalls it, with the rote, concrete elements decaying (such decay can be measured quantitatively) and being replaced by the patient's own concepts and words: a function of semantic memory.

Bowlby (1980, pp. 60–63) affords us a clinically relevant application of these two categories of memory. A patient may retrieve many positive, concrete, itemized memories of his or her behavior (episodic memory) yet retain an overall negative self-concept (semantic memory) highly dependent on parental verbal teaching (cf. the "auditive" nature of the superego, chapter 6). In psychotherapy the attempt is made to bring these two memory systems into better harmony.

Tulving does not claim that episodic and semantic memory have separate anatomical substrates nor has later research suggested this (*Quarterly Journal of Experimental Psychology*, 1986). For a highly technical updating on the construct of semantic memory, together with critiques by several recognized authorities, the reader is referred to Tulving (1984).

Categories of Memory: Short- to Long-Term; Ribot's Law

In this discussion I shall rely particularly on the formulations of Lishman (1971, 1978), Wells (1977), and Butters and Cermak (1980) as well as Tulving (Tulving and Donaldson, 1972).

The distinction between short-term (or recent) and long-term (or remote) memory is an important one for clinicians, for on this distinction depends the diagnosis of brain syndromes. In itself, however, such a distinction is too crudely black or white. Formerly it was believed that two, or at most three, stages in memory retention had to be accounted for, and represented distinct memory systems: short, medium, and long term. More recent evidence leads Tulving in particular to dispense with such stepwise staging: it is most likely that there is a completely fluid gradation of memory ages and stages, and it is unnecessary to postulate any finite number of steps, stages, or systems. Therefore, the real question is a quantitative and gradualist one. For how long, or how short a term, can a given subject retain information, or for what duration of time is there an amnesia?

Ribot's law (Lishman, 1971) states that the older a memory is (we are speaking here of episodic memory), the more likely it is that it will be preserved under conditions of brain damage. There appear to be few exceptions to this law. Butters and Cermak speak essentially of the same findings in the principle of "shrinkage": in brain-damaged states, recent information disappears rapidly, and at a rate proportional to the degree of damage. Thus, we may erect a continuum, from very short term to very long term, and may measure intervals along it. We can judge the severity of brain damage by whether a patient can retain information for 10 seconds, 3 minutes, a day, or 3 months; or by whether memories have disappeared for the past day, or week, or month, or 5 years; or by the amount of disorientation in time by half an hour, a day, 2 weeks, or a year.

Short-term memory, or "retention," is the ability to hold onto a cluster of information briefly, while manipulating it, including the decision either to forget or ignore it, or place it in longer-term storage. This ability persists in quite severely brain damaged people, provided they can recite or "rehearse" the information; for example, a list of numbers. Rehearsal is the act of subvocally repeating or reviewing the information presented. In states of brain damage such rehearsal can easily be broken by any distraction. The famous H. M. of Scoville and Milner could thus retain information for 4 to 5 minutes if he could concentrate only on it; it would inevitably be lost to him, but it would be gone instantly if he were distracted. Such short-term episodic memory can be measured quantitatively for its retention time.

G. A. Miller (1956), in a somewhat humorous approach to a serious subject, published his finding that there was a peculiar commonality in short-term memory. Regardless of what sensory modality was being tested, and regardless of the test being used, it appears that most subjects, whether bright or dull, can grasp simultaneously about seven discrete items of information: "the magic number seven, plus or minus two," and no more. Thus, "immediate memory [imposes] severe limitations on the amount of information we . . . receive, process, and remember" (p. 95). We can with practice, Miller found, stretch this number by "chunking"; clustering discrete items together so that the cluster becomes an item, then retaining seven (plus or minus two) such clusters. Miller gives the well-known example of learning Morse code. At first, the novice operator must retain patterns of dots and dashes; later, with increasing familiarity, letters become automatic and can be chunked into words, words can be chunked into phrases, and so on. Most of us, I have found, can memorize lengthy overseas telephone numbers by chunking.

This short-term memory system subserves the ability to pay attention and to grasp, for a brief time, data which are to be organized or manipulated, or handed on to long-term memory; that is, encoded, consolidated, stored for future reference. Long-term memory involves, probably, widespread circuits and depots around the various sensory cortical areas (Nielsen, 1941; Baddeley, 1986; Mishkin and Appenzeller, 1987); Lishman (1971) suggests that the essence of this storage system is that it normally resists disruption: people recover from anaesthesia, hypothermia, and convulsions with their long-term memories intact. Mishkin and Appenzeller (1987) and many others agree that the hippocampal–diencephalic–frontal lobe circuits must be intact for memories to be successfully encoded and consolidated, while these areas are not per se the repositories for long-term memory. The cholinergic system of the basal forebrain (Kopelman, 1986; Mishkin and Appenzeller, 1987) as noted above assists memory consolidation through the cortex. Also, REM or paradoxical sleep is believed to play some important part in the process of memory consolidation (Chapouthier, 1983; and see chapter 13).

Long-term memory is a storage system, for all practical purposes, of infinite capacity, unlike the 7 ± 2 capacity of short-term memory. The crucial logistic problem is how, successfully and efficiently, to retrieve from this vast data bank. A challenge for research is to devise ingenious means for discovering whether memories are being stored well or badly, or being retrieved well or badly.

Processes of Retrieval

Several categories of retrieval are established. In "free" retrieval the subject is asked to recall as many items of a list or collection as possible, without external aid. There are various techniques of "assisted" or "cued" recall, in which the subject is given direction, or stimuli to association, in the retrieval process. There is also the process of recognition, where the subject is asked to pick out, from a list, collection, or other context, certain required objects, words, pictures, and so on. This process too can be free or cued. Using such techniques, some doubt has been thrown on the previously accepted proposition that encoding or memory consolidation is the locus of impairment in brain damage. E. Miller (1975), Butters and Cermak (1980) and others cite a crucial experiment of Warrington and Weiskrantz (1970): this has strongly suggested a problem in *retrieval*. The evidence is that confused subjects (Korsakoff syndrome and temporal lobectomy) did as well as normals when a cued recall test using fragmented words was given. Hence their retrieval, rather than their storage, seems to be in question. Warrington and Weiskrantz used only 5 subjects; their experiment does not appear to have been replicated. Morris and Kopelman (1986),

reviewing the memory difficulties in Alzheimer's disease, concluded that (1) rehearsal is unimpaired; (2) "implicit" or semantic memory is likewise good; but (3) "explicit" or episodic memory is certainly impaired, with difficulties in *both* encoding and
retrieval.

A principle of economy of effort appears to be involved in
the process of retrieval. Lawson and Barker (1968) and Barker
and Lawson (1968) found that, as measured by reaction times,
words for common objects are more easily retrieved than words
for rarer ones. Based on a standard classification of occurrence
of words in English literature (frequent to rare), they found a
logarithmic relationship between the time to retrieve a word,
and its relative frequency of use.

Psychological Testing and Rating in Brain Damage

This large subject will be touched upon only briefly. The reader
may further pursue Blessed, Tomlinson, and Roth (1968), Torack (1978), Butters and Cermak (1980), Reisberg (1983), Katzman (1983), the November 1986 *Quarterly Journal of Experimental Psychology*, and Lezak's definitive monograph on neuropsychological assessment (1983).

The psychiatrist must not expect the clinical psychologist
to make the diagnosis of brain damage for him, whether in
borderline or severe chronic brain syndromes. In mild, early,
suspected cases, the patient is cooperative and testable. However, though cognitive impairment is the earliest, most sensitive
sign of brain damage, the psychiatrist is as likely, or more likely,
to pick up the crucial signs: psychological testing is unlikely to
provide crucial or incontrovertible evidence of brain damage.
In severe, advanced confusional states or acutely delirious cases,
the patient is untestable through inability to cooperate. Here
the problem is obvious, socially, clinically, to psychiatrist and
psychologist, to relatives and nurses.

What psychometrics and neuropsychology can provide
are:

1. A sophisticated variety of instruments from which to
   choose;

2. Tests, in cases where the patient is cooperative and accessible to testing;

3. Ratings, where the patient is uncooperative or incapable and observers have to be relied upon;

4. A system of quantification based on standardized norms;

5. A framework of analysis based on the attribution of neuropsychological functions to known cerebral localizations.

Let us briefly look at examples of tests used in assessing degrees and kinds of brain dysfunction.

First, the early, mild, questionable or suspected case. Here the approach is primarily intellectual and cognitive analysis, using standardized tests such as the Wechsler Adult Intelligence Scale, which taps various verbal and nonverbal skills, and has norms adjusted for sex and age groups. The analysis of subtest scores can give an index of intellectual deterioration: certain subtests, such as vocabulary, stand up well with aging and brain damage; others suffer impairment. The accuracy with which such measures will pinpoint actual brain damage is discussed critically in the references above: it is by no means 100 percent and is highly reliant on the skill and experience of the administrator. Wechsler has also developed a Memory Scale applicable to discerning amnestic problems. Again, it is unlikely to indicate specifically a condition of very early brain damage, although the greater the discrepancy between Intelligence quotient and Memory Quotient, the greater that likelihood is. H. M., Milner's famous case, with an immense global deficit in new learning and retention, scored 68 on the Wechsler Memory Scale and 112 on the Intelligence Scale.

Two instruments, one very simple and brief, the other exceedingly detailed, are applicable to mild to moderately severe (testable) cases. The Mini-Mental Status (MMS) developed by Folstein, Folstein, and McHugh (1975) is a clinical instrument and not a detailed psychological test (see also McHugh and Folstein [1979]). It is a brief set of cognitive tasks, to be used by the psychiatrist "at the bedside," and which produces a cumulative score. The highest possible score of 30 indicates an intact cerebrum with certainty; any score above 24 strongly suggests cerebral integrity and any score below 24 is progressively confirmatory of brain damage. The MMS is a compact and useful instrument which even quite inexperienced clinicians can learn to use. It has been well validated and standardized.

The most firmly established neuropsychological test instrument is certainly the Halsted–Reitan Battery. This very detailed set of tests, requiring some specific apparatus and a skilled tester, taps various cognitive and psychomotor skills, memories, and habits. The battery has never been rigidly assembled as a simple monolithic structure. Rather, elements of a collection of standard methods can be selectively applied to elucidate given problems. Quantitative scoring of the results, and a resultant sophisticated cerebral localization, are possible from the battery. For details see the references above (e.g., Wells, 1977; Lezak, 1983).

For seriously cognitively impaired patients, ratings by observers and evaluators have to be carried out. The Newcastle Group (Blessed, Tomlinson, and Roth, 1968) developed a Dementia Rating Scale based on performance of everyday activities. This scale was found to correlate well with cerebral pathology proven at autopsy, and in fact proved to be a good predictor of life expectancy. At my own university, Lawson, Rodenburg, and Dykes (1977) devised and standardized a scale which discriminates well between organic and functional disorders, though its main aim is to assess degrees of dementia in the elderly, which it does. Significantly, this rating scale fails to discriminate between organic and functional geriatric cases on the factor of emotional control (lability, catastrophic reaction, aggression), thus confirming that this factor is not a reliable index of brain damage, as was made a criterion in the DSM-I (see pp. 254–256).

Three Paradigmatic Disorders

I conclude with notes on three disorders, each of which illustrates particular points, and acts as a paradigm or model: all share the chronic brain syndrome. Korsakoff's syndrome, which, as noted earlier, logically should be called Korsakoff's disease, illustrates the amnestic syndrome (chronic brain syndrome with memory specifically and prominently disturbed) and the influence of relatively circumscribed lesions in upper brain stem and diencephalon. It also illustrates the continuity between an acute brain syndrome (Wernicke's) and a chronic one (Korsakoff's). This disorder is the subject of a model monograph by Butters and Cermak (1980) whose schema is noteworthy. Alzheimer's disease is at present the commonest cause of progressive dementia in the elderly, and is so far undefeated by research, treatment, or prevention. It illustrates a pervasive brain syndrome, with all cognitive functions eventually destroyed, and with much more widespread pathology than Korsakoff's syndrome. I review Wurtman's clear outline of models for investigation of its etiology. Finally, that semantically most confused entity, chronic brain syndrome in depression: the problems in nomenclature need not be defeating, if logically approached. This syndrome, usually in older depressed patients, is a general, vague, but pervasive cognitive impairment which may totally obscure usual depressive symptomatology. It is an example of the hopeful class of chronic brain syndromes, which can be successfully treated provided they are identified.

Korsakoff's Syndrome: A Model Approach

Butters and Cermak (1980) have published a model study, whose steps I summarize as exemplary in the presentation and analysis of a brain syndrome or disease:

1. *Delineation of the Syndrome:* the cluster of signs and symptoms; the discoverers who described it (in this instance, Korsakoff and others); its natural history (in this instance, the frequent evolution from an acute brain syndrome [Wernicke's]); the nature of an amnestic syndrome.

2. *Neuropathology and Etiology.* This entity should logically be called Korsakoff's disease, since the neuropathology is rather well established (Butters and Cermak do not deal with this point); lesions have been identified in upper brain stem and

diencephalon; causes, for the majority of cases, are found to be thiamine deficiency and the neurotoxic effects of alcohol abuse.

3. *Models for Memory and Amnesia.* The processes of short-term and long-term memory, and encoding; categories of episodic, semantic, and motor memory; problems in consolidation versus retrieval in amnestic states.

4. *Research Findings in the Syndrome.* Differential and shared features in different brain syndromes (in this instance the particular prominence of memory deficits); the curious specificities which may be found (in this instance the regular occurrence of anosmia or inability to smell, probably due to destruction of the mammillary bodies); continuities between the normal and the pathologic (in this instance, psychological similarities and differences between abstainers, problem drinkers, and actual Korsakoff sufferers).

Alzheimer's Disease: Models for Etiology

Alzheimer's disease remains the single commonest entity responsible for chronic brain syndromes in older people; its tragically progressive and irreversible course is responsible for dementia and death, and for stress and grief for families. Although brain diseases become commoner with age, Alzheimer's disease correlates so well with advancing age that it was long considered an extreme form of normal aging, though this is no longer the case (Katzman, 1985): it is clearly an independent disease entity. The challenge for the many research efforts now being mounted is to discover causes, provide treatment, and make prevention possible. The memory deficits, and their pathologic substrates, are reviewed by Morris and Kopelman (1986).

Blessed, Tomlinson, and Roth (1968) and Katzman (1979) agree that Alzheimer's disease is the commonest source of dementia, its incidence peaking in the elderly. More than 50 diseases cause senile (i.e., over 65 years) dementia: 50 percent of cases of senile dementia are related to Alzheimer's disease alone, another 10 to 15 percent to a combination of Alzheimer's with vascular or multi-infarct disease; 20 percent to multi-infarct disease alone; and the remainder to other processes, Huntington's, Korsakoff's, and Pick's syndromes, pellagra, endocrine disorder, hydrocephalus, tumors, and rarer disorders (Katzman, 1985).

There is a huge and expanding literature on such an important cause for human morbidity and mortality (Katzman, 1983; Reisberg, 1983). A number of lines of research have emerged, with a number of hypothesized models of causation for the disease, and these will be briefly summarized following Katzman (1983, 1985) and particularly Wurtman's excellent review (1985), with evidence for and against their validity:

1. *The Genetic Model.* A few cases of Alzheimer's disease are familial, showing the pattern characteristic of an autosomal dominant. Further, all cases of Down's syndrome (a chromosomal error, trisomy-21) who survive over age 40 develop the neuropathology of Alzheimer's disease. Yet, no chromosomal or enzymatic abnormality has so far been discovered for Alzheimer's disease in the commoner, previously normal, elderly cases.

2. *The Abnormal Protein Model.* The curious, double-helical filaments of the neurofibrillary tangles, and the abundance of amyloid in the senile plaques and in and around blood vessels, which are the pathological findings in Alzheimer's disease, suggest an aberrant process producing abnormal protein, and a toxic effect upon neurons. But, it is not clear whether such a process is cause or effect.

3. *The Infectious Model.* A transmissible animal disease, Scrapie, and two human diseases, Kuru and Creutzfeldt-Jakob disease, with a neuropathology somewhat like Alzheimer's disease, are now known to be due to slow viruses or peculiar viral-like organisms (prions). But so far, all evidence for transmission of Alzheimer's disease has been negative, and all attempts to transmit it to animals have been negative.

4. *The Toxic Model.* Salts of aluminum have an affinity for the neurofibrillary tangles: does this mean the disease is a poisoning from aluminum, quite possibly selectively aided by other personal contributing factors? The case is unproven.

5. *The Vascular Model.* Cerebral blood flow and glucose and oxygen uptake are reduced in Alzheimer's disease, effects which increase in correlation with increasing dementia. In normal aging, though blood flow is diminished, there is compensatory uptake of glucose and oxygen. Again, the cause–effect relationships are not clear.

6. *The Acetylcholine Model.* Acetyltransferase is grossly reduced in the hippocampus and cortex in Alzheimer's disease. Clearly the basal forebrain acetylcholine system is progressively impaired. But, so are other transmitter systems (for norepinephrine and serotonin), and there is destruction and loss of actual neurons also.

7. *"The Elephant Model."* Wurtman recalls the blind men individually examining an elephant, with reductionistic findings. He suggests that an interactional model combining several of the above may be most likely to have heuristic success.

Chronic Brain Syndrome in Depression: Detectable and Remediable

I believe it was in 1952 that I saw my first case of a chronic brain syndrome remitted by electroconvulsive treatment. The patient was a 52-year-old man, who, we thought, suffered from a dementia related to chronic alcohol abuse. Further review showed that his disorder was of quite sudden onset, and that abuse of alcohol was likewise quite recent; there was a strong element of anhedonia and retardation. He recovered to his premorbid normal state after treatment. Over several years he was readmitted twice with the same syndrome, and each time did very well on convulsive therapy. More recently, I was involved in the case (Burra, Powles, Riopelle, and Ferguson, 1980) of a late middle-aged man with a peculiar atypical psychosis responding to convulsive therapy; what was of interest to us was his presentation of primitive reflexes, which disappeared with recovery, as well as his extremely severe cognitive incompetence, which remitted.

Apparent dementia which clears up on antidepressant treatment has been a circus ring for semantic juggling. However, if we proscribe the term *dementia,* with its implication of irreversibility, then such usages as *pseudodementia* become un-necessary. A logical terminology such as chronic brain syn-drome due to major depression, or major depression, with chronic brain syndrome, would remind us once more that syn-drome simply means a consistently recurring symptom cluster.

British writers have shown the earliest and most sustained interest in pseudodementia. Kiloh (1961) included in his review many other kinds of pseudodementia in addition to the de-pressive syndrome; the Ganser state, other "twilight states," the hysterical dissociative disorders, for example. His aim was to alert clinicians not only to be careful in differential diagnosis, but to be on the alert for functional disorders masquerading as organic ones. Post (1975) reviewed the depressive organic syndrome, proposing his own simple terminology. He sug-gested as helpful a search for suggestive prodromes in cases of depression, and for clouding or fluctuation of consciousness in cases of brain damage. He notes that the syndrome tends to occur in the depressed elderly; some cognitive impairment is probably present in all severe depressions, as well as in the normally aging population. Lishman (1978) devotes a consider-able section to pseudodementia in his chapter on the senile and presenile dementias.

McAllister (1983) and Wells (1979) offer comprehensive reviews of the problems of pseudodementia of relatively recent date; these papers are recommended. The affective disorders research group at my own university has devised an ingenious, relatively simple, and certainly safe test for diagnosing de-pressive chronic brain syndrome. Letemendia, Prowse, and Southmayd (1986) describe a 40-hour sleep-deprivation vigil, during which the four depressed and confused elderly people they studied not only became euthymic, but regained cognitive competence; both depression and confusion relapsed following termination of the vigil. Psychometric testing was unsatisfactory before and after the experiment, but its results were normal at the peak of the improvement during vigil.

We shall return to this question of the pathophysiology of depression and its possible effect on cognitive functioning in chapter 14.

Bibliographic Notes: Key Readings

Three interesting overviews of mind–brain relationships are recommended. Restak's *The Brain: The Last Frontier* (1979) is eminently readable, dealing with a series of psychosocial issues related to various brain systems; regrettably, locating subjects within the book is difficult. Jason Brown, in *Mind, Brain, and Consciousness* (1977), writes in an exotic style, but offers somewhat unique Jacksonian/Piagetian orientations. Torack in *The Pathologic Physiology of Dementia* (1978) is at times chatty and discursive, at times judgmental, but his historical overview of the brain and aging is excellent.

If I must nominate one central reference base and argument-settler for the whole field of organic syndromes, it has to be Lishman's (1978) impressive text; this covers fundamental and shared organic patterns, and syndromes related to various brain problems, all in a research-based fashion. Representative of other clinician–scientist–observers is Manfred Bleuler (1951) who continued his father's work on the schizophrenias (see chapter 15) as well as the classical tradition of organic psychiatry. Wells (1978) has devoted a career to study of brain syndromes, and deserves respectful attention in this overview. Katzman (1983) and Reisberg (1983) are solid authorities on organic syndromes, with a particular expertise in Alzheimer's disease. McAllister (1983) and Wells (1979) give definitive reviews of the vexing concept of pseudodementia.

Of the neuropsychologist–clinician–investigator group, Penfield and Roberts (1959) present a small classic on neurosurgical investigation and cerebral localization. Benson and Zaidel (1985) have compiled a collection of papers by Sperry and his followers on the split brain. Butters and Cermak (1980) give a model outline for approaching all brain-disordered states in their monograph on alcoholic Korsakoff's syndrome.

Of the more directly experimental group, Lashley's (1929) classic, on the summative effects of cortical ablation and the principle of "mass-action" of the brain, remains stimulating reading. These findings from experiments with rats continue to be applicable to the human condition today. Tulving and Donaldson (1972) present principles of memory organization which are accepted today, including Tulving's own seminal constructs. Mishkin and Appenzeller (1987), in a relatively compact paper, furnish what I consider a model for viewing the anatomical substrate of human memory. The whole November issue of the *Quarterly Journal of Experimental Psychology* (1986) is devoted to the psychology of memory, a good reference source. Finally, Valzelli (1981), a pharmacologist (here studying human aggression) is notable for his clever drawings of various brain systems.

References

American Psychiatric Association (1952), *The Diagnostic and Statistical Manual of Mental Disorders*. Washington, DC: American Psychiatric Press.
—————— (1968), *The Diagnostic and Statistical Manual of Mental Disorders*, 2nd ed. Washington, DC: American Psychiatric Press.
—————— (1980), *The Diagnostic and Statistical Manual of Mental Disorders*, 3rd ed. Washington, DC: American Psychiatric Press.
—————— (1987), *The Diagnostic and Statistical Manual of Mental Disorders*, 3rd ed. rev. Washington, DC: American Psychiatric Press.
Baddeley, A. (1986), Editorial: Modularity, mass-action, and memory. *Quart. J. Experiment. Psychol.*, 38:527–533.
Barker, M. G., & Lawson, J. S. (1968), Nominal aphasia in dementia. *Brit. J. Psychiat.*, 114:1351–1356.
Benson, D. F., & Blumer, D., eds. (1975), *Psychiatric Aspects of Neurological Disease*. New York: Grune & Stratton.
*—————— Zaidel, E., eds. (1985), *The Dual Brain*. New York: Guilford Press.
Bird, J. M., Bartolucci, G., Garnett, E. S., & Cleghorn, J. M. (1985), Computerized imaging in psychiatry. *Ann. Roy. Coll. Can.*, 18:113–116.
Blessed, G., Tomlinson, B. E., & Roth, M. (1968), The association between quantitative measures of dementia and of senile change in the cerebral grey matter of elderly subjects. *Brit. J. Psychiat.*, 114:797–811.
*Bleuler, M. (1951), Psychiatry of cerebral diseases. *Brit. Med. J.*, 2:1233–1238.
Bowlby, J. (1980), An information processing approach to defense. In: *Attachment and Loss*, Vol. 3. London: Hogarth Press.
Brazier, M. A. B. (1980), Trails leading to the concept of the ascending reticular system: The state of knowledge before 1949. In: *The Reticular Formation Revisited: Specifying Function for a Non-Specific System*, ed. J. A. Hobson & M. A. B. Brazier. New York: Raven Press.
*Brown, J. (1977), *Mind, Brain, and Consciousness*. New York: Academic Press.
Burra, P., Powles, W. E., Riopelle, R. J., & Ferguson, M. (1980), Atypical psychosis with reversible primitive reflexes. *Can. J. Psychiat.*, 25:74–77.
*Butters, N., & Cermak, L. S. (1980), *Alcoholic Korsakoff's Syndrome: An Information-Processing Approach to Amnesia*. New York: Academic Press.

Chapouthier, G. (1983), Protein synthesis and memory. In: *The Physiological Basis of Memory*, 2nd ed., ed. J. A. Deutsch. New York: Academic Press.

Folstein, M. F., Folstein, S. E., & McHugh, P. R. (1975), "Mini-Mental State": A practical method for grading the cognitive state of patients for the clinician. *J. Psychiat. Res.*, 12:189–198.

Fromkin, V. A. (1985), Implications of hemispheric differences for linguistics. In: *The Dual Brain*, ed. D. F. Benson & E. Zaidel. New York: Guilford Press.

Hobson, J. A., & Brazier, M. A. B., eds. (1980), *The Reticular Formation Revisited: Specifying Function for a Non-Specific System*. New York: Raven Press.

Iversen, S. D. (1983), Brain lesions and memory in animals: A reappraisal. In: *The Physiological Basis of Memory*, 2nd ed., ed. J. A. Deutsch. New York: Academic Press.

Katzman, R., ed. (1979), *Congenital and Acquired Cognitive Disorders*. New York: Raven Press.

*——— (1983), *Biological Aspects of Alzheimer's Disease*. Banbury Report No. 15. Cold Spring Harbor, NY: Cold Spring Harbor Laboratory.

——— (1985), Current frontiers in research in Alzheimer's disease. In: *Alzheimer's Dementia: Dilemmas in Clinical Research*, ed. V. Melnick & N. N. Dubler. Clifton, NJ: Humana Press.

Kiloh, L. G. (1961), Pseudo-dementia. *Acta Psychiat. Scand.*, 37:336–351.

Kopelman, M. D. (1986), The cholinergic neurotransmitter system in human memory and dementia: *Quart. J. Experiment. Psychol.*, 38:535–573.

*Lashley, K. (1929), *Brain Mechanisms and Intelligence: A Quantitative Study of Injuries to the Brain*. New York: Hafner, 1964.

Lawson, J. S., & Barker, M. G. (1968), The assessment of nominal aphasia in dementia: The use of reaction-time measures. *Brit. J. Med. Psychol.*, 41:411–414.

——— Rodenburg, M., & Dykes, J. A. (1977), A dementia rating scale for use with psychiatric patients. *J. Gerontol.*, 32: 153–159.

Letemendia, F. J. J., Prowse, A. W., & Southmayd, S. E. (1986), Diagnostic applications of sleep deprivation. *Can. J. Psychiat.*, 31:731–736.

Lezak, M. D. (1983), *Neuropsychological Assessment*, 2nd ed. Oxford: Oxford University Press.

Lindsley, D. B., Bowden, J. W., & Magoun, H. W. (1949), Effect upon the EEG of acute injury to the brainstem activating system. *EEG Clin. Neurophysiol.*, 1:475–486.

Lipowski, Z. J. (1975), Organic brain syndromes: Overview and classification. In: *Psychiatric Aspects of Neurological Disease*, ed. D. F. Benson & D. Blumer. New York: Grune & Stratton.

——— (1984), Organic brain syndromes: New classification, concepts, and prospects. *Can. J. Psychiat.*, 29:198–204.

Lishman, W. A. (1971), Amnesic syndromes and their neuropathology. In: *Recent Developments in Psychogeriatrics*, ed. D. W. Kay & A. Walk. Ashford, Kent, UK: Headley Brothers.

*——— (1978), *Organic Psychiatry: The Psychological Consequences of Cerebral Disorder*, 2nd ed. Oxford: Blackwell, 1987.

MacLean, P. D. (1949), Psychosomatic disease and the "Visceral Brain": Recent developments bearing on the Papez theory of emotion. *Psychosom. Med.*, 11:338–353.

—————— (1952), Some psychiatric implications of physiological studies on frontotemporal portion of limbic system (visceral brain). *EEG Clin. Neurophysiol.*, 4:407–418.

—————— (1973), *A Triune Concept of the Brain and Behaviour.* Toronto: University
of Toronto Press.

*McAllister, T. W. (1983), Overview: Pseudodementia. *Amer. J. Psychiat.*, 140:
528–533.

McHugh, P., & Folstein, M. F. (1979), Psychopathology of dementia: Implications for neuropathology. In: *Congenital and Acquired Cognitive Disorders*,
ed. R. Katzman. New York: Raven Press.

Miller, E. (1975), Impaired recall and the memory disturbance in senile dementia. *Brit. J. Soc. Clin. Psychol.*, 14:73–79.

Miller, G. A. (1956), The magical number seven, plus or minus two: Some
limits on our capacity for processing information. *Psychol. Rev.*, 63:
81–97.

*Mishkin, M., & Appenzeller, T. (1987), The anatomy of memory. *Scient.
Amer.*, 256:80–89.

Moore, R. Y. (1980), The reticular formation: Monoamine neuron systems.
In: *The Reticular Formation Revisited: Specifying Function for a Non-Specific
System*, ed. J. A. Hobson & M. A. B. Brazier. New York: Raven Press.

Morris, R. G., & Kopelman, M. D. (1986), The memory deficits in Alzheimer-
type dementia: A review. *Quart. J. Experiment. Psychol.*, 38:575–600.

Moruzzi, G., & Magoun, H. W. (1949), Brain stem reticular formation and
activation of the EEG. *EEG Clin. Neurophysiol.*, 1:455–473.

Nielsen, J. M. (1941), *Textbook of Clinical Neurology*, 3rd ed. New York: Paul
B. Hoeber.

Olds, J., & Milner, P. (1954), Positive reinforcement produced by electrical
stimulation of septal area and other areas of rat brain. *J. Comp. Physiol.
Psychol.*, 47:419–427.

Papez, J. W. (1937), A proposed mechanism of emotion. *Arch. Neurol. Psychiat.*,
38:725–743.

Passingham, R. E. (1982), *The Human Primate.* Oxford: W. H. Freeman.

*Penfield, W., & Roberts, L. (1959), *Speech and Brain-Mechanisms.* Princeton,
NJ: Princeton University Press.

Post, F. (1975), Dementia, depression, and pseudo-dementia. In: *Psychiatric
Aspects of Neurological Disease*, ed. D. F. Benson & D. Blumer. New York:
Grune & Stratton.

Powles, W. E. (1944), Some methods in the management of mental diseases.
McGill Med. J., 13:61–85.

—————— (1968), A Martian psychiatrist views with alarm the current state of
the term "schizophrenia." *Dis. Nerv. Syst.*, GWAN Supplement, 29:5–10.

Quarterly Journal of Experimental Psychology, Series A (1986), 38.

Rausch, R. (1985), Differences in cognitive function with left and right temporal lobe dysfunction. In: *The Dual Brain*, ed. D. F. Benson & E. Zaidel.
New York: Guilford Press.

*Reisberg, B., ed. (1983), *Alzheimer's Disease.* New York: Free Press.

*Restak, R. M. (1979), *The Brain: The Last Frontier.* Garden City, NY: Doubleday.

Rieber, R. W., ed. (1976), *The Neuropsychology of Language.* New York: Plenum
Press.

Ropper, A. H. (1979), A rational approach to dementia. *Can. Med. Assn. J.*, 121:1175–1190.

Scheibel, A. B. (1980), Anatomical and physiological substrates of arousal: A view from the bridge. In: *The Reticular Formation Revisited: Specifying Function for a Non-Specific System*, ed. J. A. Hobson & M. A. B. Brazier. New York: Raven Press.

Scoville, W. B., & Milner, B. (1957), Loss of recent memory after bilateral hippocampal lesions. *J. Neurol. Neurosurg. Psychiat.*, 20:11–21.

Sperry, R. W. (1985), Consciousness, personal identity, and the divided brain. In: *The Dual Brain*, ed. D. F. Benson & E. Zaidel. New York: Guilford Press.

Squire, L. R., & Zola-Morgan, S. (1983), The neurology of memory: The case for correspondence between the findings for human and nonhuman primate. In: *The Physiological Basis of Memory*, 2nd ed., ed. J. A. Deutsch. New York: Academic Press.

Starzl, T. E., Taylor, C. W., & Magoun, H. W. (1951), Ascending conduction in reticular activating system, with special reference to the diencephalon. *J. Neurophysiol.*, 14:461–478.

Strayhorn, J. M. (1982), *Foundations of Clinical Psychiatry*. Chicago: Year Book Medical Publishers.

*Torack, R. M. (1978), *The Pathologic Physiology of Dementia*. Berlin: Springer-Verlag.

Tulving, E. (1984), Précis of elements of episodic memory. *Behav. & Brain Sci.*, 7:223–268.

*——— Donaldson, W., eds. (1972), *Organization of Memory*. New York: Academic Press.

*Valzelli, L. (1981), *Psychobiology of Aggression and Violence*. New York: Raven Press.

Warrington, E. K., & Weiskrantz, L. (1970), Amnesic syndrome: Consolidation or retrieval? *Nature*, 228:628–630.

Weinberger, D. R. (1984), Brain disease and psychiatric illness: When should a psychiatrist order a CAT scan? *Amer. J. Psychiat.*, 141:1521–1527.

Wells, C. E. (1971), *Dementia*, 2nd ed. Philadelphia: F. A. Davis, 1977.

*——— (1978), Chronic brain disease: An overview. *Amer. J. Psychiat.*, 135:1–12.

*——— (1979), Pseudodementia. *Amer. J. Psychiat.*, 136:895–900.

Wexler, B. E. (1980), Cerebral laterality and psychiatry: A review of the literature. *Amer. J. Psychiat.*, 137:279–291.

Wise, M. G. (1987), Delirium. In: *Textbook of Neuropsychiatry*, ed. R. E. Hales & S. C. Yudofsky. Washington, DC: American Psychiatric Press.

Wurtman, R. J. (1985), Alzheimer's disease. *Scient. Amer.*, 252:62–74.

*Recommended readings.

9

A First Homeostatic Level: Psychiatric Normality

Introduction

Overview

Psychiatric normality is the first and most desirable level of homeostasis. Though this level of homeostasis is the commonest in the population, psychiatric research and the literature generally illuminate its properties rather sparingly. No doubt such relative inattention must be explained by psychiatry's preoccupation with disordered states, and the funding of research toward unlocking the secrets of psychiatric disorders. Our diagnostic templates lack specifications for normality. There appears to be a particular deficit in understanding the psychobiological mechanisms of normality, considering how much effort has been devoted to the biology of anxiety disorders, depressions, and the schizophrenias over recent years.

The clinician must periodically make a judgment of psychiatric normality, either in a newly presenting patient, or toward the end of a course of treatment. How is this judgment to be made? How can it be predicted that a patient will remain in normal homeostasis when treatment is terminated?

There are a number of suggestive criteria which, put together, distinguish normality from disorder. Singly, such criteria as deviance from community norms, or absence of symptoms, are not wholly reliable. I hope, by the end of this chapter, to bring together such criteria as we have for judging psychiatric normality in a clinical assessment. The earlier theorists to whom we may turn, distinguished and responsible as they are, have given us somewhat abstract or "Platonic" concepts which provide little operational precision for judging the immediate individual case. Indeed, their view of normality seems more a comment on an optimal way of life than a help to here-and-now clinical assessment. This "mental health" view of normality requires a longitudinal approach, which may involve viewing the person's whole life cycle: I shall distinguish it from the cross-sectional clinical judgment of psychiatric normality. The emphasis on the longitudinal continues in the few later empirical studies we have. But no study furnishes us with clear physiological or biological referents.

The earlier theorists suggest as criteria of mental health such constructs as good adjustment, integration, and reality appreciation (M. B. Smith, 1950); dominance of conscious and preconscious over unconscious systems (Kubie, 1954); self-actualization, autonomy, and environmental mastery (Jahoda, 1958); and good intellectual, emotional, and moral development and social adaptation (Phillips, 1968).

Today we can also turn to more empirical studies which, despite their limitations (e.g., cohorts of men only) provide more clinically applicable findings as well as a good heuristic base for future investigations. Grinker and colleagues examined normal young men, from whose backgrounds and current functioning emerged a profile for the normal or "idling" state (Grinker, Grinker, and Timberlake, 1962). Vaillant (1977) has followed a remarkable sample of promising men in the many years of the Grant Study, and has developed out of this many correlates for good and poor mental health: social success, a good marriage, and mature mental mechanisms correlate remarkably with good physical and mental health; fortunate or unfortunate environmental experiences can significantly alter mental health, for good or ill. Offer and Sabshin (1966, 1984) continue to pursue the interrelationships of life cycle and mental health: mental health lies in a dynamic interaction between individual and life experience, a smooth passage between phases in the life cycle, and functioning appropriate to developmental tasks. Further, these authors review various definitions of mental health. Foulds and colleagues erected a hierarchical model of psychiatric symptoms of which psychiatric normality or nonpersonal illness (where somatic disabilities can be allowed for) is the base; absence of symptoms is particularly explored in this model (Foulds, Caine, Adams, and Owen, 1965; Foulds and Bedford, 1975). Luborsky's Health–Sickness Rating Scale (1962) is somewhat similarly based, but includes many judgments of psychosocial functioning in addition to symptoms. It offers operational criteria and clinical vignettes; levels of ideal and practical normality stand at the top of the scoring column.

From these various studies I attempt to marshal criteria which might assist the clinician in making a cross-sectional judgment of psychiatric normality. Somewhat arbitrarily, these are classified as social, phenomenologic, cognitive, and psychodynamic. Conspicuously lacking are criteria which could be placed under a physiologic heading.

Conceptual Criteria

Diagnosing Psychiatric Normality

The two central clinical questions, for which we seek help from research studies, might be put thus:

1. Is this patient sitting before me in a state of satisfactory and desirable biopsychosocial homeostasis or mental health; that is, a condition of psychiatric normality, as contrasted with psychiatric disorder?

2. Is it safe to terminate treatment with this patient, who has achieved satisfactory homeostasis of a desirable kind, and will such homeostasis persist of its own momentum?

The psychiatric diagnostician should, I submit, always consider psychiatric normality in any differential diagnostic undertaking. But what is such normality? What are its criteria, and are these research-derived or merely clinical tradition? I can still recall vividly one of the formative experiences I had as a resident. The consultant, my current preceptor, was asked to see a man on the surgical service who was being investigated (with negative results) for persistent gnawing or burning epigastric pain. Full of newfound sophistication and psychosomatic enthusiasm, I examined this middle-aged man in preparation for my "chief," finding him to be depressed, regressed, preoccupied with oral conflicts, and thus likely on positive grounds to have gastritis or undetected peptic ulcer. Much to my surprise, however, the consultant himself rendered a diagnosis of psychiatric normality, and urged further somatic investigation, from which an early gastric carcinoma was found and successfully treated. Since that experience, I have chided residents under my own supervision if they have not, at regular intervals, considered psychiatric normality in their differential diagnoses.

The clinician as therapist, be the therapy biological or psychosocial, or both, must sooner or later leave the patient to fend for herself, without professional help. But when, by what criteria, and by what indications that the state of normality achieved will persist without continued professional assistance?

There are a number of criteria which can help us with these judgments, but from a research point of view the investigation of psychiatric normality is still in its infancy.

Conceptual Criteria for Mental Health

Before we come to what research has offered, let me first list the criteria I believe most clinicians would agree to as distinguishing a psychiatric disorder from the normal state.

1. *Community as control or standard.* Psychiatric disorder is a *deviation*. This is a frail criterion in itself, failing to distinguish psychiatric disorder surely from delinquency, retardation, or genius.

2. *Life cycle or developmental curve as control or standard.* Deviation from expectable positions in the life cycle would seem a somewhat more robust, but nonetheless, in itself, an inadequate criterion.

3. *Nosological templates as control or standard.* Presence or absence of recognized symptoms, empirically matching or failing to match any recognized psychiatric syndrome: diagnosis by exclusion or inclusion.

4. *Person as own control or standard.* Personality change, discontinuity in the patient's life, particularly if accompanied by distress and disability: a necessary and useful counterbalance to the deviation criterion.

5. *Templates for psychiatric normality as control or standard control.* At present we lack any such recognized templates in our nosological schemata, and research is barely beginning to suggest criteria for such templates. Such a standard of comparison will require us to examine a patient, in a cross-sectional fashion, on social, psychologic, and biologic criteria.

The pioneer theorists on mental health have given us (as Vaillant [1977] might put it) rather "Platonic" concepts of mental health. I commence with a statement by a psychologist of considerable vision, M. Brewster Smith (1950). As guidelines for proper research he posited three "optima of mental health":

Adjustment implies the "well-being of the organism in interaction with its environmental field" (p. 504); the term is used synonymously with *adaptation,* involving both active and passive modes. *Integration,* meaning "the integrity of the organism as a complexly coordinated system" (p. 504) requiring a "degree of coordination of needs, means, and goals" (p. 505), a *resiliency;* this term is clearly synonymous with homeostasis (p. 505). Smith notes the obvious limitation or danger of such a dimension if used as a sole criterion; for example, *paranoia* is a good instance of integration at the expense of the human's social adaptation and interdependence. Accordingly, a third dimension is required, *adequacy of the individual's cognition of reality.* Smith notes two examples for this. Insight is considered an important criterion for a successful outcome of psychotherapy. Further, there is an important duality or reciprocity in that "perceptions of one's self and one's social environment go hand in hand: distortions of one are likely to imply complementary distortions in the other" (p. 505).

Lawrence Kubie (1954), a psychoanalytic theorist, presented a seminal discussion: "The Fundamental Nature of the Distinction Between Normality and Neurosis." He collates and criticizes other approaches to the question and presents his own criteria. He notes the classical and continuing debate on mental health or normality as the statistically usual versus the ideal. "Cavities in the teeth and colds in the head are universal, but they are not therefore normal; nor is health itself abnormal because it is rare" (p. 172); and "among sufferers from neurosis are those whose every moment requires a degree of discipline, high purpose, and courage which the healthy person is rarely called upon to exercise" (p. 173). Of previous approaches, Kubie comments that the phenomenologic approach notes the presence (or absence) of symptoms, but neglects underlying dynamic and organizing characterological patterns. The sociological sees neurosis in terms of social incapacity, but neglects to note that neurotic conflict can lead to creative and useful activity. The ontogenetic or anamnestic approach appraises the individual's development, but in general fails to establish criteria distinguishing the normal from the abnormal.

Normality, Kubie proposes, is an adaptive life-style based upon a major alliance between conscious and preconscious mental systems. Resultant behavior is flexible, anchored in reality, and gratifying; that is, able to satisfy and satiate needs. Contrarily, neurosis is dominated largely by the unconscious system, with stereotyped, repetitive behavior patterns which are rarely satisfying and are not amenable to change by the experiences of reality.

Marie Jahoda (1958), a distinguished social psychologist, authored a pioneering monograph commissioned by the Joint Commission on Mental Health, a government-supported but independent investigative body. Smith (1950) already expresses indebtedness to her thinking. Jahoda undertook the task of reviewing and synthesizing *Current Concepts of Positive Mental Health* (the title of the monograph) and pointing directions for further action, in this case again principally for needed empirical research. Her review and synthesis still afford useful reading. The absence of "mental disease," she finds, is not a solid criterion for mental health: empirically this is because of a lack of solid agreement as to what constitutes mental ill-health itself. Nor is a statistical definition helpful: what is "normal" or usual, or what is "normative" or desirable, both involve problems of cultural relativity and value judgment. Positive definitions of emotional well-being, such as that of the World Health Organization, beg the question of mentally healthy people suffering unavoidable and undeserved human misery.

Jahoda does develop a concept of multiple, interlocking criteria or dimensions of mental health, which should be capable of being put to empirical test. These are primarily psychological: she has already noted the lack (in 1958) of physiological correlates for mental ill-health. Briefly paraphrased, her dimensions are:

1. Attitudes to the self: self-awareness, correctness of self-perceptions, feelings about the self, sense of identity.
2. Adequacy of growth, development, and self-actualization, including motivational processes.
3. Integration and synthesizing functions: balance of forces, philosophy of life, resilience to stress.
4. Autonomy and independence of functioning, related to inner self-regulation.
5. Perception of reality: freedom from need-inspired distortion; empathy and social sensitivity.
6. Environmental mastery: ability to love, work, and play; interpersonal relations, response to situational requirements; adaptation and adjustment, problem solving, in both active and passive modes.

Phillips (1968), a psychologist, in his review monograph *Human Adaptation and its Failures*, makes several cogent points. Normality, he suggests, is a construct enabling us to *predict a person's future behavior*, particularly his or her effectiveness. The main dimensions of adaptation (practically synonymous with homeostasis) consist in (1) accepting and responding to social norms and expectations, and (2) "Flexibility and effectiveness in meeting novel and potentially disruptive conditions . . . imposing one's own direction on the course of events" (p. 2).

Phillips's principal dimensions of mental health are (1) intellectual and emotional development; (2) social adaptation, in the form of balance between independence and participation; and (3) moral development, leading to reciprocity in dealing with others.

Phillips's treatise, though it too excludes physiological or psychobiological considerations, additionally makes use of Piagetian and Kohlbergian frames of reference and deals in a major way with disorders of adaptation in terms more operational for the psychiatric clinician.

Empirically Oriented Studies

Grinker's Empirical Study

Apparently the first modern empirical study of the clinical properties of the "normal" was by Grinker et al. (1962). They studied a cohort of young men attending a college for community leaders. The research team was seeking, as controls for psychosomatic studies, subjects who were free from psychiatric disturbance, not anxious or depressed, in an "idling" phase of homeostasis, but whose responses under stress might be examined. This lengthy, engaging paper reports the sense of pleasurable shock when the psychiatric clinician actually meets a sizable number of normal young men; these subjects were modest, mundane, hard-working fellows, without lofty goals save to do the best they could and be true to themselves; not particularly introspective, but not impulsive either. Other findings included honest and accurate self-evaluations; evidence of industriousness in childhood and relatively smooth passage through puberty and adolescence; a history of firm parental discipline and strict and rigorous religious training; emotionality (fear, anger, sadness) situationally rather than interpersonally related and dealt with satisfactorily by physical activity; rather restricted sexuality with no instances of homosexuality; and coping mechanisms of muscular activity (all were in training in athletics), denial, and isolation–withdrawal.

Luborsky's Health–Sickness Rating Scale

Luborsky's (1962) Health–Sickness Rating Scale (HSRS) has been reexamined more recently (Luborsky anad Bachrach, 1974). This 100-point scale has quite good reliability, and ranks various operational definitions of mental health, with 34 illustrative case examples. The upper limit is an "ideal state of complete functioning integration, of resiliency in the face of stress, of happiness and social effectiveness" (Luborsky, 1962, p. 40; Luborsky and Bachrach, 1974, p. 293). The referents are clinical. A score of 76 to 99 represents "everyday adjustment" in persons rarely seeking treatment, through 66 to 75, mild neurosis or addiction, down to 0 to 25, clear-cut psychosis, requiring hospitalization. The ratings to be made are clinical and global, along seven dimensions: (1) the need to be protected versus autonomous functioning; (2) seriousness of symptoms; (3) degree of subjective discomfort and distress; (4) effect on the environment, danger, disruption; (5) degree of uses of abilities, especially in work; (6) quality of interpersonal relationships; (7) breadth and depth of interests.

Luborsky's work might be seen as the type or model of the transition from the conceptual to the empirical in delineating gradations from ideal normality to severe mental ill-health.

Vaillant and the Grant Study of Men

Though the attempt of this chapter is to find yardsticks for the assessment of psychiatric normality in the here-and-now (a cross-sectional approach, dynamic and homeostatic) the two major studies I shall review are heavily developmental, or longitudinal, in outlook. Perhaps their results might better illuminate the question "What is normal adult *development?*"

One of the warnings issued from the Grant Study might be paraphrased thus: although the indices of good mental health correlate well through most men's life cycles, there are significant and sobering exceptions in the lives of some who appeared mentally healthy in early years but deteriorated later; and, conversely, some who early appeared precarious but later, through fortunate experience, showed good mental health (Vaillant, 1974). By implication, this developmental approach is a commentary on Phillips's (1968) dimension of normality as prediction.

The Grant Study, summarized by Vaillant (1977) and the subject of periodic analyses and progress reports (Vaillant, 1974, 1978; Vaillant and Milofsky, 1980), has already been presented in chapters 4 and 7. A sizable cohort of college males has been prospectively followed in this study since 1939. At one stage, disadvantaged men were studied for comparison and found to have comparable life cycles and homeostatic patterns (Vaillant and Milofsky, 1980). From the homeostatic point of view, this study was designed with the recognition of the fact that life is full of discontinuities (stresses) and that adaptation to these is a central criterion of mental health. Mental health is successful adaptation, showing the strength to accept life's terms and at times positively forcing one's own terms upon life. The latter (in Piagetian terms "assimilation") is an undertaking not without risk, since it includes the possibility of progressive distortion of reality, a criterion of mental ill-health (Smith, 1950).

Vaillant concludes that mental health can be operationally defined: "inner happiness, external play, objective vocational success, mature inner defenses, good outward marriage—all correlate highly—at least as powerfully as height correlates with weight" (Vaillant, 1977, p. 373).

Mental health is variegated: there is no one stereotyped version. But again and again, in many different guises and measures, two facts stand out. Good object relations are a central hallmark of good mental health, whether this is made operational as a good and stable marriage, the ability to be a good parent, or the ability to care for and lead others in their growth (generativity); a good marriage is virtually incompatible with mental illness (Vaillant, 1978).

And, from the clinical and cross-sectional standpoint which is the main emphasis of this chapter, the adaptive mechanisms which maintain mental health appear to be of central significance. These are the well-known ego defenses of psychoanalytic theory, patterns of dealing with internal needs and external realities: patterns which may be used to defend against distress, and thus can distort reality (inner and outer) and produce symptoms; or patterns which may be used synthetically to *adapt* well to both inner need and external reality. Vaillant's (1977) schema (see also chapter 7, pp. 219–227) is based upon recognized authorities (p. 79) and proceeds by classifying such mechanisms into more or less mature, and more or less adaptively successful ranks. This hierarchical arrangement (Vaillant, 1977, pp. 383–386) may be paraphrased thus:

1. Psychotic mechanisms, used normally before age 5: delusional projection, denial of external reality (i.e., psychotic denial).
2. Immature mechanisms, common between ages 3 and 15: projection, schizoid fantasy, hypochondriasis, passive–aggressive behavior, acting out (i.e., direct expression by-passing consciousness).
3. Neurotic defenses (Vaillant's term), common between ages 3 and 90 (*sic*): intellectualization, repression, displacement, reaction formation, dissociation (or neurotic denial).
4. Mature mechanisms, used between ages 12 and 90, and popularly thought of as "virtues": altruism, humor, suppression (postponement), anticipation, sublimation (the satisfying channeling of need gratification).

Vaillant (1977, p. 87) reports a highly significant statistical correlation ($p < 0.001$) between the use of these latter mature adaptive mechanisms and other indices of personal and social happiness and success; and, conversely, between use of immature mechanisms and overall lack of happiness and success. Somewhat less highly significant correlations ($p < 0.05$–0.01) are reported between level of maturity of mechanisms and career adjustment, psychological–psychiatric adjustment, and medical adjustment (or health) and longevity.

One quite striking cluster of findings emerges when the one-third most successful men are compared with the one-third least successful. The most successful one-third show no use of immature adaptive mechanisms: of the least successful 61 percent were found to use immature mechanisms, and only 4 percent mature ones. The least successful have poorer health on all indices. They tend not to have close friends and stable marriages (a number have never married); some have never achieved independence from the family of origin, and a number have not achieved intimacy, let alone career consolidation (see chapter 4 for these constructs; and Vaillant, 1978).

In general, good relationships in childhood, rather than the absence of trauma, emerge as the best predictors of adult mental health (Vaillant, 1974). Failure to marry emerges as a predictor of serious impairment in object relations and occupational achievement. Successful career consolidation correlated remarkably with the ability to channel anger constructively.

We might note here that good early relationships and experiences, social supports in general, and the availability of a stable intimate friendship or marital relationship, have been repeatedly cited as antidotes or prophylactics for psychiatric disorder; see, for example, Brown and Harris (1978) who will be further reviewed in chapter 14 (pp. 493–499) and Werner (1989).

Offer and Sabshin: "Normatology"

Offer and Sabshin (1966) authored the first monograph devoted wholly to the study of psychiatric normality and to various criteria for defining and studying mental health. This work went into a second revised edition; and, essentially as a further sequel in the continuum of their ideas, Offer and Sabshin (1984) edited a compendium including papers of their own and of others seriously interested in the field. The 1984 work tends to revert to the conceptual and "Platonic" style noted above, although there is a considerable clinical derivation and some research input. Clearly all authors in the compendium are impressed with how little is yet solidly known of normality, and at almost every turn there is the somewhat pessimistic resort to raising questions rather than answering them. I shall focus chiefly on the orienting principles authored by Offer and Sabshin themselves.

Psychiatric normality, these workers conceive, can be approached in four ways:

1. *Normality as health*: an approach generally based on the medical model, emphasizing the absence of distress and disability, and requiring further empirical study of persons at high and at low risk for mental ill-health.

2. *Normality as statistical average:* an approach to studying the average citizen and the commonest modes of functioning, and requiring further empirical study of persons functioning adequately.

3. *Normality as utopian ideal*: a normative approach, revealing what is valued, and requiring further empirical study of the goals of human development, and of how the ideal person functions.

4. *Normality as transactional system*: a developmental–dynamic approach studying the expectable within each stage of the life cycle, the passage from stage to stage, and the homeostatic processes in the individual during these progressions.

It is clear that Offer and Sabshin are most interested in the last, developmental–homeostatic–dynamic approach, though they pay significant attention to the others. Since the work is occupied with the life cycle, the subject matter is somewhat more relevant to our chapter 3 than to this discussion. Their frame of reference is generally psychodynamic and psychosocial, somewhat psychoanalytic; that is, organized at the levels of emergence of the psychological and social, with relatively scant attention to the biological. We do not find references to "nature": genetics, sexual dimorphism, endocrinology, or normal and pathological responses to stress. There is a paucity of answers to biological questions, indeed a paucity of questions raised as needing to be answered on the biological level of emergence in psychiatric normality.

In summary (see especially Offer and Sabshin [1984, chapter 14]), psychiatric normality as seen in the majority of samples examined is seen to consist in adjusting well to the person's *expectable* environment; in coping with the additional stresses that punctuate daily living; in maintaining good relationships with the important individuals in the immediate social field; and in moving, without undue problems, from one stage in the life cycle to the next.

Such criteria actually are fulfilled by about 85 percent of the population, hence normality here meets the statistical or average approach. From this, as a practical corollary, Offer and Sabshin comment that governments and third-party insurers need not fear an avalanche of psychiatrically disordered citizens, save with the possible exception of troubles in the advanced elderly.

Summary and Synthesis

I will weave together some of the above concepts and findings under the five headings suggested above (pp. 296, 297) for criteria distinguishing psychiatric normality from psychiatric disorder.

Relationship to the Community

The term *community* will be used here in two senses: as the intimate subculture of home, church, school, and workplace in which the individual is in face-to-face interaction; and as the larger, more impersonal population which researchers use for comparison and norms of mental health and disorder. Three issues require to be dealt with: participation in the community as an index of mental health; psychiatric disorder as deviance; and ideal–Utopian versus practical–average definitions of mental health.

Almost all the theorists reviewed above believe, or discover empirically, that some type of interest and participation in the immediate community is a hallmark of mental health: a creative dialectic or harmony with the community (Jahoda, 1958; Phillips, 1968; Grinker et al., 1962; Vaillant, 1977); moral maturity and concern for others (Phillips in particular); religious participation (Grinker et al., 1962); the ability to love, work, and play

(Jahoda, 1958; Luborsky, 1962; Vaillant, 1977) and the quality of interpersonal relationships (Luborsky, 1962; Luborsky and Bachrach, 1974).

None of the literature surveyed stresses *deviance* from the immediate community, except Luborsky in his dimension of danger or disruption. Deviance is a major sociological construct but apparently too abstract or general a one to be a robust indicator of psychiatric disorders: most psychiatric disorders may represent deviance from community norms and community participation; but all deviance is by no means psychiatric, for there are geniuses, social activists, artists, criminals, the handicapped, and so on. Deviance *may* be one criterion of psychiatric disorder which can be empirically useful.

I recall a clinical conference at which the late Margaret Mead was a consultant–discussant. Our residents presented to her the case of a young man believed to suffer from an unusual paranoid psychosis with religious colorings; but he was also a member of a somewhat esoteric religious sect, thus confusing the diagnosis. Dr. Mead's comment was simple and practical: "Have you asked the members of his church whether he is a normal participant?" Needless to say, we psychiatric purists had not thought of doing so. When Dr. Mead's advice was carried out, the answer was unequivocal: "Our brother is mentally ill."

As regards the definition of mental health or psychiatric normality, it seems clear that the statistical or average (the "mode" of mental health most frequent in the community) makes the best clinical sense. Research should, of course, be directed at the tiny minority who are free of all psychopathology. But it would be absurd to suggest that the 85 percent or so of the population (Offer and Sabshin, 1984) who function well but do not enjoy *ideal* mental health are the deviants; rather, it is the small minority of completely healthy ones who are deviant (see Kubie's [1954] comment on the common cold and dental caries). Statistically, this 85 percent, as well as the completely "normal" few, manage without burdening the health care system (Offer and Sabshin, 1984). A clinical definition of psychiatric normality must then encompass the presence of small, nondisabling, degrees of psychopathology.

Relationship to Life Cycle or Developmental Curves

Most of our theorists and researchers either imply (using criteria of "maturity" or age-appropriateness) or directly address a relationship between the life cycle and mental health (see especially Vaillant [1977] and Offer and Sabshin [1984]). The person who is "on track" with reference to his or her developmental curves is likely to be mentally healthy. Such a person passes smoothly from one life stage to another, and functions within the stage he or she is traversing with relative equanimity, handling the stresses it offers with only temporary discomfort (Offer and Sabshin). Good relationships in childhood, rather than an absence of trauma, predict good adult mental health; marriage, particularly a good marriage, is also a predictor of good mental health; failure to achieve expectable developmental tasks correlates strongly with mental and physical ill-health, even a shortened life span, as does lack of social success (Vaillant, 1977). A stable, strict upbringing and childhood industriousness predict adult normality (Grinker et al., 1962).

In chapter 1 we have dealt in particular with developmental curves, and in chapter 4 with the life cycle: the construct of regression, as a falling-off from the developmental gradient, has been examined as a consistent feature of psychiatric disorder, though here too, regression will be found as a component of other conditions such as serious somatic illness or environmental hardship (starvation, concentration camps, disasters).

Relationship to Nosologic Templates

The psychiatrically disordered person can be fitted, more or less accurately, to templates in a recognized classification; the psychiatically normal person cannot. No nosological schema that I know of offers detailed templates for psychiatric normality (Foulds and Bedford, 1975; DSM-III-R, 1987). Such a diagnosis must therefore be made by exclusion; either there are no symptoms, or what symptoms there are fit no recognized syndrome. Absence of symptoms is the usual criterion (Offer and Sabshin, 1966; the "non-personal illness" of Foulds et al.

[1965] and of Foulds and Bedford, 1975). There are hierarchies of symptom patterns, from most to less severe, extrapolation of which at the less severe end gives some indication of normality (Luborsky, 1962; Foulds et al., 1965; Foulds and Bedford, 1975). May it be hoped that DSM-IV will give us templates for the recognition of psychiatric normality. In any case, the question of positive criteria for such templates will be further addressed below.

Relationship to the Person

Using the person as his or her own control may be one of the more precise criteria of psychiatric normality or disorder. This is already hinted at in the developmental approach: if the individual continues to develop smoothly, he or she is almost certainly mentally healthy.

There is little in the literature reviewed above which deals with the concept of change and discontinuity in the person, as a criterion of psychiatric disorder. But, used as his or her own control, most persons suffering psychiatric disorder have suffered a change, a shift in mode of being, usually for the worse: the person is not the same, is somehow altered. Clayton, Herjanic, Murphy, and Woodruff (1974) found this to be one reliable criterion distinguishing depression from mourning: in mourning, the person is perceived by peers as unchanged, the same person; in depression, the person is not him- or herself. In the frame of reference of this chapter, there is a distinct and persisting homeostatic shift, which therapeutic intervention will attempt to aid in shifting back to normal, to premorbid personality functioning or self.

If a person, therefore, maintains self-consistency, we are likely to be dealing with psychiatric normality. If, using the person as his or her own control, there is personality change, a shift in mode of being, the person is different or altered, there is likely to be psychiatric disorder. Such a criterion is a corrective to the criterion of deviance, and obviates also some of the problems of "labeling."

Templates for Psychiatric Normality?

Is it possible to assemble some criteria toward nosologic templates for the cross-sectional diagnosis of psychiatric normality, this first and most desirable level of homeostasis?

Of the authors reviewed above, most develop concepts of mental health based on longitudinal data; that is, mental health must be diagnosed along a historical dimension, and it is a predictor of future effectiveness (Phillips, 1968). This historical dimension includes childhood formative experiences (Grinker et al., 1962; Vaillant, 1977) and developmental progression through the life cycle (Vaillant, 1977; Offer and Sabshin, 1984); in only a few statements do we find reference to cross-sectional, here-and-now criteria.

Thus, I believe, I should return to making the fine distinction between mental health, which is historical or longitudinal in character, and psychiatric normality, which is a cross-sectional, here-and-now statement of a person's functioning at the most desirable level of homeostasis, without detailed reference to the past or to the future.

What can we extract from the above authors in the way of relatively cross-sectional criteria, such as could be marshaled during a clinical assessment? I assign the following, somewhat arbitrarily, to headings of the social, phenomenologic, cognitive, psychodynamic, and biologic:

1. *Social*: The person (or patient) is functioning appropriately or expectedly in relation to his or her position in the life cycle (Vaillant, 1977; Offer and Sabshin, 1984); demonstrates good interpersonal relationships and a breadth and depth of interests (Luborsky, 1962, 1974); is able to love, work, and play (Jahoda, 1958; Vaillant, 1977); interacts positively with social norms (Phillips, 1968); and does not appear, or feel, deviant;

2. *Phenomenologic*: Shows comfort, the "idling" state, and an absence of major or persisting symptoms (Grinker et al., 1962; Offer and Sabshin, 1984); is nondefensive (Vaillant, 1977) and demonstrates a sense of mastery (Jahoda, 1958); has not changed from his or her usual self (Clayton et al., 1974);

3. *Cognitive*: Shows good appreciation of reality, internal and external (M. B. Smith, 1950; Jahoda, 1958); is self-aware,

not dominated by need-inspired distortions (Jahoda, 1958); is intellectually and morally mature, able to empathize and reciprocate with others such as the clinician (Phillips, 1958);

4. *Psychodynamic*: Shows evidence of intrapsychic integration (M. G. Smith, 1950), harmony, balance, comfort (most authors); a lack of defensiveness (Vaillant, 1977); a preponderance of conscious and preconscious over unconscious operations (Kubie, 1954); mental mechanisms deployed are mostly mature ones, altruism, humor, suppression or postponement, anticipation, sublimation (Vaillant, 1977), muscular activity, coping with social conflict without personalizing it (Grinker et al., 1962);

5. *Biologic*: Here we are almost entirely lacking in criteria. Grinker et al. (1962) do not further elaborate on the physiological correlates of the "idling state," nor do others, somewhat surprisingly, specify such correlates for the state of comfort, integration, balance, harmony, and absence of symptoms. Thus we are left to speculate on what might be looked for cross-sectionally in the biologic sense. Can we rely on general criteria of physical fitness, exercise tolerance, stability of pulse, respiration, blood pressure, psychogalvanic response? Might it be possible to develop profiles which are norms for a variety of physiological measures: hormonal assays (cortisol, thyroid, for example); physiologic responsiveness to stress (exercise, interpersonal conflict); sleep laboratory patterns, including dreaming. In general, we will be looking for the *absence* of pathophysiologic phenomena such as will be noted in the next three chapters. But, on the other hand, may psychosocial criteria still be the most reliable indices of psychiatric normality, since this homeostatic level can exist in persons who may be somatically quite ill?

Bibliographic Notes: Key Readings

There is, as I have noted, a sparse literature on psychiatric normality, and virtually nothing on its physiologic correlates. The summation of the Grant Study, and the many interesting conclusions which can be drawn from it, *Adaptation to Life*, are presented by Vaillant (1977) and are highly recommended for their elucidation of the many correlates of mental health and ill-health. Offer and Sabshin (1984) in *Normality and the Life Cycle* continue their steps in developing a study of "normatology" together with expert contributing colleagues. This volume constantly raises questions, perhaps more questions than it has answers for.

The less recent theorists remain thought-provoking and should be pursued. I suggest M. Brewster Smith's (1950) general framework for investigations of mental health, and Jahoda's (1958) monograph produced for the Joint Commission on Mental Health, which was at that time providing an impetus to community psychiatry and preventive efforts in the United States.

I have searched without success for more recent significant publications, particularly as they might illuminate the physiological correlates of psychiatric normality. Engel's (1977, 1980) triune biopsychosocial model should, I believe, be very helpful in the continued search for the nature of normal homeostasis.

References

American Psychiatric Association (1987), *The Diagnostic and Statistical Manual of Mental Diseases,* 3rd ed. rev. Washington, DC: American Psychiatric Press.

Brown, G. W., & Harris, T. (1978), *Social Origins of Depression: A Study of Psychiatric Disorder in Women.* New York: Free Press.

Clayton, P. J., Herjanic, M., Murphy, G. E., & Woodruff, R. (1974), Mourning and depression: Their similarities and differences. *Can. Psychiat. Assn. J.,* 19:309–312.

*Engel, G. L. (1977), The need for a new medical model: A challenge for biomedicine. *Science,* 196:129–136.

*——— (1980), The clinical application of the biopsychosocial model. *Amer. J. Psychiat.,* 137:535–544.

Foulds, G. A., & Bedford, A. (1975), Hierarchy of classes of personal illness. *Psychol. Med.,* 5:181–192.

——— Caine, T. M., Adams, A., & Owen, A. (1965), *Personality and Personal Illness.* London: Tavistock.

Freud, S. (1917), Mourning and melancholia. *Standard Edition,* 14:243–258. London: Hogarth Press, 1957.

*Grinker, R. R., Sr., Grinker, R. R., Jr., & Timberlake, L. (1962), "Mentally healthy" young males (homoclites). *Arch. Gen. Psychiat.,* 6:405–453.

*Jahoda, M. (1958), *Current Concepts of Positive Mental Health*. New York: Basic Books.

Kubie, L. S. (1954), The fundamental nature of the distinction between normality and neurosis. *Psychoanal. Quart.*, 23:167–204.

Luborsky, L. (1962), Clinicians' judgments of mental health: A proposed scale. *Arch. Gen. Psychiat.*, 7:407–417.

———— Bachrach, H. (1974), Factors influencing clinicians' judgments of mental health. *Arch. Gen. Psychiat.*, 31:292–299.

Offer, D., & Sabshin, M. (1966), *Normality: Theoretical and Clinical Concepts of Mental Health*. New York: Basic Books.

*———— ———— eds. (1984), *Normality and the Life Cycle: A Critical Integration*. New York: Basic Books.

Phillips, L. (1968), *Human Adaptation and Its ·Failures*. New York: Academic Press.

*Smith, M. B. (1950), Optima of mental health: A general frame of reference. *Psychiatry*, 13:503–513.

Vaillant, G. E. (1974), Natural history of male psychological health: II. Some antecedents of healthy adult adjustment. *Arch. Gen. Psychiat.*, 31:15–22.

*———— (1977), *Adaptation to Life*. Boston: Little, Brown.

———— (1978), Natural history of male mental health: VI. Correlates of successful marriage and fatherhood. *Amer. J. Psychiat.*, 135:653–699.

———— Milofsky, E. (1980), Natural history of male psychological health: IX. Empirical evidence for Erikson's model of the life cycle. *Amer. J. Psychiat.*, 137:1348–1359.

Werner, E. E. (1989), Children of the garden island. *Scient. Amer.*, 260: 106–111.

10

A Second Homeostatic Level: Fight–Flight; The Neuroses

Introduction

Overview

As developed in chapter 7, many clinical syndromes encountered in psychiatry display the peculiar property of a stubborn autonomy and momentum which suggests that they operate as a dynamic equilibrium or homeostatic style with their own perpetuating mechanisms. The dislodging of these perpetuating mechanisms, and the return of homeostasis to a more normal level, are the tasks of much psychiatric treatment. Only a small series of major homeostatic styles are found empirically, though they embrace a large collection of clinical syndromes: psychiatric normality, fight–flight, conservation–withdrawal, disintegration, and death appear to have some lawful, sequential, or hierarchical relationship. Such a hierarchy is suggested both by some models of response to stress and by the natural history of psychiatric illness.

315

In this chapter we confront syndromes, the neuroses, organized or polarized around fight–flight psychobiology. I have adopted a rather traditional psychiatric approach to their classification, though the approach is also reasonably mirrored in taxonomies offered by behavior therapists and theorists. The neuroses either show quite frank fight–flight, in steady states (generalized anxiety disorders) or episodically (phobic and panic disorders); or they succeed partially or even wholly in staving off fight–flight psychobiology by pathological homeostatic mechanisms tending to cause bizarre symptomatology (obsessive–compulsive disorder, somatization and dissociation disorders, and paranoid disorder).

For the clinical, conceptual, and therapeutic aspects of these syndromes we are dependent on two somewhat mutually isolated or competing theoretical traditions, the psychodynamic and the behavioral. Both have shortcomings, and both have strengths; but they are barely "meshing" at the present time. The psychodynamic tradition or "camp" has been accused of nosologic and investigative slovenliness, and scorned or mourned as scientifically dying or dead. It is probably true that theoreticians of this more senior discipline suffer a complacency which blocks them from learning from other contemporary models (Bowlby is a notable exception to this malaise). Complacency, however, is not a monopoly of the psychodynamic camp: behaviorists too fail to study and learn psychodynamics. In defense of the psychodynamic tradition, however, it must be pointed out that it has accepted responsibility for treating and studying the ill and distressed, usually as persons rather than as syndromes, together with all the difficult, irreducible clusterings of whole-person homeostasis and the massive influences of the therapist–patient system.

The behaviorists, as more recent arrivals on the scene, have contributed a healthy corrective in a generally critical and objective stance, and a specification of syndromes and of the techniques used in attacking them. In doing so they have, deliberately or otherwise, made crucial exclusions, or denials of important variables. For example, they tend to treat well-organized and work-motivated people, and exclude the regressed, disorganized, and poorly motivated from treatment and study.

In doing so, they appear purposefully to neglect major pathogenic and therapeutic variables in the general organization of the patient (i.e., psychodynamics) and in the powerful influences embodied in the global treatment situation (especially the therapist–patient system).

Brief incursions into fight–flight are part of normal living for all creatures. For humans particularly, the more protracted and autonomous states which we call neuroses appear to be a maladaptive shift into a constant fight–flight condition, or to be complications and defensive and restitutive struggles against the distress of fight–flight: all these states share a common preoccupation with danger. Research has so far not made clear the relationship between acute fight–flight and these more persistent conditions. We do not know for certain whether a mood state obeys the same rules as an acute emotion. Is anxiety wholly equivalent to fear, or hostility to anger? Probably the correspondence is only partial; for example the cognitive appraisals which cause normal emotions probably follow in many instances from mood states rather than cause them. The analysis of the various components of the emotions, and of the broader homeostatic patterns involved in the neuroses and psychoses, should be important here. Most authors emphasize that there are somewhat independent components—the subjective, the cognitive, the behavioral, the physiological—which do not necessarily coexist consistently. Components such as the "defense mechanisms" certainly deserve further study. They are narrowed in repertoire in the neuroses, as befits preoccupation with danger and survival, and they both attempt to diminish distress or physiological arousal, and tend to produce irrational symptoms.

Cannon's seminal discoveries and concepts will be our main starting point. Cannon (1915) brought together a number of physiological changes which he and others had observed, and showed that these are all provoked by strong emotion, acute stress, sympathetic stimulation, or adrenalin infusion; and that, when viewed together, the whole pattern is a preparation for emergency action in doing effective battle or making swift escape, even a preparation for being wounded. Cannon reorganized current views of the autonomic nervous system and the nature of the sympathico-adrenomedullary system in particular. He did not himself coin the term *fight–flight*, which was somewhat later used by Engel (1962a,b) in a broader, clinically applicable context. Engel, collaborating later with Schmale (Schmale and Engel, 1975), added the construct of conservation–withdrawal as a second type of response to stress. (We shall attend to conservation–withdrawal in chapter 12.)

A particularly interesting animal model for emergency and stress has been constructed by Ratner (1967). This consists of the sequence of events occurring when prey interacts with predator: from tense watchfulness, to active flight, to struggle if captured or cornered, to atonic disengagement if struggle is unsuccessful. This model of an acute situation mirrors much that Cannon outlined. For more continuing stress, the model outlined by Selye (1980, 1982) as the general adaptation syndrome appears relevant: this portrays a period of acute response to stress, a period of active adaptation, and a period of fatigue, depletion, and death. It may be that this model best portrays the events of the neuroses. For humans, whose world is relatively free of predators and natural disasters, stress and danger are chiefly represented in interpersonal adaptation, conflict, and separation. Because of this, and our unique cognitive and communicational endowment, neurosis may be a rather uniquely human problem.

Research on anxiety and on hostility are rather separated in the literature. The former has tended to be the focus of study by clinicians and clinical researchers; the later has been the concern of social psychologists and those interested in human conflict, crime, and war. However, this has led to some divorce between what are essentially reciprocal emotions or moods in the fight–flight state. In the light of this reciprocity I make a tentative proposal to include "hostility neurosis" as well as "anxiety neurosis" in our nosological schemata.

After a survey of conceptual models I proceed to brief behavioral definitions of the syndromes related to fight–flight, or the neuroses. It seems appropriate to include paranoid disorder ("true paranoia," not paranoid schizophrenia) with its quintessential mood state of suspicion and its wholehearted orientation to outward dangers. The method of dissecting emotions, mood states, and homeostatic styles into their components is illustrated in the puzzling syndrome of agitated depression.

This then leads us on to examining biological aspects of the fight–flight syndromes. Research has, unfortunately, not given us here the certainties we hope for. The neuroses, particularly generalized anxiety disorder and panic disorder, are clearly familial, and a genetic basis for them has by no means been excluded. After some definitions of systems of neurotransmission, we move on to systems within the brain which are implicated in anxiety and panic disorders, then to more peripheral systems and events. The sympathico-adrenomedullary system is a rapid-acting and short-range emergency system. It interacts indirectly with the hypothalamic–pituitary–endocrine system, which comes into action more slowly but has more long-lasting operations. Although it would be hoped that events in this latter system might explain some of the autonomy and momentum of the neuroses, research findings so far are inconsistent and in some cases paradoxical.

A section is devoted to psychosocial components, starting again with questions of familial and societal variables in the neuroses. We are apparently in need of a new surge of naturalistic and observational study if we are to achieve advances in understanding these conditions. I review briefly some psychological and psychodynamic aspects of the neuroses, in the form of a taxonomy with treatment implications.

Finally, a section on treatment strategies commences with a review of the placebo phenomenon and its participation in treatment and the trial of new drugs. Again, I take up the "components" approach, in a brief look at biological and psychosocial treatment strategies for the neuroses; a critique of anxiolytic drug therapy, and drug therapy in panic disorders and obsessive–compulsive disorder. In the psychosocial area, two aspects of the psychotherapies are critically reviewed: the relatively new "brief psychotherapies," psychodynamically derived; and a schema of classification for behavioral treatment of the neuroses.

The Nature of Fight–Flight

Definitions and Problems

Fight–flight was, in its origin, a physiological or biological construct; Engel (1962a,b) has applied it as a basis for understanding clinical whole-person phenomena, thus including psychosocial dimensions. As was done in chapter 7, I shall here tease it into components. The psychosocial components include the cognitive, the appraisal of threat, danger, apprehension, and survival; defense mechanisms narrowed in range to those consonant with a state of emergency; the subjective aspects of the emotions of anger (hostility) and fear (anxiety), both reciprocal with each other and with the cognitions which give them meaning. I shall not attempt to separate the social from the psychological components. The biological components include the cluster of physiological responses as described by Cannon, and also those more recently discovered systems and events in the brain, pituitary–endocrine axis, and adrenal medulla and cortex.

Fight–flight is a more global construct than are emotion and mood, but these latter are important barometers of homeostatic style and level. Normal or adaptive fight–flight includes two alternative or reciprocal emotions, anger and fear. Its pathological, autonomous analog, in the neuroses, includes two mood states, hostility and anxiety. Fear is the emotion generated by the cognitive appraisal: "Danger, an adversary larger and more powerful than I." Fear motivates flight. The paradigmatic danger for animals is the presence and activity of a potential predator (Ratner, 1967); for humans, interpersonal threats (e.g., of separation and menace to one's personal integrity) are effective. Anger is the emotion generated by the cognitive appraisal, "My way is blocked by an adversary with whom I can successfully grapple." For animals, territorial quarrels may be the paradigm, except in the important instance of being cornered by a superior adversary, when fight gives some chance of survival. For humans, a convincing case for the frustration–aggression relationship was made long ago (Dollard,

Miller, Doob, Mowrer, and Sears, 1939): Humans become hostile when they feel thwarted by others.

Research has not made clear the relationship between emotions and mood changes, particularly pathological moods (see chapter 7). It appears likely that the same rules do not prevail for both; for example, for moods it is more likely that the mood generates the cognitions (in the case of fight–flight mood states, cognitions of being menaced or thwarted), and that subsidence of the mood state will see disappearance of the corresponding cognitions: a point of some importance in therapy. Mood states appear to be maintained by circular or feedback mechanisms, including cognitions, which it is the aim of treatment to undo. Research, unfortunately, while it has elucidated much in the physiology of emotions, has not done as well in the case of mood states; this despite 30 years of investigation of depressions and anxiety disorders. Further, research on fear and anxiety, much of it clinically oriented, has been rather divorced from research on anger and aggression, the province mainly of social psychologists, though see also a clinician such as Storr (1968), and a pharmacologist such as Valzelli (1981); undoubtedly cross-fertilization between these fields would be helpful. Theorizing on human aggression and war is obviously important; I fail to be convinced that psychobiological explanations and remedies are valid here, where a resort to social and political analysis appears more explanatory.

Cannon's Delineation of Fight–Flight

Cannon's classic, *Bodily Changes in Pain, Hunger, Fear, and Rage*, was published in 1915 and went through several reprintings; a second edition appeared in 1929 in which five chapters were added but the original chapters little changed (Cannon, 1915). Cannon's heuristic synthesis, based on the work of predecessors and colleagues, as well as his own discoveries, might be presented under three main headings:

Divisions of the Autonomic Nervous System and Their Functions. The "visceral nerves" involved in the expression of emotion, and the regulation of the *milieu intérieur*, fall into three divisions. All three are outflows from the central nervous system (CNS), but, unlike the somatic nerves, which regulate relations with the *milieu extérieur*, they synapse in ganglia *outside* the central nervous system before appropriately innervating various organs to the slower actions required of viscera compared to skeletal muscles. A cranial division, emerging anterior to the somatic nerves for the fore limbs, innervates viscera of the upper body, and appears to be responsible for "bodily conservation," intake of nourishment, and the circulatory system's resting activity. Between the somatic nerves for the fore and hind limbs, a thoraco-lumbar outflow with its chain of ganglia ("sympathetic" in the older terminology, according to Cannon) deals with emergency functions as we shall note below. Posteriorly to the somatic nerves for the hind limbs is the sacral outflow, innervating the pelvic organs and subserving various "emptying" functions including the sexual response (i.e., erection; it was recognized that the sympathetic innervates orgasm). The effects of infusing *adrenin* (Cannon's preferred term for *epinephrine* or *adrenalin*, which was a proprietary name then), stimulating the sympathetic chain, and stimulating the nerves to the adrenal medulla, were all found to be essentially the same. In fact, the adrenal medulla was found to be much like a sympathetic ganglion, as fibers came directly to it from the CNS without synapsing, and it contains nerve cells and synapses as well as secretory cells (see pp. 351–352).

Cannon's experiments were with the strong or emergency emotions, fear and rage; and with analogous stressors such as pain and asphyxia, all of which produced effects similar to infusion of adrenalin, or sympathetic or adrenal stimulation. Basically, Cannon found that what we now call the parasympathetic system (the cranial and sacral outflows) was antagonistic to the sympathetic, i.e., produced opposite states in an organ whenever the two systems were in interaction.

Strong Emotions and Sympathetic and Adrenalin Effects. A group of effects was found regularly to follow fear, rage, pain, asphyxia, sympathetic or adrenal stimulation, or adrenalin injection, effects whose adaptive significance Cannon pondered and formulated: increase in the blood sugar level, from the liver's breaking down of glycogen; improved contraction of muscles, including fatigued muscle, due both to improved blood oxygen and glucose supply and increased scavenging of metabolic products; a rise in systolic blood pressure, dilation of the arteries supplying muscles, and an increase of blood supply to the "Tripod of Life," the brain, heart, and lungs, at the expense of the supply to other viscera; a general counteraction to fatigue; a hastening of blood coagulation time; and (in the 1929 edition) an increase in circulating red blood cells. Ingenious experiments were devised to extrapolate the validity of these findings. These included painless simulation of pain in anesthetized animals, and noninvasive tests of athletes before and after their gladiatorial endeavors.

Strong Emotions and Their Interrelations. Fear, rage, and their analogs pain and asphyxia were found to have essentially identical physiological expressions, which in turn were the opposite of the effects of parasympathetic stimulation. Cannon therefore reasoned that the adaptive significance of these expressions was that "visceral change[s] . . . by way of sympathetic neurones [are] organic preparations for action . . . likely to result in flight or conflict . . . utmost struggle . . . [and they are] precisely the same" for fear, rage, pain, and asphyxia (p. 275). Despite the importance of visceral responses in strong emotion, Cannon in his 1929 edition was critical of the James-Lange theory that the perception of a more or less specific cluster of visceral sensations *is* emotion: he adduced as evidence that (1) emotions occur even when the nerves to the viscera had been cut; (2) internal viscera are in any case very insensitive; and (3) induction of changes in viscera does not generate emotion. He suggested from evidence available in 1929 that a subcortical center in the brain, probably the thalamus, accounted for the feeling tones and the involuntary nature of emotional expression, thus paving the way for Papez (1937) and MacLean (1952) and the delineation of the limbic system (see chapter 8). Marks (1987) finds that Cannon's critique of the James-Lange theory remains valid, though studies of patients with spinal cord injuries have found that subjective emotion is diminished in proportion to the severity of the lesion.

Cannon laid down the fundamental proposition that the organism under acute stress mobilizes for its survival by sympathico-adrenergic activity such as will enable it to exert maximum effort in either successful escape or physical combat, the steps 2 and 3 of Ratner's model, presented below.

Animal Models and Analogs

The Nature of Animal Models

I have referred in chapter 7 to conceptual models of a sequence of animal responses in the face of stress (Selye, 1980, 1982) and predation (Ratner, 1967). Here I wish to examine working models which are used to test in a more empirical way the nature and mechanisms of homeostatic responses and the syndromes of psychiatry. Porsolt (1985) gives an excellent review (which I follow) of the rationale and limitations of such animal models; Hanin and Usdin (1977) may also be consulted. Why are animal working models necessary or desirable? They permit rigorous investigation of mechanisms such as would be impossible or unethical to test in human subjects, including invasive and ablative approaches and even the death of the subject; even here ethical constraints apply, for in research in fight–flight and conservation–withdrawal (depression) it is necessary to stress the animal and make it miserable or even cause its death. As contrasted with humans, small animals operate on a time scale of genetics and life cycle which can be followed conveniently. Animal models and experiments generate new ideas (i.e., are heuristic) and give impetus to rethinking the human condition and hypotheses for investigating it. Trials with animals are the only justifiable route for trying out possible new treatment modalities.

But, models in general and animal working models in particular are by their very nature oversimplifications. They are never the "real thing" (McKinney and Bunney, 1969; McKinney, 1977); they cannot replicate such human dynamics as thinking, cognitive evaluation, and thought content and mental mechanisms in fear, anger, guilt, pessimism, flight of ideas, or grandiosity. We can never be sure, since we cannot ask them, how differentiated the emotional states are which animals are experiencing, and whether these are thus a reasonable replica of human experiences. On the other hand, the artificial and contrived conditions of many *human* experiments are hardly likely to evoke the kind of "strong emotions" we need to study (Carthy and Ebling, 1964). Therefore, as simplifications (McKinney and Bunney, 1969; McKinney, 1977) animal models are valid if:

1. The inducing conditions are similar to what induces the state under study in humans;
2. The animal under these conditions displays a behavioral state similar to that seen in humans;
3. The state involves physiological responses similar to those found in humans; and
4. The state responds to treatment measures as does the corresponding human one.

It appears then, that the more a human clinical syndrome contains important psychosocial components, the less reliable and valid will animal working models be in elucidating it. It may be possible to replicate behavioral states quite well in animals; it may even be possible to produce something much like an ongoing anxiety or depressive disorder in social animals such as dogs, who can signal nonverbally something of their intentions; it is far less possible to replicate reliably a paranoid or schizophrenic state in even an intelligent primate, who can communicate none of the ideational content so important in these conditions. With this stringent warning, let us proceed further with animal models and analogs.

Ratner's Generalized or Conceptual Model

Ratner's conceptual model based on the steps in response to presence of a predator (Ratner, 1967) has been previously outlined in chapter 7. The animal's response is a function of the "defensive distance" (psychological, i.e., cognitive, rather than

metric) between itself and a "threatening or predatory stimulus" (which includes stimuli such as approach and handling by
an experimenter).

1. The defensive distance is large. The stimulus may be a
    moving predator which has attracted the subject's atten-
    tion. *Response*: Subject freezes (i.e., becomes immobile
    but alert and tonic, and, by our model, goes into prepa-
    ratory fight–flight).
2. Defensive distance is closing. The stimulus is ap-
    proaching. *Response*: Subject moves away (quietly or en-
    ergetically, in the flight component of fight–flight).
3. Defensive distance closes to zero. The stimulus is at
    hand, cannot be escaped, subject is captured or cor-
    nered. *Response*: Subject struggles or fights (fight–flight,
    fight component).
4. Defensive distance continues at zero. Subject is pinned
    down or held. *Response*: Subject becomes immobile, un-
    responsive, atonic (conservation–withdrawal; to be dealt
    with further in chapter 12).

Ratner summarizes: The presence of some unfamiliar
threatening stimulus condition leads invariably, across a vast
range of animals studied, from freezing, to fleeing, to fighting,
then to immobility and unresponsiveness. Novelty or unfamil-
iarity with the stimulus cognitive component is crucial; its eliciting value is reduced upon repetition of the experience. Restraint is also a crucial initiating variable. Heightened
autonomic activity and a flattened electroencephalogram are a
typical component of the response to restraint by an unfamiliar
agent.

   This conceptual model is highly congruent with the alarm
phase of Selye's (1980, 1982) stress sequence; in fact, immobilization has been the single most successful method of producing
the stress sequence in animals, and animals will die very quickly
if kept immobilized. It is highly compatible also with Cannon's
physiological conceptions. For humans, as noted previously, the
picture of predation and immobilization is replaced by the
stress of interpersonal and intrapsychic conflict and the terrible

immobilization and helplessness which may ensue. Conflict may result not only in fight–flight psychophysiology and syndromes with a fight–flight basis (e.g., peptic ulcer) but in severe, acute instances in sudden death with cardiac diastole or ventricular fibrillation (Engel, 1980; Lown, DeSilva, Reich, and Murawski, 1980).

Animal Models for Hostility and for Aggression: Valzelli

There is a huge literature on human aggression, much of it based upon animal models; there is likewise a huge literature on anxiety, but the two do not, on the whole, interact. I refer the reader to the classic on aggression by Dollard and colleagues (1939), and to a more recent synthesis of many theses and researchers, mostly animal-based, by Valzelli (1981) whose small volume, with its lengthy reference list and ingenious drawings by the author himself, spans the gamut of evolutionary, neuroscientific, and psychosocial issues on aggression. Valzelli notes the continuum from constructive aggression to its destructive and socially disruptive forms ("violence"). The neuroanatomical and neurophysiological substrates which he elucidates so clearly (especially in his drawings) are principally based on animal models, thus rather removed from the human condition. Valzelli depicts seven types of aggression as represented in the literature.

1. *Predatory*: Dependent on both hunger and the presence of prey (of other species, i.e., interspecific) and in turn divided into the two behavioral patterns of killing and feeding.
2. *Competitive*; Characteristically male, and occurring within a species (intraspecific); related to dominance relationships, and controlled in natural settings by the establishment of stable, clear dominance hierarchies.
3. *Defensive*: Specifically related to fear as a motivant, to self-preservation as a goal; this type comes closest to our fight–flight paradigm.
4. *Irritative*: A less aimful, self-preservative form, this type has to do with frustration, and comes second closest to our paradigm.

5. *Territorial*: Related to competition over and defending of territories for feeding and breeding, and controlled in natural settings by clear definition of territories and boundaries.
6. *Maternal Protective*: The aggression shown characteristically by lactating mothers of some species who will show enormous courage in beating off intruders and potential predators.
7. *Female Social Aggression*: A rather specialized form, shown by species such as rabbits.

Valzelli's conclusions for the human condition are less related to clinical syndromes than to crime and war. He views the inherited machinery of aggression as wholly subcortical (i.e., in the paleomammalian or limbic brain) and requiring various sophisticated and quasi-therapeutic means of control, since the propensities are inborn; I read Valzelli as taking the position that destructive aggression (violence) is elicited by unbearable frustration, and probably in most human cases by social and parental deprivation as the original predisposing circumstances. He also allows for pathological cases of spontaneous and "meaningless" violence, as in schizophrenia and temporal lobe epilepsy.

Hamburg and Trudeau (1981) have edited a compendium of American origins, also biobehaviorally oriented; a chapter on our near evolutionary relatives, the chimpanzees, by Trudeau, Bergmann-Riss, and Hamburg (1981) provides suggestions on the evolutionary and genetic basis of our behavioral patterns. Those recognizable from Valzelli's classification include aggression from frustration, struggles for hierarchical dominance, territorial patrolling and fights, and differences in aggression patterns between the sexes.

Valzelli's very thoughtful and socially concerned theses might be regarded as a paradigm for the biobehavioral approach to human aggression, violence, crime, and war. This author is an expert in behavioral biology, well aware of the contributions of other experts. He is able to think in integrative dimensions: his ultimate concern, as with other concerned scientists today, is with the global devastation of nuclear holocaust.

He extracts meanings and explanations carefully, and he proposes remedial and preventive measures. Nonetheless, this type of approach poses certain difficulties of a reductionist kind.

Biobehavioral approaches fail to take into account the social level of emergence, particularly significant for the human species. An adequate explanation for violence and crime within societies, and for war between societies, together with their control and prevention, requires that we take into account complex social phenomena: the problems of poverty, hunger, social stratification, and economic exploitation within societies (analogous to intraspecific relations); and the problems of ideological paranoia and competition and of economic conquest between societies (analogous to interspecific relations, for political enemies usually describe their adversaries as nonhuman or infrahuman). Even as regards the individual, biobehavioral approaches fail to attend to the complexities of human development and learning, the effects on personality of child rearing, trauma, and social and political attitudes. From the biobehavioral perspective, wars are seen as planned and executed by angry and destructively excited men (I use the masculine pronoun deliberately). In fact, they are designed and waged by cool-headed strategists and propagandists, responding to ideological pressures and socioeconomic forces.

The predation model of violence, crime, and war is likewise vulnerable to serious criticism. It is true that man has been a skilled and effective predator and has, in fact, exterminated a number of prey species. Such predation has been motivated chiefly by economic pressures, however; our great hunts were planned coolly and deliberately, with effective social teamwork, and only in the heat of the chase could it be said that fight–flight psychophysiology likely came into play. Animal predators are not motivated by anger or competitive–destructive urges, but by hunger, the need to feed offspring, and a behavioral system for stalking and pursuing prey which is activated by these needs.

We have rubrics in our nosology for anxiety disorders, but not for "hostility disorder" or "hostility neurosis." I have had several patients, as have my colleagues, who required hospitalization for an ongoing state of anger–hostility, who meet the requirement of such a putative diagnosis. No doubt we would find many more in the hands of police, the courts, and the prisons. The following vignette is illustrative.

Mr. S. U., aged 26, was apprehended by the police and admitted to my inpatient service, after smashing in the front door of a young woman who had rejected his advances. We found him to be a self-centered and unhappily married man, the father of one child, intelligent but employed below his capacities, and who had become infatuated with a friend who was younger, prettier, and more personable than his own intelligent but homely wife. This young woman had absolutely no interest in Mr. U.'s romantic advances. For 2 weeks the patient had been building up tension, sleeping increasingly poorly, and harassing the object of his rather adolescent affections. Finally, he exploded on the evening of admission when she shut the door in his face. Mr. U. experienced no identifiable fear, anxiety, or any other mood than boiling anger quite specifically aimed at his "girl friend." Though a perfectly cooperative patient, he was tense and restless during every waking hour, with signs of central nervous system alerting. He was constantly preoccupied with vengeful and even homicidal thoughts toward the young woman. He remitted only slowly over 4 weeks, on a regimen of sedative and antipsychotic drugs, ventilatory and supportive psychotherapy, and tension-discharging and relaxant occupational and physical therapy. This case, and others I have discussed with colleagues (we have found no publications on the subject), confirm Valzelli's statement that there is no one drug which selectively controls hostility and violence: judicious combinations of stimulants, sedatives, antipsychotics, and antiandrogens appear to have helped in individual cases (Valzelli, 1981). This may be one piece of indirect evidence that the physiology of hostility differs from that of anxiety, where sedatives such as the benzodiazapines are almost specific in treatment. My colleagues and I usually prescribe methotrimeprazine as the drug of first resort in states of hostility.

Animal Models for Fear and the Anxiety Disorders: The Work of Marks

Half of Marks's encyclopedic monograph is taken up with an outline of basic science research relating to fear and avoidance

(Marks, 1987). Marks builds up from the lowest invertebrates, with their primitive avoidance responses and their sparse nervous systems, which can be elegantly studied in their simplicity and with the large size of the neurons involved. The lowest animals show responses to threat which parallel those of vertebrates up to the mammals and primates: avoidance, tactical flight strategies, including "erratic flight" such as shown by rabbits or antelopes, and distraction devices such as camouflage and deflection. It can be shown that in these simplest creatures the synapse is the locus for learning or modification of behaviors: sensitization, habituation, and conditioning all operate through modification of the synapse. In higher animals the nervous system becomes so large and complex, particularly in primates and humans, that no simple or clear mapping of the central nervous system and its functioning in fear and danger is possible, and, as we shall note below, animal models for the neuroses are less than satisfactory.

Marks (1987, p. 5) defines *fear* as the unpleasant feeling in response to realistic danger; *anxiety* as a similar emotion but without any objective danger; *phobia* as fear of a situation out of proportion to its danger, illogical and beyond voluntary control; *phobic anxiety* as the subjective emotional component of a phobia; and *panic* as a sudden upsurge of acute intense fear. He distinguishes between *trait anxiety* or *timidity*, the lasting tendency to show fearful behavior, and *state anxiety*, anxiety felt at a particular moment. Following a long tradition (see Mineka [1985]; and my previous and future comments on components in homeostatic styles) Marks divides fear into three component processes: the subjective–cognitive, the motor–behavioral, and the physiological. Many instances of human adaptive behavior and psychiatric disorder show a dissociation of these components (a kind of dècalage); that is, one or two without the presence of all three together. An interesting sidelight is Marks's conjecture that the fear of strangers, as exhibited normally by children of 8 to 24 months of age, is an evolutionary relic of a safeguard against infanticide by human males from outside the family grouping, a behavioral pattern seen in social animals such as lions and some primates, including great apes. This is to be compared with Bowlby's (see chapter 5) position that fear of the dark and loud noises, in fact separation behaviors generally, are evolutionarily a safeguard against animal predators, particularly the leopard.

Marks reviews a number of typical fear-evoking stimuli cutting across species; for example, the presentation of a hawk or even a hawklike silhouette or shadow, or a snake or snakelike object. Fear of heights can be demonstrated in human and animal infants at a very young age, using the "visual cliff." Fears of too open or too closed spaces, and of too much or too little light, and the widespread fear of snakelike objects and of staring eyes (chickens will enter tonic immobility with this latter stimulus) may well represent, Marks believes, an innate basis for human phobias.

Marks assigns fear behaviors to four categories: withdrawal (avoidance), immobility, threat, and deflection of attack. Withdrawal or avoidance represents the flight component in fight–flight, and threat the fight component. Marks appears to include emotions other than fear in the withdrawal or avoidance response; for example, distaste or disgust for repellent objects. He also includes emotions apparently other than fear in the threat response; for example, maternal aggression in defense of young, an attribution which appears somewhat subjective or anthropomorphizing. Deflection of attack includes responses such as camouflage and erratic flight. There are some real problems of terminology in the immobility category. Marks includes one pattern of "attentive immobility" which is clearly synonymous with Ratner's "freezing"; its physiology is reported to be tensional and alerting, with sympathico-adrenegic stimulation. The other principal pattern is "tonic immobility," corresponding with Ratner's step 4 of unresponsive, atonic, disengaged immobility; the physiologic shift here is to an absence of motor reactivity; to a bizarre posture, with waxy flexibility; and to paradoxical autonomic responses in which vagal action appears to predominate, with slowing of heart rate, cooling of skin, and death in diastole in extreme cases (Engel, 1980; Lown, De Silva, Reich, and Murawski, 1980). There are indeed problems of nomenclature; tonic immobility under its various synonyms, including "death feigning" will be discussed further under conservation–withdrawal in chapter 12.

Marks gives us a graphic and entertaining section, in conclusion, on the behaviors of large prey and predator animals on the East African plains.

"Minimodels" for the Anxiety Disorders: The Work of Mineka

Mineka's highly technical chapter (1985) is the most comprehensive that I have located on the subject of animal models for the clinical disorders of the fight–flight level; her theses are reviewed by Marks (1987). Mineka, as does Marks, warns us that there are no complete and satisfactory animal models, and she reviews concepts and problems associated with the models as even more important than concrete models per se. Her review is divided into analogs for the phobic disorders, for the obsessive–compulsive disorders, and for the generalized anxiety disorders, in descending order of reliability in matching animal models with human clinical conditions. While no completely satisfactory animal models mimic the human disorders, both Mineka and Marks approve of the collection of minimodels which are available; these are discrete animal behavior patterns which at least mimic steps and components in the human neuroses, and thus are of interest and heuristic value.

1. *Models for Phobic Disorders.* Mineka reports Seligman's five criteria differentiating experimental animal *fears* and avoidances from human *phobias*: phobias do not extinguish spontaneously, and often become worse with time; if phobias are initiated by trauma, this is often a one-trial initiation, whereas animal fears have to be learned over several trials; in human phobias, there is a curiously long latent period between trauma and onset of phobia; there is a highly finite class of objects for human phobias, whereas animals can be conditioned to fear almost any situation or object; conditioned fears in humans can be "talked away" successfully, whereas phobias which are irrational cannot be so treated. Classical conditioning, Mineka notes, was at first accepted as the explanation for animal fears and human phobias. Later, objections to this explanation were produced, and the newer explanation of "anxiety avoidance" supplanted it: in this explanation, the successful avoidance of a feared situation becomes in itself a reward and reinforcer of avoidance behaviors. More recently, intricate versions

of classical conditioning have returned to favor. Probably, Mineka believes, an interactive model involving a number of variables from these two explanations will be most likely to succeed in explaining human clinical problems.

A specific minimodel was reported from Mineka's own laboratory. Rhesus monkeys are known to be very frightened of snakes, even toy ones. One investigation established that monkeys who had grown up in the wild, some 20 years previously, quickly taught their laboratory-raised offspring (who were at first quite unconcerned about snakes) to become avoidant and disturbed in the presence of snakes, apparently through the processes of modeling and social observation. However, human phobias are not commonly acquired by social observation, though fears are (Marks, 1987, p. 243), and human phobias are quite difficult to produce experimentally. In another series of experiments, Tuma placed monkeys already afraid of snakes into close and steady proximity with a snake (exposure, flooding); after only a few trials, the monkeys came to reach over the snake for food, and behaviorally had overcome their fear. Nonetheless, although this behavioral component remained stable, physiological measures indicated a persisting disturbance in the presence of snakes. The results of these two sets of experiments were considered to be a reasonable model for human phobias.

2. *Models for Obsessive–Compulsive Disorders*. The gap between the complex human disorders and animal models now becomes even wider. The "avoidance model" (behavior being rewarded and perpetuated by the anxiety-reducing effect it produces) seems to be more germane here, and interruption or punishment of the disordered behaviors seems to be a more effective therapeutic component. There are several intriguing minimodels. Mineka cites work in which it was found that dogs, who have developed avoidance behaviors in an aversive situation, will show increasingly stereotyped versions of these avoidance behaviors with decreasing evidence of fear, until the behaviors appear meaningless though stereotypically driven. Rats too, who have been given the opportunity of jumping off a platform in a setting of insoluable problem presentation, continue to do this in a stereotyped way even when the problem

becomes a soluble one. Primates under continued stress begin to show "stereotypy" and "ritualistic" patterns of a locomotor kind, or sit picking their teeth or strumming on the mesh of their cage for long periods. Or, under conditions of high arousal, a number of animals exhibit "displacement" sequences, such as grooming or nesting, particularly when a conflict between drives is present; Mineka queries whether these are analogs of human tidying or washing rituals.

3. *Models for Generalized Anxiety Disorder*. Mineka notes that a general "experimental neurosis" with restlessness, autonomic overactivity, and impairment of learning was reported by Pavlov and many others, when experimental animals were stressed by insoluble discrimination problems or uncontrollable aversive stimulation; unfortunately this disorder has not been studied in its own right in a controlled manner. However, there is now a renewed interest in this syndrome as possibly the best approximation to human generalized anxiety disorder. Marks (1987) reports an experience of Pavlov with experimental dogs who were nearly drowned in a laboratory accident. Maladaptive or neurotic patterns, which had been thought to have been extinguished over time, reappeared following this trauma. Marks also points out that rather specific fear–avoidance responses learned by animals will become diffuse over time, until the animal remains generally fearful or timid, and it can no longer be discerned specifically what it fears.

Many workers have been impressed with the universality of separation (of infant animals from parents, or of peers from peers) as a model for anxiety states in animals (see Bowlby in chapter 5; Scott and Senay, 1973; McKinney 1977; Howard and Pollard, 1977). The problem with this model is its relatively short-lived course: the anxiety state either subsides, if the separation is ended, or tends to go on into the very different pattern of "despair" (i.e., conservation–withdrawal), rather than into a continuing anxiety state.

In general, it appears that something like human generalized anxiety disorder can be produced in animals by a variety of conditions which are novel, ambiguous, unpredictable, and beyond the animal's ability to solve or control. Uncontrolled, random, and inescapable punishment can over time produce a continuing "experimental neurosis," or condition of "learned helplessness" (see animal models for depression in chapter 12 below); simultaneous rewarding and aversive stimulation (e.g. food accompanied by irregular electric shocks) has much the same effect (Howard and Pollard, 1977). Mineka is inclined to conclude that this common factor of situations which are beyond the animal's control is the important variable; and that therapies (both pharmacotherapies and psychotherapies) for anxiety disorders operate by restoring a sense of mastery and control.

A curious and "unusually reliable stressor" for rats was discovered a few years ago, in the "tail pinch" (Antelman and Caggiula, 1977). Though the procedure at first sounds gruesome, pain is apparently not involved: a pressure cuff is inflated around the rat's tail, and rather promptly the animal becomes alerted, active, showing pervasive effects such as produced by administration of amphetamine, including precocious estrus and copulation. This state is rather a far cry from human anxiety disorders, but has been used consistently as a model in testing of sedative and anxiolytic drugs. The mediating mechanisms are found to be dopaminergic, interacting with the locus ceruleus; activating of serotonergic systems allays the stress response.

Human Clinical Syndromes at the Fight–Flight Level

Syndromes as Constellations of Components

Syndromes are consistently associated clusters of symptoms and signs, which are discerned, described, and entered into a nosological classification according to current views and convictions (models) and the availability and success of therapeutic measures. Syndromes contain components also which are revealed by research, and which can be classified at biological, psychological, and social levels of emergence. Marks (1987), for example, and following a long-standing tradition, separates fear into subjective–cognitive, motor–behavioral, and physiological components, which do not necessarily all coexist in a given case. Powles

(1980, 1982) drew attention to the nature of "pure" or "saturated" syndromes as having a full complement of components, while less typical syndromes have to be approached as to how closely they fit the templates for typical ones (see Figure 12.1 in chapter 12). Most clinicians would agree that for every patient with a typical syndrome we treat, there must be half a dozen who are "atypical" and not clear-cut. These we treat by clinical logic and common sense and by attacking the components or "target symptoms" which we discern. Using a superordinate category such as fight–flight or conservation–withdrawal may help us when the syndrome is highly atypical.

An example of such an "atypical" or "borderline" syndrome, to which I return repeatedly, is so-called agitated depression. Analysis of its components shows that its cognitive–subjective component is depressive (i.e., characteristic of conservation–withdrawal) with pained giving-up, helplessness, hopelessness, and attacks upon the self. Its motor-behavioral component is tensional (characteristic of fight–flight) with restlessness, stereotyped hyperactivity, and agitation. Its physiology is quite ambiguous, and clinicians empirically treat it with a mixture of sedative, antidepressant, and even antipsychotic measures (particularly if it contains a component of psychosis or disintegration). Also, one perpetuating mechanism in this syndrome may be social attention and reward, which we may have to interrupt by management deficient in sympathy.

The principal grouping of syndromes for which research is reviewed in this chapter is that of the *neuroses*, a term which I retain as a short-hand label, though its meaning has become rather battered (Knoff, 1970). Knoff's paper pays particular tribute to the Scottish physician-teacher William Cullen who coined the term "neurosis" in mid-eighteenth century. The fashion then was to attempt to classify diseases in the mode of Linnaeus. Thus, the "neuroses" were conceived of as a major Linnaean "class" of disorders not attributable to affection of a specific organ, but to generalized disturbance of the nervous system. Within this "class" were placed "genera" which in modern terminology would be called neurological, psychophysiological, psychotic, and neurotic disorders. Knoff proceeds to retrace definitions of mental disorders through Pinel, who coined the concept of "mental alienation" and "moral treatment," since psychosocial variables loomed large in his view. Through the nineteenth century, in turn, a highly medical or disease model held sway. Then, by the turn of the century, the French neurologists and Freud returned to a psychogenic and psychosexual model. Freud divided the neuroses into "actual neuroses" (anxiety neurosis and neurasthenia), with a physiological causation; and "psychoneuroses " (hysteria and obsessive–compulsive neurosis) based on psychological conflict. Meyer coined the term "reaction" to indicate that all mental disorders are a homeostatic response to multiple etiologic factors.

As I use the term *neurosis*, it is intended to indicate psychiatric disorders without major personality disorganization, in which struggles to maintain personal homeostasis (successfully to unsuccessfully) by controlling or avoiding the affects of fear and anger, are the hallmarks. Because paranoia or paranoid disorder exhibits such pure signs of fight–flight homeostasis I include it also.

A Spectrum of Syndromes in the Fight–Flight Mode

Using *The Diagnostic and Statistical Manual of Mental Disorders* (DSM-III-R) (1987) and Marks (1987) as a guide, I offer brief descriptions of the syndromes we are to include.

1. *Generalized Anxiety Disorder (GAD) or Anxiety Neurosis.* An autonomous, ongoing state typified by mildly to severely incapacitating tension and a state of fear, with their corresponding behavioral and physiological patterns, all in the context of a relatively well-organized personality (i.e., major regression is absent). Irritability and hostility often appear against the background mood of anxiety. Repression disguises the sources of intrapsychic conflict, while rationalization provides cognitions of external and internal danger. Posttraumatic stress disorder is an anxiety neurosis uncommon in peacetime; its clear onset following disaster, the presence of a startle reaction, and recurring stereotyped nightmares of the disaster, are pathognomonic.

2. *Agoraphobia with Panic Disorder*. These two patterns coexist so consistently that they appear to constitute one syndrome. Marks (1987) lists the various names given the combined syndrome, going back to Freud's time. Roth (1959) gave an early definitive description and has taken a continuing interest in the syndrome as a paradigm for the neuroses. Six percent of patients in family practice suffer from it (Katon, 1986), thus it may be the commonest neurosis.

Agoraphobia is the fear of entering places of social and commercial activity (agora = marketplace): it may be experienced as a fear of open spaces, or as a fear of being shut in and suffocated (claustrophobia). The cognitive content falls into two components: a fear of collapsing, dying, or going crazy amid uncaring strangers; and, even more significantly, a fear of being separated from a safe home base and/or a key nurturant person, whose presence often allays dread in the "agora." Thus, separation anxiety or attachment behavior is a rather concealed but crucial aspect of the syndrome.

Panic attacks are alarming, apparently spontaneous bursts of fear and dread, with physiological accompaniments of sweating, trembling, palpitation, and shortness of breath. These attacks are so frightening that they become the secondary stimulus for increasing *anticipatory* anxiety or dread.

The sufferer from this combined syndrome may become totally housebound, due to a combination of separation anxiety and anticipatory dread of the alarming panic attacks; their frightening physiological accompaniments threaten loss of control and death.

3. *Social Phobias*. Marks (1987) suggests that these are intermediate between agoraphobia–panic disorder and the very specific, circumscribed phobias. They involve fear and avoidance mechanisms for somewhat more concrete situations, such as being shamed before acquaintances, or of exhibiting specific disgraceful behaviors, or being stared at. These phobias seem to be particularly culturally determined.

Good and Kleinman (1985, pp. 315–317), in a lengthy review of transcultural correlations and definitions of anxiety and anxiety symptomatology, include a discussion of the intriguing Japanese syndrome of shinkeishitsu. Roughly synonymous with the older European construct of neurasthenia, shinkeishitsu includes chronic incapacitating anxiety and hypochondriacal concerns. What interests us here is that its various subtypes include social phobias or phobic behaviors: fear of blushing (erythrophobia), of emitting unpleasant body odor, or of direct eye contact. Such phobic concerns are rare in the west. "Morita therapy" has developed as the therapeutic attack on shinkeishitsu (see also p. 361).

4. *Specific Phobias.* These are unreasoning fears of quite specific animals or inanimate objects including certain textiles, or of clearly circumscribed situations such as heights or thunderstorms; such highly specific stimuli can be avoided in daily life by maneuvers which are not socially disruptive. Sufferers from specific phobias are for the most part rather normal people, and modern treatment can be highly successful.

5. *Obsessive–Compulsive Disorder* (OCD). There are inconsistencies of definition; probably there is a continuum from obsessive–compulsive personality traits (where defense mechanisms successfully maintain normal homeostasis) to severe, distressing, and incapacitating psychiatric disorder of relatively clear onset (where defenses are disorganized and considerable regression occurs). Mavissakalian, Turner, and Michelson (1985a) regard this disorder as "one of the most disabling, crippling, and resistant conditions in psychiatry." This pessimistic view is echoed by Salzman and Thaler (1981) who in an invited review had noted the "sparsity of theories" and "abundant therapeutic approaches," none of which has succeeded consistently, and none more effectively than leucotomy.

Two reciprocal features dominate: obsessions, which are repetitive ideas or urges, usually distressing or disgusting; and compulsions, motor rituals either carrying out the obsessions or attempting to suppress or "undo" them, and which can be as bizarre and unpalatable as the obsessions. The quality of being *forced or driven* ("compulsive") by one's own urges, against one's better judgment, is central; yet neither obsessions nor compulsions relieve or prevent intolerable distress for long (Rachman, 1985; Foa, Steketee, and Ozarow, 1985). Although authors such as Marks (1987) and Rapoport (1989) appear to regard the personality of the sufferer as well preserved, psycho-analytic observers have emphasized very considerable disorga-nization, with regression to the struggles, defense mechanisms, and developmental tasks typical of the period of learning sphincter control and sphincter morality.

6. *Somatization and Dissociation Disorders*. Marks (1987) refers to these only briefly, as outside the reach of behavior therapies; further, they cannot be considered anxiety disorders, since anx-iety may be minimal or actually absent (the phenomenon of *belle indifférence*). They are disturbances of the body image and of the patient's image of the human mind; traditional clinical wisdom was embodied in DSM-1 (1952) in viewing them as dominated by mental mechanisms which allay anxiety by dram-atizing or symbolizing human conflict through dysfunctions of bodily organs or of memory and consciousness. Such traditional wisdom has placed these disorders taxonomically together, as related to the anxiety disorders in an inverse sense, and as dynamically similar to each other. In fact, these relationships have been recognized since the time of Hippocrates (Knoff, 1970) under the label *hysteria*, a term which is today in disfavor, as imprecise, slovenly, pejorative, or even antifeminist. Krohn (1978) has made a serious effort to rehabilitate the construct of hysteria. Shapiro's (1965) brilliant essay on cognitive style in hysteria is instructive. Lishman (1971) offers an attractive hy-pothesis regarding anatomical substrates for psychogenic am-nesia. Lipowski's (1988) review of somatization is definitive.

7. *Paranoid Disorder*. I am speaking here of well-organized people who develop, suddenly or slowly, a logically consistent and unshakable belief in an *external* persecutory agency (e.g., the unfaithfulness of their nearest and dearest, or the conspir-acy of some nebulous but large and powerful organization) on which belief their whole existence and behavior turns. This is *not* the frantic and illogical restitutive attempt of a person in disintegration (i.e., paranoid schizophrenia) nor a long-term personality disorder, though these three patterns tend to be confused with one another. There is more than merely the delusional preoccupation; Shapiro's (1965) evocative study on the paranoid style shows that the subject "lives in readiness for emergency," in a total mobilization narrowly focused upon

hints and clues of danger and disaster personally directed at the subject. There is a constant, elegant, "penetrating," but stenosed and distorted attempt (never optimistic or altruistic) to "understand" what is going on *out there* (correspondingly, a total refusal or failure of introspection). This projective defense, if successful, maintains normal homeostasis in its physiologic aspects. But the subjective and cognitive components are pure examples of fight–flight: the motivational complex of suspicion permits a cold-blooded personal stance, yet one can never predict when a paranoid patient will avoid, or take flight, or explode in aggressive violence, in the manner of a cornered animal.

I have found no convincing research into the psychobiology of paranoid disorder, and will pass on with the above descriptive notes.

Biological Aspects of Fight–Flight Syndromes

Problems and Methods

I follow here the presentations of Pasnau (1984), Weiner (in Tuma and Maser [1985]), and Marks (1987); the latter two are definitive reviews. These three sources agree that there are, unfortunately, more unresolved problems and ambiguities in the biology of the anxiety disorders than there are certainties. Marks (1987) states for example that the "recent surge of biological studies has yielded little of substance; in effect, the findings are either not specific to the conditions being studied, or cannot be clearly distinguished as cause or effect" (p. 351). The following are some of the problems and difficulties:

1. The components of fear and anger do not occur together consistently; that is, the subjective–cognitive, the motor–behavioral, and the physiological. An example given by Weiner involves patients receiving flooding therapy for phobias: despite every outward evidence of intense distress, they showed little measurable physiological disturbance.

2. Nor do physiological measures show concordance with each other. Weiner presents four discrete patterns of anxiety

disorders: patients with disturbance of muscle tension; those with primarily cardiorespiratory symptoms; a cluster of upper gastrointestinal symptoms with frequency of urination; and those characterized by a sleep disturbance.

3. There is the unresolved problem of whether acute fear–anger has the same physiology as ongoing fight–flight states: do we have a recurrent "acute" physiology, or a "chronic" pattern which is different?

4. Controlled studies, using laboratory conditions and volunteer subjects, may not present authentic aspects of fight–flight emotions: the conditions are artificial, the subjects know it, and various stimuli such as unexpected loud noises, shocks, frustrations, imagining situations evoking the desired emotion, or watching films, may simply not produce the quality or quantity of emotion aimed at by the experimenter.

5. Naturalistic studies, using truly dangerous settings such as car racing, parachute jumping, or the harrowing act of landing an aircraft on a rolling aircraft carrier, are by their nature uncontrolled.

6. Until recently (Rose, 1980; Pasnau, 1984) there have been major problems of unreliability in the assay of catecholamines in body fluids, due to the unstable nature of these substances, their rapid turnover, marked differences in the rates of metabolism and excretion among individuals, and problems in assigning amounts arising from the brain and the periphery. This renders all other studies suspect, including such former impressions that noradrenalin and adrenalin were differentially responsible in the emotions of fear and anger. Recently, assays of a more reliable nature have been developed.

My overall impression in surveying the literature is that the "molecular biology" approach may have reached something of an asymptote in terms of its heuristic accomplishments, and that a broader "systems" approach will be required to guide further profitable endeavors. At the moment we are dependent on many atomistic findings derived from animal models, which need to be integrated more effectively with the human condition, particularly in a naturalistic fashion.

Nonetheless, the techniques which have been developed in the molecular approach are ingenious, sophisticated, and admirable, to say the least. Perhaps most informative has been the exploration and mapping of brain systems, tracts, nuclei, neurones, synapses, and receptors by means of pharmacologic agonists (drugs causing neurons to fire), antagonists, and blockers (drugs impeding or inhibiting neuronal action). Other intricate technical procedures have involved use of enzymes, fluorescent dyes, radioactive markers, and immune reactions. The sophisticated maps of the brain which we now have are of two kinds: a picture of localized structures such as the locus ceruleus and its connections and neurochemistry; and a kind of abstract or conceptual view of "the synapse," "the cell membrane," or "the receptor site," structures which can only be portrayed schematically (see drawings in Valzelli [1981], and in Martin, Owen, and Morihisa [1987]). Perhaps we need consciously to avoid being dazzled and bemused by the scintillating quality of these excruciatingly patient and ingenious techniques, and to retain an appropriately critical attitude toward the relative validity of their findings. It must be emphasized that, for example, it has not been solidly proven that monoamine inhibiting drugs act as such in the human brain, though they certainly do so in laboratory animals (in vivo) and in red cells or slices of brain tissue in a glass dish (in vitro). Lazarus (1986) makes a plea for considering neurochemistry as a phenomenon of a *region* or *system* (e.g., the limbic system) if we are to become more certain regarding neurotransmitter disturbances.

For the remainder of this section I shall attempt to survey what is reasonably known or proven of the syndromes and events in the fight–flight homeostatic mode. I proceed with a brief survey of familial and genetic patterns; then work outward from the brain and central events, through peripheral systems and events, out to the psychosocial level in the final section.

Familial and Genetic Patterns

Roth (1959) pioneered the modern analysis of a typical fight–flight syndrome, the Phobic Anxiety-Depersonalization

Syndrome, which in today's terms closely approaches agoraphobia/panic disorder. His subjects were 135 patients, compared with 50 patients with other neuroses and 50 normal persons. Of the sufferers from the syndrome, 93 were women, 42 men, a ratio borne up by later studies (Marks, 1987); of those under 35 years of age, 21.4 percent had a family history of "neurotic breakdown." Crowe, Noyes, Pauls, and Symen (1983) reporting a study of 41 panic disorder patients and their 278 first-degree relatives (against 41 controls and their 262 relatives) concluded that "panic disorder is a familial disease that affects women twice as frequently as men and is not associated with an increased familial risk of psychiatric conditions" (p. 1065), including generalized anxiety disorder.

I shall rely here on Marks's (1987) review of the literature (and the complexities) of familial patterns in the anxiety disorders, with their not entirely clear results. Marks reminds us how important it is to know, as a baseline, what are the actual prevalences in the community of neurosis, anxiety disorder, or even everyday anxiety symptoms; that is, to know mathematically what the risk is that close relatives of *normal* people will suffer such disorders or everyday symptoms.

I simplify Marks' findings for *patients* as follows, and return to some further discussion on pp. 355–357 below.

1. For general, diffuse anxiety disorders, 15 to 18 percent of first-degree relatives will share the same symptoms; female relatives affected will be twice as many as male; dizygotic twins will show a 4 to 9 percent concordance; and monozygotic twins a 30 to 41 percent concordance.

2. For panic disorders, 25 percent of first-degree relatives will show the disorder, 33 percent for female patients, 17 percent for male patients.

3. For agoraphobic disorders, there is a high rate of phobic and other neurotic disorders in relatives; twice as many female relatives will be affected as male. The disorder "runs in families," especially female relatives: around 33 percent of relatives will be affected as compared to 15 percent for control subjects.

4. For phobias of a more specific kind, concordance rates of 88 percent for monozygotic and 38 percent for dizygotic twins have been reported. In one adoption study reported, the

evidence, limited yet striking, was that the adoptee had inherited rather than learned the tendency to phobic disorder. As noted above (Mineka, 1985), learning by social observation does not seem an effective way of implanting phobias in humans.

5. For obsessive–compulsive disorder (which is rare enough to make statistical studies difficult) a number of investigations agree that there will be found a considerable amount of psychiatric disorder in the family, but not obsessive–compulsive disorder to a significant degree.

Central Events and Systems in Fear and Panic

Sequences in Emotion or Mood State. The modern theory of emotions relies strongly on the sequence: perception–cognitive evaluation–emotion–appropriate action. It has not been established (Weiner, 1985) how ongoing mood states are constituted, but it seems likely that a reversed sequence may also operate: mood state–cognitive rationalization of the mood state–action.

In normal living, in a situation of danger, incoming sensory experience is filtered rapidly (Bowlby, 1977; Restak, 1979) then attended to and organized into perception, through the secondary and tertiary sensory cortex and the reticular activating system; the perception is concurrently being compared with stored templates of (semantic) memory, and rapid evaluation made, here the evaluation being that of danger; cortical and subcortical mechanisms are thus mobilized; the intertwined pathways in the neomammalian brain (limbic system) for *both* memory and emotion are activated, and subjective emotion registered; the reptilian brain in the basal ganglia participates in the automatic *expression* of emotion and in other patterns of muscle tension preparatory for fight or flight; the hypothalamus, as "head ganglion" for the autonomic nervous system, rapidly activates the sympathetic network and the adrenal medulla, and somewhat later the pituitary–endocrine axis. Practically, all the important machinery for emergency and defensive emotion is subcortical (Valzelli, 1981), and beyond conscious control: it is cognitive evaluation which may be within the sway of conscious choices and less conscious defense mechanisms.

Brain Systems in Fight–Flight States. Modern mapping reveals several small but influential brain systems. A small dopaminergic system in the hypothalamus and infundibulum primes the pituitary–endocrine sequences (Martin et al., 1987). An adrenergic system is central to fear and panic responses: the tiny collection of cells making up the locus ceruleus in the lower pons, and giving the bluish tint in the floor of the fourth ventricle which names it, accounts for 50 percent of the noradrenergic neurons and 70 percent of the noradrenalin in the brain (Marks, 1987). This nucleus contains only about 400 neurons, yet has a disproportionately central and influential position. It lies in close connection with the reticular activating system, and its branchings connect widely. Marks conceives of it as an "alarm system" or panic center. It appears to function out of control in the panic disorders. The influences on this nucleus are clearly complex: serotonergic and GABA-ergic (gamma-amino-butyric acid) systems. The serotonergic system appears to soothe or calm the locus ceruleus, and the GABA system, as elsewhere in the brain, is inhibitory. Antidepressant drugs most successfully treat panic disorders; the mechanism of action on the locus ceruleus is not clearly known.

A rather recent finding is that of receptor sites scattered widely in the brain, in a pattern corresponding to no known system, which are specific for the benzodiazepine molecule (Paul and Skolnick, 1981; Pasnau, 1984; Martin et al., 1987; Marks, 1987). Diazepam labeled with radioactive hydrogen, for example, binds to these sites. This suggests that there must be naturally circulating, "endogenous" chemicals which bind to these sites in the day-to-day allaying of fear. No such substances have so far been identified. This scattered collection of benzodiazepine receptors has some connection with GABA-ergic systems, which are known to be generally inhibitory in function. Although this is an argument for the specificity or selectivity of benzodiazepines as anxiolytics, there is no agreement that benzodiazepines are superior to some older drugs in anxiolytic action (Paul and Skolnick, 1981; Marks, 1987).

An interesting line of argument connects obsessive–compulsive disorder with malfunction of the basal ganglia (Rapoport, 1989). This ancient brain center (MacLean's "reptilian brain") is concerned with stereotyped, habitual organizations, include patterns for survival and emotional expression. There is some association between incidence of obsessive–compulsive behaviors and extrapyramidal disturbances (e.g., Sydenham's chorea). Therefore obsessive–compulsive disorder might be seen as malfunctioning stereotyped survival activities; for example, in washing or cleaning rituals. Though the argument is attractive, I find Rapoport's evidence somewhat tenuous.

The following records some basic definitions of neurotransmission; adrenergic neurotransmission is prominent in fight–flight. I refer the reader for further detail to Hoffmann and Lefkowitz (1980) and Sulser (1986). Sulser offers the following two definitions:

1. A *receptor* has two functions: that of recognizing and accepting an appropriate molecule; and that of initiating a biological action in the cell (e.g., causing a neuron to "fire," or inhibiting a muscle cell from contracting) which is either stimulant or inhibitory.
2. A *binding site* recognizes and binds to a ligand (molecule accepted and bound) in a broader manner, regardless of whether any biological action ensues.

Hoffmann and Lefkowitz add these further points:

1. An *agonist* is a substance which causes a receptor to initiate a biological action; this is an all-or-nothing response, symbolized by the numerical value 1.
2. An *antagonist* interacts with a receptor so that no action is possible, symbolized by the numerical value 0.
3. A *partial agonist* carries out or impedes action so that the effect is only partial, symbolized by a numerical value somewhere between 0 and 1.
4. *Alpha adrenergic receptors* (whether in the brain or peripherally) respond to adrenalin (epinephrine, E) much more strongly than to noradrenalin (norepinephrine, NE), and generally mediate smooth muscle contraction.

Alpha-one (a1) receptors are postsynaptic, "normal" receptors; Alpha-two (a2) include atypical peripheral receptors, as in platelets, and also curious presynaptic receptors which exert negative feedback on the production of catecholamines at the synapse.

5. *Beta adrenergic receptors* are also of two types. Beta-one (b1) receptors mediate such functions as effects on heart muscle, and respond equally to E and NE. Beta-two (b2) mediate smooth muscle *relaxation* and respond much more strongly to NE than E. It is beta adrenergic receptors which become of great interest in the mechanisms of depression and its treatment (Martin et al., 1987; and see chapter 13).

Sleep Disturbance in Fight–Flight States. As compared with the depressive states, there has been a recent relative neglect of sleep disturbance in the anxiety syndromes. Williams and Karacan (1984) in reviewing the subject estimate that 35 percent of clinical sleep disturbances are related to a psychiatric problem; of these, 45 percent are attributable to an anxiety or neurotic state, and 50 percent to an affective disorder. The difficulty in anxiety states is in the initiating and maintenance of sleep. Increased sleep latency (time between going to bed and falling asleep) and decreased sleep efficiency (proportion of time spent actually asleep) are somewhat diagnostic, as contrasted with the short REM latency (time before first REM period) and early awakening in depressive states (see chapter 11). Despite the obvious fact that the anxious or fight–flight brain is alerted and the reticular activating system is influential in such alerting and in the sleep–waking cycle, actual physiological measures, including the electroencephalogram (EEG) show no reliable or consistent pattern. Williams and Karacan (1984) point to the difficulty of obtaining subjects with pure affect states: many have a mixture of anxiety, hostility, and depression. However, according to our present model, anxiety and hostility are both reciprocal aspects of the same biological state. I leave more detailed consideration of sleep and its vicissitudes to chapter 13.

Peripheral Systems and Mechanisms in Fight–Flight: The Sympathico-Adrenal

I remind the reader of Cannon's picture of physiological changes in fight–flight; these are essentially confirmed for modern times by Marks (1987). One addition however should be noted: under stress and threat, blood lipids rise quickly, attributable in part to sympathico-adrenal events and in part to pituitary-adrenal ones. Free fatty acids, triglycerides, and cholesterol in circulation increase almost immediately with the onset of fear or anxiety (Stokes, 1985; Weiner, 1985).

Mechanisms of Fight–Flight Emotions. I divide these into two functional groupings: the rapidly responding sympathico-adrenomedullary, and the more sustained hypothalamic-pituitary-adrenocortical systems. I focus on the major *shared* features in fight–flight. Marks reviews differences between fear and anger, which are small if significant at all and concludes that the argument is not settled as to whether there is a separate physiological basis for each.

Cannon established (confirmed by Marks [1987]) that in response to danger, strong emotion, and analogs such as pain and asphyxia, sympathetic activity (now known to be initiated by the hypothalamus) coordinates all vital organs in emergency action; this includes the adrenal medulla, whose secretion of adrenalin mimics all the effects of sympathetic stimulation, and provides somewhat more sustained emergency physiology through its release of adrenalin through the bloodstream.

Modern attempts to mimic the emotions through pharmacological means are reviewed by Lader and Bruce (1986), who, as do other workers, note the difficulty in producing an emotional state complete in subjective, behavioral, and physiological components. All pharmacological inductions, while they cause peripheral or physiological changes, miscarry in failing to elicit a convincing central or subjective feeling. What emerges in such inductions is an "as-if" state, suggestive, yet to the subject ambiguous and untrustworthy. The most successful induction of anxiety has been with yohimbine, which can produce some central feeling; its action is potentiated by imipramine, and muted by reserpine and amobarbital. The beta-carbolines may be more effective, but so far have not been properly tested on humans (see also Martin et al. [1987], for a discussion related to benzodiazepine receptors). Less successful have been the catecholamines and caffeine (curiously, amphetamine is not mentioned), orciprenaline, adrenalin, and noradrenalin in that order of success, with some inconsistency across subjects. Carbon dioxide inhalation, and intravenous lactate and pentylenetetrazole (formerly used in convulsive therapy) induce anxiety even more inconsistently across subjects.

These pharmacologic correlates of fight–flight agree in their effects, even if these are incomplete or subject to individual variation. The sedative–hypnotic drugs oppose or diminish fight–flight (Martin et al., 1987); with ascending dosage, they reduce anxiety and irritability ("anxiolytic" effect), produce relaxation or sedation (sedative or "tranquillization" effect), or induce sleep ("hypnotic" effect). Martin and colleagues recognize a specific anxiolytic effect at low doses in the benzodiazepines; but this effect has also been claimed for older drugs such as barbiturates; and the specific benefit of benzodiazepines has by no means been solidly established (Redmond, 1985; Marks, 1987). No drug produces natural sleep, and the search for the ideal hypnotic continues (Fleming, Bourgouin, and Hamilton, 1988).

Before we leave the phenomena of emotion, I return to Cannon's critique of the James-Lange theory of emotion which, in brief, states that an emotion *is* the perception, or specific cluster of sensations, of visceral and musculoskeletal events. In addition to affirming Cannon's criticisms (see pp. 323–324 above), Marks (1987) emphasizes that a complete experience and expression of emotion requires *both* central or subjective and peripheral or visceral events. Marks cites evidence from study of patients with spinal cord injuries: the more severe the injury, the less the patient can experience visceral sensations, and their experience of emotion is of the "as-if" variety.

The Nature of the Adrenal Glands. The adrenal glands subserve two emergency functions: an immediate but relatively short-lasting response to sympathetic stimulation, and a slower but more prolonged one through hormonal mechanisms. Each adrenal is in fact two organs, with no known direct communication between them. The medulla ("marrow") is a kind of gigantic sympathetic ganglion, and like other nervous tissues is derived from ectoderm. The cortex ("rind"), like other glandular tissues, is mesodermal in embryologic derivation. Why have the two organs come to lie in such intimate anatomic relationship (Klopper, 1964)?

The adrenal medulla is ganglionic, in receiving preganglionic sympathetic nerve fibers directly from the spinal cord. It is also an endocrine gland which synthesizes both adrenalin and noradrenalin and discharges these into the bloodstream. The chain of synthesis is from tyrosine, an amino acid, through desoxyphenylalanine (DOPA), dopamine ([DA], which is also an important synaptic transmitter in the brain), noradrenalin ([NA], or norepinephrine [NE]), to adrenalin ([A], or epinephrine [E]). The principal degradation product assayed in the urine to estimate production of noradrenalin and adrenalin is 3-methyl-4-hydroxyphenylethylene glycol (MHPG). I mention this chain here, but it should also be recalled that the same sequence applies to production and degradation of dopamine and noradrenalin in the brain (see Martin et al. [1987], for description and diagrams). As noted above (p. 343), it has been difficult to assign proportions contributed by brain and sympathico-adrenal system to the MHPG excreted in the urine (Rose, 1980; Pasnau, 1984).

The adrenal cortex is an endocrine gland, driven by secretions of the pituitary via the bloodstream. It synthesizes a remarkable variety of steroids falling generally into three classes: those which regulate electrolyte metabolism ("mineralocorticoids" such as aldosterone), those which regulate glucose metabolism and are anti-inflammatory ("glucocorticoids" such as cortisol and cortisone), and those which are androgenic or masculinizing, with properties analogous to testosterone. These steroids are released into the general blood circulation, whence they reach their various target organs.

How Do Medulla and Cortex Collaborate? Despite their intimate anatomic propinquity, and their common functions in responding to stress, there is no known direct pathway between these two organs. In the immediate, sympathico-adrenergic response to stress (Cannon's fight–flight), the hypothalamus transmits stimulation to the adrenal medulla via the sympathetic nervous system, and adrenalin and noradrenalin are released into the circulation. This response is generated within seconds, and as long as adrenalin continues circulating in the bloodstream, it persists for minutes to hours. Sympathetic stimulation alone of an organ will only result in effects persisting for seconds to minutes.

What we might call the "swift," or sympathico-adrenergic, response to stress affects the hypothalamus in a feedback loop: adrenalin in the bloodstream reactivates the hypothalamus, which then signals the pituitary to drive the adrenal cortex through the release of adrenocorticotrophic hormone (ACTH). Although the hypothalamus contains adrenergic receptors, adrenalin does not pass the blood–brain barrier. It is believed (see in general the descriptions and inferences of Klopper [1964] and Weiner [1985]) that adrenergic sensors in the carotid are what signal the hypothalamus.

The "slow" response to stress, which is generated in minutes and may persist for hours to weeks, commences as ACTH reaches the adrenal cortex, and cortisol and other products are synthesized and released into the bloodstream. Hypertrophy of the adrenals was a consistent finding in the second phase of the general adaptation syndrome (Selye, 1980, 1982). To complete yet another loop, cortisol reaching the adrenal medulla enhances synthesis of the catecholamines noradrenalin and adrenalin from their precursors.

Thus, the demonstrable connections between adrenal medulla and cortex are lengthy neurohumoral pathways through bloodstream, hypothalamus, and pituitary. These complex loops would appear to be mechanisms for successive time distributions in the collaborative efforts of short-acting and long-acting emergency response systems.

Peripheral Systems and Mechanisms: The Pituitary–Endocrine

It would seem logical to look to a slower-responding but more long-acting emergency system for biological mechanisms of the "autonomous," protracted, maladaptive fight–flight mode of the neuroses and allied disorders. These long-acting systems are well-outlined and diagrammed by Stokes (1985) as the HPE system: the component levels are hypothalamus, pituitary , and endocrines. The pituitary sends specific hormones to drive the adrenal cortex, thyroid gland, testis, and ovary, as well as more diffuse targets affected by prolactin and human growth hormone (hGH); feedback loops return to the pituitary in governing the system.

Let us therefore see what illumination the HPE system casts on events in pathological fight–flight states. Unfortunately, despite the sophistication of current research, little has become clear and firm. Weiner (1985) comments that most of the findings are disappointing, "as muddled as the clinical literature . . . very few generalizations are possible . . . [the findings are] contradictory . . . altogether anti-intuitive . . ." (p. 353). The following examples are summarized from the reviews of Stokes (1985), of Weiner (1985), and of Marks (1987), chiefly from naturalistic situations where incontrovertible stress and fear are present, but where there are major problems as to controls.

1. Older studies reported elevations in 17-ketosteroids and 17-hydroxy-cortico-steroids in flyers and athletes.
2. In the anguish of flooding treatment for phobias, where there was every outward evidence of the subjects' distress and agitation, no clear endocrine changes could be registered.
3. During serious oral and written examinations, particularly in the "most anxious" students, free fatty acids and cholesterol levels rose significantly (a cortisol effect), and serum growth hormone (hGH) rose by 33 to 40 percent.
4. Before an automobile race, the drivers' circulating free fatty acids rose 125 percent and did not return to resting levels for an hour; serum triglycerides rose steadily during the race to 111 percent above resting level; these cortisol effects correlated with a rise in catecholamine secretion.

5. During parachute jumping, with predictable variations between competent, incompetent, and novice jumpers, prolactin and thyrotropin values virtually doubled, and hGH rose tenfold.

6. In underwater demolition training, and in the equally fearsome task of landing jet fighter planes on a carrier deck, serum cortisol levels were increased threefold.

7. In officer trainees in the armed forces, the first few weeks of training correlated with "profound" fall in testosterone levels.

8. Examination fear produced a picture resembling essential hypertension, with blood pressures averaging 140/90, a picture differing from the sympathico-adrenergic pattern found by Cannon, where diastolic pressure drops.

9. Other implications for psychophysiological disorders are noted, particularly by Weiner, and will not be detailed here.

Psychosocial Aspects of Fight–Flight Syndromes

Distribution of Fight–Flight Disorders in the Community and Family

This section supplements the more biologically oriented summary in pp. 342–355 above; the line between biological and psychosocial is difficult to draw. Here we ask the questions, How frequently do anxiety disorders and other neuroses arise in the population? Do they cluster in families or social classes? Can variables such as inheritance ("nature"), child rearing, or teaching ("nurture"), and stressful life events be demonstrated to contribute to them?

One of the major problems for research has been the clear specification of these disorders: differing studies have used differing criteria. The difficulty becomes compounded when the attempt is made to assess neuroses *across cultures*, since symptomatology in this class of disorders is differentially shaped by divergent life views, customs, beliefs, and modes of thought (Good and Kleinman, 1985). Another problem noted already is a general lack of certainty on the prevalence of anxiety phenomena in the *normal* population, as controls.

The following is summarized from Weissman (1985) and Bland (1988). Weissman is a highly regarded biostatistician and epidemiologist, whose work we shall encounter several times again. She was surprised to find quite good concordance between older studies (where diagnostic specification depended on the investigator) and more recent ones (using operational and standard criteria). She found for anxiety disorders in general that the prevalence (number of ongoing cases found in a specified size of population during a specified period) averaged 4.3 cases per 100 people per year (i.e., 4.3%), the same figure as for major depressive disorders. Bland's breakdown, from a major collaborative study in which Weissman's team also participated, shows a prevalence per 100 persons per 6 month period, of 0.4 to 1.0 cases of panic disorder, 0.0 to 2.0 cases of obsessive–compulsive disorder, 1.3 to 13.4 cases of agoraphobic disorder, and 0.0 to 0.4 cases of somatization disorder.

Weissman's detailed discussion and tables should be consulted, and compared with Marks's figures given on p. 345 above. What interested Weissman greatly was the large overlap in prevalence of anxiety and depressive disorders in her research populations: patients were found who suffered major anxiety syndromes *concurrently* with a major depressive disorder; who suffered an anxiety disorder before or after a depressive one; and who suffered an anxiety disorder without any depressive one. Patients who had both syndromes, together or at separate times, had a high prevalence of pure major depression in first degree relatives (17–19 cases per 100 relatives, contrasting with 4–6 per 100 for controls).

Weissman's principal conclusions might be summarized thus: the anxiety disorders are common (prevalence 4–8 cases per 100 persons per year), heterogeneous, and familial (15 of 100 first-degree relatives are sufferers also, contrasting with 6/100 for controls). They are, as with the neuroses generally, more common in women (index cases or patients) and the female relatives of patients, than in men, by a factor of two. Younger, less well-educated, and nonwhite persons (particularly women) are most at risk: thus, influences of sex, age, and class require careful elucidation. Weissman is cautious in apportioning weight to nature and nurture (i.e., contributions of inheritance, life-style, child rearing and teaching); she does not here deal with life events. Her guarded comment is that, "No genetic hypothesis has been conclusively rejected" (p. 286). In her schema, the panic disorders are the severest of the group, judging by their highest familial prevalence; and research is required into the finding that children of persons suffering from both anxiety and depressive disorders are at high risk for developing depressive disorders, separation problems, and anxiety disorders.

Phenomenology and Natural History in Fight–Flight Disorders

I have already reviewed the basic phenomena of the various neurotic syndromes, as specified in current nosological schemata (see pp. 338–342 above). These syndromes are operationally and behaviorally defined in a way which permits valid comparisons between research efforts, and there can be little argument over the care which has gone into the classifications (Tuma and Maser, 1985; American Psychiatric Association, 1987; Marks, 1987). Current nosology tends to present such syndromes as clear-cut and mutually exclusive entities; this is in a sense a reversion to the "mental illness" model of the nineteenth century (Knoff, 1970). Thus, in the effort to be operational and empirical, something has been lost of the overall taxonomic interrelationships and adaptive significance of these disorders. Questions of this latter kind are not only out of fashion: it does not seem currently permissible to ask them (Wallace, 1988).

My arrangement of the neuroses as a continuum is based on their relationship to a model of fight–flight. Clearly, other arrangements are possible and desirable, depending upon one's aims. I place the manifest anxiety disorders at one end of a continuum: these exhibit rather pure fight–flight, as a steady or intermittent state. In an intermediate position is obsessive–compulsive disorder, where the struggle to gain relief from personal distress becomes involved with more complex and bizarre homeostatic mechanisms. Toward the other end of the continuum are somatization and dissociation disorders, whose struggle is still with conflict and the attainment of peace of mind, but whose homeostatic mechanisms may "succeed" so radically that the organism can remain in homeostatic normality; that is, in minimal to zero anxiety or fight–flight.

This arrangement fits two current trends. One is the classificatory arrangement within current nosologies; even though they do not give credit to a taxonomic principle, they do sequence the disorders in much this same way. The other is the rank order of efficacy of the behavior therapies (Tuma and Maser, 1985; Marks, 1987): the anxiety and phobic disorders are the most amenable to behavioral techniques; obsessive–compulsive disorder is beginning to be attacked with some success; and somatization and dissociation disorders seem beyond the therapeutic powers of the behavior therapies.

What we seem badly to need are questions regarding overall patterns in the neuroses, since individual syndromes are well specified. Can there be a general model of neurosis as adaptive style, homeostatic operation? Is there such a thing, in addition to a generalized or model neurosis, as a generalized neurotic predisposition in families which emerges in various syndromes? Mavissakalian, Turner, and Michelson (1985a) are inclined to believe so, in assessing studies of the wide variety of psychiatric disturbances found in the relatives of OCD sufferers.

Can naturalistic or ethological observations bring us some new light, for example by following prospectively those who are at risk for neurosis; observing the variables of family style, social class, child rearing, stressors in interaction with family or social supports; and when decompensation comes, on the natural history or evolution of each autonomous neurosis, with its prodromes and metadromes, and its worsenings and improvements? Do we need to model our methods on the observational and conceptual genius of Darwin (1872) and Cannon (1915) or more recent pioneers such as Shapiro (1965) or Brown and Harris (1978, 1986)?

Can anthropologists and transcultural psychiatrists help us strip away what is culture-bound, thereby revealing some central, common, universal picture of the adaptive and maladaptive struggle in the neurosis?

Psychology and Psychodynamics of Fight–Flight Syndromes

Contemporary theorists of all orientations agree that fear and anger are universal in sentient creatures, as a component of behavioral systems subserving personal survival. Anxiety and hostility are more quintessentially human, with their subtle gradations and cognitive apprehensions for the future. These are also the subject of much more debate and disagreement as to their properties and definitions. Mental mechanisms both generate and follow from these complex and intransitive affects; indeed, properly operating mental mechanisms can stave off or hold them quiescent for long periods, permitting homeostatic normality with or without periodic outbursts of intense feeling. No wonder then that theorists may disagree about the phenomena of anxiety and hostility states, or that one theorist may pointedly ignore data which other theorists consider important.

In general, theory divides into two camps. The behaviorist camp generally focuses on avoidant behavior, such as can be targeted in behavior therapy, and ignores subjective preoccupations and feelings, and mental mechanisms. Theorists in the psychodynamic camp are interested in more global personality functioning and inferred internal *organization* underlying behavior; they target treatment at the organizing variables.

A regrettable communication gap exists between these two camps, which either maintain a truce of silence or, at worst, engage in counterproductive armed hostilities. Examples of the problems which polarize the two camps are not hard to find. Both sides can maintain a stubborn or doctrinaire stance. Both tend to use a private technical jargon with self-satisfied or defensive failure to communicate with the other. Examples could be given of behaviorists borrowing rather well-known psychodynamic ideas or techniques, thinking them to be novel discoveries, and failing to credit their original sources (an example is shown by Foa, Steketee, and Ozarow [1985]; see p. 364 below). There is a general impression that the psychodynamic camp is the present loser in contributing to and influencing research and theory (Michels, Frances, and Shear, 1985), a feeling that "psychoanalysis is dead." The reasons are not difficult to find:

some tendency to regurgitate old insights and models as if new; generalization from single-case studies; a blurring of cause and effect which is always a problem in psychodynamics; the confounding of understanding (retrospective) with explaining (predictive); slovenliness in nosological specification, with a besetting tendency to confound personality traits with actual psychiatric disorder (an example of this may be found in Sifneos [1985]). Integrative theorists (such as Bowlby) are required who will bridge the behavioral–psychodynamic gap by using a generalized language and a variety of contemporaneous models; but they may in turn be accused by members of both "camps" of belonging to, or having defected to, the other!

The following section summarizes the psychological properties of the principal groupings of neuroses. As the reader will note, the arrangement differs from that presented above (p. 338) and again from that below (p. 377) because it is based on the explanatory features best fitting each grouping. The material represents a synthesis of Mineka (1985), Foa and Kozak (1985), and Marks (1987).

Specific or Simple Phobias. These tend to be long-term patterns, whose onset is shrouded in the mists of personal antiquity, but which often can be traced back at least to age 8 to 10. Does this apparently common time of origin relate to oedipal transactions, the development of concrete operations, the moratorium on sexual conflict of latency, or the new social world of the school child? Marks believes they may be residues from a large collection of ordinary fears which most children outgrow. Mineka and Marks both comment on the surprisingly finite range (in content or object) of these phobias. Simple phobias tend to present in quite well-organized personalities, who cope with them by simple avoidance maneuvers, and succumb to anxiety or panic only when these maneuvers are thwarted.

These phobias fit a traumatic or conditioning model well: they are most cost effectively treated by various exposure and desensitization techniques, resulting in extinguishing of the response. Only if embedded among more pervasive personality problems does more protracted psychodynamic therapy seem justified for them.

Posttraumatic Stress Disorder (or Traumatic Neurosis). I place this syndrome here as representing a classical trauma or one-trial conditioning paradigm, with onset clear and recent, symptomatology matching the trauma, and decompensation fitting the classical psychodynamic concept of overwhelming of homeostatic capacities ("psychic trauma") rather than the construct of disabling intrapsychic conflict. Such disorders are relatively uncommon in peacetime, though victims of sexual assault or civilian disasters may come to our attention. If untreated, the condition tends to drift on into a rather stubborn chronic anxiety disorder with or without a phobic component.

In its acute form, this disorder fits the conditioning model well, and calls for energetic ventilation–exposure–desensitization techniques, which may be either behavioral or verbal–psychodynamic in approach and may be with or without heavy sedation. This disorder may be also a model for studying the establishment of long-term specific or social phobias.

Social Phobias. These are intermediate in nature between specific phobias and the more global patterns of agoraphobia, panic disorder, and generalized anxiety disorder. They do not have pinpoint-specific phobic-avoidance objects; the presence of other people, familiar or strange, is important. They show a fairly clear onset in time, they are often associated with progressive and severe decompensation and disability, or they may develop into a full-blown mixed anxiety disorder; "Shinkeishitsu" (Good and Kleinman, 1985), a Japanese example of severe and incapacitating social phobic disorder, has been noted above.

Agoraphobia and Panic Disorder. As previously, I place these together as a very commonly combined syndrome, which tends to have clear onset, and can be very persistent, even lifelong. Though the disorder can be treated successfully by behavior therapy, psychodynamic issues clearly enter the picture, as behaviorists acknowledge in explaining some of their puzzling features (e.g., lack of a clear precipitating cause). Further, separation problems loom large among the psychodynamics. The following evidence needs to be considered:

1. A general predisposition to anxiety or neurosis is suggested by familial patterns, by certain animal models (Scott and Senay, 1973; Mineka, 1985), by Bowlby's (1980) "anxious attachment" syndrome, and by Brown and Harris's (1978) finding that threats of separation in childhood are conducive to neurosis.

2. Roth (1959), Katon (1986), and Michels, Frances, and Shear (1985) adduce evidence that onset of these disorders is associated with threats of separation or personal loss.

3. The clinical picture of both agoraphobia and panic attacks strongly mimics the pattern of acute separation in children.

4. In both disorders there is a clear tendency to feel safe at home, with some preferred key person (*caregiver*, to use Bowlby's terminology); or, to put it another way, the condition is *not* one of fearing being out in public so much as fearing *being away from* a source of security, of familiar and protective surroundings. This dimension has important implications for treatment, including having the therapist temporarily become the key caregiver and source of security. Many patients find they can manage the "agora" when accompanied by their preferred caregiver, or the therapist.

These conditions do not therefore fit a learning or conditioning model well: they come on too swiftly and unexplainedly to be good examples of learning (which takes a number of trials), and no overwhelmingly traumatic event can be located. The life events associated with their onset are not highly visible, and are of a symbolic kind. Thus, a life events/psychodynamic model fits best, even though dealing with the perpetuating mechanisms by behavioral techniques (exposure, desensitization, flooding, accompanied by the therapist) may work well. Marks counsels against using medication unless the patient is clearly depressed, and Ananth (1985) guardedly disagrees with the common recommendation of antidepressants for panic disorder.

Obsessive–Compulsive (OCD) and Generalized Anxiety (GAD) Disorders. Whether OCD is an anxiety disorder can be debated; it has a borderline relation to objects or situations of avoidance, which can be capitalized upon on treatment; most agree that it is "easy to diagnose and difficult to treat" (Ananth, 1985, p. 202); its compulsions can be seen to be anxiety-reducing techniques. Generalized anxiety disorder has no reference to an external avoidance object or situation; the mounting components of combined agoraphobic and panic disorder can amount to a generalized anxiety disorder (see pp. 338–339); internal perturbation accounts for almost all of the phenomena. The sufferer from OCD can never really get away from what upsets him or her: dirt or contamination are never totally washed off, nor is disarray ever reassuringly resolved; obsessions keep recurring; thus, intrapsychic dynamics must be inferred (Rachman, 1985; Foa, Steketee, and Ozarow, 1985; Marks, 1987).

I turn attention mainly to OCD because of its peculiar problems. The excellent compendium edited by Mavissakalian and colleagues (1985a) as well as Marks (1987) are recommended for further detail: both are rather behavioral in orientation. All authors agree on the distress, disability, and untreatability of this condition; it is not common, therefore statistics on it are unreliable. Its natural history is not a subject of much agreement. Rachman (1985) obviously an experienced authority, notes that the difficulty of treating it has resulted in treated and untreated cases being statistically lumped together; spontaneous remission is expectable with about as much hope as remission with treatment: despite its relatively clear onset, and a suggestion that life events precede onset, the disorder is likely to run its course as autonomously as any psychiatric disorder, little influenced by further life events, including placebos, aggressive psychotherapy, behavior therapy, or brain surgery (see Salzman and Thaler [1981]; and several chapters in Mavissakalian et al. [1985a]). The one hopeful technique of recent years has been a combination of behavioral approaches, principally "response prevention" (e.g., not allowing a patient to carry out compulsions, or arresting obsessions forcibly) and "exposure" (e.g., deliberately dirtying the hands, or having to tolerate disorder), which are successful over time in alleviating the pattern in 75 percent of cases (Marks, 1987; Foa, Steketee, and Ozarow, 1985). But there are still two large provisos: the pattern must be one which has enough of an external focus to treat behaviorally (obsessional slowness, for example, cannot be so treated); and the patient must be well enough organized and motivated to undertake systematic treatment, involving persistence and initiative on his own part. Foa and colleagues gloss over this question as one of "commitment" on the patient's part; if such is lacking, treatment will not succeed; Marks implies the same. Thus, behaviorists generally will not deal with the regressive, disorganized, frantic, ambivalent psychic state of many OCD patients, as psychodynamic theorists and clinicians since Freud's day have done; if there is too much disorganization, that is simply a tragic inconvenience.

An example of the behavioral–psychodynamic communication gap is illustrated in Foa, Steketee, and Ozarow (1985) and Rachman (1985); neither paper cites Sigmund or Anna Freud or other psychoanalytic theorists; both appear to use psychoanalytic constructs of many years' standing without giving credit for them. Both papers describe the pattern (or mental mechanism) known as "doing–undoing" in psychoanalytic literature (see chapter 7), and almost pathognomonic of obsessive–compulsive disorder. Foa and coworkers see this pattern as the generation of anxiety by obsessions, and the attempt in compulsions to undo the obsessions with their anxiety. Later they offer an even more classical psychoanalytic formulation: the OCD sufferer's "false beliefs" include (1) the necessity to be perfectly competent and achieving; (2) the inevitability of punishment for any failure of perfection; (3) the effectiveness of ruminations or magical rituals in preventing catastrophe; and (4) the power of thoughts and feelings to cause disaster and bring down punishment. This description accords extremely well with psychoanalytic constructs on regression in OCD to an early life-stage where magical thinking and a harsh and retaliatory superego precursor operate; indeed, the notion of rather pervasive regression in OCD is supported by Piaget's schemas on magical, concrete thinking, and "moral realism" in early childhood.

The premorbid personality in OCD sufferers has usually been assumed to exhibit prominent "compulsive" or perfectionistic traits. However, Marks (1987) and Rachman (1985) find otherwise: at least 30 percent of sufferers were quite "slipshod" people (Marks). This and other puzzling aspects of relatively sudden onset, extreme persistence or autonomy, and somewhat pervasive regression: all these suggest a biological problem in neurotransmission as one major perpetuating mechanism. As noted, Rapoport (1989) incriminates the basal ganglia in the pattern of symptomatology, with its greater than chance association with other extrapyramidal syndromes.

Somatization and Dissociation Disorders. Behavioral therapists and theorists tend to avoid these disorders as untreatable (Tuma and Maser, 1985; Marks, 1987) and unresearchable. The costs they incur to the community are high, but the conditions are hard to manage and prevent (Lipowski, 1988).

Lipowski's review of somatization disorders is excellent; he elects a naturalistic, descriptive level of discourse. The core of these syndromes is "the tendency to experience and communicate somatic distress in response to psychosocial stress" (p. 1358). Lipowski traces the modern medical history, going back to the famous British physician Sydenham in the seventeenth century, of the hysteria–hypochondriasis group. It seems clear that somatization and conversion disorders hold many features in common; not the least being the clash between the patients' and their physicians' cognitive assessment of their problems. Somatization disorders have three components. The experiential component includes various convincing sensations of bodily disturbance, and emotionality ranging from *belle indifférence* to panic and agitated depression. The cognitive component includes a selective focusing of attention, and a hypochondriasis which can be quantitatively estimated from mild to delusionally intense and pressureful. The behavioral component includes a characteristic type of help-seeking for bodily dysfunctions, directed toward physicians but also other helping professionals and faith healers. The causes and successful management are not well understood: a truly diagnostic approach, and commitment to long-term helping, appear essential variables in management.

I can recommend no one recent, scientifically oriented, review of the dissociation disorders. I might paraphrase Lipowski in suggesting for these a core tendency to express personal stress through dysfunction of the *mind*; that is, the patient's concept of mind. Lishman (1971, 1987) proposes an ingenious hypothesis for psychogenic amnesia, in the close association, in the limbic system, for mechanisms of both emotion and memory.

Lipowski believes that the ancient and heavily "encrusted fossil" hysteria still contains some essentially explanatory value. Krohn (1978) has made a serious attempt to rehabilitate the construct. With Shapiro (1965) he is highly interested in the cognitive style of sufferers from both somatization and dissociation disorders. The criteria of this style, as I have remarked in chapter 3, call for investigation using Piagetian constructs and norms, since it is very difficult to escape its resemblance to the "preoperational intelligence" of earlier childhood.

The psychodynamics have been consistently seen to be an amalgam of homeostatic attempts to mitigate intrapsychic distress and avoid painful insights (the "primary gain"); while a learning or behavioral component is evident in the family transactions and iatrogenic social reinforcements ("secondary gain") motivated by interest in and compassion for the patient's colorful and intriguing symptoms (Krohn, 1978; Lipowski, 1988).

Treatment Strategies in Fight–Flight Syndromes

The Placebo Effect

Camouflaged within a lengthy paragraph of Marks (1987) is the pregnant assertion that, while half of all sufferers from generalized anxiety disorder are benefited by a placebo, sufferers from obsessive–compulsive disorder are wholly placebo resistant. This comment serves as a bridge from the psychology to the treatment of the neuroses, and the placebo effect itself will be our first concern.

Lasagna and colleagues in 1954, and Beecher in 1955, unleashed an intense wave of interest in the placebo effect. While the phenomenon was well known in the medical community, and had in fact been researched at least 10 years earlier, Lasagna and Beecher initiated a new attention to it. This seems to have been because the time was ripe for the subject, for the modern psychotropic drugs were just appearing on the scene. This wave of interest and attention appears to have receded in the clinical community in the past few years, leaving our present practitioners somewhat unaware of the major impact their non-specific management strategies may have; a criticism, I believe, particularly applicable to the behavior therapists as well as pharmacotherapists. The subject is perhaps due for a revival of the kind Lasagna and Beecher launched. Meanwhile, the stringent revision of rules for drug trials, as brought about by the rediscovery of the placebo effect, has remained firmly in place.

Lasagna et al. (1954) reported two careful studies of the placebo effect, followed up by an investigation into the personalities of placebo reactors and nonreactors. In a sophisticated design, 162 patients suffering postoperative pain were given either 1 cc of sterile saline solution or 10 mg of morphine. It was found that 30 to 40 percent of pain episodes were relieved by saline alone, and about 70 percent by morphine. Therefore, it appeared, morphine was only twice as effective as placebo: morphine was neither 100 percent effective, nor was placebo 100 percent ineffective. In a second, tighter study of 93 patients, it was shown that 11 of them were always relieved of pain by placebo, 13 were never relieved, and 3 were rarely relieved. Seven of 14 with less severe pain gained relief by placebo (50%) while 20 of 54 with severe pain were so relieved (37%).

Beecher (1955) reviewed the subject of "the powerful placebo" based on an analysis of 15 previous investigations. These had found a placebo consistently and somewhat astonishingly helpful to 35.2 percent plus or minus 2.2 percent of patients with a wide variety of problems: the common cold, pain, nausea, and anxiety and depressive disorders. Beecher distinguished between "placebo" and "dummy." "Placebo," more broadly, was defined as anything (usually an inert substance) given explicitly to please or reassure a patient; "dummy," as an inert preparation given during drug trials. He settled on "placebo" as satisfactory for both uses. Placebos, Beecher concluded, are useful and effective in reassuring patients, are crucial in the testing of new drugs, and are of assistance in clarifying the mode of action of drugs generally. He noted that "toxic" or "side" effects are produced by placebos, just as by active drugs.

Beecher (1955) noted that "placebo reactors" had been identified at least 10 years earlier, and "toxic" side effects of placebos noted more recently. The collaborative study led by Lasagna et al. (1954) enquired into how placebo reactors (those helped) differed from nonreactors (not helped). This team employed a considerable battery of interviews, tests, and ratings. The aim was to attempt to identify placebo reactors by personality profiles, so that their responses could be predicted, and so that they could be excluded from drug trials as an "unsatisfactory population." Their results were not clear-cut, and a number of findings were counterintuitive. Gender and intelligence failed to discriminate reactors from nonreactors. In general, reactors were the more cooperative and appreciative patients; they minimized their pain yet were found to exhibit more symptoms and take more drugs when under stress, and to talk and weep more freely, than nonreactors; 100 percent were churchgoers. Nonreactors were found to be more complaining and less cooperative as patients, had less symptoms, took less drugs, talked and wept less easily, and only 44 percent were churchgoers. Rorschach testing gave signs of warmer, less controlled personality for the reactors.

Can certain persons be consistently identified as placebo reactors? No solid answer, pro or con, appears to have emerged. Liberman (1963) relatively early noted this uncertainty, and designed a study to try to reduce the ambiguity. He tested 52 obstetrical patients, using 30 controls, under three conditions: the pain of labor, postpartum pain, and muscle pain during work with a tourniquet applied. While placebo gave relief to pain under all three conditions, there were no patients who experienced relief under all three. Rather, their responses assumed a chance distribution. Therefore, from this study of women, no wholly consistent placebo reactors could be identified. Joyce (1959) reported an ingenious experiment with preclinical medical students in a pharmacology class. They were given rather detailed psychological assessment in a manner similar to Lasagna et al. (1954), then given a placebo (orange juice). The assessment scores of reactors in this trial were then used to predict, in a subsequent class, who would also be placebo reactors, with a very considerable proportion of success. The question of a specific placebo reactor personality remains open. Joyce believes that the tendency to react always is at one end of a continuum, with nonreactors at the other end. Thus, it seems that exact predictions with individuals cannot be made, and that we need to be on the alert for the placebo phenomenon with all our patients; further, that as Lasagna et al. originally proposed, placebo reactors cannot be excluded as a clear population in drug trials.

The placebo effect cuts across many categories of patients, illnesses, and treatments (Beecher, 1955). Beecher (1961) investigated the placebo effect in surgery and found that "surgery can evoke a placebo effect of great magnitude . . ." (p. 1105). Anxiety disorder patients are helped in 50 percent of cases. The seriously depressed (Rickels, 1986) and the acutely schizophrenic (National Institute of Mental Health, 1964) are significantly benefited. Only obsessive–compulsive disorder patients appear to be nonreactors. Besides the negative effects (or "toxic" or side effects) which placebos produce in some patients, the phenomenon of habituation or addiction to placebos is regularly reported (Rickels, 1986): patients will fight having to give up a placebo, and will experience withdrawal symptoms.

A crucial assumption had been that conscious belief in benefit (a variable of hope and trust) was crucial to the placebo effect. Park and Covi (1965) tested this assumption in a crucial pilot experiment, which apparently has not been replicated. They followed 15 new outpatients with moderately severe generalized anxiety disorder. At the end of the first, diagnostic visit each patient was given a supply of capsules containing sugar, with the careful instruction that, while it was hoped and expected these capsules would help, nonetheless that they contained no drug, only sugar. On the next visit, a week later, 14 of the patients reported marked symptom relief. This included patients who understood clearly that no active drug was involved; but also several who (it turned out) doubted the clinician's word, since the capsules had been so helpful. Only one patient had worsened. Some patients reported unpleasant side effects. Among the variables Park and Covi attended to were the patients' clear trust and reliance on their clinician, with whom they swiftly established a trusting relationship.

Many of us can still recall with amazement and amusement the events surrounding the massive promotional campaign for the new "miracle drug" chlordiazepoxide. One prominent negative side effect was to be feared: the risk that some patients would fall over backward and strike their heads. True to this announcement, a number of my colleagues' patients fell backward and struck their heads; two of my own friends experienced this frightening side effect. The reader will agree, I believe, that this negative placebo effect has long since vanished from the culture!

Two relatively recent reviews update the placebo effect. Lasagna (1986), one of the pioneer investigators, gives a chatty, discursive historical overview. He notes the peculiar etymological error which originated the term *placebo* (I shall please). He reminds us of such crucial variables as studied by Parks and Covi, of the phenomena of habituation or addiction to placebos, and of the necessity of taking into account spontaneous remission. He reports an animal model for the placebo response: animals given an active drug in a flavored solution will later show the effects of that drug when given specifically flavored water alone. Rickels (1986) emphasizes social, legal, and ethical concerns in his review. Citing Lasagna, he muses that "opponents of placebo seem to suffer from the delusion that placebos are always ineffective and experimental drugs are always safe and effective—too often the placebo-treated patients turn out to be the lucky ones" (p. 21). Rickels includes clinical vignettes: one depicts the course of an agoraphobic–panic disorder patient, the other a sufferer from major depression; each showed remarkable improvement and relapse as placebo was first given, then withdrawn. A third review by Grünbaum (1986) is dense and weighty, difficult to assimilate; curiously, Grünbaum fails to give credit to the pioneers Lasagna and Beecher.

It remains that the placebo effect benefits a proportion of patients in all nosological categories except obsessive–compulsive disorder, including the very seriously ill, such as acute schizophrenics (National Institute of Mental Health, 1964).

The Evaluation of Psychiatric Treatments

For a general guide to research design in the behavioral sciences, I can recommend Shontz (1986) whose discourse, even including exercises illustrating statistical procedures, is probably within the reach of practicing clinicians. A strict modern canon governs the evaluation of any new treatment procedure (old ones too, such as convulsive therapy). Thus, the superiority of any procedure must be demonstrated quantitatively, not over an absence of treatment, but over an appropriate placebo (Shontz, 1986; Rickels, 1986). Since it has clearly been impossible to exclude placebo reactors from treatment evaluations, as Lasagna and colleagues (1954) originally hoped, the rule is now that cohorts having similar problems shall be tested "double blind" using both placebo and active substance; that is, neither patient nor clinician must know when active treatment is being given, and when placebo or dummy. I shall not attempt to detail the variety of possible designs for such treatment evaluations, but leave the reader with a source such as Shontz (1986).

The aim of psychiatric treatment, whether pharmacologic (biological level of emergence) or psychotherapeutic (psychological and social levels) or combined, is, according to our present model, to shift the patient back to a more favorable homeostatic level. In this, we operate principally on perpetuating or maintaining mechanisms. In the present context, the emphasis is on shifting persons from fight–flight to psychiatric normality.

It is conceptually relatively easy to design evaluations of therapy with biological agents; controls, design of the trial course, an appropriate placebo, and the double-blind condition are strategically manipulable. Serious methodological difficulties arise in evaluating the effects of treatment by psychosocial means (for convulsive therapy also, see chapter 13), or psychotherapy; it is either impossible to stage a suitable "dummy" treatment, or to keep the several participants "blind," or both. For the psychotherapies, a variety of control conditions have been used. The "no treatment" or "waiting list" condition controls for spontaneous remission, one of the important issues in the placebo field; it does not provide a dummy treatment. Nonspecific first aid, as required, provides elements of support and interest in the patient not receiving specific treatment. Systematic support, or "supportive psychotherapy," is difficult to specify and execute clearly in a way that does not overlap what is going on in more strategically targeted psychotherapy. This applies particularly in the case of behavior therapy. I recall vividly hearing a tape many years ago of Dr. Wolpe administering systematic desensitization or reciprocal inhibition: my colleagues and I agreed that we had rarely heard such a kind and concerned clinician at work, a major variable we could not dissociate from the specific technique. Behavior therapy has been partially controlled by having patients do the treatment by themselves, using a booklet of instructions and/or a computer (Carr, Ghosh, and Marks, 1988). Even here, clinicians are involved, with their various degrees of concern and personal support. The problem of what constitutes a placebo for psychotherapy, and how to make the treatment as "blind" as possible, remains a thorny one.

Biological Treatment Strategies

The intricate and highly technical field of psychopharmacology suffers from some problems. Impressionistically, one sees its practitioners and investigators so preoccupied with biological variables that they forget or neglect the "art" of medicine and the inclusion of psychosocial variables (including cognizance of the placebo effect) in their work. Journeymen clinicians tend to be bemused by the sophistication and variety of drugs, and by the simplifications and claims of manufacturers as a source of guidance. Despite very useful knowledge about pharmacodynamics and modes of action, we cannot be sure that data garnered from animal experiments and animal models will reliably mirror the human condition. I therefore propose to offer some rather brief and simple comments. I shall divide these quite empirically to deal with generalized anxiety disorders, episodic anxiety disorders (panic and phobic), and obsessive–compulsive disorder (uncommon and exceptional or egregious). My sources are chiefly the reviews of Marks (1987) and Tuma and Maser's (1985) compendium.

The benzodiazepines have become established as the preeminent drugs in treatment of generalized anxiety disorder, and other states of central nervous system excitation (e.g., withdrawal reactions). This appears to be a product of skillful commercial promotion and these drugs' great *margin of safety*, for they can be ingested in large quantities without fatality. They are not less habituating or addicting than older drugs. Nor is it clear that their anxiolytic, sedative, and hypnotic properties are entirely superior to those of older drugs (alcohol, chloral hydrate, barbiturates, meprobamate) despite statements on their pharmacodynamics and influence on the sleep cycle (Ananth, 1985; Marks, 1987). It has not been established that the benzodiazepine receptors in the brain represent a natural tranquilizing system. All anxiolytic, sedative, and hypnotic drugs pose dangers, and none produces natural sleep. Rickels's (1986) comments on the good fortune of placebo responders, who receive benefit safely, is germane here.

Since generalized anxiety disorders respond with such high regularity ([50%]; see above) to placebos, it is strange that we find no investigations of a strategy for treating them with a combination of placebo and psychotherapy or behavior therapy. The older techniques of "continuous narcosis" (or drug-induced sleep lasting some days) seem to have disappeared, despite the safety of benzodiazepines for such a purpose.

For panic disorders and some phobic states, evidence is now strong that the anxiolytics are ineffective in remitting the disorder, merely offering the risks without the benefits. The antidepressants appear to offer more specific benefit, probably by "steadying" the locus ceruleus (Martin et al., 1987). Marks casts doubt on their efficacy except in patients who are also clinically depressed. Alprazolam, a benzodiazepine congener with antidepressant properties, is undergoing trials in some centers, in doses many times the anxiolytic level (Hasan and Mooney, 1986). Clear findings should be emerging for its effectiveness; it appears to be quite habituating.

For obsessive–compulsive disorder, there is ambiguity and pessimism. Rapoport (1989) is enthusiastic for the newly released clomipramine, in a high-dose range (300 mg daily). I have an impression that this drug, which has been in use outside the United States for some years, has failed to live up to its original promise as a specific. In this difficult and disabling disorder, many modalities have been tried. Ananth (1985) and Salzman and Thaler (1981) judge that none of the many drugs tried up to the time of their writing has shown clear success. The benzodiazepines offer some temporary relief, but relapse is prompt when they are discontinued. Marks is skeptical that antidepressants such as clomipramine help sufferers who are not clinically depressed. I have located no investigations of combined pharmacologic and psychosocial attack on this very stubborn and distressing disorder.

Psychosocial Treatment Strategies: The Psychotherapies

There is now a very large literature on psychotherapy research. I shall not attempt an overall review of this massive subject, though it is an important one in a day when biological psychiatry has been clearly at stage front. Here I plan simply to offer four references, in a historical progression, for further reading, and then to comment on a few focal issues.

I commence the general references with Rachman (1971) who, in the critical British academic tradition, reviewed a number of psychotherapeutic approaches, using as a springboard Eysenck's well-known and destructive attack on the psychotherapies in the early 1950s (Eysenck, 1966). Sloane (1975), with a combined British and North American background, assessed the psychodynamic therapies against the behavior therapies. Elkin, Pilkonis, Docherty, and Sotsky (1988) have most recently launched a series of communications around the topical subject of the relative effectiveness of psychotherapy and pharmacotherapy. Finally, a relatively recent monograph from the American Psychiatric Association Commission (APA, 1982) gives a good overview of the many issues of method and outcome in psychotherapy research.

The general question of whether psychotherapy "really works" has long been settled in a positive direction; stated in this form it now sounds naive in the extreme. Among evidences for the power of the psychotherapies are several indirect ones. Review of the placebo phenomenon clearly demonstrates that rather nonspecific psychosocial intervention benefits persons with a wide range of somatic and "personal" illness, even serious depressions and psychoses. The fact that a psychotherapeutic intervention has caused harm in a few cases is a somewhat paradoxical attestation to its power. It may be that some early studies, reporting a null effect from psychotherapy, studied cohorts in which people who were helped and harmed were mixed together. In general, it appears that a combination of psychosocial and biologic interventions gives more benefit than either modality when given alone. I shall refer to this in chapter 14 as the "Weissman principle."

Today the critical question for psychotherapy research is not, Does it work? That is a shotgun approach to interactions between very heterogeneous syndromes and a wide variety of psychotherapeutic interventions. The question to be addressed today is, rather, What type of psychotherapeutic intervention is most cost-effective for syndrome X? The behavior therapy movement has paid the most direct attention to this question and, understandably, is receiving favorable attention in return.

The current research-derived literature is somewhat dominated by sober to overly enthusiastic claims for the behavior therapies: the psychodynamic "camp" or "school" has lost some of its impact. For reasons which I have listed above it is easy to criticize psychodynamic theorists. However, we need to remind ourselves that it is the psychodynamic approach which has had the most lengthy experience with the neuroses; it has accepted responsibility for dealing with distressed and difficult *persons*, and with the difficult, irreducible, whole-person problems they present; it has taken full cognizance of the powerful and complex influences, for good and for ill, in the patient–therapist system. Behaviorists are vulnerable to a reciprocal criticism. Their case material is precisely specified: they treat *syndromes* defined by reference to clear templates. Their interventions are likewise well specified. But they are responsible too for three major exclusions. They tend to accept as patients those who are well organized enough to do the work; they base their conclusions on these, excluding the regressed and disorganized whom they do not treat. They pay little attention to global, whole-person variables (i.e., psychodynamics, defenses, regression, etc.) which relate the different syndromes. Finally, they appear in most cases to neglect the powerful variables in the patient–therapist system.

Two Examples of Psychosocial Intervention: Psychodynamic and Behavioral

After these general comments, I turn to two contemporary schemas as examples of advances in the two fields, psychodynamic and behavioral. The psychodynamic schema, described under various titles (Gustafson, 1984), is a short-term, time-limited, relatively aggressive analytic psychotherapy, which aims technically at exerting pressure on the patient's defenses and attacking current conflicts quite frontally, often with considerable expression of distressed emotion. Gustafson attempts to uncover and integrate the several "partial theories" currently proposed for the technique and effectiveness of this form of therapy; and to bring together (synthesize) a common, minimum set of principles for patient selection and technical intervention.

This psychotherapeutic approach is applied (and restricted) to rather mature and well-organized personalities. In the light of our developmental–structural model, it is implied that they have already attained concrete–operational intelligence and are capable of reciprocity, objective moral justice, and industry, and have a regression age no earlier than mid-childhood. The patient is held rather firmly to dealing with tasks and conflicts of early latency, particulary triangular interpersonal transactions (Sifneos, 1987). Gustafson's list of pioneers in the brief psychotherapy movement includes a loose international consortium of Malan, Davanloo, and Sifneos (see Malan, 1976; Davanloo, 1980). Sifneos (1985) contributes a chapter on treatment of obsessive–compulsive disorder to the work of Mavissakalian et al. This chapter is a reasonable illustration of the brief psychotherapy approach; but it also illustrates one of the criticisms made of the psychodynamic school, a confounding of reasonably well-organized persons who show obsessive–compulsive personality traits, with those suffering full-blown obsessive–compulsive disorder.

Quite apparently there has been a surreptitious borrowing or cross-fertilization between brief psychodynamic psychotherapy and the behavior therapies, though generally one does not see credit given to the behaviorists. The commonalities are impressive: a dealing with well-organized persons; a task orientation and pressure to work on identified problems; a challenge to habitual homeostatic mechanisms and an offer of new learning opportunities; and encouragement to express, if necessary, strong feeling, and to endure considerable discomfort in the process. Techniques in mirroring brief psychotherapy as compared with behavior therapy appear to mirror response prevention, accompanied exposure, and flooding.

It is to be hoped that these brief psychotherapies will continue to be investigated. They appear to have parallels also in the "interpersonal therapy" and "cognitive therapy" applied in depressions and on which we touch in chapter 14.

For a model of behavioral treatment strategies in the neuroses, I summarize the schema of Foa and Kozak (1985). One should note certain exclusions, such as somatization, dissociation, and paranoid disorders, in this logical taxonomy. Again, the arrangement differs from those in pp. 338–342 and pp. 372–374 above, for tactical reasons.

Foa and Kozak place the process of *exposure* conceptually at the center of the therapeutic model. Marks (1987) appears to agree. Exposure can be graded from its mildest and gentlest forms, with much support or accompaniment by the therapist, to its most demanding and disturbing. In systematic desensitization, exposure is gradual, mainly taking place in the patient's imagination; arousal is deliberately kept low. In flooding, the exposure is brutally direct, the setting is pressureful, and high arousal and emotion are deliberately sought. Foa and Kozak's schema follows:

1. *Simple phobias*: imaginal flooding and systematic desensitization are effective techniques; direct exposure to the feared stimulus is the most effective (accompaniment and support by the therapist are not discussed).

2. *Agoraphobia*: in vivo or real-life progressive exposure (accompaniment by the therapist is again not explicitly mentioned) is probably the most effective; imaginal desensitization and flooding are less effective.

3. *Obsessive–compulsive disorder*: desensitization is ineffective; flooding, with response blocking, appear to be the most effective (Marks [1987] and Foa, Steketee, and Ozarow [1985] confirm this). Behavioral techniques apply to compulsive rituals rather than obsessions (and note that only the better-organized patients can be treated).

4. *Social anxiety* (the term used by Foa and Kozak): social skills and assertion training, in combination with in vivo exposure, are most likely to be effective.

5. *Generalized anxiety disorder*: anxiety management techniques, focusing on anticipatory fear of arousal and of social rejection, are the interventions of choice. Cognitive therapy is seen by Foa and Kozak as an amalgam of approaches based on reason and the correction of erroneous belief systems, and as still (1985) in an exploratory phase for anxiety disorders.

Bibliographic Notes: Key Readings

My "review of reviews" in this chapter leans heavily on two encyclopedic books on anxiety, to which I have referred repeatedly. I recommend both, or either, as definitive resources on which one can fall back for a great deal of information. *Anxiety and the Anxiety Disorders*, edited by Tuma and Maser (1985), is a veritable library of nearly 800 pages of text, comprising 43 chapters by 60 authors, whose contributions range through basic science and animal models to clinical interventions and evaluation of these. *Fears, Phobias, and Rituals: Panic, Anxiety, and Their Disorders* is a single-author monograph of 560 pages by Marks (1987). Despite its somewhat clinical title, half the volume is occupied by basic science issues, the second half by clinical ones. There is, in fact, something of a paucity of good, integrative monographs and compendia of recent date, as compared with the literature on depression.

For a foundation, Cannon's (1915) propositions on responses to strong emotion (later termed *fight–flight* by Engel) is essential reading. The intriguing behavioral model of prey and their sequence of actions in the face of predators is outlined by Ratner (1967). The minimodels for the clinical disorders of

Mineka (1985) are basic to my argumentum, and are highly recommended in the understanding of fight–flight and its cognate clinical syndromes.

For a detailed overview of the nature of fear and anxiety, appropriate sections in both Tuma and Maser, and in Marks, are recommended. The literature on fear and anxiety is somewhat divorced from that on anger and aggression, though both are aspects of fight–flight. For a definitive social psychological study of human aggression, which in effect settled the major question of where human aggression arises, Dollard, Miller, Doob, Mowrer, and Sears (1939) should be consulted. For a biobehavioral approach to aggression, crime, and war, I recommend Valzelli (1981) whose ingenious diagrams I have already recommended in chapter 8.

Now we come to the nosology of clinical syndromes. Again, sections in both Tuma and Maser, and in Marks, deal well with anxiety disorders and phobic disorders, as well as with the more bizarre or specific syndromes. Krohn (1978) has attempted with some success to rehabilitate the abused construct of hysteria. Mavissakalian, Turner, and Michelson (1985) edit a small but incisive compendium on obsessive–compulsive disorder. Lipowski (1988) reviews competently the problem of somatization, and the syndromes dominated by that mechanism.

In regard to biological aspects and mechanisms in the neuroses, particularly disorders characterized by anxiety and panic, I recommend Martin, Owen, and Morihisa's (1987) review of neurotransmission, and Lader and Bruce's (1986) article on drug-induced emotions. Again, sections in Tuma and Maser (1985) and Marks (1987) report research on psychological aspects. This brings us to treatment issues. Shontz (1986) is a valuable guidebook to research design as applicable to treatment investigations. The placebo effect remains very important, and it is instructive to read its rediscoverers in the original: Lasagna, Masteller, von Felsinger, and Beecher (1954); Beecher (1955); as well as more recent reviews by Lasagna (1986) and Rickels (1986). Finally, among a large literature on research in psychotherapy, the monograph produced by an American Psychiatric Association commission on psychotherapy (APA, 1982) is a useful guide to methodologic issues.

References

American Psychiatric Association (1952), *The Diagnostic and Statistical Manual of Mental Disorders* (DSM-I). Washington, DC: American Psychiatric Press.

—— (1980), *The Diagnostic and Statistical Manual of Mental Disorders*, 3rd ed. (DSM-III). Washington, DC: American Psychiatric Press.

—— (1987), *The Diagnostic and Statistical Manual of Mental Disorders*, 3rd ed. rev. (DSM-III-R). Washington, DC: American Psychiatric Press.

*—— Commission on the Psychotherapies (1982), *Psychotherapy Research: Methodological and Efficacy Issues*. Washington, DC: American Psychiatric Press.

Ananth, J. (1985), Pharmacotherapy of obsessive–compulsive disorder. In: *Obsessive–Compulsive Disorder: Psychological and Pharmacological Treatment*, ed. M. Mavissakalian, S. M. Turner, & L. Michelson. New York: Plenum.

Antelman, S. M., & Caggiula, A. R. (1977), Tails (*sic*) of stress-related behavior: A neuropharmacologic model. In: *Animal Models in Psychiatry and Neurology*, ed. I. Hanin & E. Usdin. Oxford: Pergamon Press.

*Beecher, H. K. (1955), The powerful placebo. *J. Amer. Med. Assn.*, 159: 1602–1606.

—— (1961), Surgery as placebo. *J. Amer. Med. Assn.*, 176:1102–1107.

*Belmaker, R. H., & van Praag, H. M., eds. (1980), *Mania, an Evolving Concept*. New York: Spectrum.

Bland, R. C. (1988), Prevalence of mental illness. *Ann. Roy. Coll. Phys. Surg. Canada*, 21:89–93.

Bowlby, J. (1969), *Attachment and Loss, Vol. 3: Loss, Sadness, and Depressions*. London: Hogarth Press.

—— (1973), *Attachment and Loss*, Vol. 2. London: Hogarth Press.

—— (1977), *Attachment and Loss*, Vol. 3. London: Hogarth Press.

Brown, G. W., & Harris, T. (1978), *Social Origins of Depression: A Study of Psychiatric Disorder in Women*. New York: Free Press.

—— (1986), Establishing causal links: The Bedford College studies of depression. In: *Life Events and Psychiatric Disorders: Controversial Issues*, ed. H. Katschnig. Cambridge, UK: Cambridge University Press.

*Cannon, W. B. (1915), *Bodily Changes in Pain, Hunger, Fear, and Rage: An Account of Recent Researches into the Function of Emotional Excitement*, 2nd ed., 1929. Boston: Charles T. Branford Co., 1953.

Carr, A. C., Ghosh, A., & Marks, I. M. (1988), Computer-supervised exposure treatment for phobias. *Can. J. Psychiat.*, 33:112–117.

Carthy, J. D., & Ebling, F. J., eds. (1964), *The Natural History of Aggression*. New York: Academic Press.

Crowe, R. R., Noyes, R., Pauls, D. L., & Symen, D. (1983), A family study of panic disorder. *Arch. Gen. Psychiat.*, 40:1061–1069.

Darwin, C. (1872), *The Expression of the Emotions in Man and Animals*. New York: Philosophical Library, 1955.

Davanloo, H. (1980), *Short-term Dynamic Psychotherapy*. New York: Jason Aronson.

*Dollard, J., Miller, N. E., Doob, L. W., Mowrer, O. H., & Sears, R. R. (1939), *Frustration and Aggression*. New Haven, CT: Yale University Press.

Elkin, I., Pilkonis, P. A., Docherty, J. P., & Sotsky, S. M. (1988), Conceptual and methodological issues in comparative studies of psychotherapy and pharmacotherapy. I. Active ingredients and mechanisms of change. *Amer. J. Psychiat.*, 145:909–917.

Engel, G. L. (1962a), *Psychological Development in Health and Disease.* Philadelphia: W. B. Saunders.

—— (1962b), Anxiety and depression—withdrawal; the primary affects of unpleasure. *Internat. J. Psycho-Anal.*, 43:89–97.

—— (1977), The need for a new medical model: A challenge for biomedicine. *Science*, 196:129–136.

—— (1980), The clinical application of the biopsychosocial model. *Amer. J. Psychiat.*, 137:535–544.

Eysenck, H. J. (1966), *The Effects of Psychotherapy* (with comments by 17 discussants). New York: Science Publishers.

Fleming, J. A. E., Bourgouin, J., & Hamilton, P. (1988), A sleep laboratory evaluation of the long-term efficacy of zopiclone. *Can. J. Psychiat.*, 33: 103–107.

Foa, E. B., & Kozak, M. J. (1985), Treatment of anxiety disorders: Implications for psychopathology. In: *Anxiety and the Anxiety Disorders*, ed. A. H. Tuma, & J. D. Maser. Hillsdale, NJ: Lawrence Erlbaum Associates.

—— Steketee, G. S., & Ozarow, B. J. (1985), Behavior therapy with obsessive–compulsives: From theory to treatment. In: *Obsessive–Compulsive Disorder: Psychological and Pharmacological Treatment*, ed. M. Mavissakalian, S. M. Turner, & L. Michelson. New York: Plenum.

Good, B. J., & Kleinman, A. M. (1985), Culture and anxiety: Cross-cultural evidence for the patterning of anxiety disorders. In: *Anxiety and the Anxiety Disorders*, ed. A. H. Tuma & J. D. Maser. Hillsdale, NJ: Lawrence Erlbaum Associates.

Grünbaum, A. (1986), The placebo concept in medicine and psychiatry. *Psychol. Med.*, 16:19–38.

Gustafson, J. P. (1984), An integration of brief dynamic psychotherapy. *Amer. J. Psychiat.*, 141:935–944.

Hamburg, D. A., & Trudeau, M. B., eds. (1981), *Biobehavioral Aspects of Aggression.* New York: Alan R. Liss.

Hanin, I., & Usdin, E., eds. (1977), *Animal Models in Psychiatry and Neurology.* Oxford: Pergamon.

Hasan, M. K., & Mooney, R. P. (1986), Panic disorder: A review. *Comprehen. Ther.*, 12:3–7.

Hoffmann, B. B., & Lefkowitz, R. J. (1980), Alpha-adrenergic receptor subtypes. *New Eng. J. Med.*, 302:1390–1396.

Howard, J. L., & Pollard, G. T. (1977), The Geller conflict test: A model of anxiety and a screening procedure for anxiolytics. In: *Animal Models in Psychiatry and Neurology*, ed. I. Hanin & E. Usdin. Oxford: Pergamon Press.

Izard, C. E. (1977), *Human Emotions.* New York: Plenum.

Joyce, C. R. B. (1959), Consistent differences in individual reactions to drugs and dummies. *Brit. J. Pharmacol.*, 14:512–521.

Katon, W. (1986), Panic disorder: Epidemiology, diagnosis, and treatment in primary care. *J. Clin. Psychiat.*, 47:21–30.

Klein, D. F., & Rabkin, J. G. (1981), *Anxiety: New Research and Changing Concepts.* New York: Raven Press.

Klopper, A. (1964), Physiological background to aggression. In: *The Natural History of Aggression,* ed. J. D. Carthy & F. J. Ebling. New York: Academic Press.

Knoff, W. F. (1970), A history of the concept of neurosis, with a memoir of William Cullen. *Amer. J. Psychiat.,* 127:80–84.

*Krohn, A. (1978), Hysteria: the Elusive Neurosis. *Psychological Issues,* Vol. 12, Nos. 1–2. New York: International Universities Press.

*Lader, M., & Bruce, M. (1986), States of anxiety and their induction by drugs. *Brit. J. Clin. Pharmacol.,* 22:251–261.

Lasagna, L. (1986), The placebo effect. *J. Allergy Clin. Immunol.,* 78:161–165.

——— Mosteller, F., von Felsinger, J. M., & Beecher, H. K. (1954), A study of the placebo response. *Amer. J. Med.,* 16:770–779.

Lazarus, J. H. (1986), *Endocrine and Metabolic Effects of Lithium.* New York: Plenum Medical Book Co.

Liberman, R. (1963), An experimental study of the placebo response under three different situations of pain. *J. Psychiat. Res.,* 2:233–246.

Lipowski, Z. J. (1988), Somatization: The concept and its clinical application. *Amer. J. Psychiat.,* 145:1358–1368.

Lishman, W. A. (1971), Amnesic syndromes and their neuropathology. In: *Recent Developments in Psychogeriatrics,* ed. D. W. Kay & A. Walk. Ashford, Kent, UK: Headley Brothers.

——— (1987), *Organic Psychiatry: The Psychological Consequences of Cerebral Disorder.* Oxford: Blackwell.

Lown, B., DeSilva, R. A., Reich, P., & Murawski, B. J. (1980), Psychophysiologic factors in sudden cardiac death. *Amer. J. Psychiat.,* 137:1325–1335.

McKinney, W. T. (1977), Biobehavioral models of depression in monkeys. In: *Animal Models in Psychiatry and Neurology,* ed. I. Hanin & E. Usdin. Oxford: Pergamon Press.

——— Bunney,W. E. (1969), Animal model of depression: I. Review of evidence: Implications for research. *Arch. Gen. Psychiat.,* 21:240–248.

MacLean, P. D. (1952), Some psychiatric implications of physiological studies on frontotemporal portion of limbic system (visceral brain). *EEG Clin. Neurophysiol.,* 4:407–418.

Malan, D. H. (1976), *The Frontier of Brief Psychotherapy: An Example of the Convergence of Research and Clinical Practice.* New York: Plenum.

*Marks, I. M. (1987), *Fears, Phobias, and Rituals: Panic, Anxiety, and Their Disorders.* Oxford: Oxford University Press.

*Martin, M. B., Owen, C. M., & Morihisa, J. M. (1987), An overview of neurotransmitters. In: *American Psychiatric Press Textbook of Neuropsychiatry,* ed. R. E. Hales & S. C. Yudofsky. Washington DC: American Psychiatric Press.

*Mavissakalian, M., Turner, S. M., & Michelson, L. eds. (1985a), *Obsessive–Compulsive Disorder: Psychological and Pharmacological Treatment.* New York: Plenum.

——— ——— ——— (1985b), Future directions in the assessment and treatment of obsessive–compulsive disorder. In: *Obsessive–Compulsive Disorder: Psychological and Pharmacological Treatment,* ed. M. Mavissakalian & S. M. Turner. New York: Plenum.

Michels, R., Frances, A., & Shear, M. K. (1985), Psychodynamic models of anxiety. In: *Anxiety and the Anxiety Disorders,* ed. A. H. Tuma & J. D. Maser. Hillsdale, NJ: Lawrence Erlbaum Associates.

Mineka, S. (1985), Animal models of anxiety-based disorders: Their usefulness and limitations. In: *Anxiety and the Anxiety Disorders*, ed. A. H. Tuma & J. D. Maser. Hillsdale, NJ: Lawrence Erlbaum Associates.

National Institute of Mental Health, Psychopharmacology Service, Collaborative Study Group (1964), Phenothiazine treatment in acute schizophrenia. *Arch. Gen. Psychiat.*, 10:246–261.

Papez, J. W. (1937), A proposed mechanism of emotion. *Arch. Neurol. Psychiat.*, 38:725–743.

Park, L. C., & Covi, L. (1965), Nonblind placebo trial: An exploration of neurotic patients' responses to placebo when its inert content is disclosed. *Arch. Gen. Psychiat.*, 12:336–345.

Pasnau, R. O., ed. (1984), *Diagnosis and Treatment of Anxiety Disorders*. Washington, DC: American Psychiatric Press.

Paul, S. M., & Skolnick, P. (1981), Benzodiazepine receptors and psychopathological states: Toward a neurobiology of anxiety. In: *Anxiety: New Research and Changing Concepts*, ed. D. F. Klein & J. G. Rabkin. New York: Raven Press.

Porsolt, R. D. (1985), Animal models of affective disorders. In: *Pharmacotherapy of Affective Disorders: Theory and Practice*, ed. W. G. Dewhurst & G. B. Baker. London: Croom Helm.

Powles (1980), The core and the boundaries of the construct of depression: A topological model. *Psychiat. J. U. Ottawa*, 5:21–23.

——— (1982), Four perspectives on depression and the depressive illnesses. *Can. Med. Assn. J.*, 125:253–258.

Rachman, S. (1971), *The Effects of Psychotherapy*. Oxford: Pergamon.

——— (1985), Overview of clinical and research issues in obsessional–compulsive disorders. In: *Obsessive–Compulsive Disorder: Psychological and Pharmaological Treatment*, ed. M. Mavissakalian, S. M. Turner, & L. Michelson. New York: Plenum.

Rapoport, J. L. (1989), The biology of obsessions and compulsions. *Scient. Amer.*, 260:83–89.

*Ratner, S. G. (1967), Comparative aspects of hypnosis. In: *Handbook of Clinical and Experimental Hypnosis*, ed. J. E. Gordon. New York: Macmillan.

Redmond, D. E. (1985), Neurochemical basis for anxiety and anxiety disorders: Evidence from drugs which decrease human fear or anxiety. In: *Anxiety and the Anxiety Disorders*, ed. A. H. Tuma & J. D. Maser. Hillsdale, NJ: Lawrence Erlbaum Associates.

Restak, R. M. (1979), *The Brain: The Last Frontier*. Garden City, NY: Doubleday.

*Rickels, K. (1986), Use of placebo in clinical trials. *Psychopharm. Bull.*, 22:19–24.

Rose, R. M. (1980), Endocrine responses to stressful psychological events. *Psychiat. Clin. N. Amer.*, 3:251–276.

Roth, M. (1959), The phobic anxiety—depersonalization. *Proc. Roy. Soc. Med.*, 52:587–595.

Salzman, L., & Thaler, F. H. (1981), Obsessive–compulsive disorders: A review of the literature. *Amer. J. Psychiat.*, 138:286–296.

Schmale, A. H., & Engel, G. L. (1975), The role of conservation–withdrawal in depressive reactions. In: *Depression and Human Existence*, ed. E. J. Anthony & T. Benedek. Boston: Little, Brown.

Scott, J. P., & Senay, E. C., eds. (1973), *Separation and Depression: Clinical and Research Aspects.* Washington, DC: American Association for the Advancement of Science.

Selye, H. (1980), The stress concept today. In: *Handbook on Stress and Anxiety,* ed. I. L. Kutash & L. B. Schlesinger. San Francisco: Jossey Bass.

—— (1982), History and present status of the stress concept. In: *Handbook of Stress: Theoretical and Clinical Aspects,* ed. S. Breznitz & L. Goldberger. New York: Free Press.

Shapiro, D. (1965), *Neurotic Styles.* New York: Basic Books.

*Shontz, F. C. (1986), *Fundamentals of Research in the Behavioral Sciences: Principles and Practice.* Washington, DC: American Psychiatric Press.

Sifneos, P. E. (1985), Short-term dynamic psychotherapy for patients suffering from an obsessive–compulsive disorder. In: *Obsessive–Compulsive Disorder: Psychological and Pharmacological Treatment,* ed. M. Mavissakalian, S. M. Turner, & L. Michelson. New York: Plenum.

—— (1987), *Short Term Dynamic Psychotherapy: Evaluation and Technique,* 2nd ed. New York: Plenum.

Sloane, R. B. (1975), *Psychotherapy versus Behavior Therapy.* Cambridge, MA: Harvard University Press.

Stokes, P. E. (1985), The neuroendocrinology of anxiety. In: *Anxiety and the Anxiety Disorders,* ed. A. H. Tuma & J. D. Maser. Hillsdale, NJ: Lawrence Erlbaum Associates.

Storr, A. (1968), *Human Aggression.* New York: Atheneum.

Sulser, F, (1986), Update on neuroreceptor mechanisms and their implication for the pharmacotherapy of affective disorders. *J. Clin. Psychiat.,* 47(Suppl.):13–20.

Taylor, M. A., & Abrams, R. (1986), Cognitive dysfunction in mania. *Comprehen. Psychiat.,* 27:186–191.

Trudeau, M. B., Bergmann-Riss, E., & Hamburg, D. A. (1981), Towards an evolutionary perspective on aggressive behavior: The chimpanzee evidence. In: *Biobehavioral Aspects of Aggression,* ed. D. A. Hamburg & M. B. Trudeau. New York: Alan R. Liss.

*Tuma, A. H., & Maser, J. (1985), *Anxiety and the Anxiety Disorders.* Hillsdale, NJ: Erlbaum Associates.

*Valzelli, L. (1981), *Psychobiology of Aggression and Violence.* New York: Raven Press.

Wallace, E. R. (1988), What is "truth"? Some philosophical contributions to psychiatric issues. *Amer. J. Psychiat.,* 145:137–147.

Weiner, H. (1985), The psychobiology and pathophysiology of anxiety and fear. In: *Anxiety and the Anxiety Disorders,* ed. A. H. Tuma & J. D. Maser. Hillsdale, NJ: Lawrence Erlbaum Associates.

Weissman, M. M. (1985), The epidemiology of anxiety disorders: Rates, risks, and familial patterns. In: *Anxiety and the Anxiety Disorders,* ed. A. H. Tuma & J. D. Maser. Hillsdale, NJ: Lawrence Erlbaum Associates.

Williams, R. L., & Karacan, I. (1984), Anxiety and sleep. In: *Diagnosis and Treatment of Anxiety Disorders,* ed. R. O. Pasnau. Washington, DC: American Psychiatric Press.

---

*Recommended readings.

11

A Note on Mania

Understanding and Classifying the Euphoric Disorders

The spectrum of euphoric disorders, from near-normal moods to devastating psychotic mania, represents the most behavioral of psychiatric conditions: one hardly needs to discern and to understand the patient's subjective experience in order to make the diagnosis. These states are the defining component of bipolar affective disorder. Yet somehow they remain, in their causes and mechanisms, among the least confidently understood of psychiatric conditions. Further, they are difficult to fit logically into a taxonomy of homeostatic styles. Empirically and phenomenologically they are the polar opposite, in every respect, of the depressive spectrum. But they do not fit the construct of fight–flight at all well, though they are alerted and activated conditions and psychodynamically savor strongly of defensiveness and a need to escape from cruel reality.

I shall assume in mania a general homeostatic process which, in various grades, is a caricature of the "active-engaging" mode of human existence (Schmale and Engel, 1975) and of

385

the normal human emotion of pleasure or joy. This process shows the autonomy and momentum seen in other pathologic homeostatic styles such as depression. In various grades of intensity and completeness it enters into a range of clinical syndromes from near-normal mood swings to grossly psychotic schizoaffective states. At the midrange of its manifestations is the pure, intense form of severe clinical mania. This, like depression, might be thought of as neither neurotic (fight–flight) nor psychotic (disintegration) but as a legitimate independent process bridging between these (see chapter 7).

We cannot classify mania as conservation–withdrawal. In almost every conceivable clinical feature (see chapter 12, pp. 430–433) it is the exact opposite of depression. It may be homeostatically best related to schizophrenia (Belmaker and van Praag, 1980; Carlsson, 1987) judging particularly from its dopaminergic mechanisms. I choose to include it here, in a somewhat awkward taxonomic relationship to fight–flight, with which it shares certain alerted, activated, and defensive properties. But the process is not dysphoric, nor clearly geared psychobiologically to survival and self-defense: even its reduced sleep, unlike that in states of anxiety and depression, is pleasant and refreshing. Its principal defense mechanism, a massive denial of all that might be considered disturbing, appears both defensive and escapist. The principal mood state is euphoric: over this groundswell play waves of labile and transitory emotion, hostile, flirtatious, curious, sentimental, maudlin, tearful, enraged. There may be a severe form of mania (Kraepelin, 1913; Davis, Noll, and Sharma, 1986) in which a mixture of ongoing euphoric and depressive features coexist paradoxically.

The problems in researching and understanding mania only commence with problems of diagnostic criteria (Shopsin, 1979), though this situation is today improved with better operational templates. There is much hair-splitting still to be found in discussions of differential diagnosis (Davis et al., 1986; Levinson and Levitt, 1987). The authors in Georgotas and Cancro (1988), also Swann (1986), and Shopsin (1979) appear to assume that mania and cognate states are clearly delineated "Platonic entities" about which one can debate on an either–or basis (see discussion on problems of classification, chapter 12, pp.

420–424). The much-cited paper of Pope and Lipinski (1978) appears to fall under this methodological error also.

Definitive monographs and compendia on mania have been infrequent. Shopsin (1979) appears to have assembled the first modern compendium: this volume is highly biologically oriented, and somewhat outdated now. Swann (1986) edits a similarly rather narrowly biological compendium with a number of more recent emphases. Belmaker and van Praag (1980) brought together a much more comprehensive panel addressing social and psychological as well as biological issues; the book remains stimulating reading, especially as raising a number of fruitful hypotheses. Georgotas and Cancro (1988) must be considered a weighty interdisciplinary source book even if it is expectably stronger on depression than on mania. I shall cite chapters from all four of these compendia.

Phenomena and Animal Models for Mania

Carpenter and Stephens (1980) present what is still an excellent review of the clinical phenomena of mania; Lerner (1980) supplements this with fascinating and poignant self-reports by patients of their manic experiences. Initial chapters in Swann (1986) and Georgotas and Cancro (1988) do not better these descriptions. Ballenger, Reus, and Post (1982) draw attention to the difficulty of deciding whether adolescent psychotic episodes are to be considered manic or schizophrenic: as attacks continue, they tend to become more clearly differentiated with time.

Because mania can be specified so well behaviorally, it should be a good candidate for modeling in other animal species. Such is, however, by no means the case in practice. McKinney (1988) provides an up-to-date chapter on animal models in depression and mania. I prefer, however, to turn to Robbins and Sahakian (1980) for a summary of the dimensions to be modeled and the problems with them:

1. *Hyperactivity.* This is not as simple a construct as it appears. The term may denote any repetitive activity, a hyperreactivity to the environment, or a rapid shifting from one activity to another. Since the precipitating causes of mania are at present

obscure (this holds in today as it did in 1980), it seems justifiable to employ animal models regardless of what means is employed to produce them, whether drugs, brain lesions, or behavioral procedures.

2. *Elation*. Measurement of mood is impossible in animals. Therefore, some operational or behavioral definition is required; for example, reduction of the threshold for reward or reinforcement (i.e., pleasure). Intracranial self-stimulation (see chapter 8, pp. 264–268 above) is a prominent test procedure in producing such a state.

3. *Irritability*. This common component of human mania can be modeled by producing a combination of increased environmental reactivity and increased aggression.

4. *Depression* (Robbins and Sahakian's term [1980]). It is not clear to me whether this refers to the bursts of maudlin sadness manics show, or to the rather severe syndrome in which mania and some components of depression coexist. In any case, this requirement is essentially impossible to model in animals.

Animal models, used for testing antimanic drugs and for investigating the mechanisms of mania, will need to display more than one of these dimensions, a desideratum which has been difficult to meet. Amphetamine has been one of the more successful inducers of an animal model of hyperactivity and irritability. Robbins and Sahakian detail a considerable number of other methods also, with their implications for understanding the neurochemistry of mania.

Biologic Aspects of Mania

What is currently understood of the genetics of bipolar affective disorder will be dealt with in chapter 13, pp. 440–445. These disorders have long been seen to have a familial patterning: the issues are well summarized in chapters 4, 7, and 8 in Belmaker and van Praag (1980). Mania and schizophrenia do not overlap in families, thus are likely to have differing genetic contributions.

Carroll (1979) gives a still useful orientation to neuroendocrine functions in mania, commencing with the important principle that the limbic system controls both behavior (and, of course, affect) and the hypothalamic–pituitary–endocrine system, and therefore that study of neuroendocrine dysfunction generates inferences on limbic functioning. That said, we are little advanced today in terms of any specific or definitive findings for mania.

Shopsin and Annitto (1979) had to report that a "staggering array of investigations" fail to "support or confirm" a disturbance in either indoleamine or catecholamine neurotransmission in mania. Janowsky and Davis (1980) offer rather convincing suggestive evidence that an interaction between cholinergic and adrenergic systems determine mood state in both depression and mania. This line of investigation is advanced in the excellent chapter of Janowsky, Golden, Rapaport, Cain, and Gillin (1988); this discussion outlines the anatomy and pathophysiology of the several neurotransmitter systems in the brain. The argument relies in part on the balance between cholinergic (parasympathetic) and adrenergic (sympathetic) systems in *peripheral* physiology: predominance of the former is associated with resting vegetative functions, for example, in heart rate and digestion, and of the latter with excited and activated ones (fight–flight). Experimental evidence on *central* functions again suggests that cholinergic activity correlates with sedating, antimanic, and mood-depressing effects, while adrenergic activity correlates with alerting, antidepressant, and euphoriant effects (see Janowsky [1986] for case vignettes from his team's early experiments with cholinomimetics). Other workers see evidence for dopaminergic disturbance in mania; antipsychotics which are also dopamine blockers are effective in controlling mania in its severest forms (Post, 1980; Davis et al., 1986; Carlsson, 1987). Convulsive therapy is also effective in the more severe manic episodes (Davis et al., 1986).

Swann and his contributors (1986) place a strong emphasis on lithium as *the* specific medication, and essentially the defining diagnostic test for mania, as does Shopsin (1979). This has to be qualified by the finding that 20 to 30 percent of manics do not respond to lithium. It had clearly been hoped that this response would make clearer the biochemical mechanisms in mania; this has not come to pass. Lazarus (1986) must be considered the definitive author on lithium, its metabolism, and its various effects. He reviews the history of its discovery as an antimanic and prophylactic agent, noting its effectiveness as both a treatment and prophylactic agent in some cases even of unipolar depression. Post et al. (1986) devote a chapter to carbamazepine and cognate anticonvulsant drugs as antimanics. These drugs were found to be effective particularly in limbic and temporal lobe seizures and were first empirically tested for mania in Japan.

Despite a multitude of studies on the effects of these treatments and other experiments, the cerebral pathophysiology of mania remains a riddle, or more properly a collection of unresolved hypotheses. Its biological treatment remains empirically effective, lithium being the drug of choice in mild to moderate cases, and antipsychotics and convulsive therapy in more severe cases (Davis et al., 1986).

Lewis and Winokur (1987) review the puzzling and frustrating clinical phenomenon of "switching," in which, instead of the patient becoming euthymic, treatment appears to throw the mood state over into its polar opposite. It has been assumed that tricyclics are responsible for switching of depression to mania. However, these authors, studying 23 switching episodes, find that other drugs, no drugs at all, or placebos (the latter also used in other studies) were more often associated with switching. Neuroleptics and lithium are prophylactic against switching. The principal variable involved in switching, Lewis and Winokur find, is the bipolar disorder itself and not the treatment.

Psychosocial Aspects of Mania

Psychodynamic explanations of mania were prominent in the decades preceding the modern biological therapies. These are reviewed by Ginsberg (1979) and Aleksandrowicz (1980): Abraham, encouraged by Freud, studied manic-depressives and published his first ideas in 1911: these were to the effect that mania represents a massive defensive flight from dysphoria, a kind of alternative pathway to depression; and that manics showed regression to oral thematic material and cognitive style. The latter focus was elaborated by Lewin, who conceptualized manic euphoria as an analog of the dreamy bliss of the baby falling asleep after nursing. All psychoanalytic workers assumed also some genetic predisposition, without which psychodynamic factors would not cause mania. These constructs appear not so much to have been discredited (like certain other psychoanalytic constructs, they are difficult to test and refute) as left in limbo by the tide of biological psychiatry.

There has been no clear consensus regarding premorbid personality features in bipolar disorders (Waters, 1979). However, Aleksandrowicz (1980), piecing together psychoanalytic and psychological reports, suggests some traits common to subjects prone to manic episodes, traits which rather clearly differentiate them from preschizophrenic personalities. These persons are gregarious, yet rather egocentric, highly dependent upon the goodwill of others, including possibly a single key attachment figure, loss of whom (real or imagined) may, as with depressions, precipitate a manic episode. These suggestions seem highly germane to concerns with the marital relationship (see below) in bipolar disorder.

Gagrat and Spiro (1980) review a number of social, cultural, and epidemiologic issues for mania, and assess the vexed question of the contribution of life events to its genesis. Dunner and Hall (1980) review the difficulties in establishing causality of life events by retrospective and self-report studies. There is something of a persisting clinical impression that life events are more significant in precipitating manic episodes in the earlier years, whereas the impact or significance of life events becomes progressively more attenuated in the later life of the patient (Lewis and Winokur, 1987; Ambelas, 1987). I shall be pointing out (chapter 12, p. 432 and chapter 14, p. 493) that indistinctness of precipitating cause is practically a diagnostic criterion of depression. Ambelas (1987) reports what may be a crucial (also a well-designed) investigation of this whole question. He examined for life events, using Paykel's life events list, in 26 male and 24 female patients in their first manic attack; he then followed up these patients for 3 to 8 years, purposely using records rather than an interview method. The controls were 40 patients who had had more than one manic episode, and 50 age-matched surgical patients. Ambelas found that 33 (66%) of the new manic patients had had a significant life event within 4 weeks of onset (probably an underestimate because of the rigorous time limit). Mean age for these positive cases was 28 years, and for those negative for life events (17 or 34%) 48.1 years. The surgical controls showed significant life events in only 4 cases (8%). The life events found for the first-attack manics included a death, in 8 cases (24%); giving birth, in 7 women (21%), a postpartum mania; a personal separation, in five cases (15%); and assorted others, totaling 13 events. Ambelas believed it noteworthy that it was significantly older patients who failed to demonstrate life events.

De-Nour (1980) introduces three themes mirrored in other chapters in the same volume. Marital relationships and their vicissitudes appear to be highly important in the course of bipolar disorders (this suggests that disturbance of a relationship with a key attachment figure is highly pathogenic). De-Nour suggests that interpersonal relationships generally require close scrutiny in further research on bipolar patients. Perhaps De-Nour's most stimulating contribution is on the importance of including psychosocial factors in treatment intervention, and on methods for so doing.

Psychological dysfunctions during episodes of mania have not been widely studied, perhaps because the manic patient is a difficult test subject. Sackeim and Steif (1988) contribute a lengthy chapter on the neuropsychology of the affective disorders. Though it illuminates mania relatively little, and chiefly concerns depression, it is of great interest to see what a wide range of dysfunctions has been explored. Some of these are: sensation and perception, including pain perception; psychomotor functioning, including speed, spontaneous activity, and disturbance in motor laterality; learning and memory; mediational and attentional processes; profiles of intellectual functioning, including "pseudodementia"; and the general neuropsychology of emotions.

What the clinician chiefly needs to appreciate is the degree to which manic patients are intellectually or cognitively impaired. Taylor and Abrams (1986) applied a complex neuropsychological battery to 30 manic patients and 42 normal controls. Half of the manics showed moderate to severe *global* cognitive impairment. If we did not know that Taylor and Abrams are very experienced investigators of mania in its many aspects, we might think their conclusion to be esoteric: the impairments pointed to "bifrontal, non-dominant parieto-occipital" dysfunction (p. 89). This might be compared with present trends in localizing neurological dysfunctions in schizophrenia (see chapter 15, pp. 548–549, 552–554). Harrow, Grossman, Silverstein, Meltzer, and Kittering (1986) likewise found quite severe disturbance of thought in manics. They studied 34 manics during acute admission, against 30 acute schizophrenics and 30 staff members, using the Goldstein-Scheerer Object Sorting Test, the Gorham Proverbs Test, and the Comprehension Subtest of the Wechsler Adult Intelligence Scale. Both manics and schizophrenics showed severe disorder of thought content and form, the manics somewhat the more severe. At 1 year follow-up, test results showed that the total amount of disorder was greatly reduced, that the manics showed a greater reduction than the schizophrenics, but that some manics still showed significant disorder. The degree of disorder correlated well with posthospital adjustment, but had little relationship with whether patients were on medication or not.

None of the studies above involved a development–regression model explicitly, so that it would be desirable for further investigations to include children as well as normal adults in control groups. Andreasen and Powers (1976) using the Goldstein-Scheerer Object Sorting Test found that schizophrenics resembled young children in their attempts to classify, but manics did not; these authors used a regression framework, though not a Piagetian one. The reader might also refer back to descriptive comments and the case vignette on Mr. E. S. in chapter 3, pp. 87–88.

I have found no research reports evaluating formal psychotherapy with manic patients: manics are almost impossible to engage in coherent discussion, and they disrupt the treatment milieu (Bjork, Steinberg, Lindenmayer, and Pardes, 1977). An interesting evaluation of their intrusive and manipulative traits is reported by Davis et al. (1986). These authors tested the hypothesis that such traits (testing of limits, inflicting of responsibility onto others, probing the "soft spots" of others, skill in playing staff against each other, flattering behaviors, and propensity to evoke anger) were lifelong. The Janowsky Manic Interpersonal Interaction Scale was the instrument used. It transpired that the high levels of these interpersonal behaviors dwindled to normal when mania remitted, therefore were not lifelong traits. Here a regression model was not invoked, though such behaviors are certainly mindful of "difficult," anxiously attached children.

De-Nour makes a strong plea for including psychosocial interventions in treatment planning, with a specific emphasis on monitoring and correcting pathogenic marital interactions. One of the most cost-effective longer-term interventions in bipolar disorder (Powles, 1989) appears to be the lithium group; that is, group psychotherapy designed to facilitate compliance with lithium maintenance, but also to offer personal support and modification of life-style problems. The model report on this subject is that of Volkmar, Bacon, Shakir, and Pfefferbaum (1981). Members of the group reported were young and intelligent but highly incapacitated and unemployable by virtue of recurrent breakdowns and hospitalizations. At the close of the study all members were employed, and periods of hospitalization had been drastically reduced: clearly an instance of the summative or synergistic effect of combined biological and psychosocial treatments.

Bibliographic Notes: Key Readings

As with previous chapters, asterisks in the reference list denote readings which I consider to be particularly useful and significant. I have cited authors in the compendium of Belmaker and van Praag (1980) repeatedly, and several key chapters in the compendium of Georgotas and Cancro (1988). These are fine collections of resource material even though depression dominates in content in the latter. Robbins and Sahakian (1980) present an excellent review of animal models for mania and the testing of antimanic drugs, and the problems with these models. Janowsky, Golden, Rapaport, Cain, and Gillan (1988) furnish a first-rate outline of neurotransmitter theory and of cholinergic–adrenergic interactions in the bipolar affective disorders. Lazarus (1986) must be considered the definitive authority on the various aspects of lithium. De-Nour (1980) and Ambelas (1987) offer heuristic comments and findings on the puzzling problem of life events and interpersonal relations in the causation of manic episodes.

References

Aleksandrowicz, D. R. (1980), Psychoanalytic studies on mania. In: *Mania: An Evolving Concept*, ed. R. H. Belmaker & H. M. van Praag. New York: Spectrum Publications.

*Ambelas, A. (1987), Life events and mania. *Brit. J. Psychiat.*, 150:235–240.

Andreasen, N. C., & Powers, P. S. (1976), Psychosis, thought disorder, and regression. *Amer. J. Psychiat.*, 133:522–526.

Ballenger, C. M., Reus, V. I., & Post, R. (1982), The "atypical" clinical picture of adolescent mania. *Amer. J. Psychiat.*, 139:602–606.

*Belmaker, R. H., & van Praag, H. M., eds. (1980), *Mania: An Evolving Concept*. New York: Spectrum Publications.

Bjork, D., Steinberg, M., Lindenmayer, J. P., & Pardes, H. (1977), Mania and milieu: Treatment of manics in a therapeutic community. *Hosp. Commun. Psychiat.*, 28:431–436.

Carlsson, A. (1987), The dopamine hypothesis of schizophrenia 20 years later. In: *Search for the Causes of Schizophrenia*, ed. H. Hafner, W. F. Gattaz, & W. Janzarik. Berlin: Springer-Verlag.

Carpenter, W. T., Jr., & Stephens, J. H. (1980), The diagnosis of mania. In: *Mania: An Evolving Concept*, ed. R. H. Belmaker & H. M. van Praag. New York: Spectrum Publications.

Carroll, B. J. (1979), Neuroendocrine function in mania. In: *Manic Illness*, ed. B. Shopsin. New York: Spectrum Publication.

Davis, J. M., Noll, K. M., & Sharma, R. (1986), Differential diagnosis and treatment of mania. In: *Mania: New Research and Treatment*, ed. A. C. Swann. Washington, DC: American Psychiatric Press.

*De-Nour, A. K. (1980), Psychosocial aspects of the management of mania. In: *Mania: An Evolving Concept*, ed. R. H. Belmaker & H. M. van Praag. New York: Spectrum Publications.

Dunner, D. L., & Hall, K. S. (1980), Social adjustment and psychological precipitants in mania. In: *Mania: An Evolving Concept*, ed. R. H. Belmaker & H. M. van Praag. New York: Spectrum Publications.

Gagrat, D. D., & Spiro, H. R. (1980), Social, cultural, and epidemiologic aspects of mania. In: *Mania: An Evolving Concept*, ed. R. H. Belmaker & H. M. van Praag. New York: Spectrum Publications.

*Georgotas, A., & Cancro, R., eds. (1988), *Depression and Mania*. New York: Elsevier.

Ginsberg, G. L. (1979), Psychoanalytic aspects of mania. In: *Manic Illness*, ed. B. Shopsin. New York: Spectrum Publications.

Harrow, M., Grossman, L. S., Silverstein, M. L., Meltzer, H. Y., & Kettering, R. L. (1986), A longitudinal study of thought disorder in manic patients. *Arch. Gen. Psychiat.*, 43:781–785.

Janowsky, D. S. (1986), A role for acetylcholine in mania. In: *Mania: New Research and Treatment*, ed. A. C. Swann. Washington, DC: American Psychiatric Press.

———— Davis, J. M. (1980), Cholinergic mechanisms in mania and depression: Questions of specificity. In: *Mania: An Evolving Concept*, ed. R. H. Belmaker & H. M. van Praag. New York: Spectrum Publications.

*———— Golden, R. N., Rapaport, M., Cain, J. J., & Gillan, J. C. (1988), Neurochemistry of depression and mania. In: *Depression and Mania*, ed. A. Georgotas & R. Cancro. New York: Elsevier.

Kraepelin, E. (1913), *Manic–Depressive Insanity and Paranoia*. trans. R. M. Barclay. Edinburgh: E. & S. Livingstone, 1921.

*Lazarus, J. H. (1986), *Endocrine and Metabolic Effects of Lithium*. New York: Plenum Medical Book Co.

Lerner, V. (1980), The subjective experience of mania. In: *Mania: An Evolving Concept*, ed. R. H. Belmaker & H. M. van Praag. New York: Spectrum Publications.

Levinson, D. F., & Levitt, M. E. M. (1987), Schizoaffective mania reconsidered. *Amer. J. Psychiat.*, 144:415–425.

Lewis, G. L., & Winokur, G. (1987), The induction of mania: A natural history study with controls. *Psychopharm. Bull.*, 23:74–78.

McKinney, W. T. (1988), Animal models for depression and mania. In: *Depression and Mania*, ed. A. Georgotas & R. Cancro. New York: Elsevier.

Pope, H. G., & Lipinski, J. F. (1978), Diagnosis in schizophrenia and manic–depressive illness. *Arch. Gen. Psychiat.*, 35:811–828.

Post, R. M. (1980), Biochemical theories of mania. In: *Mania: An Evolving Concept*, ed. R. H. Belmaker & H. M. van Praag. New York: Spectrum Publications.

———— Uhde, T. W., Rubinow, D. R., & Weiss, S. R. B. (1986), Antimanic effects of carbamazepine: Mechanisms of action and inplications for the biochemistry of manic–depressive illness. In: *Mania: New Research and Treatment*, ed. A. C. Swann. Washington, DC: American Psychiatric Press.

Powles, W. E. (1989), Group psychotherapy with affective disorders: Critical impressions of trends and strategies. *Group Anal.*, 22:7–17.

*Robbins, T. W., & Sahakian, B. J. (1980), Animal models of mania. In: *Mania: An Evolving Concept*, ed. R. H. Belmaker & H. M. van Praag. New York: Spectrum Publications.

Sackeim, H. A., & Steif, B. L. (1988), Neuropsychology of depression and mania. In: *Depression and Mania*, ed. A. Georgotas & R. Cancro. New York: Elsevier.

Schmale, A. H., & Engel, G. L. (1975), The role of conservation–withdrawal in depressive reactions. In: *Depression and Human Existence*, ed. E. J. Anthony & T. Benedek. Boston: Little, Brown.

Shopsin, B., ed. (1979), *Manic Illness*. New York: Spectrum Publications.

———— Annitto, W. (1979), Neuropharmacology of mania. In: *Manic Illness*, ed. B. Shopsin. New York: Spectrum Publications.

Swann, A. C., ed. (1986), *Mania: New Research and Treatment*. Washington, DC: American Psychiatric Press.

Taylor, M. A., & Abrams, R. (1986), Cognitive dysfunction in mania. *Compre-hen. Psychiat.*, 27:186–191.
Volkmar, F. R., Bacon, S., Shakir, S. A., & Pfefferbaum, A. (1981), Group therapy in the management of manic-depressive illness. *Amer. J. Psy-chother.*, 35:226–234.
Waters, B. G. H. (1979), Risk to bipolar affective psychosis. In: *Manic Illness,* ed. B. Shopsin. New York: Spectrum Publications.

---

*Recommended readings.

12

A Third Homeostatic Level:
Conservation–Withdrawal; Animal Behaviors
and the Nature of Human Depression

Introduction

Overview

Three dozen years ago, the first effective antidepressant drugs ushered in a revolution in therapy and research. Today, new drugs for depression have multiplied beyond comprehension: research and its literature have burgeoned with exponential explosiveness; the intricacies of antidepressant psychopharmacology and neurochemical theory are mastered by only a handful of superspecialists.

Where does this leave us? Apparently in a state of some disquietude, for I discern two themes, explicitly stated or implied, appearing across monographs and review articles. One theme expresses an apologetic rue that there is neither time nor space to include naturalistic and psychosocial concerns in

399

the search for causes of depression. The other expresses even a hint of despair, that we are drowning in a sea of data, of new drugs, and of new hypotheses, of inferential minutiae of submicroscopic detail, from which we cry out for something new and reorienting, a redirection of our view of what depression is and means (Baldessarini, 1983).

There are variations on these pessimistic themes. One is to the effect that any consensus on the nature of depression is impossible, since the depressive disorders are so heterogeneous as to etiology, biological origins, and treatment response (Rush, 1982, chapter 1). These latter points may be true. However, that does not negate the importance of common features in all depressions, nor the concept that depression (seen as a homeostatic style or process) is a kind of final common pathway leading from many origins (Whybrow, Akiskal, and McKinney, 1984), the initiating events of which are remarkably uniform (Paykel, 1978; Brown and Harris, 1978), and the maintaining or perpetuating mechanisms of which are rather finite in number. Thus, hope for some new understanding of depression may not be wholly illusory.

In a practical approach to these concerns, I shall orient this chapter by our homeostatic–dynamic model, which views depressions (Engel and Schmale, 1972) as members of a more embracing order of processes, conservation–withdrawal. The properties of this order, quite unlike fight–flight and disintegration, are withdrawal and disengagement, an abandonment of active coping in favor of passivity and atonia, and yet withal an organized, logically consistent group of features, unlike the psychoses.

I commence this chapter with a look at three behavioral patterns observable in animals: torpor, hibernation, and "death feigning." Torpor and hibernation are precisely monitored lowerings of vital functions including, specifically, body temperature; they are responses to harsh environmental changes; and they rather resemble sleep. Death feigning is an acute response to capture by a predator; it resembles death rather than sleep. All three strategies conserve energy and maximize the chances of survival until conditions become more hopeful. I relate them to human conservation–withdrawal, whose properties were discovered, or rather rediscovered and named, by Engel.

In the second section I review attempts to define and classify depressive disorders, ending with an attempt to define depression operationally by breaking it down into component features: subjective and experiential, cognitive, behavioral, and physiological. Depression, I suggest, is an unpleasant experience which we relate to loss; the analogy is to pain which, as defined elegantly by Merskey and Spear (1967), is the unpleasant experience we associate with tissue injury. Depression is subjectively painful; paralyzing in its loss of energy, will, motivation, interest, and pleasure; stupefying in its cognitive impairment, amounting in severe cases to "pseudodementia"; it includes physiologic impairments or the "functional shift" (Pollitt, 1960) and psychomotor retardation (Widlöcher, 1983).

In the next two chapters I shall review examples of research at the biological and psychosocial levels of emergence. It is difficult to separate the psychological and the social, and relatively little research has been devoted to these recently. Global biological features include the functional shift, circadian rhythms and their disturbance, and psychomotor retardation. Sleep and its disorders have become a major research front (Borbély, 1986; Kupfer, Foster, Coble, and McPartland, 1977) and sleep deprivation has a paradoxical effect in major depressions. The most intricate and sophisticated, yet in many ways the most elusive area in biological depression research has been the quest for brain mechanisms, particularly the study of disturbed monoamine neurotransmission. I trace this field historically. Regrettably, it has not produced an accepted theory of depression as yet. We next look at biological "markers" in depression, at animal models for depression and drug testing, and the Dexamethasone Suppression Test. Finally, a few pages are devoted to research on the mechanism of convulsive therapy, and to seasonal affective disorder, a new and intriguing area in biological depression research.

Psychosocial research in depression has not produced a large literature, thus, one has to search about for significant contributions. I shall review Brown and Harris's (1978) exemplary study on the causation of depressions. This study confirms long-standing impressions that there is a high association between life events and the onset and progress of clinical depressions. I have selected Bowlby's (1980) model of attachment and separation as crucial in understanding the psychodynamics of depression, since Bowlby has also written extensively regarding the interfaces between separation experiences, mourning, and depression. The "neuropsychology," or study of cognitive disturbances in depression, has not been explored extensively; I will review several contributions, including McAllister's (1983) excellent paper on pseudodementia. Finally, the place of the psychotherapies in depressive disorders (Weissman, 1979): it now appears clear that psychotherapy is effective in the less severe and the recovering depressions, and that the combination of psychotherapy and pharmacotherapy is synergistic, more effective than either modality alone.

The following integrative summary serves several purposes. It is a brief indicator of key research sources whose evidence will be reviewed in this chapter. It should be regarded as a chain of testable hypotheses, some of which are now rather firmly accepted, but many of which require testing by replication and extension of previous studies. Though the depressive disorders are today a paradigm for the understanding and management of psychiatric disorder generally, there is as yet no firmly proposed or accepted theory of the psychobiology of depression (Akiskal and McKinney, 1973, 1975; Whybrow et al., 1984), and any attempt at conceptual order would seem to offer heuristic value. I recommend the diagrammatic model of Brown and Harris (1978) as an integrative and stimulating depiction of interacting variables in depression.

Onset of Depressions. Remarkably homogeneous variables appear to be at work in initiating depressive disorders. Personal losses and defeats, objectively or subjectively defined; "exit events" (Paykel, 1978); threats to long-term security (Brown and Harris, 1978); rejections, separations, and bereavements (Bowlby, 1980). These correlate so powerfully with depressive episodes that they must be seen as no mere nonspecific stresses or triggers, but as potent "formative effects" (Brown and Harris, 1978). It is not that all losses provoke depressions, any more than that all heavy smokers develop lung cancer (Brown and Harris), but additional variables cause affected individuals to succumb. Lack of an intimate supportive figure, death of the subject's mother before age 11, social isolation, immobilization, low socioeconomic status (Brown and Harris), and habitual defense mechanisms (Bowlby) appear to determine the "choice" of depression as a final common pathway. Normal grief and even mania are alternate pathways (Bowlby, 1980; and see chapter 11, pp. 390–392). Genetic predispositions are assumed but I can find no clear theoretical formulations on how they come to bear as mechanisms; they presumably sensitize the organism to overreact to loss. Early life experiences must be assumed to tune biological mechanisms in this direction (Bowlby, 1980), while a tendency to "giving up" more easily must be assumed to be the resultant of these mechanisms (Engel and Schmale, 1972).

Establishment of Autonomy of Depression. After a prodromal period of struggle in the fight–flight mode (or protest), despair is ushered in by the mechanism of giving up. The sequence is entirely analogous to the chain of events and behaviors in separation reactions in childhood (Bowlby, 1980). The depressive process then becomes stabilized or autonomous in characteristic fashion. This is by psychosocial and biological perpetuating mechanisms, which give the depressive episode its particular quality and severity, and which are the target for treatment strategies. Treatment shortens the natural history of the depressive episode. The process of spontaneous remission is at present not understood: hypotheses for treatment effects will be noted below.

Quality and Severity of Depression. There appears to be a continuum extending from mild, indolent ("dysthymic disorder") depressions, through complete, "saturated" major depressions, to depressions complicated and "diluted" by psychotic features (disintegration). There is a semantic problem here. Although these latter depressions are considered the "severest" (Hamilton, 1959), they are no more "typical," complete, examples of depression than are the milder ones, a concept not emphasized in the literature. The milder depressions lack a physiological functional shift or biological perpetuating mechanisms: their mechanisms are largely psychosocial, they respond to psychotherapy, and drug therapy is ineffective with them save in a placebo sense. The intermediate, pure, complete, "major" depressions with "melancholic" features are dominated by pathophysiologic perpetuating mechanisms and are ideal candidates for drug and convulsive therapy. The most severe, psychotic depressions require some admixture of antipsychotic management.

The functional shift (Pollitt, 1960) which characterizes major, typical, depressive episodes points to limbic–hypothalamic dysfunction. More recently, disturbances of circadian rhythms (Czeisler, Cronauer, Mooney, Anderson, and Allan, 1987) and particularly of sleep (Borbély, 1986; Kupfer et al., 1977) have been intensively researched. The gastrointestinal dysfunctions typical of the functional shift appear to have received scant research attention. Psychomotor retardation is a central feature of depression (Widlöcher, 1983). Cognitive difficulties are proportionate to the severity of the depressive episode and may amount to "pseudodementia" (McAllister, 1983).

The quality and severity of a depressive episode do not correlate well with the nature of the life events which initiate it (Lewis, 1934, 1938; Brown and Harris, 1978). No comprehensive or coherent theory for this exists from biological research. It appears generally assumed that bipolar and more severe unipolar depressions have genetic contributing and perpetuating causes; presumably, a sensitivity to personal loss and a heightening of the mechanisms of conservation–withdrawal in response to loss. Initial theories stemming from antidepressant treatment response postulated a relative deficiency of monoamines at limbic and hypothalamic monaminergic synapses. More recently, the complex process of "receptor down-regulation" (Baker and Dewhurst, 1985; Blier and de Montigny, 1985) has been implicated as an important biological perpetuating mechanism. Psychosocial variables correlated with the more severe depressions include: additional adverse experiences at "change points" after the depressive episode has been initiated; older age and previous depressive episodes; and loss by death in childhood. The more "dysthymic" depressions are correlated with loss by separation in childhood (Brown and Harris, 1978) and presumably they lack a strong biological or genetic diathesis.

Treatment of Depression. The concept of a continuum from mildest to severest depressive episodes also applies to their treatment. The "dysthymic" or "minor" depression spectrum responds to focal psychotherapy of a cognitive–behavioral type (Rush, 1982; Beck et al., 1979; Williams, 1984) and very little to drugs. The "melancholic" or "major" depression spectrum responds to drugs and convulsive therapy (Blier and de Montigny, 1985; Damlouji, Feighner, and Rosenthal, 1985; Kendell, 1981) and relatively little to psychotherapy, though a specific "push" approach may be effective (Wadsworth and Barker, 1976). The "psychotic" depressions require an admixture of antipsychotic treatment. It has not been clarified whether the psychotherapies operate chiefly through new learning (verbal learning is defective in depression; see McAllister [1981]) or through support and activation (Wadsworth and Barker, 1976). The combination of drug and psychotherapeutic treatment operates more effectively than either one does alone (Weissman, 1979, 1981), probably in the less seriously depressed or those already beginning remission. Psychotherapeutic approaches to the most seriously depressed are almost unresearched (Williams, 1984).

It appears important to recall that it is the *syndrome* and its perpetuating or maintaining mechanisms which are attacked in treatment, not the original "formative" causes, which are beyond recall. Part of the psychotherapeutic effort is in modifying attitudinal and life-style predisposing causes, in the interest of preventing relapse.

Animal Behavior and Human Conservation–Withdrawal

Three Adaptive Behaviors in the Animal Kingdom

In chapter 7 we have surveyed the basic nature of conservation–withdrawal and its relationship to other homeostatic modes and to the clinical syndromes of depression. Here I propose to commence with a somewhat broad base in animal behaviors, specifically those behaviors which use passivity and withdrawal as a defense against danger and stress, and as a life-preserving measure. There is a very widespread collection of such behaviors among animal taxa. One must, however, heed the warning (Lyman, Willis, Malan, and Wang, 1982) that they are not necessarily genetically related patterns, even when they occur in closely related species: they do not occur with consistency across closely related animals, and they do occur across very distantly related groups, so that parallel evolution of such behaviors is likely. It might be wiser to refer to a "collection" rather than a class of behaviors; but they are a class in terms of their survival function.

Within this broad collection or class, we shall neglect such relatively nondefensive behaviors as rest and sleep, which are regular and cyclical patterns of passivity and withdrawal. More germane are three behaviors which are responses to environmental stress and danger: hibernation, torpor, and death feigning. Climatic change in the passage of summer and winter, for example, brings threats of shortage of food and water and of chilling or scorching temperatures. More acute danger is presented in unexpected and sudden shortages of food or water, sudden chilling, or more acutely still, threat of actual capture by predators. I summarize the definitions of Lyman et al. (1982) for hibernation and torpor.

1. *Hibernation* is a radical and very precisely monitored adaptation to winter (i.e., inhospitable shifts of climate and the cutting off of food and water) by smaller terrestrial animals who cannot migrate: "active and alert on the previous day . . . [the animal is] now cold . . . moribund . . . motionless or capable of only slow, uncoordinated movements" (p. 1). Hibernation is characterized by extremely deep sleep, prolonged and fixed immobility in a sheltered place, and an energy-conserving posture. Body temperature [T(b)] by definition may be as low as 5°C, though it continues to be precisely regulated; and cardiac and respiratory rhythms are grossly slowed. Many species of rodent are habitual hibernators. Cognate processes include estivation, a withdrawal response to the heat and drying of hot

summer; for example, in fish and amphibians in East Africa and the North American desert.

2. *Torpor* is a motor and physiological sluggishness, of gradual or sudden onset, with or without a controlled drop in body temperature as far as 15°C, and from which arousal is quicker than from hibernation. Small birds use this mechanism. Bears do not truly hibernate: rather, they den up and go into a fluctuant torpor for up to 100 days, during which period their underdeveloped young are born.

3. *Death feigning* (Hunsaker, 1977), thanatosis (Edmunds, 1974), tonic immobility (Maier, 1970), animal hypnosis (Ratner, 1967), playing possum (Hartman, 1952), or sham death (further names are listed in Ratner [1967]) is an acute response to being caught by a predator, in which a state of catalepsy, with limpness and a mimicry of death, is invoked. Feigning death is recommended to humans as the defense of last resort when assaulted by a grizzly bear, though a more aggressive defense can be attempted in an attack by a black bear (Herrero, 1985). The North American opossum, *Didelphis virginiana*, is the most convincing adept at this strategy (Hartman, 1952; Maier, 1970).

Torpor, Hibernation, and Death Feigning

Lyman et al. (1982) present an integrated and recent compendium of the many dimensions in the biology of torpor and hibernation. These behaviors range across the animal kingdom. Certain fish, amphibians, and reptiles cope with the threats of summer heat and winter cold and the associated threats of dehydration, starvation, hyperthermia, and hypothermia, by digging in for the unfavorable season in hibernation or estivation. From day to day, amphibians and reptiles seek warmer or colder places to maintain the most favorable temperature. Some fish are migrators, for the same reason. Lyman believes (see his arguments) that primitive mammals must have evolved in a nocturnal ecological niche, where the range of temperatures is restricted, and that the present "standard" body temperature of around 38°C evolved as they emerged into the more variable diurnal setting.

The precise control of body temperature [or T(b)] is crucial to both birds and mammals. It has been calculated (Lyman et al., 1982, chapter 1) that, if one extrapolates the curve for metabolic rate against body mass and area, no animal can exist which is smaller than 2.5 gm. The mouse has a metabolic rate 20 times that of the sheep. Simply burning up is a constant threat for minute animals such as the shrew and the humming bird, who must eat constantly or perish. The Scylla and Charybdis of warm-blooded existence are hyperthermia (the brain begins to coagulate at 45°C) and hypothermia (animals not prepared by torpor or hibernation will die quickly by chilling). Therefore, very small animals in particular live a precarious life: they must stop foraging to sleep, and they must cope with temporary fluctuations of cold weather or cold nights or in the supply of food and drink. Clearly, some combination of acute conditions of cold and shortage of calories leads to the response of torpor, and longer-range fluctuations lead to hibernation. These are energy-conserving devices, when life cannot be sustained by any other action.

Who are the hibernators (Lyman et al., 1982)? Hummingbirds and swifts (Apodiformes), nightjars (Caprimulgiformes), African sunbirds (the ecological equivalent of the New World hummingbirds), and perhaps familiar North American wintering birds such as the chickadee and redpoll, resort to torpor on cold nights, or when food has been in short supply. *Noctivation* is a term proposed by Skutch (1973) for this type of adaptive nocturnal torpor. A fall in body temperature and a slow, sluggish arousal are involved in this strategy of conservation of energy and life. Skunks, raccoons, and badgers den up over the winter but do not enter either torpor or hibernation. Some shrews and bats enter torpor or true hibernation. Bears, as noted above, enter a fluctuant torpor; presumably because of their large body mass they do not need to utilize true hibernation. During the winter they neither eat, drink, defecate, or urinate. Nephrologists have become interested in this adaptation, since because bears consume body fat rather than protein they do not need to excrete nitrogenous wastes. Their body temperature [T(b)] falls to 31°C and metabolic rate to 50 to 60 percent of summer level; the pulse slows from the active rate of 40 to 10 per minute.

It is rodents who are the specialists and favorite research subjects in true hibernation (Lyman et al., 1982, chapters 2, 12, 14). Decline in food and water supply and cooling ambient temperature [T(a)] seem to be the stimuli preceding hibernation behavior; the pineal gland has been implicated as a link in the chain of control related to visual assessment of the decline in daylight.

Parasympathetic mechanisms including the complex and sensitive machinery of body temperature regulation (i.e., hypothalamic structures) initiate the changes of hibernation. The first is sleep, where REM patterns diminish, then disappear, and where finally even slow-wave patterns are abolished to a rather flat electroencephalogram. Body temperature drops massively and is maintained stably at a few degrees above the ambient level. A curious, intermittent, Cheyne-Stokes type of respiration carries on. The turnover of catecholamines is greatly reduced, and adrenergic activity ceases.

The recently discovered "seasonal affective disorder" may have some conceivable phylogenetic relation to mechanisms of hibernation. Czeisler et al. (1987) offer a good presentation of the construct of "photoperiod" or duration of daylight and its influence (through the optic tract, suprachiasmatic nucleus, hypothalamus, and pineal gland) on animal behavior, particularly sexual cycles. The pineal is now known to take part in producing melatonin, a neurotransmitter generally suppressive of sexual activity; it probably also mediates other photoperiod-related behaviors. It is not yet clear whether seasonal affective disorder is a proper clinical entity. Its manifestation is a rather nonspecific, indolent type of what is better called neurasthenia, or even pure conservation–withdrawal, than depression. It is remedied by exposing the subject to very strong light, much brighter than natural light or winter sunlight, several times daily (see pp. 417, 477–483).

I am unable to find clear boundaries between hibernation and torpor, partly because of problems with different terminologies. Generally, torpor and hibernation resemble sleep in body posture and what little is reported of their physiology. They show the specific component of stable fall in body temperature, and can be seen to be an energy-conserving measure. Death feigning or animal hypnosis (no name for it is completely satisfactory) has an acute or very rapid onset. Its postures are "unnatural," resembling death rather than sleep; the brain is in an alerting mode; and it is a clear response to being handled by a predator or an unfamiliar experimenter.

No primate exhibits hibernation, and only a tiny group of primitive primates, the dwarf lemurs of Madagascar, utilize torpor. Lyman notes that primates are, or originally were, residents of the tropics, and hence never had to develop a genetic adaptation to chilling. I cannot find mention of death feigning or animal hypnosis among primates, though the behavior pervades an enormous range of animal species (Ratner, 1967; Maier, 1970; Edmunds, 1974; Hartman, 1952). It is exceedingly difficult for a terrified human to feign death consciously and effectively, unless fainting has supervened (Herrero, 1985).

The hummingbird is something of a specialist at nocturnal torpor, or noctivation (Skutch, 1973). The metabolic rate of these tiny birds is extremely high, and their T(b) varies between species from 39°C to 41°C as well as fluctuating somewhat with activity in individuals. Thus they must feed constantly, like the shrews, to prevent burning up. It has been estimated (Skutch, 1973) that an adult man would have to eat 370 lb of boiled potatoes or 130 lb of bread daily to match their caloric intake; adult humans eat about 2½ lb of food daily. When the T(a) drops at night more than 7°C from that of the day (which does not happen every night), the hummingbird enters torpor: it may raise its feathers to cool down as quickly as possible; in any case its T(b) drops virtually to the T(a); it becomes sluggish and weak; it cannot fly, nor even regain its perch if removed; its breathing and pulse rates slow down; it chirps and moves feebly if handled. On recovery it regains its normal T(b) and its strength only slowly, and cannot fly until its T(b) is at least 30°C.

Death Feigning or Animal Hypnosis

Provided we do not commit the "pathetic fallacy" and assume that animals feel and think like humans, these terms will suffice for the reaction exhibited by a large range of animals, invertebrate and vertebrate, in response to being captured or experimentally restrained. The following review summarizes Ratner (1967) with contributions from Hartman (1952), Edmunds (1974), Maier ([1970], a very brief discussion), Hunsaker (1977), and Adler ([1979], a lengthy discussion on "Responses to Agression").

Ratner's (1967) interesting model of steps in predator–prey interaction and the steps of alerting–freezing, fleeing, and struggling–fighting, has been summarized in chapters 7 and 10. Here we are concerned with:

Step 4. The closure to zero continues (in effect, the subject has been cornered and seized and is being held by the predator or experimenter). *Response*: the subject becomes immobile and unresponsive, and *animal hypnosis* supervenes (Ratner's term).

Although Ratner's presentation is in the context of a work on human hypnosis, he clearly states that "animal hypnosis *is probably not* related to human hypnosis" (p. 576). It is a pattern of immobility and unresponsiveness conforming to all criteria of an innate behavior: it occurs over a large range of animal forms, it appears relevant to survival, it shows physiological components, and it appears without opportunity for learning. The response is triggered by some threatening or predatory stimulus condition, crucially an unfamiliar one; novelty and restraint are essential for its induction; it is invariably preceded by struggle. Once the situation is no longer novel, the response disappears. Birds have been the central research subjects, since the response can be elicited from almost all birds studied (the wren is an apparent exception) though insects, frogs, and reptiles have also been observed, as well as a number of mammals (rats, rabbits, dogs, coyotes, foxes; curiously, Ratner does not discuss the opossum). The little that is known of the physiology of the state suggests clearly that the animal becomes unresponsive, apparently anesthetic and analgesic, and that there is a motor inhibition. Certain reflexes are preserved. The nervous system seems to be in alerted condition, with increased heart rate but slow and shallow respiration. Posturally, the birds described either remain upright, but with drooping head and tail; or if held on their backs for 15 to 30 seconds, they then remain "feet up," the head usually turned to one side, and in some cases the legs and feet in a coarse tremor.

If we examine the survival value of this widespread behavior, and its reciprocal in the behavior of predators, it is clear that death feigning raises the probability that a predator will lose interest; as Adler (1979) states, if a mouse would only lie limp and immobile, instead of repeatedly dragging itself away after a cat's mauling, thus arousing the cat's interest all over again, it might have a much better chance of survival.

A most colorful example of death feigning is by the North American opossum, *Didelphis virginiana*, which inhabits wooded lands with water readily available, and in fact occupies the geographical area in which the whole marsupial group evolved in the late Cretaceous. This creature is well known and celebrated in folklore (Hartman, 1952) and is said to have taught the fox how to feign death. Its death feigning is particularly convincing and in consequence the attacking animal will usually leave after a few sniffs (Maier, 1970) particularly since there is evidence that anal gland secretions participate in the pattern. The African ground squirrel is said to be another expert death feigner (Edmunds, 1974). The first time I personally observed an opossum enact death feigning, our family dog was harassing one in the garden in the evening. By the time I called the dog off, I was sure that the opossum was dead, and prepared it for a decent burial, only to find it gone an hour later. On another occasion, I saw an opossum ambling along the side of a country road on an autumn afternoon, and decided to intimidate it by approaching it, shouting loudly. The opossum halted its slow walk, seemed to deflate, and fell slowly over on one side, where it lay limp and half curled up, the typical posture which will be resumed if disarranged (Hunsaker, 1977, pp. 313–316). Eyes and mouth were open, the rather menacing teeth exposed. I picked it up cautiously by the muscular tail and carried it over to our car. Its gums and tongue were cyanotic, and it drooled. I could not detect respiration. I then laid it down again, and we watched for 5 minutes. The opossum finally rose to its feet with exquisite deliberation, and glided off into the bushes in a gait mindful of a slow-motion moving picture.

This response is by no means invariable during attack by a predator (Hartman, 1952; Hunsaker, 1977). Growling, screaming, and fighting back with menacing teeth (it is a competent carnivore and omnivore) are more usual (i.e., fight–flight). When death is feigned, the animal (as I found) rolls over on its side, hunched up, tail curled under, paws extended, eyes and mouth open, quite limp and unresponsive, salivating copiously, very atonic. These postural elements are entirely unlike sleep. The behavior is also unlike "freezing" on seeing a predator at a distance: here the posture is braced and tense and readied for very swift action, whereas death feigning occurs only after actual contact with a predator; it takes some time for the animal to emerge gradually out of the state.

Relatively little has been established of physiologic changes during the time the opossum is "playing possum." It is known (Hunsaker, 1977) that the electroencephalogram is one of alerting; that the pulse is slightly accelerated; and that the electrocardiogram is unchanged from the normal or resting state (opossums always seem to be resting or moving slowly).

Conservation–Withdrawal in the Human

The adaptive–defensive pattern of disengagement and passivity in humans was discovered, or perhaps more properly rediscovered, by Engel (Engel and Schmale, 1972), who credits previous investigators such as Darwin (1884) and Hoagland (1928), as does Ratner (1967).

Darwin's (1884) posthumously published essay had evidently been conceived as part of chapter 7 on instinct in *The Origin of Species* (Darwin, 1859). In a discussion of instinctive fear he included a one-page statement on "animals feigning . . . . Death—an unknown state to each living creature" (p. 363). Darwin distinguished between 3 processes: "Fainting (I have had a Robin faint in my hands)," "the paralyzing effects of excessive fear," and "the simulation of death" (p. 363). His review and the experiments which he carried out himself were chiefly on insects. He reported examining 17 different species of spiders and insects: their attitudes during death feigning differed consistently from those in actual death.

Hoagland (1928) pointed out that animals react either actively or in a mode "surprisingly overlooked by most students of animal behavior [in which the animals] may cease all movement and remain quiescent even in the presence of violently disturbing factors" (p. 426). He cited a number of previous reports and the various names given to this extremely widespread phenomenon. Among mammals, he noted, "Foxes and opossums are said to 'feign death' " (p. 427); also, a peculiar maneuver could produce an analogous state in humans, persisting for a few seconds. Hoagland's own experiments were with lizards. In a highly technical discussion, he dealt with the influence of temperature on chemical and physiological processes, and speculated that the secretion, then degradation or excretion, of some endogenous substance (for example, adrenalin above a certain threshold) might initiate and terminate tonic immobility, whose central features are a plastic muscle tone and a lack of reactivity.

Engel's discovery was serendipitous (Engel, 1956), and took place during observation of the famous baby Monica, born with esophageal atresia, fed through a gastric fistula, and admitted to hospital for intensive study after a period of considerable emotional neglect and failure to thrive. The striking finding in this intensive single-case study, as relevant for us here, was this: in a situation much as Ainsworth's "strange situation test" (chapter 5) when her familiar doctor or nurse left her, and a stranger appeared, Monica would suddenly disengage, become unresponsive and hypotonic, and after awhile lapse into sleep; during this time her gastric mucosa would become pale and secretion would cease. She would later awake from sleep, and if the stranger were still there, would lapse back into the unresponsive and atonic condition. However, if familiar figures were there, she would express a lively joy and her gastric mucosa would secrete profusely. Engel at first termed this state *depression–withdrawal*. Later he corrected this title because the behavior did not fit the construct of depression well, and in fact seemed to be a protection against true depression. For myself, the parallel between Monica's disengaging behavior and death feigning is difficult to ignore, especially after seeing opossums play possum.

In subsequent formulations, Engel (1962a,b) pointed out that the usual sequence for a child faced with separation is to struggle and protest, and then if such behavior is ineffective, to lapse into depression—withdrawal, exhaustion, and sleep. Monica seemed to have become so sensitized to separation that she by-passed the phase of struggle and protest as futile, and proceeded directly into unresponsiveness.

From these and further observations, and joined later by his colleague Schmale, Engel elaborated the construct of conservation—withdrawal (Engel and Schmale, 1972; Schmale and Engel, 1975). All animate things cycle between activity and passivity (see also Hoagland, 1928): between the active outreach for relationships and needed nourishment, security, and comfort, the active—engaging mode; and an inactive—disengaging mode for which the prototype is sleep. Conservation—withdrawal has to be distinguished from an active disengagement from the environment, in which flight would be included. It is inactive—disengaging, passively carried out, and passively experienced: its hallmarks are a relative immobility, a quiescence, and an unresponsiveness to the environment. It has a defensive quality, however, not merely a quality of resting: its aim may be inferred to be to assure survival through disengagement and passivity, "to conserve resources," and to "assure autonomy . . . until environmental conditions are once again more compatible" (Engel and Schmale, 1972, p. 57). Although sleep is the prototype for the inactive—disengaging mode, of which conservation—withdrawal is a major example, ordinary sleep is not to be equated with conservation—withdrawal (Schmale and Engel, 1975). Rather, the type of sleep which occurs immediately after intense stimulation or profound exhaustion, and which is non-REM in pattern would be considered conservation—withdrawal. Transcendental meditation, the "alpha" state, with both lowered metabolic rate and reduced sympathico-adrenergic activity, may be regarded as an instance of conservation—withdrawal. Conservation—withdrawal, in short, allows a person or animal to carry on, in the face of inadequate or excessive stimulation, through a period of unrewarding "conditions with as little involvement, cost or risk as possible" (Schmale and Engel, 1975, p. 186). But conservation–withdrawal is not a state, it is a dynamic process.

The kind of conservation–withdrawal which we see in humans is accompanied by two characteristic and dysphoric cognitive–affective patterns which are related significantly to clinical depression, and in fact to much general ill-health. (Engel uses the term *affects* for these patterns, though he and Schmale do not describe either the subjective feeling–experience or the expressive behaviors associated with an emotion; rather, their focus is on the cognitive view of the future in these states.)

These two patterns are helplessness and hopelessness. Helplessness, whose origin and quality is in the experience of the abandoned 1- to 2-year-old child, and which can be equated with despair, relates to the dependency of young children and their need for help and protection. In helplessness, the distressed person depends (unsuccessfully) on the environment for relief, and feels personally powerless to change matters. There is still the childlike hope (as contrasted with hopelessness) that someone will do something, since the self is helpless. Hopelessness, Engel and Schmale believe, originates with the shattering of the fantasy of personal omnipotence in the oedipal period. In successful mastery of the oedipal conflict, the child, learning to identify with the parents and their strengths, becomes able to choose new objects when abandoned. But the child who learns hopelessness comes to believe that the self is inadequate, that one's own deficiencies are to blame for one's powerlessness, and that there is no hope that others will come to the rescue.

Schmale and Engel develop another major construct: the giving–up/given–up complex. With object loss ensues an unpleasant loss of ego autonomy, a loss of motivation, a reawakening of previous painful memories: this is giving up. If all goes well, there is a resolution in terms of a healthy renunciation and a taking on of new objects: this is the given up phase. However, there can be much painful and unsuccessful struggle over giving up; further, both clinical depression and many other forms of illness appear to ensue during the depletions of conservation–withdrawal, and the passively experienced dysphoria of the helplessness–hopelessness and giving-up/given-up complexes. Again, the pathophysiology of these dynamic adaptations or homeostatic readjustments is as yet poorly understood. It must be assumed that monoamine deficiencies (for depression) and changes in immune system competence (for general medical illness) will have to be invoked and further explored as explanatory mechanisms.

*Reconciliation Between Animal Behaviors and Human
Conservation–Withdrawal*

I shall be looking in chapter 13 at further animal models used to understand human depressions, as well as for the testing of antidepressant drugs: "despair" in rodents; separation reactions in young puppies and monkeys; the learned helplessness reaction in dogs; "depressions" induced by drugs such as reserpine and tetrabenazine. But here let us consolidate the argumentum so far.

I take conservation–withdrawal to be a general homeostatic and adaptive process; it is a defensive subdivision of a larger inactive–disengaging class of behaviors; in turn it forms a superordinate class which includes in humans many medical illnesses, the adaptive patterns of grief, and the maladaptive patterns of depression. Hibernation, torpor, and death feigning are cognate homeostatic processes, adaptive, defensive, and passive–disengaging. Hibernation and torpor, mimicking sleep, are adaptations to cyclical and relatively predictable environmental stress. Death feigning, mimicking death, is a response to emergency conditions where the animal cannot escape. All three are characterized primarily by atonia and profound passivity, though clearly they are finely tuned and orchestrated as physiological responses. Their aim is to give the "best chance" of survival under arid or death-dealing conditions.

There have been frequent suggestions that human depression must be related to hibernation (Pollitt, 1960), a supposition revived by recent interest in "seasonal depression" (Whybrow et al., 1984). These suggestions are researchable. The dramatic and widespread pattern of death feigning needs much physiological clarification, particularly in species closer to ourselves;

the opossum, however intriguing, is a marsupial and very far removed from humans phylogenetically.

It is necessary to recall the contrast between animal and human stress: stress, for most animals, is adaptation to impersonal environmental conditions, including climate, nutrition, and predation; while for humans, who have largely mastered environmental conditions, stress is principally interpersonal and highly dependent on personal cognitive appraisal and interpretation. Thus, we might conceive that while animals use passive, disengaging techniques to survive an arid or death-dealing alien surrounding, humans use these tactics to try to survive what is cognitively interpreted as an arid or overwhelming interpersonal situation (object loss, rejection, humiliation, and abandonment) with the cognitive estimate that the self is helpless and the future hopeless; and as the "best chance" of survival until conditions become more favorable.

The Phenomena of Depression: Classification and Definition

Early Classifications: Kraepelin; the Reactive–Endogenous Controversy

What constitutes a clinical depressive disorder? I believe we need to face problems of definition and classification before any sense can be made of researches into the meaning, the causes, and the mechanisms of the depressive disorders. The modern era begins with Kraepelin (1913), who struggled over many years with the continuum of the functional psychoses, and finally proposed that those conditions, either episodic or continuing, which produce personality deterioration, form a dementia praecox grouping; and that those conditions which are largely episodic, which have a prominent disturbance of the human sense of energy and well-being, and which typically do not eventuate in deterioration, form a manic–depressive grouping. Kraepelin, who has often, and quite wrongly, been maligned for rigidity, was astute enough to see that there is some reciprocal relation between depression and mania, conditions which previously had been classified as unrelated; his continuing effort was to make conceptual sense of a complex continuum of disorders in the functional psychoses, and he changed his views repeatedly. This continuum view of the functional psychoses is echoed in such formulations as Schneider's, to be commented on in chapter 15.

By the 1930s, attempts to classify the depressions had entered a stage of considerable controversy, which continued for 40 years. Though now of mainly historical interest, we should note the outlines of this controversy, carried out principally in Britain between research groups in Newcastle and London. It had been generally held by clinicians that the milder depressions were "reactive," that is, responses to life events; and, by contrast, that the more severe depressions were unconnected with life events and were therefore labeled "endogenous." Thus there occurred a general drift into labeling the severe depressive syndromes endogenous, regardless of their natural history, and to using the term *reactive* for any milder depression. The term *reactive* acquired an additional and different meaning: patients in milder depressions were "reactive" to environmental cues (Batchelor, 1969).

Mapother (1926) fired the first salvo in the controversy: he emphasized the "gradualist" view, later to be the main thesis of the London group: this was the empirical finding of a continuum between reactive and endogenous poles. The Newcastle group, using equally careful observation and later statistical treatment (Hamilton, 1959; Kiloh and Garside, 1963) found evidence for a clearly bimodal distribution and therefore for separate reactive and endogenous factors. Kendell (1968), then working in London, should be consulted for a review and resolution of the problem. In retrospect, one must wonder how the controversy ever arose, after reading Lewis's definitive early papers (1934, 1938) which, in exhaustive clinical presentations, showed that proper history taking would reveal a precipitating cause for even the severest depressions, and that there is very little correlation between natural history and the clinical picture. The determinants of the controversy clearly include a kind of rivalrous vendetta between energetic Northerners and the academic power base establishment in London. But these were not merely personal power struggles. Careful and skillful observations and analyses were made, but probably with inadequate attention to the clarification of natural history in the case material.

Modern Classification and Its Problems

The first properly empirical study in nosology of depressions in North America was by Grinker and colleagues (Grinker, Miller, Sabshin, Nunn, and Nunnally, 1961) on an "unselected" sample of 96 admissions to a Chicago hospital. No sample, of course, is wholly unselected: consecutive or otherwise randomized admissions are "selected" by many demographic, social, and economic pressures which determine who is admitted where, and when, and why. In this study clinical examinations were carefully separated from ratings and from complex statistical treatment. Five clusterings, indicating the influence of five factors, emerged, paraphrased as follows:

1. Dismal affect, hopelessness, loss of self-esteem, a self-image of badness; a "typical" depressive picture with various gradations of severity.
2. Almost complete concern and occupation with external problems; reactive and externalizing.
3. Strong motifs of guilt and restitution; a kind of superego and internalizing pattern.
4. A pure culture of anxiety; an anxiety–depression picture which, as I interpret it, is the result of misdiagnosis; that is, a syndrome which might more accurately be termed an anxiety disorder.
5. Pervasive feelings of being unloved, with anger and envy: the well-known hostile depression emerging from this study.

These clusterings or subtypes have been confirmed and further worked with in more recent studies; see, for example, Overall (1983).

Sedler and Dessain (1983) have translated for the first time a lecture given by Falret in Paris in 1854, thus returning us to the roots of the present unipolar–bipolar classification of the affective disorders. They recount the now rather amusing rivalry between Falret and his colleague and rival Baillarger for the honor of first identifying *folie circulaire*, or the occurrence of both manic and depressive episodes in the same patient. Sedler and Dessain appear to side with Falret against Baillarger, though the race was evidently a keen and close one. In the lecture Falret noted a greater prevalence of "folie circulaire" among women, together with the hints of genetic influence. Kahlbaum (cited by Becker, 1974, and by Lewis, 1934, 1938) later ascribed a genetic or familial influence in the more severe affective disorders, as contrasted with the less severe "cyclothymic" cases.

Today's classification, reflected in a relatively stable nomenclature, matured with Leonhard in Germany in 1962, soon supported by the independent studies of Perris in Sweden, Angst in Switzerland, and Winokur in the United States (Winokur, 1973; Dunner, 1983). Evidence rapidly emerged for a meaningful distinction between a large, heterogeneous, unipolar clustering, and a smaller, more homogeneous, Bipolar clustering, with the following features:

Unipolar
    Large heterogeneous cluster
    No manic episodes; depression(s) only
    Later age of onset; fewer episodes
    Weaker to absent family history of affective disorder
Bipolar
    Small homogeneous cluster
    Manic as well as depressive episodes, including manic episodes alone
    Earlier age of onset; more frequent episodes
    Significant family history: affected parents and two-generation linkages

As the antidepressant drugs came into use and the biological bases of depression came to be explored, the desideratum developed that a medical model of classification be followed (Andreasen, 1983); that is, that biological mechanisms or causes be used as a basis for classification. To the present date, apart from the unipolar–bipolar division, no such etiologic classification has emerged. However, efforts such as those of Schildkraut and colleagues (Schildkraut, Schatzburg, Orsulak, Mooney, and Rosenbaum, and Gudeman, 1983) are suggestive. These workers have plotted differences in excretion products of norepinephrine against various depressive phenomena, and in general they conclude that there is a clear grouping corresponding to bipolar depression, and in the unipolar depression a gradation which yields three categories: low epinephrine synthesis and release, corresponding to normal metabolism; intermediate levels suggesting normal norepinephrine output but disorder in other systems; a small group with high excretion (comparable to the bipolar group) show also a high urinary free cortisol, and may either be generating increased norepinephrine or, additionally, may have a cholinergic system derangement.

It is probably better here to review the problems in classification, and to give some illustrations of principles of classification, than to give further examples of classificatory attempts. I would recall the reader here to the principles enunciated by Beahrs (1986); namely, the inherent antithesis or inverse relationship between precision and relevance: the product of the two remains a constant. Andreason (1983) and Overall (1983) state that there is, in effect, no classification that will serve all needs. Rather, each classification has to be designed or selected to meet the needs of the work being undertaken. For researchers, precisely defined operational criteria are needed, leading to the selection of narrowly homogeneous cohorts of patients for study (examples might be patients with severely retarded depression, or with Grinker's hostile depression). Clinicians require broader, more flexible definitions and classifications (I will suggest below that their requirements may in fact include political considerations). Thus, there is an unavoidable antithesis between the "homogeneous group" approach, the narrow and exclusive definition–classification of the researcher, and the broad, inclusive, adaptable approach required for clinical work.

Andreasen reviews the types of classification that may be possible. Most commonly we think in, and use, a hierarchical classification, a branching from the largest and most inclusive class into subclasses of increasing specificity. The difficulty with this method, particularly when we are dealing with continuous and interlocking data as in psychiatry, is that we have to make forced choices between subclasses, and this use of dichotomies (Beahrs, 1986) leads us into the delusion that we are in reality dealing with sharply different, unrelated, entities, or even entities that are opposites, whereas they may be taxonomically quite closely related. The other principal classifying method is by dimensions (e.g., severity, duration, chronic versus episodic, agitated versus retarded, and so on); such a system allows combinations of variables, can become very complicated, but does allow of treatment of overlaps, and the placing of data on a continuum.

Overall (1983) reviews four classifications systems of recent evolution. The St. Louis criteria (associated particularly with the name of Feighner) give operational definitions for 16 psychiatric syndromes, aiming at "pure" groups for research purposes. Overall estimates that these would exclude about two-thirds of the patients managed for depressions in his clinical setting! The New York based Research Diagnostic Criteria (associated with Spitzer), which in effect have been incorporated into the *Diagnostic and Statistical Manual of Mental Disorders (DSM-III)*, broaden the inclusion net (APA, 1980); while the St. Louis group insisted on the centrality of dysphoric mood, the New York criteria rule that pervasive loss of interest and pleasure (anhedonia) be considered also a central feature. Overall believes that only some one-third of his hospital's depressed patients would be excluded by the New York criteria. Both the above schemata require that the patient have five of eight secondary symptoms. Overall and colleagues, in an attempt to be more inclusive, have developed a composite checklist system, which includes the St. Louis and New York criteria but adds others, with weighting for severity; only about one-fourth of "depressed" patients would escape this classificatory net. Finally, Overall reviews an international study using Grinker's and Paykel's groupings, which successfully clusters patients into four types: the anxious, retarded, agitated, and hostile. These groupings appear to succeed in including *all* patients, hence satisfy clinicians' needs to the chagrin of researchers, but Overall is not completely clear on this point; the reader can pursue the offered references.

What Is Depression?

After the discussion above, we might conclude that researchers cannot give us an answer to this key question. I submit that in fact the question and any answer to it are fundamentally the clinician's responsibility. It is the clinician's onus to make a commitment to a definition, and the researcher's to investigate that commitment.

I have suggested in previous communications (Powles 1980, 1982) and in chapter 7 of this book that conservation–withdrawal and its subclass, depression, can be helpfully regarded as broad adaptive or maladaptive patterns, final common pathways resulting from many causes and mechanisms, but pathways which share in some meaningful pattern of adaptation and survival. This "final common pathway" concept is developed by Akiskal and McKinney (1973) and Whybrow et al. (1984), though the pathway leading to depression may be a more singular and narrow one than we have believed (Brown and Harris, 1978). The spectrum of depressive disorders extends over grades of severity and many colorations, but it has clear conceptual limits, if not clear empirical ones. There are poles or boundaries to the range of depressive phenomena, where a shading into other processes takes place. There is also a central property or properties by which the spectrum itself is defined. One way to deal with this, I have suggested, is to lay out a conceptual map of the various depressive disorders, and their nosological neighbors. This "topological" arrangement would place at the center the purest, most "saturated," type of depression, "core depression," about which no diagnostic disagreement is found. Today this core syndrome would be labeled a major depressive episode, with melancholia and without psychotic features; or, following Whybrow et al. (1984), simply melancholia. Organizing the conceptual map by neu-rotic–psychotic and reactive–endogenous axes, at right angles to each other, we can place various other depressive and nonde-pressive syndromes about it, in various directions, at various distances from the center, or core depression. Grief, for exam-ple, is placed high on the reactive–endogenous axis; or schizoaf-fective psychosis between core depression and schizophrenia on the neurotic–psychotic axis.

From this arrangement it appears that core depression is neither neurotic nor psychotic, but something clearly interme-diate and distinct from both, and that as we move from core to periphery in the topological map we encounter a diminution of depressive features and increasing admixtures of nonde-pressive ones. This tends to reinforce the concept that depres-sion is a process with its own identity and intensity when in pure culture, but which diminishes in completeness when it merges with other processes. Such an assumption is testable.

Depression, seen as a process, can be teased into compo-nents, both clinical features and elements in the natural history. The more of these components are present, the more severe (conceptually speaking) is the depression. In contrast, other traditions have it that the severity of a depression is judged by the total number of features present, whether these are depressive or not. The well-known Hamilton Rating Scale (Hamilton, 1959), for example, includes many anxiety features and some psychotic ones which the rater is to add into the severity calculation. Figure 12.1 is an attempt to depict the central position of melancholia as the typical depressive syn-drome, with its full complement of features, and its interrela-tionship with its nosological neighbors, the less typical de-pressive syndromes and, at each pole of the continuum, wholly nondepressive syndromes in the neuroses and psychoses.

How Do DSM-III and DSM-III-R Define Depression?

Since classification schemata are ephemeral (they serve the needs of perhaps half a generation of clinicians and research-ers) I propose not to examine DSM-III (1980) and DSM-III-R

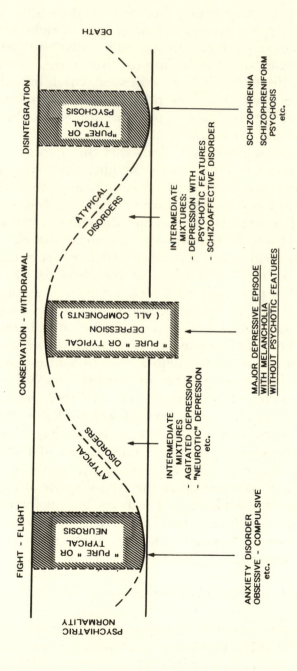

Figure 12.1. Typical and Atypical Syndromes

Major depressive disorder with melancholia is shown at center as an example of a pure, complete, or "saturated" syndrome having all the components of depression. To its right and left, we pass into atypical, mixed, incomplete depressive syndromes, until we finally reach typical examples of psychoses and neuroses.

(1987) in any detail. These nosologies are practical and intensely effort-consuming attempts to define syndromes for a heterogeneous community of practitioners, epidemiologists, and investigators; they are compromises between precision and inclusiveness (see above) and contain many elements of practical politics and consensus making; they have become increasingly ponderous in their descriptive detail.

DSM-III and DSM-III-R do not, in fact, help us with any unifying concept of depression. We have to search through a number of syndromes, which are presented as mutually exclusive; the "either–or" position noted by Overall (1983) and by Beahrs (1986). I shall scan these syndromes briefly, and attempt to relate them to each other through Figure 12.1.

Central to Figure 12.1 and to DSM-III is the major depressive episode (whether unipolar or bipolar, single or recurrent); we may add to its complexity, moving right toward the psychoses in the figure, by adding melancholia, mood-congruent psychotic features, and mood-incongruent psychotic features. We reach a limit in DSM-III: schizoaffective disorder is defined as outside the affective disorders. Moving left, in the less severe disorders, the central syndrome is dysthymic disorder, typically chronic and indolent. Its bipolar equivalent is cyclothymic disorder. Again, outside the affective disorders as DSM-III defined them, are two highly reactive syndromes, adjustment disorder with depressed affect and uncomplicated bereavement (grief) which is not considered a psychiatric illness but which may overlap major depressive episode.

The natural history of these syndromes is not (in the DSM-III and DSM-III-R) a clear diagnostic criterion. The central syndrome, major depressive episode, must have lasted at least 2 weeks, thus implying relatively acute and distinct onset; no prodromal period, nor its content, is mentioned. An adjustment disorder must develop within 1 month of a stressor, the quality of which (separation, rejection, etc.) is not specified. A dysthymic disorder or cyclothymic disorder must have been present over 2 years, implying a vague onset and chronic course; ups and downs in the symptomatology are permitted.

The cross-sectional criteria or "templates" for diagnosis in DSM-III are operational, at times superficial or sketchy on key issues, and, rarely almost disorganizing. The central, defining syndrome of major depressive episode is itself defined by two alternative central criteria and seven possible secondary ones; of these, one central and four secondary features have to be present. Dysthymic disorder is defined as less intense, consistent, more prolonged, indolent than major depression; and melancholic and psychotic features can be added, in cases of greater complexity and disability, to the major depressive episode.

What is new in DSM-III is the broadening of central criteria to include patients without dysthymia or painful dejection. The old syndrome of neurasthenia (anergia, anhedonia, aboulia, but without painful dejection) is now included in the affective disorders, and "affect" as such no longer defines the affective disorders! Put another way, DSM-III now chooses to include a larger segment of the conservation–withdrawal spectrum in the "affective" disorders.

Both DSM-III and DSM-III-R offer only rather brief and superficial descriptors for the dysthymic or dysphoric mood state. This they do, further, by focusing on the patient's colloquial words for his/her experience, as "depressed, sad, hopeless, discouraged, down in the dumps, or in terms of some other colloquial variant" (DSM-III, p. 210). DSM-III-R uses the same few colloquial descriptors, but adds that the "depressed mood can be inferred from others' observing that the person looks sad or depressed" (p. 219)—altogether a rather circular definition! European colleagues perhaps rightly criticize North Americans for being long on "rules" but short on penetrating clinical observation and description; DSM-III may be a valid target for such criticism. The dimension of agony and torment is ignored or played down in DSM-III: a depression may be merely uncomfortable, even painless, as in the more neurasthenic states.

The secondary features are not classified as to their area of dysfunction: energy and psychomotor behavior, cognitive capacity and thematic content, psychodynamic content, and physiological or vegetative dysfunction. Such elements as worthlessness and self-depreciation are now demoted to the status of secondary features. The physiological dysfunctions also are listed as merely secondary features: thus, a major depression can be without the functional shift.

Melancholia, a construct newly introduced in DSM-III, appears to be an intensification of all features of a major depressive episode, with some stress on the physiologic. It can be applied as an additional descriptor, as can the presence of psychotic features, either "mood congruent" or "mood incongruent." Mood-incongruent features violate the logical consistency of most depressive syndromes.

The approach of DSM-III and DSM-III-R is thus an attempt to diagnose and classify by the totaling of specified features, mostly clinical or cross-sectional in kind; there is only a small input from course or natural history, and no real input from a unifying concept of depression as a whole-person process with its historical, subjective, cognitive, behavioral, and pathophysiological structure.

Can Depression Be Defined? A Synthesis

Since recent nosological and research schemata tend to stress individual features of the depressive disorders, and since they tend to avoid a unifying concept or framework, can depression really be defined? I believe so, particularly if we adhere to three principles. First, the principle of relevance (Andreasen, 1983; Overall, 1983; Beahrs, 1986): what is the purpose of an attempted definition? Second, the principle of responsibility: who is responsible for the definition? Third, the principle of semantic constancy; that is, avoiding changing in some fundamental way the meaning of a term which has been in long use (e.g., Bleuler wisely coined a new term when he redefined dementia praecox, rather than shifting the meaning of the old term). My purpose here will be to indicate, operationally and testably, the central and common features of depressive syndromes, suggesting that depression is a process or consistent group of processes. My responsibility is as a clinician, writing for other clinicians, but hoping that researchers will critically examine and use the definition. I attempt to maintain semantic constancy by including under the term *depression* what it has meant in the past hundred years or more, and excluding new or contradictory content and emphasis. My definition will be seen to be influenced by the final common pathway construct of Akiskal and McKinney (1973) and also current evidence that loss is a much more regular inducer of depression than has been recognized (Brown and Harris, 1978). I propose to spell out components of depression first, then to attempt a more compact definition. This definition will indicate what the word *depression* is intended to mean in subsequent chapters in this volume.

Merskey and Spear (1967) in grappling with the definition of so elusive a phenomenon as pain, defined it as "an unpleasant experience which we primarily associate with tissue damage or describe in terms of tissue damage or both" (p. 21) By analogy, we might define depression as *an unpleasant experience which we primarily associate with irrevocable loss, or describe in such terms, or both.* This initial step in definition has two aspects: unpleasantness and loss. There is now impressive evidence that most, if not all, depressive episodes are launched by a personal loss. Equally impressive is the fact that most truly depressed patients omit to identify, or actually deny, such a loss. For grief, which is embraced by this first step in definition, all concerned agree on the visibility and importance of a personal loss.

Merskey and Tonge (1965) cite a patient who would gladly have exchanged the pain he experienced during a depressive episode for the pain of a compound fracture of the humerus he previously had suffered. Depression is unpleasant at least, agonizing at most, as is pain, and as is grief. This pain is no mere subjective abstraction, or behavioral posturing. Patients, if one spends the effort with them, can come to describe a "deep" type of pain, most commonly behind the eyes, in the throat, shoulders, chest, and abdomen. I have located no research into these pain patterns or their origins. Pain behind the eyes may be related to tension in the "pain muscle" (Darwin, 1872) and in the mechanisms which inhibit weeping. Musculoskeletal pain perhaps originates in stretching of ligaments when postural muscle tone is deficient. Visceral pain in chest and abdomen may be related to the known disorder of the gastrointestinal tract (Pollitt, 1960) with slowing of peristalsis. Darwin (1872) and Cannon (1929) have both remarked that "deep" pain is inhibitory rather than spurring to appropriate action.

The "painful dejection of spirits" shared by depression and grief (Freud [1917], whose description has not been surpassed) includes the subjective element of sadness, which has not been well researched (see chapter 7). The affects of helplessness and hopelessness (Schmale and Engel, 1975) and the silent despair of abandoned children (Bowlby, 1980) can be equated with sadness. Researchers of emotion place stress on the pained facial expression in sadness, which can be recognized regardless of culture. Weeping tends to be inhibited in depression, and may be embarassingly common in grief (Clayton, Herjanic, Murphy, and Woodruff, 1974).

Painful dejection is common to depression and grief. Part of it, or closely associated with it, is a group of psychomotor changes, yet these can exist independently too: they dominate neurasthenia, where painful dejection is absent. A paralyzed or paralyzing loss of energy (anergia), strength (asthenia), will, initiative, and motivation (aboulia), and a lack of normal interest and pleasure (anhedonia) make up this group. Widlöcher (1983) convincingly marshals evidence that psychomotor retardation is a central psychobiological feature of depression.

Depression, grief, and neurasthenia are perhaps best distinguished by their cognitive and psychodynamic content. In depression, as in grief, there is a giving-up of struggle and effort in the face of what is estimated cognitively as irrevocable loss. A sense of helplessness ensues in both states, but some hope for the future appears to be retained in grief. The sense of loss is centered on the self in depression: the self is perceived as diminished, imperfect, despicable (Freud, 1917), whereas in grief self-esteem is preserved (Freud, 1917; Clayton et al., 1974). In both processes there is a loss of interest in human relationships, particularly new objects. In depression, as in neurasthenia, there is intense self-preoccupation; in grief, intense preoccupation with the lost loved one. Suicidal ruminations, gestures, and attempts are almost specific to depressions (Clayton et al., 1974) probably expressing a mixture of self-directed hostility (Freud, 1917) with despair and bodily torment, though I have found no investigation of such a combination. The most grisly suicide I have witnessed was by a tormented middle-aged woman in a major depressive episode, who, awakening with severe depressive insomnia, virtually decapitated herself in the dark at 3 A.M. Neurasthenia lacks cognitive and psychodynamic content, apart from hypochondriacal preoccupation; hence it was classified as an "actual neurosis" rather than a psychoneurosis (see chapter 10).

Finally, the purest, most "saturated" depressive disorders (major depressive episode with melancholia) contain the elements of the physiological "functional shift": a specific sleep dysfunction, slowing of gastrointestinal peristalsis with anorexia, malnutrition, and constipation, and sexual impairment, to name the most prominent. A proportion of cases of grief show this functional shift (Clayton et al., 1974). The milder the depression, the less such biological features are present; "neurotic" depressions exhibit mainly dejection and cognitive and psychodynamic features. I have the impression that the "functional shift" fades out in the more "psychotic" depressions, but I cannot cite research evidence for this.

Two other criteria are characteristic of depression. One is a general *logical consistency* or syntonic structure to the clinical picture: mood, energy, motivation, thought efficiency and content, physiological changes, all harmonize. This is in marked contrast to the logical discordance in the psychoses, and in schizophrenia particularly.

The other is the curious but consistent inability of the patient, when depressed, to recollect any precipitating cause for the illness. I have proposed that this phenomenon, as contrasted with the great clarity of precipitating cause in grief, is a reliable criterion of depression (Powles, 1982). Many studies (Lewis, 1934; Brown and Harris, 1978; Paykel, 1978; van Praag, 1982; Rush and Altshuler, 1986) find that even severely "endogenous" cases are regularly found to have a precipitating cause, usually in a significant personal loss.

I now draw this section together in an attempt at a definition of depression for our present purposes.

Summary and Synthesis. Depression is a pathological or maladaptive variant of conservation–withdrawal, a persisting or autonomous process (or specific cluster of processes) showing high logical consistency. Its features, while varying in intensity from absent to severe along a complex continuum, can be grouped under three highly specific constellations which do not occur in any other illness:

1. *Features which are not self-evident.* An onset related to the subject's perception of irrevocable personal loss and a lack of significant personal supports; but this relation is obscured by forgetfulness, concealment, or denial.

2. *Features common to all cases in varying degrees.* A giving-up into helplessness, hopelessness, and despair, with dejection of spirits and pain of body; loss of energy, will, initiative, human interests, and normal enjoyments; self-preoccupation of a hostile quality, with reduction of self-esteem and suicidal motivation.

3. *Features particularly prominent in the most typical cases.* Psychomotor retardation together with the specific "functional shift," combining a specific sleep disturbance, impairment of appetite, digestion, elimination, and sexual drive and performance.

Thus various depressive syndromes can be classified along a continuum (as in Figure 12.1), major depressive episode with melancholia being the "type" syndrome. It can then be judged how to relate to depression a normal analog such as grief, or a pathological analog such as neurasthenia.

Research evidence for elements in this definition will now be reviewed in the following chapters.

Bibliographic Notes: Key Readings

This chapter espouses the view developed by Engel and Schmale (Engel, 1956: Engel and Schmale, 1972; Schmale and Engel, 1975) that the human depressive disorders are examples of the broad psychobiological process of conservation–withdrawal. This is the direction in which our homeostatic–dynamic model leads us. This view can be challenged, and it can be researched. It is not a view which appears prominently in much recent literature, though it would seem to promise considerable heuristic profit.

Since we have pursued a series of steps from animal behaviors (particularly, torpor, hibernation, and death feigning; other animal models produced in the laboratory will be reviewed in the next chapter) to the phenomena, definition, and classification of human depressive disorders, I recommend a recent compendium on hibernation and torpor by Lyman, Willis, Malan, and Wang (1982). Then, as a bridge into depressive disorders in humans, one should turn to the works by Engel (1956) and Engel and Schmale (1972), whose statement on conservation–withdrawal, with its appended references, I consider seminal and definitive.

There are other seminal and classical readings, from which I select Freud's 1917 work, still a valuable and cogent paper brimming with clinical and theoretical observations. Clayton, Herjanic, Murphy, and Woodruff (1974), during studies on depression and grief, produced what I believe will be a classic, replicating Freud's paper in modern terms and with modern statistics. The comparison between grief and depression ("mourning and melancholia," to echo Freud) remains a fruitful one. Kraepelin (1913) deserves to be read in the maturity of his thinking on manic-depressive insanity; I am not sure that contemporary research has greatly improved on a number of his observations. Lewis (1934) not only reviewed the phenomenology and the classification of depressive disorders with clinical illustrations, but was perhaps the first to research the high correlation between life events and depressions of all grades.

The modern era displays a kind of progressive shrinkage in integrative thinking and inclusion of psychological and social levels of emergence, together with a drift away from naturalistic animal models to the somewhat strained and sometimes implausible animal models of the laboratory. Akiskal and McKinney (1973) and Whybrow, Akiskal, and McKinney (1984) represent laudable exceptions to this progression. Anthony and Benedek (1975) may be consulted for the richest attention to naturalistic and psychosocial variables. Fann, Karacan, Pokorny, and Williams (1977) demonstrate the progressive focus on issues at the biological level, and the burgeoning of biological research on depression. This focus is best shown in the fine biologically oriented compendium of Davis and Maas (1983); a chapter in this volume by Andreasen (1983) offers an excellent discussion of the classification of depressive disorders, together with the essential principles and problems in nosological classification. Rush and Altshuler (1986) find it necessary as editors to apologize for having to exclude, due to space limitations, the psychosocial sector. One wonders whether the popular demand for understanding of biological processes in depression was an equally influential pressure. This compendium has, although compact, considerable breadth of coverage and is highly recommended.

References

Adler, N. T. (1979), On the physiological organization of social behavior: Sex and aggression. In: *Handbook of Behavioral Neurobiology*, ed. P. Marler & J. G. Vandenbergh. New York: Plenum.

*Akiskal, H. S., & McKinney, W. T. (1973), Depressive disorders: Toward a unified hypothesis. *Science*, 182:20–29.

———— (1975), Overview of recent research in depression: Integration of ten conceptual models into a comprehensive clinical frame. *Arch. Gen. Psychiat.*, 32:285–305.

American Psychiatric Association, (1980), *The Diagnostic and Statistical Manual of Mental Disorders*, 3rd ed. (DSM-III). Washington, DC: American Psychiatric Press.

——— (1987), *The Diagnostic and Statistical Manual of Mental Disorders*, 3rd ed. rev. (DMS-III-R). Washington, DC: American Psychiatric Press.

*Andreasen, N. C. (1983), The diagnosis and classsification of affective disorders. In: *The Affective Disorders*, ed. J. M. Davis & J. Maas. Washington, DC. American Psychiatric Press.

*Anthony, E. J., & Benedek, T., eds. (1975), *Depression and Human Existence*. Boston: Little, Brown.

Baker, G. B., & Dewhurst, W. G. (1985), Biochemical theories of affective disorders. In: *Pharmacotherapy of Affective Disorders: Theory and Practice*, ed. W. G. Dewhurst & G. B. Baker. London: Croom Helm.

Baldessarini, R. J. (1983), How do antidepressants work? In: *The Affective Disorders*, J. M. Davis & J. W. Maas. Washington, DC: American Psychiatric Press.

Batchelor, I. C. (1969), *Henderson and Gillespie's Textbook of Psychiatry for Students and Practitioners*, 10th ed. London: Oxford University Press.

Beahrs, J. O. (1986), *Limits of Scientific Psychiatry: The Role of Uncertainty in Mental Health*. New York: Brunner/Mazel.

Beck, A. T., Rush, A. J., Shaw, B. F., & Emery, G. (1979), *Cognitive Therapy of Depression*. New York: Guilford Press.

Becker, J. (1974), *Depression: Theory and Research*. Washington, DC: V. H. Winston.

Blier, P., & de Montigny, C. (1985), Neurological basis of antidepressant treatment. In: *Pharmacotherapy of Affective Disorders: Theory and Practice*, ed. W. G. Dewhurst & G. B. Baker. London: Croom Helm.

Borbély, A. (1986), *Secrets of Sleep*. New York: Basic Books.

Bowlby, J. (1980), *Attachment and Loss, Vol. 3: Loss, Sadness, and Depression*. London: Hogarth Press.

Brown, G. W., & Harris, T. W. (1978), *Social Origins of Depression: A Study of Psychiatric Disorder in Women*. New York: Free Press.

Cannon, W. B. (1929), *Bodily Changes in Pain, Hunger, Fear, and Rage*, 2nd ed. Boston: Charles T. Branford, 1953.

Clayton, P. J. (1983), The prevalence and course of the affective disorders. In: *The Affective Disorders*, ed. J. M. Davis & J. Maas. Washington, DC: American Psychiatric Press.

———— (1986), Prevalence and course of affective disorders. In: *Depression: Basic Mechanisms, Diagnosis, and Treatment*, ed. A. J. Rush & K. Z. Altshuler. New York: Guilford Press.

*———— Herjanic, M., Murphy, G. E., & Woodruff, R. (1974), Mourning and depression: Their similarities and differences. *Can. Psychiat. Assn. J.*, 19:309–312.

Czeisler, C. A., Kronauer, R. E., Mooney, J. J., Anderson, J. L., & Allan, J. S. (1987), Biologic rhythm disorders, depression, and phototherapy: A new hypothesis. *Psychiat. Clin. N. Amer.*, 10:687–709.

Damlouji, N. F., Feighner, J. P., & Rosenthal, M. H. (1985), Recent advances in antidepressants. In: *Pharmacotherapy of Affective Disorders: Theory and Practice*, ed. W. G. Dewhurst & G. B. Baker. London: Croom Helm.

Darwin, C. (1859), *The Origin of Species by Means of Natural Selection*, ed. J. W. Burrow. London: Penguin Books, 1968.

———— (1872), *The Expression of the Emotions in Man and Animals*. New York: Philosophical Library, 1955.

———— (1884), A posthumous essay on instinct. Appendix in: G. J. Romanes, *Mental Evolution in Animals*. New York: Appleton.

*Davis, J. M., & Maas, J., eds. (1983), *The Affective Disorders*. Washington, DC: American Psychiatric Press.

Dunner, D. L. (1983), Recent genetic studies of bipolar and unipolar depression In: *The Affective Disorders*, ed. J. M. Davis & J. Maas. Washington, DC: American Psychiatric Press.

Edmunds, M. (1974), *Defense in Animals*. Harlow, Essex, UK: Longman.

*Engel, G. L. (1956), Spontaneous and experimentally induced depressions in an infant with a gastric fistula: A contribution to the problem of depression. *J. Amer. Psychoanal. Assn.*, 4:428–452.

———— (1962a), Anxiety and depression–withdrawal: The primary affects of unpleasure. *Internat. J. Psycho-Anal.*, 43:89–97.

———— (1962b), *Psychological Development in Health and Disease*. Philadelphia: Saunders.

*———— Schmale, A. H. (1972), Conservation–withdrawal: A primary regulatory process for organismic homeostasis. In: *Physiology, Emotion, and Psychosomatic Illness* (Ciba Foundation Symposium 8, New Series). Amsterdam: Associated Scientific Publications.

*Fann, W. E., Karacan, I., Pokorny, A. D., & Williams, R. L., eds. (1977), *Phenomenology and Treatment of Depression*. New York: Spectrum.

*Freud, S. (1917), Mourning and melancholia. *Standard Edition*, 19:243–258. London: Hogarth Press, 1957.

Grinker, R. R., Sr., Miller, J., Sabshin, M., Nunn, R., & Nunnally, J. C. (1961), *The Phenomena of Depressions*. New York: Hoeber.

Hamilton, M. (1959), Clinical syndromes in depressive states. *J. Ment. Sci.*, 105:985–998.

Hartman, C. G. (1952), *Possums*. Austin: University of Texas Press, 1978.

Herrero, S. (1985), *Bear Attacks: Their Causes and Avoidance*. Piscataway, NJ: Winchester.

Hoagland, H. (1928), The mechanism of tonic immobolity ("animal hypnosis"). *J. Gen. Psychol.*, 1:426–447.

Hunsaker, D., II, ed. (1977), *The Biology of Marsupials*. New York: Academic Press.

Kendell, R. E. (1968), *The Classification of Depressive Illnesses*. London: Oxford University Press.

——— (1981), Review article: The present status of electroconvulsive therapy. *Brit. J. Psychiat.*, 139:265–283.

Kiloh, L. G., & Garside, R. F. (1963), The independence of neurotic depression and endogenous depression. *Brit. J. Psychiat.*, 109:451–463.

*Kraepelin, E. (1913), *Manic–Depressive Insanity and Paranoia*, trans. R. M. Barclay. Edinburgh: Livingstone, 1921.

Kupfer, D. J., Foster, F. G., Coble, P. A., & McPartland, R. J. (1977), EEG sleep parameters for the classification and treatment of affective disorders. *Psychopharm. Bull.*, 13:57–58.

*Lewis, A. (1934), Melancholia: A clinical review of depressive states. *J. Ment. Sci.*, 80:277–378.

——— (1938), States of depression: Their clinical and aetiological differentiation. *Brit. Med. J.*, 2:875–878.

*Lyman, C. P., Willis, J. S., Malan, A., & Wang, C. H. (1982), *Hibernation and Torpor in Animals and Birds*. New York: Academic Press.

McAllister, T. W. (1981), Cognitive functioning in the affective disorders. *Comprehen. Psychiat.*, 22:572–586.

——— (1983), Overview: Pseudodementia. *Amer. J. Psychiat.*, 140: 528–533.

Maier, R. A. (1970), *Comparative Animal Behavior*. Belmont, CA: Brooks/Cole.

Mapother, E. (1926), Discussion on manic–depressive psychosis. *Brit. Med. J.*, 2:872–876.

Merskey, H., & Spear, F. G. (1967), *Pain: Psychological and Psychiatric Aspects*. London: Bailliere.

——— Tonge, W. L. (1965), *Psychiatric Illness*. London: Bailliere.

Overall, J. (1983), Phenomenological heterogeneity of depressive disorders. In: *The Affective Disorders*, ed. J. M. Davis & J. Maas. Washington, DC: American Psychiatric Press.

Paykel, E. S. (1978), Contribution of life events to causation of psychiatric illness. *Psychol. Med.*, 8:245–253.

Pollitt, J. D. (1960), Depression and the functional shift. *Comprehen. Psychiat.*, 1:381–390.

Powles, W. E. (1980), The core and the boundaries of the construct of depression. *Psychiat. J. Univ. Ottawa*, 5:21–23.

——— (1982), Four perspectives on depression and the depressive illnesses. *Can. Med. Assn. J.*, 125:253–258.

Ratner, S. G. (1967), Comparative aspects of hypnosis. In: *Handbook of Clinical and Experimental Hypnosis*, ed. J. E. Gordon. New York: Macmillan.

Rush, A. J., ed. (1982), *Short-term Psychotherapies for Depression: Behavioral, Interpersonal, Cognitive, and Psychodynamic Approaches*. New York: Guilford Press.

————— (1986), Diagnosis of affective disorders. In: *Depression: Basic Mechanisms, Diagnosis and Treatment*, ed. A. J. Rush & K. Z. Altshuler. New York: Guilford Press.

* ————— Altshuler, K. Z., eds. (1986), *Depression: Basic Mechanisms, Diagnosis, and Treatment*. New York: Guilford Press.

Schildkraut, J. J., Schatzberg, A. F., Orsulak, P. T., Mooney, J. J. Rosenbaum, A. H., & Gudeman, J. E. (1983), Biological discrimination of subtypes of depression. In: *The Affective Disorders*, ed. J. M. Davis & J. Maas. Washington, DC: American Psychiatric Press.

Schmale, A. H., & Engel, G. L. (1975), The role of conservation–withdrawal in depressive reactions. In: *Depression and Human Existence*, ed. E. J. Anthony & T. Benedek. Boston: Little, Brown.

Scott, J. P., & Senay, E. C., eds. (1973), *Separation and Depression: Clinical and Research Aspects*. Washington, DC: American Association for the Advancement of Science.

Sedler, M. J., & Dessain, E. C. (1983), Falret's discovery: The origin of the concept of bipolar affective illness. *Amer. J. Psychiat.*, 140:1127–1133.

Seligman, M. P. (1975), *Helplessness: On Depression, Development, and Death*. San Francisco: W. H. Freeman.

Skutch, A. F. (1973), *The Life of the Hummingbird*. New York: Crown Publishers.

van Praag, H. M. (1982), A transatlantic view of the diagnosis of depressions according to the DSM-III: I. Controversies and misunderstandings in depression diagnosis. *Comprehen. Psychiat.*, 23:315–329.

Wadsworth, A. P., & Barker, H. R. (1976), A comparison of two treatments for depression: The anti-depressive programme vs. traditional therapy. *J. Clin. Psychol.*, 32:445–449.

Weissman, M. M., (1979), The psychological treatment of depression—Evidence for the efficacy of psychotherapy alone, in comparison with, and in combination with pharmacotherapy. *Arch. Gen. Psychiat.*, 36:1261–1269.

————— (1981), Psychotherapy in comparison and in combination with pharmacotherapy for the depressed outpatient. In: *The Affective Disorders*, ed. J. M. Davis & J. Maas. Washington, DC: American Psychiatric Press.

*Whybrow, P. C., Akiskal, H. S., & McKinney, W. T. (1984), *Mood Disorders: Toward a New Psychobiology*. New York: Plenum.

Widlöcher, D. (1983), Retardation: A basic emotional response. In: *The Affective Disorders*, ed. J. M. Davis & J. Maas. Washington, DC: American Psychiatric Association.

Williams, J. M. G. (1984), *The Psychological Treatment of Depression: A Guide to the Theory and Practice of Cognitive-Behavior Therapy*. New York: Free Press.

Winokur, G. (1973) Genetic aspects of depression. In: *Separation and Depression*, ed. J. P. Scott & E. C. Senay. Washington, DC: The American Association for the Advancement of Science.

---

*Recommended readings.

13

A Third Homeostatic Level:
Conservation–Withdrawal; Biological
Components of Human Depressive Disorders

Components of Depression

In the last two decades research involvement has been greatly
focused upon biological treatment and biological mechanisms.
This biological focus has taken us only so far (Becker, 1974;
Baldessarini, 1983). I have suggested that breaking down depression into component parts or part processes is of heuristic
and diagnostic usefulness, and that the more complete or "saturated" forms of depression contain the largest number of such
components. Arbitrary decisions may be required in categoriz-
ing certain of these components; for example, should psychomotor retardation be regarded as biological or psychological?
This chapter will deal with biological components of human
depressive disorders; that is, with the biological level of emergence.

439

Under the biological heading we shall examine the genetics of the affective disorders; the functional shift as a whole, and its components of psychomotor retardation and the depressive sleep disorder; the relationship of neurotransmitter disturbances to pharmacotherapy in depression; research on the mechanisms of action of convulsive therapy; and the newly defined syndrome of seasonal affective disorder.

The biological derangements, or rather their hypothesized perpetuating mechanisms, are the targets for antidepressant drugs, convulsive therapy, and more recently, phototherapy. Such biological treatments are probably wasted on patients lacking the functional shift, that is, in the less severe depressive disorders (Akiskal and McKinney, 1973; Rush, 1982; Akiskal, 1983). If drugs help such patients, particularly if they help quickly, they probably help via a placebo effect. They may in fact do potential harm in terms of unnecessary risk factors.

As to psychosocial components (it seems wise to combine psychological and social levels of emergence) we shall examine in chapter 14 research on the psychosocial causation of depressive disorders; on the neuropsychology of depression; on psychodynamic and developmental contributions to pathological grief and depression; and on the psychotherapies for depressive disorders, including the important question of combined pharmacotherapy and psychotherapy.

Familial and Genetic Aspects of Affective Disorders

I commence with some provocative orienting propositions of Becker (1974). Depression is the psychiatric disorder with the highest mortality rate, 150 percent higher than that of the general population. Depression reduces individual reproductive success, but evidently is one price we pay for our intensely social nature, our propensity to attach to other humans and to suffer when attachments are broken. Why then has depression not disappeared from the human scene, if it is determined in large part by genetic programming? Why particularly has the uniquely human behavior of suicide not long ago vanished through genetic selection? Clearly, for depression the relation between genotype and phenotype is a most complex one (Andreasen, 1983).

It was Kraepelin's wisdom to solidify a relationship between depression and mania, as well as to focus continued attention on familial predispositions, which since his time have been almost a diagnostic criterion for the affective disorders (Kraepelin, 1913). Batchelor (1969) considered that the affective disorders follow the pattern of a single dominant gene with incomplete penetrance.

Dunner (1983) summarizes the criteria for proof of a genetic contribution to any disease:

1. Clustering within families: relatives of patients are found affected;
2. Twin studies: monozygotic twins show significantly greater concordance than dizygotic;
3. Adoption studies: the illness appears despite the patient being reared in another environment;
4. Genetic markers: the illness is regularly linked with other phenomena produced by an identified gene of Mendelian-type inheritance.

Winokur (1973), Dunner (1983), and Clayton (1983, 1986) agree that the affective disorders, particularly the bipolar clustering, meet these criteria, though much further analysis of the problem is still required. The disorders *are* familial: bipolar patients' relatives are at increased risk for bipolar illness, and both bipolar and unipolar patients' relatives are at significant risk for unipolar illness. Twin studies, though not pursued energetically in recent years, are strongly suggestive; monozygotic twins have significant, though not perfect, concordance. Adoption studies favor the genetic concept. Though genetic markers have not yet been found, there is some suggestive evidence for these.

There is general agreement on the features distinguishing bipolar from unipolar affective disorder (Dunner, 1983; Clayton, 1983, 1986; Winokur, 1973; and see pp. 420–424). The definition of bipolar affective disorder has now solidified to signify any lifetime history which includes an attack of clinical mania. Unipolar now solidly signifies a lifetime history of depression only, whether of single or multiple attacks. This is another wise change of terms, as modern nosology redefines manic–depressive disorder. Bipolar disorder is characterized by a clearer familial pattern: bipolar patients tend to have unipolar as well as bipolar relatives; mothers and sisters of bipolar patients tend to be bipolar; there is an even sex distribution (unipolar disorder tends to preponderate in women); and "two-generation" pairings are common (affected parent and child, parent with several affected children, or affected child and parent). The age of onset for bipolars is generally earlier. They have more frequent illness episodes, but less chronicity. The response to biological treatment is more consistent in the bipolar than in the unipolar clustering.

Dunner (1983), on the basis of extensive studies of patients and their relatives, has further broken down the bipolar clustering into:

Bipolar I. Patients actually hospitalized for mania, a rather homogeneous group with rather clear genetic loading.

Bipolar II. Patients hospitalized for depression, but giving the history of a hypomanic episode which was not treated; these cross sectionally resemble unipolars, and in many other studies have probably been taken to be so, but pharmacologically and genetically have the same pattern as bipolar I.

Bipolar Other. Bipolars who have required only outpatient treatment.

Cyclothymic Personality. Persons who have had identifiable mood disturbances of bipolar type, but have not been patients at all, and have usually been discovered as relatives of patients.

Winokur, one of the early delineators of the unipolar–bipolar division, attracted attention by his tracing of familial patterns and the genetic inferences which he and colleagues offered (good compressed statements are found in both Anthony and Benedek [1975] and Scott and Senay [1973]). Spreading out what is evidently a continuum of cases of depression, and classifying them in a two-by-two fashion by gender and age of onset, Winokur found that the two extremes represented were the early-onset females and the late-onset males. The early-onset females proved to suffer what Winokur termed "Depression Spectrum Disease"; that is, having male relatives with sociopathy and alcoholism, the picture possibly determined by a dominant gene or genes. The late-onset males showed "Pure Depressive Illness"; that is, having relatives at low risk for alcoholism and sociopathy, again a picture suggestive of a dominant type genetic transmission. Winokur's subsequent work, based on evidence of the common association of mothers and sisters with bipolar patients, and on several pedigrees of bipolar patients whose families carried other traits, led him to propose that bipolar affective disorder is genetically determined by a dominant gene located on the X-chromosome, near the locus which also gives rise to red–green color blindness, to a disturbance in the blood Xg system, and to human lymphocyte antigen (HLA) problems (see Crowe, Campbell, Pfohl, Goeken, and Pauls, 1986, for a discussion of the latter). The work of Winokur and his successors has not been supported of late, and both Clayton and Dunner believe that, despite Winokur's intriguing suggestions, no firm Mendelian pattern has as yet been established.

Dunner (1983) reviews a large number of studies of patients and their relatives involving different approaches: blind (i.e., those examining the relatives do not know the patient's diagnosis); prospective (following cases from before their breakdown); and retrospective (examining records of past illnesses). Allowing for differences in method, Dunner calculates that:

Relatives of *any* affective disorder patient have a 15 to 20 percent risk of being affected themselves by some type of affective disorder.

Relatives of bipolar I patients have an increased risk for bipolar I illness, as compared with relatives of unipolar patients (2.8–5.3% against 0.2–3.0%).

Relatives of bipolar patients as a whole have a higher risk for unipolar than for bipolar illness (6.4–13.6% against 0.8–6.0%).

Relatives of bipolar patients have about the same risk for unipolar illness as relatives of unipolars (6.4–13.6% against 8.4–15.2%).

HUMAN DEVELOPMENT AND HOMEOSTASIS

From these figures, Dunner concludes that, while affective disorders are clearly familial and probably genetically determined, their distribution does not fit any specific Mendelian mode of inheritance.

Energetic efforts continue in the attempt to clarify the genetic contributions to affective disorders. Workers in this enterprise appear clearly to operate from a "disease" model, whereby it is hoped to isolate some specific factor(s) responsible for "causing" the illness, thereby affording both access to a specific treatment modality, and the opportunity for prevention by eliminating the incriminated factor(s) by eugenics or genetic engineering.

In the genetic search, identification of genetic markers is the objective. Crowe et al. (1986) offer a rather intricate discussion of the methodology of establishing genetic associations. "Association" is taken to mean a somewhat loose but repeated coexistence between an illness such as affective disorder and a marker, which is some trait of specifiable biological type. "Linkage" specifies a more precise association: the occurrence of the "illness" gene and the "marker" gene so close together on the chromosome that they are highly likely to be passed on as a unit, or not passed on at all, during the process of genetic information exchange between paired chromosomes during formation of the sex cells. Standards of mathematical proof for linkage have been established. The search is on, therefore, for such linkages with affective disorders. The HLA linkage search is not a dead issue (Crowe et al., 1986). Other possible linkages (Dunner, 1983) may be established for monoamine oxidase inhibitor (MAOI) enzymes and with cholinergic hypersensitivity propensities. Dunner makes the important point that a marker, to be truly useful, must be one that can be identified in the "well" state and not merely when the patient is psychiatrically ill; that is, a marker of a "trait" or persistent diathesis, rather than a "state" marker.

The present state of knowledge, for all its refinements, seems to reflect quite old impressions and opinions of careful observing clinicians such as Kraepelin (1913) or Batchelor (1969), that:

1. Genetic or hereditary patterns are strongly suggested in the affective disorders, as contributing causes.
2. This seems more distinct in the bipolar disorders.
3. The genetic mechanism most closely resembles a Mendelian dominant with incomplete penetrance (Batchelor, 1969).
4. Phenotype (the adult constitution of the person) is a resultant of genotype (inherited components) and developmental and life experiences: it expresses both vulnerabilities and also resistances to illness.

Biological Aspects: Global Physiological Impairments

The Physiological "Functional Shift"

Pollitt's seminal paper (1960) drew together and labeled the grouping of biological derangements which are a regular part of a typical depressive syndrome (melancholia, in current terminology). For many years these have been familiar to clinicians as "vegetative signs" or "depressive hypochondriasis." Pollitt's grouping included:

1. Diurnal mood variation, depressive sleep disturbance, anorexia with constipation, and sexual impotence and frigidity;
2. The inability to weep, dryness of mouth with decreased salivation and secretion of gastric juice, and diminished intestinal peristalsis;
3. Amenorrhea;
4. Lowering of metabolic rate, and delay in water excretion and glucose tolerance curve;
5. Diminished pulse rate, blood pressure, and body temperature; coldness of the extremities and disappearance of the cheek flush;
6. Disturbance of sodium, potassium, and cholesterol metabolism;
7. Stupor, inanition, and death in extreme cases.

Pollitt pointed out that this combination of disturbances has not been described in any other illness. He noted that it does not correlate 100 percent with depression, or with severity of depression, but may occur in other syndromes where affect is suppressed; Pollitt therefore pondered whether it points to a general suppression of hypothalamic function, such as in severe inhibition of emotion or in animal behaviors such as hibernation.

Pollitt's convenient title of "functional shift" does not appear to have been widely recognized and adopted in the literature, nor has the *global* pattern been systematically confirmed or pursued. Coppen (1967) and Mendels, Stern, and Frazer (1976) refer to it as an index of hypothalamic neurotransmitter disturbance. The digestive tract dysfunctions have been particularly neglected in research. Perhaps, with the recent interest in eating disorders and in overeating and carbohydrate craving in seasonal affective disorder (Boyce and Parker, 1988; Wehr and Rosenthal, 1989), this whole area will be reinvestigated. Sleep disturbance has, of course, been a field of major research activity (see pp. 450–459).

A worthy successor to Pollitt might be the excellent review of circadian rhythms and their relevance for depression by Czeisler et al. (1987). These authors outline the neural mechanisms of the circadian (*circa* = about, *dies* = day) rhythms which can be studied precisely in animals and which, centering on the suprachiasmatic nucleus (SCN), clearly relate to perception of day and night. This visually stimulated circuit, with effects on the hypothalamus and pineal gland, is also involved in seasonal animal behavioral cycles related to the length of daylight. Digestive functions are only hinted at in this study. However, a number of other functions which vary with the 24-hour cycle are, the authors hypothesize, clearly involved (cause–effect relationship being as yet obscure) in depressions. Two mechanisms are implicated: an advancement in the *phase* of the circadian rhythm, visible in early onset of REM sleep and early awakening, is one mechanism. The other, newly proposed by these authors, is a dampening down of the *amplitude* of circadian changes (e.g., in body temperature, cortisol secretion, motor activity, and neurotransmitter metabolites). The phase advance mechanisms somewhat resemble changes of advancing age, a possibility which has greatly interested Kupfer (1983) in his sleep studies.

I return to circadian rhythms briefly in a note on seasonal affective disorder (see pp. 477–483).

Psychomotor Retardation

According to our present model, immobility is an important feature of the depressive pattern, as it is of conservation–withdrawal generally. Again, there is relatively little in the research literature on this subject. Widlöcher (1983) makes a strong case for the thesis that psychomotor retardation is a central or core process in depression. The reasons, he believes, that retardation has been neglected are three in number:

1. An interest in *classification*, which has led away from study of phenomena;
2. A focus on the psychodynamics of depression;
3. A tendency to place retardation as secondary to psychic pain and the disturbance of mood.

I quote Widlöcher's conclusion: "Multi-variate analysis clearly indicates that retardation is, along with self-blame, the most common symptom of depression . . ." (p. 166); that is, that retardation surprisingly accounts for a larger proportion of variance in depression than does mood disturbance. Widlöcher reminds us that loss of motility has been shown to be typical in both monkeys and humans as a response to separation and abandonment; and that this is a phylogenetic response when fight or flight are unsuccessful. An interesting part of Widlöcher's thesis is that motor and psychic retardation can be separated: this separation is typified in agitated depressions. The two variables tend to be scattered about the outline of mental status examinations, so that retardation is dispersed and lost among other categories such as anhedonia, anergia, and loss of concentration. These items Widlöcher has shown to be correlated with a major "Factor I" which accounts for nearly 50 percent of the variance in factor analysis of 27 items found in depression. Psychic or cognitive slowing is found to be best correlated with treatment response. The Salpetrière Retardation Rating Scale, constructed out of these investigations, contains 15 categories under which motor and psychic retardation can be rated, and which range from gait and stride to patient's perception of the flow of time. Widlöcher reviews three further sets of studies on psychomotor phenomena in depressions, which give empirical leads to differential diagnosis and classification, treatment monitoring, and to the central pathophysiology of depressive states.

Greden and Carroll (1981) review the relatively few clinical and laboratory studies on the monitoring of psychomotor function in mania and depression. They note that activity is almost the defining criterion of mania (see also chapter 11); and that in depressive states certain phenomena not perceived by clinical observers can be picked up by instrumental monitoring; such as tone of facial muscles. Three areas where quantifiable observations can be usefully made are:

1. Electromyography and the facial expressions of emotion;
2. Measurement of speech phonation and pause times; and
3. Motor-activated monitoring of gross bodily motility.

Pioneering studies, particularly those of Schwartz, have been replicated by Greden's team. For example, depressed persons, when asked to imagine happy or everyday scenes, show continuing increased tone in the "grief muscle," the corrugator at the inner end of the eyebrow, this being the type of data that the clinical observer will not elicit. As to speech functions (see also Greden and Carroll [1980]; Greden, Albala, Smokler, and Gardner [1981]) depressed persons show a relatively normal amount of phonation time but an increased amount of pause time (anxious persons show high speech rates and low silent times). New wristwatch type monitors should, they believe, be promising in the study of motility of the depressed, including outpatients.

Greden, Genero, Price, Feinberg, and Levine (1986) have published a study of both "endogenous" and "nonendogenous" depressives, as against normal controls, using the affective imagery method of Schwartz. While they were asked to imagine situations making them happy or sad, muscle tone was measured in the "grief muscle" and the "smiling muscle" (zygomaticus): both groups of depressives showed less reactivity of muscle tone, with the "endogenous" showing an absolute difference from the normals, both as to general reactivity, and as to persisting tone in the corrugator during "happy" imagery and while imagining an ordinary day's activities.

Kupfer, Weiss, Foster, Detre, Delgado, and McPartland (1974) conducted a pilot study leading to the conclusion that retardation is a central feature in bipolar depressives, and that bipolars can be most effectively distinguished from unipolars by studying their sleep and motility. Bipolars show retardation and hypersomnia, unipolars agitation and insomnia; with recovery the two approach each other's patterns. Although this finding has been suggestively challenged (Greden and Carroll, 1981) it does not seem to have been either confirmed or refuted.

Weckowitz, Nutter, Cruise, and Yonge (1972) reported that both age and depression systematically slow down the performance of all psychological tests requiring speed, though not those primarily requiring power. These authors believed that a single, pervasive biological impairment could not be implicated. Later Weckowitz and colleagues (Weckowitz, Nutter, Cruise, Yonge, and Cairns, 1978) in two publications reported on a cohort of 30 depressed women and 30 control subjects. Depression was found to make a significant contribution to slowing down reaction time, tapping speed, digit symbol, writing speed, reading speed, and fluency tests. Age, as analyzed, was found to add a further component of slowing to all these tests.

Sloman, Berridge, Homatidis, Hunter, and Duck (1982) and Sloman, Pierrynowski, Berridge, Tupling, and Flowers (1987) have provided interesting evidence, from cinematography and use of a force plate, that depressives show a kind of "pulling" gait when walking, as against normals who "spring" in propelling themselves from one foot to the next. Whether this is a "state" marker, or may prove to be a "trait" marker in the nondepressed patient, remains to be established.

Widlöcher's work, and the conservation–withdrawal model, suggest strongly that psychomotor retardation is a central and defining feature of depression.

Biological Aspects: Sleep

Discoveries in the Sleep Laboratory

The huge modern literature on this subject originates with the discovery of REM sleep in the 1950s. I recommend the authoritatively based though informally written book by Borbély (1986) as a good guide to modern sleep research, and I follow his schemata. The topics covered in his review range from the norms of sleep and its stages, to sleep deprivation, to the basic organization and function of sleep, with excursions into depression and sleep deprivation. Nathaniel Kleitman, the "grandfather" of sleep research (Borbély) authored two massive texts on the whole subject of sleep which are not clinically relevant enough for us to discuss here (Kleitman, 1939, 1965).

For hundreds of years philosophers and psychologists had engaged in futile speculation over the questions of how long a dream lasts and of how internal and environmental stimuli enter into dream formation (Borbély, 1986, chapter 4). With the development of the electroencephalograph our understanding of the physiology of sleep advanced rapidly. In the very early 1950s Kleitman became interested in the slow rolling eye movements at the onset of sleep, and assigned a graduate student, Aserinsky, to elucidate them. Aserinsky found that these slow eye movements occurred not only during the onset of sleep and anesthesia, but before and after episodes of bodily movements during sleep (now called stage 1 sleep). Even more crucially, he observed rapid eye movements during sleep which had previously been unreported (Aserinsky and Kleitman, 1955). Borbély recounts how Kleitman was at first incredulous about this observation, but this proved to be the birth of the modern era of sleep and dream research. Dement, Aserinsky's successor in the project, continued the observations and introduced the relation between rapid eye movement (REM) sleep and dreaming into research annals (Dement and Kleitman, 1957); he himself continued on into a career of sleep and dream research. Kleitman (as did Magoun with the discovery of the reticular activating system) seems to have insisted that his graduate students receive credit as senior authors in these seminal revelations (Moruzzi and Magoun, 1949; Lindsley, Bowden, and Magoun, 1949). Rapid eye movement sleep was for a period entitled "paradoxical sleep" for its contradictory properties: an EEG resembling the lightest sleep stage (stage 1), but with REM never occurring at the onset of sleep; an erratic physiologic arousal, yet quite profound muscular relaxation and resistance to awakening.

But what was most noteworthy, from the psychiatrist's point of view, was the clear association between REM sleep and dreaming, and the great activity of the brain and eyes, while the rest of the body was virtually paralyzed. This breakthrough to dream research, as well as being a major stimulus to sleep research generally, finally unlocked the questions on how long dreams last, and on what part internal and external stimuli play in their content. We now must leave the large and intriguing literature on the psychodynamic aspects of sleep research (Hobson and McCarley, 1977; McCarley and Hobson, 1977) in order to pursue the relevance of sleep studies to depressive disorders.

Normal Sleep and Its Stages

Borbély proposes that two interlocking, possibly mutually inhibiting, processes or systems are involved in sleep. Process C (for cycling, circadian) is a circadian (24-hour) sleep rhythm cycle related to a number of other physiological circadian rhythms. These foster the survival and productive living of various creatures, whether small and nocturnal (i.e., vulnerable to predators should they venture out in the daylight) or large and diurnal (e.g., the large grazers, the ungulates), living in open spaces, alternately feed and have short sleeping periods over the whole 24 hours. The circadian sleep rhythm has a clear relation to the suprachiasmatic nuclei in the diencephalon ablation of which abolishes REM sleep as well as other circadian processes. Rapid eye movement sleep, Borbély concludes, is likely to be a more ancient or primitive version of sleep, which operates on a circadian rhythm (process C) little influenced by sleep deprivation. Opossums and human babies spend much time in REM sleep.

Process S (for the classical concept of a sleep "toxin" or endogenous substance accumulating during wakefulness) represents the accumulation of "pressure" for sleep which builds up during the waking hours and during sleep deprivation, and which is progressively relieved during the cycles of night sleep, until wakefulness is reached again. Non-REM sleep, comprising all the other sleep stages (light and deep), except for REM periods, is probably determined, according to Borbély, by the noncircadian process S, a more modern phylogenetic development. This probably is the sleep component disturbed in the affective disorders, a disturbance which is at least temporarily relieved by sleep deprivation in depressed subjects (Borbély and Valatx, 1984, pp. 198–200).

Normal sleep, with certain clear variations depending on age and health, is occupied by a cyclical pattern (see Figure 13.1) consisting of the following arbitrarily defined stages; the norms given are for healthy young adults (Ward, 1968; Mendels and Chernik, 1975; Kupfer, Foster, Cable, and McPartland, 1977; Borbély, 1986).

1. *Stage 1*. On passing from relaxed wakefulness to drowsing, the regular EEG alpha rhythm (8–12 per second) gives way to low voltage fast activity; muscle tone diminishes; the eyes roll in a slow (1–4-second) rhythm (Kleitman's SEM); there may be some bodily movements, and even transient dreams are reported.

2. *Stage 2*. On passing to definitive sleep, the EEG assumes larger wave forms, with brief bursts of "sleep spindles" (groups of alphalike waves, but faster) and occasional large slow waves or "K complexes"; muscle tone is further reduced, and the eyes are still. Stage 2 takes up about half the time of normal sleeping in healthy young adults.

3. *Stage 3*. The EEG shows large, slow (1–4 per second) delta waves for between 20 and 50 percent of the record; muscle tension remains low and the eyes are still.

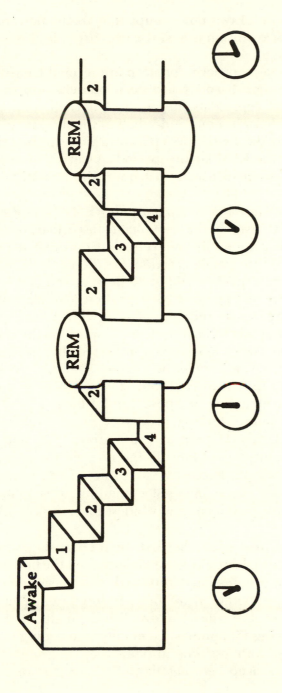

Figure 13.1. The Sleep Staircase

Borbély uses this pictorial title for his useful depiction of the first few hours of normal sleep. Sleep stages can be clearly visualized, including the special character of REM sleep. From *The Secrets of Sleep*, by Alexander Borbély. English translation Copyright © 1986 by Basic Books, Inc. Originally published in German as *Das Geheimnis des Schlafs: Neue Wege und Erkenntnisse der Forschung*. © 1984 by Deutsche Verlags-Anstalt GmbH, Stuttgart. Reprinted by permission of Basic Books, Inc.

4. *Stage 4*. The EEG is now occupied 50 to 100 percent by delta waves; muscle tension is low, the eyes are still; this is the deepest sleep stage.

These four stages or levels of sleep are termed Non-REM (NREM) sleep; stages 3 and 4 are deep or delta sleep. The above progression represents the onset of normal sleep, and occupies the first hour or hour-and-a-half of the sleeping night, a period prior to the first REM episode which can be timed quantitatively as the REM latency period. A period of stage 2 and of bodily movement usually ushers in the first REM episode.

5. *Rapid Eye Movement or Paradoxical (REM) Sleep*. Rather suddenly, the EEG assumes the low voltage, fast activity of stage 1: muscle tone is profoundly reduced; the coordinated rapid eye movements set in; penile erections occur regularly in the male; breathing rate quickens about 20 percent and heart rate and blood pressure by 10 percent, though these are inconsistent or erratic; and dreams are recovered consistently if the sleeper is awakened during this REM sleep level. It was thought at first that the direction of eye movements indicated the dimension of action in the visual imagery of the dreamer, but this hypothesis has not borne up (Borbély, 1986). There has been much speculation regarding the "purpose" and function of REM sleep: a kind of house-cleaning process, a process related to memory consolidation (Hobson and McCarley, 1977; and see chapter 8 on memory), but I have found no solidly established answer to this question. Rapid Eye Movement sleep normally occupies 20 percent of the night's sleeping time. It is, as noted above, probably the phylogenetically oldest form of sleep (Borbély, 1986).

6. *The Sleep Cycle*. After the first sleep onset stages, with the period of NREM sleep and REM latency, then the first REM period, the above progression is repeated: progressive descent into deeper sleep, another REM period, and so on. Four of these overall cycles are usual for one 7-hour night of sleep, each cycle averaging 90 minutes. Generally, succeeding cycles become less deep, with less time in delta sleep and more time in REM sleep. As sleep becomes lighter, there may be brief

awakenings, and finally the subject awakens completely, re-freshed. Figure 13.1 is Borbély's own graphic representation of the "Sleep Staircase" schematizing two cycles between 11 P.M. and 2 A.M.

There is considerable change in sleep time and the propor-tion of various sleep stages over the life cycle (Borbély, 1986, chapter 4); we shall see below how Kupfer regards the relation between depressive sleep disturbance and age.

Sleep in Major Depression

A cardinal diagnostic sign of a well-developed depressive or manic episode has been the specific pattern patients report for their sleep. The sleep laboratory, with its electroencephalo-graphic record of the sleep cycle, now lends greater objective precision, with the establishment of "sleep parameters" or quantifiable norms against which can be measured these specific patterns of disturbed sleep (Coble, Foster, and Kupfer, 1976; Kupfer, Foster, Reich, et al., 1976; Kupfer, Foster, Coble, et al., 1977). A useful overview of this subject is found in Mendels and Chernik's paper (1975). Rubin and Marder (1983) give an excellent brief summary. Kupfer (1983) shows the intricate analyses and types of differential patterns which are emerging.

I shall focus on the typical, well-developed, "core depres-sion." Kupfer has retained the terms *primary, endogenous,* and *nondelusional* for this state, and more recently (1983) has added the term *definite* (as well, he refers to secondary and psychotic or delusional categories, and to differential patterns at different stages in the disorders).

Mendels and Chernik (1975) summarize the typical de-pressive sleep pattern as a significant reduction in sleep time (though not as great a reduction as the patient, fatigued, dis-tressed, and cognitively muddled, believes) with difficulty fall-ing asleep, periods of wakening during the night, and early permanent awakening. Typically there is increased REM sleep and a striking and consistent reduction in delta or deep sleep. Kupfer (1983) emphasizes a general pattern of decrease in sleep continuity; a decrease in stage 3 and 4 sleep (though this occurs too in chronic medical illness and some other psychiatric disorders); shortened REM latency; and increased REM activity and "density" (see below). Kupfer asserts with confidence that EEG sleep measures are able to separate depressed patients both from normals and other psychiatric cases, and to differentiate primary, endogenous, secondary, and nonendogenous types of depression. A 50-minute cutoff point for REM latency can, for example, successfully identify 70 to 75 percent of primary depressions. A group of depressed persons with hypersomnia has been identified (Kupfer, 1983; Wehr and Rosenthal, 1989). Kupfer believes this pattern is likely to be characteristic of bipolar depressions; it seems a consistent feature of seasonal winter depressions. Shimizu, Hiyama, Yagasaki, Takahashi, Fujiki, and Yoshida (1979) have analyzed sleep polygraphic record of a small cohort of such patients.

Researchers in this area have developed a large number of measures and ratios for EEG sleep phenomena; for example, see Kupfer's list (1983, Figure 2). These apply to sleep onset and continuity, to components of NREM sleep, and to the intricacies of REM sleep. Following Mendels and Chernik and particularly Kupfer, I shall review briefly the more salient of these measures and ratios as they differentiate depressive states from each other and from other states. I shall also indicate Kupfer's more recent great interest in age as a variable.

1. *Sleep latency.* The time taken to get to sleep after going to bed; normally a few minutes, in "definite" depressions is about 40 minutes, and also longer in the older and in the agitated.

2. *Sleep efficiency.* The proportion of time spent actually sleeping during the night's recording session: 85.8 percent mean in younger depressed subjects and 74.7 percent in older depressives, a highly significant difference. Time spent asleep (TSA) is reduced to less than 6 hours, and is interrupted by up to half an hour of awake time, significantly more in the older and the agitated; early awakening can be measured, with a mean of half an hour, in the older group.

3. *Non-REM sleep.* Of the time depressed subjects slept, there was a mean of 4 percent in stage 3 for the younger subjects, and virtually none for the older ones; and for all, virtually no stage 4 sleep. Total delta sleep was a mean of 4.4 percent

for the younger subjects and 0.3 percent for the older. Stage 2 occupied a mean of 62 percent for both groups, as against a normal of 50 percent.

4. *REM sleep.* Compared to the normal REM latency of 60 to 90 minutes, the younger depressives had a mean of 58.7 min, and the older 44.4 min. Rapid Eye Movement sleep time averaged 70 to 80 min in both groups, a REM percent of about 24 or at the upper end of normal (20%). REM activity (the total count of bursts of rapid eye movement) and REM density (the ratio between REM activity count and total REM time) were high for both young and older groups, though the number of REM periods was slightly lower than normal, 3.5 mean periods for both groups. Thus, while total REM periods and REM time are not abnormally high, REM activity and REM density are so. Modern automated technology for counting REM activity (Kupfer, 1983) also allows for measuring the amplitude of the rapid eye movements, which appears to be high in the depressed.

Some Formulations on EEG Sleep

Kupfer's very detailed findings are representative of the intricate literature. All authors agree that the sleep disorder of core depression responds to treatment within the first two nights (Mendels and Chernik, 1975; Kupfer, Foster, Reich, et al., 1976; Cairns, Waldron, MacLean, and Knowles, 1980; Kupfer, 1983). This is not necessarily a predictor of long-term good response to treatment (Kupfer, 1983) but it does confirm the biological component in the depressive episode. The immediate favorable changes consist in a measurable shift of all the abnormal indices (sleep latency, proportion of sleep stages, and REM activity) toward the norm for the patient's age. The question then arises whether relapse can be predicted by a deterioration in sleep EEG pattern. A number of reports suggest that this is so; that a euthymic patient can nonetheless show a sleep abnormality prior to relapse, and workers at my own university (Cairns et al. [1980]; and for a manic patient, Knowles, Waldron, and Cairns [1979]) have contributed to this answer.

Kupfer (1983) makes the intriguing suggestion that the depressive sleep disorder has the same quality as premature aging: this follows from comparing depressive sleep parameters to those of normal aging. His suggestion is also that EEG sleep would be a useful diagnostic tool in differentiating depression from dementia in older patients. Finally, his tentative suggestions regarding EEG sleep and treatment planning I shall put in the form of a decision chart, as follows:

EEG Sleep Feature	Psychotic or Not	Treatment Recommended
REM latency under 20 min	+ Delusional or psychotic:	Convulsive therapy
REM Latency 21–70 min	+ Delusional or psychotic:	Tricyclics and antipsychotics
Sleep efficiency under 80%	+ Not delusional or psychotic:	Tricyclics
Sleep efficiency over 80%	+ Not delusional or psychotic:	MAO inhibitors
REM latency over 70 min	+ Not delusional or psychotic:	Require psychotherapy and psychosocial intervention
REM latency over 70 min	+ Delusional or psychotic:	May require convulsive therapy and anti-psychotics

Sleep Deprivation and Depression

Some 15 years ago the observation was made that sleep deprivation appeared to normalize the mood and psychomotor function of the definitively depressed, raising hopes for a new and relatively safe treatment (Post, Kotin, and Goodwin, 1976). More systematic studies have followed, disillusioning to the hope for a new treatment modality, but raising new theoretical questions and providing a new diagnostic tool (Knowles, Southmayd, Delva, Cairns, and Letemendia, 1979; Letemendia et al., 1986). A useful, simple review of the history of sleep deprivation research in normal people is given by Borbély (1986); more technical reviews are available by van den Hoofdakker and Beersma (1984) and other authors in Borbély and Valatx (1984), and by Gillin and Borbély (1985).

In general, sleep deprivation of the seriously depressed for two nights and one day (i.e., continuous vigil or wakefulness for about 36 hours) results, in a large minority of cases, in a return to essentially normal mood and psychomotor and cognitive functioning. However, when sleeping is resumed (usually under the "pressure" of system S and with the rapid sleep onset under this euthymic and sleep-deprived condition) there is rapid relapse into the full psychobiologic picture of depression. A few patients have been more permanently helped (Knowles, Southmayd, et al., 1979). In their single-case study, Knowles and colleagues found that: (1) recovery took place rather abruptly, between 1 and 2 A.M. on the sleep-deprived night; (2) that waking the patient at 1 to 2 A.M. during nights while clinically depressed found no sign of remission; (3) that if the patient awoke spontaneously on these nights at 1 to 2 A.M. she was clinically depressed; and (4) that varying the timing of the 36-hour vigil achieved essentially the same results—there was no evidence suggesting some influence upon a circadian rhythm.

This whole area is clearly undergoing clarification, both as to why sleep deprivation temporarily remits the depressive process, and as to how this illuminates the processes of depression more broadly (Post et al., 1976; McCarley, 1982). Borbély's schema of systems C and S has been noted above. Sleep deprivation does not, at present, promise a new, safe treatment (it would be an expensive one in terms of staff time), but it does offer a useful differential diagnostic tool, for example, in distinguishing depression from dementia; it can "suspend" depression, removing this component temporarily from a diagnostically complex case; and it can help set targets for treatment by revealing what level of function the patient is capable of reaching (Letemendia et al., 1986).

Biological Aspects: Markers and Mechanisms

Biological Markers in Diagnosis

The term *marker* has been somewhat loosely and inappropriately applied to a sign or laboratory finding associated with depression, in line with general hopes that laboratory test batteries might be developed which reliably (and inexpensively) confirm the presence of depression, and guide treatment. Strictly, the word *marker* should be restricted to mean a biological trait or predictor associated with depression-proneness in the well patient; genetic linkage has been discussed above. However, accepting this informal usage for the term, and following Rubin and Marder (1983), what are the "*state* markers" for depression? Rubin and Marder list four groupings of state markers for study:

1. Neurochemical: the study of catecholamines and indoleamines and their metabolites;
2. Neurophysiological: principally variables in sleep studies.
3. Neuroendocrine: hormonal rhythms and responses to test challenges; circadian ACTH/cortisol levels and the dexamethasone suppression test; response of thyrotropin (TSH) to thyrotropin-releasing hormone (TRH); growth hormone response to stresslike challenges; and changes in the pituitary–adrenal–gonadal axis.
4. Genetic: dexamethasone response in affective disorders families; enzyme abnormalities; the markers already noted above, the Xg blood group, red–green color blindness, and the human lymphocyte antigen (HCA) marker.

Rubin and Marder regretfully conclude that none of these categories, except for the dexamethasone suppression test, has provided tests of any conclusiveness or reliability. Kupfer's logical decision chart (see p. 458) is one example of decision making from one major category of markers. My own suggestion for following a biological test sequence draws together some of the physiological researchers already reviewed, as well as including one (stimulant challenge) not previously mentioned:

1. *Psychomotor activity*: speech pause time (Greden and Carroll, 1980, 1981), gait patterns (Sloman et al., 1987), and facial electromyography (Greden et al., 1986).
2. *Sleep patterns*: sleep efficiency, REM latency and density, plus other indices (Mendels and Chernik, 1975; Kupfer, 1977, 1983).
3. *Early therapeutic response* of 1 and 2;
4. *Sleep deprivation*: clarity of response; a negative response to this test does not rule out biological depression, but a positive response is confirmatory (Knowles, Southmayd, Delva, Cairns, and Letemendia, 1979; Letemendia, Prowse, and Southmayd, 1986); the test may helpfully distinguish depression from dementia;
5. *Stimulant challenge*: brief use of a stimulant results in improvement (in some cases) of depressive signs, and predicts response to proper antidepressants. The test is simple and inexpensive. It may or may not be solidly reliable (Fawcett and Siomopoulos, 1971; Van Kammen and Murphy, 1978; Sabelli, Fawcett, Jaraid, and Bagri, 1983; Goff, 1986).

The Dexamethasone Suppression Test (DST, DMST)

There were particularly high hopes for this marker or "first laboratory test in psychiatry," and a large literature has grown up around it (Braddock, 1986; Schlesser, 1986; APA Task Force, 1987). The APA Task Force on Laboratory Tests in Psychiatry was commissioned to review the reliability and validity of the DST, and I summarize this excellent report at length; it refers to 9 review articles and 112 other studies.

Originally, it had been noted that plasma cortisol was abnormally raised in the circadian rhythms of certain depressed patients. This led to the erroneous conclusion that in depression the organism is alerted (i.e., in fight–flight). Later it emerged that in cases of depressive disorder the normal negative feedback inhibition of adrenocorticotrophic hormone

(ACTH) in the anterior pituitary was failing, probably due to failure of the small but influential dopaminergic system in the hypothalamus which controls corticotrophin-releasing factor (CRF).

Normally, cortisol is secreted by the adrenal cortex, in response to ACTH, in half-a-dozen pulses in 24 hours, mostly during the day (or waking, active hours), secretion being inhibited during the night (or sleeping hours). Depressed patients may show higher than normal cortisol secretion. The DST is designed to aid nocturnal inhibition of cortisol secretion by administering the potent synthetic steroid dexamethasone, most commonly in a 1 mg dose at 11 P.M., a low point in the normal circadian secretion of ACTH; then blood samples are taken for assay at 8 A.M., 4 P.M., and 11 P.M. the following day. The normal feedback mechanism calls for the suppression of ACTH, but this is "escaped" in some depressions, and ACTH and thence cortisol values (the substance assayed) are not suppressed but rise above normal for the next circadian cycle.

The key question must be: In what type of depressive disorder is the DST positive? Investigators such as Kitamura, Shima, Kano, Asai, and Itoh (1985) and Benkelfat, Poirier, Leouffre, Gay, and Loo (1987) attempt to deal with the specificity question, essentially: (1) Is the DST specific for depression in the biologic sense? (2) Can it diagnose depression when clinical features may be obscured? (3) Can it separate types of depression as to their central pathophysiology, thus as to predicting treatment response and guiding the type of biological treatment to be given? Kitamura's group, in a relatively modest study, found that a positive DST correlated highly with recurrent "melancholic" depression and poorly with single-episode melancholic, or recurrent and nonmelancholic depressions. Benkelfat and colleagues, after testing the hypothesis that DST nonsuppressors are more likely to respond to noradrenergic antidepressants, and normal suppressors to serotonergic ones, report that "Actually, the DST does not have this usefulness."

To summarize the issues in the lengthy, detailed, and conceptual review of the APA Task Force (1987):

1. The DST assumes a dysfunction, specific to depression of major type, in central neural and neuroendocrine systems

of the limbic system and hypothalamus, which prevents the normal daily regulation of the pituitary–adrenal axis.

2. Many other drug and metabolic factors, for example, alcohol, sedative and anticonvulsant drugs, marked weight loss, liver disease, and chronic medical disease generally, are in fact correlated with DST nonsuppression.

3. The sensitivity of a positive DST for major depression is only modest: 30 to 70 percent, averaging only 45 percent; many clearly major depressions show a negative or normal response; sensitivity is somewhat higher (60–70%) in very severe or psychotic depressions and schizoaffective cases, but also in mania.

4. The test is thus not useful as a screening test for depressions; other indices point more efficiently to biological depression.

5. The specificity is good in identifying normal controls (90% accuracy) but poor in differentiating depression from other medical conditions; it may be positive in dementias, thus of poor differential value in dealing with "depressive pseudodementia."

6. As to treatment indications, a positive DST does not add significantly to the probability of a good response to biological treatment; nor does a negative test rule out either major depression or a good response to antidepressants; negative responders appear more likely to respond to placebo treatment.

7. Failure to convert, following clinically successful treatment, to a negative DST, may be a useful predictor of relapse and suicidal risk (see also Brown [1989]).

Pharmacologic Correlates and Animal Models of Depression

We now enter the highly intricate research area dealing with submicroscopic functions in the depressed brain, and the relation of these to the action of antidepressant drugs and convulsive therapy. We enter, in fact, the "pharmacologic detective game." I have introduced this game in chapter 10, with all its elegant tools of drugs (agonists, antagonists, blockers), enzyme studies, and histochemical, immunologic, and radioactive methods (Crow and Deakin, 1985). For depression, this sleuthing process may be said to have begun with the questioning of why modern antidepressant drugs normalize mood, soon joined with the observation that certain other drugs lower mood or conduce to depression. Thus we are also reiterating here the pharmacologic correlates of depression, or perhaps more properly, of conservation–withdrawal. The animal models used in this intricate research may in fact more closely approximate conservation–withdrawal in is broader aspects, than the more restricted construct of depression.

We turn then first to animal models used in depression research. I select the review of Porsolt (1985) as a reasonably up-to-date discussion, and certainly one which is comprehensive and informative, as the resource for this section. Porsolt outlines five classes of animal models for depression research.

1. Separation models, related to the work of Bowlby on humans and of Harlow on rhesus monkeys. The behavior of "protest" upon separation is widespread among infant precocial and altricial animals, and is counteracted by antidepressant drugs in some breeds of puppies (Scott, Stewart, and DeGhett, 1973). True "despair" behavior follows upon more prolonged separation, particularly in primates, and can be relieved by antidepressants, convulsive therapy, and alcohol.

2. Learned helplessness, a sophisticated psychological model based on the work of Seligman (1975). In this ingenious triadic design, dogs were given repeated, uncomfortable electric shocks. Those dogs who could take control of the situation escaped (fight–flight), while dogs who could have no control over the aversive stimuli developed a syndrome of general passivity, submission, and failure to effect any escape attempts (i.e., conservation–withdrawal). This syndrome has been relatively widely invoked as a model for depression. Porsolt believes that it is capable of too many interpretations (lacks parsimony); further, the syndrome responds inconsistently to antidepressant treatment. Seligman himself noted (1975, p. 24) that learned helplessness could not be produced in one-third of the dogs, and that 1 out of 20 displayed the syndrome even before the experiment, probably due to their previous life experience. While the model has been more or less successful to species

other than dogs (including humans) Porsolt weighs the evidence to conclude that this is not a good model for research at the biologic level.

3. Acute stress models, particularly the response of rats and mice to having to swim without any rescue or escape. These rodents finally "give up" and just float in "behavioral despair," a response which can be prevented or delayed by antidepressants, with norepinephrine and dopamine mechanisms being salient. This model presents a simpler behavioral picture than learned helplessness.

4. Chronic stress models, in which rodents are exhausted by running, bombarded by noxious stimuli, or socially isolated. Imipramine restores those exhausted by running, and the estrous cycle returns to females; tricyclics and MAOIs restore those bombarded by noxious stimuli; with social isolation, a fight–flight response rather than conservation–withdrawal appears to be induced. This series of models suggest strongly the broad psychobiologic response of conservation–withdrawal, though the term is not used by Seligman or the workers with rodents.

5. Drug models include the well-known effects of reserpine and related compounds, widely used to deplete dopamine, norepinephrine, and serotonin in monoaminergic neurones, and which produce behavioral effects of sedation and passivity, in effect conservation–withdrawal; these effects respond inconsistently to antidepressants, and best to the MAO inhibitors. A drug of interest is alpha-methylparatyrosine (or AMPT) which inhibits synthesis of dopamine and norepinephrine and produces "despair" in adult monkeys.

McKinney (1976, 1977) has also offered careful discussions of animal models for depression research, which remain in use. He believed at that time, and his conclusion is not refuted by Porsolt, that we still lack a wholly convincing animal model for human depression.

The Brain in Depression

Depression research at the level of molecular biology thus suffers from a triple jeopardy, and the validity of its conclusions (or rather, the hypotheses it continues to generate) must be judged against these caveats:

1. *Defining human depression.* The problem of diagnostic consistency across studies is improving rapidly, thanks to modern diagnostic criteria (e.g., the Feighner criteria, or the Research Diagnostic Criteria [Spitzer] which are mirrored in DSM-III-R).

2. *Finding an animal model or analog which replicates the selected type of human depressive disorder.* This remains a major problem, judging by experienced authorities such as McKinney and Porsolt.

3. *Conclusions from animal research.* However skilled and sophisticated the work, the end result will be only as successful as the key steps 1 and 2.

The first definitive hypothesis which attempted to explain the benefits of antidepressant drugs became known as the biogenic amine hypothesis. It had two principal protagonists, and two principal versions. Schildkraut (1965) proposed a "catecholamine hypothesis of affective disorders," to the effect that a relative deficiency of noradrenalin at the noradrenergic synapse was responsible for depression; such a deficiency could be produced experimentally, and antidepressant drugs would act by facilitating a proper supply and proper action of noradrenalin. Schildkraut and Kety (1967) published a massive review of the relationship between biogenic amines and emotion, starting from the work of Cannon on adrenalin, and concluding with the catecholamine hypothesis for depression. Coppen (1967), in an equally extensive review of biochemistry in affective disorders, took the neuron and the synapse as his starting point. He marshaled evidence that monoamine oxidase inhibitors increased a depleted "deep pool" of amines in the cell body, by inhibiting their degradation by mitochodrial enzymes; and that tricyclic antidepressants prevented the reabsorption of amines from the "superficial pool" at the synapse. Coppen favored serotonin, an indolamine, as the key biogenic amine to be inculpated, hence proposing an "indolamine hypothesis."

All three authors agreed on the importance of biogenic amines as significantly distributed in the limbic system, with the "deep" and "superficial" pools in the neuron and synapse, and on their response to drugs. All three ruled out dopamine as the significant neurotransmitter. And all three were careful and cautious in emphasizing that their respective hypotheses were tentative and oversimplified. Nonetheless, these hypotheses were seized upon rapidly as revealed truth.

Problems arose rather quickly (see several discussions in Dewhurst and Baker [1985]), the principal question being over the delay in action required for therapeutic action of antidepressants. While such drugs rapidly restored depleted monoamines in laboratory animals, and while the physiologic functional shift in humans often responds rapidly, the global syndrome of a depressive disorder requires 2 weeks and more for proper remission to commence.

Ten years later, Mendels, Stern, and Frazer (1976) reviewed the current situation, pursuing the same reasoning as Coppen. They reviewed and accepted Schildkraut's, Kety's, and Coppen's main thesis, that "depression is associated with a functional deficiency of norepinephrine or serotonin at significant receptor sites . . . mania . . . with an excess . . ." (p. 4). Emerging at this time was an interest in the postsynaptic neurone and its chemical processes in neuroreception, where possibly lithium might have an action; and in the cell membrane and receptors where possibly genetic abnormalities might be involved in the affective disorders. The "escape" of ACTH from normal inhibition with the DST had also become a subject of interest. Clearly, the apparent simplicity of the biogenic amine theory was giving way to new complexities, with the warning that depression should not be seen as a unitary process, but as having several mechanisms.

Ten years later still, no firm or embracing understanding has been established: only new and more complex theories seem to be emerging. Baker and Dewhurst (1985), in an exhaustive (400 references) review of theories, point out the problems with the norepinephrine–serotonin theory: antidepressant drugs work slowly in relieving the clinical syndrome though their neurochemical action is rapid; new drugs, which neither inhibit monoamine breakdown nor block reuptake of norepinephrine or serotonin, will relieve depression; cocaine, a potent blocker of monoamine reuptake, is not an effective antidepressant; amino acid precursors of the biogenic amines do not consistently relieve depression. These authors give a lengthy list of theories, causal or otherwise: monoamines, trace amines, amino acids; receptor changes; peptides, hormones, endorphins, and enkephalins; water, electrolyte, and carbohydrate metabolism; miscellaneous agents; sleep research; and genetic research. Clearly, none of these satisfy the authors as convincing or conclusive, nor do the writers offer any synthesis of several theories as explanatory. The "dramatic explosion in our knowledge of these disorders," of which Rush and Altshuler (1986) speak in their editorial introduction, so far has served mainly to dazzle and blind the thinking clinician! For example, two new constructs attempt to explain but also complicate the picture. It has been discovered that *presynaptic* receptors exist, which act in a feedback loop to regulate the concentration of transmitter at the synapse. Also, it now seems clear that, as transmitter levels fall, receptors multiply in number and/or increase in sensitivity; they diminish in number/sensitivity as levels rise (Blier and De Montigny, 1985), the "receptor down-regulation" hypothesis for depression.

Among the present attempts to clarify the neurochemical mechanisms in depression, data from the laboratory in testing new drugs constitutes one source. The "first generation" of antidepressants, the tricyclics and monoamine oxidase inhibitors (MAOIs), produced unpleasant side effects militating against compliance, and dangerous toxicity in overdose or suicide attempts. Imipramine and amitriptyline are examples of earlier tricyclics, and phenelzine and tranylcypromine, of earlier MAOIs. The search for drugs which lack the anticholinergic, antihistaminic, and cardiotoxic side effects has led to "second" and "third" generations, the latter in particular diverging radically from the chemical structures of prior drugs (Feighner, 1983, 1986; Damlouji, Feighner, and Rosenthal, 1985; Awad, 1987). Feighner (1983, 1986) presents useful tabular comparisons of their actions, structures, and relative influence upon adrenergic, dopaminergic, cholinergic, and serotonergic neurotransmission in the laboratory. These drugs are on the whole not more effective, but present options when older drugs fail to act desirably. They lack many of the dangerous side effects, but have introduced some new ones including (from present impressions and the popular press) perhaps a heightened suicide risk during successful treatment. In the second generation, examples include the tricyclics, trimipramine and amoxapine and the tetracyclics maprotilene, oxaprotilene, and mianserin. In the third generation of new chemical classes are a triazolopyridine, trazodone; a triazolobenzodiazepine, alprazolam; a chlorpropiophenone, bupropion; and several high-potency serotonin reuptake inhibitors of differing structures, zimelidine, fluoxetine, and fluoxamine.

The caveat should again be raised that, while laboratory evidence is convincing, we cannot be sure that the action of these drugs in the human brain is that demonstrated in laboratory preparations.

Maas (1983) reviews the evidence suggesting that noradrenergic systems are paramount in the genesis of biological depression. Blier and de Montigny (1985) on the other hand lean toward the primacy of serotonergic systems, which are strengthened by all antidepressant treatments, including convulsive therapy. All workers now agree on the principle of interacting systems, as contrasted with the older single-factor theories. McCarley (1982) collaborating with Hobson (Hobson and McCarley, 1977) has diligently developed an integrative model of cyclical interaction between monoaminergic and cholinergic systems in both sleep regulation and depression. Crow and Deakin (1985) present an intricate yet convincing picture which includes the monoaminergic correlates of reward and punishment systems in the limbic–hypothalamic area, a picture rendered the more plausible as attempting to take into account both the pleasure and pain of affective disorders. Akiskal and McKinney (1973, 1975) and Whybrow et al. (1984) have maintained the construct of depression as a psychobiologic common pathway for a number of events or processes. They correctly criticize the noncommunicating babel of voices stemming from the different disciplines, psychosocial to neurochemical, which continues to make integration difficult.

Janowsky and colleagues have since 1972 been leading proponents of the interactional viewpoint; that is, that single neurochemical systems will not be found to account for the phenomena of affective disorders, but rather the state of dynamic balance between interacting systems. Chief among these they select the noradrenergic and cholinergic brain systems (Janowsky and Risch, 1986). The review of Janowsky, Golden, Rapaport, Cain, and Gillin (1988) is, I think, one of the finest on neurochemical hypotheses I have read. These authors draw together the anatomy of the significant neurotransmitter systems (noradrenergic, cholinergic, serotonergic, dopaminergic, and a few possible others) with the physiologic activity these systems mediate. They review clearly the evidence which has undermined reliance upon disturbance in any one of these. Their own inclination is to view the balance between noradrenergic and cholinergic as crucial: relative overactivity in the noradrenergic produces mania, while the cholinergic exerts an antimanic or depression-inducing action. They are fair enough, however, to outline and give some credence to other significant theories (see also "Note on Mania," chapter 11).

Convulsive Therapy: "A Special Case in Pharmacotherapy"

The monoamine oxidase (MAO) inhibitors were discovered adventitiously during the early chemotherapy of tuberculosis, and the tricyclics during a search for better antipsychotics (Blier and de Montigny, 1985). Convulsive therapy, which is agreed to be the most specific and rapid-acting treatment for severe depression (Kendell, 1981; Weiner, 1984), arose through a mistaken assumption that epilepsy and schizophrenia were mutually exclusive. Kendell's review article gives the evolution of the method: Meduna's (1956) use of camphor injections to produce seizures produced painful abscesses; it soon appeared that seizures benefited depression rather than schizophrenia; an intravenous stimulant, pentamethylene tetrazol (metrazol), a camphor derivative turned out to be a more reliable inducer of seizures (Meduna, 1956; Cerletti, 1956); Cerletti and Bini (Cerletti, 1956) discovered through animal experiments that a proper small electric current was the most reliable producer of seizures; by the mid-1950s, the traumatic side effects of the treatment were largely overcome by using general anesthesia, muscle paralysis, and oxygenation; these measures also made clearer what therapeutic variables were crucial. From anesthetic research, an inhalant which produces seizures, Flurothyl was discovered, but has not superseded electricity (Kendell, 1981). Photoshock, the induction of seizures by stimulant medication and rhythmic pulses of light (see below) has never become a regular method of seizure induction.

A huge literature has grown up on convulsive therapy. My attempt will be to select a few publications which highlight the essential questions involved, particularly the question of mode of action. Kendell's (1981) splendid review is a good foundation, along with a brief but cogent chapter by Fink (1977) whose intriguing title I adopt for this section. For good overviews see also Martin (1986) and the brief communication including ethical issues of Hoffman (1984). The cost-effectiveness of the treatment is analyzed by Markowitz, Brown, Sweeney, and Mann (1987), and Paul, Extein, Calil, Potter, Chodoff, and Goodwin (1981).

Fink (1977) offers seven axioms; I do not think that they could be better stated, and I paraphrase them:

1. Repeated cerebral seizures (the "brain storm," might be a suitable label) change behavior specifically in the seriously depressed; not the muscular convulsion, cessation of breathing, consequent lack of oxygen, and other features of a full convulsion, which are incidental.

2. The agent initiating the cerebral seizure is irrelevant: therefore the safest and most comfortable method should be used.

3. The number of treatments required is a function of the patient and the illness, not the method of inducing seizures.

4. The time between seizures is important: the course of treatment cannot be rushed.

5. The functional shift, with its implications for diencephalic involvement, is the prime target for convulsive therapy; it improves early and remains improved in successful cases.

6. The effects of repeated seizures can be augmented or reduced by certain drugs (see Fink's discussion for details [1977], and Cronholm and Ottosson [1960] below).

7. Psychologic test deficits appearing after treatment are reversible (see also Weiner [1984], below), whereas the improvement in behavior and psychopathology is much more persistent.

How does convulsive therapy work? As with antidepressive drugs, we still have no conclusive or consensual explanation. It is probably impossible to carry out a double-blind research design, in which neither the patient nor the staff giving the treatment knows what is being given; but the results of partial attempts in this direction can be cumulated. Animal models can be used, but here we are very much at the mercy of the validity of the model. Let us piece together the accumulated evidence. First to the placebo effect, or psychosocial variables in the treatment.

Plausible psychodynamic theories have been largely relinquished as it becomes evident that the cerebral seizure is the specific therapeutic variable. These theories dealt with the fear of the treatment and fantasies that it was a punishment for guilt and a death and rebirth. But a placebo effect must be reckoned with in every treatment modality (see discussion on the placebo effect, chapter 10). My own clinical experience suggests strongly that we have passed through two eras, with vastly different colorations. When convulsive therapy was indeed horrendous, with no anesthetic, no muscle relaxant, a full convulsion, and occasional "failed convulsions" (failure to initiate a seizure with the electric stimulus) which left the patient with no protective amnesia; staff and patients alike regarded it as distasteful at best; a terrifying and a sadistic assault at worst. Both the patients receiving it, and the hospital culture more generally, shared a powerful placebo suggestion. Curiously, this sadomasochistic placebo message probably contributed to the therapeutic effect in the narcissistically preoccupied, guilt-ridden, rage-filled, delusional patients; its connotations were of explosion of affect, punishment by death, and rebirth. In the present era, when convulsive therapy is a quiet, unspectacular procedure (and I have carefully questioned patients in both eras) the placebo effect would seem to have evaporated in degree and to have become positive in sign. I personally estimate that the placebo effect now has relatively little impact compared to the neurophysiologic effects of the seizure itself; and, paradoxically, this reassuring message may even be psychodynamically antitherapeutic. Kendell (1981), who researched the subject, reports that only 18 percent of patients regard convulsive therapy negatively, whereas 49 percent thought it to be less threatening than a visit to the dentist. Kendell ascribes a mild positive therapeutic effect to present patient attitudes.

Of crucial variables in the effect of convulsive therapy, the following need to be accounted for: method of induction, particularly the electric current; the repeated unconsciousness; the cerebral seizure, and the gross motor convulsion with its huge muscular activity, apnea, and massive anoxia; and the almost invariable temporary memory loss. Animal models and experiments, for which there is always doubt as to their adequate mirroring of the human condition, generally agree with the findings in the human clinical situation (Grahame-Smith, Green, and Costain, 1978; Kendell, 1981; Weiner, 1984; Porsolt, 1985).

Ulett, Smith, and Gleser (1956) used a good design in which the patient was sedated, and unaware of most of the treatment conditions (the treatment was unpleasant and impossible to conceal), and the rating psychiatrist was blind to the treatment given. The main treatment being studied was "photoshock," convulsive therapy initiated by intravenous hexazol (a cerebral stimulant and convulsant) at subconvulsive doses, followed by photic stimulation with pulses of light to produce a seizure. This treatment, despite the advantages pointed out by these authors, has never really become established. The 84 patients with various depressive diagnoses were divided into four groups, receiving convulsive photoshock, subconvulsive photoshock (resulting in a paroxysmal EEG and generalized myoclonus but no loss of consciousness or seizure), electroshock (with sedation but no anesthesia or muscle relaxant), and a control group receiving, like the others, general ward management and sedation. A maximum of 15 treatments was given. The two nonconvulsive treatments, ward management and subconvulsive photoshock, achieved statistically similar results (33 and 38% improvement) as did the two convulsive ones, photoshock and electroshock (76 and 57%). The convulsive photoshock group showed least cyanosis and confusion as well as somewhat better clinical improvement. Most patients were protected against fear by the sedation, and the subconvulsive photoshock group, who simply had a most unpleasant experience, did least well.

This study suggests that fear, cyanosis, and confusion are not therapeutic, and relatively firmly establishes that seizure is crucial, and mode of induction is not.

Brill, Crumpton, Eiduson, Grayson, Hellman, and Richards (1959) proposed to study the electric current, unconsciousness, and motor convulsion, in 97 male patients, most of them chronic schizophrenics; the 97 were assigned randomly to five groups, given "orthodox ECT" (no anesthetic or relaxant), ECT plus Anectine (a relaxant), ECT plus Thiopental (an anesthetic), Thiopental alone with a dummy ECT procedure, and nitrous oxide alone (an anesthetic). Careful statistical analysis failed to show differences in benefit between the five procedures. Though the authors concluded that types of treatment do not differ from each other in effectiveness, nor clarify the variables involved, I believe our main conclusion has to be that convulsive therapy does not benefit chronic schizophrenics. The few true depressives included showed equivocal outcomes.

An important contribution by Cronholm and Ottosson (1960) ingeniously focused a design on the electric stimulus and the seizure itself. By this date, enough experience had accumulated with anesthesia and muscle relaxants to rule out the therapeutic effects of fear, punishment, and like motifs, and the peripheral gross muscular activity with its attendant apnea and cyanosis, as therapeutic variables. Here 65 patients with "endogenomorphic depression" were given 69 courses of convulsive therapy; treaters and raters were dissociated and the patients were unaware of the treatment condition applied. The three such conditions were: convulsive therapy with anesthesia and relaxant, initiated by a current two to three times that required to produce a seizure; anesthesia and relaxant with just the current required to initiate a seizure; and intravenous lidocaine given between the intravenous anesthetic and the intravenous muscle relaxant, thus cutting the duration of the seizure in about half, without raising the seizure threshold.

From this carefully reasoned study we conclude that the amount of current is not crucial, provided a seizure is produced; and that not only is a seizure crucial, but the actual amount of seizure time is a quantifiable therapeutic variable. The lidocaine group had approximately half the seizure time per treatment of the other two groups, and required approximately twice the number of treatments to achieve comparable benefit. About 200 seconds of seizure time in total appears to be needed to remit a major depression, a finding which I do not think has been widely assimilated. Thus, not only seizure, but total time spent in seizures, seems the crucial variable. We might note that by the date of this report it had become clear also that seizures cannot be added rapidly together with benefit: they have to be spaced apart (Kendell, 1981; Weiner, 1984; Grahame-Smith et al., 1978), and the duration of the course of treatment cannot be hurried to less than 2 to 3 weeks, a point of importance.

Freeman, Basson, and Crighton (1978) attempted one further approximation of the "double-blind" design. Their 40 patients, all severely depressed, aged 20 to 70 and in many cases on drug treatment, were assigned to a group receiving "real" treatment, and one receiving "simulated" treatment for the first two sessions of their course, following which both groups continued to receive regular convulsive therapy. As predicted, the "real" group improved in 3 to 9 treatments (mean 6) and the "simulated" in 4 to 12 (mean 7.15), with a lag in improvement proportional to the time lost in simulated treatment, though the "simulated" group caught up to the "real" in time. This study reconfirms the cruciality of the cerebral seizure. A final confirmation was from the Leicestershire trial of Brandon, Cowley, McDonald, Neville, Palmer, and Wellstood-Eason (1984) with 138 patients, of whom 28 completed a proper course of convulsive therapy and 31 of dummy treatment. Ethical and individual considerations were responsible for this attrition over the course of treatment, and benefit could be measured only for 2 and 4 weeks after the initiation of the course, since the unimproved patients had to be given follow-up treatment of various kinds.

In effect, convulsive therapy is a special case in pharmaco-therapy (Fink, (1977); if we understand the one we understand the other. The cerebral seizure, and the total amount of it, is the therapeutic agent; cerebral seizures are diencephalic in source; the diencephalic "brain storm" appears to increase monoaminergic activity, impinging upon the midbrain (sleep mechanisms), hypothalamus (other physiological changes), and the limbic system (emotion or mood state); it takes time to oper-ate cumulatively, possibly because of the progressive down reg-ulation of receptor sites (Kendell, 1981; Weiner, 1984; Blier and de Montigny, 1985).

Electroconvulsive Therapy and Brain Damage. This subject is examined most extensively and recently by Weiner (1984) whose lead paper is debated and commented upon by 22 recog-nized authorities, and followed by a massive bibliography. Weiner reviews every aspect of convulsive therapy, including the neuropathological and psychological. He concludes that temporary confusion is so common as to be a regular part of the treatment, but that there is no substantial evidence of long-term injury to brain or cognition, save in exceptional cases. Fink (1984) berates Weiner for fence-sitting, positively exonerates the treatment of all blame, and places the onus squarely on the opponents of convulsive therapy to adduce the evidence on which their case is supposed to be based. One dimension miss-ing from this debate is the "Risk–Benefit Equation": *if* there are risks in convulsive therapy, how do these balance against the distress and life-threatening position of the seriously de-pressed? The reduction of mortality by convulsive therapy is well recognized (Kendell, 1981; Weiner, 1984), but both the biological researchers and the opponents of convulsive therapy seem completely to omit reference to the disability, torment, and threat to life of the conditions with which they are dealing.

The crucial question of what ex-patients recall of their treatment experience has been researched (Kendell, 1981). The subjective complaints of memory loss and cognitive dysfunction are not borne up by objective testing in the few patients who complain of these; both the temporary amnesic effects of con-vulsive therapy and the intricate retrospective distortions of patients have to be recognized, as well as the "bad press" which still consistently dogs this treatment modality. These are a subject for psychosocial research in their own right.

The electric current used in modern convulsive therapy is the most convenient and humane form of induction so far discovered; the trappings of treatment make of it a "surgical" modality, which, one hopes, will one day be supplanted by "medical" means (as Kendell indicates) less erratic and terrifying than metrazol or flurothyl, less painful and crude and much more reliable than camphor; perhaps not quite as effective as photoshock. Only about 6 percent of the electric current flows through the brain (Kendell), the remainder traveling around the skin and skull between electrodes. Thus, if the electrodes are too close together, no current at all will pass through the brain and diencephalon. Further refinements in electrode placement will be restricted by this factor of flow. Nonetheless, though the current is not the therapeutic agent, there is a persisting clinical impression that electricity adds to the confusional effect over and above the residues of the seizure itself, which raises intracranial pressure and blood flow. Since 1960 attention has been focused on forms of current and electrode placement, in an effort to minimize any ill-effects from the current itself. Kendell and Weiner in their reviews agree that there is now a consensus that electrode placement over the nondominant or nonverbal hemisphere results in less confusion, while being somewhat less powerful therapeutically. This area is still the subject of research efforts. There appears to have been no revival of interest in photoshock as a treatment less likely to induce confusion or residual cognitive impairment.

A Note on Seasonal Affective Disorder

Persuasive medical writers, from Hippocrates to Esquirol, have claimed that climate and season influenced human well-being, and that sunlight benefited depression. Such doctrines do not appear to have been assimilated into mainstream medical theory. However, within a very few years modern biological psychiatry (in the persons, particularly, of Lewy, Rosenthal, and Wehr) has systematized these findings and proposed both a new syndrome, seasonal affective disorder (SAD), and mechanisms for it. This account follows the outline of the recent review of Wehr and Rosenthal (1989) who cover almost every conceivable dimension of the subject.

Research relating seasonality and psychiatric disorder had been mounting for a dozen years; for example, the study of admission rates for affective disorder and the rate for suicide, in relation to season. A very different line of investigation came to impinge on this research interest. Workers at the National Institute of Mental Health (Lewy, Wehr, Goodwin, Newsome, and Markey, 1980) had been studying melatonin, a substance secreted and circulated by the pineal gland in animals, and thought to be of negligible significance in humans. Melatonin was found to be suppressed by daylight and secreted mostly at night. Further, its inhibition of animal sexual activity was linked to seasonal cycles of decline in the amount of daylight and to neural circuits from the retina of the eye. The daylight suppression of melatonin in animals was prolonged by increasing their daylight hours through indoor lighting, but this did not hold for human melatonin production. Finally, it was discovered that unusually bright light induced a very prompt suppression of melatonin secretion in six human volunteers (Lewy et al., 1980).

A 63-year-old man who had suffered seasonally cycling bipolar affective disorder from age 35, who could not tolerate any antidepressants or lithium, and who had kept a careful diary for 14 years, read of the melatonin research and presented himself to the investigating team. It was he who became the first phototherapy candidate; the treatment terminated his usually prolonged winter depression in 4 days (Lewy, Kern, Rosenthal, and Wehr, 1982; Wehr and Rosenthal, 1989). A younger woman with similar difficulties was the second successful candidate (Rosenthal et al., 1982; Wehr and Rosenthal, 1989) in a pilot study by Mueller. Rosenthal and a large team of coauthors (Rosenthal, Sack, Gillin, Lewy, Goodwin, Davenport, Mueller, Newsome, and Wehr, 1982) published the first definitive paper, giving the present title to SAD, and reporting results on winter depressions from a large survey of volunteer respondents and actual patients. In this survey, persons suffering *summer* depression were also identified, and later studied. Whybrow et al. (1984) devote a section in their monograph to the status of SAD.

Meanwhile, international interest evolved rapidly, and investigations in various centers confirmed the findings of Rosenthal and colleagues. Boyce and Parker (1988) reported from the southern hemisphere. The pattern of SAD was there remarkably similar, and the results of treatment equivalent in the latitude on which Australia lies; these authors reported on winter depressions, as the syndrome had been defined, but also on a group of patients with summer depressions. I shall condense in the next paragraphs the general features of the syndrome(s) and theories attached to the characteristic response to phototherapy, working largely from Wehr and Rosenthal's (1989) review.

1. *Definition.* Seasonal affective disorder is precisely defined in DSM-III-R (1987) as a major depressive episode of recurrent type, with onset regular within a span of 60 days in late autumn, and remission within a span of 60 days in spring. A majority of cases reported have been bipolar, including patients with a spring "switch" into hypomania or mania. Summer affective disorder has apparently not yet been defined formally, or delineated as a separate syndrome. Response to phototherapy has been in part a defining criterion for winter SAD.

2. *Degree of Disability.* Seasonal affective disorder appears to be on a continuum, ranging from mild, nondisabling shifts of energy and mood through to a few severely disabled cases. Reports tend to be vague on the criterion of disability. Many, if not most, of the cases reported have continued to work despite anergia and dysphoria. The symptomatology reported suggests a preponderance of "atypical" or "neurotic" rather than classical or "endogenous" depressions. This may, as Rosenthal et al. (1982) and Boyce and Parker (1988) point out, be related to methods of case collection: these workers recruited their subjects by public advertising. It does seem clear that major depressive disorder (or episode) is now being interpreted to include many quite "minor" depressions, provided their onset and features conform to DSM-III criteria.

3. *Features of SAD Proper (Winter Depression).* The cardinal feature (see DSM-III-R, 1987) is of recurrent depression, with

onset regularly in late autumn and persisting over the winter months. Remission and maintenance of remission by phototherapy has become an important defining criterion. These depressions most commonly have been in bipolar patients, with bipolar II prominent (i.e., the index problem is depression, manic episodes being untreated), as reported by Lewy et al. (1982) and Rosenthal et al. (1982). As to symptomatology, "atypical" or "neurotic" depressions appear to be commonest, with irritability, increased sleep and appetite, and carbohydrate craving, with weight gain, in addition to anergia, dysphoria, and loss of libido; symptoms, too, tend to be worst at the close of the day (Wehr and Rosenthal, 1989). Discussion of suicidal motivation has been minimal to absent in the published reports.

4. *Features of SAD (Summer Depression).* These depressions have not received the amount of study accorded to winter depression; cases began to be noticed early in investigations of SAD. Onset is in late spring, remission in early autumn. Wehr and Rosenthal (1989) collate impressions that these depressions conform more closely to the classical, typical "endogenous" pattern: worst in the morning, with insomnia, anorexia, and weight loss. These cases do not respond to phototherapy. Boyce and Parker (1988) reported the same difference between winter and summer onset depressions, but it did not reach statistical significance. Garvey, Wesner, and Godes (1988) compared 18 SAD patients (13 winter onset, 5 summer onset), 13 nonseasonal depressed patients, and 61 normals, all carefully selected. There were statistically significant differences between SAD and non-SAD depressions: the SAD patients suffered hypersomnia and carbohydrate craving and, when in remission, a seasonal fluctuation in sleep pattern and "cloudy day dysphoria." Wehr and Rosenthal (1989) find a likely continuum between SAD sufferers and the normal population, who sleep more, eat more, put on weight, and feel sluggish in the winter, and sleep more restlessly and lose weight in the summer.

5. *Treatment of SAD.* Response to phototherapy is specific and a defining criterion for winter SAD; summer SAD does not so respond. As in the first pilot studies of Lewy (Lewy et al., 1982) and Mueller (Rosenthal et al., 1982) response is swift, within a week, to a regimen of 1/h to 2 hours each morning

with the patient working or reading in front of a bright white light of 2500 lux. A brighter light of 10,000 lux for a half-hour may be effective. Light of ordinary household brightness is ineffective. Treatment has to be maintained all winter, or relapse is prompt.

Placebo controls for phototherapy trials are difficult to impossible to devise. Most controlled studies have used yellow light of lower (300 lux) intensity, or played the light on the skin and not the eyes (Rosenthal et al., 1982; Wehr and Rosenthal, 1989).

Standard antidepressant drugs are effective in both summer and winter SAD; I find no mention of convulsive therapy, doubtless because the depressions are not extremely severe, nor of the phenomena of "switching" to mania under treatment, nor the problem of moving into rapidly cycling bipolar disorder. A combination of drugs and phototherapy is considered to be more effective than either alone, that is, synergistic.

6. *Mechanisms in SAD.* The general animal model for SAD is the annual activity cycle of animals, governed by ambient temperature and particularly by the photoperiod or amount of daily light: feeding and geographic activity, including migration cycles; hibernation and torpor for the conservation of energy; and sexual activity patterns. It is known that a retinohypothalamic tract connects with "pacemakers" for many physiologic controls and in turn to the pineal gland whose production of melatonin responds promptly to reduction in light. What is not so clear is whether, though these pathways also exist in the human, they and melatonin secretion are crucial in human behavior, as they appear to be in other warm-blooded animals.

The first hypothesis for SAD was that increased melatonin, following decrease in the daily photoperiod in the autumn, militated for depression. Results from morning and evening phototherapy tend to negate this hypothesis. A second hypothesis, again somewhat negated by phototherapy experiments, is that circadian rhythms are delayed ("phase shift") by autumn darkness, resulting in a depressive response. The most favored hypothesis today appears to be that the amplitude of circadian rhythms is dampened down by a decrease in the photoperiod ("amplitude reduction") and that the strength of circadian changes is restored by phototherapy (Czeisler et al., 1987; Wehr and Rosenthal, 1989).

7. *Evaluation and Critique.* A convincing case has so far been made for the validity of SAD as a clinical entity, with a biologic basis and a specific biologic treatment. Nonetheless problems exist which partially undermine the construct and which will need to be clarified in further research (Rosenthal et al., 1982; Wehr and Rosenthal, 1989). The epidemiology (prevalence, and incidence) of SAD are difficult to establish; its genetic contributions need to be studied; it has no natural boundaries, being apparently part of a continuum of human annual cycles. The contributions of psychosocial factors have not been well clarified; for example, recurrent annual stressors, or "anniversary reactions" (Rosenthal et al., 1982). I have noted the great difficulty in establishing psychosocial causation for affective disorders (see chapter 11, pp. 497–498; chapter 12, p. 432; chapter 14, p. 493).

Bibliographic Notes: Key Readings

Biological research on depression represents the most prolific and explosive group of contributions to the science of psychiatry in recent years, contributions which we are truly struggling to assimilate into some comprehensive theory. Thus there are major problems in what key readings to recommend. My attempt is to give some balanced combination of the non-time-bound, the historical and relatively well established, and of the swiftly moving, advancing tide of new research.

I follow here the general subject order of the chapter. For a good review on how the genetics of the affective disorders are being approached, I select Dunner (1983). Then to the global, physiological disturbance in depression, or the functional shift: the seminal paper of Pollitt (1960) remains useful reading. Two sectors in the functional shift are psychomotor retardation and depressive sleep disturbance. The former has been relatively little researched. Widlöcher (1983) reviews the concept, its various phenomena, and its central, dominant place in depression. The latter, sleep disturbance, has been the subject of a huge research literature. Here I recommend the seminal papers of Aserinsky and Kleitman (1955) and Dement and Kleitman (1957) on the discovery of REM sleep and levels of sleep; the interesting discussion of McCarley (1982) linking mechanisms of sleep and mechanisms of depression; and the presentation of Letemendia, Prowse, and Southmayd (1986) on depressive sleep and the influence of sleep deprivation.

Animal models in general, and as they apply to research on depression and antidepressant pharmacotherapy, are the subject of McKinney (1976) and Porsolt (1985). Thence we proceed into the intricate maze of depressive neurochemistry. I recommend three first-rate papers on neurotransmitter systems in the brain, each different in scope. Crow and Deakin (1985) offer the most imaginative as well as the longest and most detailed; they include their own field of interest in the reward and punishment systems within the limbic-hypothalamine area. Janowsky, Golden, Rapaport, Cain, and Gillin (1988) furnish a fine description of the several relevant neurotransmitter systems, and their accumulated experience and thinking on adrenergic–cholinergic interactions. A more compact presentation, with useful diagrams, is that of Martin, Owen, and Morihisa (1987). The intricacies of the neurotransmitter systems are also pursued in several chapters in Dewhurst and Baker (1985).

Antidepressant drugs and their analog, convulsive therapy (as Fink, 1977, suggests), are two biological aspects of treatment. Feighner (1983, 1986) offers two papers of equal value comparing the chemical structures, modes of action, and side effects of the several generations of antidepressant drugs. Damlouji, Feighner, and Rosenthal (1985) are also a good resource. The fine review paper of Kendell (1981) compresses together virtually all aspects of electroconvulsive therapy. Weiner (1984), whose paper has nearly 400 references and is commented upon by 22 peer discussants, deals in depth with the vexed question of memory deficits following convulsive therapy.

The new subject of seasonal affective disorder can be very effectively approached through Wehr and Rosenthal (1989). Czeisler et al. (1987) summarize the phenomena of the circadian rhythm and its derangement in depression.

References

Akiskal, H. S. (1983). Dysthymic disorder: Psychopathology of proposed chronic depressive subtypes. *Amer. J. Psychiat.*, 140:11–20.

———— McKinney, W. T. (1973), Depressive disorders: Toward a unified hypothesis. *Science*, 182:20–29.

American Psychiatric Association (1987), *The Diagnostic and Statistical Manual of Mental Disorders*, 3rd ed. rev. (DMS-III-R). Washington, DC: American Psychiatric Press.

Andreasen, N. C. (1983), The diagnosis and classification of affective disorders. In: *The Affective Disorders*, ed. J. M. Davis & J. Maas. Washington, DC. American Psychiatric Press.

Anthony, E. J., & Benedek, T., eds. (1975), *Depression and Human Existence*. Boston: Little, Brown.

APA Task Force (1987), The dexamethasone suppression test: An overview of its current status in psychiatry. *Amer. J. Psychiat.*, 144:1253–1262.

*Aserinsky, E., & Kleitman, N. (1955), Two types of ocular motility occurring in sleep. *J. Appl. Physiol.*, 8:1–10.

Awad, A. G. (1987), New antidepressants: The serotonin reuptake inhibitors. *Psychiat. J. Univ. Ottawa*, 12:31–34.

*Baker, G. B., & Dewhurst, W. G. (1985), Biochemical theories of affective disorders. In: *Pharmacotherapy of Affective Disorders: Theory and Practice*, ed. W. G. Dewhurst & G. B. Baker. London: Croom Helm.

Baldessarini, R. J. (1983), How do antidepressants work? In: *The Affective Disorders*, ed. J. M. Davis & J. W. Maas. Washington, DC: American Psychiatric Press.

Batchelor, I. C. (1969), *Henderson and Gillespie's Textbook of Psychiatry for Students and Practitioners*, 10th ed. London: Oxford University Press.

Becker, J. (1974), *Depression: Theory and Research*. Washington, DC: V. H. Winston.

Benkelfat, C., Poirier, M. F., Leouffre, P., Gay, C., & Loo, H. (1987), Dexamethasone suppression test and the response to antidepressant depending on their central monoaminergic action in major depression. *Can. J. Psychiat.*, 32:175–178.

Blier, P., & de Montigny, C. (1985), Neurobiological basis of antidepressant treatment. In: *Pharmacotherapy of Affective Disorders: Theory and Practice*, ed. W. G. Dewhurst & G. B. Baker. London: Croom Helm.

*Borbély, A. (1986), *Secrets of Sleep*. New York: Basic Books.

———— Valatx, J. L., eds. (1984), *Exptl. Brain Res.*, *Suppl. 8: Sleep Mechanisms*. Berlin: Springer-Verlag.

Boyce, P., & Parker, G. (1988), Seasonal affective disorder in the southern hemisphere. *Amer. J. Psychiat.*, 145:96–99.

Braddock, L. (1986), The dexamethasone suppression test: Fact and artifact. *Brit. J. Psychiat.*, 148:363–374.

Brandon, S., Cowley, P., McDonald, C., Neville, P., Palmer, R., & Wellstood-Eason, S. (1984), Electro-convulsive therapy: Results in depressive illness from the Leicestershire trial. *Brit. Med. J.*, 288:22–25.

Brill, N. Q., Crumptom, E., Eidusun, S., Grayson, H. M., Hellman, L. I., & Richards, R. A. (1959), Relative effectiveness of various components of electroconvulsive therapy. *Arch. Neurol. Psychiat.*, 81:627–635.

Brown, G. M. (1989), Psychoneuroendocrinology of depression. *Psychiat. J. Univ. Ottawa*, 14:344–348.

Cairns, J., Waldron, J., MacLean, A. W., & Knowles, J. B. (1980), Sleep and depression: A case study of EEG sleep prior to relapse. *Can. J. Psychiat.*, 25:259–263.

Cerletti, V. (1956), Electroshock therapy. In: *The Great Physiodynamic Therapies in Psychiatry*, ed. A. M. Sackler, M. D. Sackler, R. R. Sackler, & F. Marti-Ibañez. New York: Paul Hoeber.

Clayton, P. J. (1983), The prevalence and course of affective disorders. In: *The Affective Disorders*, ed. J. M. Davis & J. W. Maas. Washington, DC: American Psychiatric Press.

——— (1986), Prevalence and course of affective disorders. In: *Depression: Basic Mechanisms, Diagnosis, and Treatment*, ed. A. J. Rush & K. Z. Altshuler. New York: Guilford Press.

Coble, P., Foster, G., & Kupfer, D. J. (1976), Electroencephalographic sleep diagnosis of primary depression. *Arch. Gen. Psychiat.*, 33:1124–1127.

*Coppen, A. (1967), The biochemistry of affective disorders. *Brit. J. Psychiat.*, 113:1237–1264.

Cronholm, B., & Ottosson, J. O. (1960), Experimental studies of the therapeutic action of electroconvulsive therapy in endogenous depression. *Acta Psychiat. Scand.*, 35(Suppl. 35):69–101.

*Crow, T. J., & Deakin, J. F. W. (1985), Neurohumoral transmission, behaviour, and mental disorder. In: *The Scientific Foundations of Psychiatry*, ed. M. Shepherd. Cambridge, UK: Cambridge University Press.

Crowe, R. R., Campbell, J., Pfohl, B., Goeken, N., & Pauls, D. (1986), Genetic marker studies of HLA antigens and affective disorders: A review and report of a new pedigree. In: *Depression: Basic Mechanisms, Diagnosis, and Treatment*, ed. A. J. Rush & K. Z. Altshuler. New York: Guilford Press.

*Czeisler, C. A., Kronauer, R. E., Mooney, J. J., Anderson, J. L., & Allan, J. S. (1987), Biologic rhythm disorders, depression, and phototherapy: A new hypothesis. *Psychiat. Clin. N. Amer.*, 10:687–709.

*Damlouji, N. F., Feighner, J. P., & Rosenthal, M. H. (1985), Recent advances in antidepressants. In: *Pharmacotherapy of Affective Disorders: Theory and Practice*, ed. W. G. Dewhurst & G. B. Baker. London: Croom Helm.

*Dement, W., & Kleitman, N. (1957), Cyclic variations in EEG during sleep and their relation to eye movements, body motility, and dreaming. *EEG and Clin. Neurophys.*, 9:673–690.

*Dewhurst, W. G., & Baker, G. B. (1985), *Pharmacotherapy of Affective Disorders: Theory and Practice*. London: Croom Helm.

*Dunner, D. L. (1983), Recent genetic studies of bipolar and unipolar depression. In: *The Affective Disorders*, ed. J. M. Davis & J. W. Maas. Washington, DC: American Psychiatric Press.

Fawcett, J., & Siomopoulos, V. (1971), Dextroamphetamine response as possible predictor of improvement with tricyclic therapy in depression. *Arch. Gen. Psychiat.*, 25:247–255.

*Feighner, J. P. (1983), Second- and third-generation antidepressants: An overview. In: *Affective and Schizophrenic Disorders: New Approaches to Diagnosis and Treatment*, ed. M. R. Zales. New York: Brunner/Mazel.

*——— (1986), The new generation of antidepressants. In: *Depression: Basic Mechanisms, Diagnosis and Treatment*, ed. A. J. Rush & K. Z. Altshuler. New York: Guilford Press.

Fink, M. (1977), EST: A special case in pharmacotherapy. In: *Phenomenology and Treatment of Depression*, ed. W. F. Fann, I. Karacan, A. D. Pokorny, & R. D. Williams. New York: Spectrum.

────── (1984), ECT—verdict: Not guilty (discussion of R. T. Weiner, Does electroconvulsive therapy cause brain damage?). *Behav. Brain Sci.*, 7:26–27.

Freeman, C. P. L., Basson, J. V., & Crighton, A. (1978), Double-blind controlled trial of electroconvulsive therapy (E.C.T.) and simulated E.C.T. in depressive illness. *Lancet*, 8067:738–740.

Garvey, M. J., Wesner, R., & Godes, M. (1988), Comparison of seasonal and non-seasonal affective disorders. *Amer. J. Psychiat.*, 145:100–102.

Gillin, J. C., & Borbély, A. A. (1985), Sleep: A neurobiological window on affective disorders. *Trends in Neurosci.*, 8:537–542.

Goff, D. C. (1986), The stimulant challenge in depression. *J. Clin. Psychiat.*, 47:538–543.

Grahame-Smith, D. G., Green, A. R., & Costain, D. W. (1978), Mechanism of the antidepressant action of electroconvulsive therapy. *Lancet*, 8058:254–257.

Greden, J. F., Albala, A. A., Smokler, I. A., & Gardner, R. (1981), Speech pause time: A marker of psychomotor retardation among endogenous depressions. *Biol. Psychiat.*, 16:851–859.

────── Carroll, B. J. (1980), Decrease in speech pause time with treatment of endogenous depression. *Biol. Psychiat.*, 15:575–587.

────── ────── (1981), Psychomotor function in affective disorders: An overview of new monitoring techniques. *Amer. J. Psychiat.*, 138:1441–1448.

────── Genero, N., Price, H. L., Feinberg, M., & Levine, S. (1986), Facial electromyography in depression: Subgroup differences. *Arch. Gen. Psychiat.*, 43:269–274.

Hobson, J. A., & McCarley, R. W. (1977), The brain as a dream state generator: An activation–synthesis hypothesis of the dream process. *Amer. J. Psychiat.*, 134:1335–1348.

Hoffman, B. F. (1984), Electroconvulsive therapy—A current view. *Can. Med. Assn. J.*, 130:1123–1124.

*Janowsky, D. S., Golden, R. N., Rapaport, M., Cain, J. J., & Gillin, J. C. (1988), Neurochemistry of depression and mania. In: *Depression and Mania*, ed. A. Georgotas & R. Cancro. New York: Elsevier.

────── Risch, S. C. (1986), Adrenergic–cholinergic balance and affective disorders. *Depression: Basic Mechanisms, Diagnosis, and Treatment*, ed. A. J. Rush & K. Z. Altshuler. New York: Guilford Press.

*Kendell, R. E. (1981), Review article: The present status of electroconvulsive therapy. *Brit. J. Psychiat.*, 139:265–283.

Kitamura, T., Shima, S., Kano, S., Asai, M., & Itoh, H. (1985), Dexamethasone suppression test and subcategories of major depression. *Psychopathol.*, 18:198–200.

Kleitman, N. (1939), *Sleep and Wakefulness*. Chicago: University of Chicago Press.

────── (1965), *Sleep and Wakefulness*, 2nd ed. Chicago: University of Chicago Press.

Knowles, J. B., Southmayd, S. E., Delva, N., Cairns, J., & Letemendia, F. J. (1979), Five variations of sleep deprivation. *Brit. J. Psychiat.*, 135:403–410.

———— Waldron, J. J., & Cairns, J. (1979), Sleep preceding the onset of a manic episode. *Biol. Psychiat.*, 14:671–675.

Kraepelin, E. (1913), *Manic-Depressive Insanity and Paranoia,* trans. R. M. Barclay. Edinburgh: Livingstone, 1921.

Kupfer, D. J. (1983), Application of the sleep EEG in affective disorders. In: *The Affective Disorders,* ed. J. M. Davis & J. W. Maas. Washington, DC: American Psychiatric Press.

———— Foster, F. G., Coble, P. A., & McPartland, R. J. (1977), EEG sleep parameters for the classification and treatment of affective disorders. *Psychopharm. Bull.*, 13:57–58.

———— ———— Reich, L., Thompson, K. S., & Weiss, B. (1976), EEG sleep changes as predictors in depression. *Amer. J. Psychiat.*, 133:622–626.

———— Weiss, B. L., Foster, F. G., Detre, T. P., Delgado, J., & McPartland, R. (1974), Psychomotor activity in affective states. *Arch. Gen. Psychiat.*, 30: 765–768.

*Letemendia, F. J. J., Prowse, A. W., & Southmayd, S. E. (1986), Diagnostic applications of sleep deprivation. *Can. J. Psychiat.*, 31:731–736.

Lewy, A. J., Kern, H. A., Rosenthal, N. E., & Wehr, T. A. (1982), Bright artificial light treatment of a manic-depressive patient with a seasonal mood cycle. *Amer. J. Psychiat.,* 139:1496–1498.

———— Wehr, T. A., Goodwin, F. K., Newsome, D. A., & Markey, S. P. (1980), Light suppresses melatonin secretion in humans. *Science,* 210: 1267–1269.

Lindsley, D. B., Bowden, J. W., & Magoun, H. N. (1949), Effect upon the EEG of acute injury to the brain stem activating system. *EEG Clin. Neurophysiol.*, 1:475–486.

Maas, J. W. (1983), Norepinephrine and depression. In: *The Affective Disorders,* ed. J. M. Davis & J. W. Maas. Washington, DC: American Psychiatric Press.

Markowitz, J., Brown, R., Sweeney, J., & Mann, J. (1987), Reduced length and cost of hospital stay for major depression in patients treated with ECT. *Amer. J. Psychiat.*, 144:1025–1029.

Martin, B. A. (1986), Electroconvulsive therapy: Contemporary standards of practice. *Can. J. Psychiat.*, 31:759–771.

*Martin, M. B., Owen, C. M., & Morihisa, J. M. (1987), An overview of neurotransmitters and neuroreceptors. In: *American Psychiatric Press Textbook of Neuropsychiatry,* ed. R. E. Hales & S. C. Yudofsky. Washington, DC: American Psychiatric Press.

*McCarley, R. W. (1982), REM sleep and depression: Common neurobiological control mechanisms. *Amer. J. Psychiat.*, 139:565–570.

———— Hobson, J. A. (1977), The neurobiologic origins of psychoanalytic dream theory. *Amer. J. Psychiat.*, 134:1211–1221.

*McKinney, W. T. (1976), Animal models of depression. In: *Depression: Behavioral, Biochemical, Diagnostic, and Treatment Concepts,* ed. D. M. Gallant & G. M. Simpson. New York: Spectrum.

———— (1977), Biobehavioral models of depression in monkeys. In: *Animal Models in Neurology and Psychiatry,* ed. E. Usdin & I. Hanin. Oxford: Pergamon.

Meduna, L. J. (1956), The convulsive treatment: A reappraisal. In: *The Great Physiodynamic Therapies in Psychiatry,* ed. A. M. Sackler, M. D. Sackler, R. R. Sackler, & F. Marti-Ibañez. New York: Paul Hoeber.

Mendels, J., & Chernik, D. A. (1975), Sleep changes and affective illness. In: *The Nature and Treatment of Depression,* ed. F. F. Flach & S. C. Draghi. New York: John Wiley.

*——— Stern, S., & Frazer, A. (1976), Biochemistry of depression. *Dis. Nerv. Syst.*, 37(No. 3, Section 2):3–9.

Moruzzi, G., & Magoun, H. N. (1949), Brain stem reticular formation and activation of the EEG. *EEG Clin. Neurophysiol.*, 1:455–473.

Paul, S. M., Extein, I., Calil, H. M., Potter, W. Z., Chodoff, P., & Goodwin, F. K. (1981), Use of ECT with treatment-resistant patients at the National Institute of Mental Health. *Amer. J. Psychiat.*, 138:486–489.

*Pollitt, J. D. (1960), Depression and the functional shift. *Comprehen. Psychiat.*, 1: 381–390.

*Porsolt, R. D. (1985), Animal models of affective disorders. In: *Pharmacotherapy of Affective Disorders: Theory and Practice*, ed. W. G. Dewhurst & G. B. Baker. London: Croom Holm.

Post, R. M., Kotin, J., & Goodwin, F. K. (1976), Effects of sleep deprivation on mood and central amine metabolism in depressed patients. *Arch. Gen. Psychiat.*, 33:627–632.

Rosenthal, N. E., Sack, D. A., Gillin, J. C., Lewy, A. J., Goodwin, F. K., Davenport, Y., Mueller, P. S., Newsome, D. A., & Wehr, T. A. (1982), Seasonal affective disorder: A description of the syndrome and preliminary findings with light therapy. *Arch. Gen. Psychiat.*, 41:72–80.

Rubin, R. T., & Marder, S. R. (1983), Biological markers in affective and schizophrenic disorders: A review of contemporary research. In: *Affective and Schizophrenic Disorders: New Approaches to Diagnosis and Treatment*, ed. M. R. Zales. New York: Brunner/Mazel.

Rush, A. J., ed. (1982), *Short-term Psychotherapies for Depression: Behavioral, Interpersonal, Cognitive, and Psychodynamic Approaches.* New York: Guilford Press.

——— Altshuler, K. Z., eds. (1986), *Depression: Basic Mechanisms, Diagnosis, and Treatment,* New York: Guilford Press.

Sabelli, H. C., Fawcett, J., Jaraid, J. I., & Bagri, S. (1983), The methylphenidate test for differentiating desipramine-responsive from nortriptyline-responsive depression. *Amer. J. Psychiat.*, 140:212–214.

*Schildkraut, J. (1965), The catecholamine hypothesis of affective disorders: A review. *Amer. J. Psychiat.*, 122:509–522.

——— Kety, S. S. (1967), Biogenic amines and emotion: Pharmacological studies suggest a relationship between brain amines and affective state. *Science*, 156:21–30.

——— Schatzberg, A. F., Orsulak, P. T., Mooney, J. J., Rosenbaum, A. H., & Gudeman, J. E. (1983), Biological discrimination of subtypes of depression. In: *The Affective Disorders*, ed. J. M. Davis & J. Maas. Washington, DC: American Psychiatric Press.

Schlesser, M. A. (1986), Neuroendocrine abnormalities in affective disorders. In: *Depression: Basic Mechanisms, Diagnosis, and Treatment*, ed. A. J. Rush & K. Z. Altshuler. New York: Guilford Press.

Scott, J. P., & Senay, E. C., eds. (1973), *Separation and Depression: Clinical and Research Aspects.* Washington, DC: American Association for the Advancement of Science.

——— Stewart, J. M., & DeGhett, V. J. (1973), Separation in infant dogs: Emotional response and motivational consequences. In: *Separation and*

Depression: Clinical and Research Aspects, ed. J. P. Scott & E. C. Senay. Washington, DC: American Association for the Advancement of Science.

Seligman, M. P. (1975), *Helplessness: On Depression, Development, and Death*. San Francisco: W. H. Freeman.

Shimizu, A., Hiyama, H., Yagasaki, A., Takahashi, H., Fujiki, A., Yoshida, I. (1979), Sleep of depressed patients with hypersomnia: A 24-hour polygraphic study. *Wak. & Sleep.*, 3:335–339.

Sloman, L., Berridge, M., Homatidis, S., Hunter, D., & Duck, T. (1982), Gait patterns of depressed patients and normal subjects. *Amer. J. Psychiat.*, 139:94–97.

——— Pierrynowski, M., Berridge, M., Tupling, S., & Flowers, J. (1987), Mood, depressive illness, and gait patterns. *Can. J. Psychiat.*, 32:190–193.

Ulett, G. A., Smith, K., & Gleser, G. C. (1956), Evaluation of convulsive and subconvulsive shock therapies using a control group. *Amer. J. Psychiat.*, 112:795–802.

van den Hoofdakker, R. H., & Beersma, G. M. (1984), Sleep deprivation, mood, and sleep physiology. *Exptl. Brain Res., Suppl. 8: Sleep Mechanisms.* Berlin: Springer-Verlag, pp. 297–309.

Van Kammen, D. P., & Murphy, D. L. (1978), Prediction of imipramine antidepressant response by a one-day d-amphetamine trial. *Amer. J. Psychiat.*, 135:1179–1184.

Ward, J. A. (1968), Sleep and psychiatric disorder. *Can. Psychiat. Assn. J.*, 13: 31–48.

Weckowitz, T. E., Nutter, R. W., Cruise, D. G., & Yonge, K. A. (1972), Speed in test performance in relation to depressive illness and age. *Can. Psychiat. Assn. J.*, 17 (Special Supplement):241–250.

——— ——— ——— ——— Cairns, M. (1978), Speed in test performance in relation to depressive illness and age (an appendix). *Can. Psychiat. Assn. J.*, 23:107–109.

——— Tam, C. N. I., Mason, J., & Bay, K. S. (1978), Speed in test performance in depressed patients. *J. Abnorm. Psychol.*, 87:578–582.

*Wehr, T. A., & Rosenthal, N. E. (1989), Seasonality and affective illness. *Amer. J. Psychiat.*, 146:829–839.

*Weiner, R. T. (1984), Does electroconvulsive therapy cause brain damage? *Behav. Brain Sci.*, 7:1–53.

Whybrow, P. C. Akiskal, H. S., & McKinney, W.T. (1984), *Mood Disorders: Toward a New Psychobiology*. New York: Plenum.

*Widlöcher, D. (1983), Retardation: A basic emotional response. In: *The Affective Disorders*, ed. J. M. Davis & J. W. Maas. Washington, DC: American Psychiatry Association.

Winokur, G. (1973), Genetic aspects of depression. In: *Separation and Depression*, ed. J. P. Scott & E. C. Senay. Washington, DC: American Association for the Advancement of Science.

14

A Third Homeostatic Level:
Conservation–Withdrawal; Psychosocial
Components of Human Depressive Disorders

Psychosocial Research: Causes and Dynamics
in Depression

Sitting rather forlornly and rather alone among the accumulated riches of latter-day depression research is a neglected, undernourished, perhaps even rejected and unwanted orphan child: psychosocial research. This orphan child is hardly noticed, rarely lamented, occasionally acknowledged in an embarrassed way (Rush and Altshuler, 1986, p. vii); but perhaps she will be discovered to be beautiful and influential one day. This dearth of psychosocial research is, I submit, something like a negative scotoma. It does not "stand out": it is only noticeable when searched for. Such has been the glamorous tidal wave of biological research and psychopharmacology that clinicians may, in fact, have genuinely forgotten that there is something

491

not only interesting but very useful in understanding and managing depression psychosocially. Thus, we have rather to search about for islands of enlightenment on psychosocial issues, pinpoints of illumination in the sea of depression research literature.

How Psychogenic is Depression? Causality and Life Events

Do depressive disorders have psychosocial causes? How significant are these, balanced against predisposing genetic causes and biological mechanisms? Can depression be taught? Does the significance of psychosocial cause correlate with the severity of depressive episodes?

In a major update on *Life Events and Psychiatric Disorders* (Katschnig, 1986), a number of authors remind us that the topic is still controversial. Depression offers an excellent paradigm for wrestling with this very problem. As I have noted above, obscurity regarding a precipitating cause is practically a criterion of depressive disorders. Yet, since Lewis (1934) it has been shown repeatedly (Paykel, 1978; Brown and Harris, 1978; Lloyd, 1980; van Praag, 1982; Rush and Altshuler, 1986) that a very high proportion even of serious "endogenous" depressions reveal a clear precipitant, usually a personal loss.

Why this uncertainty or controversial quality? Perhaps because of the language barriers which divide researchers of epidemiological, psychodynamic, behavioral, and biological interests. Brown and Harris (1986), in a lengthy chapter on the methodology of establishing causal links for depression, give one simple but telling illustration of the problem:

It is known that heavy smokers get lung cancer. In fact, an extremely high proportion of persons suffering lung cancer turn out to have been heavy smokers. However, an even higher proportion of heavy smokers never do get lung cancer. Therefore, when overall statistics are assembled, the correlation between lung cancer and smoking turns out to be quite low (to the satisfaction and reassurance of the toacco lobby, it might be commented). As for depressive disorders, it is known that life events precede most depressions: but life events happen to many who in fact do not proceed to become depressed. Hence, the overall correlation between life events and depressive episodes is low. (If, in addition, I would suggest, depressed people forget or conceal defensively the precipitating event, the correlation will be lower still. Brown and Harris are able to show statistically that in fact the causal association of life events and depression is something like 73 percent or .734, a very high correlation).

The correlation of grief or mourning with life events is, of course, quite clear (i.e., essentially 100%). The relationship between grief and depression appears to be as controversial or unsettled as that for life events and depression. Abraham (1911) and Freud (1917) offered conceptual criteria for distinguishing them, largely confirmed empirically by Clayton et al. (1974). Brown and Harris, as sociologists, see little value in the distinction, though they view grief and depression as alternate expressions of loss. Bowlby (1980), Parkes (1972, 1985), and Clayton and colleagues (1974) need to be consulted as definitive investigators of grief.

The work of Paykel has been important in establishing methodology (Paykel, 1978). He has introduced the concept of the *exit event*, a term used to embrace various personal losses, and important in the genesis of depressions. His good research designs lack for the most part a prospective dimension and the in-depth exploration of causal connections which Brown and Harris demonstrate. His findings are clear. The risk of developing a depression after an exit event is raised two- to fivefold; it is raised sixfold for particularly stressful exit events.

Brown and Harris: Methodology

I devote some time to the exemplary monograph of Brown and Harris (1978) because it is far more than a research report: it is a goldmine of methodological problems and solutions to these in investigation of causality in psychiatric disorder. These authors discuss every conceivable question, concern, pitfall, and drawback which has presented in their own ongoing career research (the Bedford College Studies) and that of others, and they provide logicomathematical tools for resolving the dilemmas which are raised at various steps in the research. Let me illustrate by a few examples:

1. *Problem: Method of Enquiry.* The case study method provides in-depth information about an individual but it does not clarify what causes the disorder: in general the history of psychoanalysis illustrates this vividly. The survey or questionnaire method provides responses from larger populations of people, but the responses are usually shallow and statistical, because they are limited by their standardization; and the method yields up only correlations, not causal relationships. The solution is to combine the two methods, so that a significant data base of subjects is assembled, they are all asked the same questions, but the questions are explored in detail, and intervening variables emerge which establish cause.

2. *Problem: Establishing Causality.* How can we know that a psychosocial event was not merely a *trigger* for something that was about to happen soon, but a true cause: a "formative effect" in Brown and Harris's terminology? The solution is an ingenious logicomathematical procedure entitled "Time brought forward." A triggering effect will bring the response (depression) a week or two forward in time, slightly before it was going to happen on its own. Such a triggering effect was found in a study of life events preceding attacks of schizophrenia. But a formative effect brings the response (depression) much further forward, as much as 2 years. Such an effect, which influences the onset of depression so powerfully, can be inferred to be a major cause, as it sets in train processes which were by no means about to occur in any case.

3. *Problem: Reporting by Subjects.* How can we know that the events which the research subjects report are not multiplied or exaggerated by the mood state, distorted by time, fabricated to please the researcher, or actually diminished by forgetting? The solution lies in a number of ingenious checks and balances and statistical comparisons which are given to circumvent these. For example, including other informants, comparing response rates between depressed and nondepressed respondents, comparing respondents who remembered single events with those who remembered multiple events.

A number of design features were included to provide tight reliability and validity: clear criteria for diagnosing depression (closely conforming to the "Feighner criteria"); clearly separating causal features from natural history and the symptom picture; clear criteria for a life event, again separating the unit, or objective description of the event, from the respondent's view and emotional investment of it; the rejection of medically or psychiatrically ill persons as control subjects, since it is now abundantly clear that life events influence these conditions; a research design involving large samples, a normal control group, clearly defined independent ("adversity" as globally described) and dependent (depressions of various kinds) variables; careful training of the field investigators in the interview instruments used, resulting in high inter-interviewer reliability; and keeping interviewers and interpreters separated.

Brown and Harris: Research Subjects and Findings

The population base included only women subjects for the eminently practical reason that women suffer depression three times more often than men, and are also somewhat more likely to be found at home by investigators. The study took place in the London borough of Camberwell, in which the Maudsley Hospital is situated. By persistently contacting hospitals and physicians in the area, 114 actual psychiatric patients with depression were located, 73 being inpatients and 41 ambulatory (these 114 were termed the "patient" sample). Two random samples were drawn toward forming the control group, 458 in all, from the community; of these, 76 (17%) proved to be actual sufferers from "case" depression (the "community cases"), 37 of them "onset" cases (i.e., acute illness with onset during the research period), and 39 being chronically depressed; 87 proved to be "borderline cases" (19%); and 293 to be normals (64%) though there was a considerable prevalence of nondisabling psychiatric symptoms among these. An additional random sample, shown to be quite representative, of 154 women living on an island in the north of Scotland were studied for additional variables (rural, integrated community, etc.). Surprisingly, only a small minority of nondepressive psychiatric problems were found in this sample. In-depth interviewing, using a standard outline but permitting much individual flexibility (something like the Piagetian "clinical method") focused on the subjects' lives in the past year, on difficulties and life events, on evidences of psychiatric distress, and on points of onset of decompensation and of changes in severity ("change points").

I summarize the findings, following in sequence the major independent (adversity) and dependent (depression) variables as the authors do.

1. *Life Events.* The actual *patients* had experienced severe life events in the 48 weeks preceding onset at a rate expressed as 115 events per 100 women; the normals at a rate of 27 per 100: a 4.27-fold difference. The normal controls were asked for severe life events within 38 weeks of the investigation, since this was the *average* number of weeks preceding onset of depression in the patients. For patients, 61 percent had had one or more severe events; for the onset cases in the community, 65 percent; and for the normal controls, 20 percent. By a statistical correction which cancels out occurrence of events at the rate seen in normal controls, the patient group showed a 49 percent and the community case group a 57 percent true causal incidence of events. Multiple events did little to increase the likelihood of depression unless there were three or more events. A majority of events, 39 percent out of 57 percent, occurred within 9 weeks prior to onset. These impressive statistics suggest that *"There is no justification at all for giving priority to hereditary or constitutional factors"* (Brown and Harris, 1978, p. 121), though these of course have to be dealt with among vulnerability factors.

When a common meaning was sought among the severe events discovered, a long-term threat to the security and well-being of the subject, such as some form of loss, disappointment, or rupture of an important relationship or source of personal reward, was uncovered. However intense or shocking, threats to shorter-term security did not precede depression.

2. *Difficulties.* Since by no means all depressions were preceded by defined "events," other environmental impacts were sought, and a class of *ongoing* major stresses, termed "difficulties," was conceptualized. These made some contribution to the

onset of depression, particularly when combined with events; in some cases, difficulties and events were difficult to distinguish. Such difficulties were defined as having to be of at least 4 weeks' duration. In rates per 100 women, the patients suffered 67.5 major difficulties, the onset cases 64.9, and the normals 20.4; applying the above statistical correction, the percent of causal effect was 31 percent for patients and 35 percent for onset cases, again a powerful effect. Childbirth during a period of difficulties (in a small number of women) appeared to be a highly pathogenic combination.

Since 28 of the 114 defined patients, and 4 of the 37 community onset cases appeared to have no provoking agent (i.e., a statistically meaningful life event or difficulty), these 32 subjects were reanalyzed. Some 15 had various quite marked problems, which were not classifiable within the research rules; and all the 4 onset cases had minor difficulties or losses.

3. *Social Status.* In the search for further independent variables, social class was examined. The myth that depression is a middle-class disorder was clearly dispelled: Brown and Harris found that lower-class women in this study suffered 4 times as often as their middle-class counterparts: "the higher the class, the lower the rate" (p. 151). Working-class women were also 5 times as likely to become borderline cases. Working-class women have much chronic illness generally. Psychiatric disorder was found to be highest (prevalence 31%) in working-class women with a youngest child aged 6 or less, and lowest in those who were childless (or without any child in the home) and under 35 (12%). Having three or more children under 14 years of age at home was directly implicated as a pathogenic variable. Such families were 3 times more likely to have a severe household event. Being a working-class person and having children at home increased the risk of depression fourfold. Since these findings could not be properly explained on the basis of events and difficulties, further exploration was undertaken of vulnerability factors.

4. *Vulnerability Factors.* Since, taking life events in the community at large, only one out of five women broke down, while almost all women had severe difficulties, factors of vulnerability

to and protection from depression were analyzed. A major protective effect was found to be exerted by having a firm confiding relationship with a husband or lover; such a relationship could neutralize both the impact of events and difficulties and the other vulnerability factors. "Intimacy" is a strong protecting factor (see also chapter 9, p. 302 for a discussion of Vaillant's [1978] findings on object relations and marriage). On the other hand, the most highly vulnerable women showed a combination of less than firm intimacy, loss of mother before 11 years of age, three children or more at home, and no employment outside the home. Seemingly this combination was the lot of many lower-class women.

Although the literature, despite many well-engineered studies, is ambiguous regarding the pathogenic role of early bereavement in depression, this study revealed unequivocal findings: 43 percent of the community cases had lost a mother before 11 years, whereas only 14 percent of the noncases had had this loss. Other types of earlier personal loss did not contribute to "caseness," though, as below, they influenced the quality of depressions.

5. *Severity of Depression.* The same provoking agents cause depression in both patients and community cases, and the same vulnerability factors have a determining influence. What are the factors influencing severity and type of depression? The patients on the whole had more severe depressions, though not at onset, than the community cases. The greater severity developed later with deterioration at "change points" clearly related to additional events. Overall severity, the "neurotic–psychotic," and the "endogenous–reactive" polarities did not correlate well with each other in this study. *"Major loss in the past* is much the most significant factor in influencing severity of Depression" (Brown and Harris, 1978, p. 210) with a correlation of .45, though a previous depressive episode also correlates highly (.58): a change-point event plus a loss in the past plus a previous episode raise the correlation to .65. These losses in the past could be at any time up to early adulthood. However the groupings were arranged, events and difficulties, which were provoking factors, correlated poorly with the type or severity of depression (severe or less severe, "neurotic" or "psychotic," "endogenous" or not). Thus it is confirmed again that

provoking events are not only extremely common in the more severe depressions, but have little correlation with the ensuing clinical picture. A possible exception was the most severely "psychotic" subgroup, with an incidence of only 65 percent events–difficulties, as contrasted with 79 percent for the least severe "neurotic" group, but the difference was not statistically significant. The type of past loss suffered proved to be significant: 74 percent of the severely psychotic, as compared with 45 percent of the less severely psychotic and 16 percent of the neurotic, had suffered loss by death; whereas none of the severely psychotic, 13 percent of the less severe, and 22 percent of the neurotically depressed had suffered loss by separation. This finding was confirmed by reference to some additional case material of Kendell. The severely psychotic were significantly older (45.5 years), with a gradient down to the most neurotic (29.2 years), a finding not well explained despite multiple attempts. Unfortunately, there was no significant sample of bipolar disorder which could be analyzed, which the authors regretted; the research sample was overwhelmingly one of primary, unipolar depression.

Developmental and Psychodynamic Contributions: Bowlby

Clinical and impressionistic literature abounds for this area, but little has emerged from more controlled studies. Thus, we do not possess conclusive answers to the following questions: What developmental experiences render depression more likely, or protect against it? How do developmental experiences weigh against genetic and other biological factors, both in preventing and facilitating depression? What are the common psychodynamic features, if any, which lead into the depressive process (e.g., decisions on the nature of threats and losses, the inevitability or hopelessness of the situation)? What is the nature of giving up, and the relative importance of introjection or retroflexion of hostility? Are psychodynamic processes causes or results of dejected mood; and does this cause–effect relationship differ in different syndromes? Can depression be initiated, reinforced, or perpetuated by social reward?

Some of these questions have been answered for limited populations (e.g. Brown and Harris, who studied urban women with unipolar disorder). Can their conclusions be generalized? Mendelson's (1974) careful and extensive review of the psychoanalytic theories of depressive states, mainly clinically based, does not conclude with any unifying summary or integrative theory regarding what is crucial and common to these states. Part of the difficulty, Mendelson points out, is that different authors deal with different depressive variants, and most fail to define their clinical material precisely. Part is clearly the shortcoming of the classical in-depth case-study method, as pointed out by Brown and Harris. But Mendelson could have gone much further in attempting synthesis of the common or central or crucial dynamics of depression.

The two pioneer psychodynamic investigators of depression, Abraham (1911) and Freud (1917), both used mourning or grief as their standard of comparison. Mendelson (1974) notes their status as among the few psychodynamic writers to define their case material carefully, and to show caution in extrapolating or generalizing their hypotheses. Thus, these two authors remain good exemplars of the psychodynamic method. I shall use the mourning–grief model as a useful analytic tool here. Mourning, like depression, is an autonomous, persisting, yet normal or natural process; it shares important biological and psychosocial features with depression; it shows important dissimilarities; and both have the quality of conservation–withdrawal. Powles and Alexander (1987) summarize the classical (Freud, 1917) similarities and differences. Both mourning and depression ("melancholia") are states of painful dejection, related to object loss; in mourning, self-esteem is preserved, with a great continuing interest in the lost object; in depression, self-esteem is lowered, with great self-preoccupation of a hostile quality. Clayton and colleagues (1974), in an empirical study of mourners and depressed patients, essentially confirm these findings.

The major study which I would like to review is that of Bowlby (1980; see also Bowlby, 1960, 1961a,b) in the third volume of *Attachment and Loss*. I make this selection because Bowlby is a solid and cautious scientist who, starting from a psychoanalytic base, brings in new methods of fact-finding and theorizing, and thus provides original and corrective insights to a field which has perhaps become repetitive and circular in scope. Scott and Senay (1973) edit a compendium pursuing various themes relating separation and depression, with a somewhat more biological orientation. Bowlby's main theses might be summarized as follows:

1. Personal loss, mourning, and depression in adults involve the same process as separation reactions in children, which are a response to the rupture of an important, specific tie to an important, specific caregiver.

2. The distress, pain, pinings, pangs, and yearnings in both mourning and depression are an exact analog of the distressed "seeking" behavior of small children when separated from their mothers (or preferred caregiver).

3. There is an overlap or continuum between normal mourning, "disordered mourning" (pathological grief reactions), and clinical depression; evidence is suggestive to strong that these are all, or mostly, preceded by the rupture of an important affectional bond (Paykel's [1978] "exit event" and Brown and Harris's [1978] construct of a long-term threat to personal security).

4. The depressions which have been properly studied are found to be variants of normal mourning, determined by the use of pathogenic defenses, as well as by particular environmental impacts such as especially sudden and traumatic losses (e.g., loss of a grown child; suicide by a spouse, parent, or child), and by lack of support figures (see again Brown and Harris, 1978).

5. Normal mourning, of which there is no one "correct" form, is a process of successful relinquishment of the lost tie and redeployment of attachments. It is generally found to proceed in phases of (a) numbness of feeling; (b) grief work consisting of moratoria from pain punctuated by bursts of distress, with some personal disorganization; and (c) final restitution and reorganization.

6. Disordered mourning, which shades over into clinical depression, shows three broad patterns: (a) "chronic mourning" with turbulent, disorganized, prolonged course; (b) apathetic mourning, showing a distinct absence of conscious grief,

but with episodes of depression and various bodily ills; and (c) the antithesis of grief, euphoria, amounting in some cases to a frank manic attack (presumably in persons with a bipolar diathesis).

7. Defense mechanisms are employed by both normal and disordered mourners. These are essentially cognitive appraisals of the loss, of the lost person, and of the self, based upon formerly developed representational models in semantic and episodic memory; there can be real discordances between these appraisals, such as a self-image of badness enforced upon the child by parental injunctions, versus a child's recollections of bad parental behaviors vis-à-vis quite legitimate needs–feelings. These defenses strive to modulate the pain and distress following upon separation.

8. Defenses found only in normal mourning recognize the loss but permit a comforting sense of persisting links with the departed.

9. Defenses shared by both normal and disordered mourning, but varying in degree and fixity of defensiveness, lead to numbing and inability to reflect upon the loss; they direct attention away from painful associations to neutral or pleasant ones; or they maintain the belief (denial) that reunion is still possible.

10. Distinctly pathogenic defenses, found only in disordered mourning and depression, redirect or displace anger from an appropriate object (usually the lost person) to an inappropriate one (the self, other people); or disconnect all emotional responses from their cognitive origins. Classical terms for these include displacement, projection, repression, splitting, dissociation, and extreme denial. Bowlby does not include the term *introjection* (i.e., of hostility or blame) used in other psychodynamic studies.

11. The three broad patterns of disordered mourning correlate with three broad patterns of premorbid disturbance in secure attachment: anxious and ambivalent attachment, compulsive caregiving, and insistence on independence from emotional ties. All three are based on fear of loss and rejection and, in adulthood, the fear of being alone. Each of these patterns

come from unfavorable experiences with parenting in childhood: enforced separations without adequate substitute nurturing; critical and rejecting parental attitudes toward the child's security needs; parental threats of abandonment and particularly of suicide, an extremely pathogenic stimulus; the imposition of guilt upon the vulnerable child; demands that the child be a selfless caregiver to a sick parent. Death of a mother before 9 or 10 years of age is believed also to be pathogenic in many cases (see also Brown and Harris, 1978).

Bowlby reminds us that the attachment system is one of the great homeostatic stabilizers; that, like other such systems, it can be overwhelmed by conditions exceeding its homeostatic capacity; that the positive development of this system in childhood leads to warm peer relationships, intimacy, secure marriage, and in turn to good caregiving; and that, when the system is overwhelmed, pathogenic defenses, based on previous experiences, may be brought into play, and lead to clinical depressive disorders.

Bowlby notes a dearth of studies in two areas: study of persons coping by denial of emotional needs, and the consequences of this; and study of the more severe depressions. For the latter, he pays respectful attention to neurophysiological and neurochemical researches, but points out that (a) the causal relationships are by no means worked out in these; that (b) neurochemical processes no doubt perpetuate and increase the severity of depressive disorders; and that (c) it should by no means be assumed that genetic and prenatal factors account for all the variation in the vulnerability of neurochemical systems, since earlier life experiences can have influence in establishing the sensitivity of these systems.

Psychosocial Aspects: Neuropsychology of Depression

Disturbances in cognitive functioning during depressions have been surprisingly little noted by clinicians, except in their extreme form of "pseudodementia"; yet most clinicians would agree that they occur, probably in general proportion to the severity of depression. For some years I have used a rough but helpful test in monitoring recovery from moderate and severe depressions. Most patients in such states complain of being unable to assimilate and recall what they have seen on television, and unable to read effectively, whether from the newspapers or a novel; this has been loosely termed *disturbance in concentration*, but I believe it can be more precisely seen as a general cognitive defect, perhaps fitting the regression model and Piagetian norms. As such patients recover, they report a rather sudden return, at some point, of their ability to read or assimilate television. Some integrative process of focusing, assimilating, conceptualizing, and remembering has fallen back into place.

It seems particularly surprising that cognitive psychologists, who are proponents of cognitive therapy for depression, have not more critically examined their patients' cognitive capacities and incapacities: this in view of the impaired ability of the depressed to learn, particularly in a conceptual fashion; and of the optimistic claims for a "new learning" component in the psychotherapy of depressive disorders.

McAllister (1981) presents a useful review of cognitive impairment in depression. From the studies he marshals (his table of the studies carried out is helpful) he concludes that depression impairs memory and verbal learning; that the causes for this are, so far, obscure; and that no pathognomonic pattern of cognitive impairment has been established, apart from the recognition that cognitive capacity returns with recovery from depression. Sackeim and Steif (1988) review in great detail various neuropsychological dysfunctions in the affective disorders: sensation and perception; psychomotor functioning including disturbances in laterality; learning and memory; mediational processes; intellectual functioning; pseudodementia; and the neuropsychology of emotion.

McAllister (1983) has also very capably reviewed "pseudodementia," the semantically unfortunate but popular designation for chronic brain syndromes observed in depressive disorders (see also chapter 8). These tend to occur in older patients, hence are difficult to distinguish from senile dementia. Pseudodementia almost certainly represents the extreme end of a continuum of cognitive impairments in depressive disorders. It is particularly important to diagnose it correctly, for it is successfully treatable (Post, 1975; Letemendia, Prowse, and Southmayd, 1986; and see chapter 8).

The pioneering paper on pseudodementia (Kiloh, 1961) included many clearly psychogenic or psychodynamically determined conditions, whose clinical signs and symptoms are not those of brain damage. Since then there appears to have been a consistent duality in the use of the term *cognitive* in describing changes in depression. For cognitive therapists the focus has been on the cognitive as represented by thematic and psychodynamic content in depression; that is, a narrowed, persistent preoccupation with self-blaming, pessimistic, and nihilistic themes. Cognitive therapists (see pp. 506–512) have assumed such beliefs to be a cause of depression which needs to be remedied. An investigation of memory functions in depression by Breslow, Koesis, and Belkin (1981) found a characteristic pattern of selectivity in recalling negative elements in test stories and forgetting positive ones. Clinicians known to me have found that depressed patients give gloomy, deprived accounts of their early life, believe they have always been depressed and always will be; and then, following remission, give much more cheerful accounts of their upbringing, as well as of their probable future. This has not, to my knowledge, been researched. It would appear that the characteristic difficulty, in establishing life events at the onset of depression, relates to depressive cognitive impairment. Part of this impairment is a "neuropsychological" forgetting: part is a psychodynamic and defensive "forgetting." These are the two elements in the duality in usage of the term *cognitive*.

Psychosocial Aspects: Psychotherapy in Depression

Aims of Psychotherapy in Depressive Disorders

Psychosocial causation is now strongly implicated for many, if not most, depressive episodes. Further, pathological defense mechanisms are recognized as mediating and maintaining variables in depressive disorders. Research in psychotherapy for depression, however, a difficult endeavor at best, has been lagging far behind the spate of productive work on the biological level, and we have here more questions than answers. Some of these questions might be stated as follows:

1. Since the events provoking depression (or conservation–withdrawal) are almost invariably in the past, what is it that should be treated in psychotherapy? Whitehead (1979) suggests that the focus has to be on "maintaining" factors. In terms of our model, these are what stabilize the process of depression and keep it fixed, persistent, and autonomous. To return the patient to the state of fight-flight and then to psychiatric normality is clearly the treatment goal. Practically, this means shortening the natural history of the depressive episode, rather than "curing" the depressive diathesis.

2. Psychoanalytic therapy and theory have tended to focus on the patient's past, on vulnerability factors and the "depression-prone personality," rather than on the task of remitting syndromes of depression as such. Cognitive therapy focuses on teaching new and more wholesome beliefs as the way out of depression; that is, new learning. Can these several aims be clarified?

3. Is psychotherapy effective in remitting a depressive episode; that is, in shortening the episode and shifting the homeostatic level? What is the evidence? Is psychotherapy effective for all depressive disorders? Or, more correctly, must we ask what type of psychotherapy should be applied to what type of depressive disorder?

4. What are the differences between working to shorten a depressive episode and shift the homeostatic level, and working to deal with vulnerability factors and forestall future episodes of depressive disorder (prophylaxis)?

5. What is the interaction between psychotherapeutic and biological methods of treatment? Antagonistic? Synergistic?

Up until about 1978 the literature permitted no clear answers to these questions (Whitehead, 1979; Weissman, Prusoff, DiMascio, Neu, Goklaney, and Klerman, 1979). An extensive literature was based mainly on the case-study method, with little precision in the specification of either the syndromes being treated or the therapeutic tactics being applied, with designs and controls varying from one study to another, often featured by their conspicuous absence. However, with the advent of standardized nosological schemata and of more precisely specified and rather focal and short-term psychotherapies, better designed and controlled investigations have multiplied. At the moment of writing this, we are in a historical movement which has not yet evolved to satisfactory clarity, but there are strong suggestions now emerging which partially answer some of the questions above.

Status of the Psychotherapies: Older Strategies

The issues up to 1978 were reviewed by Whitehead (1979): no fully satisfactory study on the efficacy of psychotherapy in depressive disorders had yet emerged; there was promise in the focal, short-term therapies; there were major problems in design, for example, accounting for the high spontaneous remission rate, and for various social classes and intellectual abilities; it was maintaining rather than predisposing or precipitating factors which had to be attacked. Whitehead found 13 studies worthy of review; she divided their approaches into three categories:

1. *Psychoanalytic Based*: those stemming from the theory that depression is a result of inwardly directed aggression, which has to be externalized for remission to occur.

2. *Behavioral*: those focusing strictly upon explicit and observable phenomena which are defined as the syndrome, and which are to be extinguished and supplanted by more desirable ones (e.g., crying by laughing). This approach, she believed, was a somewhat sterile one, as its specifications were difficult to translate into more clinical terms, and it was not always clear that it was depression which was being treated.

3. *Combined Cognitive–Behavioral*: those stemming from the pioneering work of Beck (Beck, Rush, Shaw, and Emery, 1979); such approaches assumed that depression was maintained by maladaptive thoughts and attitudes as well as by maladaptive social behaviors, and specified various rather similar attacks on the problem.

Whitehead's first category, the psychoanalytic-based, is also
the oldest. Before the antidepressant drugs (up to 1955) we
had evolved detailed strategies and tactics, involving both the
hospital management of depressed patients and psychotherapy
more specifically. I believe that we applied these with some skill
and effectiveness, since convulsive therapy was our only other
resort. These psychoanalytically based tactics or strategies were
developed most explicitly at the Menninger group of hospitals.
W. C. Menninger (1936) gives an early and conceptually clear
description: all staff in contact with a patient follow a basic
approach which is designed to attack a conflict underlying the
patient's disorder. This approach operates by gratifying some
of the needs seen in the conflict, but by socially acceptable
rather than maladaptive means. Further, it provides activities
which reinforce desirable behaviors or defenses, and which
symbolically respond to the symptoms as communications. Six
such strategies are listed: outlets for aggression; encouraging
healthy identifications; facilitating atonement of guilt; affording the obtaining of love; offering means for the creative
acting out of fantasy; and offering means for creativity and
productivity. The difficult and intricate task is to sort out the
patient's dynamics, thence to prescribe the tactical applications
to various staff (nurses, occupational therapists, recreationists,
even administrators) who thereby fill out the patient's day in a
consistent and therapeutically geared manner, rather than a
random one. Many of us came to believe in this approach; tried
to use it seriously, and estimated, in the absence of controlled
studies, that it helped some quite seriously ill patients to achieve
remission. These management strategies appear to be almost
wholly forgotten today, and I can find only one controlled study
of reasonably recent date.

Wadsworth and Barker (1976) report use of the paradigm
on two cohorts of male inpatients, of mean age 40 years, moderately ("neurotic") to severely ("psychotic") depressed. These authors regret that the severity of their cases did not permit a no-
treatment control group. One cohort (28 in all, 16 neurotically
depressed and 12 psychotically depressed) was treated without
antidepressant drugs and with an antidepressive program of
hard, monotonous, boring all-day work. This was based on the

Menninger approach of kind firmness, a steadfast, no-nonsense stance prohibiting explicit reassurance and sympathy, though with an encouraging tone. The other cohort, matched for numbers and diagnostic distribution, was treated with imipramine, group psychotherapy, and a general approach of active friendliness, a much more supportive and explicitly sympathetic stance. Both cohorts improved greatly as measured in 1 and 3 weeks by two objective and self-report instruments. The 1-week improvement I find particularly impressive, since imipramine would not be expected to operate this quickly. Thus, some psychotherapeutic factor is clearly and strongly at work. What is it? While all patients improved, and the monotonous-activity program was generally the same in outcome as the pharmacologic–supportive one, the neurotic group did better on the antidepressive program. This antidepressive program had to be maintained for a mean of only 3.6 days for the neurotic group, and 5.4 for the psychotic, before mood and behavioral changes appeared, particularly in self-assertion. Then the men were rewarded by being moved out of the antidepressive program and into much more positively pleasurable occupational therapy and group psychotherapy.

Wadsworth and Barker note that these results can be interpreted behaviorally as well as psychoanalytically. One could view the patients as subjected to an aversive milieu for their depressive behavior, then rewarded as they abandon this behavior in favor of a more assertive pattern. Psychoanalytic theory would hold that their guilt was assuaged by the dreary, monotonous milieu and the firm attitude, whereupon they became able to rebel, externalized their aggression, and moved out of depression. A general factor of firm pushing toward self-activation, which I shall note several times below, is not invoked as an explanatory therapeutic variable, though it bridges behavioral and psychoanalytic views. According to our homeostatic–dynamic model, some such factor should be involved in moving from conservation–withdrawal to fight–flight. One hopes that this study will be replicated by others, with design improvements.

The Status of the Psychotherapies: The Current Scene

We must credit Myrna Weissman, research coordinator, epidemiologist, and theoretician par excellence, for the most persistent attention to our question on the therapeutic efficacy of psychotherapy in depressions. Her review (Weissman, 1979) of 17 studies on the subject, with Whitehead (1979), sets the modern stage: commencing with cost-effectiveness, noting the deficiencies of research designs to date, Weissman outlines the better specification of diagnosis and treatment strategies now possible, and reviews five broad treatment methods, with their apparent effectiveness. Cognitive therapy, behavioral approaches, and interpersonal psychotherapy have developed explicit manuals of technique, and thus specify their work operationally. Group psychotherapy and marital therapy have provided much less specific descriptions of what they do, but the 17 studies reviewed were chosen for having reasonable designs.

These studies, and the majority of the work reviewed by Weissman in subsequent publications (Weissman et al., 1979; Weissman, 1981, 1983; Weissman and Akiskal, 1984), deal with the spectrum of ambulatory or less than totally disabling depressive disorders. This is the same spectrum on which Kovacs (1980) reports that up to two-thirds of carefully selected depressed outpatients either show no response to pharmacotherapy or drop out from it: a point which is usually ignored; Akiskal (1983) alludes to it briefly. Weissman (1979) analyzes data for each psychotherapeutic modality as reported, then for the three global categories of psychotherapy alone, psychotherapy compared with drugs, and psychotherapy combined with drugs. The three focal psychotherapeutic approaches, cognitive, behavioral, and interpersonal, emerge as superior to no treatment and better than several others; in general, they improve life skills as well as help remit depression. Cognitive therapy may be more effective than imipramine, but this needs to be confirmed (it is not stated explicitly that the treatment population may be one which fails to respond to drugs). Group psychotherapy and marital therapy have a weaker but significant positive effect on the depressions reported, and also improve life skills and possibly therefore aid in preventing or delaying relapse.

Other reviews confirm Weissman's pioneering findings (e.g., Neu, Prusoff, and Klerman, 1978; Kovacs, 1980). A compact text on cognitive–behavioral therapy with research evaluations is by Williams (1984). His first two chapters on psychological models of depression and on psychological treatment of depression are excellent critical reviews. Williams upholds Weissman's earlier findings: The less severe or ambulatory depressive disorders are successfully treated by a focal, relatively short-term combined attack with cognitive (retraining in interpretations of the self, the world, and others) and behavioral (social skills and assertive training) components. The effectiveness of this method for the severe, "highly regressed," psychotic or bipolar depressive population has not been established, not because it has been proved ineffective, but because proper studies have simply not been done (Williams, 1984).

For further detail on how these focal therapies are performed, the reader can consult Rush (1982) for an excellent overview; Williams (1984) for cognitive–behavioral therapy; Klerman, Weissman, Rounsaville, and Chevron (1984) for interpersonal psychotherapy; and Beck, Rush, Shaw, and Emery (1979) for cognitive therapy. The latter two also deal with the question of combined drug and psychotherapeutic treatment, and Beck et al. offer a chapter on outcome studies. Beck is the "father" of cognitive therapy, and Rush is equally at home in biological research and psychotherapeutic treatment.

For all these focal psychotherapies, and particularly in the case of cognitive therapy, there is a theoretical and methodological problem. Rush (1982) and Beck et al. (1979) recommend that the severely depressed be helped to remit by biological means, before cognitive therapy commences, while the less disabled can start this treatment immediately. This raises a boundary question. Since the severely ill are already remitting, is it the psychotherapy in its specific technical aspects which is the effective agent for remission; or is it some more general factor which promotes remission, with the psychotherapy providing a new cognitive base for new life skills and future prevention of relapse?

This question applies too for the other focal psychotherapies. As noted on pp. 503–505, the depressed patient is a poor learner, so that a learning model may be the incorrect one to apply to the dynamics of remission. This question should not be hard to test, but it has not been tested. We need control groups based on a no-treatment condition, but also on forms of psychotherapeutic (or at least nonpharmacological) treatment which do not involve new cognitive learning. The study by Wadsworth and Barker (1976) found that a somewhat punitive "push" program moves quite severely depressed men out of their depression or conservation–withdrawal, and surprisingly quickly. Another study, on exercise for the depressed, by a Wisconsin team (Greist, Klein, Eischens, Faris, Gurman, and Morgan, 1979; Klein et al., 1985), followed a good research design. The patients were among the less disabled on the spectrum of depressions, having been recruited for research by advertising; they were divided into three groups who received running, meditation–relaxation, and cognitive–interpersonal group psychotherapy. The three groups improved to the same degree, running and meditation being slightly superior; after 9 months the improvement was maintained, and the runners now were keeping up their healthful activity, whereas members of the other treatment groups had terminated ongoing therapy.

It therefore still remains to be proved whether general factors such as personal support and, particularly, sustained push and activation (Wadsworth and Barker, 1976; Greist et al., 1979; Williams, 1984; Klein et al., 1985) are therapeutically important in remitting depressions, and to what extent new cognitive learning (however important in maintaining mental health and preventing relapse) affects actual remission.

"Combined Treatment": Drugs and Psychotherapy

Weissman (1979, 1983) and Weissman et al. (1979) have clarified this subject in a preliminary but convincing way. They find that drug treatment, as compared with psychotherapy, deals with the depressive symptom picture rather than personal and interpersonal dynamics, and drugs also help prevent relapse. Except in the case of cognitive therapy, which one study found superior to imipramine, the focal psychotherapies were about as effective as drugs, and the group and marital therapies less effective. Drugs and psychotherapy clearly produce different effects while remitting depression.

As for combined treatment with both drugs and psychotherapy, Weissman and colleagues found this to be consistently more effective than either modality alone. I think it fair to entitle their conclusions the "Weissman principles," applicable to all subsequent clinical planning, and eminently testable:

1. No combination of drugs and psychotherapy showed an antagonistic effect.
2. Each modality has a significant treatment effect, with a quality appropriate to the modality (see above).
3. Combined treatment with antidepressant drugs and psychotherapy consistently shows an additive or cumulative benefit, combining the specific benefits of each.

To the best of my knowledge, these principles have not been negated by any subsequent publications. Weissman and colleagues rightly conclude by insisting that much further work, with well-designed studies, has to be done; in particular, studies are needed on combined drug and psychotherapeutic treatment for the severely depressed.

I must in conclusion repeat a caveat at which I have hinted several times already. This concerns all drug studies (whether the drug is treatment or control condition) on ambulatory or less disabled patients. Kovacs (1980) suggests that two-thirds of depressed outpatients will fail to respond to antidepressant drugs. However, we have no precise figures, even reliable estimates, on what proportion of patients with depressive disorders will have drug therapy actually wasted upon them. The more mildly depressed may be made slightly or uncomfortably ill, or even mildly psychotic, by drugs. Or they may remit so swiftly (within a day or two) that the benefit is clearly a placebo effect. At the present time we probably have to assume that any patient lacking a functional shift will be unresponsive to pharmacotherapy, and must view with skepticism such claims as that "psychotherapy X is superior to imipramine": being better than zero is hardly a solid claim.

Case Vignette. Dr. M. F., a retired professor of biomedical engineering, is a tall, handsome, scholarly man with a gentle but intent manner and with strongly compulsive and somewhat hypochondriacal traits. He was very ill when first I met him at age 68, suffering a psychotic depression (his third in 10 years) complicated by pneumonia, urinary obstruction, and borderline glaucoma, all related to treatment with amitriptyline. He recovered quickly on convulsive therapy and medical support. Thereafter he had three further psychotic depressions, rapid in onset, responding well to convulsive therapy, over the next 6 years. We discovered that his son and only child, a teacher of physics, was a severe diabetic. Dramatic worsenings of the son's condition correlated, with pinpoint precision, with Dr. F.'s decompensations: an amputation, rapidly advancing blindness, renal failure, a coronary occlusion. We managed to train Dr. F. and his intelligent, energetic wife to contact us as soon as they received bad news. First, Dr. F. would be reasonable but generally tense and uncomfortable (fight–flight), then, within a week, gradually more agitated in a muted, mumbling way, with worries about his son shading over smoothly and progressively into delusions of his own bankruptcy, ruin, and poverty, and panic for his wife's survival. We were unable to abort full development of depression on the two occasions when he came for help early. However, he remitted rapidly in hospital each time with convulsive therapy.

His last psychotic depression developed when he learned that his son was almost certainly terminally ill. Four days after admission, and after two convulsive treatments, I had to break the news to Dr. F. that his son had died. He seemed absolutely not to hear me, continuing with his mutterings about financial ruin. Again, he remitted rapidly. During his convalescence, over a period of 6 months, we met weekly to talk about his son, his love and hopes for him, his deep sadness at the early end of his career, and the satisfaction that there were grandchildren to carry on, together with a good relationship with his daughter-in-law. After 2 months, he was shedding tears gently, no longer ashamed of his grief. His wife joined us for several of our talks.

That was Dr. F's last depression. He is now 85, frail but active. We had given him a unipolar diagnosis; however, in following up his son's death I discovered that he had had an untreated hypomanic episodic at age 48 (his first identifiable psychiatric illness) when he and his son were writing a book together. This new, bipolar II diagnosis was changed to bipolar I when he developed a full-fledged manic attack at age 77, again under interesting circumstances. He had been honored by being invited to write a series of articles for the alumni journal on the subject of new advances in biomedical engineering, began to work furiously, progressively lost sleep, then began to be a nuisance to neighbors, making noise at night and accusing them of interference. He had to be admitted as an involuntary patient, after which supportive management and antipsychotic drugs were successful in normalizing his mood and activity within three weeks. No signs of cerebral impairment were present, and he continued his writing successfully. His writing quite consciously reminded him of his earlier collaboration with his son at age 48.

This impressionistic sketch is offered for reflection on the following points:

1. Grief and depression can be distinguished and treated separately.
2. Psychotic depressions (even bipolar ones) can be highly reactive, and are an alternative pathway to grief.
3. Mania may be an alternative to grief, complicated by denial and pride, possibly triggered by loss of sleep.
4. Psychotherapy can be conducted successfully after biological treatment, even convulsive therapy ("a special case in pharmacotherapy").
5. This is so even in a bipolar depression.
6. Psychotherapy cumulates with somatic therapy and may help prevent further episodes of depression.
7. A bipolar diagnosis may clarify very late in life!

Bibliographic Notes: Key Readings

I have commented at the beginning of this chapter that recent psychosocial research on depressive disorders has to be searched out. The following, I believe, are useful examples of what is available.

Karl Abraham (1911), encouraged by Freud, was the pioneer psychoanalytic investigator of the affective disorders; his carefully thought out views remain relevant. Mendelson (1974) probably collates most thoroughly the psychoanalytic views of depression, though regrettably he does not distil, synthesize, and formulate any unified position. Bowlby (1980), using both psychodynamic or psychoanalytic approaches with modern scientific models, develops a contemporary understanding of mourning and depression.

Despite the many contributions over the years which affirm a high correlation between depressive episodes and life events, the psychogenesis of depression continues to be debated. Katschnig (1986) edits a contemporary compendium of research and theory which includes several updates on the subject. The exemplary study of Brown and Harris (1978), while limited to unipolar depression in women, is definitive in its size, detailed and convincing methodology, findings, and conclusions; one must hope that it would be replicated and extended.

Sackeim and Steif (1988) assemble a quite remarkable collection of neuropsychological functions which have been found in various studies to be adversely influenced by depression. Cognitive deficits in depression are carefully reviewed by McAllister (1981), who also (McAllister, 1983) definitively reviews "pseudodementia," or chronic brain syndrome appearing as a front for depression.

As for the nonpharmacological or psychotherapeutic approaches to treating depression, we have two very interesting examples of therapy by psychological activation. Wadsworth and Barker (1976) compare a comprehensive and successful "antidepressive program" with more traditional medication plus milieu therapy. Klein, Greist, Gurman, Neimeyer, Lesser, Bushnell, and Smith (1985) compare a program of running with two other psychotherapeutic modalities. Rush (1982) assembles four careful and evaluative studies of specific psychotherapies for depression, and Williams (1984), using an even more careful conceptual and evaluative framework, present cognitive–behavioral therapy for depression. As Williams and a number of other authors comment, most psychotherapeutic approaches have been with volunteers and ambulatory or recovering patients, so that only Wadsworth and Barker (in our sample) can be said to have dealt with more ill, hospitalized, and acute cases.

Finally, Weissman (1983) gives her most recent summary of research on the combination of antidepressant drugs with the psychotherapies, and what I have termed the "Weissman principles" on synergistic action between the two modalities.

References

*Abraham, K. (1911), Notes on the psychoanalytic investigation and treatment of manic-depressive insanity. In: *Selected Papers*. London: Hogarth Press, 1949.

Akiskal, H. S. (1983), Dysthymic disorder: Psychopathology of proposed chronic depressive subtypes. *Amer. J. Psychiat.*, 140:11–20.

Beck, A. T., Rush, A. J., Shaw, B. F., & Emery, G. (1979), *Cognitive Therapy of Depression*. New York: Guilford Press.

Bowlby, J. (1960), Grief and mourning in infancy and early childhood. *The Psychoanalytic Study of the Child*, 15:9–52. New York: International Universities Press.

——— (1961a), Processes of mourning. *Internat. J. Psycho-Anal.*, 42:317–340.

——— (1961b), Childhood mourning and its implications for psychiatry. *Amer. J. Psychiat.*, 118:481–498.

*——— (1980), *Attachment and Loss*, Vol. 3. London: Hogarth Press.

Breslow, R., Koesis, J., & Belkin, B. (1981), Contribution of the depressive perspective to memory function in depression. *Amer. J. Psychiat.*, 138:227–230.

*Brown, G. W., & Harris, T. (1978), *Social Origins of Depression: A Study of Psychiatric Disorder in Women*. New York: Free Press.

——— ——— (1986), Establishing causal links: The Bedford College studies of depression. In: *Life Events and Psychiatric Disorders*, ed. H. Katschnig. Cambridge, UK: Cambridge University Press.

Clayton, P. J., Herjanic, M., Murphy, G. E., & Woodruff, R. (1974), Mourning and depression: Their similarities and differences. *Can. Psychiat. Assn. J.*, 19:309–312.

Freud, S. (1917), Mourning and melancholia. *Standard Edition*, 14:237–258. London: Hogarth Press, 1957.

Greist, J. H., Klein, M. H., Eischens, R. R., Faris, J., Gurman, A. S., & Morgan, W. P. (1979), Running as treatment in depression. *Comprehen. Psychiat.*, 20:41–54.

*Katschnig, H., ed. (1986), *Life Events and Psychiatric Disorders: Controversial Issues.* Cambridge, UK: Cambridge University Press.

Kiloh, L. G. (1961), Pseudo-dementia. *Acta Psychiat. Scand.*, 37:336–351.

*Klein, M. H., Greist, J. H., Gurman, A. S., Neimeyer, R. A., Lesser, D. P., Bushnell, N. J., & Smith, R. E. (1985), A comparative outcome study of group psychotherapy vs. exercise treatments for depression. *Internat. J. Ment. Health*, 13:148–176.

Klerman, G. L., Weissman, M. M., Rounsaville, B. J., & Chevron, E. S. (1984), *Interpersonal Psychotherapy for Depression.* New York: Basic Books.

Kovacs, M. (1980), The efficacy of cognitive and behavioral therapies for depression. *Amer. J. Psychiat.*, 137:1495–1501.

Letemendia, F. J. J., Prowse, A. W., & Southmayd, S. E. (1986), Diagnostic applications of sleep deprivation. *Can. J. Psychiat.*, 31:71–736.

Lewis, A. (1934), Melancholia: A clinical review of depressive states. *J. Ment. Sci.*, 80:277–378.

Lloyd, C. (1980), Life events and depressive disorder reviewed: II. Events as precipitating factors. *Arch. Gen. Psychiat.*, 37:541–548.

*McAllister, T. W. (1981), Cognitive functioning in the affective disorders. *Comprehen. Psychiat.*, 22:572–586.

*——— (1983), Overview: Pseudodementia. *Amer. J. Psychiat.*, 140:528–533.

*Mendelson, M. (1974), *Psychoanalytic Concepts of Depression*, 2nd ed. Flushing, NY: Spectrum.

Menninger, W. C. (1936), Psychiatric hospital therapy designed to meet unconscious needs. *Amer. J. Psychiat.*, 32:445–449.

Neu, C., Prusoff, B., & Klerman, G. L. (1978), Measuring the interventions used in the short-term interpersonal psychotherapy of depression. *Amer. J. Orthopsychiat.*, 48:629–636.

Parkes, C. M. (1972), *Bereavement.* New York: International Universities Press.

——— (1985), Bereavement (review article). *Brit. J. Psychiat.*, 146:11–17.

Paykel, E. S. (1978), Contribution of life events to causation of psychiatric illness. *Psychol. Med.*, 8:245–253.

Post, F. (1975), Dementia, depression, and pseudo-dementia. In: *Psychiatric Aspects of Neurological Disease*, ed. D. F. Benson & D. Blumer. New York: Grune & Stratton.

Powles, W. E., & Alexander, M. G. (1987), Was Queen Victoria depressed? 1. Natural history and differential diagnosis of presenting problem. *Can. J. Psychiat.*, 32:14–19.

*Rush, A. J., ed. (1982), *Short-term Psychotherapies for Depression: Behavioral, Interpersonal, Cognitive, and Psychodynamic Approaches.* New York: Guilford Press.

——— Altshuler, K. Z. (1986), Preface. In: *Depression: Basic Mechanisms, Diagnosis, and Treatment*, ed. A. J. Rush & K. Z. Altshuler. New York: Guilford Press.

*Sackeim, H. A., & Steif, B. L. (1988), Neuropsychology of depression and mania. In: *Depression and Mania*, ed. A. Georgotos & R. Cancro. New York: Elsevier.

Scott, J. P., & Senay, E. C., eds. (1973), *Separation and Depression: Clinical and Research Aspects*. Washington, DC: American Association for the Advancement of Science.

Vaillant, G. E. (1978), Natural history of male psychological health: VI. Correlates of successful marriage and fatherhood. *Amer. J. Psychiat.*, 135: 653–699.

van Praag, H. M. (1982), A transatlantic view of the diagnosis of depressions according to the DSM-III: I. Controversies and misunderstandings in depression diagnosis. *Comprehen. Psychiat.*, 23:315–329.

*Wadsworth, A. P., & Barker, H. R. (1976), A comparison of two treatments for depression: The anti-depressive programme vs. traditional therapy. *J. Clin. Psychol.*, 32:445–449.

Weissman, M. M. (1979), The psychological treatment of depression—Evidence for the efficacy of psychotherapy alone, in comparison with, and in combination with pharmacotherapy. *Arch. Gen. Psychiat.*, 36:1261–1269.

——— (1981), Depressed outpatients: Results one year after treatment with drugs and/or interpersonal psychotherapy. *Arch. Gen. Psychiat.*, 38:51–55.

*——— (1983), Psychotherapy in comparison and in combination with pharmacotherapy for the depressed outpatient. In: *The Affective Disorders*, ed. J. M. Davis & J. Maas. Washington, DC: American Psychiatric Press.

——— Akiskal, H. S. (1984), The role of psychotherapy in chronic depressions: A proposal. *Comprehen. Psychiat.*, 25:23–31.

——— Prusoff, B. A.,DiMascio, A., Neu, C., Goklaney, M., & Klerman, G. L. (1979), The efficacy of drugs and psychotherapy in the treatment of acute depressive episodes. *Amer. J. Psychiat.*, 136:555–558.

Whitehead, A. (1979), Psychological treatment of depression: A review. *Beh. Res. Therapy*, 17:495–509.

*Williams, J. M. G. (1984), *The Psychological Treatment of Depression: A Guide to the Theory and Practice of Cognitive-Behavior Therapy*. New York: Free Press.

---

*Recommended readings.

15

A Fourth Homeostatic Level: Disintegration; the Psychoses, Delirium, and Dying

Introduction

Overview

The term *disintegration* is used in this chapter to indicate a general process or homeostatic style associated with psychotic phenomena; and also the homeostatic level at which certain serious psychiatric disorders appear to stabilize, though this style is generally unstable as well as highly threatening to personal well-being. The prototypical example of disintegration is in the schizophrenic psychoses, where multiform psychotic phenomena combine, alternate, exacerbate, and remit in a fashion which makes it impossible to divide the syndrome into a number of relatively independent entities (E. Bleuler, 1911). The most severe developmental regressions occur in the schizophrenias, and probably in other psychotic syndromes. Disintegration occurs also as a component in the more severe affective and

521

schizoaffective disorders; toxic states and deliria almost invariably also partake of this homeostatic style. One might say that
the complete picture of disintegration is seen in certain schizophrenic psychoses, with less complete forms in the others. As
previously, my suggestion will be that the less complete forms
of disintegration contain components of other processes; for
example, depression, mania, or intoxication, acute and chronic
brain syndromes.

This assumption suggests that there are two major spectra
or continua to be considered. One is a continuum reaching
from the most purely "organic" syndromes, involving identifiable brain damage; through the toxic states or deliria, whose
signs are a combination of "organic" and "functional," which as
syndromes are most often reversible, and which yield up no
tangible pathological findings; to the most purely "functional"
psychotic syndromes where no "organic" signs can be found,
nor any brain lesions (M. Bleuler, 1978; Carlsson, 1987). Some
schizophrenic syndromes are in fact found to have associated
anatomical brain changes (see below), but most are currently
believed to be associated with neurochemical and neuroreceptor disturbances.

The other major continuum spans "functional" psychoses:
from affective disorders without psychotic features, through
those with mood-congruent psychotic features, then those with
mood-incongruent ones, through the schizoaffective disorders,
to the definitive schizophrenic psychoses proper. No natural
boundaries or breaks in this continuum have been demonstrated (see Kraepelin, 1913a,b; Munro, 1987). In general,
present-day clinicians and researchers tend to operate from the
"syndrome" rather than the "continuum" approach to psychiatric disorders. *The Diagnostic and Statistical Manual of Mental Disorders* (1980, 1987) (DSM-III, DSM-III-R) exemplifies this tendency, and the risks it engenders. These risks are that
taxonomically very closely related syndromes (i.e., close neighbors along a continuum) will appear to be distinct or unrelated
entities, or even mutually exclusive or antithetical ones; see
discussion in chapter 12, p. 423.

The construct of disintegration is drawn together from
Lehmann (1961) and from Foulds and Bedford (1975) and

other sources; Manfred Bleuler (1972, 1978) reflects the concept. Disintegration is promoted by psychotomimetics and mental integration is restored by neuroleptics. For further discussion on disintegration see chapter 7.

Carlsson (1987), reviewing the status of the "dopamine hypothesis," points out that excessive central action of dopamine will produce multiform psychotic pictures: delirious, manic, paranoid, schizophreniform; and that dopamine blockers dramatically relieve these. Therefore, a dopamine hypothesis of psychosis (i.e., rather than of schizophrenia) is suggested. Neuroleptics are antipsychotic, not antischizophrenic drugs: they do not act specifically on schizophrenia. It is of some interest that Lehmann and Hanrahan (1954), in the first North American publication on chlorpromazine, were impressed with the wide usefulness of this drug for various psychotic, delirious, and agitated states; they considered it particularly helpful in mania. Later, Lehmann (1961) saw the principal mode of action of antipsychotic drugs to be the restoration of "mental integration." Therefore (Carlsson suggests) the dopamine hypothesis for schizophrenia is merely one logical possibility. Schneider's "first-rank symptoms of schizophrenia" are likewise not entirely specific for schizophrenia, being found in a variety of psychoses (Carpenter, 1987). My own reading of Schneider (1959) is that he by no means insisted that these symptoms (including audible thoughts, voices commenting and arguing, influences playing on the body, thought-withdrawal and interferences with thought, the ominous "delusional perception," and conviction of the malign influence of others) were central or pathognomonic for schizophrenia; rather he saw them as the most important psychotic or disintegrative features one could select in the differential diagnosis of schizophrenia from cyclothymia or manic–depressive psychosis. His small treatise is a rich collection of clinical observations and vignettes, interweaving the major functional psychoses in the chapter in question (Schneider, 1959, pp. 88–144).

Pope and Lipinski (1978), in a frequently quoted paper which suffers from some of the weaknesses of the rigid syndrome approach to differential diagnosis, nonetheless suggest a wide distribution of psychotic or disintegrative phenomena among the continua of functional psychoses. Ballenger, Reus, and Post (1982) debate the well-known finding that, in the first or second attack of functional psychosis in adolescents, it may be very difficult to assign the disorder to affective or schizophrenic categories, and not until later attacks can the diagnosis be crystallized into one of these patterns: again, some generalized psychotic process appears to be at work. Munro (1987) continues the debate on how to label syndromes falling between the classically schizophrenic and affective.

Thus, in reviewing research, we may be unwise to seek premature closure by focusing on specific syndromes; rather, better heuristic value might be attained by a focus on a general process, in this case psychosis or disintegration, and its components. This will be my frame of reference in the present chapter. Even though almost exclusive attention will be paid to research on the schizophrenias, this will be because they are the prototypes or purest forms of disintegration, a process also manifested in delirium, severe affective disorder, and, apparently, in the passage of dying.

I therefore ask the reader to keep a kind of dual perspective: to think of disintegration during discussions of schizophrenia, and to think of schizophrenia as a paradigm when assessing general processes of psychosis or disintegration.

I commence by reviewing the contributions of Eugen Bleuler (1911) and Manfred Bleuler (1972, 1978) in developing the construct of schizophrenia, followed by some key authors and sources in more recent years. I briefly review other syndromes of disintegration, into which proper research is difficult, and on which the literature is somewhat clinical and descriptive: delirium, mutism, lethal catatonia, the postpsychotic deficit syndromes of schizophrenia, and the experience of nearly dying. This latter appears to be the link between disintegration and death, the last and final cessation of human homeostasis, or its fifth level.

As in previous chapters, sections on biological and psychosocial aspects of research into schizophrenia will follow; since we have covered most issues of research method and content in previous chapters, this chapter is rather brief. Animal models become even more difficult to produce in mimicking human disintegration. Familial and genetic patterns are only modestly well worked out. Brain dysfunctions and neurotransmitter theory, as in the affective disorders, are still rather incompletely illuminated, but the dopamine hypothesis of psychosis is well supported. Borderline states (or borderline personality disorder) have been investigated chiefly by clinicians. Attentional and cognitive deficits are central to the functional psychoses, particularly the schizophrenias; hallucinosis has been surprisingly little investigated. Life events and experiences in the genesis of schizophrenia are, like brain dysfunctions, still being actively clarified for significance. A final, somewhat reflective, section ponders the present state of treatment methods in the schizophrenias, which may be seen as the cancers among psychiatric disorders.

Phenomena and Classification of the Schizophrenias

Eugen Bleuler's Definitions

As the originator of the construct of schizophrenia, we must pay very careful attention to Eugen Bleuler in his major work *Dementia Praecox or the Group of Schizophrenias*, written between 1908 and 1911 and, surprisingly (for his ideas had become highly influential), published in English only in 1950 (E. Bleuler, 1911).

Bleuler reviewed the evolution of his concepts from the late nineteenth century. He, like Kraepelin (1913a), credits Morel with introducing the name "Démence Précoce" for a disabling psychosis of youthful onset, Kahlbaum (1873) with describing "catatonia," with its stages, from any one of which except the last the patient could recover: melancholia, mania, stupor, confusion, and dementia (an interesting forerunner of the "staging" of schizophrenic psychoses which I have noted in chapter 7). He also credits Hecker with describing hebephrenia, which Kahlbaum then invited him to include as closely allied with catatonia. Bleuler gave abundant credit to Emil Kraepelin, to Freud and to psychoanalytically oriented colleagues at his own university's Burghölzli Hospital, Abraham and Jung. He acknowledged Kraepelin's wisdom in drawing together a group of functional psychoses sharing the feature of progressive deterioration as dementia praecox, and separating them from the also episodic but nondeteriorating manic–depressive grouping. Bleuler considered Kraepelin's textbook, in its fifth edition of 1896, to be the "cradle" of his own ideas.

Bleuler apologized for having to coin a new term, *schizophrenia*, since in effect he fully accepted the validity of Kraepelin's constructs. Nevertheless, he chose the new term because (1) by no means all cases had early onset; (2) the term could be used adjectivally; and (3) it expressed the central feature of splitting up of personality functions.

Zinkin's excellent translation of Bleuler gives the following definition of the schizophrenias: A "group of psychoses which can stop or retrograde (sic) at any stage, but does not permit a full *restitutio ad integrum* (i.e., return to complete premorbid normality) . . . characterized by a specific type of alteration of thinking, feeling, and relation to the external world which appears nowhere else . . . a more or less clear-cut splitting of the psychic functions" (p. 9).

These disorders could range from mildest temperamental or "latent" versions (most recently conceptualized as the borderline states) through insidious and progressively worsening cases, through acute and intermittent forms, to the most florid and malignant patterns. What welded the whole nosological concept together was that, in effect, any case could potentially develop any form of the disorder at any stage, and that in every case a central cluster of dysfunctions could be found, even in persons who had apparently recovered and returned to social competence. What are these central, fundamental, or permanent features?

1. *Fundamental or permanent features.* First, an absence of the signs of *organic psychoses* (Bleuler's term); that is, of any "primary disturbances of perception, orientation, or memory . . . ," even in highly disturbed people (E. Bleuler, 1911, p. 9). Then, the changes remembered by the somewhat hackneyed "A's" which medical students have been taught: association, affectivity, ambivalence, autism, attention, and activity, as well as changes in the will and the person, and dementia. These

represent disturbances in three "simple" functions and six "compound" ones, as follows.

Disturbance in Association is the most crucial problem:

[The] personality loses its unity . . . integration appears insufficient . . . ideas are only partly worked out . . . are "split off" . . . fragments of ideas are connected in an illogical way . . . concepts lose their completeness . . . associations [become] incorrect, bizarre, and strictly unpredictable . . . [there is blocking, and there enter] new ideas [irrelevant to the] previous stream of thought [p. 9].

Affective expressions are "completely lacking . . . to extremely exaggerated . . . qualitatively abnormal; that is, inadequate to the intellectual processes involved" (p. 10).

Ambivalence endows "the most diverse psychisms" with "both positive and negative indicators" at one and the same time, this finding applying to thoughts and volitions as well, in the condition of "*Ambi-Tendenz*" (p. 53). Ambivalence may be a factor in thought blocking and in problems of the will.

As for the more complex or "compound" functions, autism is the powerful tendency to turn inward in resort to fantasy, the denial or distortion of reality, and withdrawal from it; this loosening of reality considerations and judgments gives free rein to "internal complexes" and is a direct consequence of the schizophrenic splitting of the psyche (p. 379). There are problems in attention: the modern sensory overload hypothesis is presaged here (McGhie, 1969). The will is impaired, with "abulia" (lack of will), "hyperbulia" (too strong or impulsive will), vacillation, and blocking. The person is changed and diminished: "the ego is never entirely intact" (p. 71). "Schizophrenic dementia," always to be carefully distinguished from "imbecility" and "amnesia" (loss of memory) is at least potentially reversible. It includes an "endless variety" of deficits of both cognitive (association) and motivational (affectivity) types (pp. 71–90). Finally, activity and behavior are bizarre, often stereotypically so, and related to the other dysfunctions.

2. *Secondary or accessory features.* "We assume the presence of a process, which directly produces the primary symptoms; the secondary symptoms are partly psychic functions operating under altered conditions, and partly the results of more or less

successful attempts at adaptation to the primary disturbances" (p. 461). What are these secondary symptoms, indeed what is the process whose influence is assumed? The secondary features are "hallucinations, delusions, confusion, stupor, mania and melancholic fluctuations, and catatonic symptoms" (E. Bleuler, 1911, p. 10).

3. *Tentative grouping of the schizophrenias*. These appear to have become so well accepted as to be the main divisions used for the next 70 years by clinicians and teachers. Bleuler viewed them as related to predominance or absence of secondary–accessory symptoms:

a. *The paranoid group*. Acute to chronic and fluctuant, dominated by delusions and hallucinations, with suspiciousness and litigiousness, explosiveness, and auditory hallucinations common; always the central deteriorating process;

b. *Catatonia*. Often very acute, with "the usual schizophrenic excitements"; dominated by motor or behavioral features, stupor, catalepsy, hyperkinesis, irregular alterations from manic to melancholic, confusional to violent, with bizarre postures and acts;

c. *Hebephrenia*. "There are no specific symptoms for this group" (p. 234), that is, central schizophrenic features, general deterioration, and senselessness are dominant, rather than the coloration being by specific "accessory symptoms";

3. *The process*. Bleuler ponders deeply as to what the process must be which causes the central features of the schizophrenias, and leads to deterioration. This process does not cause "organic" signs; the clinical features are in fact more like "severe versions of the neuroses." The withdrawal from reality is often quite understandable, though clear life events are not regularly associated with onset. Sexual problems (e.g., masturbation) are probably result rather than cause. Brain abnormalities are found in some, particularly long-standing, cases, such as dilatation of the ventricles (a subject of interest today; see pp. 548–550). But however subtle the findings, there is the inexorable deterioration: therefore it must be a cerebral disease, "the schizophrenic cerebral disease" (E. Bleuler, 1911, p. 349), with the crucial effect of splitting the various mental functions, and undoing the coherence of personality. "The symptomatology

of this disease differs basically from that of any other known organic toxic disorder" (p. 462). Bleuler cites Sommer's conception of a "disturbance of conduction" as a differential accounting for the symptoms, a prophetic footnote: "Complete justice to all these factors can only be done by a concept of the disease which assumes the presence of (anatomic or chemical) (Bleuler's parenthesis) disturbances of the brain" (p. 463).

The uncertainty regarding causes is mirrored in Bleuler's somewhat slim section on treatment, much of it occupied by now-discredited forms of intervention. Chiefly, relief from stress, the avoidance of hospitalization if possible, and a considerable emphasis on psychotherapeutic approaches to confront the withdrawal from reality, are recommended.

Manfred Bleuler Continues Defining Schizophrenia

Manfred Bleuler, the son of Eugen, after a period of general practice, trained in psychiatry in Switzerland and the United States, thus giving him a wider than usual experience and understanding in the field. He finally assumed his father's work at the Burghölzli. His remarkable volume, *The Schizophrenic Disorders: Long-Term Patient and Family Studies* (1972), was published in English in 1978. It is an in-depth follow-up of 208 schizophrenic patients admitted between 1942 and 1943, every one of them known to the author, with additional data from his other clinical experiences in Zürich, Boston, and New York. Rather than attempt to summarize from this massive study, I shall chiefly paraphrase his conclusions in a later paper "On Schizophrenic Psychoses" (1978), which may be thought of as updating, some 60 years later, the original constructs of Bleuler, Sr.:

1. Schizophrenic psychoses are "disintegrations of the most important, most vital functions of human life, which in healthy men and women are highly organized. . . . This disintegration extends to life itself in many cases . . . through starvation or exhaustion, for instance" (p. 1403).

2. Life expectancy is reduced: one-third of the 1942 to 1943 cases had died by the time of their 20-year follow-up (Bleuler, 1972).
3. Progression toward deterioration is not required to make the diagnosis.
4. Hereditary and environmental influences are interwoven in the pathogenesis; Bleuler doubts that the genetic code contributes causally.
5. Decisive causal significance has not been found for the many metabolic errors discovered.
6. "[N]early 30% of schizophrenics recover without neuroleptics and 10% remain severely sick in spite of long-term neuroleptic treatment" (p. 1407). This led Bleuler to doubt a specific metabolic disturbance.
7. "Nearly a third of schizophrenics recover for good" (p. 1407).
8. "In general, the psychosis does not progress after five years from its outbreak but, rather, improves" (p. 1407).
9. A good knowledge of and good relationship with patients is vital; they have suffered contradictory personality traits, a weak ego, and an inharmonious social environment.

Thus, we see that in some 60 years modifications had been made to the construct: the inevitable deterioration is no longer a central feature; progression does not seem inevitable, but a "burning out" of the psychotic process can occur; satisfactory remissions and even permanent recovery are quite common; neuroleptic treatment does not correlate completely with recovery. Bleuler's work was the last great study on the natural history of the schizophrenias, being based on patients admitted prior to the neuroleptic era. Thus, its relatively optimistic aspects deserve very serious consideration. A major difficulty today is that there are virtually no untreated patients whose course can be followed over time.

Statements from the Bleulers' Time to the Present

What have been the nosological developments between 1911 and the contemporary scene? Adolf Meyer was the cornerstone of American psychiatric learning in the first half of this century. His roots were in Europe, and his views were carried back to Britain by Sir Aubrey Lewis. Meyer found Kraepelin's principles to be both useful and questionable: useful in the sense that broad groupings of a meaningful kind were newly synthesized; questionable because a rigid disease model (based on general paralysis or the syndrome of tertiary syphilitic brain disease) appeared to lurk behind these (Meyer, Jelliffe, and Hoch, 1911). Meyer could find no consistent neuropathological patterns (he moved to psychiatry from neuropathology) in the cases he had examined or found reported, but he, with Hoch (Meyer, Jelliffe, and Hoch, 1911), was impressed by the consistent behavioral or mental aspects, which led him to see the disorders as based on failures of homeostasis in the psychobiological sense. Hoch in his paper (Meyer, Jelliffe, and Hoch, 1911) pointed out that delusions can very often be understood empathically and psychodynamically; he indicated what we would call today defense mechanisms of wish fulfillment, projection, and introjection, and opined that dementia praecox is an overgrowth of compensatory trends at the expense of the main, well-adapted interests of the personality.

Kraepelin's final statement was in his *Textbook of Psychiatry*, 8th Edition, Volume 3, of which part II has been translated as *Dementia Praecox and Paraphrenia* (Kraepelin, 1913a). Kraepelin's superb clinical descriptions need to be read to be appreciated; his classification is descriptive, and he never claimed that it was final; he outlines the symptom-pictures in great detail, with chapters on course, prognosis, end-stages, causes, neuropathology, and treatment. It is clear that Kraepelin had assimilated the views of Bleuler by this time, although he places his main ideas from 1896: a group of psychoses without impairment of perception, orientation, consciousness, or retention, but with a "peculiar [progressive] destruction of the internal connections of the psychic personality [involving] the emotional and volitional spheres of mental life . . . [evidently] a single morbid process though [clinical pictures] often diverge very far from one another . . . these peculiar dementias seem to stand in near relation to the period of youth" (p. 4). He therefore adopted the name *dementia praecox*, giving credit to Morel, who had first used the term "démence précoce" in 1860. However, by 1913 Kraepelin had found that some cases recover completely, and that the relation to youth was not consistent or pathognomonic. He therefore groped for a new title: "a name that as far as possible said nothing would be preferable, as 'dysphrenia' " (p. 4). He wondered which of several current labels, including Bleuler's "schizophrenia," would be adopted.

We now seek a retrospective view of the half-century since Kraepelin's last statement. For this retrospective, I have selected a veteran clinician–investigator, an integrator of nosological and psychoanalytic constructs, Bellak, who had set himself in 1948 the task of a major review of schizophrenia every ten years (Bellak, 1979). Summing up the points important to himself in his compendium of advances in both research and clinical aspects of *The Schizophrenic Spectrum*, Bellak distils the following:

We no longer see in our psychiatric wards the bizarre, regressed, queer, and dilapidated people on whose behavior the classicists based their ideas. Stepping into a modern (1979) ward it is even hard to discriminate patients from staff; there are no frozen catatonics, no dishevelled hair-pickers or hair-swallowers, no-one is babbling outrageously, or lying in a pool of excrement. What has happened? There are very few untreated schizophrenics today. The combination of neuroleptic drugs and community psychiatry, though both have failed a number of patients, contrasts greatly with the sensory deprivation and social isolation which in older days were iatrogenic influences contributing to bizarre regressions. Yet, if we approach these normal-appearing patients of today, we find the same fundamental disorder of thought, feeling, and motivation, the "schizophrenic spectrum." This construct implies a collection of many etiologic and pathogenic subgroups, but with a final common pathway of disordered process. Bellak plays philosophically with the conception of "spectrum": the human condition itself, he avers, is a spectrum disorder, of which schizophrenia is a part.

A symposium of world experts was held for the 600th anniversary of the founding of Heidelberg University, whence so much seminal work on the schizophrenias has emanated: Kraepelin (1913a,b), Jaspers (1913), and Schneider (1959), to name the best known, worked there. Its proceedings, *Search for the Causes of Schizophrenia*, edited by Häfner, Gattaz, and Janzarik (1987), draws strongly upon German, Scandinavian, and British sources. I present general trends from the symposium here and specific citations below. There is some criticism of the American preoccupation with "rules" for diagnosis, as contrasted with the European insistence on careful, reliable, in-depth observation and description. Problems with definition remain, rendering difficult the comparison of one investigation with another; here the more recent (American) operational criteria are helpful. The narrower American definitions are contrasted with more liberal European criteria, by which the schizophrenias are seen as more hopeful in course and prognosis. The symposium has a tendency to criticize the "disease" model, and to view "schizophrenia" as a useful shorthand title for a complex and potentially serious disturbance of human adaptation. The search for an "inviolable Platonic entity is most unlikely to succeed," though hypotheses based on a disease model can be heuristically useful (Wing, 1987, p. 40).

The prognosis for the schizophrenias is seen as more hopeful than in Kraepelinian days, even though Kraepelin found that 17 percent of his patients recovered (see particularly Shepherd [1987]): 10 percent of patients recover without disability; 30 percent have several episodes, but without subsequent impairment; 10 percent suffer long-term impairment after their first attack, but no further deterioration after subsequent episodes; and 47 percent have successive attacks or exacerbations, with disability increasing with each episode, and no return to normality (Shepherd, 1987).

The classical division is maintained between "active" or "positive" symptoms (roughly equivalent to Bleuler's "Secondary Symptoms") which can now be effectively eliminated by modern treatment; and "negative," "deficit," or "type II" symptoms, which are by no means amenable to easy change, but which may be psychosocially influenced both for good and ill (see particularly Carpenter [1987]).

Schizophrenia, which affects about 1 percent of the population, is unique among human disorders in the evenness with which it is distributed across societies and nations (Sartorius,

Jablensky, Ernberg, Leff, Korten, and Gulbinat, 1987): "this would put schizophrenia into a class all by itself and raise the question of whether indeed it is a disorder" (Zubin, 1987, p. 114). While this suggests a genetic contribution, heredity accounts for only a part of its causation, and therefore other influences must be sought.

I shall return to other contributions in Häfner, Gattaz, and Janzarik (1987). Meanwhile, we need to scan the definitive and influential criteria of the most recent *Diagnostic and Statistical Manual of Mental Disorders* (DSM-III-R) (1987) of the American Psychiatric Association. Schizophrenia, by these templates, has its usual onset in adolescence or early adulthood, though late onset can occur. Its course must span at least 6 months, including prodromes, an active psychotic phase, and residuals (*metadromes* as I term them in chapter 7); the active psychotic phase must persist at least one week if untreated. Functioning below the highest premorbid level, in work, social relations, and self-care, is an important criterion, though full recovery is permitted by the templates. There must be no disturbance of sensorium; organic illness must be excluded. Affective disorder too must be excluded: any distinct affective symptoms render the diagnosis of schizophrenia invalid. Of the multiple psychological disturbances, no one is pathognomonic: usually there are combinations of disturbance in thought content, thought form (coherent organization), perception, sense of self, volition, interpersonal function, and psychomotor behavior. These criteria appear to have been made somewhat more liberal and flexible than those in DSM-III (1980); the difficult task of rationalizing "soft" data and a polymorphous process has been grappled with rather effectively. A hint of the exclusionary or either–or position shows up particularly in the differential diagnostic statements regarding organic and affective disorders, as well as in dividing schizophrenia from schizoaffective and schizophreniform syndromes. These latter are given separate status, one as having an admixture of affective features, the other as having duration of less than 6 months.

The schizophrenias remain the "cancers" among psychiatric disorders: they are potentially malignant in every case, prognosis is always uncertain; overall morbidity and mortality is high; the presenting syndrome is to be attacked aggressively and as comprehensively as humanly possible, even though it "might" be self-limited and spontaneously remitting; chronic disability, with its human wastage and misery, its economic costliness, and the problems it poses in successful management, remains a public health problem of the highest rank.

My own clinical experience, not to mention the personal circle of my family and friends, has presented one jolting surprise after another, some of these, fortunately, being happy and encouraging ones even as others are bleak and chilling. One bright young professional man, with florid, late-onset disorder, appeared actually to be heading for excellent remission. Instead, 15 years later, he is a disabled, dishevelled, deteriorated bum in the core city. A university student of good premorbid personality appeared to be developing the most malignant, "metastasizing" schizophrenic process, perhaps crucially related to the breakup of her family. Yet, just the other day, a cheerful young woman greeted me walking across the campus. I did not recognize her, for I had only known a very ill, disordered girl, in and out of hospital, and obviously condemned to chronic deterioration and disability. Five years later, she was doing well in her studies and personal life.

Perhaps, as in the case of oncology, we may develop computer-assisted diagnostic and treatment strategies from collaborative study programs. It is hoped that these may help revolutionize prognosis as they have done for some of the cancers.

Other Syndromes of Disintegration

Delirium

The literature on delirium is descriptive and statistical; controlled studies are virtually impossible due to the nature of the syndrome. I follow Wise (1987) in this review, with additional comments from the major discussion of Lishman (1987) and from the DSM-III-R (1987) criteria. I have suggested that there is a continuum of clinical pictures from organic to schizophrenic, with delirium being the bridge between these. Because of its acute onset and its nature as a metabolic disturbance, delirium is frequently characterized by psychotic or disintegrative phenomena; that is, features of serious personality disorganization, behind which the etiologic processes have to be discerned. Lishman's fundamental picture of delirium is as a drowsy, dreamy state, though he includes agitated and psychotic forms. Wise holds to the more turbulent picture. The syndrome was formerly (see chapter 8) conceptualized as acute brain syndrome with or without neurotic, psychotic, or behavioral disturbances.

Delirium is probably the commonest psychiatric syndrome found on the medical and surgical wards of general hospitals. Its morbidity and mortality surpass those of all other psychiatric disorders. Its course and symptoms are highly variable (in fact variability and fluctuation are its hallmarks) but the following combination of "organic" and "functional" features is typical (Wise, 1987; DSM-III-R, 1987).

1. *Course.* Onset is rapid, with initial restlessness, anxiety, irritability, and sleep disruption; duration is usually brief.

2. *Clouding of Consciousness.* A combination of difficulties with attention, arousal, concentration, and registration of information, highly characteristic of this condition. Lishman points out that clouding of consciousness is not to be seen as fluctuation up and down a continuum from wakefulness to sleep: it is fluctuation along a continuum from normal alertness and attention to coma. DSM-III-R stresses difficulties in maintaining and shifting attention.

3. *Impaired Memory and Orientation.* This applies primarily to time and space.

4. *Disturbance of Sleep–Waking Rhythm.* The patient is often hyperalert at night and somnolent by day.

5. *Disorganization of Thinking and Speech.* Bizarre answers to questions and solutions to test problems; rambling, irrelevant, and incoherent speech.

6. *Emotional Lability.* This spans all emotions.

7. *Illusions, Hallucinations.* These are particularly visual; auditory and tactile hallucinations often turn out to be misinterpretations of actual stimuli, or illusions.

8. *EEG Findings*. These findings are highly correlated with the severity of the condition as monitored by the mental state examination; principally slowing.

All of the above tend to come and go inconsistently, the patient often jumping rapidly from apparent lucidity to bizarre, out-of-contact behavior.

The causes of delirium are legion, and have to be identified and treated specifically; however, generalized antipsychotic treatment (see pp. 521–525) is usually effective when the cause has not yet been identified (Wise, 1987). This contributes to the concept that delirium is one of a range of syndromes involving some central process of psychosis (M. Bleuler, 1978; Carlsson, 1987) or disintegration.

Mutism

This syndrome, an "inability or unwillingness to speak, and resulting in an absence or marked paucity of verbal output" (Altshuler, Cummings, and Mills, 1986, p. 1409) should not be equated with catatonic schizophrenia, though that disorder may include mutism. Drugs of many kinds; neurological conditions including stroke, encephalitis, frontal lesions, the fascinating syndrome of akinetic mutism (Lishman, 1971), and metabolic and toxic medical illness have to be looked for in its causation. Catatonic signs (waxy flexibility, etc.) are not of differential diagnostic value. I mention this major symptom picture here as tangentially related to both the schizophrenias and deliria. The paper of Altshuler et al. includes 22 new cases as well as a good literature review.

Lethal Catatonia

This mysterious and deadly syndrome has been recognized for many years. I recall following two cases through to a fatal outcome, despite heroic measures, 45 years ago in my first mental hospital rotation. Mann et al. (1986) review this life-threatening febrile illness with its multiple underlying causes, both organic and functional; in many cases the cause never becomes clear.

The clinical description is remarkably constant: it is a true syndrome. After a prodromal phase of about 2 weeks with labile mood, insomnia, and anorexia, uninterrupted motor excitement sets in, with destructive violence, suicidal attempts, bizarre delusions and hallucinations, and incoherent speech. This phase lasts a week or more, with rising fever, and many metabolic and autonomic signs; terminally there develop stuporous exhaustion, extreme hyperthermia, cardiovascular collapse, coma, and death. Mann et al. have collected 265 cases from the foreign literature and 27 from the American, published since 1960. They believe that severe affective disorder may be the most common form. Convulsive therapy, given early, holds out the best hope, even in clearly organic cases; corticosteroids appear promising.

Prodromal and Postpsychotic Syndromes

Psychotic syndromes in the disintegration mode do not erupt, fully developed, upon the unsuspecting patient and his attendants. Rather, a prodromal period, with symptoms too diffuse to be recognized as a known disorder, regularly precedes the first symptom of psychosis (e.g., the first hallucination). A few days or hours of restlessness and sleep disruption usher in delirium (Wise, 1987; Lishman, 1987). Some 2 weeks of emotional lability, insomnia, and anorexia precede the deadly syndrome of lethal catatonia (Mann et al., 1986).

For the schizophrenias the prodromal period is even longer: it may unfold over months. I have already reviewed, in chapter 7, two studies on the natural history of stages in onset (Donlon and Blacker, 1973) and both onset and restitution (Docherty, van Kammen, Siris, and Marder, 1978) of schizophrenic psychoses. These studies suggest that disintegration only supervenes after a lawful progression through fight–flight and conservation–withdrawal, and that restitution proceeds in the reverse order. Clearly, these studies need to be replicated. If they are confirmed, the neurochemistry of the steps in the natural history will have to be reexamined critically.

A number of studies report and comment on the regularity with which diffuse depressive symptoms appear as the psychotic phase of schizophrenia resolves (De Alarcon and Carney, 1969; Hoedemaker, 1970; Roth, 1970; Stern, Pillsburg and Sonnenburg, 1972; Rada and Donlon, 1975; McGlashan and Carpenter, 1976; Jeffries, 1977; Siris, Harmon, and Endicott, 1981). None comes to firm conclusions about its nature and treatment. Some regard this "metadrome" as transient; others view it as intractable, and with pessimism. Clinical teams on which I have worked have learned to applaud the development of depression, even with its suicidal risk, as a phase in restitution from psychosis. I have had no experience myself with intractable postpsychotic depression. On this subject also, see chapter 7, pp. 206–208.

Crow, Taylor, and Tyrell (1986) outline the two principal syndromes of schizophrenia, on which division there is widespread agreement (see several authors in Häfner, Gattaz, and Janzarik, 1987). The type I or acute psychotic syndrome is characterized by "positive," active symptoms (delusions and hallucinations, the secondary symptoms of Bleuler) and a turbulent course. Following resolution of the active phase, a type II or postpsychotic deficit syndrome may set in, characterized by "negative" symptoms of flat affect, poverty of speech and thought, an amotivational state, and disorder of thinking (the residual classical "central" symptoms of Bleuler). This phase may be described as depression (as in the above studies) of an intractable kind.

When the patient remains in the type II postpsychotic state there is a major challenge to treatment today. The active, type I syndrome is on the whole well controlled by modern antipsychotic management, but not so the type II syndrome. This phase represents the classical deterioration or failure of a *restitutio ad integrum* of Bleuler and Kraepelin. Various causes are currently being sought for it. Crow, Taylor, and Tyrrell (1986) favor cell loss and structural change in the brain, including a viral hypothesis. A hypodopaminergic condition, as contrasted with dopaminergic hyperactivity for the psychotic phase, has been postulated (Crow, Taylor, and Tyrell, 1986; Carlsson, 1987). Psychosocial factors may maintain this syndrome (Carpenter, 1987; Häfner, 1987; Shepherd, 1987) or it may be seen as a resultant of shock and shame at being psychotic (Jeffries, 1977). I return to this type II syndrome several times below.

The Experience of Nearly Dying

Death represents the failure and cessation of homeostasis, and the conceptual fifth level of homeostasis in our present schema (see Figure 7.1 in chapter 7). I have been unable to find any data or theory to suggest that any level intervening between disintegration and death should be included in this model. One somewhat confirmatory piece of evidence lies in the remarkably consistent experiences reported by patients who in recent years have, in effect, died and been revived by cardiopulmonary resuscitation. These experiences fit the disintegration construct quite well; that is, they are analogous to psychotic or delirious experiences. A somewhat softer form of evidence (which today does not often occur) was the not infrequent unexplained death of psychotics in former years, either in excited states (see lethal catatonia above) or in chronic, anergic, withdrawn ones, with no clear pathological findings accounting for the cause of death. The "experience of nearly dying" (Hunter, 1967) or "near-death experience" (NDE) (Morse, Castillo, Venecia, Milstein, and Tyler, 1986) was first reported when modern resuscitation techniques were developed for cardiac arrest. There followed for some years a steady succession of publications on the subject. These were descriptive and even anecdotal, since the phenomenon can hardly be put to controlled investigation. Nevertheless, what has been reported is so consistent, even across many cultures (Osis and Haraldsson, 1977; *Lancet* Editorial, 1978; Stevenson and Greyson, 1979) that there can be no doubt of its validity and reliability. More recently there has been a mere trickle of reports, because, perhaps, no new dimensions remain to be uncovered. The early review of Noyes (1972) is informative, though it also includes a wholly different phenomenon, the experience of acute anticipation of death in the conscious state, for example, in mountain-climbing falls, where the instantaneous review of one's whole life is often reported. The largest collection of cases, transculturally based, and somewhat anecdotal in reportage, is by Osis and Haraldsson (1977). These authors do give some impression of subjectivity or cultural naiveté; for example, they show surprise at, and find bizarre, the experience of a Hindu patient who dreamed while dying of riding to heaven on a cow. Nonetheless, their overall findings show strong internal consistency.

Morse and colleagues (1986), who add to the literature the near-death experiences of quite young children and adolescents (these differ in no way from those of adults), summarize the basic features of this "syndrome." The great majority of NDEs are pleasant, only a few being horrifying (see also Osis and Haraldsson, 1977). They are pervaded by a characteristic transcendental or cosmic consciousness. As in ordinary dreams, their content is ego syntonic and hallucinatory, with visual phenomena greatly predominating; the experience is completely convincing; images of going through a great tunnel, or in some other way to the far side of some great divide or gulf, are common; meeting with friendly spirits, angels, friends who have predeceased the dying one, is a consistent theme. The "out-of-body" experience is regularly reported, where the subject is detached from the soma, and is looking on, often in an autoscopic way, and from above, upon his or her own body and the surroundings. The subject may indeed report in great detail what was going on in the emergency room or hospital ward during the death and resuscitation crisis, as seen from his or her floating position. Stevenson and Greyson (1979) remind us with great objectivity not to ignore, for research purposes, the possible hypothesis that these experiences indicate a passage into immortality. This reminds me that in this discussion I may be committing the reductionistic fallacy of treating dying as a *merely* psychiatric, indeed psychotic, phenomenon. I do not wish or intend to ignore existential, philosophic, and religious aspects, but in this context I limit my view to that of a scientist considering psychobiologic homeostasis.

Biological Aspects

Animal Models for Schizophrenia

The nature and validity of animal models has already been reviewed in chapters 10 to 13. I shall therefore limit this discussion to review of a single publication, that of McKinney and Moran (1981) on the principles and limitations of animal models for schizophrenia. An animal model can never be exactly the same as the "real" condition being modeled: it remains a simplified compromise intended to aid in understanding something more complete or complex. It is particularly difficult to be sure just what animal behavior is to be interpreted as psychotic. In other words, there is a serious danger of prematurely labeling animal behavioral states as equivalent to human symptoms in these conditions. In particular, no animal preparation replicates properly for auditory hallucinations, flatness of affect, thought alienation, delusions of control, neologisms, associative disorders, ambivalence, or incongruous affect, all key psychotic or schizophrenic features.

As in the case of the other major groups of disorders (e.g., in our discussion of mania in chapter 11), animal models can be divided into categories induced by drugs, and by nondrug means such as social manipulation and cerebral stimulation. Amphetamine has been used consistently to induce a state of hypervigilance, with stereotyped behaviors, based on the similarity in humans of amphetamine psychosis and paranoid schizophrenia: the congruence with human psychosis is not very complete. Phenylethylene produces virtually the same behaviors, perhaps more convincingly, as does 6-hydroxydopamine. The latter is believed to affect noradrenergic reward systems. Hallucinogens do not produce convincing pictures in animals. Somewhat more hopeful as a model is interfering with arousal by implantation of electrodes in the reticular activating system, based on the construct of disorders of attention as central to schizophrenia: the disturbance thus induced is reversed by chlorpromazine and other antipsychotics. The "glaring social deficits" produced by social isolation, particularly in primates, have been taken as a model for schizophrenia also.

These are helped by antipsychotics, but it is not at all clear what human condition is really being modeled, whether it is an affective disorder or psychosis.

McKinney and Moran conclude that "there is as yet no compelling animal model of schizophrenia" (p. 482). These authors believe that further "ethological" attention to human schizophrenic patients is needed; that is, careful behavioral observation and analysis, in order to generate animal models of a more convincing kind. It thus appears that, the further we descend the ladder of homeostatic styles, the more difficult it becomes to model human disorders using animal species. It may be relatively easy to model states of fear and aggression; it is harder to achieve valid animal models for states of despondency and elation; and harder still to model psychotic disintegration with reliability and validity. Yet, a huge range of drugs has been developed and tested against the latter animal models.

Genetics and Schizophrenia

Since Bleuler (1911) and Kraepelin (1913a), interest in discerning a genetic basis for the schizophrenias has stemmed from an impression that they showed a vaguer familial incidence than the affective disorders. However, a conviction that they were in some way hereditary has persisted. This peaked in the 1960s with the excitement of Kallmann's discovery, based on extensive studies of twins, that 86 percent of monozygotic (MZ or identical) twins with schizophrenia showed concordance in the cotwin, as against 15 percent for dizygotic (DZ or nonidentical) twin pairs (Kringlen, 1987). Modern studies, however, now reduce the importance of hereditary factors to a much less determinate position, as errors in Kallmann's data searches and determinations of zygosity have emerged (Baron, 1986a; Häfner, 1987).

On the status of genetics in schizophrenia I select a small sample of recent reviews for discussion. Kringlen (1987) reviews studies on twin pairs and relatives of schizophrenics and the conclusions that may be inferred from these. Baron (1986a, b), in two rather technical papers, surveys statistical methods for analyzing family relationships and genetic possibilities, and the more recent approaches of seeking vulnerability trait associations and genetic markers (Baron [1987] also contributes a chapter in Häfner, Gattaz, and Janzarik [1987]). Mendlewicz and Sevy (1986) give us a somewhat more compact review of genetic associations. Venables (1987) in addition to contemporary theory reports an ongoing prospective study of children at risk. Häfner (1987) briefly summarizes the present state of this field.

Scandinavia, particularly Denmark, with its meticulous vital statistics, has been a prime source for epidemiological data. Therefore I select Kringlen (1987), a Scandinavian researcher, for particular mention. Kringlen reviews the various uses of twin and family analyses and what these then indicate about contributions to the schizophrenias from genetic and environmental factors. Studies of concordance between twin pairs (the dizygotic twins should be of the same sex) control for genetic influences and indicate how much influence must be attributed to life experiences. It is now agreed that Kallmann's original figures were inflated by imperfections in method: today, 30 to 40 percent concordance in MZ twins and 10 to 20 percent in DZ appear credible. Examination of the nonschizophrenic cotwin, Kringlen points out, is of great interest in solving the nature–nurture equation. In one study he carried out he found a concordance of 31 percent for schizophrenia in MZ twins; however, in this study, 31 percent of cotwins of the schizophrenic subjects were found to be psychiatrically completely normal, an impressive figure. The remaining 38 percent of the cotwins showed a range of neurotic and character disorders. This finding renders untenable the concept of schizophrenia as a disease which is transmitted genetically. Rather it suggests the transmission of personality vulnerabilities which can be compensated for by good upbringing. Only seven monozygotic twin pairs reared apart have been studied: Kringlen was impressed by the "very miserable upbringings" these separated twins experienced, though a high concordance rate (57%) was found. The offspring of discordant twin pairs should further indicate heritable factors. A study of these gave a suggestive, but not statistically significant, indication of heritability, but an even stronger suggestion of environmental influences. An analysis of offspring of schizophrenic parents who had been adopted could only suggest interactions between nature and nurture. These parents, who were currently psychotic, or developed schizophrenic psychoses later, in fact begot children with a surprising range of characteristics, from the highly gifted to the mentally retarded, and from psychiatrically normal to character disordered, as compared with controls. As for relatives of schizophrenic patients who had themselves been adopted, a significantly higher incidence of schizoid and borderline disorders was found among their biological, as compared with their adoptive, relatives. In the case of "cross-fostering," no differences were found between the incidence of schizophrenic psychosis among children of normals brought up by schizophrenics (about 10%) and children of schizophrenics fostered by normals.

Examination of a number of MZ twin pairs indicated that the twin who eventually developed schizophrenic psychosis was from birth the smaller, more submissive twin, dependent upon the parents and tending to engender concern, worry, and overprotectiveness in them.

Kringlen, supported by Strömgren (1987), concludes that:

1. The more careful the data gathering and analysis, the lower are the found concordance rates in twin pairs.
2. Twin studies prove that environmental factors are significant, but suggest that genetic ones are important too.
3. Adoption studies prove the existence of genetic factors and also suggest that environmental ones are important.
4. Genes in themselves are insufficient to produce schizophrenia.
5. It has not yet been shown that adverse environmental experiences can produce schizophrenia in themselves, although this seems likely.
6. A multifactorial, polygenic hypothesis best explains the spectrum of disorders seen in the families of schizophrenics.

Baron (1986a) outlines three possible statistical models for estimating genetic contributions to schizophrenia. These need to be tested simultaneously against each other in the search for significance. The single major locus (SML) model assumes that a single, autosomal (i.e., not on a sex chromosome) gene transmits schizophrenia. The multifactorial-polygenic model (MFP) assumes a number of genes with interacting and additive effects. A "mixed" model permits some relaxation of the rigor of the first two by combining their assumptions. Essentially, all such models assume that genetic factors are *contributing* causes, requiring formative and precipitating causes of other origins for the initiation of psychosis. One mixed model proposes a "primary" genetic factor plus an interacting "contributing" one; to this interaction random environmental events add further causal effects. Thus, an algebraic sum of vulnerability factors, protective factors, and random events in the milieu become the matrix for development of schizophrenia.

Baron's (1986b) lengthy list of vulnerability traits and possible (none has been proven) genetic markers includes attentional, neurophysiological, and neuropathological deficits and disorders. Possible actual genetic markers include such categories as immune response mechanisms and biogenic amine enzyme systems. Such markers must be "state-independent"; that is, found in patients who are not currently psychotic, and in their healthy relatives. Some attentional deficits hold promise for research, since they are both heritable and stably persistent in well family members and also in ill patients.

Venables (1987) reports an ingenious prospective study on a cohort of children in Mauritius. These children are not yet old enough to develop schizophrenia. But they carry three assumed vulnerability traits, two of these clearly heritable. They display increased electrodermal sensitivity; and they have a problem with smooth visual tracking reported in up to 86 percent of schizophrenics as well as in members of their families. In addition, they are of below average intelligence. Venables (1987) and Crow (1987) hypothesize that schizophrenia is a function of deficits in screening the experiences of life, and that below average intelligence impairs effective screening. This cohort of children will be followed for emergence of cases of clinical schizophrenia.

Baron (1986b) and many others stress the usefulness of studying persons and families with manifest biological problems. The whole universe of the schizophrenias probably gives a bleached-out, averaged effect for biological and genetic factors, so that concentration on the more clearly biologically predisposed is more likely to elucidate genetic variables.

Zubin (1987) and Strömgren (1987) summarize our present knowledge of genetic contributions to schizophrenia, and the research problems still remaining. The schizophrenic disorders are atypical in having a rather uniform incidence across the societies studied. One interpretation of this finding, clearly, is that cultural factors are minor contributions to it. On the other hand, calculations of the genetic contribution indicate that it plays a minor, though statistically significant, role. In Zubin's example, whatever model is employed, the genetic contribution accounts for only about 26 percent of causal effects. Kringlen's (1987) suggestion is that schizophrenia is not an inherited disease proper, but follows from inherited vulnerabilities in appropriate cases. This parallels Bellak's (1979) rather philosophical proposition that the spectrum of disorders culminating in schizophrenic psychosis itself represents only an extreme portion of the "spectrum disorder" of human existence itself.

If schizophrenia is a disease with a genetic contribution, why has it not long ago faded out of the human breeding population since it places its victims at a clear reproductive disadvantage (Baron, 1986a)? Even if it is assumed, as it should be, that the rather small statistical contribution of genetics to the schizophrenias is an effect of averaging a very heterogeneous population; and even if somewhat atypical, biologically predisposed families could be sequestered and properly studied; it remains today that, for the schizophrenias as a whole, "the mode of inheritance remains elusive" (Baron, 1986a, p. 1051), "none of the models solves the problem of transmission in schizophrenia" (Mendlewicz and Sevy, 1986, p. 9), and it behooves us to continue an energetic search also for nongenetic causes (Crow, 1987).

Brain Dysfunction in the Schizophrenias

Particularly because of the deteriorating courses of a number of cases, a neuropathologic component in the schizophrenias has long been postulated, despite the absence of "organic" deficits in sensorium, memory, and orientation. Bleuler (1911) listed the pathologic findings recognized in his day, a list which remains very topical. Yet no consistent pattern, nor clear cause–effect relationships, has so far been established. The reader might compare Bleuler's review with that of Heinrichs and Buchanan (1988), Shelton, Karson, Doran, Pickar, Bigelow, and Weinberger (1988), or Berman, Weinberger, Shelton, and Zec (1987). The intuitive hypothesis guiding ongoing research is that fine tissue changes determine particularly the postpsychotic deficit state.

There is general agreement (Shepherd, 1987; Carpenter, 1987; Hirsch, 1987) on the two principal clusterings of schizophrenic symptomatology into an active psychotic phase and a postpsychotic deficit state. The active psychotic phase with its "positive" or type I symptoms is successfully managed by modern therapy. Dopaminergic overactivity and treatment with dopamine blockers provide a principal hypothesis in explanation of the active psychotic phase (Carlsson, 1987). Modern therapy is so far ineffective in the postpsychotic deficit phase with its "negative" or type II symptoms, and its chronic conservation–withdrawal quality (see chapter 7). For this phase, a deficit in dopamine neurotransmission has been postulated, but here particularly the relevance of brain changes is today being carefully reinvestigated with modern techniques.

Not only do neuropathologic changes have relevance to the understanding and more successful management of the type II condition, but this subject is closely related to the search for genetic markers and trait associations in the schizophrenias. M. Seeman (1988) reviews trait associations and putative markers correlated with the schizophrenias. They fall under four general headings: psychological, neurobehavioral, neurophysiologic, and neuroanatomic–neuropathologic. Although modern imaging techniques now lend great sophistication to the search for biologic abnormalities (Garber, Weilburg, Buananno, Manschreck, and New, 1988) Seeman states that, so far, no replicable findings specific to schizophrenia have emerged.

Most interesting of the neurobehavioral anomalies is the smooth-pursuit eye tracking dysfunction. To test for this, the subject is asked to follow an object such as a swinging pendulum. The smooth visual pursuit is interrupted in positively affected individuals by nystagmuslike jumps or "saccades." We have noted Venables's (1987) prospective study of children showing the anomaly. Seeman reports that this pattern is reported to be present in 50 to 85 percent of schizophrenic patients and in 34 percent of patients' parents. It thus approaches the status of a state-independent biologic marker.

Seeman notes that abnormalities in skin conductance (also used as a variable by Venables), in dichotic listening, in visual hemifield and tactile discrimination tasks, and in general electroencephalographic findings as well as evoked potentials, point to some left cerebral hemisphere problem. She (see also Carlsson [1987]) points out, however, that these findings are applicable to psychosis generally (i.e., disintegration), with only some specificity for schizophrenia.

Various studies are currently in progress attempting to assess the causal meaning of neuropathologic findings. Heinrichs and Buchanan (1988) give a good review of general neurological signs in schizophrenia. Shelton et al. (1987) studied, in a chronic population, the interrelations between ventricular size, cerebral blood flow, and attentional and conceptual problems. These studies confirm an ongoing impression that cerebral atrophy (as measured by computer-assisted scans and formulas for calculating loss of brain tissue):

1. fails to correlate with severity of illness;
2. correlates positively with duration of disability;
3. relates positively with negative symptoms and the defect state;
4. suggests some localization of pathology in the left and prefrontal areas.

Crow and Deakin (1985) include in their extensive chapter a good review of neuropathologic issues and tentative current conclusions from these. Intriguing hypotheses continue to be put forth, such as that of Crow (1987) for a slow-virus encephalitis (see also Hirsch [1987]).

Neurochemical Theories of Schizophrenia

It is small wonder that the affinities between schizophrenia and delirium have suggested a toxic or metabolic derangement in the schizophrenias. Thus, a search for possible exogenous or endogenous toxic substances has accompanied the history of the construct of schizophrenia. E. Bleuler (1911), Arieti (1974), and Crow and Deakin (1985) outline the steps in this historical search. Bleuler speculated on "endogenous toxins"; "auto-intoxication" theories spawned a succession of bizarre treatment approaches; more recently, modern biochemical theories have incriminated such factors as hallucinogenic abnormally methylated monoamine neurotransmitters. None of these theories has been upheld. Most recently, and despite Bellak's (1979) mourning that neurotransmitter theories were already "fading in hope," theories of abnormality in central neurotransmission are dominant.

Crow and Deakin (1985) are again an excellent source of explication of this field. In general, the neurotransmitter hypothesis might be stated thus: due to an inherited defect, or to antenatal or early postnatal influences, significant neurotransmitter systems are vulnerable to breakdown, which precedes the onset of active psychosis. The hypothesis that relative dopaminergic hyperactivity mediates type I schizophrenia is probably the currently dominant one. Carlsson (1987) as well as Hirsch (1987) remind us that vulnerability and breakdown in neurotransmitter systems mediates psychosis generally (i.e., disintegration, in our present model) and not schizophrenia alone: application of the dopamine hypothesis to schizophrenia represents a focal use of a more general theory.

Carlsson, who was highly influential in developing the dopamine theory of psychosis (Carlsson, 1975), reviews the current evidence for the hypothesis as follows (Carlsson, 1987). I simplify his argument in the following steps. P. Seeman (1985) has been an early and continuing investigator of dopaminergic dysfunction in schizophrenia also; I have partially incorporated his constructs.

1. Drugs which increase dopamine activity (e.g., the dopamine precursor l-DOPA used in treatment of Parkinsonism, and the amphetamines) induce a variety of psychoses: paranoid, manic, delirious, and schizophreniform. Amphetamine produces a condition almost exactly mimicking paranoid schizophrenia.

2. Reserpine, which depletes monoamine storage, is antipsychotic.

3. Effective antipsychotics are dopamine blockers, some of them powerfully and specifically so. This blockade has two major effects. One is on the extrapyramidal dopamine system (substantia nigra to corpus striatum), producing dystonic symptoms. The other is on the mesolimbic-forebrain dopamine system, the antipsychotic action. (The third, small, tubero-infundibular dopamine system does not enter the argument.)

4. The same problem arises for this hypothesis as for the antidepressant drugs in affective disorders (see chapter 13, pp. 465–470 above): dopamine blockade is swift, while antipsychotic action is much slower. Therefore, complex refinements to the theory are necessary, such as assuming interactions between dopamine and other monoamine systems, and dynamic shifts in number and sensitivity of receptor sites (as we have discussed in chapter 13).

Carlsson thus goes on to warn against using the dopamine hypothesis simplistically; rather, an interactional view is required. The brain, he points out, is no mere chemical factory. It is a "complex cell hierarchy" (he did not use the computer as analogy) in which relatively limited disturbance of synaptic contacts can have devastating effects. He notes that the dopamine systems are newcomers in the evolutionary sense, their task being to integrate neocortical and paleocortical structures; and, like all newer evolutionary developments, the dopamine systems have problems of redundancy and inefficiency (and, we might add, by the Jacksonian principles enunciated in chapter 7, differential vulnerability to injury).

For a review of the several other neurotransmitter theories, Crow and Deakin (1985) should be consulted. Crow and Deakin (as noted in chapter 13) themselves contribute a plausible explanation in the involvement of the limbic system and its reward and punishment centers in the adrenergic transmitter disturbance, a hypothesis mainly relevant to affective disorders but also to schizophrenia. Hirsch (1987) reviews various attempts to localize the disruptive effects of dopaminergic disturbance; I return to these in the next section. A number of rather exotic hypotheses need to be pursued, though they seem implausible a priori. For example, Hirsch reviews one which locates the neuropathology of schizophrenia in the left amygdala. And, as noted earlier, Crow (1987) proposes that a slow virus may cause, essentially, a general encephalitis; but, it cannot be detected, nor experimentally transmitted, since it has merged so subtly into the host cells and probably altered their genetic code. Can such a hypothesis even be tested?

A Summary of Present Hypotheses

There is risk in trusting explanations of a pervasive disorder such as psychosis (schizophrenia) to anatomically localizing hypotheses. Schizophrenia as defined has always lacked the signs of organic brain damage. Nonetheless, it is true that relatively localized brain lesions can be highly disruptive. In recent research, two trends appear to be converging: the study of neurotransmitter system disturbances, principally in acute, psychotic phases of the disorder; and the study of premorbid traits and markers and brain changes in the chronic deficit state. Convergence of these studies has brought attention to the limbic and frontal areas of the brain.

Let me return, before summarizing recent trends, to some prophetic statements offered by the interdisciplinary team of Miller, Galanter, and Pribram (1960) three decades ago. These workers viewed the "core" of the forebrain, the limbic system, and its frontal connections, as mediating the motivational aspects of information processing; the hippocampus as protecting the amygdala from irrelevant information; and the frontal association areas as the "working memory" system which maintains an orderly plan as information is processed. The following brief summary of current trends might, then, be assessed against this presage of things to come.

It is recognized that noradrenergic and serotonergic nuclei in the brain stem are small, but have most extensive ramifications to the reticular activating system and cerebral hemispheres (Hornykiewycz, 1986). The same applies to the three rather limited-appearing dopaminergic systems, the mesolimbic-forebrain system apparently being of greatest relevance in the psychoses (Carlsson, 1975, 1987). All three monoamine systems (as well as the acetylcholine system) interlock and interact in the regulation of attention, information processing, and motivation, and all must interdependently be affected in psychosis (Crow and Deakin, 1985; Carlsson, 1987). Recent studies converge to suggest some particular localization of pathology in the left hemisphere and frontal lobes. Berman et al. (1987), investigating a chronic population, are able to relate loss of brain tissue in the left hemisphere and both prefrontal areas to length of disability and negative symptoms. Hirsch (1987) referring to the dopaminergic disturbance in more acute states, is drawn to the left hemisphere and frontal areas also; he postulates maturational problems in the brain predating actual clinical illness. Cohen and Borst (1987) attribute the information-processing deficit in schizophrenic states to disruption of the left amygdala and perturbation of the left hemisphere. Thus, present research trends appear to incriminate both anatomical and functional (neurotransmitter disturbances) variables localizable to the left limbic area and both frontal lobes in the disintegration of psychosis (Carlsson, 1987; Hirsch, 1987; Shelton et al., 1988) and its paradigmatic syndrome, schizophrenia.

Liddle (1987) has proposed a conceptual model which appears somewhat difficult to test but even so to have heuristic merit. He outlines three patterns which, in the schizophrenias, may appear singly or in combination. A pattern of psychomotor poverty, which he refers to disturbance of the dorsolateral frontal areas, has important implications for global psychosocial deterioration. A pattern of disorganization, referable to the orbital frontal area, bears on vocational deterioration. And a pattern of reality distortion can, he believes, be referred to disruption of temporal-limbic connections.

Psychosocial Aspects

Borderline States

The rather elusive personality disorder termed *borderline* has been a target of clinical curiosity and concern, and not truly a research-derived construct. Further, its original relation to schizophrenia, psychosis, or disintegration was metaphorical. Nonetheless, because of the current popularity of the diagnosis I include a brief review of the subject here, and because it may ultimately prove to have a relation to familial and genetic components of the schizophrenias. The construct originated in the course of psychotherapy and psychoanalysis, where certain patients were found to present unpredicted difficulties, and the explanatory resort was to Eugen Bleuler's (1911) nosological category of "latent schizophrenia." Stern (1938) was the first to publish a paper on the therapy of the "border line group of neuroses"; Zilboorg (1941) spoke of "ambulatory schizophrenia"; Deutsch (1942) of the "as if personality"; Federn (1947) of "latent schizophrenia"; Hoch and Polatin (1949) of "pseudo-neurotic schizophrenia"; Eisenstein (1951) and Knight (1953) of "borderline states"; and Kernberg (1967) of "borderline personality organization." All authors were psychoanalytically oriented, grappling with puzzling common features in a class of patients who on initial examination appeared relatively normal or maturely socially competent, but who, usually soon after systematic psychotherapy commenced, showed unusually sudden and turbulent transference phenomena, lapses in accepting the realities and limits of the treatment contract, difficulties in impulse control, queer and regressive thinking, and bursts of unexplained and unacknowledged emotion, most often hostile and depressive. When offered projective psychological tests, their responses were often bizarre. Stern's concept of "border line," quickly shared by others, suggested that these individuals hovered somewhere between normality and psychosis. Problematically, and this became a defining feature of the construct, they never did develop a clear-cut, persisting psychosis, nor even a classical psychoneurosis, yet their problems appeared pervasive, unpredictable, and frequently alarming.

Grinker, Weble, and Drye (1968) were the first and so far only researchers to examine a sizable cohort of such patients empirically and in detail; their book is a model of methodology for research into personality organization. The patients proved to be a rather heterogeneous group, clustering into four general types: the "psychotic border"; the "core borderline syndrome"; the adapted, affectless, defended "as-if" personality; and the "border with the neuroses." Further clinical and conceptual reviews are those of Gunderson and Singer (1975); Perry and Klerman (1978); Links (1982); and Reiser and Levenson (1984). Perry and Klerman issued a ringing challenge to clinicians to halt the torrent of descriptive, even anecdotal publications, and to undertake serious hypothesis testing. Reiser and Levenson warned of the serious possibilities for abuse of the diagnosis, particularly by inexperienced clinicians, or as a countertransference distortion. Links and others have wrestled with the diagnostic validity and reliability of the diagnosis. DSM-III (1980) and DSM-III-R (1987) have attempted operational specification, clearly following Gunderson and Singer and the early work of Grinker. In so doing, diagnostic specificity has bleached out the qualities of inconsistency, unpredictability, and polymorphous and elusive presentation which have so long intrigued and challenged clinicians.

The construct, in my own experience, is of value as a kind of supplementary warning label to be attached to other more formal personality diagnoses (Powles, 1989). Such a warning label acts as a guide in planning the strategy and tactics of psychotherapy. It often comes as a mirror of hindsight in understanding unpredicted, bizarre, and difficult happenings in the therapist–patient relationship, which might have been mitigated or avoided by an earlier diagnosis. Borderline states do not appear to be muted versions of schizophrenia, as Bleuler originally suggested. They may prove to have genetic roots and to be, after all, a part of the "schizophrenic spectrum" (Bellak, 1979).

Attentional Deficits

Since Bleuler's original descriptions, problems in attention have been considered central to the schizophrenias: distractibility, inability to focus steadily on a problem, difficulties in selecting what is to be attended to from what is, for healthy people, background "noise." The depressed patient (see chapter 14) apparently suffers such problems to a degree. However, the psychotic or schizophrenic apparently suffers a more precisely identifiable problem: the inability to screen the oncoming stream of experience, so that the large proportion of ordinarily irrelevant stimuli cannot be shut out in the focus upon the relevant; in addition, the ability to shift attention and frames of reference is impaired. Reality testing is, in fact, disturbed in a number of objectively assessable dimensions, some of which relate to Piagetian developmental principles.

I follow McGhie (1969) whose relatively early work remains a good keystone of understanding on the subject. The schizophrenic patient, because of certain cognitive deficits, becomes a passive target of experience, often drowning in the flood of stimuli taken in by intact sense organs but unmanageable to his perceptual apparatus. When the environment does not bombard him mercilessly, his own hallucinations do. Thus, the phenomenon of social withdrawal has one explanation as an attempt to protect the self from this flooding of stimulation. McGhie gives poignant self-reports of patients undergoing such experiences.

This difficulty in organizing perception correlates not only with hallucinosis and misperception generally. It correlates with inability to estimate size, distance, and perspective visually: the world assumes for the patient terrifying shapes, insecure slopes, and cavernous yawnings. Optical illusions and embedded forms presented to such patients are mishandled.

This group of phenomena, based on Broadbent's "filter" and "information flow" model (McGhie, 1969), became subsumed under the rubric of "sensory overload" as central to schizophrenia. Whether the overload phenomenon is a cause, a result, or an epiphenomenon of psychosis, McGhie did not clarify. Hemsley (1987) more recently judged that the failure to screen reality is central and explanatory of many clinical findings. A failure of semantic memory is implied in McGhie's findings: when stored judgments cannot be brought to bear, relevance and irrelevance themselves become irrelevant. Hemsley gives several implications for failure of screening; for example, withdrawal in the face of "high expressed emotion" relatives (see pp. 560–562 below); and hallucinations and delusions as unscreened intrusions from long-term memory stores (Hemsley, 1987). Cohen and Borst (1987) also view the information-processing deficit as central. They relate this problem to over-activity of the left hemisphere, secondary to dopamine neurotransmitter disruption which causes the right hemisphere and the left amygdala (a most important information coordinator) to malfunction.

Psychodynamically oriented clinicians (Arieti, 1974) had for many years hypothesized that at least some of the above cognitive problems were defensive or purposive, serving to deal with unbearable conflict and hurtful interpersonal impingements. Such a position seems to have receded, as the more properly neuropsychological aspects of schizophrenia, and their accessibility to drug treatment, have gained prominence. The psychoanalytic theory of psychosis has also included attention to the way in which people and ideas are cathected; that is, experiences are welded together. Such cathexis or welding was believed to break down in the psychoses, a theory not far from present neuropsychological understanding.

Many of the neuropsychological phenomena (as well as motivational and other aspects) of schizophrenia fit a model of severe regression very well. Again, psychoanalysts have long seen psychosis as a severe regression to forms of experience and of need systems appropriate to very early childhood.

Disorders of Thought and Perception

This is a major field of investigation, for which I propose to include a sampling of studies on schizophrenic thought disorder, on problems of conceptual organization, and on the mechanisms of auditory hallucinations. By Bleuler's criteria, disorders of thought association were the central feature of the schizophrenias. This has proven an elusive construct for researchers: the validity and the definition of the "schizophrenic thought disorder" continues to be debated. The usual method of examining for formal thought disorder is linguistic analysis (Reed, 1970; Rabin, Doneson, and Jentons, 1979). It is difficult to separate a disorder in *formal* thought process from allied cognitive problems such as regression in the faculties of attention, conceptualization, and classification. But perhaps the key difficulty today is that we are simply running out of subjects to test: the classical dilapidated schizophrenic hardly exists today, and new cases come rapidly under modern treatment (Bellak, 1979; Zubin, 1987). In any case, Reed (1970) found serious disagreement among investigators as to what actually constitutes the formal thought disorder. He believed it to stem from an amalgam of concreteness and overinclusion. Concreteness centers on an inability to guide thinking by higher principles and to shift frames of reference appropriately; overinclusion, an inability to maintain boundaries or hierarchies, thus allowing unrelated thoughts to interpenetrate inappropriately. Berman et al. (1987) used an instrument designed to measure the shifting of attention in their study of brain dysfunction in chronic schizophrenias (see pp. 548–550): this was the Wisconsin Card Sorting Test. Their understanding was that measures by this test are independent of other global cognitive capacities, and that attention shifting is processed in the prefrontal area. The Goldstein-Scheerer Object Sorting Test (Andreasen and Powers, 1976; Harrow, Grossman, Silverstein, Meltzer, and Kettering, 1986) is used to measure ability to classify and for bizarre, idiosyncratic thinking.

Harrow et al. (1986) included 30 schizophrenics as part of a control group in testing for thought disorder in mania (see chapter 11, p. 393). The subjects were examined during an acute admission, and again a year after discharge, for bizarre, idiosyncratic thinking (i.e., thought *content* as well as thought *form*). The manics were somewhat more severely thought-disordered than the schizophrenics during the acute admission; and though both groups showed considerable reduction in thought disorder at follow-up, there was a larger reduction of the disorder in the manic group. Both groups, compared with normal controls, showed severe thought disorder during the acute admission.

Thought disorder has been sometimes confused with problems in conceptual thinking. Kay and Singh (1975) and Kay, Singh, and Smith (1975) devised three perceptual–conceptual tests based on Piagetian developmental categories, and with them tested a mixed schizophrenic cohort, with nonpsychotic adults as controls. These tests clearly separated normals from psychotics. Further, they discriminated subgroups of schizophrenics: an acute–subacute–paranoid subgroup, while inferior to normals, scored generally in the concrete-operations range, and their performance improved with drug treatment; a chronic group scored in the preoperational range generally, with some primitive responses being of sensorimotor quality, and these patients did not improve with treatment. These authors deduced that a *psychophysiological* group of variables, responsive to treatment, could be contrasted with a *developmental* group, unresponsive to treatment. They did not use the term *regression*. It would be of great interest to have had normal children of various ages included as controls.

Andreasen and Powers (1976) used the Goldstein-Scheerer on schizophrenics, young children, and normal adults. Though these authors did not use Piagetian concepts as such, they found the performances of schizophrenics and young children to be quite similar, both groups distinctly differentiated from normal adults.

We now leave this somewhat unsatisfactory subject, to look at one psychotic symptom which is capable of rather more precise specification. It is surprising that such reasonably specifiable dysfunctions of perception, including estimation of size and perspective, have not been more diligently pursued.

An ingenious study was reported by Bick and Kinsbourne (1987) on auditory hallucinosis. These authors hypothesized that auditory hallucinations are formed by "subvocal speech," used regularly in normal thinking, but in the case of psychosis projected outwardly as audible speech. Eighteen hallucinating patients were asked to carry out various maneuvers including holding the mouth open wide. Only during this maneuver, when the speech organs were immobilized, did 14 of them report that their hallucinations disappeared. The investigators were somewhat disappointed that the patients had no interest in exploiting this knowledge to control their hallucinations, which in most instances were unpleasant and distressing. An interesting feature of the study was in using volunteer college students as controls: under hypnosis, they were induced to hallucinate voices, which again were arrested by the mouth-opening maneuver. The conclusion reached was that what would otherwise be a normal component of thinking (subvocal speech) was projected due to loss of normal inhibitory control. This study can be seen to be in harmony with Hemsley's ideas noted above, in which failure of normal filtering conduces to many psychotic phenomena including hallucinations.

Life Experiences and Causation

There was for some time a great interest in the influence of the family, and more specifically the key role of the mother, in forming personal vulnerabilities and contributing to the actual onset of clinical psychosis (Arieti, 1974; Mosher and Gunderson, 1979). The evidence for these influences came mostly from single-case and descriptive studies, with their known deficiencies. The interesting hypotheses which these studies generated have not been put to controlled and prospective testing, and appear presently to have faded in popularity, partly because they appear pejorative of women. Most clinicians I know have met parents whose interaction with the identified patient appears pathological and possibly pathogenic. I have personally identified some fathers whose behavior toward the patient appears highly personally disruptive; these have usually been teamed with kindly, inoffensive, rather helpless mothers. The field is in need of a revival of study. Prospective investigations alone will clarify whether there is a cause–effect relationship here.

A familial construct of *expressed emotion* (EE) has recently become rather clearly established. Koenigsberg and Handley (1986) offer a capable review of this whole subject. They credit the term to G. W. Brown (collaborator with Harris in depression studies) who, working with Wing in studying postdischarge adjustment of schizophrenic patients, found that patients returning to their families fared more poorly than those placed with relatives or boarding homes. The criterion variable was of relapse within a year of discharge. An initial prospective study suggested strongly that high levels of emotionality within a family, particularly of a hostile quality, favored deterioration in the patient's condition. A series of further studies replicated and confirmed this finding, while standardized ratings of family emotionality were developed. Koenigsberg and Handley review eight further studies. They define "expressed emotion" (EE) as the manner in which relatives, at interview, voice critical, hostile, overinvolved, and intrusive feelings toward the patient. Brown (Koenigsberg and Handley, 1986) discovered that any emotion directed toward the patient, including hostility, and also hostile interactions between relatives and between relatives and patient, are the relevant variables. Several of the reviewed studies tested causal relationships by intervening therapeutically, aiming to decrease hostile interactions. Such interventions included family therapy and the teaching of interpersonal skills to the patient. Decreasing high EE was found to influence the patient's course favorably, thus confirming the causal link. A thought-provoking paper by Strauss (1987) deals with a possibly neglected element in the equation between life experiences and schizophrenia: the patient, and the patient's own homeostatic resources and strengths. Leff (1987) found that patients in high EE families were three times as likely to relapse as those in low EE families. His formula for rate of relapse includes the factors of high EE and unfavorable life events interacting with prophylactic medication.

The life events literature for the schizophrenias indicates a relatively weak relationship between defined life events and onset of clinical episodes. In this area, the search for nongenetic variables has been as disappointing as the search for genetic ones. Let me remind the reader of the formulation of Brown and Harris (1978) and Katschnig (1986) for unipolar depression. Women suffering unipolar depressions were found significantly to have experienced an adverse life event, or a cluster of difficulties. However, *most* persons experiencing similar problems did not succumb to depression, thanks to mitigating variables. The strong causal association between adverse events and onset of depression was expressed as a "time brought forward" of up to 2 years. By contrast, the episodes of schizophrenia Brown and Harris studied showed a "time brought forward" of only about 2 weeks; that is, a weak, "triggering" effect for an illness which likely would have developed soon in any case.

Shepherd's (1987) model includes a contribution from life stresses. He cites collateral evidence from transcultural studies: in "developing" countries there is a better prognosis, with 25 percent of cases recovering completely without subsequent episodes. Causes for this difference remain conjectural but may include differences in personality structure and family support systems. Zubin (1987) calculates that life experiences influence time of onset, maintenance of the psychotic episode, and processes of both recovery and relapse. Häfner (1987) concludes that life experiences may have a formative influence on "negative" or deficit symptoms. Dohrenwend, Shrout, Link, and Skodol (1987) agree with many other authors on the rather weak association between life events and schizophrenic breakdown, as does Katschnig (1986, 1987).

Reflections on Treatment in Schizophrenia

Models for the Schizophrenias and Their Treatment

The schizophrenias are the cancers of the psychiatric world. Each acute case is (like its relatives in the disintegration style, the severer affective and schizoaffective disorders, delirium, and lethal catatonia) a clinical emergency: the threat to life calls for urgent, concerted, unremitting modern treatment. In the chronic form, soul-destroying, socially costly and disrupting, each case calls for steadfast and unflinching care. Our task is to do battle with these malignant disorders up to the point where we can simply do no more with the weapons we have today, and then not give up. For this task, research can give us only statistical help. In the individual case, clinical judgment, skill, faith, and hope have to be brought to bear. We must sacrifice our scientific curiosity in the acute case, using all treatment modalities, without holding back because this *might* be a self-limited episode. If we are defeated, and the case merges into chronicity, we keep fighting. Surprises, both inspiring and depressing, greet our efforts (see pp. 530–535): cases recover which we had deemed hopeless, and cases which we had deemed hopeful go downhill.

This metaphor of the malignant neoplasm stresses as its first treatment priority the survival of the affected individual. Realistically, the subsequent course and ultimate outcome will vary with the type of "neoplasm," the resources of the patient, and relatively unpredicted environmental events, both favorable and antitherapeutic. In this model, the clinician is bound during the acute psychotic phase to assume a worst scenario position, and to treat accordingly; we will never know, scientifically speaking, what proportion of patients did not actually require total and radical therapy. And yet, how radical and total the therapy has to be balanced (as in cancer treatment) against both the potential seriousness of the disease *and* the quality of life remaining to the patient if survival is assured by initial treatment.

In the longer-term management of the schizophrenias, a second metaphor becomes relevant. This metaphor applies to all psychiatric disorders ranked by our homeostatic–dynamic model: it is cardiac decompensation. The first duty of the clinician is to shift a complex system (such as the cardiovascular) into a more favorable style of homeostasis, then to take stock. It may be possible to correct faults in the system (e.g., by cardiac surgery) so that return to normality is possible. On the other hand, it may be necessary to leave a defective heart in its defective state; or, relatively irreversible changes in the system may have resulted during the decompensation process. In this case, we move into rehabilitation rather than causally directed treatment. The issue becomes one of tailoring a life-style which is maximally productive, geared to continuing disability, but taking advantage of all the strengths which the patient retains; and, of course, motivating the patient to continue any specific treatment modalities which are likely to help.

Philosophy and Methods of Treatment

Considering the gravity of the subject and the large size of the literature, I shall summarize only a brief sample of research-derived articles on treatment. It is divided essentially into two groupings: acute and chronic management. Clearly, as the above suggests, philosophical value judgments as well as clear conceptual models enter into the treatment of these most malignant of psychiatric disorders.

The anchors of modern treatment for disintegration are the antipsychotic drugs. Their arrival on the psychiatric scene in the early 1950s was dramatic, not to say revolutionary, and they probably are the crucial ingredient in restoring mental integration (Lehmann, 1961). We shall probably never know whether they were the most important variable in the mental hospital reforms of the 1950s and 1960s, for they were but one major factor in a dialectical movement involving new methods, new hopes, and a humanizing of the mental hospital milieu by the new learning stemming from psychiatric advances during World War II. My own experience tends to cast doubt on the sole credit often accorded antipsychotic drugs in this movement. I am a group psychotherapist who enthusiastically took part in new methods of milieu therapy and the literature and word-of-mouth communication on this subject. I am aware of at least two major hospitals where the abolition of locks and bars, the expectation that patients were humans and that they should be treated and could act as such, a burgeoning of interest in group management, help to families, and active rehabilitation, the opening of hospital doors, and the reduction in hospital overcrowding, had all commenced just before the antipsychotic drugs came into regular use.

Nonetheless, it would be foolish to deny the enormous impact of these new drugs and their catalytic effects on mental hospitals, their staffs, and their patients. It would be unethical today to deny these drugs to any psychotic patient even if this deprives us, scientifically speaking, of important information on the natural history of the disorders. It is less clearly evident that we have lost many of our psychosocial management methods and skills, so vital for the chronic population, and that there is an ever-present danger that we resort to a mechanistic reliance on drugs alone as centrally effective.

Arieti (1974) and Lipton and Burnett (1979) review the history of modern antipsychotic drugs; Klein (1981) extends the discussion of other modern psychotropics. Most texts include some historical comments (Bellack, 1984; Menuck and Seeman, 1985; Bebbington and McGuffin, 1988). The phenothiazines had been in use in the dyeing industry and as antiparasitic remedies in animal and human medicine. On being discovered to have antihistaminic and sedative properties, several of the compounds were tested as potentiators for general anesthesia and to stop the shivering which was an obstacle in surgical hypothermia. Thence it was a short step to trials with psychiatric patients showing psychomotor excitement. Chlorpromazine was assessed first in France, then in Canada (Lehmann and Hanrahan, 1954); within a few years it was clear that the drug has a potent, specific, antipsychotic action.

Confusion in terminology and models of action ensued. Because chlorpromazine and reserpine were sedative, and because psychodynamic theory held that psychosis resulted from intolerable conflict, the drugs were termed "major tranquillizers" (Klein, 1981) even though the known sedatives or "minor tranquillizers" could be pushed to the point of coma without remitting psychosis. The European term "neuroleptic" arose to describe the important subcortical actions of these drugs. At the present time "antipsychotic" and "neuroleptic" have become virtually synonymous terms.

The search for more effective drugs with fewer side effects engendered a family of "typical" neuroleptics (Stahl and Wets, 1988), all dopamine blockers, and all tending to extrapyramidal side effects and even irreversible disfiguring and disabling tardive dyskinesias: examples include the phenothiazines of differing side chains such as thioridazine and trifluoperazine; the thioxanthene flupenthixol; and the butyrophenone haloperidol. The search continues for "new" or "atypical" neuroleptics which will be effective, safe, and without extrapyramidal effects. Meanwhile, in the early search for chemical analogs, there emerged serendipitously the first generation of tricyclic antidepressant drugs (Klein, 1981). Imipramine sedated depressed patients, and more slowly relieved depression; the sedation failed to remit anxiety disorders. I refer the reader back to chapter 13 for further discussion of the antidepressants.

In an early collaborative study of antipsychotic drugs (National Institute of Mental Health, 1964) it was found that 75 percent of acute cases of schizophenia were significantly helped by hospitalization and phenothiazine drugs; and that 25 percent were helped by hospitalization and placebo. For the acute case, the tripod of acute treatment consisting of hospitalization, general supportive management, and modern antipsychotic drugs (Carlsson, 1987; Shepherd, 1987) give excellent results.

While treatment of the acute psychotic phase, with its positive or type I symptoms, is today quite successful, the same cannot be said of the postpsychotic deficit states with their negative or type II symptoms. The great challenge lies therefore now in the chronic progressive phase of the schizophrenias. Angermeyer (1987) and May (1986), the latter referring to "Bleuler's disease," summarize the treatment issues for this phase. The essence of the approach must be attention to multiple, relatively nonspecific variables, not a focus on any one specific pathogenic agent; that is, a true, comprehensive, biopsychosocial approach. The total equation (Katschnig, 1987) involves reducing *both* the patient's vulnerabilities *and* the nature of external stresses.

Angermeyer's findings included, perhaps surprisingly, one that "labeling" schizophrenia openly was very helpful to some patients, and did no harm in any instance. Relapse prevention by drugs, he finds, does not increase negative symptoms. Patients for whom family intervention is given require less drugs. But families grow old, and die; therefore training the patient in social skills may even be life-saving.

May analyzed outcomes of single and combined treatments for both the acute hospital phase of schizophrenia ("Bleuler's disease") and at 3- to 5-year follow-up. Patients receiving drugs, with or without psychotherapy, left hospital soonest, and those receiving convulsive therapy, the least expensive modality, next soonest. Patients receiving milieu care and psychotherapy remained longest in hospital, and this was the most expensive treatment combination. Those receiving drugs and psychotherapy attained the best insight at relatively small extra cost. Some patients did well on all of the modalities given singly.

At follow-up, some patients had done well and some very poorly, whether on any single treatment or on combinations. Drugs or convulsive therapy given alone provided the best outcomes, and psychotherapy alone the poorest. All modalities tended to "wear out" in their effects, and overall the outcomes were "far from reassuring." May (1986) believed that the best predictor for a given treatment regimen is the early response to it. As to psychotherapy, he had the impression that a focus on the body and self-image may be most useful. The combination of drugs and psychotherapy, in agreement with other studies, proved to be the most reliable overall.

We are left with the thorny problem of helping patients who appear to have lost cerebral tissue, and in whom negative symptoms predominate (Berman et al., 1987). These probably represent quintessentially the classical Bleulerian and Kraepelinian deterioration, though fortunately they are represented less in our hospitals today (Bellak, 1979; Zubin, 1987). Here there is still hope in the rehabilitative concept. Though these unfortunate persons are diminished, they can be sheltered against too great stimulation and stress, for their filtering may be permanently damaged (Katschnig, 1987). They can ideally be offered sheltered employment, and, if their families remain available, family intervention. Katschnig's interactional formula for vulnerability involves the person, the social network, and accidental stressful events. When all else fails, humane protective custody of these wholly disabled citizens must be the resort. At the present time psychosurgery is in deep disfavor: surely there must be cautious revival of investigations of this modality, for we do not hesitate to undertake radical surgery for cancer patients if that will help their chances for a better life. I think too that some further focused attention to psychobiological processes in conservation–withdrawal may shine additional helpful and hopeful light on this currently discouraging picture.

Bibliographic Notes: Key Readings

The problems of selection are nowhere better typified than in this attempt to recommend a sample of key contributions to the literature on psychosis or disintegration. However, I commence with some confidence at least. One thing we do need to cover is the resort to original sources: I submit that no one is entitled to argue, for example, about Kraepelin, Freud, or Bleuler, who has not read these pioneers in the original or a good translation.

I commence therefore urging a reading of Eugen Bleuler (1911), who, among a number of voices, emerged as a dominant formulator of constructs on dementia praecox or "the group of schizophrenias." Kraepelin (1913a,b), evidently having assimilated Bleuler's ideas, gave his mature presentation; it is clear that he was a master describer and a flexible thinker. Schneider's (1959) little book and its short section on the functional psychoses likewise impress by their original and creative tone. Manfred Bleuler (1978) joins both sides of the Atlantic as he carries on clarification of the construct of schizophrenia from his vast store of clinical observations.

Then we move to the modern era, though I have cited several authors in this chapter who represent research and thinking of the intermediate years; that is, the years coming after generalized introduction of psychotropic drugs. In defining psychosis (particularly schizophrenia) today, debate continues. Pope and Lipinski (1978) demonstrate the either–or approach to differential diagnosis which remains so common in the literature (Kraepelin, the Bleulers, and Schneider never fell into this trap, it should be noted). Munro (1987) wrestles with the "gradualist" view in examining the spectrum of syndromes extending from the affective disorders to frank schizophrenia.

Regarding some other syndromes at the disintegration level of human homeostasis, I recommend review articles by Wise (1987) on delirium and by Mann, Caroff, Bleier, Welz, Kling, and Hayashida (1986) on lethal catatonia. From the latter it is a logical step to examine recent updating of the phenomena of near-death or dying by Morse, Castillo, Venecia, Milstein, and Tyler (1986). The important but currently neglected subject of the natural history of schizophrenic episodes is represented by Donlon and Blacker (1973) with stages in the development of the illness (prodromes) and its recovery (metadromes); and by McGlashan and Carpenter (1976) on postpsychotic depression.

A most important book, I believe, is the compendium on schizophrenia edited by Häfner, Gattaz, and Janzarik (1987) celebrating the 600th anniversary of Heidelberg University, from whence many seminal ideas on schizophrenia were propagated. I cite a number of authors and papers from this volume, as recent thinking by outstanding investigators. Häfner (1987) attempts a summary, in a closing chapter, of the present state of research into the causes of schizophrenia. Three relatively compact, recent, research-oriented compendia can be recommended: Bellack (1984), Menuck and Seeman (1985), and Bebbington and McGuffin (1988).

As to research into biological aspects of the psychoses, I again note with approval the three fine presentations on neurotransmitter systems of Crow and Deakin (1985); Martin, Owen, and Morihisa (1987); and Janowsky, Golden, Rapaport, Cain, and Gillin (1988). I recommend too the review of animal models for schizophrenia research by McKinney and Moran (1981); I have the impression that animal modeling has not significantly improved since their publication. Berman, Weinberger, Shelton, and Zec (1987) and Heinrichs and Buchanan (1988) bring together quite recent findings on the relationship between brain changes and the chronic phase of schizophrenia. Baron (1986a,b) presents a technical survey of statistical models used in assessing the contribution of genetic factors and the establishment of genetic markers. Kringlen (1987) presents as interesting a review of the methods and meanings of twin studies as I have come across. Carlsson (1987), a principal originator of the dopaminergic disturbance theory for schizophrenia, updates the current status of this still dominant construct.

As for psychosocial issues, Gunderson and Singer (1975) remain probably the single most influential reviewers of the concept of borderline personality disorder, a subject requiring hard-nosed research. Katschnig (1986) edits an important volume of studies on the relationship between life events and psychiatric breakdown, including papers on schizophrenia. McGhie (1969) was a pioneer on the attentional deficits apparently central to the psychology of psychosis and on the sensory overload hypothesis for schizophrenia. Hemsley (1987) updates this subject in a contemporary model combining attention, perception, and thought disorders and their role in producing schizophrenic symptoms. Koenigsberg and Handley (1986) review the relatively recent construct of expressed emotion (EE) and its role in the natural history of schizophrenia.

I devote relatively brief attention to treatment in schizophrenia, the cancer among psychiatric disorders. A relatively old paper from the National Institute of Mental Health (1964) analyzes the relative effect of various treatment components, including a significant placebo effect. May (1986) more recently reviews the interactions between treatment modalities. Carlsson (1987) may be referred to again here. The truly thorny problem today is the treatment of chronic schizophrenia, or the type II, postpsychotic, impaired state. Angermeyer (1987) presents a very interesting discussion of a combined treatment approach to chronic schizophrenia; May (1986) may also be consulted. Strauss (1987) draws attention to a somewhat neglected element in the treatment equation: the patient's own person, with its vulnerabilities and strengths.

References

Altshuler, L. J., Cummings, J. L., & Mills, M. J. (1986), Mutism: Review, differential diagnosis, and report of 22 cases. *Amer. J. Psychiat.*, 143: 1409–1414.

American Psychiatric Association. (1980), *The Diagnostic and Statistical Manual of Mental Disorders*, 3rd ed. (DSM-III). Washington, DC: American Psychiatric Press.

——— (1987), *The Diagnostic and Statistical Manual of Mental Disorders*, 3rd ed. rev. Washington, DC: American Psychiatric Press.

Andreasen, N. C., & Powers, P. S. (1976), Psychosis, thought disorder, and regression. *Amer. J. Psychiat.*, 133:522–526.

*Angermeyer, M. C. (1987), Theoretical implications of psychosocial intervention studies on schizophrenia. In: *Search for the Causes of Schizophrenia*, ed. H. Häfner, W. F. Gattaz, & W. Janzarik. Berlin: Springer Verlag.

Arieti, S. (1974), *Interpretation of Schizophrenia*, 2nd ed. New York: Basic Books.

Ballenger, C. M., Reus, V. I., & Post, R. (1982), The "atypical" clinical picture of adolescent mania. *Amer. J. Psychiat.*, 5:602–606.

*Baron, M. (1986a), Genetics of schizophrenia: I. Familial patterns and mode of inheritance. *Biol. Psychiat.*, 21:1051–1066.

*———— (1986b), Genetics of schizophrenia: II. Vulnerability traits and gene markers. *Biol. Psychiat.*, 21:1189–1211.

———— (1987), Genetic models and the transmission of schizophrenia. In: *Search for the Causes of Schizophrenia*, ed. H. Häfner, W. F. Gattaz, & W. Janzarik. Berlin: Springer Verlag.

*Bebbington, P. & McGuffin, P., eds. (1988), *Schizophrenia: The Major Issues*. Oxford: Heinemann.

*Bellack, A. S., ed. (1984), *Schizophrenia: Treatment, Management, Rehabilitation*. New York: Grune & Stratton.

Bellak, L. (1979), Introduction: An idiosyncratic overview. In: *Disorders of the Schizophrenic Syndrome*, ed. L. Bellak. New York: Basic Books.

*Berman, K. F., Weinberger, D. R., Shelton, R. C., & Zec, R. F. (1987), A relationship between anatomical and physiological brain pathology in schizophrenia: Lateral cerebral ventricular size predicts cortical blood flow. *Amer. J. Psychiat.*, 144:1277–1282.

Bick, P. A., & Kinsbourne, M. (1987), Auditory hallucinations and subvocal speech in schizophrenic patients. *Amer. J. Psychiat.*, 144:222–225.

*Bleuler, E. (1911), *Dementia Praecox or the Group of Schizophrenias*, trans. J. Zinkin. New York: Basic Books, 1950.

Bleuler, M. (1972), *The Schizophrenic Disorders: Long-Term Patient and Family Studies*, trans. S. M. Clemens. New Haven, CT: Yale University Press, 1978.

*———— (1978), On schizophrenic psychoses. *Amer. J. Psychiat.*, 136: 1403–1409.

Brown, G. W., & Harris, T. (1978), *Social Origins of Depression: A Study of Psychiatric Disorder in Women*. New York: Free Press.

Carlsson, A. (1975), Pharmacological approach to schizophrenia. In: *Schizophrenia: Biological and Psychological Perspectives*, ed. G. Usdin. New York: Basic Books.

*———— (1987), The dopamine hypothesis of schizophrenia 20 years later. In: *Search for the Causes of Schizophrenia*, ed. H. Häfner, W. F. Gattaz, & W. Janzarik. Berlin: Springer Verlag.

Carpenter, W. T., Jr. (1987), Psychological and psychophysiological models of schizophrenia: Discussion. In: *Search for the Causes of Schizophrenia*, ed. H. Häfner, W. F. Gattaz, & W. Janzarik. Berlin: Springer Verlag.

Cohen, R., & Borst, U. (1987), Psychological models of schizophrenia impairments. In: *Search for the Causes of Schizophrenia*, ed. H. Häfner, W. F. Gattaz, & W. Janzarik. Berlin: Springer Verlag.

Crow, T. J. (1987), The retrovirus/transposon hypothesis of schizophrenia. In: *Search for the Causes of Schizophrenia*, ed. H. Häfner, W. F. Gattaz, & W. Janzarik. Berlin: Springer Verlag.

*———— Deakin, J. F. W. (1985), Neurohumoral transmission, behaviour, and mental disorders. In: *The Scientific Foundations of Psychiatry*, ed. M. Shepherd. Cambridge, UK: Cambridge University Press.

———— Taylor, G. R., & Tyrrell, D. A. J. (1986), Two syndromes in schizophrenia and the viral hypothesis. *Prog. Brain Res.*, 65:17–27.

De Alarcon, R., & Carney, M. W. P. (1969), Severe depressive mood changes following slow-release intramuscular fluphenazine injection. *Brit. Med. J.*, 3:564–567.

Deutsch, H. (1942), Some forms of emotional disturbance and their relationship to schizophrenia. *Psychoanal. Quart.*, 11:301–321.

Docherty, J. P., van Kammen, D. P., Siris, S. G., & Marder, S. R. (1978), Stages of onset of schizophrenic psychosis. *Amer. J. Psychiat.*, 135:420–426.

Dohrenwend, B. P., Shrout, B. P., Link, B. G., & Skodol, A. E. (1987), Social and psychologic risk factors for episodes of schizophrenia. In: *Search for Causes of Schizophrenia*, ed. H. Häfner, W. F. Gattaz, & W. Janzarik. Berlin: Springer Verlag.

*Donlon, P. J., & Blacker, K. H. (1973), Stages of schizophrenic decompensation and reintegration. *J. Nerv. Ment. Dis.*, 157:200–209.

Eisenstein, V. (1951), Differential psychotherapy of borderline states. *Psychiat. Quart.*, 25:379–401.

Federn, P. (1947), Principles of psychotherapy in latent schizophrenia. *Amer. J. Psychother.*, 1:129–144.

Foulds, G. A., & Bedford, A. (1975), Hierarchy of classes of personal illness. *Psychol. Med.*, 5:181–192.

Garber, H. J., Weilburg, J. B., Buananno, F. S., Manschreck, T. C., & New, P. F. J. (1988), Use of magnetic resonance imaging in psychiatry. *Amer. J. Psychiat.*, 145:164–171.

Grinker, R. R., Sr., Weble, B., & Drye, R. C. (1968), *The Borderline Syndrome*. New York: Basic Books.

*Gunderson, J. G., & Singer, M. T. (1975), Defining borderline patients: An overview. *Amer. J. Psychiat.*, 132:1–10.

*Häfner, H. (1987), Search for the causes of schizophrenia: Summary and outlook. In: *Search for Causes of Schizophrenia*, ed. H. Häfner, W. F. Gattaz, & W. Janzarik. Berlin: Springer Verlag.

*——— Gattaz, W. F., & Janzarik, W. eds. (1987), *Search for the Causes of Schizophrenia*. Berlin: Springer Verlag.

Harrow, M., Grossman, L. S., Silverstein, M. L., Meltzer, H. Y., & Kettering, R. L. (1986), A longitudinal study of thought disorder in manic patients. *Arch. Gen. Psychiat.*, 43:781–785.

*Heinrichs, D. W., & Buchanan, R. W. (1988), Significance and meaning of neurological signs in schizophrenia. *Amer. J. Psychiat.*, 145:11–18.

*Hemsley, D. R. (1987), An experimental psychological model for schizophrenia. In: *Search for Causes of Schizophrenia*, ed. H. Häfner, W. F. Gattaz, & W. Janzarik. Berlin: Springer Verlag.

Hirsch, S. (1987), Biological hypotheses of schizophrenia: Discussion. In: *Search for Causes of Schizophrenia*, ed. H. Häfner, W. F. Gattaz, & W. Janzarik. Berlin: Springer Verlag.

Hoch, P., & Polatin, P. (1949), Pseudoneurotic forms of schizophrenia. *Psychiat. Quart.*, 23:248–276.

Hoedemaker, F. S. (1970), Psychotic episodes and postpsychotic depression in young adults. *Amer. J. Psychiat.*, 127:606–610.

Hornykiewycz, O. (1986), Brain noradrenaline and schizophrenia. *Prog. Brain Res.*, 65:29–39.

Hunter, R. C. A. (1967), On the experience of nearly dying. *Amer. J. Psychiat.*, 124:84–88.

*Janowsky, D. S., Golden, R. N., Rapaport, M., Cain, J. J., & Gillin, J. C. (1988), Neurochemistry of depression and mania. In: *Depression and Mania*, ed. A. Georgotas & R. Cancro. New York: Elsevier.

Jaspers, K. (1913), *General Psychopathology*, 7th ed., trans. J. Hoenig & M. W. Hamilton. Chicago: University of Chicago Press, 1963.

Jeffries, J. J. (1977), The trauma of being psychotic: A neglected area in the management of chronic schizophrenia. *Can. Psychiat. Assn. J.*, 22: 199–206.

Kahlbaum, K. L. (1873), *Catatonia*, trans. Y. Levij & T. Pridan. Baltimore: Johns Hopkins University Press, 1973.

*Katschnig, H., ed. (1986), *Life Events and Psychiatric Disorders*. New York: Cambridge University Press.

———— (1987), Vulnerability and trigger models/rehabilitation: Discussion. In: *Search for the Causes of Schizophrenia*, ed. H. Häfner, W. F. Gattaz, & W. Janzarik. Berlin: Springer Verlag.

Kay, S. R., & Singh, M. M. (1975), A developmental approach to delineate components of cognitive dysfunction in schizophrenia. *Brit. J. Soc. Clin. Psychol.*, 14:387–399.

———— ———— Smith, J. M. (1975), Color form representation test: A developmental method for the study of cognition in schizophrenia. *Brit. J. Soc. Clin. Psychol.*, 14:401–411.

Kernberg, O. (1967), Borderline personality organization. *J. Amer. Psychoanal. Assn.*, 15:641–685.

Klein, D. F. (1981), Anxiety reconceptualized. In: *Anxiety: New Research and Changing Concepts*, ed. D. F. Klein & J. G. Rabkin. New York: Raven Press.

Knight, R. P. (1953), Borderline states. *Bull. Menn. Clin.*, 17:1–12.

*Koenigsberg, H. W., & Handley, R. (1986), Expressed emotion: From predictive index to clinical construct. *Amer. J. Psychiat.*, 143:1361–1373.

*Kraepelin, E. (1913a), *Dementia Praecox and Paraphrenia*, trans. R. M. Barclay. Edinburgh: E. & S. Livingstone, 1919.

———— (1913b), *Manic–Depressive Insanity and Paranoia*, trans. R. M. Barclay. Edinburgh: E. & S. Livingstone, 1921.

*Kringlen, E. (1987), Contributions of genetic studies on schizophrenia. In: *Search for Causes of Schizophrenia*, ed. H. Häfner, W. F. Gattaz, & W. Janzarik. Berlin: Springer Verlag.

Lancet Editorial (1978), The experience of dying. *Lancet*, 1:1347–1348.

Leff, J. (1987), A model of schizophrenic vulnerability to environmental factors. In: *Search for Causes of Schizophrenia*, ed. H. Häfner, W. F. Gattaz, & W. Janzarik. Berlin: Springer Verlag.

Lehmann, H. E. (1961), New drugs in psychiatric therapy. *Can. Med. Assn. J.*, 85:1145–1151.

———— Hanrahan, G. E. (1954), Chlorpromazine, new inhibiting agent for psychomotor excitement and manic states. *Arch. Neurol. Psychiat.*, 71: 227–237.

Liddle, P. F. (1987), Schizophrenic syndromes, cognitive performance, and neurological dysfunction. *Psychol. Med.*, 17:49–57.

Links, P. S. (1982), The existence of the borderline diagnosis: Studies on diagnostic validity. *Can. J. Psychiat.*, 27:585–592.

Lipton, M. A., & Burnett, G. B. (1979), Pharmacological treatment of schizo-
    phrenia. In: *Disorders of the Schizophrenic Syndrome*, ed. L. Bellak. New
    York: Basic Books.
Lishman, W. A. (1971), Amnesic syndromes and their neuropathology. In:
    Recent Developments in Psychogeriatrics, ed. D. W. Kay & A. Walk. Ashford,
    Kent, UK: Headley Brothers.
——— (1987), *Organic Psychiatry: The Psychological Consequences of Cerebral Dis-
    order*, 2nd ed. Oxford: Blackwell.
*Mann, S. C., Caroff, S. N., Bleier, H. R., Welz, W. K. R., Kling, M. A., &
    Hayashida, M. (1986), Lethal catatonia. *Amer. J. Psychiat.*,
    143:1374–1381.
*Martin, M. B., Owen, C. M., & Morihisa, J. M. (1987), An overview of
    neurotransmitters and neuroreceptors. In: *The American Psychiatric Press
    Textbook of Neuropsychiatry*, ed. R. E. Hales & S. C. Yudofsky. Washing-
    ton, DC: American Psychiatric Press.
*May, P. R. A. (1986), Some research relating to the treatment of Bleuler's
    disease (schizophrenia). *Psychiat. J. Univ. Ottawa*, 11:117–126.
*McGhie, A. (1969), *Pathology of Attention*. Harmondsworth, Middlesex, UK:
    Penguin Books.
*McGlashan, T. H., & Carpenter, W. T. (1976), An investigation of the post-
    psychotic depressive syndrome. *Amer. J. Psychiat.*, 133:14–19.
*McKinney, W. J., & Moran, E. C. (1981), Animal models for schizophrenia.
    Amer. J. Psychiat., 138:478–483.
Mendlewicz, J., & Sevy, S. (1986), Genetic and immunological factors in af-
    fective disorders and schizophrenia. *Prog. Brain. Res.*, 65:1–15.
*Menuck, M. N., & Seeman, M. V., eds. (1985), *New Perspectives in Schizophre-
    nia*. New York: Macmillan.
Meyer, A., Jelliffe, S. E., & Hoch, A. (1911), *Dementia Praecox: A Monograph*.
    Boston: Richard G. Badger/Gorham Press.
Miller, G. A., Galanter, E., & Pribram, K. H. (1960), *Plans and the Structure of
    Behavior*. New York: Henry Holt.
*Morse, M., Castillo, P., Venecia, D., Milstein, J., & Tyler, D. C. (1986),
    Childhood near-death experiences. *Amer. J. Dis. Child.*, 140:1110–1114.
Mosher, L. R., & Gunderson, J. G. (1979), Group, family, milieu, and commu-
    nity support systems treatment for schizophrenia. In: *Disorders of the
    Schizophrenic Spectrum*, ed. L. Bellak. New York: Basic Books.
*Munro, A. (1987), Neither lions nor tigers: Disorders which lie between
    schizophrenia and affective disorder. *Can. J. Psychiat.*, 32:296–297.
*National Institute of Mental Health Psychopharmacology Service Center,
    Collaborative Study Group (1964), Phenothiazine treatment in acute
    schizophrenia. *Arch. Gen. Psychiat.*, 10:246–261.
Noyes, R., Jr. (1972), The experience of dying. *Psychiat.*, 35:174–184.
Osis, K., & Haraldsson, E. (1977), *What They Saw at the Hour of Death*. New
    York: Avon Books.
Perry, J. C., & Klerman, G. L. (1978), The borderline patient: A comparative
    analysis of four sets of diagnostic criteria. *Arch. Gen. Psychiat.*,
    35:141–150.
*Pope, H. G., & Lipinski, J. F. (1978), Diagnosis in schizophrenia and manic-
    depressive illness. *Arch. Gen. Psychiat.*, 35:811–828.
Powles, W. E. (1989), Problems in diagnosis and group treatment design with
    borderline personalities: Can focal conflict theory help? In: *The Difficult*

Patient in Group: Group Psychotherapy with Borderline and Narcissistic Disorders, ed. B. E. Roth, W. N. Stone, & H. D. Kibel. Madison, CT: International Universities Press.

Rabin, A. I., Doneson, S. L., & Jentons, R. L. (1979), Studies of psychological functions in schizophrenia. In: *Disorders of the Schizophrenic Spectrum*, ed. L. Bellak. New York: Basic Books.

Rada, R. T., & Donlon, P. J. (1975), Depression and the acute schizophrenic process. *Psychosom.*, 16:116–119.

Reed, J. L. (1970), Schizophrenic thought disorder: A review and hypothesis. *Comprehen. Psychiat.*, 11:403–432.

Reiser, D. E., & Levenson, H. (1984), Abuses of the borderline diagnosis: A clinical problem with teaching opportunities. *Amer. J. Psychiat.*, 141:1528–1532.

Roth, S. (1970), The seemingly ubiquitous depression following acute schizophrenic episodes, a neglected area of clinical discussion. *Amer. J. Psychiat.*, 127:51–58.

Sartorius, N., Jablensky, J., Ernberg, N., Leff, J., Korten, A., & Gulbinat, W. (1987), Course of schizophrenia in different countries: Some results of a WHO international comparative 5-year follow-up study. In: *Search for Causes of Schizophrenia*, ed. H. Häfner, W. F. Gattaz, & W. Janzarik. Berlin: Springer Verlag.

*Schneider, K. (1959), *Clinical Psychopathology*, trans. M. W. Hamilton. New York: Grune & Stratton.

Seeman, M. V. (1988), Schizophrenia: Search for the elusive biological marker. *Can. Psychiat. Assn. Newsletter*, Spring:12–14.

Seeman, P. (1985), Brain dopamine receptors in schizophrenia. In: *New Perspectives in Schizophrenia*, ed. M. N. Menuck & M. V. Seeman. New York: Macmillan.

Shelton, R. C., Karson, C. N., Doran, A. R., Pickar, D., Bigelow, L. B., & Weinberger, D. (1988), Cerebral structural pathology in schizophrenia: Evidence for a selective prefrontal cortical defect. *Amer. J. Psychiat.*, 145:154–163.

Shepherd, M. (1987), Formulation of new research strategies on schizophrenia. In: *Causes of Schizophrenia*, ed. H. Häfner, W. F. Gattaz, & W. Janzarik. Berlin: Springer Verlag.

Siris, S. G., Harmon, G. K., & Endicott, J. (1981), Postpsychotic depressive syndrome. *Arch. Gen. Psychiat.*, 38:1122–1123.

Stahl, S. M., & Wets, K. M. (1988), Clinical pharmacology of schizophrenia. In: *Schizophrenia: The Major Issues*, ed. P. Bebbington & P. McGuffin. Oxford: Heinemann.

Stern, A. (1938), Psychoanalytic investigation of and therapy in the border line group of neuroses. *Psychoanal. Quart.*, 7:467–489.

Stern, M. J., Pillsburg, J. A., & Sonnenburg, S. M. (1972), Postpsychotic depression in schizophrenics. *Comprehen. Psychiat.*, 13:591–598.

Stevenson, I., & Greyson, B. (1979), Near-death experiences: Relevance to the question of survival after death. *J. Amer. Med. Assn.*, 242:265–267.

*Strauss, J. S. (1987), Processes of healing and chronicity in schizophrenia. In: *Search for Causes of Schizophrenia*, ed. H. Häfner, W. F. Gattaz, & W. Janzarik. Berlin: Springer Verlag.

Strömgren, E. (1987), The genetics of schizophrenia: Discussion. In: *Search for the Causes of Schizophrenia*, ed. H. Häfner, W. F. Gattaz, & W. Janzarik. Berlin: Springer Verlag.

Venables, P. H. (1987), Cognitive and attentional disorders in the development of schizophrenia. In: *Search for the Causes of Schizophrenia*, ed. H. Häfner, W. F. Gattaz, & W. Janzarik. Berlin: Springer Verlag.

Wing, J. K. (1987), History, classification, and research strategies: Discussion. In: *Search for Causes of Schizophrenia*, ed. H. Häfner, W. F. Gattaz, & W. Janzarik. Berlin: Springer Verlag.

*Wise, M. G. (1987), Delirium. In: *American Psychiatric Press Textbook of Neuropsychiatry*, ed. R. E. Hales & S. C. Yudovsky. Washington, DC: American Psychiatric Press.

Zilboorg, G. (1941), Ambulatory schizophrenia. *Psychiatry*, 4:149–155.

Zubin, J. (1987), Epidemiology and course of schizophrenia: Discussion. In: *Search for Causes of Schizophrenia*, ed. H. Häfner, W. F. Gattaz, & W. Janzarik. Berlin: Springer Verlag.

---

*Recommended readings.

Name Index

Note: r denotes bibliographic reference
         * denotes recommended reading

Abraham, K., 27, 29r, 107–108, 128, 129r, 493, 500, 516*, 517r*
Abrams, R., 392–393, 397r
Adams, A., 194, 207, 245r, 295, 312r
Adler, N. T., 204, 209, 244r, 411–412, 435r
Ainsworth, M. D. S., 145, 147–148, 150–151, 158*, 158r
Akiskal, H. S., 400, 402, 424, 430, 434*, 435r*, 438r*, 469, 484r, 489r, 510, 517r, 519r
Aleksandrowicz, D. R., 390–391, 395r
Alexander, F., 17, 29r
Alexander, M. G., 500, 518r
Allan, J. S., 404, 436r
Altshuler, K. Z., 432, 435*, 436r, 438r*, 491–492, 518r, 537, 570r
Ambelas, A., 391, 395*, 395r*
American Psychiatric Association, 251, 289r, 308, 312r, 338, 341, 357, 374, 379*, 380r*, 423, 425–429, 435r, 522,

534–536, 555, 570r
Ananth, J., 362–363, 373–374, 380r
Anderson, J. L., 404, 436r
Andreasen, N. C., 393, 395r, 421, 422–423, 429, 435*, 435r*, 558–559, 570r
Angermeyer, M. C., 566, 570*, 570r*
Annitto, W., 388, 396r
Antelman, S. M., 336, 380r
Anthony, E. J., 247r, 383r, 434*, 435r*
Appenzeller, T., 251–252, 270, 278–279, 289*, 291r*
Argyle, M., 228–229, 231, 239, 244*, 244r*
Arieti, S., 550, 557, 560, 565, 571r
Aring, C. D., 226, 244r
Arlow, J. A., 165–166, 189r
Auerbach, A. H., 246r

Bachrach, H., 301, 307, 313r
Bacon, S., 394, 397r
Baddeley, A., 250, 252, 270,

577

Subject Index

Bold page numbers indicate definitions. Italic page numbers indicate illustrations.